The Asheville Reader

The Modern World

EDITED BY

Edward J. Katz
Tracey Rizzo

Copley Custom Publishing Group
Acton, Massachusetts 01720

ISBN 1-58152-268-1

Acknowledgments:

pp. 4–8: From *Discoveries and Opinions of Galileo* by Galileo Galilei, translated by Stillman Drake. Copyright © 1957 by Stillman Drake. Used by permission of Doubleday, a division of Random House, Inc.

pp. 10–18: From *Thoughts* by Blaise Pascal. Copyright © Everyman's Library/David Campbell Publishers. Reprinted by permission of the publisher.

pp. 38–42: From *Emperor of China* by Jonathan D. Spence. Copyright © 1974 by Jonathan D. Spence. Used by permission of Alfred A. Knopf, a division of Random House, Inc.

pp. 61–66: From *The Philosophy of Kant* by Immanuel Kant, translated by Carl Friedrich. Copyright © 1949 by Random House, Inc. Used by permission of Random House, Inc.

pp. 124–134: From *The Portable Enlightenment Reader* edited by Isaac Kramnick. Copyright © 1995 by Penguin Books USA Inc. Used by permission of Viking Penguin, a division of Penguin Group (USA) Inc.

pp. 144–147: From *Letters from a Peruvian Woman* by Françoise de Graffigny. Copyright © 1993 by Modern Language Association of America. Reprinted by permission of the publisher.

pp. 252–255: As appeared in *Women, the Family, and Freedom*, Vol. One. Translated by Giselle Pincetl. Copyright © by Giselle Pincetl. Reprinted by permission of the translator.

pp. 300–303: From *Noli Me Tangere* by José Rizal, translated by León Ma. Guerrero. Copyright © 1961 by Indiana University Press. Reprinted by permission of the publisher.

pp. 322–326: From *Indian Home Rule* by Mahatma Gandhi. Copyright © by Navajivan Trust. Reprinted by permission.

pp. 328–332: From *Sources of Japanese Tradition* edited by William Theodore de Bary. Copyright © 1958 by Columbia University Press. Reprinted by permission of the publisher via the Copyright Clearance Center.

pp. 334–338: From *Imperialism: The Highest Stage of Capitalism* by Vladimir Lenin. Copyright © International Publishers. Reprinted by permission of the publishers.

To the memory of Deryl Howard,
whose spirit and vision lie
at the heart of this collection

Contents

II. The Late Enlightenment: Revolutions in Society and Politics

III. Neoclassical and Romantic Art and Social Ideas

IV. The Politics of Slavery and Gender in the Eighteenth and Nineteenth Centuries

V. Social, Economic, and Political Thought in the Nineteenth Century

VI. Imperialism and the Conflict of Cultures

VII. Race and Politics in Modern America

VIII. Intellectual Uncertainty and the Rise of Modernism

IX. Crisis in the Years of World War

X. World War II, the Holocaust Experience, and the Response of Existentialism

Appendix

Acknowledgments

Assembling a collection of primary documents such as those comprising *The Modern World* would be daunting, if not impossible, without the help of others. We would like to thank the following contributors to this second edition for their valuable work, both in text selection and in the writing of introductions: Charles James, Doug Jones, Sarah Judson, Jeff Konz, Bruce Larson, John McClain, Jeanne McGlinn, and Dan Pierce. In addition, we would like to thank the following individuals for their contributions to the first edition of this text: Mary Alm, Joy Bulluck, Peter Caulfield, Michael Gillum, Deborah James, Michael Ridgway Jones, Susan McMichaels, Merritt Moseley, Dwight Mullen, Pamela Nickless, Mike Ruiz, William Spellman, Sheryl Sawin, and Lee Tatum. Tracey Rizzo translated the excerpts from the *Declaration of the Rights of Man and Citizen* and de Gouges' *Declaration of the Rights of Woman and Citizen*. We want to express our gratitude as well to Cindy Ho, Director of the UNCA Humanities Program, who offered us support both material and moral. Thanks also to Lucy Miskin and the staff at Copley Custom Publishing Group for their energy and expertise.

General Introduction

The editors of this Asheville Reader volume, *The Modern World,* have designed the text with the aim of exposing students to the diversity of thought and expression that has shaped their modern experience. In opening our collection with writings from the Scientific Revolution and the Enlightenment, and concluding with selections that reflect upon the meaning of World War II and the Holocaust, we hoped to capture a sense of the intellectual vitality and courage that characterize the leading intellectuals and artists of this period of history. The writings of political leaders and of ordinary people—from Europe and the United States, from Asia, Africa, and South America—help us to see our world in new ways and often reveal to us the prejudices that cloud our understanding. From the optimism of the Age of Reason to the darkness of the mid-twentieth century, we have witnessed the shift away from certainty, from the comforts of a purpose-oriented worldview, to a sense of the human condition as fragmented, dehumanized, and alienated. In crafting this collection, we did not want to turn away from the barbarism of the modern age or to deny the critical failures that have plagued humanity over the last three centuries. In his long essay *The Myth of Sisyphus,* the French philosopher Albert Camus wrote, "Beginning to think is beginning to be undermined"; that is to say, by thinking critically we risk challenging the values and beliefs we hold most dearly. And yet, Camus goes on to argue, it is only by taking on the burden of critical and deeply self-reflective inquiry that we are able to assess our reality and to envision ways to transform it. Though many of the readings offered in this volume center on the West and its systems of belief, we have included the work of women and people of color who write from a wide range of cultural traditions and practices. Their depth of insight and breadth of outlook, we believe, will serve us as intellectual and spiritual resources in the next millennium.

Each reading selection is preceded by a short introduction that conveys the important biographical details of the writer's life, the cultural and intellectual background that influenced his or her thought, and a set of questions designed to stimulate further reflection. The writings gathered here engage the difficulties of coming to terms with our changing sense of self and others, of nature and culture, of God and humankind. We intend these readings to challenge our own ideas and traditions, so that we might come to know more powerfully our responsibility and our potential as we engage modernity.

I. The Scientific Revolution
and the Early Enlightenment

Galileo Galilei

1564–1642

Galileo Galilei was a central figure of the Scientific Revolution, which had begun in controversy with the publication of Nicolas Copernicus's *On the Revolution of the Heavenly Spheres* in 1543. Copernicus had argued that placing the Sun, rather than the Earth, at the center of the universe provided a simpler picture for explaining observed astronomical phenomena. His arguments were also based on tenets of the neoplatonists, who gave central importance to the Sun as the giver of life. One of the first to recognize the contradiction between the Copernican universe and the biblical model was Martin Luther, the leader of the Protestant Reformation in Germany. Thus, he referred to Joshua 10:13, where the Sun and Moon stopped for a time by an act of God: "And the Sun stood still, and the Moon stayed." For Luther, then, the Bible indicates that, except for a miracle such as this one, the Sun and Moon move.

Nonetheless, it wasn't until the painstaking observations of the astronomer Tycho Brahe in the later sixteenth century that massive amounts of planetary data were collected. Johannes Kepler analyzed this data and found that the planets orbit the Sun in ellipses. It was around this time that Galileo heard of the invention of the telescope and, in 1610, he constructed his own. With the aid of this new device, Galileo directly observed several features of the universe that supported the Copernican model. He discovered four moons, now called the Galilean moons, circling Jupiter. He also discovered the phases of Venus, which were more easily explained within the context of the heliocentric model. The craters he viewed on the moon and sunspots on the Sun also opposed the model of the day, which presented the heavens as perfect and unchanging. Subsequently, Galileo's strong support of the heliocentric model led him into conflict with the Inquisition of the Roman Catholic Church, which condemned him for heresy in 1633. He was forced to recant his heretical views and was placed under house arrest for the remaining years of his life.

"The Letter to the Grand Duchess Christina" (1615) is an eloquent essay in which Galileo argues that both Scripture and science can be right. He points out that science helps us understand the true meaning of the Bible, the spiritual message, and that this can never be contradicted by science. Imagine yourself in the time of Galileo. Essentially all priests, preachers, and ministers interpret the Bible to categorically state that the Earth is the center of the universe.

It was only after Galileo's death that biblical views did change in light of scientific truth. Like science, biblical interpretation is dynamic and changing. Refinements are made in both scientific and religious thinking that enable one to get to the deeper meaning of each. What are the key elements of Galileo's argument in this excerpt? Can you find other historical examples where science and religion are in conflict? How would Galileo resolve these?

from "The Letter to the Grand Duchess Christina" (1615)

Galileo Galilei to the most serene Grand Duchess Mother:

Some years ago, as Your Serene Highness well knows, I discovered in the heavens many things that had not been seen before our own age. The novelty of these things, as well as some consequences which followed from them in contradiction to the physical notions commonly held among academic philosophers, stirred up against me no small number of professors—as if I had placed these things in the sky with my own hands in order to upset nature and overturn the sciences. They seemed to forget that the increase of known truths stimulates the investigation, establishment, and growth of the arts; not their diminution or destruction.

Showing a greater fondness for their own opinions than for truth, they sought to deny and disprove the new things which, if they had cared to look for themselves, their own senses would have demonstrated to them. To this end they hurled various charges and published numerous writings filled with vain arguments, and they made the grave mistake of sprinkling these with passages taken from places in the Bible which they had failed to understand properly, and which were ill suited to their purposes.

• • •

I hope to show that I proceed with much greater piety than they do, when I argue not against condemning this book, but against condemning it in the way they suggest—that is, without understanding it, weighing it, or so much as reading it. For Copernicus never discusses matters of religion or faith, nor does he use arguments that depend in any way upon the authority of sacred writings which he might have interpreted erroneously. He stands always upon physical conclusions pertaining to the celestial motions, and deals with them by astronomical and geometrical demonstrations, founded primarily upon sense experiences and very exact observations. He did not ignore the Bible, but he knew very well that if his doctrine were proved, then it could not contradict the Scriptures when they were rightly understood.

• • •

Such are the people who labor to persuade us that an author like Copernicus may be condemned without being read, and who produce various

4

authorities from the Bible, from theologians, and from Church Councils to make us believe that this is not only lawful but commendable. Since I hold these to be of supreme authority, I consider it rank temerity for anyone to contradict them—when employed according to the usage of the holy Church. Yet I do not believe it is wrong to speak out when there is reason to suspect that other men wish, for some personal motive, to produce and employ such authorities for purposes quite different from the sacred intention of the holy Church.

• • •

The reason produced for condemning the opinion that the earth moves and the sun stands still is that in many places in the Bible one may read that the sun moves and the earth stands still. Since the Bible cannot err, it follows as a necessary consequence that anyone takes an erroneous and heretical position who maintains that the sun is inherently motionless and the earth movable.

With regard to this argument, I think in the first place that it is very pious to say and prudent to affirm that the holy Bible can never speak untruth—whenever its true meaning is understood. But I believe nobody will deny that it is often very abstruse, and may say things which are quite different from what its bare words signify. Hence in expounding the Bible if one were always to confine oneself to the unadorned grammatical meaning, one might fall into error. Not only contradictions and propositions far from true might thus be made to appear in the Bible, but even grave heresies and follies. Thus it would be necessary to assign to God feet, hands, and eyes, as well as corporeal and human affections, such as anger, repentance, hatred, and sometimes even the forgetting of things past and ignorance of those to come. These propositions uttered by the Holy Ghost were set down in that manner by the sacred scribes in order to accommodate them to the capacities of the common people, who are rude and unlearned. For the sake of those who deserve to be separated from the herd, it is necessary that wise expositors should produce the true senses of such passages, together with the special reasons for which they were set down in these words. This doctrine is so widespread and so definite with all theologians that it would be superfluous to adduce evidence for it.

Hence I think that I may reasonably conclude that whenever the Bible has occasion to speak of any physical conclusion (especially those which are very abstruse and hard to understand), the rule has been observed of avoiding confusion in the minds of the common people which would render them contumacious toward the higher mysteries. Now the Bible, merely to condescend to popular capacity, has not hesitated to obscure some very important pronouncements, attributing to God himself some qualities extremely remote from (and even contrary to) His essence. Who, then, would positively declare that this principle has been set aside, and the Bible has confined itself rigorously to the bare and restricted sense of its words, when speaking but casually of the earth, of water, of the sun, or of any other created thing? Especially in view of the fact that these things in no way concern the primary purpose of the sacred writings, which is the service of God and the salvation of souls—matters infinitely beyond the comprehension of the common people.

This being granted, I think that in discussions of physical problems we ought to begin not from the authority of scriptural passages, but from sense-experiences and necessary demonstrations; for the holy Bible and the phenomena of nature proceed alike from the divine Word, the former as the dictate of the Holy Ghost and the latter as the observant executrix of God's commands. It is necessary for the Bible, in order to be accommodated to the understanding of every man, to speak many things which appear to differ from the absolute truth so far as the bare meaning of the words is concerned. But Nature, on the other hand, is inexorable and immutable; she never transgresses the laws imposed upon her, or cares a whit whether her abstruse reasons and methods of operation are understandable to men. For that reason it appears that nothing physical which sense-experience sets before our eyes, or which necessary demonstrations prove to us, ought to be called in question (much less condemned) upon the testimony of biblical passages which may have some different meaning beneath their words. For the Bible is not chained in every expression to conditions as strict as those which govern all physical effects; nor is God any less excellently revealed in Nature's actions than in the sacred statements of the Bible. Perhaps this is what Tertullian[1] meant by these words:

"We conclude that God is known first through Nature, and then again, more particularly, by doctrine; by Nature in His works, and by doctrine in His revealed word."

From this I do not mean to infer that we need not have an extraordinary esteem for the passages of holy Scripture. On the contrary, having arrived at any certainties in physics, we ought to utilize these as the most appropriate aids in the true exposition of the Bible and in the investigation of those meanings which are necessarily contained therein, for these must be concordant with demonstrated truths. I should judge that the authority of the Bible was designed to persuade men of those articles and propositions which, surpassing all human reasoning, could not be made credible by science, or by any other means than through the very mouth of the Holy Spirit.

Yet even in those propositions which are not matters of faith, this authority ought to be preferred over that of all human writings which are supported only by bare assertions or probable arguments, and not set forth in a demonstrative way. This I hold to be necessary and proper to the same extent that divine wisdom surpasses all human judgment and conjecture.

But I do not feel obliged to believe that that same God who has endowed us with senses, reason, and intellect has intended to forgo their use and by some other means to give us knowledge which we can attain by them. He would not require us to deny sense and reason in physical matters which are set before our eyes and minds by direct experience or necessary demonstrations. This must be especially true in those sciences of which but the faintest trace (and that consisting of conclusions) is to be found in the Bible. Of astronomy, for instance, so little is found that none of the planets except Venus are so much as mentioned, and this only once or twice under the name of "Lucifer." If the sacred scribes had had any intention of teaching people certain arrangements and motions of the heavenly bodies, or had they wished us to derive such knowledge from the Bible, then in my opinion they would not have spoken of these matters so sparingly in comparison with the infinite number of admirable conclusions which are demonstrated in that science. Far from pretending to teach us the constitution and motions of the heavens and the stars, with their shapes, magnitudes, and distances, the authors of the Bible intentionally forbore to speak of these things, though all were quite well known to them. Such is the opinion of the holiest and most learned Fathers, and in St. Augustine we find the following words:

"It is likewise commonly asked what we may believe about the form and shape of the heavens according to the Scriptures, for many contend much about these matters. But with superior prudence our authors have forborne to speak of this, as in no way furthering the student with respect to a blessed life—and, more important still, as taking up much of that time which should be spent in holy exercises. What is it to me whether heaven, like a sphere, surrounds the earth on all sides as a mass balanced in the center of the universe, or whether like a dish it merely covers and overcasts the earth? Belief in Scripture is urged rather for the reason we have often mentioned; that is, in order that no one, through ignorance of divine passages, finding anything in our Bibles or hearing anything cited from them of such a nature as may seem to oppose manifest conclusions, should be induced to suspect their truth when they teach, relate, and deliver more profitable matters. Hence let it be said briefly, touching the form of heaven, that our authors knew the truth but the Holy Spirit did not desire that men should learn things that are useful to no one for salvation."

The same disregard of these sacred authors toward beliefs about the phenomena of the celestial bodies is repeated to us by St. Augustine in his next chapter. On the question whether we are to believe that the heaven moves or stands still, he writes thus:

"Some of the brethren raise a question concerning the motion of heaven, whether it is fixed or moved. If it is moved, they say, how is it a firmament? If it stands still, how do these stars which are held fixed in it go round from east to west, the more northerly performing shorter circuits near the pole, so that the heaven (if there is another pole unknown to us) may seem to revolve upon some axis, or (if there is no other pole) may be thought to move as a discus? To these men I reply that it would require many subtle and profound reasonings to find out which of these things is actually so; but to undertake this and discuss it is consistent neither with my leisure nor with the duty of those whom I desire to instruct in essential matters more directly conducing to their salvation and to the benefit of the holy Church."

From these things it follows as a necessary consequence that, since the Holy Ghost did not intend to teach us whether heaven moves or stands still, whether its shape is spherical or like a discus or extended in a plane, nor whether the earth is located at its center or off to one side, then so much the less was it intended to settle for us any other conclusion of the same kind. And the motion or rest of the earth and the sun is so closely linked with the things just named, that without a determination of the one, neither side can be taken in the other matters. Now if the Holy Spirit has purposely neglected to teach us propositions of this sort as irrelevant to the highest goal (that is, to our salvation), how can anyone affirm that it is obligatory to take sides on them, and that one belief is required by faith, while the other side is erroneous? Can an opinion be heretical and yet have no concern with the salvation of souls? Can the Holy Ghost be asserted not to have intended teaching us something that does concern our salvation? I would say here something that was heard from an ecclesiastic[2] of the most eminent degree: "That the intention of the Holy Ghost is to teach us how one goes to heaven, not how heaven goes." . . .

Notes

[1] An early church father (c. 200).
[2] Attributed to Cardinal Baronius (1538–1607).

Blaise Pascal

1623–1662

Blaise Pascal was the son of a high-level French tax official. He received his education from his father and was a child prodigy in mathematics. In the course of his relatively short life, Pascal accomplished several major achievements, any one of which would be enough to earn him a place in history for all time. Working in probability theory, he constructed the famous *Pascal Triangle*, commonly encountered today in algebra classes. He discovered how pressure increases as one descends lower and lower in a fluid, which in physics is known as *Pascal's Law*. He also built a mechanical calculating machine to assist his father's computing tasks. The computer language *PASCAL* (c. 1970) is named in his honor.

Pascal suffered from frail health throughout most of his life. During a period of illness in 1654, he had a mystical experience, after which he turned to writing about philosophy and religion. *Pensées (Thoughts)*, published after his death in 1670, is a collection of nearly one thousand reflections (grouped into 14 chapters) on life and the transcendent. Pascal believed in the limitation of human reason in the study of the spiritual. He privileged the personal mystical experience over dogma in truly understanding God: that is, he argued, we come to know God through the "heart." Though Pascal writes within the context of the Christian religion—Catholicism, in particular—his profound thinking has value for all.

In the following selection, Pascal uses mathematical reasoning to convince us and his gambling friends at the time that probability dictates we make the wager that God exists. This "leap of faith" has similarities to twentieth-century existential thought, where personal choice and affirmation of one's belief are of fundamental importance. Once this initial step is taken, what do Pascal's ideas imply about our approach to daily life experiences and challenges? How does Pascal's thinking about belief compare to Galileo's ideas of faith and its relation to reason?

from *Thoughts* (1670)

Section I
Thoughts on Mind and on Style

3

Those who are accustomed to judge by feeling do not understand the process of reasoning, for they would understand at first sight, and are not used to seek for principles. And others, on the contrary, who are accustomed to reason from principles, do not at all understand matters of feeling, seeking principles and being unable to see at a glance.

• • •

Section II
The Misery of Man without God

66

One must know oneself. If this does not serve to discover truth, it at least serves as a rule of life, and there is nothing better.

67

The vanity of the sciences.—Physical science will not console me for the ignorance of morality in the time of affliction. But the science of ethics will always console me for the ignorance of the physical sciences.

• • •

72

Man's disproportion. . . . Let man then contemplate the whole of nature in her full and grand majesty, and turn his vision from the low objects which surround him. Let him gaze on that brilliant light, set like an eternal lamp to illumine the universe; let the earth appear to him a point in comparison with the vast circle described by the sun; and let him wonder at the fact that this vast circle is itself but a very fine point in comparison with that described by the stars in their revolution round the firmament. But if our view be arrested there, let our imagination pass beyond; it will sooner exhaust the power of conception than nature that of supplying material for conception. The whole visible world is only an imperceptible atom in the ample bosom of nature. No idea approaches it. We may enlarge our conceptions beyond all imaginable space; we only produce atoms in comparison with the reality of things. It is an infinite sphere, the centre of which is everywhere, the circumference nowhere. In short, it is the greatest sensible mark of the almighty power of God, that imagination loses itself in that thought.

Returning to himself, let man consider what he is in comparison with all existence; let him regard himself as lost in this remote corner of nature; and from the little cell in which he finds himself lodged, I mean the universe, let him estimate at their true value the earth, kingdoms, cities, and himself. What is a man in the Infinite?

•   •   •

For in fact what is man in nature? A Nothing in comparison with the Infinite, an All in comparison with the Nothing, a mean between nothing and everything. Since he is infinitely removed from comprehending the extremes, the end of things and their beginning are hopelessly hidden from him in an impenetrable secret; he is equally incapable of seeing the Nothing from which he was made, and the Infinite in which he is swallowed up.

•   •   •

Our intellect holds the same position in the world of thought as our body occupies in the expanse of nature. Limited as we are in every way, this state which holds the mean between two extremes is present in all our impotence. Our senses perceive no extreme. Too much sound deafens us; too much light dazzles us; too great distance or proximity hinders our view. Too great length and too great brevity of discourse tend to obscurity; too much truth is paralysing (I know some who cannot understand that to take four from nothing leaves nothing). First principles are too self-evident for us; too much pleasure disagrees with us. Too many concords are annoying in music; too many benefits irritate us; we wish to have the wherewithal to over-pay our debts. *Beneficia eo usque laeta sunt dum videntur exsolvi posse; ubi multum antevenere, pro gratia odium redditur.*[1] We feel neither extreme heat nor extreme cold. Excessive qualities are prejudicial to us and not perceptible by the senses; we do not feel but suffer them. Extreme youth and extreme age hinder the mind, as also too much and too little education. In short, extremes are for us as though they were not, and we are not within their notice. They escape us, or we them.

This is our true state; this is what makes us incapable of certain knowledge and of absolute ignorance. We sail within a vast sphere, ever drifting in uncertainty, driven from end to end. When we think to attach ourselves to any point and to fasten to it, it wavers and leaves us; and if we follow it, it eludes our grasp, slips past us, and vanishes for ever. Nothing stays for us. This is our natural condition, and yet most contrary to our inclination; we burn with desire to find solid ground and an ultimate sure foundation whereon to build a tower reaching to the Infinite. But our whole groundwork cracks, and the earth opens to abysses.

Let us therefore not look for certainty and stability. Our reason is always deceived by fickle shadows; nothing can fix the finite between the two Infinites, which both enclose and fly from it.

• • •

And what completes our incapability of knowing things, is the fact that they are simple, and that we are composed of two opposite natures, different in kind, soul and body. For it is impossible that our rational part should be other than spiritual; and if any one maintain that we are simply corporeal, this would far more exclude us from the knowledge of things, there being nothing so inconceivable as to say that matter knows itself. It is impossible to imagine how it should know itself.

So if we are simply material, we can know nothing at all; and if we are composed of mind and matter, we cannot know perfectly things which are simple, whether spiritual or corporeal. Hence it comes that almost all philosophers have confused ideas of things, and speak of material things in spiritual terms, and of spiritual things in material terms. For they say boldly that bodies have a tendency to fall, that they seek after their centre, that they fly from destruction, that they fear the void, that they have inclinations, sympathies, antipathies, all of which attributes pertain only to mind. And in speaking of minds, they consider them as in a place, and attribute to them movement from one place to another; and these are qualities which belong only to bodies.

Instead of receiving the ideas of these things in their purity, we colour them with our own qualities, and stamp with our composite being all the simple things which we contemplate.

Who would not think, seeing us compose all things of mind and body, but that this mixture would be quite intelligible to us? Yet it is the very thing we least understand. Man is to himself the most wonderful object in nature; for he cannot conceive what the body is, still less what the mind is, and least of all how a body should be united to a mind. This is the consummation of his difficulties, and yet it is his very being. *Modus quo corporibus adhaerent spiritus comprehendi ab hominibus non potest, et hoc tamen homo est.*[2] . . .

77

I cannot forgive Descartes. In all his philosophy he would have been quite willing to dispense with God. But he had to make Him give a fillip to set the world in motion; beyond this, he has no further need of God. . . .

146

Man is obviously made to think. It is his whole dignity and his whole merit; and his whole duty is to think as he ought. Now, the order of thought is to begin with self, and with its Author and its end.

Now, of what does the world think? Never of this, but of dancing, playing the lute, singing, making verses, running at the ring, etc., fighting, making oneself king, without thinking what it is to be a king and what to be a man.

• • •

162

He who will know fully the vanity of man has only to consider the causes and effects of love. The cause is a *je ne sais quoi* (Corneille),[3] and the effects are dreadful. This *je ne sais quoi*, so small an object that we cannot recognise it, agitates a whole country, princes, armies, the entire world.

Cleopatra's nose: had it been shorter, the whole aspect of the world would have been altered.

• • •

Section III
Of the Necessity of the Wager

206

The eternal silence of these infinite spaces frightens me.

207

How many kingdoms know us not!

208

Why is my knowledge limited? Why my stature? Why my life to one hundred years rather than to a thousand? What reason has nature had for giving me such, and for choosing this number rather than another in the infinity of those from which there is no more reason to choose one than another, trying nothing else?

• • •

230

It is incomprehensible that God should exist, and it is incomprehensible that He should not exist; that the soul should be joined to the body, and that we should have no soul; that the world should be created, and that it should not be created, etc.; that original sin should be, and that it should not be.

• • •

233

. . . Let us then examine this point, and say, "God is, or He is not." But to which side shall we incline? Reason can decide nothing here. There is an infinite chaos which separated us. A game is being played at the extremity of this infinite distance where heads or tails will turn up. What will you wager? According to reason, you can do neither the one thing nor the other; according to reason, you can defend neither of the propositions.

Do not then reprove for error those who have made a choice; for you know nothing about it. "No, but I blame them for having made, not this choice, but a choice; for again both he who chooses heads and he who chooses tails are equally at fault, they are both in the wrong. The true course is not to wager at all."

Yes; but you must wager. It is not optional. You are embarked. Which will you choose then? Let us see. Since you must choose, let us see which interests you least. You have two things to lose, the true and the good; and two things to stake, your reason and your will, your knowledge and your happiness; and your nature has two things to shun, error and misery. Your reason is no more shocked in choosing one rather than the other, since you must of necessity choose. This is one point settled. But your happiness? Let us weigh the gain and the loss in wagering that God is. Let us estimate these two chances. If you gain, you gain all; if you lose, you lose nothing. Wager, then, without hesitation that He is.—"That is very fine. Yes, I must wager; but I may perhaps wager too much."—Let us see. Since there is an equal risk of gain and of loss, if you had only to gain two lives, instead of one, you might still wager. But if there were three lives to gain, you would have to play (since you are under the necessity of playing), and you would be imprudent, when you are forced to play, not to chance your life to gain three at a game where there is an equal risk of loss and gain. But there is an eternity of life and happiness. And this being so, if there were an infinity of chances, of which one only would be for you, you would still be right in wagering one to win two, and you would act stupidly, being obliged to play, by refusing to stake one life against three at a game in which out of an infinity of chances there is one for you, if there were an infinity of an infinitely happy life to gain. But there is here an infinity of an infinitely happy life to gain, a chance of gain against a finite number of chances of loss, and what you stake is finite. It is all divided; wherever the infinite is and there is not an infinity of chances of loss against that of gain, there is no time to hesitate, you must give all. And thus, when one is forced to play, he must renounce reason to preserve his life, rather than risk it for infinite gain, as likely to happen as the loss of nothingness.

For it is no use to say it is uncertain if we will gain, and it is certain that we risk, and that the infinite distance between the *certainty* of what is staked and the *uncertainty* of what will be gained, equals the finite good which is certainly staked against the uncertain infinite. It is not so, as every player stakes a certainty to gain an uncertainty, and yet he stakes a finite certainty to gain a finite uncertainty, without transgressing against reason. There is not an infinite distance between the certainty staked and the uncertainty of the gain; that is untrue. In truth, there is an infinity between the certainty of gain and the certainty of loss. But the uncertainty of the gain is proportioned to the certainty of the stake according to the proportion of the chances of gain and loss. Hence it comes that, if there are as many risks on one side as on the other, the course is to play even; and then the certainty of the stake is equal to the uncertainty of the gain, so far is it from fact that there is an infinite distance between them. And so our proposition is of infinite force, when there is the finite to stake in a game where there are equal risks of gain and of loss, and the infinite to gain. This is demonstrable; and if men are capable of any truths, this is one.

"I confess it, I admit it. But, still, is there no means of seeing the faces of the cards?"—Yes, Scripture and the rest, etc. "Yes, but I have my hands tied and my mouth closed; I am forced to wager, and am not free. I am not released, and am so made that I cannot believe. What, then, would you have me do?"

True. But at least learn your inability to believe, since reason brings you to this, and yet you cannot believe. Endeavour then to convince yourself, not by increase of proofs of God, but by the abatement of your passions. You would like to attain faith, and do not know the way; you would like to cure yourself of unbelief, and ask the remedy for it. Learn of those who have been bound like you, and who now stake all their possessions. These are people who know the way which you would follow, and who are cured of an ill of which you would be cured. Follow the way by which they began; by acting as if they believed, taking the holy water, having masses said, etc. Even this will naturally make you believe, and deaden your acuteness.—"But this is what I am afraid of."—And why? What have you to lose?

But to show you that this leads you there, it is this which will lessen the passions, which are your stumbling-blocks.

The end of this discourse.—Now, what harm will befall you in taking this side? You will be faithful, honest, humble, grateful, generous, a sincere friend, truthful. Certainly you will not have those poisonous pleasures, glory and luxury; but will you not have others? I will tell you that you will thereby gain in this life, and that, at each step you take on this road, you will see so great certainty of gain, so much nothingness in what you risk, that you will at last recognise that you have wagered for something certain and infinite, for which you have given nothing.

"Ah! This discourse transports me, charms me," etc.

If this discourse pleases you and seems impressive, know that it is made by a man who has knelt, both before and after it, in prayer to that Being, infinite and without parts, before whom he lays all he has, for you also to lay before Him all you have for your own good and for His glory, that so strength may be given to lowliness.

•   •   •

Section IV
Of the Means of Belief

273

If we submit everything to reason, our religion will have no mysterious and supernatural element. If we offend the principles of reason, our religion will be absurd and ridiculous.

277

The heart has its reasons, which reason does not know. We feel it in a thousand things. I say that the heart naturally loves the Universal Being, and also itself naturally, according as it gives itself to them; and it hardens itself against one or the other at its will. You have rejected the one, and kept the other. Is it by reason that you love yourself?

278

It is the heart which experiences God, and not the reason. This, then, is faith: God felt by the heart, not by the reason.

•   •   •

Section VI
The Philosophers

339

I can well conceive a man without hands, feet, head (for it is only experience which teaches us that the head is more necessary than feet). But I cannot conceive man without thought; he would be a stone or a brute.

•   •   •

346

Thought constitutes the greatness of man.

347

Man is but a reed, the most feeble thing in nature; but he is a thinking reed. The entire universe need not arm itself to crush him. A vapour, a drop of water suffices to kill him. But, if the universe were to crush him, man would still be more noble than that which killed him, because he knows that he dies and the advantage which the universe has over him; the universe knows nothing of this.

All our dignity consists, then, in thought. By it we must elevate ourselves, and not by space and time which we cannot fill. Let us endeavour, then, to think well; this is the principle of morality.

●　●　●

379

It is not good to have too much liberty. It is not good to have all one wants.

●　●　●

Section VII
Morality and Doctrine

436

Weakness.—Every pursuit of men is to get wealth; and they cannot have a title to show that they possess it justly, for they have only that of human caprice; nor have they strength to hold it securely. It is the same with knowledge, for disease takes it away. We are incapable both of truth and goodness.

437

We desire truth, and find within ourselves only uncertainty.

We seek happiness, and find only misery and death.

We cannot but desire truth and happiness, and are incapable of certainty or happiness. This desire is left to us, partly to punish us, partly to make us perceive where from we are fallen.

438

If man is not made for God, why is he only happy in God? If man is made for God, why is he so opposed to God?

Notes

[1] "Kindnesses are pleasant only insofar as they appear able to be repaid; when they are too excessive hatred results instead of gratitude" (Tacitus, c. 100).

[2] "The manner in which the spirit clings to the body cannot be understood by humans and this, nevertheless, is a human being" (Augustine, c. 400).

[3] Literally, "I don't know what," i.e., something indescribable. Pierre Corneille (1606–1684), dramatist.

Sir Isaac Newton

1642–1727

Isaac Newton was born in Woolsthorpe, Lincolnshire, England. On the Julian calendar, which was in use in England, he was born on Christmas day 1642, but on the Gregorian calendar used in Europe, his birth date was 4 January 1643. During his early life, people recognized Newton's mechanical aptitude and brilliance. Newton entered Trinity College, Cambridge, when he was eighteen, but an outbreak of the black plague closed the school in 1665. While at home from Cambridge, he independently developed calculus, which he called "fluxions," and formulated his famous Law of Gravitation. The issue of who was first to discover calculus—the philosopher and mathematician Gottfried Wilhelm Leibniz is also now credited with this discovery— embroiled Newton in controversy for most of his life. In 1684, beginning with a question about planetary motion, he started the work that was to become the *Philosophiae Naturalis Principia Mathematica* (*The Mathematical Principles of Natural Philosophy*). Andrew Mott did the first American translation in 1729, which is used here; in 1756, Gabrielle-Émile Marquise du Châtelet completed a French translation, which in turn influenced the *philosophes*. Newton hated controversy and the *Principia* had its share. Robert Hooke, of the Royal Society, claimed credit for some of the work's ideas. In response to his critics, Newton threatened not to publish Book III of the *Principia* and had to be encouraged to publish the entire work by Edmond Halley, who paid to have it printed. Newton had only a few friends, although even those he could let go of suddenly. He often discussed science, religion, and politics with John Locke, whose friendship he did maintain throughout his life. Newton served as a Member of Parliament, as warden of the English Mint and eventually as head of the Royal Society. Newton's interests went well beyond mathematics, cosmology, and physics; for much of his life he made forays into alchemy, and his theological studies continued until his death in 1727.

The *Principia* first appeared, written in Latin, in 1687. Newton wrote it in order to present the underlying mathematical structure of the forces and motion of bodies in the universe. However, those who read the *Principia*, and in some cases those who only heard about the book, saw in it a worldview that changed art, philosophy and religion. The following selections demonstrate Newton's assumption, shared by others at the time, that observable and predictable patterns in the world could be understood using mathematics. These excerpts highlight the questions he felt were worth asking about the nature of the world and the answers he thought were best suited to solving them.

What was the difference for Newton between rational and practical mechanics? When Newton stated the rules for understanding the universe in Book III, what might he have been saying about earlier conceptions? Why might Newton have assumed that mathematics could be applied to understanding nature? The acceptance of the *Principia* represents a change in how the people of that time saw the world. What were the changes? To whom is Newton writing? What do Newton's comments about his critics reveal? Why did he not write Book III in a more popular style?

from *Principia* (1684)

Newton's Preface to the First Edition

Since the ancients (as we are told by *Pappus*), made great account of the science of mechanics in the investigation of natural things; and the moderns, lying aside substantial forms and occult qualities, have endeavoured to subject the phænomena of nature to the laws of mathematics, I have in this treatise cultivated mathematics so far as it regards philosophy. The ancients considered mechanics in a twofold respect; as rational, which proceeds accurately by demonstration; and practical. To practical mechanics all the manual arts belong, from which mechanics took its name. But as artificers do not work with perfect accuracy, it comes to pass that mechanics is so distinguished from geometry, that what is perfectly accurate is called geometrical; what is less so, is called mechanical. But the errors are not in the art, but in the artificers. He that works with less accuracy is an imperfect mechanic; and if any could work with perfect accuracy, he would be the most perfect mechanic of all; for the description of right lines and circles, upon which geometry is founded, belongs to mechanics. Geometry does not teach us to draw these lines, but requires them to be drawn; for it requires that the learner should first be taught to describe these accurately, before he enters upon geometry; then it shows how by these operations problems may be solved. To describe right lines and circles are problems, but not geometrical problems. The solution of these problems is required from mechanics; and by geometry the use of them, when so solved, is shown; and it is the glory of geometry that from those few principles, brought from without, it is able to produce so many things. Therefore geometry is founded in mechanical practice, and is nothing but that part of universal mechanics which accurately proposes and demonstrates the art of measuring. But since the manual arts are chiefly conversant in the moving of bodies, it comes to pass that geometry is commonly referred to their magnitudes, and mechanics to their motion. In this sense rational mechanics will be the science of motions resulting from any forces whatsoever, and of the forces required to produce any motions, accurately proposed and demonstrated. This part of mechanics was cultivated by the ancients in the five powers which relate to manual arts, who considered gravity (it not being a manual power), no otherwise than as it moved weights by those powers. Our design not respecting arts, but philosophy, and our subject not manual but natural powers, we consider chiefly those things which relate to gravity, levity, elastic force, the resistance of fluids, and the like forces, whether attractive or impulsive; and therefore we offer this work as the mathematical principles of philosophy; for all the difficulty of philosophy seems to consist in this—from the phænomena of motions to investigate the forces of nature, and then from these forces to demonstrate the other phænomena; and to this end the general propositions in the first and second book are directed. In the third book we give an example of this in the explication of the System of the World; for by the propositions mathematically demonstrated in the former books, we in the third derive from the celestial phænomena the forces of gravity with which bodies tend to the sun and the several planets. Then from these forces, by other propositions which are also mathematical, we deduce the motions of the planets, the comets, the moon, and the sea. I wish we could derive the rest of the phænomena of nature by the same kind of reasoning from mechanical principles; for I am induced by many reasons to suspect that they may all depend upon certain forces by which the particles of bodies, by some causes hitherto unknown, are either mutually impelled towards each other, and cohere in regular figures, or are repelled and recede from each other; which forces being unknown, philosophers have hitherto attempted the search of nature in vain; but I hope the principles here laid down will afford some light either to this or some truer method of philosophy.

In the publication of this work the most acute and universally learned Mr. Edmund Halley not only assisted me with his pains in correcting the press and taking care of the schemes, but it was to his solicitations that its becoming public is owing; for when he had obtained of me my demonstrations of the figure of the celestial orbits, he continually pressed me to communicate the same to the *Royal Society*, who afterwards, by their kind encouragement and entreaties, engaged me to think of publishing them. But after I had begun to consider the inequalities of the lunar motions, and had entered upon some other things relating to the laws and measures of gravity, and other forces; and the figures that would be described by bodies attracted according to given laws; and the motion of several bodies moving among themselves; the motion of bodies in resisting mediums; the forces, densities, and motions, of mediums; the orbits of the comets, and such like; deferred that publication till I had made a search into those matters, and could put forth the whole together. What relates to the lunar motions (being imperfect), I have put all together in the corollaries of Prop. 66, to avoid being obliged to propose and distinctly demonstrate the several things there contained in a method more prolix than the subject deserved, and interrupt the series of the several propositions. Some things, found out after the rest, I chose to insert in places less suitable, rather than change the number of the propositions and the citations. I heartily beg that what I have here done may be read with candour; and that the defects in a subject so difficult be not so much reprehended as kindly supplied, and investigated by new endeavours of my readers.

Isaac Newton
Cambridge, Trinity College, May 8, 1686

Book III
The System of the World

In the preceding Books I have laid down the principles of philosophy, principles not philosophical, but mathematical: such; to wit, as we may build our reasonings upon in philosophical inquiries. These principles are the laws and conditions of certain motions, and powers or forces, which chiefly have respect to philosophy; but, lest they should have appeared of themselves dry and barren, I have illustrated them here and there with some philosophical scholiums, giving an account of such things as are of more general nature, and which philosophy seems chiefly to be founded on; such as the density and the resistance of bodies, spaces void of all bodies, and the motion of light and sounds. It remains that, from the same principles, I now demonstrate the frame of the System of the World. Upon this subject I had, indeed, composed the third Book in a popular method, that it might be read by many; but afterward, considering that such as had not sufficiently entered into the principles could not easily discern the strength of the consequences, nor lay aside the prejudices to which they had been many years accustomed, therefore, to prevent the disputes which might be raised upon such accounts, I chose to reduce the substance of this Book into the form of Propositions (in the mathematical way), which should be read by those only who had first made themselves masters of the principles established in the preceding Books: not that I would advise any one to the previous study of every Proposition of those Books; for they abound with such as might cost too much time, even to readers of good mathematical learning. It is enough if one carefully read the Definitions, the Laws of Motion, and the first three Sections of the first Book. He may then pass on to this Book, and consult such of the remaining Propositions of the first two Books, as the references in this, and his occasions, shall require.

Rules of Reasoning in Philosophy

Rule I.

We are to admit no more causes of natural things than such as are both true and sufficient to explain their appearances.

To this purpose the philosophers say that Nature does nothing in vain, and more is in vain when less will serve; for Nature is pleased with simplicity, and affects not the pomp of superfluous causes.

Rule II.

Therefore to the same natural effects we must, as far as possible, assign the same causes.

As to respiration in a man and in a beast; the descent of stones in *Europe* and in *America*; the light of our culinary fire and of the sun; the reflection of light in the earth, and in the planets.

Rule III.

The qualities of bodies, which admit neither intension nor remission of degrees, and which are found to belong to all bodies within the reach of our experiments, are to be esteemed the universal qualities of all bodies whatsoever.

For since the qualities of bodies are only known to us by experiments, we are to hold for universal all such as universally agree with experiments; and such as are not liable to diminution can never be quite taken away. We are certainly not to relinquish the evidence of experiments for the sake of dreams and vain fictions of our own devising; nor are we to recede from the analogy of Nature, which uses to be simple, and always consonant to itself. We no other way know the extension of bodies than by our senses, nor do these reach it in all bodies; but because we perceive extension in all that are sensible, therefore we ascribe it universally to all others also. That abundance of bodies are hard, we learn by experience; and because the hardness of the whole arises from the hardness of the parts, we therefore justly infer the hardness of the undivided particles not only of the bodies we feel but of all others. That all bodies are impenetrable, we gather not from reason, but from sensation. The bodies which we handle we find impenetrable, and thence conclude impenetrability to be an universal property of all bodies whatsoever. That all bodies are moveable, and endowed with certain powers (which we call the *vires inertiæ*) of persevering in their motion, or in their rest we only infer from the like properties observed in the bodies which we have seen. The extension, hardness, impenetrability, mobility, and *vis inertiæ* of the whole, result from the extension hardness, impenetrability, mobility, and *vires inertiæ* of the parts; and thence we conclude the least particles of all bodies to be also all extended, and hard and impenetrable, and moveable, and endowed with their proper *vires inertiæ*. And this is the foundation of all philosophy. Moreover, that the divided but contiguous particles of bodies may be separated from one another, is matter of observation; and, in the particles that remain undivided, our minds are able to distinguish yet lesser parts, as is mathematically demonstrated. But whether the parts so distinguished, and not yet divided, may, by the powers of Nature, be actually divided and separated from one another, we cannot certainly determine. Yet, had we the proof of but one experiment that any undivided particle, in breaking a hard and solid body, offered a division, we might by virtue of this rule conclude that the undivided as well as the divided particles may be divided and actually separated to infinity.

Lastly, if it universally appears, by experiments and astronomical observations, that all bodies about the earth gravitate towards the earth, and that in proportion to the quantity of matter which they severally contain, that the moon likewise, according to the quantity of its matter, gravitates towards the earth; that, on the other hand, our sea gravitates towards the moon; and all the planets mutually one towards another; and the comets in like manner towards the sun; we must, in consequence of this rule, universally allow that all bodies whatsoever are endowed with a principle of mutual gravitation. For the argument from the appearances concludes with more force for the universal gravitation of all bodies that for their impenetrability; of which, among those in the celestial regions, we have no experiments, nor any manner of observation. Not that I affirm gravity to be essential to bodies: by their *vis insita* I mean nothing but their *vis inertiæ*. This is immutable. Their gravity is diminished as they recede from the earth.

Rule IV.

In experimental philosophy we are to look upon propositions collected by general induction from phænomena as accurately or very nearly true, notwithstanding any contrary hypotheses that may be imagined, till such time as other phænomena occur, by which they may either be made more accurate, or liable to exceptions.

This rule we must follow, that the argument of induction may not be evaded by hypotheses.

John Locke

1632–1704

The son of an attorney and middle-class landowner in the district of
Somerset near Bristol, John Locke was raised in the religious and cultural
milieu of seventeenth-century Puritanism. When he was fourteen, his father
sent him to the Westminster School, where he studied for six years before
entering Christ Church, Oxford, graduating with a B.A. in 1656. His religious
liberalism led him away from a future in the Church and instead he indulged
an interest in the physical sciences and medicine; he lectured at the college in
Greek and rhetoric until 1665. In 1683, he left England as a political exile,
returning in 1689 following the Glorious Revolution and the accession of
William and Mary to the throne.

With the publication of *Two Treatises of Government* and *Essay
Concerning Human Understanding* in 1690, Locke's reputation as one of the
Enlightenment's greatest thinkers was secured. In his *Two Treatises*, Locke
argues that, in order for government to be just and adequate to the human
condition, we must reject divine-right monarchy and look instead to natural
rights and social contract theory. Locke argues, in agreement with the position
outlined in Hobbes's *Leviathan* (1651), that the need for a social contract
emerges as a response to the dangers posed by human passions and material
desires. However, Locke diverges from Hobbes's darkly pessimistic view of
humankind, stressing instead basic human goodness, the establishment of
rational limits for government, and the possibility of dissolving governments
that have descended into tyranny. In these ways, particularly, Locke's political
theories resonated deeply with the colonial American revolutionaries of the
eighteenth century and, in 1776, Thomas Jefferson employed Lockean rhetoric when it came time to draft the Declaration of Independence.

In reading the selection which follows, consider that for Locke the state
of nature confers liberty and equality upon all human beings, but that he
describes the condition of slavery to be one of war, in which both freedom and
equality no longer apply. It is also worth considering that Locke's conception
of political society is guided by "consent of the majority." What dangers inhere
in government by majority rule? What responsibilities lie with the individual
in Locke's political model? In what ways are the analogies Locke draws
between political and "paternal" power problematic or inadequate?

from *Two Treatises of Government* (1690)

Chapter II
Of the State of Nature

• • •

6. But though this be a *State of Liberty*, yet it is *not a State of Licence*, though Man in that State have an uncontroleable Liberty, to dispose of his Person or Possessions, yet he has not Liberty to destroy himself, or so much as any Creature in his Possession, but where some nobler use, than its bare Preservation calls for it. The *State of Nature* has a Law of Nature to govern it, which obliges every one: And Reason, which is that Law, teaches all Mankind, who will but consult it, that being all equal and independent, no one ought to harm another in his Life, Health, Liberty, or Possessions. For Men being all the Workmanship of one Omnipotent, and infinitely wise Maker; All the Servants of one Sovereign Master, sent into the World by his order and about his business, they are his Property, whose Workmanship they are, made to last during his, not one anothers Pleasure. And being furnished with like Faculties, sharing all in one Community of Nature, there cannot be supposed any such *Subordination* among us, that may Authorize us to destroy one another, as if we were made for one anothers uses, as the inferior ranks of Creatures are for ours. Every one as he is *bound to preserve himself*, and not to quit his Station wilfully; so by the like reason when his own Preservation comes not in competition, ought he, as much as he can, *to preserve the rest of Mankind*, and may not unless it be to do Justice on an Offender, take away, or impair the life, or what tends to the Preservation of the Life, the Liberty, Health, Limb or Goods of another.

7. And that all Men may be restrained from invading others Rights, and from doing hurt to one another, and the Law of Nature be observed, which willeth the Peace and *Preservation of all Mankind*, the *Execution* of the Law of Nature is in that State, put into every Mans hands, whereby every one has a right to punish the transgressors of that Law to such a Degree, as may hinder its Violation. For the *Law of Nature* would, as all other Laws that concern Men in this World, be in vain, if there were no body that in the State of Nature, had a *Power to Execute* that Law, and thereby preserve the innocent and restrain offenders, and if any one in the State of Nature may punish another, for any evil he has done, every one may do so. For in that *State of perfect Equality*, where naturally

27

there is no superiority or jurisdiction of one, over another, what any may do in Prosecution of that Law, every one must needs have a Right to do.

8. And thus in the State of Nature, *one Man comes by a Power over another*; but yet no Absolute or Arbitrary Power, to use a Criminal when he has got him in his hands, according to the passionate heats, or boundless extravagancy of his own Will, but only to retribute to him, so far as calm reason and conscience dictates, what is proportionate to his Transgression, which is so much as may serve for *Reparation* and *Restraint*. For these two are the only reasons, why one Man may lawfully do harm to another, which is that we call *punishment*. In transgressing the Law of Nature, the Offender declares himself to live by another Rule, than that of *reason* and common Equity, which is that measure God has set to the actions of Men, for their mutual security: and so he becomes dangerous to Mankind, the tye, which is to secure them from injury and violence, being slighted and broken by him. Which being a trespass against the whole Species, and the Peace and Safety of it, provided for by the Law of Nature, every man upon this score, by the Right he hath to preserve Mankind in general, may restrain, or where it is necessary, destroy things noxious to them, and so may bring such evil on any one, who hath transgressed that Law, as may make him repent the doing of it, and thereby deter him, and by his Example others, from doing the like mischief. And in this case, and upon this ground, every *Man hath a Right to punish the Offender, and be Executioner of the Law of Nature.*

• • •

Chapter IV
Of Slavery

22. The *Natural Liberty of Man* is to be free from any Superior Power on Earth, and not to be under the Will or Legislative Authority of Man, but to have only the Law of Nature for his Rule. The *Liberty of Man, in Society*, is to be under no other Legislative Power, but that established, by consent, in the Common-wealth, nor under the Dominion of any Will, or Restraint of any Law, but what that Legislative shall enact, according to the Trust put in it. . . .

23. This *Freedom* from Absolute, Arbitrary Power, is so necessary to, and closely joyned with a Man's Preservation, that he cannot part with it, but by what forfeits his Preservation and Life together. For a Man, not having the Power of his own Life, *cannot*, by Compact, or his own Consent, *enslave himself* to any one, nor put himself under the Absolute, Arbitrary Power of another, to take away his Life, when he pleases. No body can give more Power than he has himself; and he that cannot take away his own Life, cannot give another power over it. Indeed having, by his fault, forfeited his own Life, by some

Act that deserves Death; he, to whom he has forfeited it, may (when he has him in his Power) delay to take it, and make use of him to his own Service, and he does him no injury by it. For, whenever he finds the hardship of his Slavery out-weigh the value of his Life, 'tis in his Power, by resisting the Will of his Master, to draw on himself the Death he desires.

24. This is the perfect condition of *Slavery*, which *is* nothing else, but *the State of War continued, between a lawful Conqueror, and a Captive*. For, if once *Compact* enter between them, and make an agreement for a limited Power on the one side, and Obedience on the other, the State of War and *Slavery* ceases, as long as the Compact endures. For, as has been said, no Man can, by agreement, pass over to another that which he hath not in himself, a Power over his own Life.

• • •

Chapter VI
Of Paternal Power

54. Though I have said above, Chap. II, *That all Men by Nature are equal*, I cannot be supposed to understand all sorts of *Equality: Age* or *Virtue* may give Men a just Precedency: *Excellency of Parts and Merit* may place others above the Common Level: *Birth* may subject some, and *Alliance* or *Benefits* others, to pay an Observance to those to whom Nature, Gratitude or other Respects may have made it due; and yet all this consists with the *Equality*, which all Men are in, in respect of Jurisdiction or Dominion one over another, which was the *Equality* I there spoke of, as proper to the Business in hand, being that *equal Right* that every Man hath, *to his Natural Freedom*, without being subjected to the Will or Authority of any other Man.

55. *Children*, I confess are not born in this full state of *Equality*, though they are born to it. Their Parents have a sort of Rule and Jurisdiction over them when they come into the World, and for some time after, but 'tis but a temporary one. The Bonds of this Subjection are like the Swadling Cloths they are wrapt up in, and supported by, in the weakness of their Infancy. Age and Reason as they grow up, loosen them till at length they drop quite off, and leave a Man at his own free Disposal.

• • •

63. The *Freedom* then of Man and Liberty of acting according to his own Will, is *grounded on* his having *Reason*, which is able to instruct him in that Law he is to govern himself by, and make him know how far he is left to the freedom of his own will. To turn him loose to an unrestrain'd Liberty, before he has Reason to guide him, is not the allowing him the privilege of his Nature,

to be free; but to thrust him out amongst Brutes, and abandon him to a state as wretched, and as much beneath that of a Man, as theirs. This is that which puts the *Authority* into the *Parents* hands to govern the *Minority* of their Children. God hath made it their business to imploy this Care on their Off-spring, and hath placed in them suitable Inclinations of Tenderness and Concern to temper this power, to apply it as his Wisdom designed it, to the Childrens good, as long as they should need to be under it.

64. But what reason can hence advance this Care of the *Parents* due to their Off-spring into an *Absolute Arbitrary Dominion* of the Father, whose power reaches no farther, than by such a Discipline as he finds most effectual to give such strength and health to their Bodies, such vigour and rectitude to their Minds, as may best fit his Children to be most useful to themselves and others; and, if it be necessary to his Condition, to make them work when they are able for their own Subsistence. But in this power the *Mother* too has her share with the *Father*.

65. Nay, this *power* so little belongs to the *Father* by any peculiar right of Nature, but only as he is Guardian of his Children, that when he quits his Care of them, he loses his power over them, which goes along with their Nourishment and Education, to which it is inseparably annexed, and it belongs as much to the *Foster-Father* of an exposed Child, as to the Natural Father of another: So little power does the bare *act of begetting* give a Man over his Issue, if all his Care ends there, and this be all the Title he hath to the Name and Authority of a Father. And what will become of this *Paternal Power* in that part of the World where one Woman hath more than one Husband at a time? Or in those parts of *America* where when the Husband and Wife part, which happens frequently, the Children are all left to the Mother, follow her, and are wholly under her Care and Provision? If the Father die whilst the Children are young, do they not naturally every where owe the same Obedience to their *Mother*, during their Minority, as to their Father were he alive? And will any one say, that the *Mother* hath a Legislative Power over her Children? that she can make standing Rules, which shall be of perpetual Obligation, by which they ought to regulate all the Concerns of their Property, and bound their Liberty all the course of their Lives? Or can she inforce the observation of them with Capital Punishments? For this is the proper *power of the Magistrate*, of which the Father hath not so much as the shadow. His Command over his Children is but temporary, and reaches not their Life or Property. It is but a help to the weakness and imperfection of their Nonage, a Discipline necessary to their Education: And though a *Father* may dispose of his own Possessions as he pleases, when his Children are out of danger of perishing for want, yet *his power* extends not to the Lives or Goods, which either their own industry, or anothers bounty has made theirs; nor to their Liberty neither, when they are

once arrived to the infranchisement of the years of discretion. The *Father's Empire* then ceases, and he can from thence forwards no more dispose of the liberty of his Son, than that of any other Man: And it must be far from an absolute or perpetual Jurisdiction, from which a Man may withdraw himself, having Licence from Divine Authority to *leave Father and Mother and cleave to his Wife.*

• • •

Chapter VII
Of Political and Civil Society

77. God having made Man such a Creature, that, in his own Judgment, it was not good for him to be alone, put him under strong Obligations of Necessity, Convenience, and Inclination to drive him into *Society*, as well as fitted him with Understanding and Language to continue and enjoy it. The *first Society* was between Man and Wife, which gave beginning to that between Parents and Children; to which, in time, that between Master and Servant came to be added: And though all these might, and commonly did meet together, and make up but one Family, wherein the Master or Mistress of it had some sort of Rule proper to a Family; each of these, or all together came short of *Political Society*, as we shall see, if we consider the different Ends, Tyes, and Bounds of each of these.

78. *Conjugal Society* is made by a voluntary Compact between Man and Woman: and tho' it consist chiefly in such a Communion and Right in one anothers Bodies, as is necessary to its chief End, Procreation; yet it draws with it mutual Support, and Assistance, and a Communion of Interest too, as necessary not only to unite their Care and Affection, but also necessary to their common Off-spring, who have a Right to be nourished and maintained by them, till they are able to provide for themselves.

79. For the end of *conjunction between Male and Female*, being not barely Procreation, but the continuation of the Species, this conjunction betwixt Male and Female ought to last, even after Procreation, so long as is necessary to the nourishment and support of the young Ones, who are to be sustained by those that got them, till they are able to shift and provide for themselves. This Rule, which the infinite wise Maker hath set to the Works of his hands, we find the inferiour Creatures steadily obey. In those vivaparous Animals which feed on Grass, the *conjunction between Male and Female* lasts no longer than the very Act of Copulation: because the Teat of the Dam being sufficient to nourish the Young, till it be able to feed on Grass, the Male only begets, but concerns not himself for the Female or Young, to whose Sustenance he can contribute nothing. But in Beasts of Prey the *conjunction* lasts longer: because the Dam not

being able well to subsist her self, and nourish her numerous Off-spring by her own Prey alone, a more laborious, as well as more dangerous way of living, than by feeding on Grass, the Assistance of the Male is necessary to the Maintenance of their common Family, which cannot subsist till they are able to prey for themselves, but by the joynt Care of Male and Female. The same is to be observed in all Birds (except some domestick ones, where plenty of food excuses the Cock from feeding, and taking care of the young Brood) whose Young needing Food in the Nest, the Cock and Hen continue Mates, till the Young are able to use their wing, and provide for themselves.

80. And herein I think lies the chief, if not the only reason, *why the Male and Female in Mankind are tyed to a longer conjunction* than other Creatures, *viz.* Because the Female is capable of conceiving, and *de facto* is commonly with Child again, and Brings forth too a new Birth long before the former is out of a dependency for support on his Parents help, and able to shift for himself, and has all the assistance is due to him from his Parents: whereby the Father, who is bound to take care for those he hath begot, is under an Obligation to continue in Conjugal Society with the same Woman longer than other Creatures, whose Young being able to subsist of themselves, before the time of Procreation returns again, the Conjugal Bond dissolves of it self, and they are at liberty, till *Hymen,*[1] at his usual Anniversary Season, summons them again to chuse new Mates. Wherein one cannot but admire the Wisdom of the great Creatour, who having given to Man foresight and an Ability to lay up for the future, as well as to supply the present necessity, hath made it necessary, that *Society of Man and Wife should be more lasting,* than of Male and Female amongst other Creatures; that so their Industry might be encouraged, and their Interest better united, to make Provision, and lay up Goods for their common Issue, which uncertain mixture, or easie and frequent Solutions of Conjugal Society would mightily disturb.

81. But though these are Ties upon *Mankind,* which make the *Conjugal Bonds* more firm and lasting in Man, than the other Species of Animals; yet it would give one reason to enquire, why this *Compact,* where Procreation and Education are secured, and Inheritance taken care for, may not be made determinable, either by consent, or at a certain time, or upon certain Conditions, as well as any other voluntary Compacts, there being no necessity in the nature of the thing, nor to the ends of it, that it should always be for Life; I mean, to such as are under no Restraint of any positive Law, which ordains all such Contracts to be perpetual.

82. But the Husband and Wife, though they have but one common Concern, yet having different understandings, will unavoidably sometimes have different wills too; it therefore being necessary, that the last Determination, *i.e.* the Rule, should be placed somewhere, it naturally falls to

the Man's share, as the abler and the stronger. But this reaching but to the things of their common Interest and Property, leaves the Wife in the full and free possession of what by Contract is her peculiar Right, and gives the Husband no more power over her Life, than she has over his. The *Power of the Husband* being so far from that of an absolute Monarch, that the *Wife* has, in many cases, a Liberty to *separate* from him; where natural Right, of their Contract allows it, whether that Contract be made by themselves in the state of Nature, or by the Customs or Laws of the Countrey they live in; and the Children upon such Separation fall to the Father or Mother's Lot, as such Contract does determine.

83. For all the ends of *Marriage* being to be obtained under Politick Government, as well as in the state of Nature, the Civil Magistrate doth not abridge the Right, or Power of either naturally necessary to those ends, *viz.* Procreation and mutual Support and Assistance whilst they are together; but only decides any Controversie that may arise between Man and Wife about them. If it were otherwise, and that absolute *Sovereignty* and Power of Life and Death naturally belong'd to the Husband, and were *necessary to the Society between Man and Wife*, there could be no Matrimony in any of those Countries where the Husband is allowed no such absolute Authority. But the ends of Matrimony requiring no such Power in the Husband, the Condition of *Conjugal Society* put it not in him, it being not at all necessary to that state. *Conjugal Society* could subsist and obtain its ends without it; nay, Community of Goods, and the Power over them, mutual Assistance, and Maintenance, and other things belonging to *Conjugal Society*, might be varied and regulated by that Contract, which unites Man and Wife in that Society, as far as may consist with Procreation and the bringing up of Children till they could shift for themselves; nothing being necessary to any Society, that is not necessary to the ends for which it is made.

•　　•　　•

Chapter VIII
Of the Beginning of Political Societies

96. For when any number of Men have, by the consent of every individual, made a *Community*, they have thereby made that *Community* one Body, with a Power to Act as one Body, which is only by the will and determination of the *majority*. For that which acts any Community, being only the consent of the individuals of it, and it being necessary to that which is one body to move one way; it is necessary the Body should move that way whither the greater force carries it, which is the *consent of the majority*: or else it is impossible it should act or continue one Body, *one Community*, which the consent of

every individual that united into it, agreed that it should; and so every one is bound by that consent to be concluded by the *majority*. And therefore we see that in Assemblies impowered to act by positive Laws where no number is set by that positive Law which impowers them, the *act of the Majority* passes for the act of the whole, and of course determines, as having by the Law of Nature and Reason, the power of the whole.

97. And thus every Man, by consenting with others to make one Body Politick under one Government, puts himself under an Obligation to every one of that Society, to submit to the determination of the *majority*, and to be concluded by it; or else this *original Compact*, whereby he with others incorporates into *one Society*, would signifie nothing, and be no Compact, if he be left free, and under no other ties, than he was in before in the State of Nature. For what appearance would there be of any Compact? What new Engagement if he were no farther tied by any Decrees of the Society, than he himself thought fit, and did actually consent to? This would be still as great a liberty, as he himself had before his Compact, or any one else in the State of Nature hath, who may submit himself and consent to any acts of it if he thinks fit.

98. For if *the consent of the majority* shall not in reason, be received, as *the act of the whole*, and conclude every individual; nothing but the consent of every individual can make any thing to be the act of the whole: But such a consent is next impossible ever to be had, if we consider the Infirmities of Health, and Avocations of Business, which in a number, though much less than that of a Common-wealth, will necessarily keep many away from the publick Assembly. To which if we add the variety of Opinions, and contrariety of Interests, which unavoidably happen in all Collections of Men, the coming into Society upon such terms, would be only like *Cato's*[2] coming into the Theatre, only to go out again. Such a Constitution as this would make the mighty *Leviathan*[3] of a shorter duration, than the feeblest Creatures; and not let it outlast the day it was born in: which cannot be suppos'd, till we can think, that Rational Creatures should desire and constitute Societies only to be dissolved. For where the *majority* cannot conclude the rest, there they cannot act as one Body, and consequently will be immediately dissolved again.

99. Whosoever therefore out of a state of Nature unite into a *Community*, must be understood to give up all the power, necessary to the ends for which they unite into Society, to the *majority* of the Community, unless they expressly agreed in any number greater than the majority. And this is done by barely agreeing to *unite into one Political Society*, which is *all the Compact* that is, or needs be, between the Individuals, that enter into, or make up a *Commonwealth*. And thus that, which begins and actually *constitutes any Political Society*, is nothing but the consent of any number of Freemen capable of a majority to unite and incorporate into such a Society. And this is that, and that

only, which did, or could give *beginning* to any *lawful Government* in the World.

• • •

Chapter XI
Of the Extent of the Legislative Power

134. The great end of Mens entring into Society, being the enjoyment of their Properties in Peace and Safety, and the great instrument and means of that being the Laws establish'd in that Society; the *first and fundamental positive Law* of all Common-wealths, *is the establishing of the Legislative* Power; as the *first and fundamental natural Law*, which is to govern even the Legislative it self, is *the preservation of the Society*, and (as far as will consist with the pub- ˙ lick good) of every person in it. This *Legislative* is not only the *supream power* of the Common-wealth, but sacred and unalterable in the hands where the Community have once placed it; nor can any Edict of any Body else, in what Form soever conceived, or by what Power soever backed, have the force and obligation of a *Law*, which has not its *Sanction from* that *Legislative*, which the publick has chosen and appointed. For without this the Law could not have that, which is absolutely necessary to its being a Law, *the consent of the Society*, over whom no Body can have a power to make Laws, but by their own consent, and by Authority received from them; and therefore all the *Obedience*, which by the most solemn Ties any one can be obliged to pay, ultimately terminates in this *Supream Power*, and is directed by those Laws which it enacts: nor can any Oaths to any Foreign Power whatsoever, or any Domestick Subordinate Power, discharge any Member of the Society from his *Obedience to the Legislative*, acting pursuant to their trust, nor oblige him to any Obedience contrary to the Laws so enacted, or farther than they do allow; it being ridiculous to imagine one can be tied ultimately to *obey* any *Power* in the Society, which is not the *Supream*.

Chapter XIX
Of the Dissolution of Governments

222. The Reason why Men enter into Society, is the preservation of their Property; and the end why they chuse and authorize a Legislative, is, that there may be Laws made, and Rules set as Guards and Fences to the Properties of all the Members of the Society, to limit the Power, and moderate the Dominion of every Part and Member of the Society. For since it can never be supposed to be the Will of the Society, that the Legislative should have a Power to destroy that, which every one designs to secure, by entering into Society, and for which

the People submitted themselves to Legislators of their own making; whenever the *Legislators endeavour to take away, and destroy the Property of the People,* or to reduce them to Slavery under Arbitrary Power, they put themselves into a state of War with the People, who are thereupon absolved from any farther Obedience, and are left to the common Refuge, which God hath provided for all Men, against Force and Violence. Whensoever therefore the *Legislative* shall transgress this fundamental Rule of Society; and either by Ambition, Fear, Folly or Corruption, *endeavour to grasp* themselves, *or put into the hands of any other an Absolute Power* over the Lives, Liberties, and Estates of the People; By this breach of Trust they *forfeit the Power,* the People had put into their hands, for quite contrary ends, and it devolves to the People, who have a Right to resume their original Liberty, and, by the Establishment of a new Legislative (such as they shall think fit) provide for their own Safety and Security, which is the end for which they are in Society.

Notes

[1] Greek god of marriage.

[2] Roman statesman, also called Cato the Elder (234–149 B.C.).

[3] Thomas Hobbes's term for the commonwealth (Leviathan, 1651).

Emperor K'ang-hsi (Kangxi)

Reign: 1661–1722

K'ang-hsi was Manchurian and the second of the Qing emperors. Though the Qing regime was initially intolerant of traditional Chinese beliefs and practices, K'ang-hsi gradually blended Manchu and Chinese cultural forms, helping achieve a necessary stability in ethnic relations. His policies and those of his immediate successors made the eighteenth century in China one of the most glorious in terms of the extent of empire, agricultural productivity, and literary and artistic achievement. Indeed, K'ang-hsi was a patron of knowledge who contributed to this cultural flourish. Like some of his counterparts in Europe, K'ang-hsi sponsored the compilation of impressive tomes, including a 5,000 volume dictionary and a 36,000 volume anthology of literary works. K'ang-hsi himself was a prolific writer, though his collected writings were not published in English until 1974 when the historian Jonathan Spence assembled them to present a self-portrait of K'ang-hsi.

In Spence's *Emperor of China*, K'ang-hsi expounds upon governance above all else, though for him this was an expansive process entailing reflection on family matters, religion, nature, and even diet. In his self-presentation, he is certainly the model emperor, possessing the Confucian qualities of balance, uprightness, benevolence, and harmony, fit for a ruler exercising the mandate of heaven from his celestial throne, and believed to be the head of the entire human race. Such power required occasional cruelty, but also impeccable personal virtue and a fatherly love for his people. These ideals, while distinctively Chinese, also appealed to some Europeans. Indeed, his grandson, Qianlong, was seen by Enlightenment thinkers like Voltaire as the perfect philosopher-king.

In these selections, K'ang-hsi offers his answers to timeless human questions: the source of knowledge, filial duty, religious toleration, and cultural relativism. How do K'ang-hsi's ideas relate to the intellectual and cultural ferment in Europe known as the Scientific Revolution and the Enlightenment? How are they distinctly Chinese? In what ways was European presence in China already a threat to its autonomy?

from *Self Portrait of K'ang-hsi*
(Early Eighteenth Century)

Too many people claim to know things when, in fact, they know nothing about them. Since my childhood I have always tried to find things out for myself and not to pretend to have knowledge when I was ignorant. Whenever I met older people I would ask them about the experiences they had had, and remember what they said. Keep an open mind, and you'll learn things; you will miss other people's good qualities if you just concentrate on your own abilities. It's my nature to enjoy asking questions, and the crudest or simplest people have something of value to say, something one can check through to the source and remember.

• • •

If you want to really know something you have to observe or experience it in person; if you claim to know something on the basis of hearsay, or on happening to see it in a book, you'll be a laughingstock to those who really know.

• • •

Sometimes an exact answer is hard to find, as with the morning and evening tides. Whenever I was on the seashore—whether in Shan-hai-kuan, or Tientsin, or near the mouth of the Yangtze River—I would observe when the tides rose and fell. But when I would question the locals they generally all gave different answers, and the records of the times kept in different places were also different. Later I found that even water in springs and wells fluctuates slightly in level, though again one can't be precise about the time. I questioned Westerners and ocean sailors; they all disagreed. Clearly Chu Hsi was right that there is a relationship between tides and the moon's waxing and waning, but it's hard to get clearer than that.

So we draw our idea of "principle" from experience rather than from study, though we need to keep aware of both. Many people, after all, call old porcelain vessels "antiques"; but if we think of vessels from the view of principle, then we know that once they were meant to be used. Only now are they grubby-looking and unsuitable for us to drink from, so we end up putting them on our desks or on bookshelves, and look at them once in a while. On the other hand, we can change the function of a given object and thus change its nature, as I did by converting a rustless sword that the Dutch once gave me into a measuring stick that I kept on my desk. As the Jesuit Antoine Thomas observed, this was converting something that gave fear into something that gave pleasure. The rare can become common, as with the lions and other animals that foreign ambassadors like to give us and my children are now accustomed to; though when something new appears, I always take a close look at it, as with the sea lion that the Korean king gave me once on a Northern Tour. I immediately sent riders back to Peking for a copy of the book in which the Westerners said this creature could be identified.

Western skills are a case in point: in the late Ming Dynasty,[1] when the Westerners first brought the gnomon,[2] the Chinese thought it a rare treasure until they understood its use. And when the Emperor Shun-chih got a small chiming clock in 1653, he kept it always near him; but now we have learned to balance the springs and to adjust the chimes and finally to make the whole clock, so that my children can have ten chiming clocks each to play with, if they want them. Similarly, we learned in a short time to make glassware that is superior to that made in the West, and our lacquer would be better than theirs, too, were it not that their wet sea climate gives a better sheen than the dry and dusty Chinese climate ever could.

•　•　•

I told Chang Ying once, on a Southern Tour, that there is no need to visit a temple again if you've already been there several times, and I myself like to go to different shrines, whether to the temples in the South, to Wu-t'ai-shan (where I wrote a eulogy in Manchu and had it carved on stone), or to the top of Mount T'ai (where Confucius once stood and surveyed the world below). On that journey, in 1684, I refused my retainers' requests that we visit the precipices where people sometimes killed themselves, hoping that by offering up their own lives they might save those of their dying parents. I refused to condone such acts by visiting the place where they occurred; for even if the suicide was committed in the name of filial piety, by killing himself the victim cut off forever all chances of helping his parents. Instead, I proceeded to Confucius' home at Ch'ü-fu, made the ritual prostrations and offerings, heard the ritual music, and listened to the ritual lectures on the *Great Learning* and the *Book of Changes*. Then I told Confucius' descendant, the Yen-sheng duke, K'ung Yü-ch'i, and his clansman K'ung Shang-jen to show me around.

•　•　•

The temple grounds were so extensive: where was the Sage's own dwelling? Behind the hall where I heard the lectures were the Lu wall ruins, where Confucius had his home. So I leaned over the railings of Confucius' well and, admiring, drew some water and tasted it. I asked about the ruins, and they said it was in this wall that the ninth-generation descendant of Confucius hid the *Classics* when the Emperor Ch'in Shih-huang burned the books. They were rediscovered when Emperor Han Ching-ti's fifth son started to pull down the buildings to make way for his own palace [*c.* A.D. 150]. I had them point out the actual places, and looked them over carefully.

Trees and grasses grew on Confucius' tomb, and I faced north and kowtowed before it, offering three libations from the golden bowl of wine that Mingju held. "What are those trees and grasses growing on the tomb? What are the *k'ai* trees used for? Isn't there any *chih* grass? Bring me some to look at. If fifty blades are growing in one clump of *chih* grass, the divinations you make with it will be fulfilled. Is there any of that kind here or not?" Not at present, they said, but some would surely grow in honor of the Emperor's visit. So I had them hunt for what there was, and when they found some I took a double handful and inhaled its strange fragrance.

• • •

I realized, too, that Western mathematics has its uses. I first grew interested in this subject shortly after I came to the throne, during the confrontations between the Jesuit Adam Schall and his Chinese critic, Yang Kuang-hsien, when the two men argued the merits of their respective techniques by the Wu-men Gate and none of the great officials there knew what was going on. Schall died in prison, but after I had learned something about astronomy I pardoned his friend Verbiest in 1669 and gave him an official position, promoting him in 1682. In 1687 I let the newly arrived Jesuit Fontaney and the others come to Peking, although they had come to China illegally on a Chinese merchant vessel and the Board of Rites had recommended their deportation; and throughout the 1680s I discussed Western skills in Manchu with Verbiest, and I made Grimaldi and Pereira learn the language as well, so they could converse with me.

• • •

But I was careful not to refer to these Westerners as "Great Officials," and corrected Governor Liu Yin-shu when he referred to the Jesuits Régis and Fridelli—whom I had dispatched to make a geographical survey of his province—as if they were honored imperial commissioners. For even though some of the Western methods are different from our own, and may even be an improvement, there is little about them that is new. The principles of mathematics all derive from the *Book of Changes*, and the Western methods are Chinese in origin: this algebra—"A-erh-chu-pa-erh"—springs from an Eastern word. And though it was indeed the Westerners who showed us something our ancient calendar experts did not know—namely how to calculate the angles of the northern pole—this but shows the truth of what Chu Hsi arrived at through his investigation of things: the earth is like the yolk within an egg. The Westerners seem to have principles found in the *Book of Changes*, echoing that book with four axes and four points; and they have magic squares like those in the *Ho-t'u lo-shu*, a sequence of the numbers one, three, nine, seven moving around from the left, and the number five stationary in the center, representing the sum of three for heaven and two for earth—the harmony of mankind.

4	9	2
3	5	7
8	1	6

I did praise their work, saying "the 'new methods' of calculating make basic errors impossible" and "the general principles of Western calendrical science are without error." But I added that they still cannot prevent small errors from occurring, and that over the decades these small errors mount up.

After all, they know only a fraction of what I know, and none of the Westerners is really conversant with Chinese literature—except perhaps for the Jesuit Bouvet, who has read a great deal, and developed the ability to undertake serious study of the *Book of Changes*. Often one can't keep from smiling when they start off on a discussion. How can they presume to talk about "the great principles of China"? Sometimes they act wrongly because they are not used to our ways, sometimes they are misled by ignorant Chinese fellows—the papal legate de Tournon used wrongly elevated characters on his memorials, employed improper phrases, implied that the word "emperor" [*huang*] was also used among his own people, wrote his memorials on paper decorated with five-clawed dragons, and so on.

●   ●   ●

On the question of the Chinese Rites that might be practiced by the Western missionaries, de Tournon would not speak, though I sent messages to him repeatedly. I had agreed with the formulation the Peking fathers had drawn up in 1700: that Confucius was honored by the Chinese as a master, but his name was not invoked in prayer for the purpose of gaining happiness, rank, or wealth; that worship of ancestors was an expression of love and filial remembrance, not intended to bring protection to the worshiper; and that there was no idea, when an ancestral tablet was erected, that the soul of the ancestor dwelt in that tablet. And when sacrifices were offered to Heaven it was not the blue existent sky that was addressed, but the lord and creator of all things. If the ruler Shang-ti was sometimes called Heaven, *T'ien*, that had no more significance than giving honorific names to the emperor.

If de Tournon didn't reply, the Catholic Bishop Maigrot did, coming to Jehol and telling me that Heaven is a material thing and should not be worshiped, and that one should invoke only the name "Lord of Heaven" to show the proper reverence. Maigrot wasn't merely ignorant of Chinese literature, he couldn't even recognize the simplest Chinese characters; yet he chose to discuss the falsity of the Chinese moral system. Sometimes, as I pointed out, the emperor is addressed honorifically as "under the steps of the throne"; would Maigrot say this was reverence to a set of steps made by some artisan? I am addressed as "Wan-sui, Ten Thousand Years"; obviously that too is not literal—since from the beginnings of history to the present day only 7,600 years have passed. Even little animals mourn their dead mothers for many days; these Westerners who want to treat their dead with indifference are not even equal to animals. How could they be compared with Chinese? We venerate Confucius because of his doctrines of respect for virtue, his system of education, his inculcation of love for superiors and ancestors. Westerners venerate their own saints because of their actions. They paint pictures of men with wings and say, "These represent heavenly spirits, swift as if they had wings, though in reality there are no men with wings." I do not find it appropriate to dispute this doctrine, yet with superficial knowledge Maigrot discussed Chinese sanctity. He talked for days, with his perverse reason, his poorly concealed anger, and fled the country when he could not get his way, a sinner against the Catholic teaching and a rebel to China. As my son Yin-jeng said to Bouvet on another occasion, "If Buddha and other idols are shown in clothes does that prevent you from wearing clothes? They have temples, yet you build them also to your god. One doesn't blame your attachment to your religion, but one does blame—and rightly—your obstinacy on matters of which you know nothing."

Every country must have spirits that it reveres. This is true for our dynasty, as for Mongols of Mohammedans, Miao or Lolo, or other foreigners. Just as everyone fears something, some snakes but not toads, some toads but not snakes; and as all countries have different pronunciations and different alphabets. But in this Catholic religion, the Society of Peter quarrels with the Jesuits, Bouvet quarrels with Mariani, and among the Jesuits the Portuguese want only their own nationals in their church while the French want only French in theirs. This violates the principles of religion. Such dissension cannot be inspired by the Lord of Heaven but by the Devil, who, I have heard the Westerners say, leads men to do evil since he can't do otherwise.

Notes

[1] 1368–1644.

[2] Pin on a sundial that casts a shadow indicating the time of day.

David Hume

1711–1776

Considered the leading figure of the Scottish Enlightenment, David Hume was an accomplished philosopher, historian, economist, and essayist. Unlike Locke, whose ideas influenced or inspired many of his inquiries, Hume was a secular humanist, an avowed atheist, and a professional academic whose heterodoxy cost him chairs of philosophy at both the University of Edinburgh (Scotland) and the University of Glasgow (Scotland). Hume was, by all accounts, a "man of the Enlightenment" whose theories concerning human perception and understanding enjoyed wide acceptance among the European and British American elite. Thomas Jefferson was said to have been particularly fond of Hume.

Hume wrote *A Treatise of Human Nature* in 1739–1740 while in France. Though he later repudiated it as "juvenile," it is nonetheless an excellent representation of his philosophical skepticism and empirical method, as he sought to formulate a more complete system for explaining, what we would later call, cognition. How are his conclusions more fully developed than those of Locke, and what do they tell us about the maturation or development of Enlightenment thought during the mid-eighteenth century?

from *A Treatise of Human Nature* (1739–1740)

• • •

'Tis evident, that all the sciences have a relation, greater or less, to human nature; and that however wide any of them may seem to run from it, they still return back by one passage or another. Even *Mathematics, Natural Philosophy, and Natural Religion,* are in some measure dependent on the science of Man; since they lie under the cognizance of men, and are judged of by their powers and faculties. 'Tis impossible to tell what changes and improvements we might make in these sciences were we thoroughly acquainted with the extent and force of human understanding, and cou'd explain the nature of the ideas we employ, and of the operations we perform in our reasonings. And these improvements are the more to be hoped for in natural religion, as it is not content with instructing us in the nature of superior powers, but carries its views farther, to their disposition towards us, and our duties towards them; and consequently we ourselves are not only the beings, that reason, but also one of the objects, concerning which we reason.

If therefore the sciences of Mathematics, Natural Philosophy, and Natural Religion, have such a dependence on the knowledge of man, what may be expected in the other sciences, whose connexion with human nature is more close and intimate? The sole end of logic is to explain the principles and operations of our reasoning faculty, and the nature of our ideas: morals and criticism regard our tastes and sentiments: and politics consider men as united in society, and dependent on each other. In these four sciences of *Logic, Morals, Criticism and Politics,* is comprehended almost every thing, which it can any way import us to be acquainted with, or which can tend either to the improvement or ornament of the human mind.

Here then is the only expedient, from which we can hope for success in our philosophical researches, to leave the tedious lingering method, which we have hitherto followed, and instead of taking now and then a castle or village on the frontier, to march up directly to the capital or center of these sciences, to human nature itself; which being once masters of, we may every where else hope for an easy victory. From this station we may extend our conquests over all those sciences, which more intimately concern human life, and may afterwards proceed at leisure to discover more fully those, which are the objects of pure curiosity. There is no question of importance, whose decision is not compriz'd in the science of man; and there is none, which can be decided with any certainty, before we become acquainted with that science. In pretending there-

44

fore to explain the principles of human nature, we in effect propose a compleat system of the sciences built on a foundation almost entirely new, and the only one upon which they can stand with any security. . . .

Of the Origin of Our Ideas

All the perceptions of the human mind resolve themselves into two distinct kinds, which I shall call IMPRESSIONS and IDEAS. The difference betwixt these consists in the degrees of force and liveliness, with which they strike upon the mind, and make their way into our thought or consciousness. Those perceptions, which enter with most force and violence, we may name *impressions*; and under this name I comprehend all our sensations, passions and emotions, as they make their first appearance in the soul. By *ideas* I mean the faint images of these in thinking and reasoning; such as, for instance, are all the perceptions excited by the present discourse, excepting only, those which arise from the sight and touch, and excepting the immediate pleasure or uneasiness it may occasion. I believe it will not be very necessary to employ many words in explaining this distinction. Every one of himself will readily perceive the difference betwixt feeling and thinking. The common degrees of these are easily distinguished; tho' it is not impossible but in particular instances they may very nearly approach to each other. Thus in sleep, in a fever, in madness, or in any very violent emotions of soul, our ideas may approach to our impressions: As on the other hand it sometimes happens, that our impressions are so faint and low, that we cannot distinguish them from our ideas. But notwithstanding this near resemblance in a few instances, they are in general so very different, that no-one can make a scruple to rank them under distinct heads, and assign to each a peculiar name to mark the difference.[1]

There is another division of our perceptions, which it will be convenient to observe, and which extends itself both to our impressions and ideas. This division is into SIMPLE and COMPLEX. Simple perceptions or impressions and ideas are such as admit of no distinction nor separation. The complex are the contrary to these, and may be distinguished into parts. Tho' a particular colour, taste, and smell are qualities all united together in this apple, 'tis easy to perceive they are not the same, but are at least distinguishable from each other.

Having by these divisions given an order and arrangement to our objects, we may now apply ourselves to consider with the more accuracy their qualities and relations. The first circumstance, that strikes my eye, is the great resemblance betwixt our impressions and ideas in every other particular, except their degree of force and vivacity. The one seem to be in a manner the reflexion of the other; so that all the perceptions of the mind are double, and appear both as impressions and ideas. When I shut my eyes and think of my chamber, the ideas I form are exact representations of the impressions I felt; nor is there any circumstance of the one, which is not to be found in the other. In running over my other perceptions, I find still the same resemblance and representation. Ideas and impressions appear always to correspond to each other. This circumstance seems to me remarkable, and engages my attention for a moment.

Upon a more accurate survey I find I have been carried away too far by the first appearance, and that I must make use of the distinction of perceptions into *simple* and *complex*, to limit this general decision, *that all our ideas and impressions are resembling*. I observe, that many of our complex ideas never had impressions, that corresponded to them, and that many of our complex impressions never are exactly copied in ideas. I can imagine to myself such a city as the *New Jerusalem*, whose pavement is gold and walls are rubies, tho' I never saw any such. I have seen *Paris*; but shall I affirm I can form such an idea of that city, as will perfectly represent all its streets and houses in their real and just proportions?

I perceive, therefore, that tho' there is in general a great resemblance betwixt our *complex* impressions and ideas, yet the rule is not universally true, that they are exact copies of each other. We may next consider how the case stands with our *simple* perceptions. After the most accurate examination, of which I am capable, I venture to affirm, that the rule here holds without any exception, and that every simple idea has a simple impression, which resembles it; and every simple impression a correspondent idea. That idea of red, which we form in the dark, and that impression, which strikes our eyes in sunshine, differ only in degree, not in nature. That the case is the same with all our simple impressions and ideas, 'tis impossible to prove by a particular enumeration of them. Every one may satisfy himself in this point by running over as many as he pleases. But if any one should deny this universal resemblance, I know no way of convincing him, but by desiring him to shew a simple impression, that has not a correspondent idea, or a simple idea, that has not a correspondent impression. If he does not answer this challenge, as 'tis certain he cannot, we may from his silence and our own observation establish our conclusion.

Thus we find, that all simple ideas and impressions resemble each other; and as the complex are formed from them, we may affirm in general, that these two species of perception are exactly correspondent. Having discover'd this relation which requires no farther examination, I am curious to find some other of their qualities. Let us consider how they stand with regard to their existence, and which of the impressions and ideas are causes, and which effects.

The *full* examination of this question is the subject of the present treatise; and therefore we shall here content ourselves with establishing one general proposition, *That all our simple ideas in their first appearance are deriv'd from simple impressions, which are correspondent to them, and which they exactly represent.*

In seeking for phaenomena to prove this proposition, I find only those of two kinds; but in each kind the phaenomena are obvious, numerous, and conclusive. I first make myself certain, by a new review, of what I have already asserted, that every simple impression is attended with a correspondent idea, and every simple idea with a correspondent impression. From this constant conjunction of resembling perceptions I immediately conclude, that there is a great connexion betwixt our correspondent impressions and ideas, and that the existence of the one has a considerable influence upon that of the other. Such a constant conjunction, in such an infinite number of instances, can never arise from chance; but clearly proves a dependence of the impressions on the ideas, or of the ideas on the impressions. That I may know on which side this dependence lies, I consider the order of their *first appearance*; and find by constant experience, that the simple impressions always take the precedence of their correspondent ideas, but never appear in the contrary order. To give a child an idea of scarlet or orange, of sweet or bitter, I present the objects, or in other words, convey to him these impressions; but proceed not so absurdly, as to endeavour to produce the impressions by exciting the ideas. Our ideas upon their appearance produce not their correspondent impressions, nor do we perceive any colour, or feel any sensation merely upon thinking of them. On the other hand we find, that any impressions either of the mind or body is constantly followed by an idea, which resembles it, and is only different in the degrees of force and liveliness. The constant conjunction of our resembling perceptions, is a convincing proof, that the one are the causes of the other; and this priority of the impressions is an equal proof, that our impressions are the causes of our ideas, not our ideas of our impressions.

To confirm this I consider another plain and convincing phaenomenon; which is, that where-ever by any accident the faculties, which give rise to any impressions, are obstructed in their operations, as when one is born blind or deaf; not only the impressions are lost, but also their correspondent ideas; so that there never appear in the mind the least traces of either of them. Nor is this only true, where the organs of sensation are entirely destroy'd, but likewise where they have never been put in action to produce a particular impression. We cannot form to ourselves a just idea of the taste of a pineapple, without having actually tasted it.

There is however one contradictory phaenomenon, which may prove, that 'tis not absolutely impossible for ideas to go before their correspondent impressions. I believe it will readily be allow'd, that the several distinct ideas of colours, which enter by the eyes, or those of sounds, which are convey'd by the hearing, are really different from each other, tho' at the same time resembling.

Now if this be true of different colours, it must be no less so of the different shades of the same colour, that each of them produces a distinct idea, independent of the rest. For if this shou'd be deny'd, 'tis possible, by the continual gradation of shades, to run a colour insensibly into what is most remote from it; and if you will not allow any of the means to be different, you cannot without absurdity deny the extremes to be the same. Suppose therefore a person to have enjoyed his sight for thirty years, and to have become perfectly well acquainted with colours of all kinds, excepting one particular shade of blue, for instance, which it never has been his fortune to meet with. Let all the different shades of that colour, except that single one, be plac'd before him, descending gradually from the deepest to the lightest; 'tis plain, that he will perceive a blank, where that shade is wanting, and will be sensible, that there is a greater distance in that place betwixt the contiguous colours, than in any other. Now I ask, whether 'tis possible for him, from his own imagination, to supply this deficiency, and raise up to himself the idea of that particular shade, tho' it had never been conveyed to him by his senses? I believe there are few but will be of opinion that he can; and this may serve as a proof, that the simple ideas are not always derived from the correspondent impressions; tho' the instance is so particular and singular, that 'tis scarce worth our observing, and does not merit that for it alone we should alter our general maxim.

But besides this exception, it may not be amiss to remark on this head, that the principle of the priority of impressions to ideas must be understood with another limitation, *viz.* that as our ideas are images of our impressions, so we can form secondary ideas, which are images of the primary; as appears from this very reasoning concerning them. This is not, properly speaking, an exception to the rule so much as an explanation of it. Ideas produce the images of themselves in new ideas; but as the first ideas are supposed to be derived from impressions, it still remains true, that all our simple ideas proceed either mediately or immediately, from their correspondent impressions.

This then is the first principle I establish in the science of human nature; nor ought we to despise it because of the simplicity of its appearance. For 'tis remarkable, that the present question concerning the precedency of our impressions or ideas, is the same with what has made so much noise in other terms, when it has been disputed whether there be any *innate ideas*, or whether all ideas be derived from sensation and reflexion. We may observe, that in order to prove the ideas of extension and colour not to be innate, philosophers do nothing but shew, that they are conveyed by our senses. To prove the ideas of passion and desire not to be innate, they observe that we have a preceding experience of these emotions in ourselves. Now if we carefully examine these arguments, we shall find that they prove nothing but that ideas are preceded by other more lively perceptions, from which they are derived, and which they represent. I hope this clear stating of the question will remove all disputes concerning it, and will render this principle of more use in our reasonings, than it seems hitherto to have been.

Note

[1] I here make use of these terms, *impression and idea*, in a sense different from what is usual, and I hope this liberty will be allowed me. Perhaps I rather restore the word, idea, to its original sense, from which Mr *Locke* had perverted it, in making it stand for all our perceptions. By the terms of impression I would not be understood to express the manner, in which our lively perceptions are produced in the soul, but merely the perceptions themselves; for which there is no particular name either in the *English* or any other language, that I know of.

Jean Jacques Rousseau

(1712–1778)

Rousseau's life and thought typified the Enlightenment at times and challenged it at others. In his personal relationships with the *philosophes*, Rousseau, a Swiss, was the *bête noir* of salon society, unconventional and unpredictable in his behavior. Especially uneasy in his relations with women, Rousseau revealed all of his own idiosyncrasies in his *Confessions* (1770) and made public those of his former comrades. In his obsession with the self in all of its non-rational incarnations, Rousseau thus glimpses Romanticism, even as he rightly belongs to the pantheon of philosophes who constituted the Age of Reason.

Author of hundreds of treatises, essays, and dramatic pieces, Rousseau's most widely known work today was one of his lesser known works in his own time. *The Social Contract* is his discourse on the place of the individual in community, individual liberty must be exercised only in the context of the whole. For Rousseau, early men exercised complete natural liberty in an anarchic state of nature. The need to protect property necessitated the sacrifice of natural liberty for civil liberty. The "right" to do whatever one wanted was replaced by "rights" within a delimited context. The possession of these rights was predicated on the sacrifice of selfish interest to the general will.

Few ideas have been so widely discussed, applied, and misunderstood as Rousseau's enigmatic "general will." Scholars agree that modern political systems from anarchism to totalitarianism can be derived from Rousseau's concept. Developing Locke's idea that the legitimacy of government depends on the consent of the governed, Rousseau pondered the individual's capacity for consent. He believed that individual wills, always self-interested, could not be the basis for peaceful governance; only the sum total of the best of those wills could be the foundation of law. The general will constituted an entity above individual; an entity, however, of their own making, and one they would readily surrender their natural liberty to for the good of the whole. It is only within this context that the individual can be free. In one of the more troubling passages which follows, individuals who do not recognize their participation in the general will as freedom would be compelled to do so.

Beginning with the Jacobins in 1789, revolutionaries found much inspiration in Rousseau's ideas. During the era of Revolutions which followed the Enlightenment many proposals for governing free men would be put forward. Which of the following dilemmas identified by Rousseau plagued every

50

attempt to create a government based on consent: dissenters, the power of the sovereign, liberty's limits, self-interest? How do Rousseau's views differ from those of Locke? Jefferson? How can surrender to the general will be considered proto-romantic?

from *The Social Contract* (1763)

Chapter I
Subject of the First Book

Man is born free; and everywhere he is in chains. One thinks himself the master of others, and still remains a greater slave than they. How did this change come about? I do not know. What can make it legitimate? That question I think I can answer.

• • •

Chapter II
The First Societies

The most ancient of all societies, and the only one that is natural, is the family: and even so the children remain attached to the father only so long as they need him for their preservation. As soon as this need ceases, the natural bond is dissolved. The children, released from the obedience they owed to the father, and the father, released from the care he owed his children, return equally to independence. If they remain united, they continue so no longer naturally, but voluntarily; and the family itself is then maintained only by convention.

This common liberty results from the nature of man. His first law is to provide for his own preservation, his first cares are those which he owes to himself; and, as soon as he reaches years of discretion, he is the sole judge of the proper means of preserving himself, and consequently becomes his own master.

The family then may be called the first model of political societies: the ruler corresponds to the father, and the people to the children; and all, being born free and equal, alienate their liberty only for their own advantage. The whole difference is that, in the family, the love of the father for his children repays him for the care he takes of them, while, in the State, the pleasure of commanding takes the place of the love which the chief cannot have for the peoples under him.

• • •

Chapter III
The Rights of the Strongest

The strongest is never strong enough to be always the master, unless he transforms strength into right, and obedience into duty. Hence the right of the strongest, which, though to all seeming meant ironically, is really laid down as a fundamental principle. But are we never to have an explanation of this phrase? Force is a physical power, and I fail to see what moral effect it can have. To yield to force is an act of necessity, not of will—at the most, an act of prudence. In what sense can it be a duty?

Suppose for a moment that this so-called "right" exists. I maintain that the sole result is a mass of inexplicable nonsense. For, if force creates right, the effect changes with the cause: every force that is greater than the first succeeds to its right. As soon as it is possible to disobey with impunity, disobedience is legitimate; and, the strongest being always in the right, the only thing that matters is to act so as to become the strongest. But what kind of right is that which perishes when force fails? If we must obey perforce, there is no need to obey because we ought; and if we are not forced to obey, we are under no obligation to do so. Clearly, the word "right" adds nothing to force: in this connection, it means absolutely nothing.

Obey the powers that be. If this means yield to force, it is a good precept, but superfluous: I can answer for its never being violated. All power comes from God, I admit; but so does all sickness: does that mean that we are forbidden to call in the doctor? A brigand surprises me at the edge of a wood: must I not merely surrender my purse on compulsion; but, even if I could withhold it, am I in conscience bound to give it up? For certainly the pistol he holds is also a power.

Let us then admit that force does not create right, and that we are obliged to obey only legitimate powers. In that case, my original question recurs.

Chapter IV
Slavery

Since no man has a natural authority over his fellow, and force creates no right, we must conclude that conventions form the basis of all legitimate authority among men.

•   •   •

To renounce liberty is to renounce being a man, to surrender the rights of humanity and even its duties. For him who renounces everything no indemnity is possible. Such a renunciation is incompatible with man's nature; to remove all liberty from his will is to remove all morality from his acts. Finally, it is an empty and contradictory convention that sets up, on the one side, absolute authority, and, on the other, unlimited obedience. Is it not clear that we can be under no obligation to a person from whom we have the right to exact everything? Does not this condition alone, in the absence of equivalence or exchange, in itself involve the nullity of the act? For what right can my slave have against me, when all that he has belongs to me, and, his right being mine, this right of mine against myself is a phrase devoid of meaning?

Grotius[1] and the rest find in war another origin for the so-called right of slavery. The victor having, as they hold, the right of killing the vanquished, the latter can buy back his life at the price of his liberty; and this convention is the more legitimate because it is to the advantage of both parties.

But it is clear that this supposed right to kill the conquered is by no means deducible from the state of war. Men, from the mere fact that, while they are living in their primitive independence, they have no mutual relations stable enough to constitute either the state of peace or the state of war, cannot be naturally enemies. War is constituted by a relation between things, and not between persons; and, as the state of war cannot arise out of simple personal relations, but only out of real relations, private war, or war of man with man, can exist neither in the state of nature, where there is no constant property, nor in the social state, where everything is under the authority of the laws.

Individual combats, duels and encounters, are acts which cannot constitute a state; while the private wars, authorised by the Establishments of Louis IX, King of France, and suspended by the Peace of God, are abuses of feudalism, in itself an absurd system if ever there was one, and contrary to the principles of natural right and to all good polity.

War then is a relation, not between man and man, but between State and State, and individuals are enemies only accidentally, not as men, nor even as citizens, but as soldiers; not as members of their country, but as its defenders. Finally, each State can have for enemies only other States, and not men; for between things disparate in nature there can be no relation.

● ● ●

Chapter VI
The Social Compact

. . . "The problem is to find a form of association which will defend and protect with the whole common force the person and goods of each associate, and in which each, while uniting himself with all, may still obey himself alone, and remain as free as before." This is the fundamental problem of which the

Social Contract provides the solution.

The clauses of this contract are so determined by the nature of the act that the slightest modification would make them vain and ineffective; so that, although they have perhaps never been formally set forth, they are everywhere the same and everywhere tacitly admitted and recognised, until, on the violation of the social compact, each regains his original rights and resumes his natural liberty, while losing the conventional liberty in favour of which he renounced it.

These clauses, properly understood, may be reduced to one—the total alienation of each associate, together with all his rights, to the whole community; for, in the first place, as each gives himself absolutely, the conditions are the same for all; and, this being so, no one has any interest in making them burdensome to others.

Moreover, the alienation being without reserve, the union is as perfect as it can be, and no associate has anything more to demand: for, if the individuals retained certain rights, as there would be no common superior to decide between them and the public, each, being on one point his own judge, would ask to be so on all; the state of nature would thus continue, and the association would necessarily become inoperative or tyrannical.

Finally, each man, in giving himself to all, gives himself to nobody; and as there is no associate over whom he does not acquire the same right as he yields others over himself, he gains an equivalent for everything he loses, and an increase of force for the preservation of what he has.

If then we discard from the social compact what is not of its essence, we shall find that it reduces itself to the following terms—

"Each of us puts his person and all his power in common under the supreme direction of the general will, and, in our corporate capacity, we receive each member as an indivisible part of the whole."

At once, in place of the individual personality of each contracting party, this act of association creates a moral and collective body, composed of as many members as the assembly contains votes, and receiving from this act its unity, its common identity, its life and its will. This public person, so formed by the union of all other persons formerly took the name of *city*, and now takes that of *Republic* or *body politic*; it is called by its members *State* when passive, *Sovereign* when active, and *Power* when compared with others like itself. Those who are associated in it take collectively the name of *people*, and severally are called *citizens*, as sharing in the sovereign power, and *subjects*, as being under the laws of the State. But these terms are often confused and taken one for another: it is enough to know how to distinguish them when they are being used with precision.

Chapter VII
The Sovereign

This formula shows us that the act of association comprises a mutual undertaking between the public and the individuals, and that each individual, in making a contract, as we may say, with himself, is bound in a double capacity; as a member of the Sovereign he is bound to the individuals, and as a member of the State to the Sovereign. But the maxim of civil right, that no one is bound by undertakings made to himself, does not apply in this case; for there is a great difference between incurring an obligation to yourself and incurring one to a whole of which you form a part.

Attention must further be called to the fact that public deliberation, while competent to bind all the subjects to the Sovereign, because of the two different capacities in which each of them may be regarded, cannot, for the opposite reason, bind the Sovereign to itself; and that it is consequently against the nature of the body politic for the Sovereign to impose on itself a law which it cannot infringe. Being able to regard itself in only one capacity, it is in the position of an individual who makes a contract with himself; and this makes it clear that there neither is nor can be any kind of fundamental law binding on the body of the people—not even the social contract itself. This does not mean that the body politic cannot enter into undertakings with others, provided the contract is not infringed by them; for in relation to what is external to it, it becomes a simple being, an individual.

But the body politic or the Sovereign, drawing its being wholly from the sanctity of the contract, can never bind itself, even to an outsider, to do anything derogatory to the original act, for instance, to alienate any part of itself, or to submit to another Sovereign. Violation of the act by which it exists would be self-annihilation; and that which is itself nothing can create nothing.

As soon as this multitude is so united in one body, it is impossible to offend against one of the members without attacking the body, and still more to offend against the body without the members resenting it. Duty and interest therefore equally oblige the two contracting parties to give each other help; and the same men should seek to combine, in their double capacity, all the advantages dependent upon that capacity.

Again, the Sovereign, being formed wholly of the individuals who compose it, neither has nor can have any interest contrary to theirs; and consequently the sovereign power need give no guarantee to its subjects, because it is impossible for the body to wish to hurt all its members. We shall also see later on that it cannot hurt any in particular. The Sovereign, merely by virtue of what it is, is always what it should be.

This, however, is not the case with the relation of the subjects to the Sovereign, which, despite the common interest, would have no security that they would fulfil their undertakings, unless it found means to assure itself of their fidelity.

In fact, each individual, as a man, may have a particular will contrary or dissimilar to the general will which he has as a citizen. His particular interest may speak to him quite differently from the common interest: his absolute and naturally independent existence may make him look upon what he owes to the common cause as a gratuitous contribution, the loss of which will do less harm to others than the payment of it is burdensome to himself; and, regarding the moral person which constitutes the State as a *persona ficta*, because not a man, he may wish to enjoy the rights of citizenship without being ready to fulfil the duties of a subject. The continuance of such an injustice could not but prove the undoing of the body politic.

In order then that the social compact may not be an empty formula, it tacitly includes the undertaking, which alone can give force to the rest, that whoever refuses to obey the general will shall be compelled to do so by the whole body. This means nothing less than that he will be forced to be free; for this is the condition which, by giving each citizen to his country, secures him against all personal dependence. In this lies the key to the working of the political machine; this alone legitimises civil undertakings, which, without it, would be absurd, tyrannical, and liable to the most frightful abuses.

Chapter VIII
The Civil State

The passage from the state of nature to the civil state produces a very remarkable change in man, by substituting justice for instinct in his conduct, and giving his actions the morality they had formerly lacked. Then only, when the voice of duty takes the place of physical impulses and right of appetite, does man, who so far had considered only himself, find that he is forced to act on different principles, and to consult his reason before listening to his inclinations. Although, in this state, he deprives himself of some advantages which he got from nature, he gains in return others so great, his faculties are so stimulated and developed, his ideas so extended, his feelings so ennobled, and his whole soul so uplifted, that, did not the abuses of this new condition often degrade him below that which he left, he would be bound to bless continually the happy moment which took him from it for ever, and, instead of a stupid and unimaginative animal, made him an intelligent being and a man.

Let us draw up the whole account in terms easily commensurable. What man loses by the social contract is his natural liberty and an unlimited right to everything he tries to get and succeeds in getting; what he gains is civil liberty and the proprietorship of all he possesses. If we are to avoid mistake in weighing one against the other, we must clearly distinguish natural liberty, which is bounded only by the strength of the individual, from civil liberty, which is limited by the general will; and possession, which is merely the effect of force or the right of the first occupier, from property, which can be founded only on a positive title.

We might, over and above all this, add, to what man acquires in the civil state, moral liberty, which alone makes him truly master of himself; for the mere impulse of appetite is slavery, while obedience to a law which we prescribe to ourselves is liberty. But I have already said too much on this head, and the philosophical meaning of the word liberty does not now concern us.

Note

[1] Hugo Grotius, Dutch statesman and jurist (1583–1645).

Immanuel Kant

1724–1804

Born in 1724, in Königsberg, Prussia, Immanuel Kant was the fourth of nine children, but soon found himself the eldest surviving child of the family. His father was a saddler, and his mother, though not formally educated, was known for the sharpness of her intellect. Kant was raised in his parents' Lutheran Pietism, a Protestant denomination characterized by simplicity, moral obedience, and a notable absence of theological dogmatism. At eight years old, Kant entered a Pietist Latin grammar school, where he studied a curriculum grounded in the classics. In 1740, he began his studies at the University of Königsberg, where he was to concentrate on theology, but soon turned to mathematics, physics, and philosophy. Kant left university for a time to become a private family tutor, but he returned in 1755 to take his degree. Thereafter, he became a University lecturer at Königsberg, where he taught and wrote about subjects as diverse as logic, metaphysics, ethics, geography, mathematics, geology, and astronomy. His contributions in the sciences were significant, if little known outside Königsberg; his work in philosophy, in contrast, was wide-ranging and controversial.

In 1770, Kant was appointed Chair of Logic and Metaphysics, and began a period of exhaustive intellectual work and prolific writing. In 1781, he published his *Critique of Pure Reason*, which examined how knowledge about the outside world is constructed and on what grounds we are able to make theoretical judgments. Turning to ethics, Kant published the *Critique of Practical Reason* (1788), an examination of the role of reason in moral life, in which he engaged such concepts as duty, freedom, and good will. It was in this work that he formulated his famous Categorical Imperative: that we should, in his words, "Act only on that maxim by which you can at the same time will that it should become a universal law." In 1789, he published his third great work, the *Critique of Judgment*, a study of aesthetic and teleological judgment. Kant's other important works include *Prolegomena to Any Future Metaphysics* (1783); *Idea for a Universal History* (1784); *Foundations of the Metaphysics of Morals* (1785); *Religion within the Limits of Reason Alone* (1793); and *Metaphysics of Ethics* (1793).

Kant's essay "What is Enlightenment?" (1784) asks what it means to be a free and enlightened person in a society that often inspires only intellectual laziness and cowardice. Kant argues that Enlightenment is a matter of intellectual independence, and human reason is the tool we use to acquire this virtue. Enlightenment, thus construed, is a public responsibility. Agreeing with Rousseau, Kant notes that our freedom is always restricted, but for him this is something that we do to ourselves because of our failure to "make public use of our reason." In thinking through the assertions Kant puts forward, what do you think are the responsibilities of an enlightened citizenry? What are the forces that limit our intellectual independence? In what ways and for what reasons might we persist in our own intellectual cowardice, our "self-incurred . . . tutelage"?

What Is Enlightenment? (1784)

Enlightenment is man's leaving his self-caused immaturity. Immaturity is the incapacity to use one's intelligence without the guidance of another. Such immaturity is self-caused if it is not caused by lack of intelligence, but by lack of determination and courage to use one's intelligence without being guided by another. *Sapere Aude!* Have the courage to use your own intelligence! is therefore the motto of the enlightenment.

Through laziness and cowardice a large part of mankind, even after nature has freed them from alien guidance, gladly remain immature. It is because of laziness and cowardice that it is so easy for others to usurp the role of guardians. It is so comfortable to be a minor! If I have a book which provides meaning for me, a pastor who has conscience for me, a doctor who will judge my diet for me and so on, then I do not need to exert myself. I do not have any need to think; if I can pay, others will take over the tedious job for me. The guardians who have kindly undertaken the supervision will see to it that by far the largest part of mankind, including the entire "beautiful sex," should consider the step into maturity, not only as difficult but as very dangerous.

After having made their domestic animals dumb and having carefully prevented these quiet creatures from daring to take any step beyond the lead-strings to which they have fastened them, these guardians then show them the danger which threatens them, should they attempt to walk alone. Now this danger is not really so very great; for they would presumably learn to walk after some stumbling. However, an example of this kind intimidates and frightens people out of all further attempts.

It is difficult for the isolated individual to work himself out of the immaturity which has become almost natural for him. He has even become fond of it and for the time being is incapable of employing his own intelligence, because he has never been allowed to make the attempt. Statutes and formulas, these mechanical tools of a serviceable use, or rather misuse, of his natural faculties, are the ankle-chains of a continuous immaturity. Whoever threw it off would make an uncertain jump over the smallest trench because he is not accustomed to such free movement. Therefore there are only a few who have pursued a firm path and have succeeded in escaping from immaturity by their own cultivation of the mind.

But it is more nearly possible for a public to enlighten itself: this is even inescapable if only the public is given its freedom. For there will always be some people who think for themselves, even among the self-appointed guardians of

61

the great mass who, after having thrown off the yoke of immaturity themselves, will spread about them the spirit of a reasonable estimate of their own value and of the need for every man to think for himself. It is strange that the very public, which had previously been put under this yoke by the guardians, forces the guardians thereafter to keep it there if it is stirred up by a few of its guardians who are themselves incapable of all enlightenment. It is thus very harmful to plant prejudices, because they come back to plague those very people who themselves (or whose predecessors) have been the originators of these prejudices. Therefore a public can only arrive at enlightenment slowly. Through revolution, the abandonment of personal despotism may be engendered and the end of profit-seeking and domineering oppression may occur, but never a true reform of the state of mind. Instead, new prejudices, just like the old ones, will serve as the guiding reins of the great, unthinking mass.

All that is required for this enlightenment is *freedom*; and particularly the least harmful of all that may be called freedom, namely, the freedom for man to make *public* use of his reason in all matters. But I hear people clamor on all sides: Don't argue! The officer says: Don't argue, drill! The tax collector: Don't argue, pay! The pastor: Don't argue, believe! (Only a single lord in the world says: *Argue*, as much as you want to and about what you please, *but obey!*) Here we have restrictions on freedom everywhere. Which restriction is hampering enlightenment, and which does not, or even promotes it? I answer: The *public use* of a man's reason must be free at all times, and this alone can bring enlightenment among men: while the private use of a man's reason may often be restricted rather narrowly without thereby unduly hampering the progress of enlightenment.

I mean by the public use of one's reason, the use which a scholar makes of it before the entire reading public. Private use I call the use which he may make of this reason in a civic post or office. For some affairs which are in the interest of the commonwealth a certain mechanism is necessary through which some members of the commonwealth must remain purely passive in order that an artificial agreement with the government for the public good be maintained or so that at least the destruction of the good be prevented. In such a situation it is not permitted to argue; one must obey. But in so far as this unit of the machine considers himself as a member of the entire commonwealth, in fact even of world society; in other words, he considers himself in the quality of a scholar who is addressing the true public through his writing, he may indeed argue without the affairs suffering for which he is employed partly as a passive member. Thus it would be very harmful if an officer who, given an order by his superior, should start, while in the service, to argue concerning the utility or appropriateness of that command. He must obey, but he cannot equitably be prevented from making observations as a scholar concerning the mistakes in the military service nor from submitting these to the public for its judgment. The citizen cannot refuse to pay the taxes imposed upon him. Indeed, a rash criticism of such taxes, if they are the ones to be paid by him, may be punished as a scandal which might cause general resistance. But the same man does not act contrary to the duty of a citizen if, as a scholar, he utters publicly his thoughts against the undesirability or even the injustice of such taxes. Likewise a clergyman is obliged to teach his pupils and his congregation according to the doctrine of the church which he serves, for he has been accepted on that condition. But as a scholar, he has full freedom, in fact, even the obligation, to communicate to the public all his diligently examined and well-intentioned thoughts concerning erroneous points in that doctrine and concerning proposals regarding the better institution of religious and ecclesiastical matters. There is nothing in this for which the conscience could be blamed. For what he teaches according to his office as one authorized by the church, he presents as something in regard to which he has no latitude to teach according to his own preference. . . . He will say: Our church teaches this or that, these are the proofs which are employed for it. In this way he derives all possible practical benefit for his congregation from rules which he would not himself subscribe to with full conviction. But he may nevertheless undertake the presentation of these rules because it is not entirely inconceivable that truth may be contained in them. In any case, there is nothing directly contrary to inner religion to be found in such doctrines. For, should he believe that the latter was not the case he could not administer his office in good conscience; he would have to resign it. Therefore the use which an employed teacher makes of his reason before his congregation is merely a private use since such a gathering is always only domestic, no matter how large. As a priest (a member of an organization) he is not free and ought not to be, since he is executing someone else's mandate. On the other hand, the scholar speaking through his writings to the true public which is the world, like the clergyman making public use of his reason, enjoys an unlimited freedom to employ his own reason and to speak in his own person. For to suggest that the guardians of the people in spiritual matters should always be immature minors is a non-sense which would mean perpetuating forever existing non-sense.

But should a society of clergymen, for instance an ecclesiastical assembly, be entitled to commit itself by oath to a certain unalterable doctrine in order to perpetuate an endless guardianship over each of its members and through them over the people? I answer that this is quite inconceivable. Such a contract which would be concluded in order to keep humanity forever from all further enlightenment is absolutely impossible, even should it be confirmed by the highest authority through parliaments and the most solemn peace treaties. An age cannot conclude a pact and take an oath upon it to commit the succeeding age to a situation in which it would be impossible for the latter to enlarge even its most important knowledge, to eliminate error and altogether to progress in enlightenment. Such a thing would be a crime against human nature, the original destiny of which consists in such progress. Succeeding generations are entirely justified in discarding such decisions as unauthorized and criminal. The touchstone of all this to be agreed upon as a law for people is to be found in the question whether a people could impose such a law upon itself. Now it might be possible to introduce a certain order for a definite short period as if in anticipation of a better order. This would be true if one permitted at the same time each citizen and especially the clergyman to make his criticisms in his quality as a scholar. . . . In the meantime, the provisional order might continue until the insight into the particular matter in hand has publicly progressed to the point where through a combination of voices (although not, perhaps, of all) a proposal may be brought to the crown. Thus those congregations would be protected which had agreed to (a changed religious institution) according to their own ideas and better understanding, without hindering those who desired to allow the old institutions to continue. . . .

A man may postpone for himself, but only for a short time, enlightening himself regarding what he ought to know. But to resign from such enlightenment altogether either for his own person or even more for his descendants means to violate and to trample underfoot the sacred rights of mankind. Whatever a people may not decide for themselves, a monarch may even less decide for the people, for his legislative reputation rests upon his uniting the entire people's will in his own. If the monarch will only see to it that every true or imagined reform (of religion) fits in with the civil order, he had best let his subjects do what they consider necessary for the sake of their salvation; that is not his affair. His only concern is to prevent one subject from hindering another by force, to work according to each subject's best ability to determine and to promote his salvation. In fact, it detracts from his majesty if he interferes in such matters and subjects to governmental supervision the writings by which his subjects seek to clarify their ideas (concerning religion). This is true whether he does it from his own highest insight, for in this case he exposes himself to the reproach: *Caesar non est supra grammaticos*; it is even more true when he debases his highest power to support the spiritual despotism of some tyrants in his state against the rest of his subjects.

The question may now be put: Do we live at present in an enlightened age? The answer is: No, but in an age of enlightenment. Much still prevents men from being placed in a position or even being placed into position to use their own minds securely and well in matters of religion. But we do have very definite indications that this field of endeavor is being opened up for men to work freely and reduce gradually the hindrances preventing a general enlightenment and an escape from self-caused immaturity. In this sense, this age is the age of enlightenment and the age of Frederick (the Great).

A prince should not consider it beneath him to declare that he believes it to be his duty not to prescribe anything to his subjects in matters of religion but to leave to them complete freedom in such things. In other words, a prince who refuses the conceited title of being "tolerant," is himself enlightened. He deserves to be praised by his grateful contemporaries and descendants as the man who first freed humankind of immaturity, at least as far as the government is concerned and who permitted everyone to use his own reason in all matters of conscience. Under his rule, venerable clergymen could, regardless of their official duty, set forth their opinions and views even though they differ from the accepted doctrine here and there; they could do so in the quality of scholars, freely and publicly. The same holds even more true of every other person who is not thus restricted by official duty. This spirit of freedom is spreading even outside (the country of Frederick the Great) to places where it has to struggle with the external hindrances imposed by a government which misunderstands its own position. For an example is illuminating them which shows that such freedom (public discussion) need not cause the slightest worry regarding public security and the unity of the commonwealth. Men raise themselves by and by out of backwardness if one does not purposely invent artifices to keep them down.

I have emphasized the main point of enlightenment, that is of man's release from his self-caused immaturity, primarily *in matters of religion*. I have done this because our rulers have no interest in playing the guardian of their subjects in matters of arts and sciences. Furthermore immaturity in matters of religion is not only most noxious but also most dishonorable. But the point of view of a head of state who favors freedom in the arts and sciences goes even farther; for he understands that there is no danger in legislation permitting his subjects to make public use of their own reason and to submit *publicly* their thoughts regarding a better framing of such laws together with a frank criticism of existing *legislation*. We have a shining example of this; no prince excels him whom we admire. Only he who is himself enlightened does not fear spectres when he at the same time has a well-disciplined army at his disposal as a guarantee of public peace. Only he can say what (the ruler of a) free state dare not say: *Argue as much as you want and about whatever you want but obey!* Thus we see here as elsewhere an unexpected turn in human affairs just as we observe that almost everything therein is paradoxical. A great degree of civic freedom seems to be advantageous for the freedom of the *spirit* of the people and yet it establishes impassable limits. A lesser degree of such civic freedom provides additional space in which the spirit of a people can develop to its full capacity. Therefore nature has cherished, within its hard shell, the germ of the inclination and need for free *thought*. This free thought gradually acts upon the mind of the people and they gradually become more capable of acting in freedom. Eventually, the government is also influenced by this free thought and thereby it treats man, who is now more than a machine, according to his dignity.

Koenigsberg, September 30, 1784

II. THE LATE ENLIGHTENMENT: REVOLUTIONS IN SOCIETY AND POLITICS

Adam Smith

1723–1790

Born in Kirkcaldy, Scotland, and educated both at Glasgow University and at Balliol College, Oxford, Adam Smith became a leading intellectual of the Scottish Enlightenment of the eighteenth century. In 1748 he accepted a lectureship in rhetoric and belles-lettres at Edinburgh, and was later appointed professor of logic and moral philosophy at Glasgow. His first major publication was *The Theory of Moral Sentiments* (1759), in which he wrote about human sympathy, the ability to "feel alongside" the experience of others, as the foundation for the social bond. In 1764, Smith left Glasgow University and traveled to Paris, where he met Voltaire and made the acquaintance of the physiocrats, a school of political economists who stressed the importance of natural laws, property rights, and freedom of industry.

In *An Inquiry into the Nature and Causes of the Wealth of Nations* (1776), Smith argued for a *laissez-faire* approach to political economy, contending that the enlightened self-interest of individuals would lead most efficiently to the accumulation of capital and most directly to the social good. At the heart, therefore, of Smith's economic theory is the idea of the autonomous Enlightenment individual, for whom reason will serve as the path to personal and social transformation, to material and moral progress. Still, as the selection below demonstrates, Smith was aware that, even though individuals are most often the best judges of what lies in their interest, at times it becomes necessary for government to intervene in the economic relations of its industries. *Laissez faire*, then, is a principle to which we should aspire, but it is not inviolable; it is only in more recent times that *laissez faire* has been advanced as ideology.

The selection below raises a host of critical questions: To what extent is the individual's success a product of his or her industry alone? Is reason enough to ensure our economic progress as individuals or as a society? Can materialism truly bring about social or moral transformation, as Smith suggests? Does enlightened self-interest—the pursuit of that which will benefit the individual—just as often lead us away from the social good?

from *The Wealth of Nations* (1776)

Book I

Of the Causes of Improvement in the productive Powers of Labour, and of the Order according to which its Produce is naturally distributed among the different Ranks of People.

Chapter I
Of the Division of Labour

The greatest improvement in the productive powers of labour, and the greater part of the skill, dexterity, and judgment with which it is any where directed, or applied, seem to have been the effects of the division of labour.

The effects of the division of labour, in the general business of society, will be more easily understood, by considering in what manner it operates in some particular manufactures. It is commonly supposed to be carried furthest in some very trifling ones; not perhaps that it really is carried further in them than in others of more importance: but in those trifling manufactures which are destined to supply the small wants of but a small number of people, the whole number of workmen must necessarily be small; and those employed in every different branch of the work can often be collected into the same work-house, and placed at once under the view of the spectator. In those great manufactures, on the contrary, which are destined to supply the great wants of the great body of the people, every different branch of the work employs so great a number of workmen, that it is impossible to collect them all into the same workhouse. We can seldom see more, at one time, than those employed in one single branch. Though in such manufactures, therefore, the work may really be divided into a much greater number of parts, than in those of a more trifling nature, the division is not near so obvious, and has accordingly been much less observed.

To take an example, therefore, from a very trifling manufacture; but one in which the division of labour has been very often taken notice of, the trade of the pin-maker; a workman not educated to this business (which the division of labour has rendered a distinct trade), nor acquainted with the use of the machinery employed in it (to the invention of which the same division of labour has probably given occasion), could scarce, perhaps, with his utmost industry, make one pin in a day, and certainly could not make twenty. But in the way in which this business is now carried on, not only the whole work is a peculiar trade, but it is divided into a number of branches, of which the greater part are likewise peculiar trades. One man draws out the wire, another straights it, a third cuts it, a fourth points it, a fifth grinds it at the top for receiving the head; to make the head requires two or three distinct operations; to put it on, is a peculiar business, to whiten the pins is another; it is even a trade by itself to put them into the paper; and the important business of making a pin is, in this manner, divided into about eighteen distinct operations, which, in some manufactories, are all performed by distinct hands, though in others the same man will sometimes perform two or three of them. I have seen a small manufactory of this kind where ten men only were employed, and where some of them consequently performed two or three distinct operations. But though they were very poor, and therefore but indifferently accommodated with the necessary machinery, they could, when they exerted themselves, make among them about twelve pounds of pins in a day. There are in a pound upwards of four thousand pins of a middling size. Those ten persons, therefore, could make among them upwards of forty-eight thousand pins in a day. Each person, therefore, making a tenth part of forty-eight thousand pins, might be considered as making four thousand eight hundred pins in a day. But if they had all wrought separately and independently, and without any of them having been educated to this peculiar business, they certainly could not each of them have made twenty, perhaps not one pin in a day; that is, certainly, not the two hundred and fortieth, perhaps not the four thousand eight hundredth part of what they are at present capable of performing, in consequence of a proper division and combination of their different operations.

In every other art and manufacture, the effects of the division of labour are similar to what they are in this very trifling one; though, in many of them, the labour can neither be so much subdivided, nor reduced to so great a simplicity of operation. The division of labour, however, so far as it can be introduced, occasions, in every art, a proportionable increase of the productive powers of labour. The separation of different trades and employments from one another, seems to have taken place in consequence of this advantage. This separation, too, is generally called furthest in those countries which enjoy the highest degree of industry and improvement; what is the work of one man in a rude state of society, being generally that of several in an improved one. In every improved society, the farmer is generally nothing but a farmer; the manufacturer, nothing but a manufacturer. The labour too which is necessary to produce any one complete manufacture, is almost always divided among a great number of hands. How many different trades are employed in each branch of the linen and woollen manufactures, from the growers of the flax and the wool, to the bleachers and smoothers of the linen, or to the dyers and dressers of the cloth!

•　　•　　•

This great increase of the quantity of work, which, in consequence of the division of labour, the same number of people are capable of performing, is owing to three different circumstances; first, to the increase of dexterity in every particular workman; secondly, to the saving of the time which is commonly lost in passing from one species of work to another; and lastly, to the invention of a great number of machines which facilitate and abridge labour, and enable one man to do the work of many.

First, the improvement of the dexterity of the workman necessarily increases the quantity of the work he can perform; and the division of labour, by reducing every man's business to some one simple operation, and by making this operation the sole employment of his life, necessarily increases very much the dexterity of the workman. A common smith, who, though accustomed to handle the hammer, has never been used to make nails, if upon some particular occasion he is obliged to attempt it, will scarce, I am assured, be able to make above two or three hundred nails in a day, and those too very bad ones. A smith who has been accustomed to make nails, but whose sole or principal business has not been that of a nailer, can seldom with his utmost diligence make more than eight hundred or a thousand nails in a day. I have seen several boys under twenty years of age who had never exercised any other trade but that of making nails, and who, when they exerted themselves, could make, each of them, upwards of two thousand three hundred nails in a day. The making of a nail, however, is by no means one of the simplest operations. The same person blows the bellows, stirs or mends the fire as there is occasion, heats the iron, and forges every part of the nail: In forging the head too he is obliged to change his tools. The different operations into which the making of a pin, or of a metal button, is subdivided, are all of them much more simple, and the dexterity of the person, of whose life it has been the sole business to perform them, is usually much greater. The rapidity with which some of the operations of those manufactures are performed, exceeds what the human hand could, by those who had never seen them, be supposed capable of acquiring.

Secondly, the advantage which is gained by saving the time commonly lost in passing from one sort of work to another, is much greater than we should at first view be apt to imagine it. It is impossible to pass very quickly from one kind of work to another, that is carried on in a different place, and with quite different tools. A country weaver, who cultivates a small farm, must lose a good deal of time in passing from his loom to the field, and from the field to his loom. When the two trades can be carried on in the same workhouse, the loss of time is no doubt much less. It is even in this case, however, very considerable. A man commonly saunters a little in turning his hand from one sort of employment to another. When he first begins the new work he is seldom very keen and hearty; his mind, as they say, does not go to it, and for some time he rather trifles than applies to good purpose. The habit of sauntering and of indolent careless application, which is naturally, or rather necessarily acquired by every country workman who is obliged to change his work and his tools every half hour, and to apply his hand in twenty different ways almost every day of his life; renders him almost always slothful and lazy, and incapable of any vigorous application even on the most pressing occasions. Independent, therefore, of his deficiency in point of dexterity, this cause alone must always reduce considerably the quantity of work which he is capable of performing.

Thirdly, and lastly, every body must be sensible how much labour is facilitated and abridged by the application of proper machinery. It is unnecessary to give any example. I shall only observe, therefore, that the invention of all those machines by which labour is so much facilitated and abridged, seems to have been originally owing to the division of labour. Men are much more likely to discover easier and readier methods of attaining any object, when the whole attention of their minds is directed towards that single object, than when it is dissipated among a great variety of things. But in consequence of the division of labour, the whole of every man's attention comes naturally to be directed towards some one very simple object. It is naturally to be expected, therefore, that some one or other of those who are employed in each particular branch of labour should soon find out easier and readier methods of performing their own particular work, wherever the nature of it admits of such improvement. A great part of the machines made use of in those manufactures in which labour is most subdivided, were originally the inventions of common workmen, who, being each of them employed in some very simple operation, naturally turned their thoughts towards finding out easier and readier methods of performing it. Whoever has been much accustomed to visit such manufactures must frequently have been shewn very pretty machines, which were the inventions of such workmen in order to facilitate and quicken their own particular part of the work. In the first fire-engines, a boy was constantly employed to open and shut alternately the communication between the boiler and the cylinder, according as the piston either ascended or descended. One of those boys, who loved to play with his companions, observed that, by tying a string from the handle of the valve which opened this communication to another part of the machine, the valve would open and shut without his assistance, and leave him at liberty to divert himself with his play-fellows. One of the greatest improvements that has been made upon this machine, since it was first invented, was in this manner the discovery of a boy who wanted to save his own labour.

All the improvements in machinery, however, have by no means been the inventions of those who had occasion to use the machines. Many improvements have been made by the ingenuity of the makers of the machines, when to make them became the business of a peculiar trade; and some by that of those who are called philosophers or men of speculation, whose trade it is not to do any thing, but to observe every thing; and who, upon that account, are often capable of combining together the powers of the most distant and dissimilar objects. In the progress of society, philosophy or speculation becomes, like every other employment, the principal or sole trade and occupation of a particular class of citizens. Like every other employment too, it is subdivided into a great number of different branches, each of which affords occupation to a peculiar tribe or class of philosophers; and this subdivision of employment in philosophy, as well as in every other business, improves dexterity, and saves time. Each individual becomes more expert in his own peculiar branch, more work is done upon the whole, and the quantity of science is considerably increased by it.

It is the great multiplication of the productions of all the different arts, in consequence of the division of labour, which occasions, in a well-governed society, that universal opulence which extends itself to the lowest ranks of the people. Every workman has a great quantity of his own work to dispose of beyond what he himself has occasion for; and every other workman being exactly in the same situation, he is enabled to exchange a great quantity of his own goods for a great quantity, or, what comes to the same thing, for the price of a great quantity of theirs. He supplies them abundantly with what they have occasion for, and they accommodate him as amply with what he has occasion for, and a general plenty diffuses itself through all the different ranks of the society.

•　•　•

BOOK IV

Chapter II
Of Restraints Upon the Importation from Foreign Countries of Such Goods as Can Be Produced at Home

. . . But the annual revenue of every society is always precisely equal to the exchangeable value of the whole annual produce of its industry, or rather is precisely the same thing with that exchangeable value. As every individual, therefore, endeavours as much as he can both to employ his capital in the support of domestic industry, and so to direct that industry that its produce may be of the greatest value; every individual necessarily labours to render the annual revenue of the society as great as he can. He generally, indeed, neither intends to promote the public interest, nor knows how much he is promoting it. By preferring the support of domestic to that of foreign industry, he intends only his own security; and by directing that industry in such a manner as its produce may be of the greatest value, he intends only his own gain, and he is in this, as in many other cases, led by an invisible hand to promote an end which was no part of his intention. Nor is it always the worse for the society that it was no part of it. By pursuing his own interest he frequently promotes that of the society more effectually than when he really intends to promote it. I have never known much good done by those who affected to trade for the public good. It is an affectation, indeed, not very common among merchants, and very few words need be employed in dissuading them from it.

What is the species of domestic industry which his capital can employ, and of which the produce is likely to be of the greatest value, every individual, it is evident, can, in his local situation, judge much better than any statesman or lawgiver can do for him. The statesman, who should attempt to direct private people in what manner they ought to employ their capitals, would not only load himself with a most unnecessary attention, but assume an authority which could safely be trusted, not only to no single person, but to no council or senate whatever, and which would nowhere be so dangerous as in the hands of a man who had folly and presumption enough to fancy himself fit to exercise it.

To give the monopoly of the home-market to the produce of domestic industry, in any particular art or manufacture, is in some measure to direct private people in what manner they ought to employ their capitals, and must, in almost all cases, be either a useless or a hurtful regulation. If the produce of domestic can be brought there as cheap as that of foreign industry, the regulation is evidently useless. If it cannot, it must generally be hurtful. It is the maxim of every prudent master of a family, never to attempt to make at home what it will cost him more to make than to buy. The taylor does not attempt to make his own shoes, but buys them of the shoemaker. The shoemaker does not attempt to make his own clothes, but employs a taylor. The farmer attempts to make neither the one nor the other, but employs those different artificers. All of them find it for their interest to employ their whole industry in a way in which they have some advantage over their neighbours, and to purchase with a part of its produce, or what is the same thing, with the price of a part of it, whatever else they have occasion for.

What is prudence in the conduct of every private family, can scarce be folly in that of a great kingdom. If a foreign country can supply us with a commodity cheaper than we ourselves can make it, better buy it of them with some part of the produce of our own industry, employed in a way in which we have some advantage. The general industry of the country, being always in proportion to the capital which employs it, will not thereby be diminished, no more than that of the above-mentioned artificers; but only left to find out the way in which it can be employed with the greatest advantage. It is certainly not employed to the greatest advantage when it is thus directed towards an object which it can buy cheaper than it can make. The value of its annual produce is certainly more or less diminished, when it is thus turned away from producing commodities evidently of more value than the commodity which it is directed to produce. According to the supposition, that commodity could be purchased from foreign countries cheaper than it can be made at home. It could, therefore, have been purchased with a part only of the commodities, or, what is the same thing, with a part only of the price of the commodities, which the industry employed by an equal capital would have produced at home, had it been left to follow its natural course. The industry of the country, therefore, is thus turned away from a more, to a less advantageous employment, and the exchangeable value of its annual produce, instead of being increased, according to the intention of the lawgiver, must necessarily be diminished by every such regulation. . . .

Thomas Jefferson

1743–1826

Thomas Jefferson, the principal author of the Declaration of Independence, was one of the most remarkable men of the eighteenth century. Born into a Virginia planter family, he was educated at the College of William and Mary, studied law, and practiced as a lawyer. At the Continental Congress, he was chosen—along with John Adams, Benjamin Franklin, and two others—to serve as a member of the committee to draft the Declaration of Independence. Jefferson's gifts were recognized immediately and he was given primary responsibility for the document. Jefferson was also one of the finest American architects of his time, inaugurating the neoclassical revival in America with his designs of the Virginia State Capitol, his home at Monticello, and the campus of the University of Virginia, which he founded in 1819. To this day, contemporary interpretation of neoclassical design reflects the influence of Jefferson's Enlightenment sensibility, gracing government and university buildings in Washington and other American cities.

The aim of the Declaration was to declare independence from British rule and to explain the reasoning of the revolutionaries for committing themselves to this action. As well as this informative function, the Declaration had a persuasive aim that was equally important: to convince undecided colonists to support the revolution and to encourage foreign governments, particularly France, to lend their support. In this effort, Jefferson and the Congress wrote a powerful argument, reasoning deductively from "self-evident" truths. Based in large part on Locke, these truths are a central expression of eighteenth-century Enlightenment thought. Jefferson altered Locke's statement of man's rights—life, liberty, and estate—to life, liberty, and the pursuit of happiness. From this major premise follows the principles underlying the formation of government. Through the social contract, government is instituted to protect the rights of the citizen.

No one at the time realized the power and scope of Jefferson's statement on individual rights. Since the time of the American Constitution, which followed in 1789, several amendments have been added to extend the basic rights of the individual to all citizens. The struggle for equal rights, regardless of sex or race, and the efforts to preserve these rights continue to this day. Jefferson's great legacy can be summarized in a phrase from a letter he wrote when he was unable to attend the fiftieth-anniversary celebration of the Declaration of

Independence: that we all should "assume the blessings and security of self-government." He died only a few days later, exactly fifty years after the signing of the Declaration of Independence.

According to the Declaration, what should be done if the established government fails to guard the rights of the individual? What are some of the reasons Jefferson gives for the failure of the British colonial government?

The Declaration of Independence (1776)

When, in the course of human events, it becomes necessary for one people to dissolve the political bands which have connected them with another,
and to assume, among the powers of the earth, the separate and equal station
to which the laws of nature and of nature's God entitle them, a decent respect
to the opinions of mankind requires that they should declare the causes which
impel them to the separation.

We hold these truths to be self-evident, that all men are created equal;
that they are endowed by their Creator with certain unalienable rights; that
among these are life, liberty, and the pursuit of happiness. That, to secure these
rights, governments are instituted among men, deriving their just powers from
the consent of the governed; that, whenever any form of government becomes
destructive of these ends, it is the right of the people to alter or to abolish it,
and to institute a new government, laying its foundation on such principles,
and organizing its powers in such form, as to them shall seem most likely to
effect their safety and happiness. Prudence, indeed, will dictate that governments long established should not be changed for light and transient causes;
and accordingly, all experience hath shown, that mankind are more disposed
to suffer, while evils are sufferable, than to right themselves by abolishing the
forms to which they are accustomed. But, when a long train of abuses and
usurpations, pursuing invariably the same object, evinces a design to reduce
them under absolute despotism, it is their right, it is their duty, to throw off
such government, and to provide new guards for their future security. Such has
been the patient sufferance of these colonies, and such is now the necessity
which constrains them to alter their former systems of government. The history of the present King of Great Britain is a history of repeated injuries and
usurpations, all having, in direct object, the establishment of an absolute tyranny over these states. To prove this, let facts be submitted to a candid world:

He has refused his assent to laws the most wholesome and necessary for
the public good.

He has forbidden his governors to pass laws of immediate and pressing
importance, unless suspended in their operation till his assent should be
obtained; and, when so suspended, he has utterly neglected to attend to them.

He has refused to pass other laws for the accommodation of large districts
of people, unless those people would relinquish the right of representation in
the legislature; a right inestimable to them, and formidable to tyrants only.

He has called together legislative bodies at places unusual, uncomfortable, and distant from the depository of their public records, for the sole purpose of fatiguing them into compliance with his measures.

He has dissolved representative houses repeatedly, for opposing, with manly firmness, his invasions on the rights of the people.

He has refused, for a long time after such dissolutions, to cause others to be elected; whereby the legislative powers, incapable of annihilation, have returned to the people at large for their exercise; the state remaining, in the meantime, exposed to all the dangers of invasion from without, and convulsions within.

He has endeavored to prevent the population of these States; for that purpose, obstructing the laws for naturalization of foreigners, refusing to pass others to encourage their migrations hither, and raising the conditions of new appropriations of lands.

He has obstructed the administration of justice, by refusing his assent to laws for establishing judiciary powers.

He has made judges dependent on his will alone, for the tenure of their offices, and the amount and payment of their salaries.

He has erected a multitude of new offices, and sent hither swarms of officers to harass our people, and eat out their substance.

He has kept among us, in times of peace, standing armies, without the consent of our legislatures.

He has affected to render the military independent of, and superior to, the civil power.

He has combined, with others, to subject us to a jurisdiction foreign to our Constitution, and unacknowledged by our laws; giving his assent to their acts of pretended legislation:

For quartering large bodies of armed troops among us:

For protecting them by a mock trial, from punishment, for any murders which they should commit on the inhabitants of these States:

For cutting off our trade with all parts of the world:

For imposing taxes on us without our consent:

For depriving us, in many cases, of the benefit of trial by jury:

For transporting us beyond seas to be tried for pretended offenses:

For abolishing the free system of English laws in a neighboring province,[1] establishing therein an arbitrary government, and enlarging its boundaries, so as to render it at once an example and fit instrument for introducing the same absolute rule into these colonies:

For taking away our charters, abolishing our most valuable laws, and altering, fundamentally, the forms of our governments:

For suspending our own legislatures, and declaring themselves invested with power to legislate for us in all cases whatsoever.

He has abdicated government here, by declaring us out of his protection, and waging war against us.

He has plundered our seas, ravaged our coasts, burnt our towns, and destroyed the lives of our people.

He is, at this time, transporting large armies of foreign[2] mercenaries to complete the works of death, desolation, and tyranny, already begun, with circumstances of cruelty and perfidy scarcely paralleled in the most barbarous ages, and totally unworthy the head of a civilized nation.

He has constrained our fellow-citizens, taken captive on the high seas, to bear arms against their country, to become the executioners of their friends and brethren, or to fall themselves by their hands.

He has excited domestic insurrections amongst us, and has endeavored to bring on the inhabitants of our frontiers, the merciless Indian savages, whose known rule of warfare is an undistinguished destruction of all ages, sexes, and conditions.

In every stage of these oppressions, we have petitioned for redress, in the most humble terms; our repeated petitions have been answered only by repeated injury. A prince, whose character is thus marked by every act which may define a tyrant, is unfit to be the ruler of a free people.

Nor have we been wanting in attentions to our British brethren. We have warned them, from time to time, of attempts by their legislature to extend an unwarrantable jurisdiction over us. We have reminded them of the circumstances of our emigration and settlement here. We have appealed to their native justice and magnanimity, and we have conjured them, by the ties of our common kindred, to disavow these usurpations, which would inevitably interrupt our connections and correspondence. They, too, have been deaf to the voice of justice and of consanguinity. We must, therefore, acquiesce in the necessity which denounces our separation, and hold them, as we hold the rest of mankind, enemies in war, in peace, friends.

We, therefore, the representatives of the United States of America, in general Congress assembled, appealing to the Supreme Judge of the world for the rectitude of our intentions, do, in the name, and by the authority of the good people of these colonies, solemnly publish and declare, that these united colonies are, and of right ought to be, free and independent states; that they are absolved from all allegiance to the British Crown, and that all political connection between them and the state of Great Britain is, and ought to be, totally dissolved; and that, as free and independent states, they have full power to levy war, conclude peace, contract alliances, establish commerce, and to do all other acts and things which independent states may of right do. And, for the support of this declaration, with a firm reliance on the protection of Divine Providence, we mutually pledge to each other our lives, our fortunes, and our sacred honour.

Notes

[1] Quebec

[2] German

Thomas Jefferson

A Bill Establishing Religious Freedom (1786)

Thomas Jefferson originally drafted this document in 1779. One of the chief ideals of the Enlightenment was that of secularism. For Jefferson and others this meant that religion ought to be a matter of individual conscience, that the state should neither compel allegiance to a particular religion—through taxes or restrictive legislation—nor prevent individuals from freely exercising their religious beliefs. James Madison, another advocate of the secular state, actually moved this act through the Virginia Legislature in the face of attempts to assess a tax to support certain Protestant denominations in Virginia. The Statute became the basis of similar acts passed by other states and of the religion clause of the First Amendment to the U.S. Constitution.

What does Jefferson say about "truth" in this work? What relationship does Jefferson envision between church and state? How might restrictions against the establishment of religion by the state and the free exercise of religion by the individual come into conflict?

A Bill for Establishing
Religious Freedom (1786)

SECTION I. Well aware that the opinions and belief of men depend not on their own will, but follow involuntarily the evidence proposed to their minds; that Almighty God hath created the mind free, and manifested his supreme will that free it shall remain by making it altogether insusceptible of restraint; that all attempts to influence it by temporal punishments, or burthens, or by civil incapacitations, tend only to beget habits of hypocrisy and meanness, and are a departure from the plan of the holy author of our religion, who being lord both of body and mind, yet chose not to propagate it by coercions on either, as was in his Almighty power to do, but to exalt it by its influence on reason alone; that the impious presumption of legislators and rulers, civil as well as ecclesiastical, who, being themselves but fallible and uninspired men, have assumed dominion over the faith of others, setting up their own opinions and modes of thinking as the only true and infallible, and as such endeavoring to impose them on others, hath established and maintained false religions over the greatest part of the world and through all time: That to compel a man to furnish contributions of money for the propagation of opinions which he disbelieves and abhors, is sinful and tyrannical; that even the forcing him to support this or that teacher of his own religious persuasion, is depriving him of the comfortable liberty of giving his contributions to the particular pastor whose morals he would make his pattern, and whose powers he feels most persuasive to righteousness; and is withdrawing from the ministry those temporary rewards, which proceeding from an approbation of their personal conduct, are an additional incitement to earnest and unremitting labours for the instruction of mankind; that our civil rights have no dependence on our religious opinions, any more than our opinions in physics or geometry; that therefore the proscribing any citizen as unworthy the public confidence by laying upon him an incapacity of being called to offices of trust and emolument, unless he profess or renounce this or that religious opinion, is depriving him injuriously of those privileges and advantages to which, in common with his fellow citizens, he has a natural right; that it tends also to corrupt the principles of that very religion it is meant to encourage, by bribing, with a monopoly of worldly honours and emoluments, those who will externally profess and conform to it; that though indeed these are criminals who do not withstand such temptation, yet neither are those innocent who lay the bait in their way;

that the opinions of men are not the object of civil government, nor under its jurisdiction; that to suffer the civil magistrate to intrude his powers into the field of opinion and to restrain the profession or propagation of principles on supposition of their ill tendency is a dangerous fallacy, which at once destroys all religious liberty, because he being of course judge of that tendency will make his opinions the rule of judgment, and approve or condemn the sentiments of others only as they shall square with or differ from his own; that it is time enough for the rightful purposes of civil government for its officers to interfere when principles break out into overt acts against peace and good order; and finally, that truth is great and will prevail if left to herself; that she is the proper and sufficient antagonist to error, and has nothing to fear from the conflict unless by human interposition disarmed of her natural weapons, free argument and debate; errors ceasing to be dangerous when it is permitted freely to contradict them.

SECTION II. We the General Assembly of Virginia do enact that no man shall be compelled to frequent or support any religious worship, place, or ministry whatsoever, nor shall be enforced, restrained, molested, or burthened in his body or goods, nor shall otherwise suffer, on account of his religious opinions or belief; but that all men shall be free to profess, and by argument to maintain, their opinions in matters of religion, and that the same shall in no wise diminish, enlarge, or affect their civil capacities.

SECTION III. And though we well know that this Assembly, elected by the people for the ordinary purposes of legislation only, have no power to restrain the acts of succeeding Assemblies, constituted with powers equal to our own, and that therefore to declare this act irrevocable would be of no effect in law; yet we are free to declare, and do declare, that the rights hereby asserted are of the natural rights of mankind, and that if any act shall be hereafter passed to repeal the present or to narrow its operation, such act will be an infringement of natural right.

James Madison

1751–1836

Alexander Hamilton

c. 1755–1804

After the revolutionary war of the American colonists came to a successful
end in 1781 and the official treaty was signed in 1783, the independent states
faced a challenging set of problems. The states opposed a strongly centralized
federal government, having already endured the tyranny of British rule.
Therefore, a loose confederation emerged under the Articles of Confederation
in 1781. This arrangement proved to be a failure as the confederation depended on voluntary contributions from the states for revenue and troops; moreover,
confederation offered no central regulation of commerce.

The Federalist Papers (1787–1788), eighty-five essays appearing in New
York newspapers, called for a strong federal government. The proponents of
federalism believed that such a government could be designed with safeguards,
such as the separation of the legislative, executive, and judicial branches of government, in order to prevent tyranny (the "Leviathan" of Thomas Hobbes).
Most of the federalist essays were written by Alexander Hamilton, about a fifth
of them by James Madison, and a few by John Jay (1745–1829). The
American Constitution, in reflecting the ideas of such Enlightenment thinkers
as Locke and Montesquieu, is an example of applying "enlightened" reason to
the political arena. As a product of the Enlightenment, the United States has
survived for over two centuries since its official inception in 1789 as one of history's longest-lived democracies.

In reading the selection below, consider the following questions: What
are factions according to Madison and what causes them? Is a faction always a
minority? How can the mischiefs of factions be cured? What is the difference
between a democracy and a republic? What advantages or disadvantages accrue
to a nation as a result of its geographical size? What does Madison mean by his
assertion that "Ambition must be made to counteract ambition"?

from *The Federalist Papers* (1787–1788)

The Federalist No. 10

To the People of the State of New York:

Among the numerous advantages promised by a well-constructed Union, none deserves to be more accurately developed than its tendency to break and control the violence of faction.

• • •

By a faction, I understand a number of citizens, whether amounting to a majority or a minority of the whole, who are united and actuated by some common impulse of passion, or of interest, adverse to the rights of other citizens, or to the permanent and aggregate interests of the community.

There are two methods of curing the mischiefs of faction: the one, by removing its causes; the other, by controlling its effects.

There are again two methods of removing the causes of faction: the one, by destroying the liberty which is essential to its existence; the other, by giving to every citizen the same opinions, the same passions, and the same interests.

It could never be more truly said than of the first remedy, that it is worse than the disease. Liberty is to faction what air is to fire, an aliment without which it instantly expires. But it could not be less folly to abolish liberty, which is essential to political life, because it nourishes faction, than it would be to wish the annihilation of air, which is essential to animal life, because it imparts to fire its destructive agency.

The second expedient is as impracticable as the first would be unwise. As long as the reason of man continues fallible, and he is at liberty to exercise it, different opinions will be formed. As long as the connection subsists between his reason and his self-love, his opinions and his passions will have a reciprocal influence on each other; and the former will be objects to which the latter will attach themselves. The diversity in the faculties of men, from which the rights of property originate, is not less an insuperable obstacle to a uniformity of interests. The protection of these faculties is the first object of government. From the protection of different and unequal faculties of acquiring property, the possession of different degrees and kinds of property immediately results; and from the influence of these on the sentiments and views of the respective proprietors, ensues a division of the society into different interests and parties.

The latent causes of faction are thus sown in the nature of man; and we see them everywhere brought into different degrees of activity, according to the different circumstances of civil society. A zeal for different opinions concerning religion, concerning government, and many other points, as well of speculation as of practice; an attachment to different leaders ambitiously contending for preeminence and power; or to persons of other descriptions whose fortunes have been interesting to the human passions, have, in turn, divided mankind into parties, inflamed them with mutual animosity, and rendered them much more disposed to vex and oppress each other than to co-operate for their common good. So strong is this propensity of mankind to fall into mutual animosities, that where no substantial occasion presents itself, the most frivolous and fanciful distinctions have been sufficient to kindle their unfriendly passions and excite their most violent conflicts. But the most common and durable source of factions has been the various and unequal distribution of property. Those who hold and those who are without property have ever formed distinct interests in society. Those who are creditors, and those who are debtors, fall under a like discrimination. A landed interest, a manufacturing interest, a mercantile interest, a moneyed interest, with many lesser interests, grow up of necessity in civilized nations, and divide them into different classes, actuated by different sentiments and views. The regulation of these various and interfering interests forms the principal task of modern legislation, and involves the spirit of party and faction in the necessary and ordinary operations of the government.

• • •

From this view of the subject it may be concluded that a pure democracy, by which I mean a society consisting of a small number of citizens, who assemble and administer the government in person, can admit of no cure for the mischiefs of faction. A common passion or interest will, in almost every case, be felt by a majority of the whole; a communication and concert result from the form of government itself; and there is nothing to check the inducements to sacrifice the weaker party or an obnoxious individual. Hence it is that such democracies have ever been spectacles of turbulence and contention; have ever been found incompatible with personal security or the rights of property; and have in general been as short in their lives as they have been violent in their deaths. Theoretic politicians, who have patronized this species of government, have erroneously supposed that by reducing mankind to a perfect equality in their political rights, they would, at the same time, be perfectly equalized and assimilated in their possessions, their opinions, and their passions.

A republic, by which I mean a government in which the scheme of representation takes place, opens a different prospect, and promises the cure for which we are seeking. Let us examine the points in which it varies from pure democracy, and we shall comprehend both the nature of the cure and the efficacy which it must derive from the Union.

The two great points of difference between a democracy and a republic are: first, the delegation of the government in the latter to a small number of citizens elected by the rest; secondly, the greater number of citizens and greater sphere of country over which the latter may be extended.

The effect of the first difference is, on the one hand, to refine and enlarge the public views, by passing them through the medium of a chosen body of citizens, whose wisdom may best discern the true interest of their country, and whose patriotism and love of justice will be least likely to sacrifice it to temporary or partial considerations. Under such a regulation, it may well happen that the public voice, pronounced by the representatives of the people, will be more consonant to the public good than if pronounced by the people themselves, convened for the purpose. On the other hand, the effect may be inverted. Men of factious tempers, of local prejudices, or of sinister designs, may by intrigue, by corruption, or by other means, first obtain the suffrages, and then betray the interests of the people. The question resulting is, whether small or extensive republics are more favorable to the election of proper guardians of the public weal; and it is clearly decided in favor of the latter by two obvious considerations.

In the first place, it is to be remarked that, however small the republic may be, the representatives must be raised to a certain number in order to guard against the cabals of a few; and that, however large it may be, they must be limited to a certain number in order to guard against the confusion of a multitude. Hence, the number of representatives in the two cases not being in proportion to that of the two constituents, and being proportionally greater in the small republic, it follows that, if the proportion of fit characters be not less in the large than in the small republic, the former will present a greater option and consequently a greater probability of a fit choice.

In the next place, as each representative will be chosen by a greater number of citizens in the large than in the small republic, it will be more difficult for unworthy candidates to practise with success the vicious arts by which elections are too often carried; and the suffrages of the people being more free, will be more likely to centre in men who possess the most attractive merit and the most diffusive and established characters.

It must be confessed that in this, as in most other cases, there is a mean, on both sides of which inconveniences will be found to lie. By enlarging too much the number of electors, you render the representative too little acquainted with all their local circumstances and lesser interests: as by reducing it too much, you render him unduly attached to these, and too little fit to comprehend and pursue great and national objects. The federal Constitution forms a happy combination in this respect; the great and aggregate interests being referred to the national, the local and particular to the State legislatures.

• • •

Hence, it clearly appears that the same advantage which a republic has over a democracy in controlling the effects of faction is enjoyed by a large over a small republic,—is enjoyed by the Union over the States composing it.

• • •

The Federalist No. 51

To the People of the State of New York:

To what expedient, then, shall we finally resort for maintaining in practice the necessary partition of power among the several departments as laid down in the Constitution? The only answer that can be given is, that as all these exterior provisions are found to be inadequate, the defect must be supplied by so contriving the interior structure of the government as that its several constituent parts may, by their mutual relations, be the means of keeping each other in their proper places. Without presuming to undertake a full development of this important idea, I will hazard a few general observations, which may perhaps place it in a clearer light, and enable us to form a more correct judgment of the principles and structure of the government planned by the convention.

In order to lay a due foundation for that separate and distinct exercise of the different powers of government, which to a certain extent is admitted on all hands to be essential to the preservation of liberty, it is evident that each department should have a will of its own; and consequently should be so constituted that the members of each should have as little agency as possible in the appointment of the members of the others. Were this principle rigorously adhered to, it would require that all the appointments for the supreme executive, legislative, and judiciary magistracies should be drawn from the same fountain of authority, the people, through channels having no communication whatever with one another. Perhaps such a plan of constructing the several departments would be less difficult in practice than it may in contemplation appear. Some difficulties, however, and some additional expense would attend the execution of it. Some deviations, therefore, from the principle must be admitted. In the constitution of the judiciary department in particular, it might be inexpedient to insist rigorously on the principle: first, because peculiar qualifications being essential in the members, the primary consideration ought to be to select that mode of choice which best secures these qualifications; secondly, because the permanent tenure by which the appointments are held in that department must soon destroy all sense of dependence on the authority conferring them.

• • •

Ambition must be made to counteract ambition. The interest of the man must be connected with the constitutional rights of the place. It may be a reflection on human nature, that such devices should be necessary to control the abuses of government. But what is government itself, but the greatest of all reflections on human nature? If men were angels, no government would be necessary. If angels were to govern men, neither external nor internal controls on government would be necessary. In framing a government which is to be administered by men over men, the great difficulty lies in this: you must first enable the government to control the governed; and in the next place oblige it to control itself. A dependence on the people is, no doubt, the primary control on the government; but experience has taught mankind the necessity of auxiliary precautions.

•   •   •

National Assembly of France

1787–1788

Some contemporary observers of the French Revolution, as well as later critics, believed that the ideas of the Enlightenment influenced the tumultuous events of 1789. Indeed, social contract theories which transformed subjects into citizens and unleashed the idea of rights were promoted by some of the philosophes, albeit with considerable limitations. Even more generally, Enlightenment criticism of religion as well as social and political institutions certainly weakened the Old Regime. Successful reform efforts, the abolition of torture for example, encouraged people to demand more.

These demands culminated in the following document. Though it lasted for only four years in this form, the Declaration of the Rights of Man and Citizen, more than any other from the Revolution, has had a major impact on world history, even serving as the model for the United Nations' Universal Declaration of Human Rights. An amalgam of Enlightenment political thought, with its emphasis on natural law, and Old Regime constitutionalism, the declaration guaranteed rights to liberty, property, and freedom from oppression. Similar to its American predecessor, it also provided for a strict separation of powers. It was replaced in 1793, which in turn was replaced in 1795 by "The Declaration of the Rights and Duties of Man and Citizen." Yet, its general principles were rarely disavowed by future governments in France.

How does the declaration compare with that offered by Jefferson? de Gouges (see p. 175)? What Enlightenment sources can be identified as influences? What are its limitations?

Declaration of the Rights
of Man and Citizen (1789)

The Representatives of the French people, organized in National Assembly, considering that ignorance, forgetfulness or contempt of the rights of man, are the sole causes of the public miseries and of the corruption of governments, have resolved to set forth in a solemn declaration the natural, inalienable, and sacred rights of man, in order that this declaration, being ever present to all members of the social body, may unceasingly remind them of their rights and their duties; in order that the acts of the legislative power and those of the executive power may be each moment compared with the aim of every political institution and thereby may be more respected; and in order that the demands of the citizens, grounded henceforth upon simple and incontestable principles, may always take the direction of maintaining the constitution and welfare of all.

In consequence, the National Assembly recognizes and declares, in the presence and under the auspices of the Supreme Being, the following rights of man and citizen.

1. Men are born free and remain equal in rights. Social distinctions can be based only on public utility.

2. The aim of every political association is the preservation of the natural and imprescriptible rights of man. These rights are liberty, property, security, and resistance to oppression.

3. The source of all sovereignty is essentially in the nation; no body, no individual can exercise authority that does not proceed from it in plain terms.

4. Liberty consists in the power to do anything that does not injure others; accordingly, the exercise of the rights of each man has no limits except those that secure to the other members of society the enjoyment of these same rights. These limits can be determined only by law.

5. The law has only the right to forbid such actions as are injurious to society. Nothing can be forbidden that is not interdicted by the law, and no one can be constrained to do that which it does not order.

6. Law is the expression of the general will. All citizens have the right to take part personally, or by their representatives, in its formation. It must be the same for all, whether it protects or punishes. All citizens being equal in its eyes, are equally eligible to all public dignities, places, and employments, according to their capacities, and without other distinction than that of their virtues and talents.

7. No man can be accused, arrested, or detained, except in the cases determined by the law and according to the forms it has prescribed. Those who procure, expedite, execute, or cause to be executed, arbitrary orders ought to be punished: but every citizen summoned or seized in virtue of the law ought to render instant obedience; he makes himself guilty by resistance.

8. The law ought only to establish penalties that are strict and obviously necessary, and no one can be punished except in virtue of a law established and promulgated prior to the offense and legally applied.

9. Every man being presumed innocent until he has been pronounced guilty, if it is thought indispensable to arrest him, all severity that may not be necessary to secure his person ought to be strictly suppressed by law.

10. No one should be disturbed on account of his opinion, even religious, provided their manifestation does not derange the public order established by law.

11. The free communication of ideas and opinions is one of the most precious of the rights of man; every citizen can then freely speak, write, and print, subject to responsibility for the abuse of this freedom in the cases determined by law.

12. The guarantee of the rights of man and citizen requires a public force; this force then is instituted for the advantage of all and not for the personal benefit of those to whom it is entrusted.

13. For the maintenance of the public force and for the expenses of administration a general tax is indispensable; it ought to be equally apportioned among all citizens according to their means.

14. All citizens have the right to ascertain, by themselves or by their representatives, the necessity of the public tax, to consent to it freely, to follow the employment of it, and to determine the quota, the assessment, the collection, and the duration of it.

15. Society has the right to call for an account of his administration of every public agent.

16. Any society in which the guarantee of the rights is not secured, or the separation of powers not determined, has no constitution at all.

17. Property being a sacred and inviolable right, no one can be deprived of it, unless a legally established public necessity evidently demands it, under the condition of a just and prior indemnity.

French Constitution

The National Assembly, wishing to establish the French constitution upon the principles which it has just recognized and declared, abolishes irrevocably the institutions that have injured liberty and the equality of rights.

There is no longer nobility, nor peerage, nor hereditary distinctions, nor distinctions of orders, nor feudal regime, nor patrimonial jurisdictions, nor any titles, denominations, or prerogatives derived therefrom, nor any order of chivalry, nor any corporations or decorations which demanded proof of nobility or that were grounded upon distinctions of birth, nor any superiority other than that of public officials in the exercise of their functions.

There is no longer sale or inheritance of any public office.

There is no longer for any part of the nation nor for any individual any privilege or exception to the law that is common to all Frenchmen.

There are no longer "jurandes," nor corporations of professions, arts, and crafts.

The law no longer recognizes religious vows, nor any other obligation which may be contrary to natural rights or the constitution.

Jeremy Bentham

1748–1832

Bentham was a precocious boy who entered Oxford University at age 12; his father had high expectations and intended for him to pursue a career in law. At Oxford, Bentham studied under Blackstone, whose authoritative *Commentaries* (1765–1769) formed the first synthesis of English law and jurisprudence. Blackstone held that the essential law of England was based on cases and rulings of the past, and the justification for law is its acceptance through accumulated tradition and precedent. Contrary to the English legal tradition, and to Blackstone, Bentham argued that English law had no valid philosophical foundation and was adhered to through mysticism and tradition rather than reason. Similarly, Bentham dismissed abstract explanations of Natural Law and Natural Rights as not only lacking a scientific, rational foundation, but as "nonsense on stilts," because they are held up as foundational, but lack foundation themselves. In 1789, Bentham published his *Introduction to Principles of Morals and Legislation*, which sought to provide a *rational* basis for not only the law, but for ethics and all social institutions, founded on the basis of utility.

Philosophically, Bentham was a radical, but not in the modern sense. "Radical" comes from the Latin *radix*, which means "root"; Bentham and his followers proposed to go to the foundations of reason and construct an ethical system from the root motivations of human behavior which could be used to optimally design institutions. In this way, Bentham sought to establish a scientific, rational basis for the law, the penal code, the political structure, and all human institutions, a philosophy known today as Utilitarianism. He formulated the Principle of Utility, which is commonly reduced to the idea that every action or policy that we make ought to have the "greatest good for the greatest number" as its objective. Even today, contemporary institutions, including democracy, free markets, property rights, and free expression are often justified on utilitarian grounds. The rest of his life was devoted to elaborating on the idea of Utilitarianism and educating others of the wisdom of his system. This devotion to Utilitarianism lasted up to his death: his will stipulated that his body should be dissected to promote scientific knowledge, and that his skeleton, dressed in his clothes, should be displayed at University College, London, as a model for others to remember his lessons. His remains are on display there to this day.

Utilitarianism is held to provide an objective, scientific basis for judging the rightness and wrongness of actions—a scientific ethics—that follows from Bentham's assessment of human psychology as being self-interested. How does Bentham's introduction illustrate the application of the scientific method to the social sphere that characterizes the Enlightenment? Is it appropriate to derive an ethical worldview and principles of moral action from a statement based on empirical observation? Bentham dismisses abstract natural rights, such as those delineated by Locke, as "nonsense on stilts." Is there really greater validity in a scientific basis for determining rights and action, such as Utilitarianism, than in abstract argument?

from *The Introduction to the Principles of Morals and Legislation* (1789)

Chapter 1
Of the Principle of Utility

I. Nature has placed mankind under the governance of two sovereign masters, *pain* and *pleasure*. It is for them alone to point out what we ought to do, as well as to determine what we shall do. On the one hand the standard of right and wrong, on the other the chain of causes and effects, are fastened to their throne. They govern us in all we do, in all we say, in all we think: every effort we can make to throw off our subjection, will serve but to demonstrate and confirm it. In words a man may pretend to abjure their empire: but in reality he will remain subject to it all the while. The *principle of utility*[1] recognises this subjection, and assumes it for the foundation of that system, the object of which is to rear the fabric of felicity by the hands of reason and of law. Systems which attempt to question it, deal in sounds instead of sense, in caprice instead of reason, in darkness instead of light.

But enough of metaphor and declamation: it is not by such means that moral science is to be improved.

II. The principle of utility is the foundation of the present work: it will be proper therefore at the outset to give an explicit and determinate account of what is meant by it. By the principle[2] of utility is meant that principle which approves or disapproves of every action whatsoever, according to the tendency it appears to have to augment or diminish the happiness of the party whose interest is in question: or, what is the same thing in other words, to promote or to oppose that happiness. I say of every action whatsoever; and therefore not only of every action of a private individual, but of every measure of government.

III. By utility is meant that property in any object, whereby it tends to produce benefit, advantage, pleasure, good, or happiness, (all this in the present case comes to the same thing) or (what comes again to the same thing) to prevent the happening of mischief, pain, evil, or unhappiness to the party whose interest is considered: if that party be the community in general, then the happiness of the community: if a particular individual, then the happiness of that individual.

IV. The interest of the community is one of the most general expressions that can occur in the phraseology of morals: no wonder that the meaning of it is often lost. When it has a meaning, it is this. The community is a fictitious *body*, composed of the individual persons who are considered as constituting as it were its *members*. The interest of the community then is, what?—the sum of the interests of the several members who compose it.

V. It is in vain to talk of the interest of the community, without understanding what is the interest of the individual.[3] A thing is said to promote the interest, or to be *for* the interest, of an individual, when it tends to add to the sum total of his pleasures: or, what comes to the same thing, to diminish the sum total of his pains.

VI. An action then may be said to be conformable to the principle of utility, or, for shortness sake, to utility, (meaning with respect to the community at large) when the tendency it has to augment the happiness of the community is greater than any it has to diminish it.

VII. A measure of government (which is but a particular kind of action, performed by a particular person or persons) may be said to be conformable to or dictated by the principle of utility, when in like manner the tendency which it has to augment the happiness of the community is greater than any which it has to diminish it.

VIII. When an action, or in particular a measure of government, is supposed by a man to be conformable to the principle of utility, it may be convenient, for the purposes of discourse, to imagine a kind of law or dictate, called a law or dictate of utility: and to speak of the action in question, as being conformable to such law or dictate.

IX. A man may be said to be a partizan of the principle of utility, when the approbation or disapprobation he annexes to any action, or to any measure, is determined by and proportioned to the tendency which he conceives it to have to augment or to diminish the happiness of the community: or in other words, to its conformity or unconformity to the laws or dictates of utility.

X. Of an action that is conformable to the principle of utility one may always say either that it is one that ought to be done, or at least that it is not one that ought not to be done. One may say also, that it is right it should be done; at least that it is not wrong it should be done: that it is a right action; at least that it is not a wrong action. When thus interpreted, the words *ought*, and *right* and *wrong*, and others of that stamp, have a meaning: when otherwise, they have none.

XI. Has the rectitude of this principle been ever formally contested? It should seem that it had, by those who have not known what they have been meaning. Is it susceptible of any direct proof? it should seem not: for that which is used to prove every thing else, cannot itself be proved: a chain of proofs must have their commencement somewhere. To give such proof is as impossible as it is needless.

XII. Not that there is or ever has been that human creature breathing, however stupid or perverse, who has not on many, perhaps on most occasions of his life, deferred to it. By the natural constitution of the human frame, on most occasions of their lives men in general embrace this principle, without thinking of it: if not for the ordering of their own actions, yet for the trying of their own actions, as well as of those of other men. There have been, at the same time, not many, perhaps, even of the most intelligent, who have been disposed to embrace it purely and without reserve. There are even few who have not taken some occasion or other to quarrel with it, either on account of their not understanding always how to apply it, or on account of some prejudice or other which they were afraid to examine into, or could not bear to part with. For such is the stuff that man is made of: in principle and in practice, in a right track and in a wrong one, the rarest of all human qualities is consistency.

XIII. When a man attempts to combat the principle of utility, it is with reasons drawn, without his being aware of it, from that very principle itself.[4] His arguments, if they prove any thing, prove not that the principle is *wrong*, but that, according to the applications he supposes to be made of it, it is *misapplied*. Is it possible for a man to move the earth? Yes; but he must first find out another earth to stand upon.

XIV. To disprove the propriety of it by arguments is impossible; but, from the causes that have been mentioned, or from some confused or partial view of it, a man may happen to be disposed not to relish it. Where this is the case, if he thinks the settling of his opinions on such a subject worth the trouble, let him take the following steps, and at length, perhaps, he may come to reconcile himself to it.

1. Let him settle with himself, whether he would wish to discard this principle altogether; if so, let him consider what it is that all his reasonings (in matters of politics especially) can amount to?

2. If he would, let him settle with himself, whether he would judge and act without any principle, or whether there is any other he would judge and act by?

3. If there be, let him examine and satisfy himself whether the principle he thinks he has found is really any separate intelligible principle; or whether it be not a mere principle in words, a kind of phrase, which at bottom expresses neither more nor less than the mere averment of his own unfounded sentiments; that is, what in another person he might be apt to call caprice?

4. If he is inclined to think that his own approbation or disapprobation, annexed to the idea of an act, without any regard to its consequences, is a sufficient foundation for him to judge and act upon, let him ask himself whether his sentiment is to be a standard of right and wrong, with respect to every other

man, or whether every man's sentiment has the same privilege of being a standard to itself?

5. In the first case, let him ask himself whether his principle is not despotical, and hostile to all the rest of human race?

6. In the second case, whether it is not anarchial, and whether at this rate there are not as many different standards of right and wrong as there are men? and whether even to the same man, the same thing, which is right to-day, may not (without the least change in its nature) be wrong to-morrow? and whether the same thing is not right and wrong in the same place at the same time? and in either case, whether all argument is not at an end? and whether, when two men have said, 'I like this,' and 'I don't like it,' they can (upon such a principle) have any thing more to say?

7. If he should have said to himself, No: for that the sentiment which he proposes as a standard must be grounded on reflection, let him say on what particulars the reflection is to turn? if on particulars having relation to the utility of the act, then let him say whether this is not deserting his own principle, and borrowing assistance from that very one in opposition to which he sets it up: or if not on those particulars, on what other particulars?

8. If he should be for compounding the matter, and adopting his own principle in part, and the principle of utility in part, let him say how far he will adopt it?

9. When he has settled with himself where he will stop, then let him ask himself how he justifies to himself the adopting it so far? and why he will not adopt it any farther?

10. Admitting any other principle than the principle of utility to be a right principle, a principle that it is right for a man to pursue; admitting (what is not true) that the word *right* can have a meaning without reference to utility, let him say whether there is any such thing as a *motive* that a man can have to pursue the dictates of it: if there is, let him say what that motive is, and how it is to be distinguished from those which enforce the dictates of utility: if not, then lastly let him say what it is this other principle can be good for?

Notes

[1] Note by the Author, July 1822.

To this denomination has of late been added, or substituted, the *greatest happiness* or *greatest felicity* principle: this for shortness, instead of saying at length *that principle* which states the greatest happiness of all those whose interest is in question, as being the right and proper, and only right and proper and universally desirable, end of human action: of human action in every situation, and in particular in that of a functionary or set of functionaries exercising the powers of Government. The word *utility* does not so clearly point to the ideas of *pleasure* and *pain* as the words *happiness* and *felicity* do: nor does it lead us to the consideration of the *number*, of the interests affected; to the *number*, as being the circumstance, which contributes, in the largest proportion, to the formation of the standard here in question; the *standard of right and wrong*, by which alone the propriety of human conduct, in every situation, can with propriety be tried. This want of a sufficiently manifest connexion between the ideas of *happiness* and *pleasure* on the one hand, and the idea of *utility* on the other, I have every now and then found operating, and with but too much efficiency, as a bar to the acceptance, that might otherwise have been given, to this principle.

2 The word principle is derived from the Latin principium: which seems to be compounded of the two words *primus*, first, or chief, and *cipium*, a termination which seems to be derived from *capio*, to take, as in *mancipium, municipium*; to which are analogous, *auceps, forceps*, and others. It is a term of very vague and very extensive signification: it is applied to any thing which is conceived to serve as a foundation or beginning to any series of operations: in some cases, of physical operations; but of mental operations in the present case.

The principle here in question may be taken for an act of the mind; a sentiment; a sentiment of approbation; a sentiment which, when applied to an action, approves of its utility, as that quality of it by which the measure of approbation or disapprobation bestowed upon it ought to be governed.

3 Interest is one of those words, which not having any superior *genus*, cannot in the ordinary way be defined.

4 'The principle of utility, (I have heard it said) is a dangerous principle: it is dangerous on certain occasions to consult it.' This is as much as to say, what? that it is not consonant to utility, to consult utility: in short, that it is *not* consulting it, to consult it.

Addition by the Author, July 1822.

Not long after the publication of the Fragment on Government, anno 1776, in which, in the character of an all-comprehensive and all-commanding principle, the principle of *utility* was brought to view, one person by whom observation to the above effect was made was *Alexander Wedderburn*, at that time Attorney or Solicitor General, afterwards successively Chief Justice of the Common Pleas, and Chancellor of England, under the successive titles of Lord Loughborough and Earl of Rosslyn. It was made—not indeed in my hearing, but in the hearing of a person by whom it was almost immediately communicated to me. So far from being self-contradictory, it was a shrewd and perfectly true one. By that distinguished functionary, the state of the Government was thoroughly understood: by the obscure individual, at that time not so much as supposed to be so: his disquisitions had not been as yet applied, with any thing like a comprehensive view, to the field of Constitutional Law, nor therefore to those features of the English Government, by which the greatest happiness of the ruling *one* with or without that of a favoured few, are now so plainly seen to be the only ends to which the course of it has at any time been directed. The *principle of utility* was an appellative, at that time employed by me, as it had been by others, to designate that which, in a more perspicuous and instructive manner, may, as above, be designated by the name of the *greatest happiness principle*. 'This principle (said Wedderburn) is a dangerous one.' Saying so, he said that which, to a certain extent, is strictly true: a principle, which lays down, as the only *right* and justifiable end of Government, the greatest happiness of the greatest number—how can it be denied to be a dangerous one? dangerous it unquestionably is, to every government which has for its actual end or object, the greatest happiness of a certain *one*, with or without the addition of some comparatively small number of others, whom it is matter of pleasure or accommodation to him to admit, each of them, to a share in the concern, on the footing of so many junior partners. *Dangerous* it therefore really was, to the interest—the sinister interest—of all those functionaries, himself included, whose interest it was, to maximize delay, vexation, and expense, in judicial and other modes of procedure, for the sake of the profit, extractible out of the expense. In a Government which had for its end in view the greatest happiness of the greatest number, Alexander Wedderburn might have been Attorney General and then Chancellor: but he would not have been Attorney General with £15,000 a year, nor Chancellor, with a peerage with a veto upon all justice, with £25,000 a year, and with 500 sinecures at his disposal, under the name of Ecclesiastical Benefices, besides *et cæteras*.

Edmund Burke

1729–1797

Edmund Burke was born in Dublin, Ireland; his father was a middle-class Protestant attorney and his mother a Roman Catholic. Sickly as a youth, Burke was sent to a Catholic school in Ballyduff, his mother's former home, and then with his brothers to a boarding school in Ballitore. At the age of fifteen he was admitted to Trinity College, Dublin, where he studied philosophy, literature, and history, until his graduation in 1749. Moving to London in 1750, Burke followed his father into the law, entering the Middle Temple (one of London's legal societies), but after starting his preparations for the Bar, he found himself drawn to the life of the literati, frequenting the coffeehouses and theaters. In 1757, Burke published his famous *Philosophical Inquiry into the Origin of Our Ideas of the Sublime and the Beautiful,* in which he offered an examination of the psychological foundations of aesthetics; his approach was rigorously empirical, based on facts he derived from a study of sense experience. He began his career in politics, working as a private secretary to the Marquis of Rockingham, and in 1766 was elected to the House of Commons, where he served until 1795. Burke opposed British policy toward the American colonies, publishing *On American Taxation* in 1774 and *On Conciliation with the Colonies* in 1775, in which he argued that England was guilty of abusing its colonial power.

In 1790, as a response to a speech by the dissenting minister Dr. Richard Price, who praised the French Revolution as comparable to Britain's Glorious Revolution of 1688, Burke wrote and published *Reflections on the Revolution in France.* Within a short time, as many as thirty thousand copies were in print. Many English readers approved of Burke's conservatism and his admonition to consider well the value of tradition, before embarking on a program of change; still, other intellectuals, such as Thomas Paine in America, thought that Burke's objection to the French experiment was proof of a sympathy for absolutist monarchy and religious oppression.

In the excerpt below, consider Burke's claim that convention and history must be taken into account in shaping a form of government adequate to our needs. What are the limits of reason alone in the creation of new political systems? What are the benefits and costs of relying on tradition and historical precedent for future political development?

from *Reflections on the Revolution in France* (1790)

. . . You will observe that from Magna Charta[1] to the Declaration of Right[2] it has been the uniform policy of our constitution to claim and assert our liberties as an *entailed inheritance* derived to us from our forefathers, and to be transmitted to our posterity—as an estate specially belonging to the people of this kingdom, without any reference whatever to any other more general or prior right. By this means our constitution preserves a unity in so great a diversity of its parts. We have an inheritable crown, an inheritable peerage, and a House of Commons and a people inheriting privileges, franchises, and liberties from a long line of ancestors.

This policy appears to me to be the result of profound reflection, or rather the happy effect of following nature, which is wisdom without reflection, and above it. A spirit of innovation is generally the result of a selfish temper and confined views. People will not look forward to posterity, who never look backward to their ancestors. Besides, the people of England well know that the idea of inheritance furnishes a sure principle of conservation and a sure principle of transmission, without at all excluding a principle of improvement. It leaves acquisition free, but it secures what it acquires. Whatever advantages are obtained by a state proceeding on these maxims are locked fast as in a sort of family settlement, grasped as in a kind of mortmain forever. By a constitutional policy, working after the pattern of nature, we receive, we hold, we transmit our government and our privileges in the same manner in which we enjoy and transmit our property and our lives. The institutions of policy, the goods of fortune, the gifts of providence are handed down to us, and from us, in the same course and order. Our political system is placed in a just correspondence and symmetry with the order of the world and with the mode of existence decreed to a permanent body composed of transitory parts, wherein, by the disposition of a stupendous wisdom, molding together the great mysterious incorporation of the human race, the whole, at one time, is never old or middle-aged or young, but, in a condition of unchangeable constancy, moves on through the varied tenor of perpetual decay, fall, renovation, and progression. Thus, by preserving the method of nature in the conduct of the state, in what we improve we are never wholly new; in what we retain we are never wholly obsolete. By adhering in this manner and on those principles to our forefathers, we are guided not by the superstition of antiquarians, but

104

by the spirit of philosophic analogy. In this choice of inheritance we have given to our frame of polity the image of a relation in blood, binding up the constitution of our country with our dearest domestic ties, adopting our fundamental laws into the bosom of our family affections, keeping inseparable and cherishing with the warmth of all their combined and mutually reflected charities our state, our hearths, our sepulchres, and our altars.

Through the same plan of a conformity to nature in our artificial institutions, and by calling in the aid of her unerring and powerful instincts to fortify the fallible and feeble contrivances of our reason, we have derived several other, and those no small, benefits from considering our liberties in the light of an inheritance. Always acting as if in the presence of canonized forefathers, the spirit of freedom, leading in itself to misrule and excess, is tempered with an awful gravity. This idea of a liberal descent inspires us with a sense of habitual native dignity which prevents that upstart insolence almost inevitably adhering to and disgracing those who are the first acquirers of any distinction. By this means our liberty becomes a noble freedom. It carries an imposing and majestic aspect. It has a pedigree and illustrating ancestors. It has its bearings and its ensigns armorial. It has its gallery of portraits, its monumental inscriptions, its records, evidences, and titles. We procure reverence to our civil institutions on the principle upon which nature teaches us to revere individual men: on account of their age and on account of those from whom they are descended. All your sophisters[3] cannot produce anything better adapted to preserve a rational and manly freedom than the course that we have pursued, who have chosen our nature rather than our speculations, our breasts rather than our inventions, for the great conservatories and magazines of our rights and privileges.

● ● ●

The Chancellor of France, at the opening of the states, said, in a tone of oratorical flourish, that all occupations were honorable. If he meant only that no honest employment was disgraceful, he would not have gone beyond the truth. But in asserting that anything is honorable, we imply some distinction in its favor. The occupation of a hairdresser or of a working tallow-chandler cannot be a matter of honor to any person—to say nothing of a number of other more servile employments. Such descriptions of men ought not to suffer oppression from the state; but the state suffers oppression if such as they, either individually or collectively, are permitted to rule. In this you think you are combating prejudice, but you are at war with nature.

I do not, my dear Sir, conceive you to be of that sophistical, captious spirit, or of that uncandid dulness, as to require, for every general observation or sentiment, an explicit detail of the correctives and exceptions which reason will presume to be included in all the general propositions which come from reasonable men. You do not imagine that I wish to confine power, authority, and distinction to blood and names and titles. No, Sir. There is no qualification for government but virtue and wisdom, actual or presumptive. Wherever they are actually found, they have, in whatever state, condition, profession, or trade, the passport of Heaven to human place and honor. Woe to the country which would madly and impiously reject the service of the talents and virtues, civil, military, or religious, that are given to grace and to serve it, and would condemn to obscurity everything formed to diffuse luster and glory around a state. Woe to that country, too, that, passing into the opposite extreme, considers a low education, a mean contracted view of things, a sordid, mercenary occupation as a preferable title to command. Everything ought to be open, but not indifferently, to every man. No rotation; no appointment by lot; no mode of election operating in the spirit of sortition or rotation can be generally good in a government conversant in extensive objects. Because they have no tendency, direct or indirect, to select the man with a view to the duty or to accommodate the one to the other. I do not hesitate to say that the road to eminence and power, from obscure condition, ought not to be made too easy, nor a thing too much of course. If rare merit be the rarest of all rare things, it ought to pass through some sort of probation. The temple of honor ought to be seated on an eminence. If it be opened through virtue, let it be remembered, too, that virtue is never tried but by some difficulty and some struggle.

• • •

It is said that twenty-four millions ought to prevail over two hundred thousand. True; if the constitution of a kingdom be a problem of arithmetic. This sort of discourse does well enough with the lamp-post for its second; to men who *may* reason calmly, it is ridiculous. The will of the many and their interest must very often differ, and great will be the difference when they make an evil choice. A government of five hundred country attornies and obscure curates is not good for twenty-four millions of men, though it were chosen by eight and forty millions, nor is it the better for being guided by a dozen of persons of quality who have betrayed their trust in order to obtain that power. At present, you seem in everything to have strayed out of the high road of nature.

• • •

If civil society be the offspring of convention, that convention must be its law. That convention must limit and modify all the descriptions of constitution which are formed under it. Every sort of legislative, judicial, or executory power are its creatures. They can have no being in any other state of things;

and how can any man claim under the conventions of civil society rights which do not so much as suppose its existence—rights which are absolutely repugnant to it? One of the first motives to civil society, and which becomes one of its fundamental rules, is *that no man should be judge in his own cause.* By this each person has at once divested himself of the first fundamental right of uncovenanted man, that is, to judge for himself and to assert his own cause. He abdicates all right to be his own governor. He inclusively, in a great measure, abandons the right of self-defense, the first law of nature. Men cannot enjoy the rights of an uncivil and of a civil state together. That he may obtain justice, he gives up his right of determining what it is in points the most essential to him. That he may secure some liberty, he makes a surrender in trust of the whole of it.

Government is not made in virtue of natural rights, which may and do exist in total independence of it, and exist in much greater clearness and in a much greater degree of abstract perfection; but their abstract perfection is their practical defect. By having a right to everything they want everything. Government is a contrivance of human wisdom to provide for human *wants.* Men have a right that these wants should be provided for by this wisdom. Among these wants is to be reckoned the want, out of civil society, of a sufficient restraint upon their passions. Society requires not only that the passions of individuals should be subjected, but that even in the mass and body, as well as in the individuals, the inclinations of men should frequently be thwarted, their will controlled, and their passions brought into subjection. This can only be done *by a power out of themselves,* and not, in the exercise of its function, subject to that will and to those passions which it is its office to bridle and subdue. In this sense the restraints on men, as well as their liberties, are to be reckoned among their rights. But as the liberties and the restrictions vary with times and circumstances and admit to infinite modifications, they cannot be settled upon any abstract rule; and nothing is so foolish as to discuss them upon that principle.

The moment you abate anything from the full rights of men, each to govern himself, and suffer any artificial, positive limitation upon those rights, from that moment the whole organization of government becomes a consideration of convenience. This it is which makes the constitution of a state and the due distribution of its powers a matter of the most delicate and complicated skill. It requires a deep knowledge of human nature and human necessities, and of the things which facilitate or obstruct the various ends which are to be pursued by the mechanism of civil institutions. The state is to have recruits to its strength, and remedies to its distempers. What is the use of discussing a man's abstract right to food or medicine? The question is upon the method of procuring and administering them. In that deliberation I shall always advise to call in the aid of the farmer and the physician rather than the professor of metaphysics.

The science of constructing a commonwealth, or renovating it, or reforming it, is, like every other experimental science, not to be taught *a priori*. Nor is it a short experience that can instruct us in that practical science, because the real effects of moral causes are not always immediate; but that which in the first instance is prejudicial may be excellent in its remoter operation, and its excellence may arise even from the ill effects it produces in the beginning. The reverse also happens: and very plausible schemes, with very pleasing commencements, have often shameful and lamentable conclusions. In states there are often some obscure and almost latent causes, things which appear at first view of little moment, on which a very great part of its prosperity or adversity may most essentially depend. The science of government being therefore so practical in itself and intended for such practical purposes—a matter which requires experience, and even more experience than any person can gain in his whole life, however sagacious and observing he may be—it is with infinite caution that any man ought to venture upon pulling down an edifice which has answered in any tolerable degree for ages the common purposes of society, or on building it up again without having models and patterns of approved utility before his eyes.

These metaphysic rights entering into common life, like rays of light which pierce into a dense medium, are by the laws of nature refracted from their straight line. Indeed, in the gross and complicated mass of human passions and concerns the primitive rights of men undergo such a variety of refractions and reflections that it becomes absurd to talk of them as if they continued in the simplicity of their original direction. The nature of man is intricate; the objects of society are of the greatest possible complexity; and, therefore, no simple disposition or direction of power can be suitable either to man's nature or to the quality of his affairs. When I hear the simplicity of contrivance aimed at and boasted of in any new political constitutions, I am at no loss to decide that the artificers are grossly ignorant of their trade or totally negligent of their duty. The simple governments are fundamentally defective, to say no worse of them. If you were to contemplate society in but one point of view, all these simple modes of polity are infinitely captivating. In effect each would answer its single end much more perfectly than the more complex is able to attain all its complex purposes. But it is better that the whole should be imperfectly and anomalously answered than that, while some parts are provided for with great exactness, others might be totally neglected or perhaps materially injured by the over-care of a favorite member.

The pretended rights of these theorists are all extremes; and in proportion as they are metaphysically true, they are morally and politically false. The rights of men are in a sort of *middle*, incapable of definition, but not impossible to be discerned. The rights of men in governments are their advantages; and these are often in balances between differences of good, in compromises sometimes between good and evil, and sometimes between evil and evil. Political reason is a computing principle: adding, subtracting, multiplying, and dividing, morally and not metaphysically or mathematically, true moral denominations.

By these theorists the right of the people is almost always sophistically confounded with their power. The body of the community, whenever it can come to act, can meet with no effectual resistance; but till power and right are the same, the whole body of them has no right inconsistent with virtue, and the first of all virtues, prudence. Men have no right to what is not reasonable and to what is not for their benefit.

• • •

I hear, and I rejoice to hear, that the great lady,[4] the other object of the triumph, has borne that day (one is interested that beings made for suffering should suffer well), and that she bears all the succeeding days, that she bears the imprisonment of her husband,[5] and her own captivity, and the exile of her friends, and the insulting adulation of addresses, and the whole weight of her accumulated wrongs, with a serene patience, in a manner suited to her rank and race, and becoming the offspring of a sovereign distinguished for her piety and her courage; that, like her, she has lofty sentiments; that she feels with the dignity of a Roman matron; that in the last extremity she will save herself from the last disgrace; and that, if she must fall, she will fall by no ignoble hand.

It is now sixteen or seventeen years since I saw the queen of France, then the dauphiness,[6] at Versailles, and surely never lighted on this orb, which she hardly seemed to touch, a more delightful vision. I saw her just above the horizon, decorating and cheering the elevated sphere she just began to move in—glittering like the morning star, full of life and splendor and joy. Oh! what a revolution! and what a heart must I have to contemplate without emotion that elevation and that fall! Little did I dream when she added titles of veneration to those of enthusiastic, distant, respectful love, that she should ever be obliged to carry the sharp antidote against disgrace concealed in that bosom; little did I dream that I should have lived to see such disasters fallen upon her in a nation of gallant men, in a nation of men of honor and of cavaliers. I thought ten thousand swords must have leaped from their scabbards to avenge even a look that threatened her with insult. But the age of chivalry is gone. That of sophisters, economists; and calculators has succeeded; and the glory of Europe is extinguished forever. Never, never more shall we behold that generous loyalty to rank and sex, that proud submission, that dignified obedience, that subordination of the heart which kept alive, even in servitude itself, the spirit of an exalted freedom. The unbought grace of life, the cheap defense of nations, the nurse of manly sentiment and heroic enterprise, is gone! It is gone, that sensibility of principle, that chastity of honor which felt a stain like a wound, which inspired courage whilst it mitigated ferocity, which ennobled whatever it touched, and under which vice itself lost half its evil by losing all its grossness.

• • •

We know, and what is better, we feel inwardly, that religion is the basis of civil society and the source of all good and of all comfort. In England we are so convinced of this, that there is no rust of superstition with which the accumulated absurdity of the human mind might have crusted it over in the course of ages, that ninety-nine in a hundred of the people of England would not prefer to impiety. We shall never be such fools as to call in an enemy to the substance of any system to remove its corruptions, to supply its defects, or to perfect its construction. If our religious tenets should ever want a further elucidation, we shall not call on atheism to explain them. We shall not light up our temple from that unhallowed fire. It will be illuminated with other lights. It will be perfumed with other incense than the infectious stuff which is imported by the smugglers of adulterated metaphysics. If our ecclesiastical establishment should want a revision, it is not avarice or rapacity, public or private, that we shall employ for the audit, or receipt, or application of its consecrated revenue. Violently condemning neither the Greek nor the Armenian, nor, since heats are subsided, the Roman system of religion, we prefer the Protestant, not because we think it has less of the Christian religion in it, but because, in our judgment, it has more. We are Protestants, not from indifference, but from zeal.

We know, and it is our pride to know, that man is by his constitution a religious animal; that atheism is against, not only our reason, but our instincts; and that it cannot prevail long. But if, in the moment of riot and in a drunken delirium from the hot spirit drawn out of the alembic of hell, which in France is now so furiously boiling, we should uncover our nakedness by throwing off that Christian religion which has hitherto been our boast and comfort, and one great source of civilization amongst us and amongst many other nations, we are apprehensive (being well aware that the mind will not endure a void) that some uncouth, pernicious, and degrading superstition might take place of it.

• • •

To avoid, therefore, the evils of inconstancy and versatility, ten thousand times worse than those of obstinacy and the blindest prejudice, we have consecrated the state, that no man should approach to look into its defects or corruptions but with due caution, that he should never dream of beginning its reformation by its subversion, that he should approach to the faults of the state as to the wounds of a father, with pious awe and trembling solicitude. By this wise prejudice we are taught to look with horror on those children of their country who are prompt rashly to hack that aged parent in pieces and put him into the kettle of magicians, in hopes that by their poisonous weeds and wild incantations they may regenerate the paternal constitution and renovate their father's life.

Society is indeed a contract. Subordinate contracts for objects of mere occasional interest may be dissolved at pleasure—but the state ought not to be considered as nothing better than a partnership agreement in a trade of pepper and coffee, calico, or tobacco, or some other such low concern, to be taken up for a little temporary interest, and to be dissolved by the fancy of the parties. It is to be looked on with other reverence, because it is not a partnership in things subservient only to the gross animal existence of a temporary and perishable nature. It is a partnership in all science; a partnership in all art; a partnership in every virtue and in all perfection. As the ends of such a partnership cannot be obtained in many generations, it becomes a partnership not only between those who are living, but between those who are living, those who are dead, and those who are to be born. Each contract of each particular state is but a clause in the great primeval contract of eternal society, linking the lower with the higher natures, connecting the visible and invisible world, according to a fixed compact sanctioned by the inviolable oath which holds all physical and all moral natures, each in their appointed place. This law is not subject to the will of those who by an obligation above them, and infinitely superior, are bound to submit their will to that law. The municipal corporations of that universal kingdom are not morally at liberty at their pleasure, and on their speculations of a contingent improvement, wholly to separate and tear asunder the bands of their subordinate community and to dissolve it into an unsocial, uncivil, unconnected chaos of elementary principles. It is the first and supreme necessity only, a necessity that is not chosen but chooses, a necessity paramount to deliberation, that admits no discussion and demands no evidence, which alone can justify a resort to anarchy. This necessity is no exception to the rule, because this necessity itself is a part, too, of that moral and physical disposition of things to which man must be obedient by consent or force; but if that which is only submission to necessity should be made the object of choice, the law is broken, nature is disobeyed, and the rebellious are outlawed, cast forth, and exiled from this world of reason, and order, and peace, and virtue, and fruitful penitence, into the antagonist world of madness, discord, vice, confusion, and unavailing sorrow. . . .

Notes

[1] Charter of liberties signed by King John of England in 1215.

[2] Parliamentary document forming the basis for England's contribution, accepted by William and Mary in 1689.

[3] Fallacious reasoners.

[4] Marie Antionette, Queen of France.

[5] Louis XVI, King of France (reigned 1774–1792).

[6] Wife of the eldest son of the King of France, at this time Louis XV who reigned from 1715 to 1774.

Benjamin Banneker

1731–1806

Benjamin Banneker was the epitome of the Enlightenment man. Growing up in humble circumstances on a Maryland tobacco farm, the largely self-taught Banneker early on showed a streak of genius. He taught himself the flute and violin, devised an elaborate irrigation system at the age of 15 that kept his family farm flourishing even in drought, and at 21 carved a wooden clock that struck precisely on the hour for more than forty years. Maryland industrialist Joseph Ellicott heard about Banneker's accomplishments and took him under his wing, lending him books on astronomy and mathematics and instruments to conduct his own observations and experiments. While Banneker remained on the family farm, like other Enlightenment figures, he undertook a lifelong and serious study of mathematics, astronomy and other sciences. He predicted a solar eclipse for 14 April 1789, successfully contradicting better-known scientists of the day. He also published acclaimed studies of bees and the life-cycle of the seventeen-year locust.

Banneker is best known for his accomplishments later in life, however. In 1791, President George Washington appointed him to help survey the site for the District of Columbia under the leadership of Major Andrew Ellicott (Joseph's cousin). The pair worked closely with temperamental architect Pierre L'Enfant in creating the design for the new capital. When L'Enfant was fired and took all of his plans with him, Banneker redrew them from memory, single-handedly salvaging the project. In the same year, he followed in the footsteps of another Enlightenment intellectual, Benjamin Franklin, and published his *Almanac and Ephemeris*. Observers favorably compared Banneker's almanac to Franklin's *Poor Richard's Almanac*.

In one important aspect, however, Benjamin Banneker differed dramatically from other Enlightenment figures: he was African-American. Indeed, another of Banneker's lifelong projects was the abolition of slavery and the recognition of the intellectual accomplishments and potential of African peoples. He especially sought to dispel Enlightenment notions of the inherent inferiority of persons of African descent.Banneker responds to these notions in this letter to Thomas Jefferson, Enlightenment hero, author of the Declaration of Independence, Virginia slaveholder and one of the chief American disseminators of the ideology of black racial inferiority.

What arguments did Banneker use to challenge Jefferson's, and other Enlightenment thinkers', contentions of African inferiority? Why did Banneker send Jefferson a copy of his almanac? What do you think of Jefferson's response?

Letter from Benjamin Banneker

Maryland, Baltimore County, Near Ellicott's Lower Mills

August 19th: 1791

Sir,

I am fully sensible of the greatness of that freedom which I take with you on the present occasion; a liberty which Seemed to me scarcely allowable, when I reflected on that distinguished, and dignified station in which you Stand, and the almost general prejudice and prepossession which is so prevalent in the world against those of my complexion.

I suppose it is a truth too well attested to you, to need a proof here, that we are a race of Beings who have long labored under the abuse and censure of the world, that we have long been looked upon with an eye of contempt, and that we have long been considered rather as brutish than human, and scarcely capable of mental endowments.

Sir I hope I may Safely admit, in consequence of that report which hath reached me, that you are a man far less inflexible in Sentiments of this nature, than many others, that you are measurably friendly and well disposed toward us, and that you are willing and ready to Lend your aid and assistance to our relief from those many distresses and numerous calamities to which we are reduced.

Now Sir if this is founded in truth, I apprehend you will readily embrace every opportunity to eradicate that train of absurd and false ideas and oppinions which so generally prevails with respect to us, and that your Sentiments are concurrent with mine, which are that one universal Father hath given being to us all, and that he hath not only made us all of one flesh, but that he hath also without partiality afforded us all the Same Sensations and endued us all with the same faculties and that however variable we may be in Society or religion, however diversified in Situation or colour, we are all of the Same Family, and Stand in the Same relation to him.

Sir, if these are Sentiments of which you are fully persuaded, I hope you cannot but acknowledge, that it is the indispensible duty of those who maintain for themselves the rights of human nature, and who possess the obligations of Christianity, to extend their power and influence to the relief of every part of the human race, from whatever burthen or oppression they may unjustly labor under, and this I apprehend a full conviction of the truth and obligation of these principles should lead all to.

Sir, I have long been convinced, that if your love for your Selves, and for those inestimable laws which preserved to you the rights of human nature, was founded on Sincerity, you could not but be Solicitous, that every Individual, of whatsoever rank or distinction, might with you equally enjoy the blessings thereof, neither could you rest Satisfyed short of the most active diffusion of your exertions, in order to their promotion from any State of degradation, to which the unjustifyable cruelty and barbarism of men may have reduced them.

Sir I freely and Chearfully acknowledge, that I am of the African race, and in that colour which is natural to them of the deepest dye, and it is under a Sense of the most profound gratitude to the Supreme Ruler of the universe, that I now confess to you, that I am not under that State of tyrannical thraldom, and inhuman captivity, to which too many of my brethren are doomed; but that I have abundantly tasted of the fruition of those blessings which proceed from that free and unequalled liberty with which you are favoured and which I hope you will willingly allow you have received from the immediate hand of that Being, from whom proceedeth every good and perfect gift.

Sir, Suffer me to recall to your mind that time in which the Arms and tyranny of the British Crown were exerted with every powerful effort in order to reduce you to a State of Servitude, look back I intreat you on the variety of dangers to which you were exposed, reflect on that time in which every human aid appeared unavailable, and in which even hope and fortitude wore the aspect of inability to the Conflict, and you cannot but be led to a Serious and grateful Sense of your miraculous and providential preservation; you cannot but acknowledge, that the present freedom and tranquility which you enjoy you have mercifully received, and that it is the peculiar blessing of Heaven.

This, Sir, was a time when you clearly saw into the injustice of a State of Slavery, and in which you had just apprehensions of the horrors of its condition, it was now that your abhorrence thereof was so excited, that you publickly held forth this true and invaluable doctrine, which is worthy to be recorded and remember'd in all Succeeding ages. "We hold these truths to be Self evident, that all men are created equal, and that they are endowed by their creator with certain unalienable rights, that among these are life, liberty, and the pursuit of happyness."

Here Sir, was a time in which your tender feelings for your selves had engaged you thus to declare, you were then impressed with proper ideas of the great valuation of liberty, and the free possession of those blessings to which you were entitled by nature; but Sir how pitiable is it to reflect, that altho you were so fully convinced of the benevolence of the Father of mankind, and of his equal and impartial distribution of those rights and privileges which he hath conferred upon them, that you should at the Same time counteract his mercies, in detaining by fraud and violence so numerous a part of my brethren under groaning captivity and cruel oppression, that you should at the Same time be found guilty of that most criminal act, which you professedly detested in others, with respect to yourselves.

Sir, I suppose that your knowledge of the situation of my brethren is too extensive to need a recital here; neither shall I presume to prescribe methods by which they may be relieved; otherwise than by recommending to you and all others, to wean yourselves from those narrow prejudices which you have imbibed with respect to them, and as Job proposed to his friends "Put your Soul in their Souls stead" thus shall your hearts be enlarged with kindness and benevolence toward them, and thus shall you need neither the direction of myself or others in what manner to proceed herein.

And now, Sir, although my Sympathy and affection for my brethren hath caused my enlargement thus far, I ardently hope that your candour and generosity will plead with you in my behalf, when I make known to you, that it was not originally my design; but that having taken up my pen in order to direct to you as a present, a copy of an Almanack which I have calculated for the Succeeding year, I was unexpectedly and unavoidably led thereto.

This calculation, Sir, is the production of my arduous Study in this my advanced Stage of life; for having long had unbounded desires to become acquainted with the Secrets of nature, I have had to gratify my curiosity herein thro my own assiduous application to Astronomical Study, in which I need not to recount to you the many difficulties and disadvantages which I have had to encounter.

And altho I had almost declined to make my calculation for the ensuing year, in consequence of that time which I had allotted therefor being taking up at the Federal Territory by the request of Mr. Andrew Ellicott, yet finding myself under Several engagements to printers of this state to whom I had communicated my design, on my return to my place of residence, I industriously apply'd myself thereto, which I hope I have accomplished with correctness and accuracy; a copy of which I have taken the liberty to direct to you, and which I humbly request you will favourably receive, and altho you may have the opportunity of perusing it after its publication, yet I chose to send it to you in manuscript previous thereto, that thereby you might not only have an earlier inspection, but that you might also view it in my own hand writing.—And now Sir, I shall conclude and Subscribe my Self, with the most profound respect your most Obedient humble Servant,

Benjamin Banneker

To Benjamin Banneker

Philadelphia Aug. 30. 1791.

Sir,

I thank you sincerely for your letter of the 19th. instant and for the Almanac it contained. No body wishes more than I do to see such proofs as you exhibit, that nature has given to our black brethren, talents equal to those of the other colours of men, and that the appearance of a want of them is owing merely to the degraded condition of their existence both in Africa and America. I can add with truth that no body wishes more ardently to see a good system commenced for raising the condition both of their body and mind to what it ought to be, as fast as the imbecillity of their present existence, and other circumstances which cannot be neglected, will admit.—I have taken the liberty of sending your almanac to Monsieur de Condorcet, Secretary of the Academy of sciences at Paris, and member of the Philanthropic society because I considered it as a document to which your whole colour had a right for their justification against the doubts which have been entertained of them. I am with great esteem, Sir Your most obedt. humble servt.,

Th: Jefferson

Emperor Ch'ien-lung

Reign: 1736–1796

The grandson of K'ang-hsi, Ch'ien-lung is the most famous of the Qing emperors. It was during his reign that China achieved its greatest geographic extent and its population doubled. Praised by Voltaire in France as the ideal philosopher-king, Ch'ien-lung continued his grandfather's patronage of the arts and sciences.

Ch'ien-lung increased restrictions on Western activity in China. K'ang-hsi had already expressed nervousness about the proliferation of Western missionaries; he tolerated their presence but sought to limit their influence on the general population. Ch'ien-lung was more concerned with the economic impact of Western commerce, British trade in particular. Only government-appointed Chinese merchants could trade with British companies, and all transactions had to occur outside city walls. Already with a foothold in India, the British sought to expand Asian trade. One of their envoys, sent in 1759, was imprisoned for three years because he violated Ch'ien-lung's prohibitions which also included learning Chinese. In 1792, George III sent another envoy, this time in a heavily armed warship bearing gifts for the emperor and a personal letter requesting an easing of China's restrictions. What follows is Ch'ien-lung's response.

This letter is important because it illustrates China's traditional disdain for Europeans and its self-sufficiency. It also reveals the clash of cultures which would mark all of Europe's imperialist overtures. Ch'ien-lung rejected England's request. One consequence was a worsening in the balance of trade between China and England which would inspire England to take more drastic measures (the Opium wars of the mid-nineteenth century). On what basis does Ch'ien-lung reject both British goods and British "civilization?" How was China better able to resist European domination than the civilizations of the Americas? What would Voltaire have thought about this clash with the British?

119

Letter to King George III (1793)

"Chu Kuei (Viceroy of Canton) memorialises Us that the King of England has forwarded a memorial with tribute. Two years ago, on the occasion of the tribute mission from the King coming to Peking, We conferred upon him many valuable presents, so he has now dispatched a further memorial with offerings of tribute, thus indicating his loyal sincerity. We raise absolutely no objection to the fact of his having omitted to send a mission on this occasion, and are graciously pleased to accept his offerings. In addition, We bestow upon him the following mandate: "Your nation is inaccessible, lying far beyond the dividing seas, but you sent a mission with a memorial and tribute to pay homage at our Court, and We, in recognition of your loyal sincerity, conferred upon you our mandate and valuable gifts, as evidence of our satisfaction. Now, O King, you have again prepared a memorial and offerings, which have been conveyed by your barbarian vessels to Canton and transmitted to Us. Your reverent submission to Our person is manifest. Our Celestial dynasty, which sways the wide world, attaches no value to the costly presents which are offered at Our Court: what We appreciate is the humble spirit of the offerers. We have commanded Our Viceroy to accept your tribute in order that your reverence may be duly recognised.

"As regarding Our sending of a punitive expedition to Nepal, Our Commander-in-chief marched at the head of a great army into that country, occupied the chief strategic points, and terrified the Ghoorkas into grovelling submission to Our majestic Empire. Our Commander-in-chief duly memorialised Us, and We, whose Imperial clemency is world-wide, embracing Chinese and foreigners alike, could not endure the thought of exterminating the entire population of the country. Accordingly We accepted their surrender. At that time Our Commander-in-chief duly informed Us of your having dispatched a mission into Tibet, with a petition to Our Resident, stating that you had advised the Nepalese to surrender. But at the time of your petition Our troops had already gained a complete victory and the desired end had been attained. We were not obliged to trouble your troops to render assistance. You allude to this matter in your present memorial, but are doubtless ignorant of the precise course of events in Nepal, as your tribute mission was on its way to Peking at the time of these occurrences. Nevertheless, O King, you entertained a clear perception of your duty towards Us, and your reverent acknowledgment of Our dynasty's supremacy is highly praiseworthy.

"We therefore now bestow upon you various costly gifts. Do you, O King, display even more energetic loyalty in future and endeavour to deserve for ever Our gracious affection, so that we may conform to Our earnest resolve to pacify distant tribes and to manifest Our Imperial clemency.

"Chu Kuei is to hand this mandate to your Agent, for transmission to yourself, in order that you may be encouraged to display still greater gratitude and reverent submission hereafter, in acknowledgment of Our indulgence.

"It is contrary to Our dynastic ordinances for Our officials to enter into social relations with barbarians, and Chu Kuei acted therefore quite properly in returning the presents which were sent to the former Viceroy and Superintendent of Customs at Canton."

Marquis de Condorcet

1743–1794

Marie-Jean-Antoine-Nicolas de Caritat, Marquis de Condorcet, was a noted mathematician, historian of science, political theorist, and feminist. He served as the perpetual secretary of the *Académie des Sciences*, and a member of the even more prestigious *Académie française* in the latter decades of his life, thus indicating the degree to which he was a central figure of the institutional Enlightenment. Through his friendships with noted philosophes Voltaire and D'Alembert, he was also central to the more radical and subversive Enlightenment; this was facilitated in part by his marriage to Sophie de Grouchy whose salon was one of the most famous in the period. Unlike many of his philosophe counterparts, he played a major role in the early phase of the French Revolution when he drew up plans for universal free education and argued, as an elected member of the National Assembly, on behalf of the rights of women. Defending the idea of a liberal constitution, he incurred the wrath of the Jacobins under the radical Republic, and fled once his arrest warrant was issued during the Reign of Terror. Two days after his arrest in March 1794, he was found dead in his prison cell. The cause of death is unknown.

After the fall of the Jacobins on 9 Thermidor (July 1794), Condorcet's moderation was vindicated by the Convention, whose members claimed him as their philosophical inspiration (the Jacobins had claimed Rousseau), and which eventually implemented his plan for universal education. Though his plan was later dismantled by Napoleon, his reputation as a liberal and his influence on a new generation was assured. Madame de Condorcet contributed to spread her husband's ideas and posthumous writings through her salon which met regularly until her death in 1822. Many liberal luminaries frequented her salon, leading one scholar to conclude that "modern liberalism has owed much to Condorcet's philosophy of liberty and progress."

Condorcet's most thorough and passionate treatise on progress is his "Outline of a Historical Portrait of the Progress of the Human Spirit," completed while he was in hiding and published in 1795. Even at the close of the century, more than one hundred years after the publication of Newton's *Principia*, and after the frightful experiences of the Revolution, Condorcet could avow that the "general laws" directing the universe apply to the "development of the intellectual and moral faculties of man." Through the spread of scientific knowledge across the globe, he alleged, native and African savages

122

would be lifted out of their barbarism, and free commerce would guarantee universal peace. This Eurocentric call for universal uplift makes Condorcet an apologist for capitalism as well as for imperialism: he suggests that North Americans will, because of the inexorability of progress, either "civilize or peacefully remove the savage nations," and that Europeans shall become for Africans and Asians "the beneficent instruments of their freedom."

Even Europeans will be shaped by universal progress, according to Condorcet. Anticipating Malthus and Darwin, he argues that man himself will be perfected as the species adapts to poverty and other environmental circumstances, and even that the lessons of animal breeding should not be lost on those seeking human perfection. Condorcet, then, glimpses many of the later developments of the nineteenth century, thus revealing the degree to which the Enlightenment emphasis on progress had pernicious consequences. Can the Enlightenment therefore be blamed for the excesses of militant imperialism? Eugenics? Was Condorcet's philosophy inherently racist? In what ways was he a founder of modern liberalism, evincing the best of liberal faith in humanity? How is any advocacy of universal progress, even in the guise of universal human rights (which Condorcet advocated), an imperialist act?

The Future Progress of the
Human Mind (1795)

If man can, with almost complete assurance, predict phenomena when he knows their laws, and if, even when he does not, he can still, with great expectation of success, forecast the future on the basis of his experience of the past, why, then, should it be regarded as a fantastic undertaking to sketch, with some pretence to truth, the future destiny of man on the basis of his history? The sole foundation for belief in the natural sciences is this idea, that the general laws directing the phenomena of the universe, known or unknown, are necessary and constant. Why should this principle be any less true for the development of the intellectual and moral faculties of man than for the other operations of nature? Since beliefs founded on past experience of like conditions provide the only rule of conduct for the wisest of men, why should the philosopher be forbidden to base his conjectures on these same foundations, so long as he does not attribute to them a certainty superior to that warranted by the number, the constancy, and the accuracy of his observations?

Our hopes for the future condition of the human race can be subsumed under three important heads: the abolition of inequality between nations, the progress of equality within each nation, and the true perfection of mankind. Will all nations one day attain that state of civilization which the most enlightened, the freest and the least burdened by prejudices, such as the French and the Anglo-Americans, have attained already? Will the vast gulf that separates these peoples from the slavery of nations under the rule of monarchs, from the barbarism of African tribes, from the ignorance of savages, little by little disappear?

Is there on the face of the earth a nation whose inhabitants have been debarred by nature herself from the enjoyment of freedom and the exercise of reason?

Are those differences which have hitherto been seen in every civilized country in respect of the enlightenment, the resources, and the wealth enjoyed by the different classes into which it is divided, is that inequality between men which was aggravated or perhaps produced by the earliest progress of society, are these part of civilization itself, or are they due to the present imperfections of the social art? Will they necessarily decrease and ultimately make way for a real equality, the final end of the social art, in which even the effects of the natural differences between men will be mitigated and the only kind of inequality to persist will be that which is in the interests of all and which favors the

124

progress of civilization, of education, and of industry, without entailing either poverty, humiliation, or dependence? In other words, will men approach a condition in which everyone will have the knowledge necessary to conduct himself in the ordinary affairs of life, according to the light of his own reason, to preserve his mind free from prejudice, to understand his rights and to exercise them in accordance with his conscience and his creed; in which everyone will become able, through the development of his faculties, to find the means of providing for his needs; and in which at last misery and folly will be the exception, and no longer the habitual lot of a section of society?

Is the human race to better itself, either by discoveries in the sciences and the arts, and so in the means to individual welfare and general prosperity; or by progress in the principles of conduct or practical morality; or by a true perfection of the intellectual, moral, or physical faculties of man, an improvement which may result from a perfection either of the instruments used to heighten the intensity of these faculties and to direct their use or of the natural constitution of man?

In answering these three questions we shall find in the experience of the past, in the observation of the progress that the sciences and civilization have already made, in the analysis of the progress of the human mind and of the development of its faculties, the strongest reasons for believing that nature has set no limit to the realization of our hopes.

If we glance at the state of the world today we see first of all that in Europe the principles of the French Constitution are already those of all enlightened men. We see them too widely propagated, too seriously professed, for priests and despots to prevent their gradual penetration even into the hovels of their slaves; there they will soon awaken in these slaves the remnants of their common sense and inspire them with that smoldering indignation which not even constant humiliation and fear can smother in the soul of the oppressed.

As we move from nation to nation, we can see in each what special obstacles impede this revolution and what attitudes of mind favor it. We can distinguish the nations where we may expect it to be introduced gently by the perhaps belated wisdom of their governments, and those nations where its violence intensified by their resistance must involve all alike in a swift and terrible convulsion.

Can we doubt that either common sense or the senseless discords of European nations will add to the effects of the slow but inexorable progress of their colonies, and will soon bring about the independence of the New World? And then will not the European population in these colonies, spreading rapidly over that enormous land, either civilize or peacefully remove the savage nations who still inhabit vast tracts of its land?

Survey the history of our settlements and commercial undertakings in Africa or in Asia, and you will see how our trade monopolies, our treachery, our murderous contempt for men of another color or creed, the insolence of our usurpations, the intrigues or the exaggerated proselytic zeal of our priests, have destroyed the respect and goodwill that the superiority of our knowledge and the benefits of our commerce at first won for us in the eyes of the inhabitants. But doubtless the moment approaches when, no longer presenting ourselves as always either tyrants or corrupters, we shall become for them the beneficent instruments of their freedom.

The sugar industry, establishing itself throughout the immense continent of Africa, will destroy the shameful exploitation which has corrupted and depopulated that continent for the last two centuries.

Already in Great Britain, friends of humanity have set us an example; and if the Machiavellian government of that country has been restrained by public opinion from offering any opposition, what may we not expect of this same spirit, once the reform of a servile and venal constitution has led to a government worthy of a humane and generous nation? Will not France hasten to imitate such undertakings dictated by philanthropy and the true self-interest of Europe alike? Trading stations have been set up in the French islands, in Guiana and in some English possessions, and soon we shall see the downfall of the monopoly that the Dutch have sustained with so much treachery, persecution and crime. The nations of Europe will finally learn that monopolistic companies are nothing more than a tax imposed upon them in order to provide their governments with a new instrument of tyranny.

So the peoples of Europe, confining themselves to free trade, understanding their own rights too well to show contempt for those of other peoples, will respect this independence, which until now they have so insolently violated. Their settlements, no longer filled with government hirelings hastening, under the cloak of place or privilege, to amass treasure by brigandry and deceit, so as to be able to return to Europe and purchase titles and honor, will now be peopled with men of industrious habit, seeking in these propitious climates the wealth that eluded them at home. The love of freedom will retain them there, ambition will no longer recall them, and what have been no better than the counting houses of brigands will become colonies of citizens propagating throughout Africa and Asia the principles and the practice of liberty, knowledge and reason, that they have brought from Europe. We shall see the monks who brought only shameful superstition to these peoples, and aroused their antagonism by the threat of yet another tyranny, replaced by men occupied in propagating amongst them the truths that will promote their happiness and in teaching them about their interests and their rights. Zeal for the truth is also one of the passions, and it will turn its efforts to distant lands, once there are no longer at home any crass prejudices to combat, any shameful errors to dissipate. . . .

The progress of these peoples is likely to be more rapid and certain than our own because they can receive from us everything that we have had to find out for ourselves, and in order to understand those simple truths and infallible methods which we have acquired only after long error, all that they need to do is to follow the expositions and proofs that appear in our speeches and writings. If the progress of the Greeks was lost to later nations, this was because of the absence of any form of communication between the different peoples, and for this we must blame the tyrannical domination of the Romans. But when mutual needs have brought all men together, and the great powers have established equality among societies as well as among individuals and have raised respect for the independence of weak states and sympathy for ignorance and misery to the rank of political principles, when maxims that favor action and energy have ousted those which would compress the province of human faculties, will it then be possible to fear that there are still places in the world inaccessible to enlightenment, or that despotism in its pride can raise barriers against truth that are insurmountable for long?

The time will therefore come when the sun will shine only on free men who know no other master but their reason; when tyrants and slaves, priests and their stupid or hypocritical instruments, will exist only in works of history and on the stage; and when we shall think of them only to pity their victims and their dupes; to maintain ourselves in a state of vigilance by thinking on their excesses; and to learn how to recognize and so to destroy, by force of reason, the first seeds of tyranny and superstition, should they ever dare to reappear amongst us.

In looking at the history of societies we shall have had occasion to observe that there is often a great difference between the rights that the law allows its citizens and the rights that they actually enjoy, and, again, between the equality established by political codes and that which in fact exists amongst individuals: and we shall have noticed that these differences were one of the principal causes of the destruction of freedom in the ancient republics, of the storms that troubled them, and of the weakness that delivered them over to foreign tyrants.

These differences have three main causes: inequality in wealth; inequality in status between the man whose means of subsistence are hereditary and the man whose means are dependent on the length of his life, or, rather, on that part of his life in which he is capable of work; and, finally, inequality in education.

We therefore need to show that these three sorts of real inequality must constantly diminish without, however, disappearing altogether: for they are the result of natural and necessary causes, which it would be foolish and dangerous to wish to eradicate; and one could not even attempt to bring about the entire disappearance of their effects without introducing even more fecund sources of inequality, without striking more direct and more fatal blows at the rights of man.

It is easy to prove that wealth has a natural tendency to equality, and that any excessive disproportion could not exist, or at least would rapidly disappear, if civil laws did not provide artificial ways of perpetuating and uniting fortunes; if free trade and industry were allowed to remove the advantages that accrued wealth derives from any restrictive law or fiscal privilege; if taxes on covenants, the restrictions placed on their free employment, their subjection to tiresome formalities, and the uncertainty and inevitable expense involved in implementing them did not hamper the activity of the poor man and swallow up his meager capital; if the administration of the country did not afford some men ways of making their fortune that were closed to other citizens; if prejudice and avarice, so common in old age, did not preside over the making of marriages; and if, in a society enjoying simpler manners and more sensible institutions, wealth ceased to be a means of satisfying vanity and ambition, and if the equally misguided notions of austerity, which condemn spending money in the cultivation of the more delicate pleasures, no longer insisted on the hoarding of all one's earnings.

Let us turn to the enlightened nations of Europe, and observe the size of their present populations in relation to the size of their territories. Let us consider, in agriculture and industry, the proportion that holds between labor and the means of subsistence, and we shall see that it would be impossible for those means to be kept at their present level, and consequently for the population to be kept at its present size, if a great number of individuals were not almost entirely dependent for the maintenance of themselves and their family either on their own labor or on the interest from capital invested so as to make their labor more productive. Now both these sources of income depend on the life and even on the health of the head of the family. They provide what is rather like a life annuity, save that it is more dependent on chance: and in consequence there is a very real difference between people living like this and those whose resources are not at all subject to the same risks, who live either on revenue from land, or on the interest on capital, which is almost independent of their own labor.

Here then is a necessary cause of inequality, of dependence and even of misery, which ceaselessly threatens the most numerous and most active class in our society.

We shall point out how it can be in great part eradicated by guaranteeing people in old age a means of livelihood produced partly by their own savings and partly by the savings of others who make the same outlay, but who die before they need to reap the reward; or, again, on the same principle of compensation, by securing for widows and orphans an income which is the same and costs the same for those families which suffer an early loss and for those which suffer it later; or again by providing all children with the capital necessary for the full use of their labor, available at the age when they start work and found a family, a capital which increases at the expense of those whom premature death prevents from reaching this age. It is to the application of the calculus to the probabilities of life and the investment of money that we owe the idea of these methods which have already been successful, although they have not been applied in a sufficiently comprehensive and exhaustive fashion to render them really useful, not merely to a few individuals, but to society as a whole, by making it possible to prevent those periodic disasters which strike at so many families and which are such a recurrent source of misery and suffering.

We shall point out that schemes of this nature, which can be organized in the name of the social authority and become one of its greatest benefits, can also be the work of private associations, which will be formed without any real risk, once the principles for the proper working of these schemes have been widely diffused and the mistakes which have been the undoing of a large number of these associations no longer hold terrors for us. . . .

So we might say that a well-directed system of education rectifies natural inequality in ability instead of strengthening it, just as good laws remedy natural inequality in the means of subsistence, and just as in societies where laws have brought about this same equality, liberty, though subject to a regular constitution, will be more widespread, more complete, than in the total independence of savage life. Then the social art will have fulfilled its aim, that of assuring and extending to all men enjoyment of the common rights to which they are called by nature.

The real advantages that should result from this progress, of which we can entertain a hope that is almost a certainty, can have no other term than that of the absolute perfection of the human race; since, as the various kinds of equality come to work in its favor by producing ampler sources of supply, more extensive education, more complete liberty, so equality will be more real and will embrace everything which is really of importance for the happiness of human beings.

It is therefore only by examining the progress and the laws of this perfection that we shall be able to understand the extent or the limits of our hopes.

No one has ever believed that the mind can gain knowledge of all the facts of nature or attain the ultimate means of precision in the measurement, or in the analysis of the facts of nature, the relations between objects and all the possible combinations of ideas. Even the relations between magnitudes, the mere notion of quantity or extension, taken in its fullest comprehension, gives rise to a system so vast that it will never be mastered by the human mind in its entirety, that there will always be a part of it, always indeed the larger part of it, that will remain forever unknown. People have believed that man can never know more than a part of the objects that the nature of his intelligence allows him to understand, and that he must in the end arrive at a point where the number and complexity of the objects that he already knows have absorbed all his strength so that any further progress must be completely impossible.

But since, as the number of known facts increases, the human mind learns how to classify them and to subsume them under more general facts, and, at the same time, the instruments and methods employed in their observation and their exact measurement acquire a new precision; since, as more relations between various objects become known, man is able to reduce them to more general relations, to express them more simply, and to present them in such a way that it is possible to grasp a greater number of them with the same degree of intellectual ability and the same amount of application; since, as the mind learns to understand more complicated combinations of ideas, simpler formulae soon reduce their complexity; so truths that were discovered only by great effort, that could at first only be understood by men capable of profound thought, are soon developed and proved by methods that are not beyond the reach of common intelligence. If the methods which have led to these new combinations of ideas are ever exhausted, if their application to hitherto unsolved questions should demand exertions greater than either the time or the capacity of the learned would permit, some method of a greater generality or simplicity will be found so that genius can continue undisturbed on its path. The strength and the limits of man's intelligence may remain unaltered; and yet the instruments that he uses will increase and improve, the language that fixes and determines his ideas will acquire greater breadth and precision, and, unlike mechanics, where an increase of force means a decrease of speed, the methods that lead genius to the discovery of truth increase at once the force and the speed of its operations.

Therefore, since these developments are themselves the necessary consequences of progress in detailed knowledge, and since the need for new methods in fact only arises in circumstances that give rise to new methods, it is evident that, within the body of the sciences of observation, calculation and experiment, the actual number of truths may always increase, and that every part of this body may develop, and yet man's faculties be of the same strength, activity and extent.

If we apply these general reflections to the various sciences, we can find in each of them examples of progressive improvement that will remove any doubts about what we may expect for the future. We shall point out in particular the progress that is both likely and imminent in those sciences which prejudice regards as all but exhausted. We shall give examples of the manner and extent of the precision and unity which could accrue to the whole system of human knowledge as the result of a more general and philosophical application of the sciences of calculation to the various branches of knowledge. We shall show how favorable to our hopes would be a more universal system of education by giving a greater number of people the elementary knowledge which could awaken their interest in a particular branch of study, and by providing conditions favorable to their progress in it; and how these hopes would be further raised if more men possessed the means to devote themselves to these studies, for at present even in the most enlightened countries scarcely one in fifty of the people who have natural talents receives the necessary education to develop them; and how, if this were done, there would be a proportionate increase in the number of men destined by their discoveries to extend the boundaries of science.

We shall show how this equality in education and the equality which will come about among the different nations would accelerate the advance of these sciences whose progress depends on repeated observations over a large area; what benefits would thereby accrue to mineralogy, botany, zoology and meteorology; and what a vast disproportion holds in all these sciences between the poverty of existing methods, which have nevertheless led to useful and important new truths, and the wealth of those methods which man would then be able to employ.

We shall show how even the sciences in which discovery is the fruit of solitary meditation would benefit from being studied by a greater number of people, in the matter of those improvements in detail which do not demand the intellectual energy of an inventor but suggest themselves to mere reflection.

If we turn now to the arts, whose theory depends on these same sciences, we shall find that their progress, depending as it does on that of theory, can have no other limits; that the procedures of the different arts can be perfected and simplified in the same way as the methods of the sciences; new instruments, machines and looms can add to man's strength and can improve at once the quality and the accuracy of his productions, and can diminish the time and labor that has to be expended on them. The obstacles still in the way of this progress will disappear, accidents will be foreseen and prevented, the insanitary conditions that are due either to the work itself or to the climate will be eliminated.

A very small amount of ground will be able to produce a great quantity of supplies of greater utility or higher quality; more goods will be obtained for a smaller outlay; the manufacture of articles will be achieved with less wastage in raw materials and will make better use of them. Every type of soil will produce those things which satisfy the greatest number of needs; of several alternative ways of satisfying needs of the same order, that will be chosen which satisfies the greatest number of people and which requires least labor and least expenditure. So, without the need for sacrifice, methods of preservation and economy in expenditure will improve in the wake of progress in the arts of producing and preparing supplies and making articles from them.

So not only will the same amount of ground support more people, but everyone will have less work to do, will produce more, and satisfy his wants more fully.

With all this progress in industry and welfare, which establishes a happier proportion between men's talents and their needs, each successive generation will have larger possessions, either as a result of this progress or through the preservation of the products of industry; and so, as a consequence of the physical constitution of the human race, the number of people will increase. Might there not then come a moment when these necessary laws begin to work in a contrary direction; when, the number of people in the world finally exceeding the means of subsistence, there will in consequence ensue a continual diminution of happiness and population, a true retrogression, or at best an oscillation between good and bad? In societies that have reached this stage, will not this oscillation be a perennial source of more or less periodic disaster? Will it not show that a point has been attained beyond which all further improvement is impossible, that the perfectibility of the human race has after long years arrived at a term beyond which it may never go?

There is doubtless no one who does not think that such a time is still very far from us; but will it ever arrive? It is impossible to pronounce about the likelihood of an event that will occur only when the human species will have necessarily acquired a degree of knowledge of which we can have no inkling. And who would take it upon himself to predict the condition to which the art of converting the elements to the use of man may in time be brought?

But even if we agree that the limit will one day arrive, nothing follows from it that is in the least alarming as far as either the happiness of the human race or its indefinite perfectibility is concerned. If we consider that, before all this comes to pass, the progress of reason will have kept pace with that of the sciences, and that the absurd prejudices of superstition will have ceased to corrupt and degrade the moral code by its harsh doctrines instead of purifying and elevating it, we can assume that by then men will know that, if they have a duty towards those who are not yet born, that duty is not to give them existence but to give them happiness; their aim should be to promote the general welfare of the human race or of the society in which they live or of the family to which they belong, rather than foolishly to encumber the world with useless and wretched beings. It is, then, possible that there should be a limit to the amount of food that can be produced, and, consequently, to the size of the population of the world, without this involving that untimely destruction of some of those creatures who have been given life, which is so contrary to nature and to social prosperity. . . .

Organic perfectibility or deterioration amongst the various strains in the vegetable and animal kingdom can be regarded as one of the general laws of nature. This law also applies to the human race. No one can doubt that, as preventive medicine improves and food and housing become healthier, as a way of life is established that develops our physical powers by exercise without ruining them by excess, as the two most virulent causes of deterioration, misery and excessive wealth, are eliminated, the average length of human life will be increased and a better health and a stronger physical constitution will be ensured. The improvement of medical practice, which will become more efficacious with the progress of reason and of the social order, will mean the end of infectious and hereditary diseases and illnesses brought on by climate, food, or working conditions. It is reasonable to hope that all other diseases may likewise disappear as their distant causes are discovered. Would it be absurd, then, to suppose that this perfection of the human species might be capable of indefinite progress; that the day will come when death will be due only to extraordinary accidents or to the decay of the vital forces, and that ultimately the average span between birth and decay will have no assignable value? Certainly man will not become immortal, but will not the interval between the first breath that he draws and the time when in the natural course of events, without disease or accident, he expires, increase indefinitely? Since we are now speaking of a progress that can be represented with some accuracy in figures or on a graph, we shall take this opportunity of explaining the two meanings that can be attached to the word *indefinite.*

In truth, this average span of life, which we suppose will increase indefinitely as time passes, may grow in conformity either with a law such that it continually approaches a limitless length but without ever reaching it, or with a law such that through the centuries it reaches a length greater than any determinate quantity that we may assign to it as its limit. In the latter case such an increase is truly indefinite in the strictest sense of the word, since there is no term on this side of which it must of necessity stop. In the former case it is equally indefinite in relation to us if we cannot fix the limit it always approaches without ever reaching, and particularly if, knowing only that it will never stop, we are ignorant in which of the two senses the term *indefinite* can be applied to it. Such is the present condition of our knowledge as far as the perfectibility of the human race is concerned; such is the sense in which we may call it indefinite.

So, in the example under consideration, we are bound to believe that the average length of human life will forever increase unless this is prevented by physical revolutions; we do not know what the limit is which it can never exceed. We cannot tell even whether the general laws of nature have determined such a limit or not.

But are not our physical faculties and the strength, dexterity and acuteness of our senses, to be numbered among the qualities whose perfection in the individual may be transmitted? Observation of the various breeds of domestic animals inclines us to believe that they are, and we can confirm this by direct observation of the human race.

Finally may we not extend such hopes to the intellectual and moral faculties? May not our parents, who transmit to us the benefits or disadvantages of their constitution, and from whom we receive our shape and features, as well as our tendencies to certain physical affections, hand on to us also that part of the physical organization which determines the intellect, the power of the brain, the ardor of the soul or the moral sensibility? Is it not probable that education, in perfecting these qualities, will at the same time influence, modify and perfect the organization itself? Analogy, investigation of the human faculties and the study of certain facts, all seem to give substance to such conjectures, which would further push back the boundaries of our hopes.

These are the questions with which we shall conclude this final stage. How consoling for the philosopher, who laments the errors, the crimes, the injustices which still pollute the earth, and of which he is often the victim, is this view of the human race, emancipated from its shackles, released from the empire of fate and from that of the enemies of its progress, advancing with a firm and sure step along the path of truth, virtue and happiness! It is the contemplation of this prospect that rewards him for all his efforts to assist the progress of reason and the defense of liberty. He dares to regard these strivings as part of the eternal chain of human destiny; and in this persuasion he is filled with the true delight of virtue and the pleasure of having done some lasting good, which fate can never destroy by a sinister stroke of revenge, by calling back the reign of slavery and prejudice. Such contemplation is for him an asylum, in which the memory of his persecutors cannot pursue him; there he lives in thought with man restored to his natural rights and dignity, forgets man tormented and corrupted by greed, fear, or envy; there he lives with his peers in an Elysium created by reason and graced by the purest pleasures known to the love of mankind.

III. Neoclassical and Romantic Art and Social Ideas

Alexander Pope

1688–1744

Born to a London linen merchant, Alexander Pope was raised in the Roman Catholic faith and lived for most of his youth at Bonfield, in Windsor Forest, Berkshire. When he was twelve, Pope took ill with a tubercular spinal infection which stunted his growth dramatically and caused his health to suffer throughout adulthood. Primarily self-educated, he began composing poetry at an early age and, despite the social and political difficulties he experienced due to his religious affiliation, he became the foremost poet of the neoclassical period in England. Pope's "Essay on Criticism" (1711) and his "Essay on Man" (1734) are both written in heroic couplets—pairs of rhymed lines in iambic pentameter—a form he used in many of his works.

Pope's art reflects the values and attitudes of the Enlightenment. To him, the Greco-Roman period and its literature had achieved the creative and intellectual heights to which all modern poets should aspire. By studying and imitating the classics, by applying reason to the pursuit of aesthetic principles, Pope believed, an artist might escape the limitations of his particular time and taste, and capture something universal, good, and true.

In the selections below, Pope articulates the idea that poetry—indeed, all art—is a matter of applying rules, particularly those tested by time and handed down to us through history. Without such rules, what we have is not really art, but chaos. In thinking that we can shape great art or come to know deep truths without appealing to the wisdom of the past, we indulge ourselves in moral and intellectual arrogance. What are the costs and benefits of Pope's orientation to history and tradition? To what extent is the expression of truth in art possible if our primary concern is to accommodate conventions and rules? What do artists and intellectuals give up by trying to break free from the past? What do they gain?

from *Essay on Criticism* (1711)

•   •   •

First follow Nature, and your judgment frame
By her just standard, which is still the same:
Unerring NATURE, still divinely bright,
One clear, unchang'd, and universal light,
Life, force, and beauty, must to all impart,
At once the source, and end, and test of Art.
Art from that fund each just supply provides,
Works without show, and without pomp presides:
In some fair body thus th' informing soul
With spirits feeds, with vigour fills the whole,
Each motion guides, and ev'ry nerve sustains;
Itself unseen, but in th' effects, remains.
Some, to whom Heav'n in wit has been profuse,
Want as much more, to turn it to its use;
For wit and judgment often are at strife,
Tho' meant each other's aid, like man and wife.
'Tis more to guide, than spur the Muse's steed;
Restrain his fury, than provoke his speed;
The winged courser, like a gen'rous horse,
Shows most true mettle when you check his course.
      Those RULES of old discovered, not devis'd,
Are Nature still, but Nature methodiz'd;
Nature, like liberty, is but restrain'd
By the same laws which first herself ordain'd.
      Hear how learn'd Greece her useful rules indites,
When to repress, and when indulge our flights:
High on Parnassus'[1] top her sons she show'd,
And pointed out those arduous paths they trod;
Held from afar, aloft, th' immortal prize,
And urg'd the rest by equal steps to rise.
Just precepts thus from great examples giv'n,
She drew from them what they deriv'd from Heav'n.
The gen'rous Critic fann'd the Poet's fire,
And taught the world with reason to admire.

•   •   •

When first young Maro[2] in his boundless mind
A work t' outlast immortal Rome design'd,
Perhaps he seem'd above the critic's law,
And but from Nature's fountains scorn'd to draw:
But when t' examine ev'ry part he came,
Nature and Homer were, he found, the same.
Convinc'd, amaz'd, he checks the bold design;
And rules as strict his labour'd work confine,
As if the Stagirite[3] o'erlook'd each line.
Learn hence for ancient rules a just esteem;
To copy nature is to copy them.

•   •   •

A *little learning* is a dang'rous thing;
Drink deep, or taste not the Pierian[4] spring:
There shallow draughts intoxicate the brain,
And drinking largely sobers us again.

•   •   •

Some to *Conceit* alone their taste confine,
And glitt'ring thoughts struck out at ev'ry line;
Pleas'd with a work where nothing's just or fit;
One glaring Chaos and wild heap of wit.
Poets, like painters, thus, unskill'd to trace
The naked nature and the living grace,
With gold and jewels cover ev'ry part,
And hide with ornaments their want of art.
True Wit is Nature to advantage dress'd,
What oft was thought, but ne'er so well express'd,
Something, whose truth convinc'd at sight we find,
That gives us back the image of our mind.
As shades more sweetly recommend the light,
So modest plainness sets off sprightly wit.
For works may have more wit than does 'em good,
As bodies perish thro' excess of blood.
Others for *Language* all their care express,
And value books, as women men, for Dress:
Their praise is still,—the Style is excellent:
The Sense, they humbly take upon content.
Words are like leaves; and where they most abound,

Much fruit of sense beneath is rarely found,
False Eloquence, like the prismatic glass,
Its gaudy colours spreads on ev'ry place;
The face of Nature we no more survey,
All glares alike, without distinction gay:
But true expression, like th' unchanging Sun,
Clears and improves whate'er it shines upon,
It gilds all objects, but it alters none.
Expression is the dress of thought, and still
Appears more decent, as more suitable;

. . .

To what base ends, and by what abject ways,
Are mortals urg'd thro' sacred lust of praise!
Ah ne'er so dire a thirst of glory boast,
Nor in the Critic let the Man be lost.
Good-nature and good-sense must ever join;
To err is human, to forgive, divine.

. . .

Notes

[1] Greek mountain, sacred to Apollo and the Muses.

[2] Virgil, Roman poet (70–19 B.C.), author of the epic poem "The Aeneid."

[3] Aristotle.

[4] A spring sacred to the Muses.

from *Essay on Man* (1734)

Epistle I

• • •

    I. Say first, of God above, or Man below,
What can we reason, but from what we know?
Of Man, what we see but his station here,
From which to reason, or to which refer?
Thro' worlds unnumber'd tho' the God be known,
'Tis ours to trace him only in our own.
He, who thro' vast immensity can pierce,
See worlds on worlds compose one universe,
Observe how system into system runs,
What other planets circle other suns,
What vary'd Being peoples ev'ry star,
May tell why Heav'n has made us as we are.
But of this frame the bearings, and the ties,
The strong connexions, nice dependencies,
Gradations just, has thy pervading soul
Look'd thro'? or can a part contain the whole?
    Is the great chain, that draws all to agree,
And drawn supports, upheld by God, or thee?
    II. Presumptuous Man! the reason wouldst thou find,
Why form'd so weak, so little, and so blind?
First, if thou canst, the harder reason guess,
Why form'd no weaker, blinder, and no less?
Ask of thy mother earth, why oaks are made
Taller or shorter than the weeds they shade?
Or ask of yonder argent fields above,
Why JOVE'S satellites are less than JOVE?
Of Systems possible, if 'tis confest
That Wisdom infinite must form the best,
Where all must full or not coherent be,
And all that rises, rise in due degree;
Then, in the scale of reas'ning life, 'tis plain,
There must be, somewhere, such as rank as Man:
And all the question (wrangle e'er so long)

Is only this, if God has plac'd him wrong?
      Respecting Man, whatever wrong we call,
May, must be right, as relative to all.
In human works, tho' labour'd on with pain,
A thousand movements scarce one purpose gain;
In God's, one single can its end produce;
Yet serves to second too some other use.
So Man, who here seems principal alone,
Perhaps acts second to some sphere unknown,
Touches some wheel, or verges to some goal;
'Tis but a part we see, and not the whole.
      When the proud steed shall know why Man restrains
His fiery course, or drives him o'er the plains:
When the dull Ox, why now he breaks the clod,
Is now a victim, and now Ægypt's God;
Then shall Man's pride and dulness comprehend
His actions', passions', being's, use and end;
Why doing, suff'ring, check'd, impell'd; and why
This hour a slave, the next a deity.
      Then say not Man's imperfect, Heav'n in fault;
Say rather, Man's as perfect as he ought:
His knowledge measur'd to his state and place;
His time a moment, and a point in space.
If to be perfect in a certain sphere,
What matter, soon or late, or here or there?
The blest to day is as completely so,
As who began a thousand years ago.
      III. Heav'n from all creatures hides the book of Fate,
All but the page prescrib'd, their present state:
From brutes what men, from men what spirits know:
Or who could suffer Being here below?
The lamb thy riot dooms to bleed to-day,
Had he thy Reason, would he skip and play?
Pleas'd to the last, he crops the flow'ry food,
And licks the hand just rais'd to shed his blood.
Oh blindness to the future! kindly giv'n,
That each may fill the circle mark'd by Heav'n:
Who sees with equal eye, as God of all,
A hero perish, or a sparrow fall,
Atoms or systems into ruin hurl'd,
And now a bubble burst, and now a world.

Hope humbly then; with trembling pinions soar;
Wait the great teacher Death; and God adore!
What future bliss, he gives not thee to know,
But gives that Hope to be thy blessing now.
Hope springs eternal in the human breast:
Man never Is, but always to be blest:
The soul, uneasy and confin'd from home,
Rests and expatiates in a life to come.
Lo, the poor Indian! whose untutor'd mind
Sees God in clouds, or hears him in the wind;
His soul, proud Science never taught to stray
Far as the solar walk, or milky way;
Yet simple Nature to his hope has giv'n,
Behind the cloud-topt hill, an humbler heav'n;
Some safer world in depth of woods embrac'd,
Some happier island in the watry waste,
Where slaves once more their native land behold,
No fiends torment, no Christians thirst for gold.
To Be, contents his natural desire,
He asks no Angel's wing, no Seraphs's fire;
But thinks, admitted to that equal sky,
His faithful dog shall bear him company.
    IV. Go, wiser thou! and, in thy scale of sense,
Weigh thy Opinion against Providence;
Call imperfection what thou fancy'st such,
Say, here he gives too little, there too much:
Destroy all Creatures for thy sport or gust,
Yet cry, If Man's unhappy, God's unjust;
If Man alone engross not Heav'n's high care,
Alone made perfect here, immortal there:
Snatch from his hand the balance and the rod,
Re-judge his justice, be the GOD of GOD.
In Pride, in reas'ning Pride, our error lies;
All quit their sphere, and rush into the skies.
Pride still is aiming at the blest abodes,
Men would be Angels, Angels would be Gods.
Aspiring to be Gods, if Angels fell,
Aspiring to be Angels, Men rebel:
And who but wishes to invert the laws
Of ORDER, sins against th' Eternal Cause.

● ● ●

Françoise de Graffigny

1695–1758

Zilia, the fictional heroine of Françoise de Graffigny's best-seller, *Letters of a Peruvian Woman*, was an Inca princess destined to marry her brother, Aza, at the time of her capture by the Spaniards. Her letters, which make up most of the book, were written to him as she struggled to keep in touch with the world that was lost to her. Basing her account of the destruction of the Incan Empire in the mid-sixteenth century on surviving narratives, Graffigny used Zilia to inspire sympathy for the native peoples whose lives and cultures were destroyed by Spanish imperialism. Graffigny also constructed Zilia as the "noble savage" whose innocence enabled her to critique European mores once she arrived in France after being captured yet again during a pirate's raid.

Graffigny employed the popular literary devices of her day. The epistolary novel was already a well-established genre by the time she took up her pen. Moreover, her work resembled Montesquieu's *Persian Letters* in which the exotic traveller is used to voice the author's social criticism, an important feature of Enlightenment thought. Unlike Montesquieu, however, Graffigny's heroine is female and her experience of the strange world of Paris is explicitly gendered. For example, she shows a great deal of concern over the relatively low status of women in eighteenth-century France. This reflects Graffigny's own concerns as the survivor of an abusive marriage which left her penniless. She was one of a handful of women authors at the time who could live by her pen.

In the following excerpt, Zilia exemplifies a foundational feature of Enlightenment thought. A virtual "tabula rasa" thrown against her will into a world completely alien to her, Zilia is eager to reflect on the multitude of sensory experiences in order to achieve understanding. Her evolution towards accepting aspects of French identity, including dress, proves that the "blank slate" of human nature could be pressed into new molds. As she negotiates her way between two very different cultures, she ponders whether or not human nature is universal. *Letters of a Peruvian Woman* introduces key moral questions which only become harder to answer in the nineteenth century: What is the relationship between "civilized" and "primitive" cultures? How can individuals construct an identity as they are forced to move between several of them? Can the displaced individual find community in an alien, if not hostile, land? Was European civilization good for Zilia? If so, is Graffigny justifying imperialism?

from *Letters from a Peruvian Woman* (1747)

IX

Now reassured in regard to [her captor, Déterville's] religion, I am not entirely so with respect to the country from which he hails. His language and his clothes are so different from ours that often my confidence is shaken. Upsetting reflections at times cloud my fondest hopes. I pass in turn from fear to joy and from joy to worry.

Fatigued by my mind's confusion, disheartened by the uncertainties that are tearing me apart, I had resolved not to think anymore, but how is one to slow the movement of a soul deprived of all communication that is acting only upon itself and is spurred to reflection by such strong interests? I am incapable of it, dearest Aza; I seek enlightenment with an urgency that consumes me, yet I continually find myself in the deepest darkness. I knew that being deprived of one sense can mislead in several respects, but I am surprised to see that the use of mine ushers me from one error to the next. Would the comprehension of languages also be that of the soul? Oh dear Aza! How my misfortunes make me glimpse upsetting truths! But let these sad thoughts leave me, for we are reaching land. The light of my days will dispel in a moment the shadows that surround me.

X

I have finally reached this land that had been the object of my desires, dearest Aza, but I have not yet seen anything here that presages the happiness I had been expecting. Everything that is offered to my eyes strikes, surprises, and astonishes me, leaving me with only a vague impression and a dumb-founded sense of confusion from which I do not even seek to deliver myself. My mistakes stifle my judgment, and I remain unsure, practically doubting even what I see.

Scarcely had we left the floating house when we entered a city built upon the seaside. The people who swarmed after us looked to me to be of the same nation as the *Cacique*,[1] but the houses bear no resemblance to those in the cities of the Sun. If those cities possess houses of greater beauty thanks to the richness of their decoration, these are superior by virtue of the many marvels with which they are filled.

As I entered the room Déterville has made my lodging, my heart trembled, for in one of the corners I saw a young person dressed in the manner of a Virgin of the Sun. I ran to her with open arms. What a surprise, dearest Aza, what a great surprise it was to find nothing but an impenetrable resistance there where I saw a human figure moving about in a most extensive space! My amazement held me transfixed, eyes locked onto that shadow when Déterville drew my attention to his own figure next to the one with which I was completely preoccupied. I touched him, I spoke to him, and I saw him at once very near and very far from me.

These marvels disturb the mind and offend reason. What is one to think of this country's inhabitants? Must one fear them? Must one love them? I shall be careful to reserve judgment in this matter.

The *Cacique* gave me to understand that the figure I saw was my own, but what does that tell me? Is the marvel any less great? Am I any less mortified at finding only error and ignorance in my mind? I observe with sorrow, dearest Aza, that the least clever inhabitants of this Region are more learned than all our *Amautas*.

The *Cacique* has given me a most lively young *China*,[2] and it is indeed a great comfort to me again to see women and be served by them. Several others hasten to attend to my needs, which I would rather they not do as their presence awakens my fears. From the way they look at me, I see clearly that they have never been to Cuzco. For the moment I am still unable to reach any firm conclusions: my spirit continues to float on a sea of uncertainties, my lonely, unwavering heart desires, expects, and awaits only a happiness without which all can be nothing but hardship.

XI

Although I have taken care to do everything in my power to shed some light on my situation, dearest Aza, I am no better informed of it than I was three days ago. I have been able to observe only that the savages of this region seem to be as good and humane as the *Cacique*: they sing and dance as if they had fields to plow every day. If, to understand my current circumstances, I relied primarily on the differences between their customs and those of our nation, I would lose all hope. But I recall that your august father subjugated quite distant provinces whose peoples bore no more relation to ours than do these: why should this not be one of them? The Sun, purer and more beautiful than I have ever seen, seems pleased to illuminate this land, and I am pleased to give myself over to the confidence he inspires in me. My only remaining worry concerns how much time will have to pass before I will be able to enlighten myself regarding our interests, for I am now convinced, dearest Aza, that use of the language of the land alone will inform me of the truth and bring my worries to an end.

I allow no opportunity to learn it slip away and avail myself of all moments when Déterville lets me do what I will to take lessons from my

China. This is a feeble resource for, not being able to make her understand my thoughts, I cannot reason with her. At times the *Cacique's* signs are more useful to me. Habit has made of them a kind of language for us that at least serves us as a way to express our wishes. Yesterday he took me to a house where, without this mutual understanding, I would have conducted myself quite badly.

We entered a chamber much larger and more ornate than the one in which I live. Many people had gathered there. I was displeased by the general amazement shown at the sight of me. The excessive laughter that several young girls attempted to keep back and that started again when they looked upon me stirred in my heart a feeling so disturbing that I would have taken it for shame had I felt myself guilty of some offense. Finding only great repugnance at the thought of remaining with them, however, I was about to retrace my steps when a sign from Déterville held me back.

I understood that I would be committing an offense if I left and was quite careful to do nothing worthy of the blame being assigned me without cause; accordingly, I stayed and, focusing all my attention on those women, thought myself to have discerned that the singularity of my clothes alone caused the surprise of some and the offensive laughter of others. I felt pity for their weakness and from then on thought only of convincing them by my bearing that my soul did not differ so much from theirs as my clothing did from their finery.

A man whom I would have taken for a *Curacas*[3] had he not been dressed in black, came and took my hand in an affable manner, then led me over to a woman whose proud air made me take her for the region's *Pallas*.[4] He uttered several words that I know from having heard Déterville say them a thousand times: "How beautiful she is! What lovely eyes! . . ." Another man replied, "What grace! The figure of a nymph! . . ." Apart from the women, who said nothing, everyone kept repeating more or less the same words. I do not know their meaning yet, but they surely convey pleasant ideas, for their utterance is always accompanied by a beaming countenance.

The *Cacique* appeared extremely satisfied with what was being said. He remained forever at my side, or, if he moved off to speak with someone, his eyes never lost sight of me, and his signs advised me of what I should do. For my part, I was quite careful to observe him so as not to insult the customs of a nation so little aware of our own.

I know not, dearest Aza, if I will be able to make you understand how extraordinary these savages' manners appeared to me.

They are full of such an impatient liveliness that words do not satisfy their desire to express themselves, so they speak as much through the movements of their bodies as by the sounds of their voices. What I have seen of their ceaseless commotion has fully convinced me of the minor import of those displays by the *Cacique* that caused me such consternation and about which I entertained so many false conjectures.

Yesterday he kissed the hands of the *Pallas* as well as those of all the other women, even kissing them on the face. And there was another thing I had not seen before: men came up to him and embraced him as well. Some took him by the hand, others pulled at his clothing, and all of it with a swiftness of which we have absolutely no notion.

Judging their minds by the liveliness of their gestures, I am sure that our measured expressions and the sublime comparisons that so naturally express our tender feelings and affectionate thoughts would appear insipid to them. They would take our modest, serious demeanor for stupidity and the gravity of our gait for dullness. You will hardly believe it, dearest Aza, but despite their imperfections, if you were here, I would be quite content in their company. A certain air of affability infusing all that they do makes them likeable, and if my soul were happier, I would take pleasure from the variety of objects that are successively presented to my eyes. But the slight relation they have with you erases the charms of their novelty. You are my sole source of benefit and pleasures.

XII

I have gone quite some time, dearest Aza, without being able to devote a single moment to my favorite occupation; however, I have quite a number of extraordinary things to tell you. I shall take advantage of a bit of leisure to try to inform you of them.

The day after my visit to the home of the *Pallas*, Déterville had me brought a most beautiful garment of the customary sort in this country. After my little *China* had settled it upon me to her liking, she led me to that ingenious device that duplicates objects. Much as I should have grown accustomed to its effects, I could not help being surprised at seeing myself as if I were standing opposite myself.

Notes

[1] Provincial magistrate.

[2] Servant.

[3] Minor regional servant.

[4] Princess.

François Marie Arouet de Voltaire

1694–1778

No *philosophe* is more exemplary of the Enlightenment than Voltaire. Best known today for his satirical work, *Candide*, Voltaire was the author of hundreds of treatises, essays, and plays. His strident critiques of French absolutism and Catholicism forced him in and out of jail and exile. He was eventually immortalized by the French government during the Revolution when his ashes were the first to be transferred to the Pantheon in 1790, a former church in which the remains of all of France's men of genius would eventually come to rest.

Throughout his life, Voltaire advocated religious toleration and the secularization of society and politics. He favored individual liberty in thought and action, but stopped short of promoting democracy; like most *philosophes*, he was a reformer, not a revolutionary. Similarly, while he left few of society's institutions unscathed by his fierce pen, he did not argue for equality or rights for slaves, Jews, or women. As can be seen below, however, Voltaire did not believe anyone should be subject to brutality or persecution. Moreover, the freedom of thought Voltaire championed in both his life and work provided later inspiration to generations who would push the Enlightenment project of reform further.

In the *Philosophical Dictionary*, originally published in 1734, Voltaire authored alphabetical entries treating hundreds of different topics. His essay on "fanaticism" is included here because no subject preoccupied Voltaire more. He found all peoples guilty of fanatical intolerance towards those whose beliefs, especially religious, differed from their own. From the continual persecution of Jews to the depopulation of the Americas, Voltaire sought to raise awareness of fanaticism's lethal consequences. Of course, the only remedy for such a malignancy on the human race was philosophy. Only rationality and moderation could triumph where laws and religion failed. In this admonition to educate minds, Voltaire offers one of the chief legacies of the Enlightenment for future generations: progress is only possible through moral and rational education. In his opinion, can believers refrain from spurning those who reject their beliefs? Why is law ineffective against fanaticism? How does he distinguish between the many perpetrators of fanaticism?

148

from *Philosophical Dictionary* (1764)

Fanaticism

Section I

Fanaticism is the effect of a false conscience, which makes religion subservient to the caprices of the imagination, and the excesses of the passions.

It arises, in general, from legislators entertaining too narrow views, or from their extending their regulations beyond the limits within which alone they were intended to operate. Their laws are made merely for a select society. When extended by zeal to a whole people, and transferred by ambition from one climate to another, some changes of institution should take place, some accommodation to persons, places and circumstances. But what, in fact, has been the case? Certain minds, constituted in a great degree like those of the small original flock, have received a system with equal ardor, and become its apostles, and even its martyrs, rather than abate a single iota of its demands. Others, on the contrary, less ardent, or more attached to their prejudices of education, have struggled with energy against the new yoke, and consented to receive it only after considerable softenings and mitigations: hence the schism between rigorists and moderates, by which all are urged on to vehemence and madness—the one party for servitude and the other for freedom.

• • •

But let us turn our attention to other frenzies and other spectacles. All Europe passes into Asia by a road inundated with the blood of Jews, who commit suicide to avoid falling into the hands of their enemies. This epidemic depopulates one-half of the inhabited world: kings, pontiffs, women, the young and the aged, all yield to the influence of the holy madness which, for a series of two hundred years, instigated the slaughter of innumerable nations at the tomb of a god of peace. Then were to be seen lying oracles, and military hermits, monarchs in pulpits, and prelates in camps. All the different states constitute one delirious populace; barriers of mountains and seas are surmounted; legitimate possessions are abandoned to enable their owners to fly to conquests which were no longer, in point of fertility, the land of promise; manners become corrupted under foreign skies; princes, after having exhausted their respective kingdoms to redeem a country which had never been theirs, complete the ruin of them for their personal ransom; thousands of soldiers, wandering under the banners of many chieftains, acknowledge the authority of none and hasten their defeat by their desertion; and the disease terminates only to be succeeded by a contagion still more horrible and desolating.

The same spirit of fanaticism cherished the rage for distant conquests: scarcely had Europe repaired its losses when the discovery of a new world hastened the ruin of our own. At that terrible injunction, "Go and conquer," America was desolated and its inhabitants exterminated; Africa and Europe were exhausted in vain to repeople it; the poison of money and of pleasure having enervated the species, the world became nearly a desert and appeared likely every day to advance nearer to desolation by the continual wars which were kindled on our continent, from the ambition of extending its power to foreign lands.

Let us now compute the immense number of slaves which fanaticism has made, whether in Asia, where uncircumcision was a mark of infamy, or in Africa, where the Christian name was a crime, or in America, where the pretext of baptism absolutely extinguished the feelings of humanity. Let us compute the thousands who have been seen to perish either on scaffolds in the ages of persecution, or in civil wars by the hands of their fellow citizens, or by their own hands through excessive austerities, and maceration. Let us survey the surface of the earth, and glance at the various standards unfurled and blazing in the name of religion; in Spain against the Moors, in France against the Turks, in Hungary against the Tartars; at the numerous military orders, founded for converting infidels by the point of the sword, and slaughtering one another at the foot of the altar they had come to defend. Let us then look down from the appalling tribunal thus raised on the bodies of the innocent and miserable, in order to judge the living, as God, with a balance widely different, will judge the dead.

In a word, let us contemplate the horrors of fifteen centuries; all frequently renewed in the course of a single one; unarmed men slain at the feet of altars; kings destroyed by the dagger or by poison; a large state reduced to half its extent by the fury of its own citizens; the nation at once the most warlike and the most pacific on the face of the globe, divided in fierce hostility against itself; the sword unsheathed between the sons and the father; usurpers, tyrants, executioners, sacrilegious robbers, and bloodstained parricides violating, under the impulse of religion, every convention divine or human—such is the deadly picture of fanaticism.

Section II

• • •

Fanaticism is, in reference to superstition, what delirium is to fever, or rage to anger. He who is involved in ecstasies and visions, who takes dreams for realities, and his own imaginations for prophecies, is a fanatical novice of great hope and promise, and will probably soon advance to the highest form, and kill man for the love of God.

• • •

There is no other remedy for this epidemical malady than that spirit of philosophy, which, extending itself from one to another, at length civilizes and softens the manners of men and prevents the access of the disease. For when the disorder has made any progress, we should, without loss of time, fly from the seat of it, and wait till the air has become purified from contagion. Law and religion are not completely efficient against the spiritual pestilence. Religion, indeed, so far from affording proper nutrition to the minds of patients laboring under this infectious and infernal distemper, is converted, by the diseased process of their minds, into poison. These malignant devotees have incessantly before their eyes the example of Ehud, who assassinated the king of Eglon; of Judith, who cut off the head of Holofernes while in bed with him; of Samuel, hewing in pieces King Agag; of Jehoiada the priest, who murdered his queen at the horse-gate. They do not perceive that these instances, which are respectable in antiquity, are in the present day abominable. They derive their fury from religion, decidedly as religion condemns it.

Laws are yet more powerless against these paroxysms of rage. To oppose laws to cases of such a description would be like reading a decree of council to a man in a frenzy. The persons in question are fully convinced the Holy Spirit which animates and fills them is above all laws; that their own enthusiasm is, in fact, the only law which they are bound to obey.

What can be said in answer to a man who says he will rather obey God than men, and who consequently feels certain of meriting heaven by cutting your throat?

When once fanaticism has gangrened the brain of any man the disease may be regarded as nearly incurable.

William Blake

1757–1827

The son of a London hosier and dissenting Protestant, William Blake was for the most part self-taught, reading widely in works of poetry, religion, and mysticism. Even as early as four years of age, Blake's unusual imaginative powers revealed themselves in a series of visions: he claimed once to have seen God looking in on him at his window, and a short time later he said that he had seen the prophet Ezekiel and a host of angels in a field near his home. Blake began writing verse at the age of twelve and in 1783 published his first collection, entitled *Poetical Sketches*. As a young boy, he also knew that he wanted to become a painter and, when he turned 14, was apprenticed to the engraver James Basire, under whom he worked and studied for seven years. Blake then studied for a very brief time at the Royal Academy, but left in disagreement with the aesthetic principles of Academy's president, the great neoclassical painter Sir Joshua Reynolds. Among his closest friends Blake counted the neoclassical sculptor John Flaxman and the Swiss painter Johann Heinrich Fuseli, whose paintings of nightmarish visions Blake found evocative of deep human truths.

In 1789, Blake published his *Songs of Innocence*, a collection of engravings and poetry which convey his interest in pushing the boundaries of accepted artistic convention, and his *Book of Thel*, the first of his extensively symbolic "prophetic" works. Following these works, in 1793 and 1794, he published four more prophetic books—*Visions of the Daughters of Albion, America: A Prophecy, Europe: A Prophecy*, and *The First Book of Urizen*—and another important collection, his *Songs of Experience*. In these works and others, Blake put forth his critique of Enlightenment materialism and rationalism, seeing the glory of man and God alike in the power of the creative imagination. In his poem "Milton" (1804–1808), named after the poet who in the seventeenth century wrote the epic *Paradise Lost*, Blake advises us "To cast off Rational Demonstration. . . ./To cast off the rotten rags of Memory by Inspiration/To cast off Bacon, Locke, and Newton." To him, the philosophies of these thinkers merely limited human potential and subjugated us to a world of things.

Given his susceptibility to visions throughout his lifetime and the uniqueness of his artistic approach, Blake was undeniably an eccentric, but his values reflect a serious engagement with the issues of his day. His works reveal an abiding concern for religious freedom, sexual liberation, pacifism, and political and economic justice. In the selections below, how does Blake evoke a romantic sensibility? In "London," how does the poet represent the problems of child labor and economic oppression? His intensely challenging poem "The Sick Rose" presents the reader with a number of possible narratives, from the literal to the highly symbolic. What narratives do you see at work in the text? What attitudes seem to be in play?

London (1794)

I wander thro' each charter'd street,
Near where the charter'd Thames does flow,
And mark in every face I meet
Marks of weakness, marks of woe.

In every cry of every Man,
In every Infant's cry of fear,
In every voice, in every ban,
The mind-forg'd manacles I hear.

How the chimney-sweeper's cry
Every black'ning church appals;
And the hapless soldier's sigh
Runs in blood down palace walls.

But most thro' midnight streets I hear
How the youthful harlot's curse
Blasts the new-born infant's tear,
And blights with plagues the marriage hearse.

The Sick Rose (1794)

O Rose, thou art sick!
The invisible worm,
That flies in the night,
In the howling storm,

Has found out thy bed
Of crimson joy;
And his dark secret love
Does thy life destroy.

Robert Owen

1771–1858

Robert Owen was a Welsh inventor, industrialist and manufacturer whose attempts at reforming the rapidly industrializing society of early nineteenth century Britain earned him a reputation as one of the most influential utopian socialists of his time. He is best known for the introduction of a range of social and industrial welfare programs at his experimental mill town, New Lanark, in southwestern Scotland. His work and philosophy inspired other utopian communities as far away as New Harmony, Indiana.

In what might be considered a tone of gentle admonition, Owen was addressing his fellow industrialists and British policy makers with his series of essays, "A New View of Society" (1813–1814). His emphasis on child welfare, education, decent housing, and working conditions was reflected in his reform efforts at New Lanark and the establishment of his Institute for the Formation of Character there in 1816.

It is important to note that Owen never criticized or abandoned the profit motive, only the abuses that it caused when managers and industrialists did not show the proper regard for their workers. Moreover, Owen argued that profit, productivity, and worker welfare could be achieved simultaneously. By focusing on the latter at New Lanark, he demonstrated that investments in the welfare of the society at large have a direct relation to that society's productivity. As a utopian, Owen believed that these investments, in both welfare of workers and their children, could address many of the social ills that rapid industrialization had aggravated. How is his appeal similar to that of Enlightenment thinkers, and how does it compare to the ethos that guided other contemporary industrialists?

from *A New View of Society*

Or, Essays on the Principle of the Formation of the Human Character, and the Application of the Principle to Practice (1813–1814)

To the superintendents of manufactories, and to those individuals generally, who, by giving employment to an aggregated population, may easily adopt the means to form the sentiments and manners of such a population

Like you, I am a manufacturer for pecuniary profit, but having for many years acted on principles the reverse in many respects of those in which you have been instructed, and having found my procedure beneficial to others and to myself, even in a pecuniary point of view, I am anxious to explain such valuable principles, that you and those under your influence may equally partake of their advantages. . . .

Many of you have long experienced in your manufacturing operations the advantages of substantial, well-contrived, and well-executed machinery.

Experience has also shown you the difference of the results between mechanism which is neat, clean, well-arranged, and always in a high state of repair; and that which is allowed to be dirty, in disorder, without the means of preventing unnecessary friction, and which therefore becomes, and works, much out of repair.

In the first case the whole economy and management are good; every operation proceeds with ease, order, and success. In the last, the reverse must follow, and a scene be presented of counteraction, confusion, and dissatisfaction among all the agents and instruments interested or occupied in the general process, which cannot fail to create great loss.

If, then, due care as to the state of your inanimate machines can produce such beneficial results, what may not be expected if you devote equal attention to your vital machines, which are far more wonderfully constructed?

When you shall acquire a right knowledge of these, of their curious mechanism, of their self-adjusting powers; when the proper mainspring shall be applied to their varied movements you will become conscious of their real value, and you will readily be induced to turn your thoughts more frequently from your inanimate to your living machines; you will discover that the latter may be easily trained and directed to procure a large increase of pecuniary gain, while you may also derive from them high and substantial gratification.

Will you then continue to expend large sums of money to procure the best devised mechanism of wood, brass, or iron; to retain it in perfect repair; to provide the best substance for the prevention of unnecessary friction, and to save it from falling into premature decay?—Will you also devote years of intense application to understand the connection of the various parts of these lifeless machines, to improve their effective powers, and to calculate with mathematical precision all their minute and combined movements?—And when in these transactions you estimate time by minutes, and the money expended for the chance of increased gain by fractions, will you not afford some of your attention to consider whether a portion of your time and capital would not be more advantageously applied to improve your living machines? From experience which cannot deceive me, I venture to assure you, that your time and money so applied, if directed by a true knowledge of the subject, would return you, not five, ten, or fifteen per cent for your capital so expended, but often fifty, and in many cases a hundred per cent.

I have expended much time and capital upon improvements of the living machinery; and it will soon appear that time and the money so expended in the manufactory at New Lanark, even while such improvements are in progress only, and but half their beneficial effects attained, are now producing a return exceeding fifty per cent, and will shortly create profits equal to cent per cent on the original capital expended in them.

Indeed, after experience of the beneficial effects from due care and attention to the mechanical implements, it became easy to a reflecting mind to conclude at once, that at least equal advantages would arise from the application of similar care and attention to the living instruments. And when it was perceived that inanimate mechanism was greatly improved by being made firm and substantial; that it was the essence of economy to keep it neat, clean, regularly supplied with the best substance to prevent unnecessary friction, and by proper provision for the purpose to preserve it in good repair, it was natural to conclude that the more delicate, complex, living mechanism would be equally improved by being trained to strength and activity and that it would also prove true economy to keep it neat and clean; to treat it with kindness, that its mental movements might not experience too much irritating friction; to endeavour by every means to make it more perfect; to supply it regularly with a sufficient quantity of wholesome food and other necessaries of life, that the body might be preserved in good working condition, and prevented from being out of repair, or falling prematurely to decay.

These anticipations are proved by experience to be just.

Since the general introduction of inanimate mechanism into British manufactories, man, with few exceptions, has been treated as a secondary and inferior machine; and far more attention has been given to perfect the raw materials of wood and metals than those of body and mind. Give but due reflection to the subject, and you will find that man, even as an instrument for the creation of wealth, may be still greatly improved.

But, my friends, a far more interesting and gratifying consideration remains. Adopt the means which ere long shall be rendered obvious to every understanding, and you may not only partially improve those living instruments, but learn how to impart to them such excellence as shall make them infinitely surpass those of the present and all former times.

Here, then, is an object which truly deserves your attention; and, instead of devoting all your faculties to invent improved inanimate mechanism, let your thoughts be, at least in part, directed to discover how to combine the more excellent materials of body and mind which, by a well-devised experiment, will be found capable of progressive improvement.

Thus seeing with the clearness of noonday light, thus convinced with the certainty of conviction itself, let us not perpetuate the really unnecessary evils which our present practices inflict on this large proportion of our fellow subjects. Should your pecuniary interests somewhat suffer by adopting the line of conduct now urged, many of you are so wealthy that the expense of founding and continuing at your respective establishments the institutions necessary to improve your animate machines would not be felt, but when you may have ocular demonstration, that, instead of any pecuniary loss, a well-directed attention to form the character and increase the comforts of those who are so entirely at your mercy, will essentially add to your gains, prosperity, and happiness, no reasons, except those founded on ignorance of your self-interest, can in future prevent you from bestowing your chief care on the living machines which you employ. And by so doing you will prevent an accumulation of human misery, of which it is now difficult to form an adequate conception.

That you may be convinced of this most valuable truth, which due reflection will show you is founded on the evidence of unerring acts, is the sincere wish of

The Author

First Essay

Any general character, from the best to the worst, from the most ignorant to the most enlightened, may be given to any community, even to the world at large, by the application of proper means; which means are to a great extent at the command and under the control of those who have influence in the affairs of men.

According to the last returns under the Population Act, the poor and working classes of Great Britain and Ireland have been found to exceed fifteen millions of persons, or nearly three-fourths of the population of the British Islands.

The characters of these persons are now permitted to be very generally formed without proper guidance or direction, and, in many cases, under circumstances which directly impel them to a course of extreme vice and misery; thus rendering them the worst and most dangerous subjects in the empire; while the far greater part of the remainder of the community are educated upon the most mistaken principles of human nature, such, indeed, as cannot fail to produce a general conduct throughout society, totally unworthy of the character of rational beings.

The first thus unhappily situated are the poor and the uneducated profligate among the working classes, who are now trained to commit crimes, for the commission of which they are afterwards punished.

The second is the remaining mass of the population, who are now instructed to believe, or at least to acknowledge, that certain principles are unerringly true, and to act as though they were grossly false; thus filling the world with folly and inconsistency, and making society, throughout all its ramifications, a scene of insincerity and counteraction.

In this state the world has continued to the present time; its evils have been and are continually increasing; they cry aloud for efficient corrective measures, which if we longer delay, general disorder must ensue.

'But,' say those who have not deeply investigated the subject, 'attempts to apply remedies have been often made, yet all of them have failed. The evil is now of a magnitude not to be controlled; the torrent is already too strong to be stemmed; and we can only wait with fear or calm resignation to see it carry destruction in its course, by confounding all distinctions of right and wrong.'

Such is the language now held, and such are the general feelings on this most important subject.

These, however, if longer suffered to continue, must lead to the most lamentable consequences. Rather than pursue such a course, the character of legislators would be infinitely raised, if, forgetting the petty and humiliating contentions of sects and parties, they would thoroughly investigate the subject, and endeavour to arrest and overcome these mighty evils. . . .

Emily Brontë

1818–1848

Emily Brontë was one of the three famous Brontë sisters, who are known for their contributions to the tradition and development of the English novel. Their father was an Irish clergyman who was educated in England. Two of the six Brontë children died in their youth and Emily's mother herself died in 1821. The three sisters and their brother Branwell grew up in the moorlands of Yorkshire in northern England. Emily received virtually all of her early education at home. Later, the eldest sister, Charlotte, hoped to establish a school for girls where the family could work together, but this idea was abandoned in 1845. The Brontës then concentrated on becoming authors and, in 1847, a trio of novels appeared: Emily's *Wuthering Heights*, Anne's *Agnes Grey*, and Charlotte's *Jane Eyre*. However, Emily's career was cut short in 1848, at the age of 30. For over a year, she had experienced a difficult time caring for her brother, who by this time was an alcoholic and opium addict. At his funeral in September, she caught a cold that quickly developed into a serious inflammation of the lungs. She refused medical treatment and lived on stoically until her death in December.

Emily Brontë's imaginative force ran counter to the sensibilities of Victorian England. In *Wuthering Heights*, Emily's striking treatment of love, passion, and hatred against the backdrop of the Yorkshire moors successfully integrated elements of realism and the romantic. In her poems, there is dynamic tension between romantic desire and a sense of alienation from the social conventions of the day. This theme of alienation, evident in Brontë's "The Night-Wind" (1840), will become more dominant as we pass from the early nineteenth-century romanticism, through mid-century realism, to the modernism of the early twentieth century. What elements of romanticism and alienation does "The Night-Wind" illustrate? What conflicting emotions does the poem seem to represent? What meanings does the wind evoke in the poem?

The Night-Wind (1840)

In summer's mellow midnight,
A cloudless moon shone through
Our open parlour window
And rosetrees wet with dew.

I sat in silent musing,
The soft wind waved my hair:
It told me Heaven was glorious,
And sleeping Earth was fair.

I needed not its breathing
To bring such thoughts to me,
But still it whispered lowly,
"How dark the woods will be!

"The thick leaves in my murmur
Are rustling like a dream,
And all their myriad voices
Instinct[1] with spirit seem."

I said, "Go, gentle singer,
Thy wooing voice is kind,
But do not think its music
Has power to reach my mind.

"Play with the scented flower,
The young tree's supple bough,
And leave my human feelings
In their own course to flow."

The wanderer would not leave me;
Its kiss grew warmer still—
"O come," it sighed so sweetly,
"I'll win thee 'gainst thy will.

"Have we not been from childhood friends?
Have I not loved thee long?
As long as thou hast loved the night
Whose silence wakes my song.

161

"And when thy heart is laid at rest
Beneath the church-yard stone
I shall have time enough to mourn
And thou to be alone."

September 11, 1840

Note

[1] Permeated.

Ralph Waldo Emerson

1803–1882

Ralph Waldo Emerson was the leading figure in the school of American romanticism called Transcendentalism. Born into an old Boston family with a long tradition of ministry, he attended Boston Latin School, Harvard University and the Harvard Divinity School, earning his license to preach in 1826. He was ordained as a Unitarian minister in 1829 and became the pastor at the Second Church in Boston. In 1829 he married, but when his young wife died in 1831, his doubts about Christian doctrine intensified. His encounter at Harvard with the Newtonian view of the world and the Lockean conception of the mind caused him many difficulties in integrating his various religious studies. The determinism of classical physics along with Locke's shaping of the mind through the sensation of the environment left little room for free will. This cause-and-effect understanding of natural law challenged the very concept of the miraculous. He resigned from the Church in 1832.

Emerson was a prolific writer: his major works include *Nature* (1836), *Essays* (1841 and 1844), *Representative Men* (1850), *English Traits* (1856), and *The Conduct of Life* (1860). In his quest to understand the spiritual, he came to the conclusion that transcendence of the mechanical world is possible, but only with the recognition that the transcendent lies deep within the individual. Each of us possesses the divine, an inner wisdom, and a power of insight and moral awareness. We should rely on this inner spirit to guide our lives, Emerson argues, but most of us refuse to listen to it. We willingly accept our mediocrity, because conforming to social expectations is safer than trusting ourselves. In "Self-Reliance" (1841), Emerson anticipates the existentialists of the twentieth century, asking us to decide whether meaning, value, and truth reside within the individual or within social conventions. Why do we fail ourselves and others, even when we know the right course of action? What are some of the arguments Emerson gives to convince us of the reality and power of inner experience? What other writers or schools of thought does Emerson's essay evoke?

from "Self-Reliance" (1841)

. . . . To believe your own thought, to believe that what is true for you in your private heart is true for all men—that is genius. Speak your latent conviction, and it shall be the universal sense; for the inmost in due time becomes the outmost, and our first thought is rendered back to us by the trumpets of the Last Judgment. Familiar as the voice of the mind is to each, the highest merit we ascribe to Moses, Plato and Milton is that they set at naught books and traditions, and spoke not what men but what *they* thought. A man should learn to detect and watch that gleam of light which flashes across his mind from within, more than the lustre of the firmament of bards and sages. Yet he dismisses without notice his thought, because it is his. In every work of genius we recognize our own rejected thoughts; they come back to us with a certain alienated majesty. Great works of art have no more affecting lesson for us than this. They teach us to abide by our spontaneous impression with good-humored inflexibility then most when the whole cry of voices is on the other side. Else, to-morrow a stranger will say with masterly good sense precisely what we have thought and felt all the time, and we shall be forced to take with shame our own opinion from another.

There is a time in every man's education when he arrives at the conviction that envy is ignorance; that imitation is suicide; that he must take himself for better for worse as his portion; that though the wide universe is full of good, no kernel of nourishing corn can come to him but through his toil bestowed on that plot of ground which is given to him to till. The power which resides in him is new in nature, and none but he knows what that is which he can do, nor does he know until he has tried.

• • •

Trust thyself: every heart vibrates to that iron string. Accept the place the divine providence has found for you, the society of your contemporaries, the connection of events. Great men have always done so, and confided themselves childlike to the genius of their age, betraying their perception that the absolutely trustworthy was seated at their heart, working through their hands, predominating in all their being. And we are now men, and must accept in the highest mind the same transcendent destiny; and not minors and invalids in a protected corner, not cowards fleeing before a revolution, but guides, redeemers, and benefactors, obeying the Almighty effort, and advancing on Chaos and the Dark.

• • •

These are the voices which we hear in solitude, but they grow faint and inaudible as we enter into the world. Society everywhere is in conspiracy against the manhood of every one of its members. Society is a joint-stock company, in which the members agree, for the better securing of his bread to each shareholder, to surrender the liberty and culture of the eater. The virtue in most request is conformity. Self-reliance is its aversion. It loves not realities and creators, but names and customs.

Whoso would be a man must be a nonconformist. He who would gather immortal palms must not be hindered by the name of goodness, but must explore if it be goodness. Nothing is at last sacred but the integrity of your own mind. Absolve you to yourself, and you shall have the suffrage of the world. I remember an answer which when quite young I was prompted to make to a valued adviser who was wont to importune[1] me with the dear old doctrines of the church. On my saying, "What have I to do with the sacredness of traditions, if I live wholly from within?" my friend suggested—"But these impulses may be from below, not from above." I replied, "They do not seem to me to be such; but if I am the Devil's child, I will live then from the Devil." No law can be sacred to me but that of my nature. Good and bad are but names very readily transferable to that or this; the only right is what is after my constitution, the only wrong what is against it. A man is to carry himself in the presence of all opposition as if every thing were titular and ephemeral but he. I am ashamed to think how easily we capitulate to badges and names, to large societies and dead institutions.

• • •

What I must do is all that concerns me, not what the people think. This rule, equally arduous in actual and in intellectual life, may serve for the whole distinction between greatness and meanness. It is the harder because you will always find those who think they know what is your duty better than you know it. It is easy in the world to live after the world's opinion; it is easy in solitude to live after our own; but the great man is he who in the midst of the crowd keeps with perfect sweetness the independence of solitude.

The objection to conforming to usages that have become dead to you is that it scatters your force. It loses your time and blurs the impression of your character. If you maintain a dead church, contribute to a dead Bible-society, vote with a great party either for the government or against it, spread your table like base housekeepers—under all these screens I have difficulty to detect the precise man you are and, of course so much force is withdrawn from your proper life. But do your work, and I shall know you. Do your work, and you shall reinforce yourself. A man must consider what a blind-man's-bluff is this game of conformity. If I know your sect I anticipate your argument. I hear a preacher announce for his text and topic the expediency of one of the institutions of his church. Do I not know beforehand that not possibly can he say a new and spontaneous word? Do I not know that with all this ostentation of examining the grounds of the institution he will do no such thing? Do I not know that he is pledged to himself not to look but at one side, the permitted side, not as a man, but as a parish minister? He is a retained attorney, and these airs of the bench are the emptiest affectation. Well, most men have bound their eyes with one or another handkerchief, and attached themselves to some one of these communities of opinion. This conformity makes them not false in a few particulars, authors of a few lies, but false in all particulars. Their every truth is not quite true. Their two is not the real two, their four not the real four; so that every word they say chagrins us and we know not where to begin to set them right. Meantime nature is not slow to equip us in the prison-uniform of the party to which we adhere. We come to wear one cut of face and figure, and acquire by degrees the gentlest asinine expression. There is a mortifying experience in particular, which does not fail to wreak itself also in the general history; I mean "the foolish face of praise," the forced smile which we put on in company where we do not feel at ease, in answer to conversation which does not interest us. The muscles, not spontaneously moved but moved by a low usurping wilfulness, grow tight about the outline of the face with the most disagreeable sensation.

• • •

The other terror that scares us from self-trust is our consistency; a reverence for our past act or word because the eyes of others have no other data for computing our orbit than our past acts, and we are loth[2] to disappoint them.

• • •

A foolish consistency is the hobgoblin of little minds, adored by little statesmen and philosophers and divines. With consistency a great soul has simply nothing to do. He may as well concern himself with his shadow on the wall. Speak what you think now in hard words and to-morrow speak what to-morrow thinks in hard words again, though it contradict every thing you said to-day.—'Ah, so you shall be sure to be misunderstood.'—Is it so bad then to be misunderstood? Pythagoras was misunderstood, and Socrates, and Jesus, and Luther, and Copernicus, and Galileo, and Newton, and every pure and wise spirit that ever took flesh. To be great is to be misunderstood.

• • •

Check this lying hospitality and lying affection. Live no longer to the expectation of these deceived and deceiving people with whom we converse. Say to them, 'O father, O mother, O wife, O brother, O friend, I have lived with you after appearances hitherto. Henceforward I am the truth's. Be it known unto you that henceforward I obey no law less than the eternal law. I will have no covenants but proximities. I shall endeavour to nourish my parents, to support my family, to be the chaste husband of one wife—but these relations I must fill after a new and unprecedented way. I appeal from your customs. I must be myself. I cannot break myself any longer for you, or you. If you can love me for what I am, we shall be the happier. If you cannot, I will still seek to deserve that you should. I will not hide my tastes or aversions. I will so trust that what is deep is holy, that I will do strongly before the sun and moon whatever inly rejoices me and the heart appoints. If you are noble, I will love you; if you are not, I will not hurt you and myself by hypocritical attentions. If you are true, but not in the same truth with me, cleave to your companions; I will seek my own. I do this not selfishly but humbly and truly. It is alike your interest, and mine, and all men's, however long we have dwelt in lies, to live in truth. Does this sound harsh to-day? You will soon love what is dictated by your nature as well as mine, and, if we follow the truth, it will bring us out safe at last.'—But so you may give these friends pain. Yes, but I cannot sell my liberty and my power, to save their sensibility. Besides, all persons have their moments of reason, when they look out into the region of absolute truth; then will they justify me and do the same thing.

• • •

And truly it demands something godlike in him who has cast off the common motives of humanity and has ventured to trust himself for a taskmaster. High be his heart, faithful his will, clear his sight, that he may in good earnest be doctrine, society, law, to himself, that a simple purpose may be to him as strong as iron necessity is to others!

If any man consider the present aspects of what is called by distinction *society*, he will see the need of these ethics. The sinew and heart of man seem to be drawn out, and we are become timorous, desponding whimperers. We are afraid of truth, afraid of fortune, afraid of death, and afraid of each other. Our age yields no great and perfect persons. We want men and women who shall renovate life and our social state, but we see that most natures are insolvent, cannot satisfy their own wants, have an ambition out of all proportion to their practical force and do lean and beg day and night continually. Our housekeeping is mendicant, our arts, our occupations, our marriages, our religion we have not chosen, but society has chosen for us. We are parlour soldiers. We shun the rugged battle of fate, where strength is born.

• • •

Insist on yourself; never imitate. Your own gift you can present every moment with the cumulative force of a whole life's cultivation; but of the adopted talent of another you have only an extemporaneous, half possession. That which each can do best, none but his Maker can teach him. No man yet knows what it is, nor can, till that person has exhibited it. Where is the master who could have taught Shakespeare? Where is the master who could have instructed Franklin, or Washington, or Bacon, or Newton? Every great man is a unique.

• • •

Nothing can bring you peace but yourself. Nothing can bring you peace but the triumph of principles.

Notes

[1] Urge.

[2] Loath.

IV. The Politics of Slavery and Gender in the Eighteenth and Nineteenth Centuries

Abigail Adams

1744–1818

John Adams

1735–1826

Abigail Adams was one of the most progressive women during the early history of the United States. In spite of a lack of formal education, typical for women of her generation, she developed keen "enlightened" ideas, many of which were ahead of her time. A prolific correspondent—we have over 2000 of her letters—she frequently wrote of her views to friends and family. She wrote frequently to her husband, John Adams, when his political career required him to travel and live elsewhere. The letters included here were written in 1776, during John Adams's term as delegate to the first Continental Congress. Abigail was one of the earliest supporters of American independence, an opponent of slavery, and a strong proponent of women's rights. She had a brilliant flair for expressing her ideas in the most straightforward and clearly conceived way.

John Adams became the first vice president of the United States and later followed George Washington as the country's second president. As first lady, Abigail continued to prove herself an insightful political partner for her husband throughout his presidency. She accompanied him on diplomatic missions and shared ideas through correspondence when he was away. Their son, John Quincy, became the nation's sixth president in 1825; however, Abigail died a few years before his election. Both John Adams and Thomas Jefferson died in 1826, only hours apart, fifty years to the day after the signing of the Declaration of Independence.

In this excerpt from one of her letters, Abigail urges her husband to "remember the ladies" as he plans legislation following the Declaration of Independence. Here, she argues, is an opportunity to formulate new laws that are fair to women. She challenges him to "be more generous and favorable to them than your ancestors." Her warnings foretell the women's rights movement of the next century and beyond. How does Abigail use the concepts of political representation and tyranny that were employed by the colonists in their rebellion against England? Are there other parallels between her thinking and that of the revolutionaries? What is the tone and content of John's response? What does he seem afraid of? Compare John's exchange of views with his wife to those in his correspondence with a male colleague, James Sullivan.

An Exchange of Letters (1776)

91. Abigail Adams
Braintree, 31 March, 1776.

• • •

I have sometimes been ready to think that the passion for liberty cannot be equally strong in the breasts of those who have been accustomed to deprive their fellow-creatures of theirs. Of this I am certain, that it is not founded upon that generous and Christian principle of doing to others as we would that others should do unto us.

• • •

I long to hear that you have declared an independency. And, by the way, in the new code of laws which I suppose it will be necessary for you to make, I desire you would remember the ladies and be more generous and favorable to them than your ancestors. Do not put such unlimited power into the hands of the husbands. Remember, all men would be tyrants if they could. If particular care and attention is not paid to the ladies, we are determined to foment a rebellion, and will not hold ourselves bound by any laws in which we have no voice or representation.

That your sex are naturally tyrannical is a truth so thoroughly established as to admit of no dispute; but such of you as wish to be happy willingly give up the harsh title of master for the more tender and endearing one of friend. Why, then, not put it out of the power of the vicious and the lawless to use us with cruelty and indignity with impunity? Men of sense in all ages abhor those customs which treat us only as the vassals of your sex; regard us then as beings placed by Providence under your protection, and in imitation of the Supreme Being make use of that power only for our happiness.

• • •

94. John Adams.
14 April, 1776.

• • •

As to your extraordinary code of laws, I cannot but laugh. We have been told that our struggle has loosened the bonds of government everywhere; that children and apprentices were disobedient; that schools and colleges were grown turbulent; that Indians slighted their guardians, and negroes grew insolent to their masters. But your letter was the first intimation that another tribe, more numerous and powerful than all the rest, were grown discontented. This is rather too coarse a compliment, but you are so saucy, I won't blot it out. Depend upon it, we know better than to repeal our masculine systems. Although they are in full force, you know they are little more than theory. We dare not exert our power in its full latitude. We are obliged to go fair and softly, and, in practice, you know we are the subjects. We have only the name of masters, and rather than give up this, which would completely subject us to the despotism of the petticoat, I hope General Washington and all our brave heroes would fight; I am sure every good politician would plot, as long as he would against despotism, empire, monarchy, aristocracy, oligarchy, or ochlocracy. A fine story, indeed! I begin to think the ministry as deep as they are wicked. After stirring up Tories, land-jobbers, trimmers, bigots, Canadians, Indians, negroes, Hanoverians, Hessians, Russians, Irish Roman Catholics, Scotch renegadoes, at last they have stimulated the ———— to demand new privileges and threaten to rebel.

From John Adams to James Sullivan

Philadelphia, 26 May, 1776.

. . . It is certain, in theory, that the only moral foundation of government is, the consent of the people. But to what an extent shall we carry this principle? Shall we say that every individual of the community, old and young, male and female, as well as rich and poor, must consent, expressly, to every act of legislation? No, you will say, this is impossible. How, then does the right arise in the majority to govern the minority, against their will? Whence arises the right of the men to govern the women, without their consent? Whence the right of the old to bind the young, without theirs?

But let us first suppose that the whole community, of every age, rank, sex, and condition, has a right to vote. This community is assembled. A motion is made, and carried by a majority of one voice. The minority will not agree to this. Whence arises the right of the majority to govern, and the obligation of the minority to obey?

From necessity, you will say, because there can be no other rule.

But why exclude women?

You will say, because their delicacy renders them unfit for practice and experience in the great businesses of life, and the hardy enterprises of war, as well as the arduous cares of state. Besides, their attention is so much engaged with the necessary nurture of their children, that nature has made them fittest for domestic cares. And children have not judgment or will of their own. True. But will not these reasons apply to others? Is it not equally true, that men in general, in every society, who are wholly destitute of property, are also too little acquainted with public affairs to form a right judgment, and too dependent upon other men to have a will of their own? If this is a fact, if you give to every man who has no property, a vote, will you not make a fine encouraging provision for corruption, by your fundamental law? Such is the frailty of the human heart, that very few men who have no property, have any judgment of their own. They talk and vote as they are directed by some man of property, who has attached their minds to his interest. . . .

Your idea that those laws which affect the lives and personal liberty of all, or which inflict corporal punishment, affect those who are not qualified to vote, as well as those who are, is just. But so they do women, as well as men; children, as well as adults. What reason should there be for excluding a man of twenty years eleven months and twenty-seven days old, from a vote, when you admit one who is twenty-one? The reason is, you must fix upon some period in life, when the understanding and will of men in general, is fit to be trusted by the public. Will not the same reason justify the state in fixing upon some certain quantity of property, as a qualification?

The same reasoning which will induce you to admit all men who have no property, to vote, with those who have, for those laws which affect the person, will prove that you ought to admit women and children; for, generally speaking, women and children have as good judgments, and as independent minds, as those men who are wholly destitute of property; these last being to all intents and purposes as much dependent upon others, who will please to feed, clothe, and employ them, as women are upon their husbands, or children on their parents. . . .

Depend upon it, Sir, it is dangerous to open so fruitful a source of controversy and altercation as would be opened by attempting to alter the qualifications of voters; there will be no end of it. New claims will arise; women will demand a vote; lads from twelve to twenty-one will think their rights not enough attended to; and every man who has not a farthing, will demand an equal voice with any other, in all acts of state. It tends to confound and destroy all distinctions, and prostrate all ranks to one common level.

Olympe de Gouges

1748–1793

Olympe de Gouges was a butcher's daughter from Montauban who managed to educate herself, move to Paris, and live by her pen. She wrote plays and treatises on many subjects, including the abolition of slavery as well as women's rights. Though her position on women's issues was quite radical, she remained a royalist in the midst of the French Revolution, even going so far as to address her political writings to royal patrons, including the queen herself. This was the ostensible reason for her execution during the Reign of Terror in 1793, though her agitation on behalf of women's rights cannot have been irrelevant.

De Gouges' declaration includes a preamble and postamble as well as seventeen articles which echo those issued by the French government in 1789. In some, de Gouges merely adds "woman" alongside "man." Others are expanded to include issues with special relevance for women, especially article 11 which guaranties free speech. Though the declaration is addressed to the Queen, de Gouges also aims to appeal to men who have imbibed Enlightenment precepts. In the context of natural law, so revered by the philosophes, she asks on what basis the subordination of women can be justified. However, in addition to blaming the negligence of the queen, and the prejudices of men, de Gouges also points to the complicity of elite women whose "nocturnal administration" has corrupted France.

De Gouges' feminism must be seen in context. With the outbreak of the Revolution, French women enjoyed an unprecedented role in political life, forming political clubs, leading rallies and marches, hosting salons, and informing the decisions of the powerful men with whom they were associated. Moreover, the discussion of women's rights was becoming an international phenomenon with participation from American Abigail Adams and Englishwoman Mary Wollstonecraft among many others. In what way did Enlightenment thought foster the growth of feminist ideas? Are these ideas properly designated "feminist"? How does revolutionary ferment enable an expanded role for women?

Declaration of the Rights of Woman and Citizen (1791)

To the Queen

Madame,

Little skilled in the language appropriate to addressing royalty, I will not employ a courtesan's adulation to pay you homage with this unique work. Madame, my purpose is to speak to you frankly. I have not awaited the epoch of liberty to express myself thus; I displayed as much energy in a time when the blindness of despots punished such noble audacity.

When the whole empire accused you and held you responsible for its calamities, I alone in a time of trouble and storm, I alone had the strength to take up your defense. I have never been able to persuade myself that a princess raised in the midst of grandeur had all the vices of baseness.

•   •   •

Madame, may a nobler function [than plotting against the government] characterize you, excite your ambition, and fix your attention. It belongs to one whom chance has elevated to an eminent place to give weight to the progress of the Rights of Woman, and to hasten its success. If you were less well informed, Madame, I would fear that your individual interests would outweigh those of your sex. You love glory: consider, madame, that the greatest crimes become immortal like the greatest virtues, but what a different fame in the annals of history. One is ceaselessly cited as an example, the other is eternally the execration of the human race.

It will never be a crime for you to work for the restoration of morals, to give to your sex all the credit it is due. This is not the work of one day, unfortunately for the new regime. This revolution will happen only when all women fathom the depth of their deplorable fate, and of the rights they have lost in society. Undertake, madame, such a beautiful cause; defend this unfortunate sex and you will soon have one half the kingdom on your side, and at least one third of the other half.

Madame, with the deepest respect I am your most humble and obedient servant.

The Rights of Woman

Man, are you capable of being just? It is a woman who poses the question; at least you will not take away this right. Tell me, what has given you the sovereign empire to oppress my sex? Your strength? Your talents? Observe the Creator in his wisdom; look at nature in all her grandeur, with whom you seem to want to be in harmony, and give me, if you dare, an example of this tyrannical empire.

Go back to the animals, consult the elements, study plants, finally cast a glance over all the modifications of organized matter, and submit to the evidence when I offer it to you; search, probe and distinguish, if you can, the sexes in the administration of nature. Everywhere you will find them mingled, everywhere they cooperate with a unity harmonious to the immortal masterpiece.

Man alone has dressed up this exception as a principle. Bizarre, blind, bloated with science and degenerated—in the century of light and wisdom— in the crassest ignorance, he wants to command as a despot this sex which has received all intellectual faculties; he pretends to enjoy the revolution and reclaim his rights to equality only to say nothing more about it.

Declaration of the Rights of Woman and Citizen

Preamble

Mothers, daughters, sisters, representatives of the Nation, demand to be constituted into a national assembly. Considering that ignorance, forgetfulness, or scorn for the rights of woman are the sole causes of public misfortune and corrupt government, [women] have resolved to expose in a solemn declaration the natural, inalienable, and sacred rights of woman in order that this declaration, constantly presented to all members of society, will ceaselessly recall them to their rights and duties; in order that the powerful acts of women and the powerful acts of men can be compared at each instant with the purpose of every political institution, in being more respected, so that the demands of female citizens, henceforth founded on simple and incontestable principles, turn always towards the maintenance of the constitution, good morals, and the happiness of everyone.

Consequently, the sex that is superior in beauty as in the courage of maternal suffering recognizes and declares in the presence and under the auspices of the Supreme Being, the following rights of woman and of female citizens:

Article One

Woman is born free and lives equal to man in her rights. Social distinctions may be founded only upon common utility.

Article Two

The purpose of any political association is the conservation of the natural and imprescriptible rights of woman and man; these rights are liberty, property, security, and above all resistance to oppression.

Article Three

The principle of all sovereignty essentially resides in the Nation, which is nothing more than the union of woman and man: no body, no individual can exercise authority which does not emanate from it.

Article Four

Liberty and justice consist in rendering all that belongs to others; thus the exercise of the natural rights of woman has only been limited by the perpetual tyranny that man opposes to it; these limits should be reformed by the laws of nature and reason.

Article Five

The laws of nature and reason prohibit all actions harmful to society: anything that is not prohibited by these wise and divine laws cannot be prevented, and no one can be constrained to do that which they do not order.

Article Six

The law should be the expression of the general will; all female and male citizens should concur personally, or by their representatives, in its formation; it should be the same for all: all female and male citizens, being equal in its eyes, should be equally admissible to every honor, position, and public employment, according to their capacities, and without any distinction than those of their virtues and talents.

Article Seven

No woman is excepted; she is accused, arrested, and detained in cases determined by law. Women, like men, obey this rigorous law.

Article Eight

The law should only establish those penalties strictly and obviously necessary, and no one can be punished except by a law established and promulgated prior to the crime and legally applicable to women.

Article Nine

Any woman found guilty [is subject to] every rigor of the law.

Article Ten

No one should be disquieted for holding basic opinions; woman has the right to mount the scaffold; she should equally have the right to mount the podium, provided that her demonstrations do not trouble the public order established by law.

Article Eleven

The free communication of thoughts and opinions is one of the most precious rights of woman, since that liberty assures the legitimacy of children *vis-á-vis* their fathers. Every citizen should be able to say freely, "I am the mother of the child who belongs to you," without being forced by a barbarous prejudice to hide the truth; [an exception may be made] to respond to the abuse of this liberty in cases determined by law.

Article Twelve

The guarantee of the rights of woman and citizen entails a major benefit; this guarantee should be instituted for the advantage of all, and not for the particular benefit of those to whom it is entrusted.

Article Thirteen

For the support of the public force, and for the expenses of administration, the contributions of woman and man are equal; she shares a part in all duties and difficult tasks; she should thus have the same share in the distribution of positions, employment, offices, honors, and jobs.

Article Fourteen

Female and male citizens have the right to verify by themselves, or by their representatives, the necessity of the public contribution. Women can adhere to this only by the admission of an equal share, not only of wealth, but of public administration, and in the determination of the proportion, base, the collection, and the duration of the tax.

Article Fifteen

The mass of women, joined for tax purposes to men, has the right to demand of any public agent an account of his administration.

Article Sixteen

No society in which the guarantee of rights is not assured, nor the separation of powers determined, has a constitution; the constitution is null if the majority of individuals who constitute the Nation has not participated in drafting it.

Article Seventeen

Property belongs to both sexes whether united or separate; it is for everyone an inviolable and sacred right; no one can be deprived of it as it is the veritable patrimony of nature, unless public necessity, legally constituted, obviously needs it, and under the condition of a just and prior indemnity.

Postamble

Women, wake up; the tocsin[1] of reason is heard throughout the whole universe; recognize your rights. The powerful empire of nature is no longer surrounded by prejudice, fanaticism, superstition, and lies. The flame of truth has dissipated all the clouds of folly and usurpation. Enslaved man has multiplied his forces, and needs recourse to yours to break his chains. Having become free, he has become unjust towards his companion. O women, women, when will you cease to be blind? What are the advantages you have received from the revolution? A more marked scorn, a more pronounced disdain. In the centuries of corruption you have reigned only over the weaknesses of men. Your empire is destroyed; what remains for you?

• • •

Women have done more harm than good. Constraint and dissimulation have been their portion. That which force ravished from them ruse returned to them; they had recourse to all the resources of their charms, and the most irreproachable could not resist them. Poison and the sword were both subject to them; they commanded in crime as in virtue. The French government, above all, depended for centuries on the nocturnal administration of women; the cabinet kept no secret from their indiscretion; ambassadorial post, command, ministry, presidency, pontificate, cardinalate; finally anything which characterizes the stupidity of men, profane and sacred, all have been submitted to the cupidity and ambition of this sex, formerly contemptible yet respected, and since the revolution respectable and scorned.

Note

[1] An alarm bell, used as a signal or warning.

Olaudah Equiano

c. 1745–1797

Born into a family of considerable status in the Ibo society of Benin (modern-day Nigeria), Olaudah Equiano was kidnapped by slave traders at the age of ten and forced to endure the terrors of the middle passage. After a short stay in Barbados, Equiano was then taken on a slave ship to the North American colonies, where he was finally sold to the owner of a Virginia plantation. In 1757, he was sold again, this time to a British navy lieutenant, under whom he served as valet, powder boy, and finally gunmate in the Royal Navy. For much of the Seven Years' War (1756–63), Equiano fought in many of Britain's most important battles against France, including the final assault on the citadel of Belle Isle in 1761. After his master's service to the Navy came to an end, Equiano was sold twice, finally to the Quaker Robert King, for whom he worked as a small-goods trader and a clerk aboard slave ships that sailed between the West Indies and the chief ports of North America. On 11 July 1766, Equiano purchased his freedom from King with money he had earned over the years, but he continued to work for him until 1767, when he moved to London as a free man.

It was in England that Equiano began to seek religious experiences that might help him understand his spiritual condition and his former life as a slave. By 1775, Equiano had converted to Christianity, becoming a follower of the English Methodist minister George Whitefield, who had traveled and worked extensively in America. Many black writers of Equiano's time were drawn to the teachings of Whitefield rather than those of the more famous John Wesley, because Whitefield advocated more rigorous conceptions of predestination and divine election. This doctrinal position stood in contrast with Wesley's belief that, with active preparation and methodical study, redemption was possible for all people of faith. To former slaves, this idea of salvation gave meaning to their suffering and liberation.

From the late-1770s to the end of his life, Equiano worked for the material benefit and political freedom of blacks in England and in Africa. In 1789, he published *The Interesting Narrative of the Life of Olaudah Equiano . . . the African*, which was reprinted numerous times until 1837, when it all but disappeared from the booksellers lists. In the selection below, Equiano offers his solution to the slave trade: in an echo of Adam Smith's *Wealth of Nations*, he calls on Europe and America to recognize the value of Africa as a manufacturing civilization, rather than merely as a source of slaves: allow the people of Africa to develop a modern system of industry, and all the nations of the world will benefit. Thus, Equiano takes his place at the front of a long line of black intellectuals—including Booker T. Washington, Marcus Garvey, and Malcolm X—who insist on the importance of developing black economic institutions as a means of achieving political equality.

In reading Equiano's narrative, consider how he appropriates Western strategies to contend with the experience of slavery and its aftermath. What is the tone of this selection? Why might Equiano have chosen to write it as he did? How might his ideas have appealed to progressive Enlightenment thinkers? How might his ideas have been threatening?

See p. 533 for accompanying map.

from *The Interesting Narrative of the Life of Olaudah Equiano or Gustavus Vassa, the African* (1789)

． ． ．

I hope to have the satisfaction of seeing the renovation of liberty and justice resting on the British government, to vindicate the honour of our common nature. These are concerns which do not perhaps belong to any particular office: but, to speak more seriously to every man of sentiment, actions like these are the just and sure foundation of future fame; a reversion, though remote, is coveted by some noble minds as a substantial good. It is upon these grounds that I hope and expect the attention of gentlemen in power. These are designs consonant to the elevation of their rank and the dignity of their stations: they are ends suitable to the nature of a free and generous government; and, connected with views of empire and dominion, suited to the benevolence and solid merit of the legislature. It is a pursuit of substantial greatness.—May the time come—at least the speculation to me is pleasing—when the sable people shall gratefully commemorate the auspicious era of extensive freedom. Then shall those persons particularly be named with praise and honour, who generously proposed and stood forth in the cause of humanity, liberty, and good policy; and brought to the ear of the legislature designs worthy of royal patronage and adoption. May Heaven make the British senators the dispersers of light, liberty, and science, to the uttermost parts of the earth: then will be glory to God on the highest, on earth peace, and good-will to men:—Glory, honour, peace, etc. to every soul of man that worketh good, to the Britons first, (because to them the Gospel is preached) and also to the nations. 'Those that honour their Maker have mercy on the poor.' 'It is righteousness exalteth a nation; but sin is a reproach to any people; destruction shall be to the workers of iniquity, and the wicked shall fall by their own wickedness.' May the blessings of the Lord be upon the heads of all those who commiserated the cases of the oppressed negroes, and the fear of God prolong their days; and may their expectations be filled with gladness! 'The liberal devise liberal things, and by liberal things shall stand,' Isaiah xxxii. 8. They can say with pious Job, 'Did not I weep for him that was in trouble? was not my soul grieved for the poor?' Job xxx. 25.

As the inhuman traffic of slavery is to be take into the consideration of the British legislature, I doubt not, if a system of commerce was established in Africa, the demand for manufactures would most rapidly augment, as the

183

native inhabitants will insensibly adopt the British fashions, manners, customs, etc. In proportion to the civilization, so will be the consumption of British manufactures.

The wear and tear of a continent, nearly twice as large as Europe, and rich in vegetable and mineral production, is much easier conceived than calculated.

A case in point. It cost the Aborigines of Britain, little or nothing in clothing, etc. The difference between their forefathers and the present generation, in point of consumption, is literally infinite. The supposition is most obvious. It will be equally immense in Africa. The same cause, viz. civilization, will ever have the same effect.

It is trading upon safe grounds. A commercial intercourse with Africa opens an inexhaustible source of wealth to the manufacturing interests of Great Britain, and to all which the slave trade is an objection.

If I am not misinformed, the manufacturing interest is equal, if not superior, to the landed interest, as to the value, for reasons which will soon appear. The abolition of slavery, so diabolical, will give a most rapid extension of manufactures, which is totally and diametrically opposite to what some interested people assert.

The manufactures of this country must and will, in the nature and reason of things, have a full and constant employ by supplying the African markets.

Population, the bowels and surface of Africa, abound in valuable and useful returns; the hidden treasures of centuries will be brought to light and into circulation. Industry, enterprise, and mining, will have their full scope, proportionably as they civilize. In a word, it lays open an endless field of commerce to the British manufacturer and merchant adventurer. The manufacturing interest and the general interests are synonymous. The abolition of slavery would be in reality an universal good.

Tortures, murder, and every other imaginable barbarity and iniquity, are practised upon the poor slaves with impunity. I hope the slave trade will be abolished. I pray it may be an event at hand. The great body of manufacturers, uniting in the cause, will considerably facilitate and expedite it; and as I have already stated, it is most substantially their interest and advantage, and as such the nation's at large, (except those persons concerned in the manufacturing neck-yokes, collars, chains, handcuffs, leg-bolts, drags, thumb-screws, iron muzzles, and coffins; cats, scourges, and other instruments of torture used in the slave trade.) In a short time one sentiment alone will prevail from motives of interest as well as justice and humanity. Europe contains one hundred and twenty millions of inhabitants. Query—How many millions doth Africa contain? Supposing the Africans, collectively and individually, to expend 5*l.* a head in raiment and furniture, yearly, when civilized, etc. an immensity beyond the reach of imagination!

This I conceive to be a theory founded upon facts, and therefore an infallible one. If the blacks were permitted to remain in their own country, they would double themselves every fifteen years. In proportion to such increase, will be the demand for manufactures. Cotton and indigo grow spontaneously in most parts of Africa; a consideration this of no small consequence to the manufacturing towns of Great Britain. It opens a most immense, glorious, and happy prospect—the clothing, etc. of a continent ten thousand miles in circumference, and immensely rich in productions of every denomination in return for manufactures.

I have only therefore to request the reader's indulgence and conclude. I am far from the vanity of thinking there is any merit in this narrative: I hope censure will be suspended when it is considered that it was written by one who was as unwilling as unable to adorn the plainness of truth by the colouring of imagination. My life and fortune have been extremely chequered and my adventures various. Even those I have related are considerably abridged. If any incident in this little work should appear uninteresting and trifling to most readers, I can only say as my excuse, for mentioning it that almost every event of my life made an impression on my mind and influenced my conduct. I early accustomed myself to look for the hand of God in the minutest occurrence and to learn from it a lesson of morality and religion, and in this light every circumstance I have related was to me of importance. After all, what makes any event important, unless by its observation we become better and wiser, and learn 'to do justly, to love mercy, and to walk humbly before God'? To those who are possessed of this spirit there is scarcely any book of incident trifling that does not afford some profit, while to others the experience of ages seems of no use; and even to pour out to them the treasures of wisdom is throwing the jewels of instruction away.

Mary Wollstonecraft

1759–1797

Mary Wollstonecraft was one of the most insightful women of the Enlightenment, able to transcend the limited thinking of her time and to push the analytical powers of reason to their logical conclusion concerning human rights and gender. She was born in London, the daughter of a weaver who later became an unsuccessful farmer. After an unhappy childhood, she moved to London and made a career as a writer and teacher. In 1792, she left England for Paris, describing herself to others as the wife of American captain Gilbert Imlay, in order to observe firsthand the revolution in France. The political and intellectual atmosphere Wollstonecraft encountered was tumultuous: she had been in Paris when Louis XVI fell to the guillotine and, only a year earlier, Olympe de Gouges had written her *Declaration of the Rights of Woman and Citizen*, arguing for the extension of the rights of the citizen to women. The violent political and social transformations she witnessed in France seemed at last to promise enfranchisement and equality for all.

Wollstonecraft returned to England in 1794 and, in May of that year, she gave birth to her first daughter, Fanny Imlay, but was soon deserted by the child's father. Back at home, she renewed her friendship with William Godwin, a leading radical political thinker and novelist. In March 1797 they married, though they continued to maintain separate dwellings. On August 30, their daughter Mary was born, and 11 days later Mary Wollstonecraft died from complications in childbirth. Years later, her daughter Mary would marry the poet Percy Shelley and write the famous and popular novel Frankenstein.

In *A Vindication of the Rights of Woman* (1792), Wollstonecraft gives us a comprehensive analysis of the causes of gender inequality. Reaching beyond the social conventions of her time, she argues that human rights are not based on a person's sex. In other words, there is no fundamental difference between men and women that would justify denying women equal rights. Understanding the difficulty in getting her message across to men, she presents her arguments through a rigorous Enlightenment rhetoric, even suggesting that the reader conduct this scientific experiment: "Let [women's] faculties have room to unfold, and their virtues to gain strength, and then determine where the whole sex must stand in the intellectual scale." What, according to Wollstonecraft, are the causes that enslave women? How does Wollstonecraft use the example of a military soldier to describe the condition of women? What is wrong with referring to women as the "weaker sex," based on physical constitution, according to Wollstonecraft? In what ways do the inequities and problems she observes in the eighteenth century persist today? Are the causes of contemporary gender inequity the same as those of Wollstonecraft's day?

from *A Vindication of the Rights of Woman* (1792)

Chapter II
The Prevailing Opinion of a Sexual Character Discussed

To account for, and excuse the tyranny of man, many ingenious arguments have been brought forward to prove, that the two sexes, in the acquirement of virtue, ought to aim at attaining a very different character; or, to speak
explicitly, women are not allowed to have sufficient strength of mind to
acquire what really deserves the name of virtue. Yet it should seem, allowing
them to have souls, that there is but one way appointed by Providence to lead
mankind to either virtue or happiness.

If then women are not a swarm of ephemeron triflers,[1] why should they
be kept in ignorance under the specious name of innocence? Men complain,
and with reason, of the follies and caprices of our sex, when they do not keen-
ly satirise our headstrong passions and grovelling vices. Behold, I should
answer, the natural effect of ignorance! The mind will ever be unstable that has
only prejudices to rest on, and the current will run with destructive fury when
there are no barriers to break its force. Women are told from their infancy, and
taught by the example of their mothers, that a little knowledge of human
weakness, justly termed cunning, softness of temper, *outward* obedience, and
a scrupulous attention to a puerile kind of propriety, will obtain for them the
protection of man; and should they be beautiful, everything else is needless, for
at least twenty years of their lives.

Thus Milton describes our first frail mother; though when he tells us that
women are formed for softness and sweet attractive grace, I cannot comprehend his meaning, unless, in the true Mahometan[2] strain, he meant to deprive
us of souls, and insinuate that we were beings only designed by sweet attractive grace, and docile blind obedience, to gratify the senses of man when he
can no longer soar on the wing of contemplation.

How grossly do they insult us who thus advise us only to render ourselves
gentle, domestic brutes! For instance, the winning softness so warmly and frequently recommended, that governs by obeying. What childish expressions,
and how insignificant is the being—can it be an immortal one?—who will
condescend to govern by such sinister methods! "Certainly," says Lord Bacon,
"man is of kin to the beasts by his body; and if he be not of kin to God by his

spirit, he is a base and ignoble creature!" Men, indeed, appear to me to act in a very unphilosophical manner, when they try to secure the good conduct of women by attempting to keep them always in a state of childhood. Rousseau was more consistent when he wished to stop the progress of reason in both sexes, for if men eat of the tree of knowledge, women will come in for a taste; but, from the imperfect cultivation which their understandings now receive, they only attain a knowledge of evil.

Children, I grant, should be innocent; but when the epithet is applied to men, or women, it is but a civil term for weakness. For if it be allowed that women were destined by Providence to acquire human virtues, and, by the exercise of their understandings, that stability of character which is the firmest ground to rest our future hopes upon, they must be permitted to turn to the fountain of light, and not forced to shape their course by the twinkling of a mere satellite. Milton, I grant, was of a very different opinion; for he only bends to the indefeasible right of beauty, though it would be difficult to render two passages which I now mean to contrast, consistent. But into similar inconsistencies are great men often led by their senses:

To whom thus Eve with *perfect beauty* adorn'd.
My author and disposer, what thou bids't
Unargued I obey; so God ordains;
God is *thy law, thou mine:* to know no more
Is woman's *happiest* knowledge and her *praise.*

These are exactly the arguments that I have used to children; but I have added, your reason is now gaining strength, and, till it arrives at some degree of maturity, you must look up to me for advice,—then you ought to *think*, and only rely on God.

Yet in the following lines Milton seems to coincide with me, when he makes Adam thus expostulate with his Maker:

Hast Thou not made me here Thy substitute,
And these inferior far beneath me set?
Among *unequals* what society
Can sort, what harmony or true delight?
Which must be mutual, in proportion due
Given and received; but in *disparity*
The one intense, the other still remiss
Cannot well suit with either, but soon prove
Tedious alike: of *fellowship* I speak
Such as I seek, fit to participate
All rational delight—

In treating therefore of the manners of women, let us, disregarding sensual arguments, trace what we should endeavour to make them in order to co-operate, if the expression be not too bold, with the Supreme Being.

By individual education, I mean, for the sense of the word is not precisely defined, such an attention to a child as will slowly sharpen the senses, from the temper, regulate the passions as they begin to ferment, and set the understanding to work before the body arrives at maturity; so that the man may only have to proceed, not to begin, the important task of learning to think and reason.

To prevent any misconstruction, I must add, that I do not believe that a private education can work the wonders which some sanguine writers have attributed to it. Men and women must be educated, in a great degree, by the opinions and manners of the society they live in. In every age there has been a stream of popular opinion that has carried all before it, and given a family character, as it were, to the century. It may then fairly be inferred, that, till society be differently constituted, much cannot be expected from education. It is, however, sufficient for my present purpose to assert that, whatever effect circumstances have on the abilities, every being may become virtuous by the exercise of its own reason; for if but one being was created with vicious inclinations, that is positively bad, what can save us from atheism? or if we worship a God, is not that God a devil?

Consequently, the most perfect education, in my opinion, is such an exercise of the understanding as is best calculated to strengthen the body and form the heart. Or, in other words, to enable the individual to attain such habits of virtue as will render it independent. In fact, it is a farce to call any being virtuous whose virtues do not result from the exercise of its own reason. This was Rousseau's opinion respecting men; I extend it to women, and confidently assert that they have been drawn out of their sphere by false refinement, and not by an endeavour to acquire masculine qualities. Still the regal homage which they receive is so intoxicating, that until the manners of the times are changed, and formed on more reasonable principles, it may be impossible to convince them that the illegitimate power which they obtain by degrading themselves is a curse, and that they must return to nature and equality if they wish to secure the placid satisfaction that unsophisticated affections impart. But for this epoch we must wait—wait perhaps till kings and nobles, enlightened by reason, and, preferring the real dignity of man to childish state, throw off their gaudy hereditary trappings; and if then women do not resign the arbitrary power of beauty—they will prove that they have *less* mind than man.

I may be accused of arrogance; still I must declare what I firmly believe, that all the writers who have written on the subject of female education and manners, from Rousseau to Dr. Gregory,[3] have contributed to render women more artificial, weak characters, than they would otherwise have been; and consequently, more useless members of society. I might have expressed this conviction in a lower key, but I am afraid it would have been the whine of affectation, and not the faithful expression of my feelings, of the clear result which experience and reflection have led me to draw. When I come to that division of the subject, I shall advert to the passages that I more particularly disapprove of, in the works of the authors I have just alluded to; but it is first necessary to observe that my objection extends to the whole purport of those books, which tend, in my opinion, to degrade one-half of the human species, and render women pleasing at the expense of every solid virtue.

Though, to reason on Rousseau's ground, if man did attain a degree of perfection of mind when his body arrived at maturity, it might be proper, in order to make a man and his wife *one*, that she should rely entirely on his understanding; and the graceful ivy, clasping the oak that supported it, would form a whole in which strength and beauty would be equally conspicuous. But, alas! husbands, as well as their helpmates, are often only overgrown children,—nay, thanks to early debauchery, scarcely men in their outward form,—and if the blind lead the blind, one need not come from heaven to tell us consequence.

Many are the causes that, in the present corrupt state of society, contribute to enslave women by cramping their understandings and sharpening their senses. One, perhaps, that silently does more mischief than all the rest, is their disregard of order.

To do every thing in an orderly manner is a most important precept, which women, who, generally speaking, receive only a disorderly kind of education, seldom attend to with that degree of exactness that men, who from their infancy are broken into method, observe. This negligent kind of guess-work—for what other epithet can be used to point out the random exertions of a sort of instinctive common sense, never brought to the test of reason?—prevents their generalising matters of fact; so they do to-day what they did yesterday, merely because they did it yesterday.

This contempt of the understanding in early life has more baneful consequences than is commonly supposed; for the little knowledge which women of strong minds attain is, from various circumstances, of a more desultory kind than the knowledge of men, and it is acquired more by sheer observations on real life than from comparing what has been individually observed with the results of experience generalised by speculation. Led by their dependent situation and domestic employments more into society, what they learn is rather by snatches; and as learning is with them in general only a secondary thing, they do not pursue any one branch with that persevering ardour necessary to give vigour to the faculties and clearness to the judgment. In the present state of society, a little learning is required to support the character of a gentleman, and boys are obliged to submit to a few years of discipline. But in the education of women, the cultivation of the understanding is always subordinate to the acquirement of some corporeal accomplishment. Even when enervated by confinement and false notions of modesty, the body is prevented from attaining that grace and beauty which relaxed half-formed limbs never exhibit. Besides, in youth their faculties are not brought forward by emulation; and having no serious scientific study, if they have natural sagacity, it is turned too soon on life and manners. They dwell on effects and modifications, without tracing them back to causes; and complicated rules to adjust behaviour are a weak substitute for simple principles.

As a proof that education gives this appearance of weakness to females, we may instance the example of military men, who are, like them, sent into the world before their minds have been stored with knowledge, or fortified by principles. The consequences are similar; soldiers acquire a little superficial knowledge, snatched from the muddy current of conversation, and from continually mixing with society, they gain what is termed a knowledge of the world; and this acquaintance with manners and customs has frequently been confounded with a knowledge of the human heart. But can the crude fruit of casual observation, never brought to the test of judgment, formed by comparing speculation and experience, deserve such a distinction? Soldiers, as well as women, practise the minor virtues with punctilious politeness. Where is then the sexual difference, when the education has been the same? All the difference that I can discern, arises from the superior advantage of liberty which enables the former to see more of life.

• • •

It may be further observed that officers are also particularly attentive to their persons, fond of dancing, crowded rooms, adventures, and ridicule. Like the *fair* sex, the business of their lives is gallantry; they were taught to please, and they only live to please. Yet they do not lose their rank in the distinction of sexes, for they are still reckoned superior to women, though in what their superiority consists, beyond what I have just mentioned, it is difficult to discover.

The great misfortune is this, that they both acquire manners before morals, and a knowledge of life before they have from reflection any acquaintance with the grand ideal outline of human nature. The consequence is natural. Satisfied with common nature, they become a prey to prejudices, and taking all their opinions on credit, they blindly submit to authority. So that if they have any sense, it is a kind of instinctive glance that catches proportions, and decides with respect to manners, but fails when arguments are to be pursued below the surface, or opinions analysed.

May not the same remark be applied to women? Nay, the argument may be carried still further, for they are both thrown out of a useful station by the unnatural distinctions established in civilised life. Riches and hereditary honours have made cyphers of women to give consequence to the numerical figure; and idleness has produced a mixture of gallantry and despotism into society, which leads the very men who are the slaves of their mistresses to tyrannise over their sisters, wives, and daughters. This is only keeping them in rank and file, it is true. Strengthen the female mind by enlarging it, and there will be an end to blind obedience; but as blind obedience is ever sought for by power, tyrants and sensualists are in the right when they endeavour to keep woman in the dark, because the former only want slaves, and the latter a plaything. The sensualist, indeed, has been the most dangerous of tyrants, and women have been duped by their lovers, as princes by their ministers, whilst dreaming that they reigned over them.

• • •

Women are therefore to be considered either as moral beings, or so weak that they must be entirely subjected to the superior faculties of men.

Let us examine this question. Rousseau declares that a woman should never for a moment feel herself independent, that she should be governed by fear to exercise her *natural* cunning, and made a coquettish slave in order to render her a more alluring object of desire, a *sweeter* companion to man, whenever he chooses to relax himself. He carries the arguments, which he pretends to draw from the indications of nature, still further, and insinuates that truth and fortitude, the corner-stones of all human virtue, should be cultivated with certain restrictions, because, with respect to the female character, obedience is the grand lesson which ought to be impressed with unrelenting rigour.

What nonsense! When will a great man arise with sufficient strength of mind to puff away the fumes which pride and sensuality have thus spread over the subject! If women are by nature inferior to men, their virtues must be the same in quality, if not in degree, or virtue is a relative idea; consequently their conduct should be founded on the same principles, and have the same aim.

Connected with man as daughters, wives, and mothers, their moral character may be estimated by their manner of fulfilling those simple duties; but the end, the grand end, of their exertions should be to unfold their own faculties, and acquire the dignity of conscious virtue. They may try to render their road pleasant; but ought never to forget, in common with man, that life yields not the felicity which can satisfy an immortal soul. I do not mean to insinuate that either sex should be so lost in abstract reflections or distant views as to forget the affections and duties that lie before them, and are, in truth, the means appointed to produce the fruit of life; on the contrary, I would warmly recommend them, even while I assert, that they afford most satisfaction when they are considered in their true sober light.

Probably the prevailing opinion that woman was created for man, may have taken its rise from Moses' poetical story; yet as very few, it is presumed, who have bestowed any serious thought on the subject ever supposed that Eve was, literally speaking, one of Adam's ribs, the deduction must be allowed to fall to the ground, or only be so far admitted as it proves that man, from the remotest antiquity, found it convenient to exert his strength to subjugate his companion, and his invention to show that she ought to have her neck bent under the yoke, because the whole creation was only created for his convenience or pleasure.

Let it not be concluded that I wish to invert the order of things. I have already granted that, from the constitution of their bodies, men seemed to be designed by Providence to attain a greater degree of virtue. I speak collectively of the whole sex; but I see not the shadow of a reason to conclude that their virtues should differ in respect to their nature. In fact, how can they, if virtue has only one eternal standard? I must therefore, if I reason consequentially, as strenuously maintain that they have the same simple direction as that there is a God.

It follows then that cunning should not be opposed to wisdom, little cares to great exertions, or insipid softness, varnished over with the name of gentleness, to that fortitude which grand views alone can inspire.

I shall be told that woman would then lose many of her peculiar graces, and the opinion of a well-known poet might be quoted to refute my unqualified position. For Pope has said, in the name of the whole male sex:

Yet ne'er so sure our passion to create,
As when she touch'd the brink of all we hate.

In what light this sally places men and women I shall leave to the judicious to determine. Meanwhile, I shall content myself with observing, that I cannot discover why, unless they are mortal, females should always be degraded by being made subservient to love or lust.

To speak disrespectfully of love is, I know, high treason against sentiment and fine feelings; but I wish to speak the simple language of truth, and rather to address the head than the heart. To endeavor to reason love out of the world would be to out-Quixote Cervantes, and equally offend against common sense; but an endeavor to restrain this tumultuous passion, and to prove that it should not be allowed to dethrone superior powers, or to usurp the sceptre which the understanding should ever coolly wield, appears less wild.

Youth is the season for love in both sexes; but in those days of thought-less enjoyment provision should be made for the more important years of life, when reflection takes place of sensation. But Rousseau, and most of the male writers who have followed his steps, have warmly inculcated that the whole tendency of female education ought to be directed to one point—to render them pleasing.

Let me reason with the supporters of this opinion who have any knowl-edge of human nature. Do they imagine that marriage can eradicate the habi-tude of life? The woman who has only been taught to please will soon find that her charms are oblique sunbeams, and that they cannot have much effect on her husband's heart when they are seen every day, when the summer is passed and gone. Will she then have sufficient native energy to look into herself for comfort, and cultivate her dormant faculties? or is it not more rational to expect that she will try to please other men, and, in the emotions raised by the expectation of new conquests, endeavor to forget the mortification her love or pride has received? When the husband ceases to be a lover, and the time will inevitably come, her desire of pleasing will then grow languid, or become a spring of bitterness; and love, perhaps, the most evanescent of all passions, gives place to jealously or vanity.

I now speak of women who are restrained by principle or prejudice. Such women, though they would shrink from an intrigue with real abhorrence, yet, nevertheless, wish to be convinced by the homage of gallantry that they are cruelly neglected by their husbands; or, days and weeks are spent in dreaming of the happiness enjoyed by congenial souls, till their health is undermined and their spirits broken by discontent. How then can the great art of pleasing be such a necessary study? it is only useful to a mistress. The chaste wife, and seri-ous mother should only consider her power to please as the polish of her virtues, and the affection of her husband as one of the comforts that render her task less difficult and her life happier. But, whether she be loved or neglected, her first wish should be to make herself respectable, and not to rely for all her happiness on a being subject to like infirmities with herself.

The worthy Dr. Gregory fell into a similar error. I respect his heart, but entirely disapprove of his celebrated *Legacy to his Daughters*.

He advises them to cultivate a fondness for dress, because a fondness for dress, he asserts, is natural to them. I am unable to comprehend what either he or Rousseau mean when they frequently use this indefinite term. If they told us that in a pre-existent state the soul was fond of dress, and brought this inclination with it into a new body, I should listen to them with a half-smile, as I often do when I hear a rant about innate elegance. But if he only meant to say that the exercise of the faculties will produce this fondness, I deny it. It is not natural; but arises, like false ambition in men, from a love of power.

Dr. Gregory goes much further; he actually recommends dissimulation, and advises an innocent girl to give the lie to her feelings, and not dance with spirit, when gaiety of heart would make her feet eloquent without making her gestures immodest. In the name of truth and common sense, why should not one woman acknowledge that she can take more exercise than another? or, in other words, that she has a sound constitution; and why, to damp innocent vivacity, is she darkly to be told that men will draw conclusions which she little thinks of? Let the libertine draw what inference he pleases; but, I hope, that no sensible mother will restrain the natural frankness of youth by instilling such indecent cautions. Out of the abundance of the heart the mouth speaketh; and a wiser than Soloman hath said that the heart should be made clean, and not trivial ceremonies observed, which it is not very difficult to fulfil with scrupulous exactness when vice reigns in the heart.

Women ought to endeavor to purify their heart; but can they do so when their uncultivated understandings make them entirely dependent on their senses for employment and amusement, when no noble pursuits set them above the little vanities of the day, or enables them to curb the wild emotions that agitate a reed, over which every passing breeze has power? To gain the affections of a virtuous man, is affectation necessary? Nature has given woman a weaker frame than man; but, to ensure her husband's affections, must a wife, who, by the exercise of her mind and body whilst she was discharging the duties of a daughter, wife, and mother, has allowed her constitution to retain its natural strength, and her nerves a healthy tone,—is she, I say, to condescend to use art, and feign a sickly delicacy, in order to secure her husband's affection? Weakness may excite tenderness, and gratify the arrogant pride of man; but the lordly caresses of a protector will not gratify a noble mind that pants for and deserves to be respected. Fondness is a poor substitute for friendship!

In a *seraglio*, I grant, that all these arts are necessary; the epicure must have his palate tickled, or he will sink into apathy; but have women so little ambition as to be satisfied with such a condition? Can they supinely dream life away in the lap of pleasure, or the languor of weariness, rather than assert their claim to pursue reasonable pleasures, and render themselves conspicuous by practising the virtues which dignify mankind? Surely she has not an immortal soul who can loiter life away merely employed to adorn her person, that she may amuse the languid hours, and soften the cares of a fellow-creature who is willing to be enlivened by her smiles and tricks, when the serious business of life is over.

Besides, the woman who strengthens her body and exercises her mind will, by managing her family and practising various virtues, become the friend, and not the humble dependent of her husband; and if she, by possessing such substantial qualities, merit his regard, she will not find it necessary to conceal her affection, nor to pretend to an unnatural coldness of constitution to excite her husband's passions. In fact, if we revert to history, we shall find that the women who have distinguished themselves have neither been the most beautiful nor the most gentle of their sex.

Nature, or, to speak with strict propriety, God, has made all things right; but man has sought him out many inventions to mar the work. I now allude to that part of Dr. Gregory's treatise, where he advises a wife never to let her husband know the extent of her sensibility or affection. Voluptuous precaution, and as ineffectual as absurd. Love, from its very nature, must be transitory. To seek for a secret that would render it constant, would be as wild a search as for the philosopher's stone, or the grand panacea; and the discovery would be equally useless, or rather pernicious, to mankind. The most holy band of society is friendship. It has been well said, by a shrewd satirist, "that rare as true love is, true friendship is still rarer."

This is an obvious truth, and, the cause not lying deep, will not elude a slight glance of inquiry.

Love, the common passion, in which chance and sensation take place of choice and reason, is, in some degree, felt by the mass of mankind; for it is not necessary to speak, at present, of the emotions that rise above or sink below love. This passion, naturally increased by suspense and difficulties, draws the mind out of its accustomed state, and exalts the affections; but the security of marriage, allowing the fever of love to subside, a healthy temperature is thought insipid only by those who have not sufficient intellect to substitute the calm tenderness of friendship, the confidence of respect, instead of blind admiration, and the sensual emotions of fondness.

This is, must be, the course of nature. Friendship or indifference inevitably succeeds love. And this constitution seems perfectly to harmonise with the system of government which prevails in the moral world. Passions are spurs to action, and open the mind; but they sink into mere appetites, become a personal and momentary gratification when the object is gained, and the satisfied mind rests in enjoyment. The man who had some virtue whilst he was struggling for a crown, often becomes a voluptuous tyrant when it graces his brow; and, when the lover is not lost in the husband, the dotard, a prey to childish caprices and fond jealousies, neglects the serious duties of life, and the caresses which should excite confidence in his children are lavished on the overgrown child, his wife.

In order to fulfil the duties of life, and to be able to pursue with vigour the various employments which form the moral character, a master and mistress of a family ought not to continue to love each other with passion. I mean to say that they ought not to indulge those emotions which disturb the order of society, and engross the thoughts that should be otherwise employed. The

mind that has never been engrossed by one object wants vigour,—if it can long
be so, it is weak.

• • •

I own it frequently happens, that women who have fostered a romantic
unnatural delicacy of feeling, waste their lives in *imagining* how happy they
should have been with a husband who could love them with a fervid increasing affection every day, and all day. But they might as well pine married as single and would not be a jot more unhappy with a bad husband than longing
for a good one. That a proper education, or, to speak with more precision, a
well-stored mind, would enable a woman to support a single life with dignity,
I grant; but that she should avoid cultivating her taste, lest her husband should
occasionally shock it, is quitting a substance for a shadow. To say the truth, I
do not know of what use is an improved taste, if the individual be not rendered
more independent of the casualties of life; if new sources of enjoyment, only
dependent on the solitary operations of the mind, are not opened. People of
taste, married or single, without distinction, will ever be disgusted by various
things that touch not less observing minds. On this conclusion the argument
must not be allowed to hinge; but in the whole sum of enjoyment is taste to
be denominated a blessing?

The question is, whether it procures most pain or pleasure? The answer
will decide the propriety of Dr. Gregory's advice, and show how absurd and
tyrannic it is thus to lay down a system of slavery, or to attempt to educate
moral beings by any other rules than those deduced from pure reason, which
apply to the whole species.

Gentleness of manners, forbearance and long-suffering, are such amiable
Godlike qualities, that in sublime poetic strains the Deity had been invested
with them; and, perhaps, no representation of His goodness so strongly fastens
on the human affections as those that represent Him abundant in mercy and
willing to pardon. Gentleness, considered in this point of view, bears on its
front all the characteristics of grandeur, combined with the winning graces of
condescension; but what a different aspect it assumes when it is the submissive
demeanour of dependence, the support of weakness that loves, because it
wants protection; and is forbearing, because it must silently endure injuries;
smiling under the lash at which it dare not snarl. Abject as this picture appears,
it is the portrait of an accomplished woman, according to the received opinion of female excellence, separated by specious reasoners from human excellence. Or, they kindly restore the rib, and make one moral being of a man and
woman; not forgetting to give her all the "submissive charms."

How women are to exist in that state where there is neither to be marrying nor giving in marriage, we are not told. For though moralists have agreed

that the tenor of life seems to prove that *man* is prepared by various circumstances for a future state, they constantly concur in advising *woman* only to provide for the present. Gentleness, docility, and a spaniel-like affection are, on this ground, consistently recommended as the cardinal virtues of the sex; and, disregarding the arbitrary economy of nature, one writer has declared that it is masculine for a woman to be melancholy. She was created to be the toy of man, his rattle, and it must jingle in his ears whenever, dismissing reason, he chooses to be amused.

• • •

As a philosopher, I read with indignation the plausible epithets which men use to soften their insults; and, as a moralist, I ask what is meant by such heterogeneous associations, as fair defects, amiable weaknesses, etc.? If there be but one criterion of morals, but one architype for man, women appear to be suspended by destiny, according to the vulgar tale of Mahomet's coffin; they have neither the unerring instinct of brutes, nor are allowed to fix the eye of reason on a perfect model. They were made to be loved, and must not aim at respect, lest they should be hunted out of society as masculine.

But to view the subject in another point of view. Do passive indolent women make the best wives? Confining our discussion to the present moment of existence, let us see how such weak creatures perform their part? Do the women who, by the attainment of a few superficial accomplishments, have strengthened the prevailing prejudice, merely contribute to the happiness of their husbands? Do they display their charms merely to amuse them? And have women, who have early imbibed notions of passive obedience, sufficient character to manage a family or educate children? So far from it, that, after surveying the history of woman, I cannot help agreeing with the severest satirist, considering the sex as the weakest as well as the most oppressed half of the species. What does history disclose but marks of inferiority, and how few women have emancipated themselves from the galling yoke of sovereign man? So few that the exceptions remind me of an ingenious conjecture respecting Newton that he was probably a being of superior order, accidentally caged in a human body. Following the same train of thinking, I have been led to imagine that the few extraordinary women who have rushed in eccentrical directions out of the orbit prescribed to their sex, were *male* spirits, confined by mistake in female frames. But if it be not philosophical to think of sex when the soul is mentioned, the inferiority must depend on the organs; or the heavenly fire, which is to ferment the clay, is not given in equal portions.

But avoiding, as I have hitherto done, any direct comparison of the two sexes collectively, or frankly acknowledging the inferiority of woman, according to the present appearance of things, I shall only insist that men have increased that inferiority till women are almost sunk below the standard of rational creatures. Let their faculties have room to unfold, and their virtues to gain strength, and then determine where the whole sex must stand in the intellectual scale. Yet let it be remembered, that for a small number of distinguished women I do not ask a place.

It is difficult for us purblind mortals to say to what height human discoveries and improvements may arrive when the gloom of despotism subsides, which makes us stumble at every step; but, when morality shall be settled on a more solid basis, then, without being gifted with a prophetic spirit, I will venture to predict that woman will be either the friend or slave of man. We shall not, as at present, doubt whether she is a moral agent, or the link which unites man with brutes. But should it then appear that like the brutes they were principally created for the use of man, he will let them patiently bite the bridle, and not mock them with empty praise; or, should their rationality be proved, he will not impede their improvement merely to gratify his sensual appetites. He will not, with all the graces of rhetoric, advise them to submit implicitly their understanding to the guidance of man. He will not, when he treats of the education of women, assert that they ought never to have the free use of reason, nor would he recommend cunning and dissimulation to beings who are acquiring, in like manner as himself, the virtues of humanity.

• • •

These may be termed Utopian dreams. Thanks to that Being who impressed them on my soul, and gave me sufficient strength of mind to dare to exert my own reason, till, becoming dependent only on Him for the support of my virtue, I view, with indignation, the mistaken notions that enslave my sex.

I love man as my fellow; but his sceptre, real or usurped, extends not to me, unless the reason of an individual demands my homage; and even then the submission is to reason, and not to man. In fact, the conduct of an accountable being must be regulated by the operations of its own reason; or on what foundation rests the throne of God?

It appears to me necessary to dwell on these obvious truths, because females have been insulated, as it were; and, while they have been stripped of the virtues that should clothe humanity, they have been decked with artificial graces that enable them to exercise a short-lived tyranny. Love, in their bosoms, taking place of every nobler passion, their sole ambition is to be fair, to raise emotion instead of inspiring respect; and this ignoble desire, like the servility in absolute monarchies, destroys all strength of character. Liberty is the mother of virtue, and if women be, by their very constitution, slaves, and not allowed to breathe the sharp invigorating air of freedom, they must ever languish like exotics, and be reckoned beautiful flaws in nature.

As to the argument respecting the subjection in which the sex has ever been held, it retorts on man. The many have always been enthralled by the few; and monsters, who scarcely have shown any discernment of human excellence, have tyrannised over thousands of their fellow-creatures. Why have men of superior endowments submitted to such degradation? For, is it not universally acknowledged that kings, viewed collectively, have ever been inferior, in abilities and virtue, to the same number of men taken from the common mass of mankind—yet have they not, and are they not still treated with a degree of reverence that is an insult to reason? China is not the only country where a living man has been made a God. *Men* have submitted to superior strength to enjoy with impunity the pleasure of the moment; *women* have only done the same, and therefore till it is proved that the courtier, who servilely resigns the birthright of a man, is not a moral agent, it cannot be demonstrated that woman is essentially inferior to man because she has always been subjugated.

Chapter IX.
Of the Pernicious Effects Which Arise from the Unnatural Distinctions Established in Society

• • •

Besides, when poverty is more disgraceful than even vice, is not morality cut to the quick? Still to avoid misconstruction, though I consider that women in the common walks of life are called to fulfil the duties of wives and mothers, by religion and reason, I cannot help lamenting that women of a superior cast have not a road open by which they can pursue more extensive plans of usefulness and independence. I may excite laughter, by dropping an hint, which I mean to pursue, some future time, for I really think that women ought to have representatives, instead of being arbitrarily governed without having any direct share allowed them in the deliberations of government.

Notes

[1] Individuals who engage in short-lived trivialities.

[2] Muslim.

[3] Author of *A Father's Legacy to His Daughters* (1774), a popular book of the day on women and education.

Angelina E. Grimké

1805–1879

Angelina Grimké and her older sister Sarah (1792–1873) were leading figures of the nineteenth-century abolition movement. They spoke out against slavery and also argued for equality between men and women. Born into an aristocratic slaveholding family in Charleston, South Carolina, they rejected the racial views dominant in the Deep South and, instead, strongly believed that slaves had an inalienable right to their freedom. It was out of this conviction that Sarah, when still just a child, secretly taught her young waiting-maid to read, for which her parents sternly reprimanded her after discovering the transgression.

When Angelina was born in 1805, her parents agreed to twelve-year-old Sarah's persistent requests to be made Angelina's godmother. An early bond was established between the two that would grow later into a profound commitment to social equality. In 1821, Sarah left Charleston and also turned away from the Episcopal Church due its stance on slavery. Angelina joined her sister in Philadelphia shortly afterwards and the two became Quakers. The Grimké sisters, and especially Angelina, earned a reputation for their speeches on the abolition of slavery and on women's rights. Their political activity caused a considerable stir, since it was not socially acceptable for women of that time to engage themselves in such dominant public roles. In fact, for women speakers to appear before audiences of men and women was regarded by many as shocking behavior and such gatherings were considered to be "promiscuous." Yet Angelina mesmerized her audiences with a sincerity and eloquence that profoundly touched the hearts of her listeners.

In 1836, Angelina wrote her pamphlet *Appeal to the Christian Women of the South*, a document unique in that it is the only antislavery work written by a southern woman to other southern women. When the printed pamphlets arrived in Charleston, the postmaster burned them in public. Angelina's family informed her that she should not return to Charleston for fear of imprisonment and mob violence. In Grimké's *Appeal,* which of her arguments are grounded in principles of the Enlightenment? Which teachings of Christianity does she draw upon to convince the Christian women of the South that slavery must end? What role had women played in the fight for the end of slavery up to that time? Why might it have been especially urgent for women of the South to become active in the abolition movement?

from *Appeal to the Christian Women of the South* (1836)

. . . It will be, and that very soon, clearly perceived and fully acknowledged by all the virtuous and the candid, that in *principle* it is as sinful to hold
a human being in bondage who has been born in Carolina, as one who has
been born in Africa. All that sophistry of argument which has been employed
to prove, that although it is sinful to send to Africa to procure men and
women as slaves, who have never been in slavery, that still, it is not sinful to
keep those in bondage who have come down by inheritance, will be utterly
overthrown. We must come back to the good old doctrine of our forefathers
who declared to the world, "this self evident truth that *all* men are created
equal, and that they have certain *inalienable* rights among which are life, *liberty*, and the pursuit of happiness." It is even a greater absurdity to suppose a
man can be legally born a slave under *our free Republican* Government, than
under the petty despotisms of barbarian Africa. If then, we have no right to
enslave an African, surely we can have none to enslave an American; if it is a
self evident truth that *all* men, every where and of every color are born equal,
and have an *inalienable right to liberty*, then it is equally true that *no* man can
be born a slave, and no man can ever *rightfully* be reduced to *involuntary*
bondage and held as a slave, however fair may be the claim of his master or
mistress through will and title-deeds.

•   •   •

But some slaveholders have said, "we were never in bondage to any man,"
and therefore the yoke of bondage would be insufferable to us, but slaves are
accustomed to it, their backs are fitted to the burden. Well, I am willing to
admit that you who have lived in freedom would find slavery even more
oppressive than the poor slave does, but then you may try this question in
another form—Am I willing to reduce *my little child* to slavery? You know that
if it is brought up a slave it will never know any contrast, between freedom and
bondage, its back will become fitted to the burden just as the negro child's
does—not *by nature*—but by daily, violent pressure, in the same way that the
head of the Indian child becomes flattened by the boards in which it is bound.
It has been justly remarked that "*God never made a slave*," he made man
upright; his back was *not* made to carry burdens, nor his neck to wear a yoke,
and the *man* must be crushed within him, before *his* back can be *fitted* to the
burden of perpetual slavery; and that his back is *not* fitted to it, is manifested

203

by the insurrections that so often disturb the peace and security of slavehold-ing countries. Who ever heard of a rebellion of the beasts of the field; and why not? simply because *they* were all placed *under the feet of man*, into whose hand they were delivered; it was originally designed that they should serve him, therefore their necks have been formed for the yoke, and their backs for the burden; but *not so with man*, intellectual, immortal man! I appeal to you, my friends, as mothers; Are you willing to enslave *your* children? You start back with horror and indignation at such a question. But why, if slavery is *no wrong* to those upon whom it is imposed? why, if as has often been said, slaves are happier than their masters, free from the cares and perplexities of providing for themselves and their families: why not place *your children* in the way of being supported without your having the trouble to provide for them, or they for themselves? Do you not perceive that as soon as this golden rule of action is applied to *yourselves* that you involuntarily shrink from the test; as soon as your actions are weighed in *this* balance of the sanctuary that *you are found wanting*? Try yourselves by another of the Divine precepts, "Thou shalt love thy neigh-bor as thyself." Can we love a man *as* we love *ourselves*[;] if we do, and contin-ue to do unto him, what we would not wish any one to do to us? Look too, at Christ's example, what does he say of himself, "I came *not* to be ministered unto, but to minister." Can you for a moment imagine the meek, and lowly, and compassionate Saviour, *a Slaveholder*? do you not shudder at this thought as much as at that of his being a *warrior*? But why, if slavery is not sinful?

•   •   •

And what, I would ask in conclusion, have *women* done for the great and glorious cause of Emancipation? Who wrote that pamphlet which moved the heart of Wilberforce[1] to pray over the wrongs, and his tongue to plead the cause of the oppressed African? It was a *woman*, Elizabeth Heyrick. Who labored assiduously to keep the sufferings of the slave continually before the British public? They were *women*. And how did they do it? By their needles, paint brushes and pens, by speaking the truth, and petitioning Parliament for the abolition of slavery. And what was the effect of their labors? Read it in the Emancipation bill of Great Britain. Read it, in the present state of her West India Colonies. Read it, in the impulse which has been given to the cause of freedom in the United States of America. Have English women then done so much for the negro, and shall American women do nothing? Oh no! Already are there sixty female Anti-Slavery Societies in operation. These are doing just what the English women did, telling the story of the colored man's wrongs, praying for his deliverance, and presenting his kneeling image constantly before the public eye on bags and needle-books, card-racks, pen-wipers, pin-cushions, &c. Even the children of the north are inscribing on their handy work, "May the points of our needles prick the slaveholder's conscience." Some of the reports of these Societies exhibit not only considerable talent, but a deep sense of religious duty, and a determination to persevere through evil as well as good report, until every scourge, and every shackle, is buried under the feet of the manumitted[2] slave.

• • •

Northern women may labor to produce a correct public opinion at the North, but if Southern women sit down in listless indifference and criminal idleness, public opinion cannot be rectified and purified at the South. It is manifest to every reflecting mind, that slavery must be abolished; the era in which we live, and the light which is overspreading the whole world on this subject, clearly show that the time cannot be distant when it will be done. Now there are only two ways in which it can be effected, by moral power or physical force, and it is for *you* to choose which of these you prefer. Slavery always has, and always will produce insurrections wherever it exists, because it is a violation of the natural order of things, and no human power can much longer perpetuate it. The opposers of abolitionists fully believe this; one of them remarked to me not long since, there is no doubt there will be a most terrible overturning at the South in a few years, such cruelty and wrong, must be visited with Divine vengeance soon. Abolitionists believe, too, that this must inevitably be the case if you do not repent, and they are not willing to leave you to perish without entreating you, to save yourselves from destruction.

• • •

Notes

[1] William Wilberforce (1759–1833), British abolitionist.
[2] Freed.

Frederick Douglass

1817–1895

Frederick Douglass was born into slavery in eastern Maryland; his mother was a slave, and his father, his biographers are generally agreed, was his mother's slaveowner. In his slave narrative, Douglass tells us that he rarely saw his mother as a child and then only at night, without his master's knowledge. For his first seven years, he lived on the plantation of Colonel Edward Lloyd, but was then relocated to the Baltimore home of Hugh Auld, an in-law of Lloyd's. Douglass's experience in the fields of the Lloyd plantation had exposed him to all the cruelties of the slave's life; once in Baltimore, he began to sense what might be accomplished in freedom. While still a boy, he was taught to read and write by Sophia Auld, his new master's wife, but when Hugh Auld put an end to this he was forced to finish his education on his own. In 1833, when he was sixteen years old, Douglass was turned over to Edward Covey, a sadistic and ill-tempered man, known for his abilities in breaking the spirits of slaves. After only six months, Douglass had endured enough of Covey's cruel treatment and, in what becomes a primary thematic episode in his narrative, he rebelled physically against his tormenter. Covey never again laid hands on him; for Douglass this was an early taste of freedom.

After a failed escape in 1835, Douglass returned to Baltimore, where Hugh Auld put him to work as a caulker. He began assiduously to cultivate the knowledge and skills necessary to liberate himself and, in 1838, he did win his freedom, fleeing to New York and finally settling in New Bedford, Massachusetts. There, he married Anna Murray, a free black woman who had helped to finance his escape from Baltimore. Within a short time, Douglass became deeply involved in the black abolition movement, speaking at anti-slavery conventions and lecturing for the Massachusetts Anti-Slavery Society. In 1845, Douglass published the *Narrative of the Life of Frederick Douglass, An American Slave*, which became a success nearly overnight: within just three years, 11,000 copies were in print, in nine editions, with translations appearing in both France and Holland. In 1846, Douglass received his legal emancipation: Anna and Ellen Richardson, two English women whom he had met during a two-year lecture tour there, bought his freedom from his former master for a sum of seven hundred dollars. Moving to Rochester, New York, in 1847, Douglass embarked on a career as a newspaper publisher. In 1859, he had to leave the United States, first moving to Canada and then to England, wrongfully implicated in John Brown's raid at Harper's Ferry, West Virginia. At the start of the Civil War, Douglass became involved in efforts to allow blacks to serve in the Union army and then to recruit black enlistees. Until his death, Douglass worked tirelessly as an advocate for racial equality, women's suffrage, and economic opportunity for the poor.

In the excerpt of the *Narrative*, Douglass compels us to examine the dehumanizing effects of slavery not only on slaves, but also on their masters. What were the strategies employed by slaveowners to dehumanize the slave? How does Douglass describe the ways in which slavery transforms the natures of slaveowners? What, according to Douglass, are the means by which he—and by extension, other slaves as well—might escape this dehumanized condition? What points of contact might exist between Douglass's analysis of his experience as a slave and the ideas advanced by writers of the Enlightenment and Romantic works?

from *Narrative of the Life of Frederick Douglass, an American Slave* (1845)

Chapter I

I was born in Tuckahoe, near Hillsborough, and about twelve miles from Easton, in Talbot county, Maryland. I have no accurate knowledge of my age, never having seen any authentic record containing it. By far the larger part of the slaves know as little of their ages as horses know of theirs, and it is the wish of most masters within my knowledge to keep their slaves thus ignorant. I do not remember to have ever met a slave who could tell of his birthday. They seldom come nearer to it than planting-time, harvest-time, cherry-time, spring-time, or fall-time. A want of information concerning my own was a source of unhappiness to me even during childhood. The white children could tell their ages. I could not tell why I ought to be deprived of the same privilege. I was not allowed to make any inquiries of my master concerning it. He deemed all such inquiries on the part of a slave improper and impertinent, and evidence of a restless spirit. The nearest estimate I can give makes me now between twenty-seven and twenty-eight years of age. I come to this, from hearing my master say, some time during 1835, I was about seventeen years old.

My mother was named Harriet Bailey. She was the daughter of Isaac and Betsey Bailey, both colored, and quite dark. My mother was of a darker complexion than either my grandmother or grandfather.

My father was a white man. He was admitted to be such by all I ever heard speak of my parentage. The opinion was also whispered that my master was my father; but of the correctness of this opinion, I know nothing; the means of knowing was withheld from me. My mother and I were separated when I was but an infant—before I knew her as my mother. It is a common custom, in the part of Maryland from which I ran away, to part children from their mothers at a very early age. Frequently, before the child has reached its twelfth month, its mother is taken from it, and hired out on some farm a considerable distance off, and the child is placed under the care of an old woman, too old for field labor. For what this separation is done, I do not know, unless it be to hinder the development of the child's affection toward its mother, and to blunt and destroy the natural affection of the mother for the child. This is the inevitable result.

I never saw my mother, to know her as such, more than four or five times in my life; and each of these times was very short in duration, and at night.

She was hired by a Mr. Stewart, who lived about twelve miles from my home. She made her journeys to see me in the night, travelling the whole distance on foot, after the performance of her day's work. She was a field hand, and a whipping is the penalty of not being in the field at sunrise, unless a slave has special permission from his or her master to the contrary—a permission which they seldom get, and one that gives to him that gives it the proud name of being a kind master. I do not recollect of ever seeing my mother by the light of day. She was with me in the night. She would lie down with me, and get me to sleep, but long before I waked she was gone. Very little communication ever took place between us. Death soon ended what little we could have while she lived, and with it her hardships and suffering. She died when I was about seven years old, on one of my master's farms, near Lee's Mill. I was not allowed to be present during her illness, at her death, or burial. She was gone long before I knew any thing about it. Never having enjoyed, to any considerable extent, her soothing presence, her tender and watchful care, I received the tidings of her death with much the same emotions I should have probably felt at the death of a stranger.

Called thus suddenly away, she left me without the slightest intimation of who my father was. The whisper that my master was my father, may or may not be true; and, true or false, it is of but little consequence to my purpose whilst the fact remains, in all its glaring odiousness, that slaveholders have ordained, and by law established, that the children of slave women shall in all cases follow the condition of their mothers; and this is done too obviously to administer to their own lusts, and make a gratification of their wicked desires profitable as well as pleasurable; for by this cunning arrangement, the slaveholder, in cases not a few, sustains to his slaves the double relation of master and father.

I know of such cases; and it is worthy of remark that such slaves invariably suffer greater hardships, and have more to contend with, than others. They are, in the first place, a constant offence to their mistress. She is ever disposed to find fault with them; they can seldom do any thing to please her; she is never better pleased than when she sees them under the lash, especially when she suspects her husband of showing to his mulatto children favors which he withholds from his black slaves. The master is frequently compelled to sell this class of his slaves, out of deference to the feelings of his white wife; and, cruel as the deed may strike any one to be, for a man to sell his own children to human flesh-mongers, it is often the dictate of humanity for him to do so; for, unless he does this, he must not only whip them himself, but must stand by and see one white son tie up his brother, of but few shades darker complexion than himself, and ply the gory lash to his naked back; and if he lisp one word of disapproval, it is set down to his parental partiality, and only makes a bad matter worse, both for himself and the slave whom he would protect and defend.

Every year brings with it multitudes of this class of slaves. It was doubtless in consequence of a knowledge of this fact, that one great statesman of the south predicted the downfall of slavery by the inevitable laws of population. Whether this prophecy is ever fulfilled or not, it is nevertheless plain that a very different-looking class of people are springing up at the south, and are now held in slavery, from those originally brought to this country from Africa; and if their increase do no other good, it will do away the force of the argument, that God cursed Ham, and therefore American slavery is right. If the lineal descendants of Ham are alone to be scripturally enslaved, it is certain that slavery at the south must soon become unscriptural; for thousands are ushered into the world, annually, who, like myself, owe their existence to white fathers, and those fathers most frequently their own masters.

•   •   •

Chapter 6

My new mistress proved to be all she appeared when I first met her at the door,—a woman of the kindest heart and finest feelings. She had never had a slave under her control previously to myself, and prior to her marriage she had been dependent upon her own industry for a living. She was by trade a weaver; and by constant application to her business, she had been in a good degree preserved from the blighting and dehumanizing effects of slavery. I was utterly astonished at her goodness. I scarcely knew how to behave towards her. She was entirely unlike any other white woman I had ever seen. I could not approach her as I was accustomed to approach other white ladies. My early instruction was all out of place. The crouching servility, usually so acceptable a quality in a slave, did not answer when manifested toward her. Her favor was not gained by it; she seemed to be disturbed by it. She did not deem it impudent or unmannerly for a slave to look her in the face. The meanest slave was put fully at ease in her presence, and none left without feeling better for having seen her. Her face was made of heavenly smiles, and her voice of tranquil music.

But, alas! this kind heart had but a short time to remain such. The fatal poison of irresponsible power was already in her hands, and soon commenced its infernal work. That cheerful eye, under the influence of slavery, soon became red with rage; that voice, made all of sweet accord, changed to one of harsh and horrid discord; and that angelic face gave place to that of a demon.

Very soon after I went to live with Mr. and Mrs. Auld, she very kindly commenced to teach me the A, B, C. After I had learned this, she assisted me in learning to spell words of three or four letters. Just at this point of my progress, Mr. Auld found out what was going on, and at once forbade Mrs. Auld to instruct me further, telling her, among other things, that it was unlawful, as well as unsafe, to teach a slave to read. To use his own words, further, he said, "If you give a nigger an inch, he will take an ell. A nigger should know nothing but to obey his master—to do as he is told to do. Learning would *spoil* the best nigger in the world. Now," said he, "if you teach that nigger (speaking of myself) how to read, there would be no keeping him. It would forever unfit him to be a slave. He would at once become unmanageable, and of no value to his master. As to himself, it could do him no good, but a great deal of harm. It would make him discontented and unhappy." These words sank deep into my heart, stirred up sentiments within that lay slumbering, and called into existence an entirely new train of thought. It was a new and special revelation, explaining dark and mysterious things, with which my youthful understanding had struggled, but struggled in vain. I now understood what had been to me a most perplexing difficulty—to wit, the white man's power to enslave the black man. It was a grand achievement, and I prized it highly. From that moment, I understood the pathway from slavery to freedom. It was just what I wanted, and I got it at a time when I the least expected it. Whilst I was saddened by the thought of losing the aid of my kind mistress, I was gladdened by the invaluable instruction which, by the merest accident, I had gained from my master. Though conscious of the difficulty of learning without a teacher, I set out with high hope, and a fixed purpose, at whatever cost of trouble, to learn how to read. The very decided manner with which he spoke, and strove to impress his wife with the evil consequences of giving me instruction, served to convince me that he was deeply sensible of the truths he was uttering. It gave me the best assurance that I might rely with the utmost confidence on the results which, he said, would flow from teaching me to read. What he most dreaded, that I most desired. What he most loved, that I most hated. That which to him was a great evil, to be carefully shunned, was to me a great good, to be diligently sought; and the argument which he so warmly urged, against my learning to read, only served to inspire me with a desire and determination to learn. In learning to read, I owe almost as much to the bitter opposition of my master, as to the kindly aid of my mistress. I acknowledge the benefit of both.

I had resided but a short time in Baltimore before I observed a marked difference, in the treatment of slaves, from that which I had witnessed in the country. A city slave is almost a freeman, compared with a slave on the plantation. He is much better fed and clothed, and enjoys privileges altogether unknown to the slave on the plantation. There is a vestige of decency, a sense of shame, that does much to curb and check those outbreaks of atrocious cruelty so commonly enacted upon the plantation. He is a desperate slaveholder, who will shock the humanity of his non-slaveholding neighbors with the cries of his lacerated slave. Few are willing to incur the odium attaching to the reputation of being a cruel master; and above all things, they would not be known as not giving a slave enough to eat. Every city slaveholder is anxious to have it known of him, that he feeds his slaves well; and it is due to them to say, that most of them do give their slaves enough to eat. There are, however, some painful exceptions to this rule. Directly opposite to us, on Philpot Street, lived Mr. Thomas Hamilton. He owned two slaves. Their names were Henrietta and Mary. Henrietta was about twenty-two years of age, Mary was about fourteen; and of all the mangled and emaciated creatures I ever looked upon, these two were the most so. His heart must be harder than stone, that could look upon these unmoved. The head, neck, and shoulders of Mary were literally cut to pieces. I have frequently felt her head, and found it nearly covered with festering sores, caused by the lash of her cruel mistress. I do not know that her master ever whipped her, but I have been an eye-witness to the cruelty of Mrs. Hamilton. I used to be in Mr. Hamilton's house nearly every day. Mrs. Hamilton used to sit in a large chair in the middle of the room, with a heavy cowskin always by her side, and scarce an hour passed during the day but was marked by the blood of one of these slaves. The girls seldom passed her without her saying, "Move faster, you *black gip!*" at the same time giving them a blow with the cowskin over the head or shoulders, often drawing the blood. She would then say, "Take that, you *black gip!*"—continuing, "If you don't move faster, I'll move you!" Added to the cruel lashings to which these slaves were subjected, they were kept nearly half-starved. They seldom knew what it was to eat a full meal. I have seen Mary contending with the pigs for the offal thrown into the street. So much was Mary kicked and cut to pieces, that she was oftener called "*pecked*" than by her name.

Elizabeth Cady Stanton

1815–1902

The following document, a "Declaration of Sentiments," marks the formal beginning of a national women's rights movement in the U.S. While the discussion of women's rights dates back to the founding of the Republic, only at Seneca Falls, New York, was an organized platform for change promulgated. The two organizers of the meeting, Elizabeth Cady Stanton and Lucretia Mott, had determined to organize on behalf of women's rights after their participation in the London Anti-slavery Convention of 1840 was limited because of their gender (all women were required to maintain silence and sit behind a curtain). Both Quakers, each woman's life spanned most of the nineteenth century and included principled participation in a variety of causes, especially abolition.

Clearly inspired by Olympe de Gouges's declaration which echoed that of the French government, over one hundred Seneca women and twelve men drafted a document which echoes the Declaration of Independence. Like de Gouges, the Seneca group was also writing in the midst of revolutionary ferment when normal social conventions were relaxed. In 1848, over fifty revolutions swept across continental Europe creating the possibility for dramatic change. French women early in that year, for example, agitated for women's suffrage and even (illegally) ran candidates for office.

The document was considered scandalous by many, especially pundits writing in mainstream newspapers. The audacity of the Seneca group to paraphrase the Declaration of Independence bordered on sacrilege according to some. Applying Jefferson's logic to the condition of women enabled the writers to expose the oppression of women in sweeping terms. How do the two declarations compare? Why, in light of the innumerable disadvantages under which women lived, did obtaining the suffrage become the focal point of the women's movement? Does the Seneca declaration represent some women's interests more than others?

Declaration of Sentiments (1848)

When, in the course of human events, it becomes necessary for one portion of the family of man to assume among the people of the earth a position different from that which they have hitherto occupied, but one to which the laws of nature and of nature's God entitle them, a decent respect to the opinions of mankind requires that they should declare the causes that impel them to such a course.

We hold these truths to be self-evident: that all men and women are created equal; that they are endowed by their Creator with certain inalienable rights; that among these are life, liberty, and the pursuit of happiness; that to secure these rights governments are instituted, deriving their just powers from the consent of the governed. Whenever any form of government becomes destructive of these ends, it is the right of those who suffer from it to refuse allegiance to it, and to insist upon the institution of a new government, laying its foundation on such principles, and organizing its powers in such form, as to them shall seem most likely to effect their safety and happiness. Prudence indeed, will dictate that governments long established should not be changed for light and transient causes; and accordingly all experience hath shown that mankind are more disposed to suffer, while evils are sufferable, than to right them selves by abolishing the forms to which they were accustomed. But when a long train of abuses and usurpations, pursuing invariably the same object evinces a design to reduce them under absolute despotism, it is their duty to throw off such government, and to provide new guards for their future security. Such has been the patient sufferance of the women under this government, and such is now the necessity which constrains them to demand the equal station to which they are entitled.

The history of mankind is a history of repeated injuries and usurpations on the part of man toward woman, having in direct object the establishment of an absolute tyranny over her. To prove this, let facts be submitted to a candid world.

He has never permitted her to exercise her inalienable right to the elective franchise.

He has compelled her to submit to laws, in the formation of which she had no voice.

He has withheld from her rights which are given to the most ignorant and degraded men—both natives and foreigners.

Having deprived her of this first right of a citizen, the elective franchise, thereby leaving her without representation in the halls of legislation, he has oppressed her on all sides.

He has made her, if married, in the eye of the law, civilly dead.

He has taken from her all right in property, even to the wages she earns.

He has made her, morally, an irresponsible being, as she can commit many crimes with impunity, provided they be done in the presence of her husband. In the covenant of marriage, she is compelled to promise obedience to her husband, he becoming, to all intents and purposes, her master—the law giving him power to deprive her of her liberty, and to administer chastisement.

He has so framed the laws of divorce, as to what shall be the proper causes, and in case of separation, to whom the guardianship of the children shall be given, as to be wholly regardless of the happiness of women—the law, in all cases, going upon a false supposition of the supremacy of man, and giving all power into his hands.

After depriving her of all rights as a married woman, if single, and the owner of property, he has taxed her to support a government which recognizes her only when her property can be made profitable to it.

He has monopolized nearly all the profitable employments, and from those she is permitted to follow, she receives but a scanty remuneration. He closes against her all the avenues to wealth and distinction which he considers most honorable to himself. As a teacher of theology, medicine, or law, she is not known.

He has denied her the facilities for obtaining a thorough education, all colleges being closed against her.

He allows her in Church, as well as State, but a subordinate position, claiming Apostolic authority for her exclusion from the ministry, and, with some exceptions, from any public participation in the affairs of the Church.

He has created a false public sentiment by giving to the world a different code of morals for men and women, by which moral delinquencies which exclude women from society, are not only tolerated, but deemed of little account in man.

He has usurped the prerogative of Jehovah himself, claiming it as his right to assign for her a sphere of action, when that belongs to her conscience and to her God.

He has endeavored, in every way that he could, to destroy her confidence in her own powers, to lessen her self-respect, and to make her willing to lead a dependent and abject life.

Now, in view of this entire disfranchisement of one-half the people of this country, their social and religious degradation—in view of the unjust laws above mentioned, and because women do feel themselves aggrieved, oppressed, and fraudulently deprived of their most sacred rights, we insist that they have immediate admission to all the rights and privileges which belong to them as citizens of the United States.

In entering upon the great work before us, we anticipate no small amount of misconception, misrepresentation, and ridicule; but we shall use every instrumentality within our power to effect our object. We shall employ agents, circulate tracts, petition the State and National legislatures, and endeavor to enlist the pulpit and the press in our behalf. We hope this Convention will be followed by a series of Conventions embracing every part of the country.

The following resolutions were discussed by Lucretia Mott, Thomas and Mary Ann McClintock, Amy Post, Catharine A. F. Stebbins, and others, and were adopted:

WHEREAS, The great precept of nature is conceded to be, that "man shall pursue his own true and substantial happiness." Blackstone in his Commentaries remarks, that this law of Nature being coeval with mankind, and dictated by God himself, is of course superior in obligation to any other. It is binding over all the globe, in all countries, and at all times; no human laws are of any validity if contrary to this, and such of them as are valid, derive all their force, and all their validity, and all their authority, mediately and immediately, from this original; therefore;

Resolved, That such laws as conflict, in any way, with the true and substantial happiness of woman, are contrary to the great precept of nature and of no validity, for this is "superior in obligation to any other."

Resolved, That all laws which prevent woman from occupying such a station in society as her conscience shall dictate, or which place her in a position inferior to that of man, are contrary to the great precept of nature, and therefore of no force or authority.

Resolved, That woman is man's equal—was intended to be so by the Creator, and the highest good of the race demands that she should be recognized as such.

Resolved, That the women of this country ought to be enlightened in regard to the laws under which they live, that they may no longer publish their degradation by declaring themselves satisfied with their present position, nor their ignorance by asserting that they have all the rights they want.

Resolved, That inasmuch as man, while claiming for himself intellectual superiority, does accord to woman moral superiority, it is preeminently his duty to encourage her to speak and teach, as she has an opportunity, in all religious assemblies.

Resolved, That the same amount of virtue, delicacy, and refinement of behavior that is required of woman in the social state, should also be required of man, and the same transgressions should be visited with equal severity on both man and woman.

Resolved, That the objection of indelicacy and impropriety, which is so often brought against woman when she addresses a public audience, comes with a very ill-grace from those who encourage, by their attendance, her appearance on the stage, in the concert, or in feats of the circus.

Resolved, That woman has too long rested satisfied in the circumscribed limits which corrupt customs and a perverted application of the Scriptures have marked out for her, and that it is time she should move in the enlarged sphere which her great Creator has assigned her.

Resolved, That it is the duty of the women of this country to secure to themselves their sacred right to the elective franchise.

Resolved, That the equality of human rights results necessarily from the fact of the identity of the race in capabilities and responsibilities.

Resolved, therefore, That, being invested by the Creator with the same capabilities, and the same consciousness of responsibility for their exercise, it is demonstrably the right and duty of woman, equally with man, to promote every righteous cause by every righteous means; and especially in regard to the great subjects of morals and religion, it is self-evidently her right to participate with her brother in teaching them, both in private and in public, by writing and by speaking, by any instrumentalities proper to be used, and in any assemblies proper to be held; and this being a self-evident truth growing out of the divinely implanted principles of human nature, any custom or authority adverse to it, whether modern or wearing the hoary sanction of antiquity, is to be regarded as a self-evident falsehood, and at war with mankind.

At the last session Lucretia Mott offered and spoke to the following resolution:

Resolved, That the speedy success of our cause depends upon the zealous and untiring efforts of both men and women, for the overthrow of the monopoly of the pulpit, and for the securing to woman an equal participation with men in the various trades, professions, and commerce.

Sojourner Truth

1797–1883

What we know of the life of Sojourner Truth is very incomplete. She was born Isabella Baumfree, so named by her slaveowner, in Ulster County, New York. She married another slave by the name of Thomas and together they had five children. In 1827, just before slavery was abolished in the state of New York, she escaped to freedom. While working in New York City as a domestic servant, she brought legal action to win the freedom of one of her sons, who had illegally been sold to a Southern slaveowner; as a result of her tenacity and intelligence, she won her case and her son was returned to her. She became involved in the evangelical movement and, in 1843, she renamed herself "Sojourner Truth," following a mystical experience during which she was instructed to go forth and advocate for God and abolition.

Truth was praised for her insight and oratorical power by white anti-slavery activists such as George W. Benson and William Lloyd Garrison. She spoke in support of women's suffrage at the request of Elizabeth Cady Stanton, and, anticipating the black nationalism of Marcus Garvey, she was a proponent of forming a "Negro State." Sojourner Truth died in 1883 in Battle Creek, Michigan.

In both speeches offered below, Truth insists on the fundamental equality of the races and compels us to examine the moral arrogance that served to support the slaveholding mentality for so long. What are the common foundations of her anti-slavery stance and her position on suffrage? On what intellectual traditions does she draw in her oratory? What are the sources of her rhetorical power?

A'n't I a Woman (1851)

Well, children, where there is so much racket there must be somethin' out o'kilter. I think that 'twixt the Negroes of the North and the South and the women at the North, all talkin' 'bout rights, the white men will be in a fix pretty soon. But what's all this here talkin' 'bout?

That man over there say that women needs to be helped into carriages, and lifted over ditches, and to have the best place everywhere. Nobody ever helps me into carriages, or over mud-puddles, or give me any best place! And ain't I a woman? Look at me? Look at my arm! I have ploughed, and planted, and gathered into barns, and no man could head me! And ain't I a woman? I could work as much and eat as much as a man—when I could get it—and bear the lash as well! And ain't I a woman? I have borne thirteen children, and seen em mos' all sold off to slavery, and when I cried out with my mother's grief, none but Jesus heard me! And ain't I a woman?

Then they talk about this thing in the head; what's this they call it? ["Intellect," whispered some one near.] That's it honey. What's that got to do with women's rights or Negro's rights? If my cup won't hold but a pint and yours holds a quart, wouldn't you be mean not to let me have my little half measure full?

Then that little man in black there, he says women can't have as much rights as men, 'cause Christ wasn't a woman! Where did your Christ come from? Where did your Christ come from? From God and a woman! Man had nothin' to do with Him.

If the first woman God ever made was strong enough to turn the world upside down all alone, these women together ought to be able to turn it back, and get it right side up again? And now they is asking to do it, they better let 'em. 'Bliged to you for hearin' me, and now ole Sojourner hasn't got nothin' more to say.

Akron, Ohio, May 29, 1851

Address to the First Annual Meeting of the American Equal Rights Association (1867)

My friends, I am rejoiced that you are glad, but I don't know how you will feel when I get through. I come from another field—the country of the slave. They have got their liberty—so much good luck to have slavery partly destroyed; not entirely. I want it root and branch destroyed. Then we will all be free indeed. I feel that if I have to answer for the deeds done in my body just as much as a man, I have a right to have just as much as a man. There is a great stir about colored men gettin' their rights, but not a word about the colored women; and if colored men get their rights, and not colored women theirs, you see the colored men will be masters over the women, and it will be just as bad as it was before. So I am for keeping the thing going while things are stirring; because if we wait till it is still, it will take a great while to get it going again. White women are a great deal smarter, and know more than colored women, while colored women do not know scarcely anything. They go out washing, which is about as high as a colored woman gets, and their men go about idle, strutting up and down; and when the women come home, they ask for their money and take it all, and then scold because there is no food. I want you to consider on that, chil'n. I call you chil'n; you are somebody's chil'n, and I am old enough to be mother of all that is here. I want women to have their rights. In the courts women have no right, no voice; nobody speaks for them. I wish woman to have her voice there among the pettifoggers.[1] If it is not a fit place for women, it is unfit for men to be there.

I am above eighty years old; it is about time for me to be going. I have been forty years a slave and forty years free, and would be here forty years more to have equal rights for all. I suppose I am kept here because something remains for me to do; I suppose I am yet to help to break the chain. I have done a great deal of work; as much as a man, but did not get so much pay. I used to work in the field and bind grain, keeping up with the cradler; but men doing no more, go twice as much pay; so with the German women. They work in the field and do as much work, but do not get the pay. We do as much, we eat as much, we want as much. I suppose I am about the only colored woman that goes about to speak for the rights of the colored women. I want to keep the thing stirring, now that the ice is cracked. What we want is a little money. You men know that you get as much again as women when you write, or for what you do. When we get our rights we shall not have to come to you for money, for then we shall have money enough in our own pockets; and may be you will ask us for money. But help us now until we get it. It is a good consolation to know that when we have got this battle once fought we shall not be coming to you any more. You have been having our rights so long, that you think, like a slave-holder, that you own us. I know that it is hard for one who has held the rein for so long to give up; it cuts like a knife. It will feel all the better when it closes up again. I have been in Washington about three years, seeing about these colored people. Now colored men have the right to vote. There ought to be equal rights now more than ever, since colored people have got their freedom. . . .

I am glad to see that men are getting their rights, but I want women to get theirs, and while the water is stirring I will step into the pool. Now that there is a great stir about colored men's getting their rights is the time for women to step in and have theirs. I am sometimes told that "Women ain't fit to vote. Why, don't you know that a woman had seven devils in her: and do you suppose a woman is fit to rule the nation?" Seven devils ain't no account; a man had a legion in him. The devils didn't know where to go; and so they asked that they might go into the swine. They thought that was as good a place as they came out from. They didn't ask to go into the sheep—no, into the hog; that was the selfish beast; and man is so selfish that he has got women's rights and his own too, and yet he won't give women their rights. He keeps them all to himself. . . .

I have lived on through all that has taken place these forty years in the anti-slavery cause, and I have plead with all the force I had that the day might come that the colored people might own their soul and body. Well, the day has come, although it came through blood. It makes no difference how it came— it did come. I am sorry it came in that way. We are now trying for liberty that requires no blood—that women shall have their rights—not rights from you. Give them what belongs to them; they ask it kindly too. I ask it kindly. Now, I want it done very quick. It can be done in a few years. How good it would be. I would like to go up to the polls myself. I own a little house in Battle Creek, Michigan. Well, every year I got a tax to pay. Taxes, you see, be taxes. Well, a road tax sounds large. . . . There was women there that had a house as well as I. They taxed them to build a road, and they went on the road and worked. It took 'em a good while to get a stump up. Now, that shows that women can work. If they can dig up stumps they can vote. It is easier to vote than dig stumps. It doesn't seem hard work to vote, though I have seen some men that had a hard time of it. . . . I don't want to take up your time, but I calculate to live. Now, if you want me to get out of the world, you had better get the women votin' soon. I shan't go till I can do that.

New York, May 9, 1867

Note

[1] Lawyer who handles petty cases.

John Stuart Mill

1806–1873

John Stuart Mill was the son of James Mill, a leading radical philosopher and reformer in England. Jeremy Bentham, an advocate of philosophical reform, founded with James Mill the school of thought known as Utilitarianism, which desired to produce "the greatest happiness for the greatest number." The young Mill was given an intense and strict education by his father, learning Greek at age three and Latin at age eight, along with studies in algebra and geometry. By the age of ten, he had completed a study of the classics typically taught at the college level. At twenty, he underwent a severe psychological crisis, which he later attributed to his sternly practical education, which did not allow for the full development of feelings and the creative sensibility. He cured himself, in part, by reading the romantic poetry of Wordsworth. Later, he made significant contributions to Utilitarianism by adding a more humane dimension, insisting on the values of the nineteenth-century progressive liberal—that is, one who advocates intellectual freedom and autonomy for the individual.

In 1830 he met Harriet Taylor, a married woman and mother of three children, developing with her an unconventional and passionate friendship, finally marrying twenty-one years later when Taylor's husband died. Mill credited his wife for her significant role in all his later work: she helped him revise his book *On Liberty* (1859), published the year after her death, and in Mill's view she was "the inspirer, . . .in part the author, of all that is best in my writings." Though completed in 1861, Mill delayed the publication of *The Subjection of Women*, believing that the climate was not right for its release. He served three years in the House of Commons, where he voted as a radical and supported women's suffrage, making him unpopular in the eyes of his male colleagues. After his work supporting women's rights in Parliament, he felt the time had come to publish *The Subjection of Women*, which he did in 1869.

In *The Subjection of Women*, how does Mill support his position that equal rights and freedom should be extended to women? In what sense is Mill correct when he argues that men want women to be not only obedient, but *willing* slaves?

from *The Subjection of Women* (1869)

Chapter I

The object of this Essay is to explain as clearly as I am able, the grounds of an opinion which I have held from the very earliest period when I had formed any opinions at all on social or political matters, and which, instead of being weakened or modified, has been constantly growing stronger by the progress of reflection and the experience of life. That the principle which regulates the existing social relations between the two sexes—the legal subordination of one sex to the other—is wrong in itself, and now one of the chief hindrances to human improvement; and that it ought to be replaced by a principle of perfect equality, admitting no power or privilege on the one side, nor disability on the other.

• • •

It is one of the characteristic prejudices of the reaction of the nineteenth century against the eighteenth, to accord to the unreasoning elements in human nature the infallibility which the eighteenth century is supposed to have ascribed to the reasoning elements. For the apotheosis[1] of Reason we have substituted that of Instinct; and we call everything instinct which we find in ourselves and for which we cannot trace any rational foundation. This idolatry, infinitely more degrading than the other, and the most pernicious of the false worships of the present day, of all of which it is now the main support, will probably hold its ground until it gives way before a sound psychology laying bare the real root of much that is bowed down to as the intention of Nature and the ordinance of God. As regards the present question, I am willing to accept the unfavourable conditions which the prejudice assigns to me. I consent that established custom, and the general feeling, should be deemed conclusive against me, unless that custom and feeling from age to age can be shown to have owed their existence to other causes than their soundness, and to have derived their power from the worse rather than the better parts of human nature. I am willing that judgment should go against me, unless I can show that my judge has been tampered with. The concession is not so great as it might appear; for to prove this, is by far the easiest portion of my task.

• • •

In the first place, the opinion in favour of the present system, which entirely subordinates the weaker sex to the stronger, rests upon theory only; for

223

there never has been trial made of any other: so that experience, in the sense in which it is vulgarly opposed to theory, cannot be pretended to have pronounced any verdict. And in the second place, the adoption of this system of inequality never was the result of deliberation, or forethought, or any social ideas, or any notion whatever of what conduced to the benefit of humanity or the good order of society. It arose simply from the fact that from the very earliest twilight of human society, every woman (owing to the value attached to her by men, combined with her inferiority in muscular strength) was found in a state of bondage to some man. Laws and systems of polity always begin by recognising the relations they find already existing between individuals. They convert what was a mere physical fact into a legal right, give it the sanction of society, and principally aim at the substitution of public and organised means of asserting and protecting these rights, instead of the irregular and lawless conflict of physical strength. . . . No presumption in its favour, therefore, can be drawn from the fact of its existence. The only such presumption which it could be supposed to have, must be grounded on its having lasted till now, when so many other things which came down from the same odious source have been done away with. And this, indeed, is what makes it strange to ordinary ears, to hear it asserted that the inequality of rights between men and women has no other source than the law of the strongest.

• • •

But, it will be said, the rule of men over women differs from all these others in not being a rule of force: it is accepted voluntarily; women make no complaint, and are consenting parties to it. In the first place, a great number of women do not accept it. Ever since there have been women able to make their sentiments known by their writings (the only mode of publicity which society permits to them), an increasing number of them have recorded protests against their present social condition: and recently many thousands of them, headed by the most eminent women known to the public, have petitioned Parliament for their admission to the Parliamentary Suffrage. The claim of women to be educated as solidly, and in the same branches of knowledge, as men, is urged with growing intensity, and with a great prospect of success; while the demand for their admission into professions and occupations hitherto closed against them, becomes every year more urgent. Though there are not in this country, as there are in the United States, periodical conventions and an organised party to agitate for the Rights of Women, there is a numerous and active society organised and managed by women, for the more limited object of obtaining the political franchise. Nor is it only in our own country and in America that women are beginning to protest, more or less collectively, against the disabilities under which they labour. France, and Italy, and

Switzerland, and Russia now afford examples of the same thing. How many more women there are who silently cherish similar aspirations, no one can possibly know; but there are abundant tokens how many *would* cherish them, were they not so strenuously taught to repress them as contrary to the proprieties of their sex. It must be remembered, also, that no enslaved class ever asked for complete liberty at once. When Simon de Montfort[2] called the deputies of the commons to sit for the first time in Parliament, did any of them dream of demanding that an assembly, elected by their constituents, should make and destroy ministries, and dictate to the king in affairs of State? No such thought entered into the imagination of the most ambitious of them. The nobility had already these pretensions; the commons pretended to nothing but to be exempt from arbitrary taxation, and from the gross individual oppression of the king's officers. It is a political law of nature that those who are under any power of ancient origin, never begin by complaining of the power itself, but only of its oppressive exercise. There is never any want of women who complain of ill-usage by their husbands. There would be infinitely more, if complaint were not the greatest of all provocatives to a repetition and increase of the ill-usage. It is this which frustrates all attempts to maintain the power but protect the woman against its abuses. In no other case (except that of a child) is the person who has been proved judicially to have suffered an injury, replaced under the physical power of the culprit who inflicted it. Accordingly wives, even in the most extreme and protracted cases of bodily ill-usage, hardly ever dare avail themselves of the laws made for their protection: and if, in a moment of irrepressible indignation, or by the interference of neighbours, they are induced to do so, their whole effort afterwards is to disclose as little as they can, and to beg off their tyrant from his merited chastisement.

All causes, social and natural, combine to make it unlikely that women should be collectively rebellious to the power of men. They are so far in a position different from all other subject classes, that their masters require something more from them than actual service. Men do not want solely the obedience of women, they want their sentiments. All men, except the most brutish, desire to have, in the woman most nearly connected with them, not a forced slave but a willing one, not a slave merely, but a favourite. They have therefore put everything in practice to enslave their minds. The masters of all other slaves rely, for maintaining obedience, on fear; either fear of themselves, or religious fears. The masters of women wanted more than simple obedience, and they turned the whole force of education to effect their purpose. All women are brought up from the very earliest years in the belief that their ideal of character is the very opposite to that of men; not self-will, and government by self-control, but submission, and yielding to the control of other. All the moralities tell them that it is the duty of women, and all the current sentimentalities that it is their nature, to live for others; to make complete abnegation of themselves, and to have no life but in their affections. And by their affections are meant the only ones they are allowed to have—those to the men with whom they are connected, or to the children who constitute an additional and indefeasible tie between them and a man. When we put together three things—first, the natural attraction between opposite sexes; secondly, the wife's entire dependence on the husband, every privilege or pleasure she has being either his gift, or depending entirely on his will; and lastly, that the principal object of human pursuit, consideration, and all objects of social ambition, can in general be sought or obtained by her only through him, it would be a miracle if the object of being attractive to men had not become the polar star of feminine education and formation of character. And, this great means of influence over the minds of women having been acquired, an instinct of selfishness made men avail themselves of it to the utmost as a means of holding women in subjection, by representing to them meekness, submissiveness, and resignation of all individual will into the hands of a man, as an essential part of sexual attractiveness. Can it be doubted that any of the other yokes which mankind have succeeded in breaking, would have subsisted till now if the same means had existed, and had been so sedulously used, to bow down their minds to it? If it had been made the object of the life of every young plebeian to find personal favour in the eyes of some patrician, of every young serf with some seigneur; if domestication with him, and a share of his personal affections, had been held out as the prize which they all should look out for, the most gifted and aspiring being able to reckon on the most desirable prizes; and if, when this prize had been obtained, they had been shut out by a wall of brass from all interests not centring in him, all feelings and desires but those which he shared or inculcated; would not serfs and seigneurs, plebeians and patricians, have been as broadly distinguished at this day as men and women are? and would not all but a thinker here and there, have believed the distinction to be a fundamental and unalterable fact in human nature?

• • •

Neither does it avail anything to say that the *nature* of the two sexes adapts them to their present functions and position, and renders these appropriate to them. Standing on the ground of common sense and the constitution of the human mind, I deny that anyone knows, or can know, the nature of the two sexes, as long as they have only been seen in their present relation to one another. If men had ever been found in society without women, or women without men, or if there had been a society of men and women in which the women were not under the control of the men, something might have been positively known about the mental and moral differences which may be inherent in the nature of each. What is now called the nature of women is an eminently artificial thing—the result of forced repression in some directions, unnatural stimulation in others. It may be asserted without scruple, that no other class of dependents have had their character so entirely distorted from its natural proportions by their relation with their masters; for, if conquered and slave races have been, in some respects, more forcibly repressed, whatever in them has not been crushed down by an iron heel has generally been let alone, and if left with any liberty of development, it has developed itself according to its own laws; but in the case of women, a hot-house and stove cultivation has always been carried on of some of the capabilities of their nature, for the benefit and pleasure of their masters. Then, because certain products of the general vital force sprout luxuriantly and reach a great development in this heated atmosphere and under this active nurture and watering, while other shoots from the same root, which are left outside in the wintry air, with ice purposely heaped all round them, have a stunted growth, and some are burnt off with fire and disappear; men, with that inability to recognise their own work which distinguishes the unanalytic mind, indolently believe that the tree grows of itself in the way they have made it grow, and that it would die if one half of it were not kept in a vapour bath and the other half in the snow.

• • •

Chapter III

It will be said, perhaps, that the greater nervous susceptibility of women is a disqualification for practice, in anything but domestic life, by rendering them mobile, changeable, too vehemently under the influence of the moment, incapable of dogged perseverance, unequal and uncertain in the power of using their faculties. I think that these phrases sum up the greater part of the objections commonly made to the fitness of women for the higher class of serious business. Much of all this is the mere overflow of nervous energy run to waste, and would cease when the energy was directed to a definite end. Much is also the result of conscious or unconscious cultivation; as we see by the almost total disappearance of "hysterics" and fainting-fits, since they have gone out of fashion. Moreover, when people are brought up, like many women of the higher classes (though less so in our own country than in any other), a kind of hot-house plants, shielded from the wholesome vicissitudes of air and temperature, and untrained in any of the occupations and exercises which give stimulus and development to the circulatory and muscular system, while their nervous system, especially in its emotional department, is kept in unnaturally active play; it is no wonder if those of them who do not die of consumption, grow up with constitutions liable to derangement from slight causes, both internal and external, and without stamina to support any task, physical or mental, requiring continuity of effort. But women brought up to work for their livelihood show none of these morbid characteristics, unless indeed they are chained to an excess of sedentary work in confined and unhealthy rooms. Women who in their early years have shared in the healthful physical education and bodily freedom of their brothers, and who obtain a sufficiency of pure air and exercise in after-life, very rarely have any excessive susceptibility of nerves which can disqualify them for active pursuits.

Notes

[1] Deification.

[2] Simon de Montfort (1208–1265), Earl of Leicester, England.

V. SOCIAL, ECONOMIC, AND POLITICAL THOUGHT IN THE NINETEENTH CENTURY

Simón Bolívar

1783–1830

Simón Bolívar was born in Caracas, Venezuela, the son of a wealthy Creole aristocrat. By the time he was six, both his mother and father had died and he went to live with his uncle, Esteban Palacios, who cared well for him and made sure that he received an education. Though he was a temperamental and high-spirited child, he displayed a powerful intellect and profound sense of justice. Bolívar was tutored by Simón Carreño Rodríguez, who was a disciple of Rousseau. The young Bolívar's introduction to the political thought of eighteenth-century European writers influenced him deeply and at the age of sixteen he continued his schooling in Europe, where he studied the writings of Hobbes, Locke, Montesquieu, and Voltaire.

In 1807, Bolívar returned to Venezuela, after a visit to the United States, in order to participate in the Latin-American independence movement, which had been ignited by Napoleon's campaign against the Iberian peninsula. Bolívar joined the military in 1811 and within one year was placed in control of Puerto Cabello, Venezuela's most vital port. Early in 1812, Bolívar left Venezuela for Cartegena, New Grenada (modern-day Colombia), where he raised a militia in order to liberate Venezuela from Spanish rule. On 6 August 1813, he rode into Caracas and proclaimed himself Liberator, assuming dictatorial powers. After three years of military successes and failures, Bolívar had managed to end Spanish control in the region and in 1819 he addressed the congress of Angostura, where he was made president of the newly formed republic of Gran Columbia. In 1827, however, civil war erupted and by 1829 Gran Columbia had fallen into irreparable disarray. In the fall of 1829, Venezuela seceded from Colombia and in September 1830 Ecuador withdrew from Colombia as well. Bolívar's dream of a unified republic had been dashed.

In the excerpt of his address below, Bolívar observes that the people of Gran Colombia do not have experience in freedom and self-rule. Further, in an echo of Burke in *Reflections of the Revolution in France*, Bolívar argues that no other governmental model—not even that of America to the north—offers a political structure adequate to accommodate Venezuelan culture and tradition. If Burke is right in his claim that governments are best developed out of an awareness of history and tradition, what is Bolívar to do? On what resources can he draw in order to provide his people with a lasting political order? Can a people ever escape history and emerge from oppression?

Message to the Congress of Angostura (1819)

And, now that by this act of adherence to the Liberty of Venezuela, I can aspire to the glory of being counted among her most faithful lovers, permit me, Sirs, to state with the frankness of a true republican, my respectful opinion regarding the scope of this *Project of a Constitution*, which I take the liberty to submit, as a token of the sincerity and candor of my sentiments. As this is a question involving the welfare of all, I venture to believe that I have the right to be heard by the Representatives of the people. Well I know that in your wisdom you have no need of counsel; I am also aware that my *project* may perhaps appear to you erroneous and impracticable. But, Sirs, receive with benevolence this work which is a tribute of my sincere submission to Congress rather than the outcome of a presumptuous levity. On the other hand, your functions being the creation of a body politic, and, one might say, the creation of an entire community surrounded by all the difficulties offered by a situation—a most peculiar and difficult one—the voice of a citizen may perhaps point out a hidden or unknown danger.

By casting a glance over the past, we shall see what is the basic element of the Republic of Venezuela.

America, on becoming separated from the Spanish monarchy, found itself like the Roman Empire, when that enormous mass fell to pieces in the midst of the ancient world. Each dismembered portion formed then an independent nation in accordance with its situation or its interests, the difference being that those members established anew their former associations. We do not even preserve the vestiges of what once we were; we are not Europeans, we are not Indians, but an intermediate species between the aborigines and the Spaniards—Americans by birth and Europeans in right, we are placed in the dilemma of disputing with the natives our titles of possession and maintaining ourselves in the country where we were born, against the opposition of the invaders. Thus, ours is a most extraordinary and complicated case. Moreover, our part has always been a purely passive one; our political existence has always been null, and we find ourselves in greater difficulties in attaining our liberty than we ever had when we lived on a plane lower than servitude, because we had been robbed not only of liberty but also of active and domestic tyranny. Allow me to explain this paradox.

In an absolute régime, authorized power does not admit any limits. The will of the despot is the extreme law, arbitrarily executed by the subordinates who participate in the organized oppression according to the measure of the authority they enjoy.

They are intrusted with civil, political, military and religious functions; but in the last analysis, the Satraps of Persia are Persians, the Pashas of the Great Master are Turks, the Sultans of Tartary are Tartars. China does not send for her Mandarins to the land of Genghis-khan, her conqueror. America, on the contrary, received all from Spain, which had really deprived her of true enjoyment and exercise of active tyranny, by not permitting us to share in our own domestic affairs and interior administration. This deprivation had made it impossible for us to become acquainted with the course of public affairs; neither did we enjoy that personal consideration which the glamour of power inspires in the eyes of the multitude, so important in the great revolutions. I will say, in short, we were kept in estrangement, absent from the universe and all that relates to the science of government.

The people of America having been held under the triple yoke of ignorance, tyranny and vice, have not been in a position to acquire either knowledge, power or virtue. Disciples of such pernicious masters, the lessons we have received and the examples we have studied, are most destructive. We have been governed more by deception than by force, and we have been degraded more by vice than by superstition. Slavery is the offspring of Darkness; an ignorant people is a blind tool, turned to its own destruction; ambition and intrigue exploit the credulity and inexperience of men foreign to all political, economical or civil knowledge; mere illusions are accepted as reality, license is taken for liberty, treachery for patriotism, revenge for justice. Even as a sturdy blind man who, relying on the feeling of his own strength, walks along with the assurance of the most wide-awake man and, striking against all kinds of obstacles, can not steady his steps.

A perverted people, should it attain its liberty, is bound to lose this very soon, because it would be useless to try to impress upon such people that happiness lies in the practice of righteousness; that the reign of law is more powerful than the reign of tyrants, who are more inflexible, and all ought to submit to the wholesome severity of the law; that good morals, and not force, are the pillars of the law and that the exercise of justice is the exercise of liberty. Thus, Legislators, your task is the more laborious because you are to deal with men misled by the illusions of error, and by civil incentives. Liberty, says Rousseau, is a succulent food, but difficult to digest. Our feeble fellow-citizens will have to strengthen their mind much before they will be ready to assimilate such wholesome nourishment. Their limbs made numb by their fetters, their eyesight weakened in the darkness of their dungeons and their forces wasted away through their foul servitude, will they be capable of marching with a firm step towards the august temple of Liberty? Will they be capable of coming close to it, and admiring the light it sheds, and of breathing freely its pure air?

Consider well your decision, Legislators. Do not forget that you are about to lay the foundations of a new people, which may some day rise to the heights that Nature has marked out for it, provided you make those foundations proportionate to the lofty place which that people is to fill. If your selection be not made under the guidance of the Guardian Angel of Venezuela, who must inspire you with wisdom to choose the nature and form of government that you are to adopt for the welfare of the people; if you should fail in this, I warn you, the end of our venture would be slavery.

The annals of past ages display before you thousands of governments. Recall to mind the nations which have shone most highly on the earth and you will be grieved to see that almost the entire world has been, and still is, a victim of bad government. You will find many systems of governing men, but all are calculated to oppress them, and if the habit of seeing the human race, led by shepherds of peoples, did not dull the horror of such a revolting sight, we would be astonished to see our social species grazing on the surface of the globe, even as lowly herds destined to feed their cruel drivers.

Nature, in truth, endows us at birth with the instinctive desire for liberty; but whether because of negligence, or because of an inclination inherent in humanity, it remains still under the bonds imposed on it. And as we see it in such a state of debasement we seem to have reason to be persuaded that the majority of men hold as a truth the humiliating principle that it is harder to maintain the balance of liberty than to endure the weight of tyranny. Would to God that this principle, contrary to the morals of Nature, were false! Would to God that this principle were not sanctioned by the indolence of man as regards his most sacred rights!

Many ancient and modern nations have cast off oppression; but those which have been able to enjoy a few precious moments of liberty are most rare, as they soon relapsed into their old political vices; because it is the people more often than the government, that bring on tyranny. The habit of suffering domination makes them insensible to the charms of honor and national prosperity, and leads them to look with indolence upon the bliss of living in the midst of liberty, under the protection of laws framed by their own free will. The history of the world proclaims this awful truth!

Only democracy, in my opinion, is susceptible of absolute freedom. But where is there a democratic government that has united at the same time power, prosperity and permanence? Have we not seen, on the contrary, aristocracy, monarchy, rearing great and powerful empires for centuries and centuries? What government is there older than that of China? What republic has exceeded in duration that of Sparta, that of Venice? The Roman Empire, did it not conquer the world? Does not France count fourteen centuries of monarchy? Who is greater than England? These nations, however, have been, or still are, aristocracies and monarchies.

Notwithstanding such bitter reflections, I am filled with unbounded joy because of the great strides made by our republic since entering upon its noble career. Loving that which is most useful, animated by what is most just and aspiring to what is most perfect, Venezuela in separating from the Spanish Nation has recovered her independence, her freedom, her equality, her national sovereignty. In becoming a democratic republic, she proscribed monarchy, distinctions, nobility, franchises and privileges; she declared the rights of man, the liberty of action, of thought, of speech, of writing. These preeminently liberal acts will never be sufficiently admired for the sincerity by which they are inspired. The first Congress of Venezuela has impressed upon the annals of our legislation with indelible characters the majesty of the people, so fittingly expressed in the consummation of the social act best calculated to develop the happiness of a Nation.

I need to gather all my strength in order to feel with all the reverence of which I am capable, the supreme goodness embodied in this immortal Code of our rights and our laws! But how can I venture to say it! Shall I dare profane by my censure the sacred tablets of our laws? There are sentiments that no lover of liberty can hold within his breast; they overflow stirred by their own violence, and notwithstanding the efforts of the one harboring such sentiments, an irresistible force will disclose them. I am convinced that the Government of Venezuela must be changed, and while many illustrious citizens will feel as I do, not all possess the necessary boldness to stand publicly for the adoption of new principles. This consideration compels me to take the initiative in a matter of the gravest concern, although there is great audacity in my pretending to give advice to the Counsellors of the People.

The more I admire the excellence of the Federal Constitution of Venezuela, the more I am persuaded of the impossibility of its application in our State. And, in my opinion, it is a wonder that its model in North America may endure so successfully, and is not upset in the presence of the first trouble or danger. Notwithstanding the fact that that people is a unique model of political virtues and moral education; notwithstanding that it has been a cradle of liberty, that it has been reared in freedom and lives on pure liberty, I will say more, although in many respects that people is unique in the history of humanity, it is a prodigy, I repeat, that a system so weak and complicated as the federal system should have served to govern that people in circumstances as difficult and delicate as those which have existed. But, whatever the case may be, as regards the American Nation, I must say that nothing is further from my mind than to try to assimilate the conditions and character of two nations as different as the Anglo-American and the Spanish-American. Would it not be extremely difficult to apply to Spain the Code of political, civil and religious liberty of England? It would be even more difficult to adapt to Venezuela the laws of North America. Does not *The Spirit of the Laws*[1] state that they must be suited to the people for whom they are made; that it is a great coincidence when the laws of one nation suit another; that the laws must bear relation to the physical features of a country, its climate, its soil, its situation, extension and manner of living of the people; that they must have reference to the degree of liberty that their constitution may be able to provide for the religion of the inhabitants, their inclinations, wealth, number, trade, customs and manners? Such is the Code that we should consult, not that of Washington!

•　•　•

Note

[1] Montesquieu's *The Spirit of the Laws* (1748), which offers analyses of forms of government, separation of powers, and the effect of regionalism on politics.

Alexis de Tocqueville

1805–1859

French politician, historian, and political philosopher, Alexis de Tocqueville was born into an aristocratic family. His father supported the restored monarchy following the fall of Napoleon. Typical of the aristocratic class of his day, Tocqueville sought a career in politics and studied law. He did not, however, share the conservative royalist sympathies of his family. Rather, he was fascinated by and favored (in theory) the liberalism proposed by the Enlightenment. For young European aristocrats, liberty, equality, and fraternity were intellectual abstractions whose application during the French Revolution and under Napoleon had been uneven and violent. Wanting to see the modern experiment of these principles at play elsewhere, Tocqueville turned toward North America, specifically the United States.

In May 1831 he arrived in New York City with his colleague Gustave de Beaumont. They had received a commission from the French government for their study, *On the Penitentiary System in the United States and Its Application in France* (1833). In nine months they traveled all over the country: they reached the "frontier" region of the Great Lakes after visiting Buffalo (and spent two weeks in French Canada, seeing Montreal). From Boston, they visited Baltimore, Philadelphia, Cincinnati, Louisville, Nashville, Memphis and New Orleans—much of this travel by river. From New Orleans they went by stagecoach to Washington D.C., then back to New York City. They left the United States in February 1832. Their investigation of the penal system did not interfere with Tocqueville's primary task: a first-hand experience of the democratic version of the Enlightenment presented by America—in all of its aspects, regions, and ways of life: urban, rural, and frontier. His experiences, and analyses of them, resulted in the work he is known for today, the two-volume *Democracy in America* (1835–1840).

In volume two of *Democracy in America*, from which our excerpts are taken, Tocqueville describes the democratic culture he found in the United States. To him it is a culture full of paradox: Americans are astonishing in their determination and energy regarding the pursuit of personal achievement. Nevertheless, *what* they hope to achieve and *how* they do it are remarkably similar. In fact, Americans are often conformists. "Equality" is based on a dominant standard of personal worth, material wealth. This standard "equalizes" at a narrow intellectual level all those willing to participate, or simply

236

buys participation (e.g., slaves), or marginalizes everyone else (e.g., Indians). Indeed, "individualism" really seems to mean "independence" in economic pursuits. "Liberty" is freedom for personal accumulation. This goal isolates individuals as it encourages innovation to beat the competition. All other interests—religious affiliation, education, political preference—are filtered via the lens of the monetary. In the name of equality and liberty, materialism is the winner.

Alexis de Tocqueville wrote *Democracy in America* over 160 years ago. Is he describing today? What resources does a democratic culture have that can foster alternative notions of individuality and freedom? Can equality and liberty be otherwise defined? Should they be?

from *Democracy in America* (1835–1840)

Second Book
Influence of Democracy on the Feelings of the Americans

Chapter I
Why Democratic Nations Show a More Ardent and
Enduring Love of Equality than of Liberty

The first and most intense passion which is engendered by the equality of conditions is, I need hardly say, the love of that same equality. My readers will therefore not be surprised that I speak of it before all others. Everybody has remarked that in our time, and especially in France, this passion for equality is every day gaining ground in the human heart. It has been said a hundred times that our contemporaries are far more ardently and tenaciously attached to equality than to freedom; but as I do not find that the causes of the fact have been sufficiently analyzed, I shall endeavor to point them out.

It is possible to imagine an extreme point at which freedom and equality would meet and be confounded together. Let us suppose that all the members of the community take a part in the government, and that each one of them has an equal right to take a part in it. As none is different from his fellows, none can exercise a tyrannical power: men will be perfectly free, because they will all be entirely equal; and they will all be perfectly equal, because they will be entirely free. To this ideal state democratic nations tend. Such is the completest form that equality can assume upon earth; but there are a thousand others which, without being equally perfect, are not less cherished by those nations.

The principle of equality may be established in civil society, without prevailing in the political world. Equal rights may exist of indulging in the same pleasures, of entering the same professions, of frequenting the same places—in a word, of living in the same manner and seeking wealth by the same means, although all men do not take an equal share in the government. A kind of equality may even be established in the political world, though there should be no political freedom there. A man may be the equal of all his countrymen save one, who is the master of all without distinction, and who selects equally from among them all the agents of his power. Several other combinations might be easily imagined, by which very great equality would be united to institutions more or less free, or even to institutions wholly without freedom. Although men cannot become absolutely equal unless they be entirely free, and consequently equality, pushed to its furthest extent, may be confounded with freedom, yet there is good reason for distinguishing the one from the other. The taste which men have for liberty, and that which they feel for equality, are, in fact, two different things; and I am not afraid to add that, amongst democratic nations, they are two unequal things.

Upon close inspection, it will be seen that there is in every age some peculiar and preponderating fact with which all others are connected; this fact almost always gives birth to some pregnant idea or some ruling passion, which attracts to itself, and bears away in its course, all the feelings and opinions of the time: it is like a great stream, towards which each of the surrounding rivulets seems to flow. Freedom has appeared in the world at different times and under various forms; it has not been exclusively bound to any social condition, and it is not confined to democracies. Freedom cannot, therefore, form the distinguishing characteristic of democratic ages. The peculiar and preponderating fact which marks those ages as its own is the equality of conditions; the ruling passion of men in those periods is the love of this equality. Ask not what singular charm the men of democratic ages find in being equal, or what special reasons they may have for clinging so tenaciously to equality rather than to the other advantages which society holds out to them: equality is the distinguishing characteristic of the age they live in; that, of itself, is enough to explain that they prefer it to all the rest.

But independently of this reason there are several others, which will at all times habitually lead men to prefer equality to freedom. If a people could ever succeed in destroying, or even in diminishing, the equality which prevails in its own body, this could only be accomplished by long and laborious efforts. Its social condition must be modified, its laws abolished, its opinions superseded, its habits changed, its manners corrupted. But political liberty is more easily lost; to neglect to hold it fast is to allow it to escape. Men therefore not only cling to equality because it is dear to them; they also adhere to it because they think it will last forever.

That political freedom may compromise in its excesses the tranquillity, the property, the lives of individuals, is obvious to the narrowest and most unthinking minds. But, on the contrary, none but attentive and clear-sighted men perceive the perils with which equality threatens us, and they commonly avoid pointing them out. They know that the calamities they apprehend are remote, and flatter themselves that they will only fall upon future generations, for which the present generation takes but little thought. The evils which freedom sometimes brings with it are immediate; they are apparent to all, and all are more or less affected by them. The evils which extreme equality may produce are slowly disclosed; they creep gradually into the social frame; they are only seen at intervals, and at the moment at which they become most violent habit already causes them to be no longer felt. The advantages which freedom brings are only shown by length of time; and it is always easy to mistake the cause in which they originate. The advantages of equality are instantaneous, and they may constantly be traced from their source. Political liberty bestows exalted pleasures, from time to time, upon a certain number of citizens. Equality every day confers a number of small enjoyments on every man. The charms of equality are every instant felt, and are within the reach of all; the noblest hearts are not insensible to them, and the most vulgar souls exult in them. The passion which equality engenders must therefore be at once strong and general. Men cannot enjoy political liberty unpurchased by some sacrifices, and they never obtain it without great exertions. But the pleasures of equality are self-proffered: each of the petty incidents of life seems to occasion them, and in order to taste them nothing is required but to live.

Democratic nations are at all times fond of equality, but there are certain epochs at which the passion they entertain for it swells to the height of fury. This occurs at the moment when the old social system, long menaced, completes its own destruction after a last intestine struggle, and when the barriers of rank are at length thrown down. At such times men pounce upon equality as their booty, and they cling to it as to some precious treasure which they fear to lose. The passion for equality penetrates on every side into men's hearts, expands there, and fills them entirely. Tell them not that by this blind surrender of themselves to an exclusive passion they risk their dearest interests: they are deaf. Show them not freedom escaping from their grasp, whilst they are looking another way: they are blind—or rather, they can discern but one sole object to be desired in the universe.

What I have said is applicable to all democratic nations: what I am about to say concerns the French alone. Amongst most modern nations, and especially amongst all those of the Continent of Europe, the taste and the idea of freedom only began to exist and to extend themselves at the time when social conditions were tending to equality, and as a consequence of that very equality. Absolute kings were the most efficient levellers of ranks amongst their subjects. Amongst these nations equality preceded freedom: equality was therefore a fact of some standing when freedom was still a novelty: the one had already created customs, opinions, and laws belonging to it, when the other, alone and for the first time, came into actual existence. Thus the latter was still only an affair of opinion and of taste, whilst the former had already crept into the habits of the people, possessed itself of their manners, and given a particular turn to the smallest actions of their lives. Can it be wondered that the men of our own time prefer the one to the other?

I think that democratic communities have a natural taste for freedom: left to themselves, they will seek it, cherish it, and view any privation of it with regret. But for equality, their passion is ardent, insatiable, incessant, invincible: they call for equality in freedom; and if they cannot obtain that, they still call for equality in slavery. They will endure poverty, servitude, barbarism—but they will not endure aristocracy. This is true at all times, and especially true in our own. All men and all powers seeking to cope with this irresistible passion, will be overthrown and destroyed by it. In our age, freedom cannot be established without it, and despotism itself cannot reign without its support.

Chapter II
Of Individualism in Democratic Countries

I have shown how it is that in ages of equality every man seeks for his opinions within himself: I am now about to show how it is that, in the same ages, all his feelings are turned towards himself alone. Individualism[1] is a novel expression, to which a novel idea has given birth. Our fathers were only acquainted with egotism. Egotism is a passionate and exaggerated love of self, which leads a man to connect everything with his own person, and to prefer himself to everything in the world. Individualism is a mature and calm feeling, which disposes each member of the community to sever himself from the mass of his fellow-creatures; and to draw apart with his family and his friends; so that, after he has thus formed a little circle of his own, he willingly leaves society at large to itself. Egotism originates in blind instinct: individualism proceeds from erroneous judgment more than from depraved feelings; it originates as much in the deficiencies of the mind as in the perversity of the heart. Egotism blights the germ of all virtue; individualism, at first, only saps the virtues of public life; but, in the long run, it attacks and destroys all others, and is at length absorbed in downright egotism. Egotism is a vice as old as the world, which does not belong to one form of society more than to another: individualism is of democratic origin, and it threatens to spread in the same ratio as the equality of conditions.

Amongst aristocratic nations, as families remain for centuries in the same condition, often on the same spot, all generations become as it were contemporaneous. A man almost always knows his forefathers, and respects them: he thinks he already sees his remote descendants, and he loves them. He willingly imposes duties on himself towards the former and the latter; and he will frequently sacrifice his personal gratifications to those who went before and to those who will come after him. Aristocratic institutions have, moreover, the effect of closely binding every man to several of his fellow-citizens. As the classes of an aristocratic people are strongly marked and permanent, each of them is regarded by its own members as a sort of lesser country, more tangible and more cherished than the country at large. As in aristocratic communities all the citizens occupy fixed positions, one above the other, the result is that each of them always sees a man above himself whose patronage is necessary to him, and below himself another man whose co-operation he may claim. Men living in aristocratic ages are therefore almost always closely attached to something placed out of their own sphere, and they are often disposed to forget themselves. It is true that in those ages the notion of human fellowship is faint, and that men seldom think of sacrificing themselves for mankind; but they often sacrifice themselves for other men. In democratic ages, on the contrary, when the duties of each individual to the race are much more clear, devoted service to any one man becomes more rare; the bond of human affection is extended, but it is relaxed.

Amongst democratic nations new families are constantly springing up, others are constantly falling away, and all that remain change their condition; the woof of time is every instant broken, and the track of generations effaced. Those who went before are soon forgotten; of those who will come after no one has any idea: the interest of man is confined to those in close propinquity to himself. As each class approximates to other classes, and intermingles with them, its members become indifferent and as strangers to one another. Aristocracy had made a chain of all the members of the community, from the peasant to the king: democracy breaks that chain, and severs every link of it. As social conditions become more equal, the number of persons increases who, although they are neither rich enough nor powerful enough to exercise any great influence over their fellow-creatures, have nevertheless acquired or retained sufficient education and fortune to satisfy their own wants. They owe nothing to any man, they expect nothing from any man; they acquire the habit of always considering themselves as standing alone, and they are apt to imagine that their whole destiny is in their own hands. Thus not only does democracy make every man forget his ancestors, but it hides his descendants, and separates his contemporaries from him; it throws him back forever upon himself alone, and threatens in the end to confine him entirely within the solitude of his own heart.

Chapter XIII
Causes of the Restless Spirit of the Americans in the Midst of Their Prosperity

In certain remote corners of the Old World you may still sometimes stumble upon a small district which seems to have been forgotten amidst the general tumult, and to have remained stationary whilst everything around it was in motion. The inhabitants are for the most part extremely ignorant and poor; they take no part in the business of the country, and they are frequently oppressed by the government; yet their countenances are generally placid, and their spirits light. In America I saw the freest and most enlightened men, placed in the happiest circumstances which the world affords: it seemed to me as if a cloud habitually hung upon their brow, and I thought them serious and almost sad even in their pleasures. The chief reason of this contrast is that the former do not think of the ills they endure—the latter are forever brooding over advantages they do not possess. It is strange to see with what feverish ardor the Americans pursue their own welfare; and to watch the vague dread that constantly torments them lest they should not have chosen the shortest path which may lead to it. A native of the United States clings to this world's goods as if he were certain never to die; and he is so hasty in grasping at all within his reach, that one would suppose he was constantly afraid of not living long enough to enjoy them. He clutches everything, he holds nothing fast, but soon loosens his grasp to pursue fresh gratifications.

In the United States a man builds a house to spend his latter years in it, and he sells it before the roof is on: he plants a garden, and lets it just as the trees are coming into bearing: he brings a field into tillage, and leaves other men to gather the crops: he embraces a profession, and gives it up: he settles in a place, which he soon afterwards leaves, to carry his changeable longings elsewhere. If his private affairs leave him any leisure, he instantly plunges into the vortex of politics; and if at the end of a year of unremitting labor he finds he has a few days' vacation, his eager curiosity whirls him over the vast extent of the United States, and he will travel fifteen hundred miles in a few days, to shake off his happiness. Death at length overtakes him, but it is before he is weary of his bootless chase of that complete felicity which is forever on the wing.

At first sight there is something surprising in this strange unrest of so many happy men, restless in the midst of abundance. The spectacle itself is however as old as the world; the novelty is to see a whole people furnish an exemplification of it. Their taste for physical gratifications must be regarded as the original source of that secret inquietude which the actions of the Americans betray, and of that inconstancy of which they afford fresh examples every day. He who has set his heart exclusively upon the pursuit of worldly welfare is always in a hurry, for he has but a limited time at his disposal to reach it, to grasp it, and to enjoy it. The recollection of the brevity of life is a constant spur to him. Besides the good things which he possesses, he every instant fancies a thousand others which death will prevent him from trying if he does not try them soon. This thought fills him with anxiety, fear, and regret, and keeps his mind in ceaseless trepidation, which leads him perpetually to change his plans and his abode. If in addition to the taste for physical well-being a

social condition be superadded, in which the laws and customs make no condition permanent, here is a great additional stimulant to this restlessness of
temper. Men will then be seen continually to change their track, for fear of
missing the shortest cut to happiness. It may readily be conceived that if men,
passionately bent upon physical gratifications, desire eagerly, they are also easily discouraged: as their ultimate object is to enjoy, the means to reach that
object must be prompt and easy, or the trouble of acquiring the gratification
would be greater than the gratification itself. Their prevailing frame of mind
then is at once ardent and relaxed, violent and enervated. Death is often less
dreaded than perseverance in continuous efforts to one end.

The equality of conditions leads by a still straighter road to several of the
effects which I have here described. When all the privileges of birth and fortune
are abolished, when all professions are accessible to all, and a man's own energies may place him at the top of any one of them, an easy and unbounded career
seems open to his ambition, and he will readily persuade himself that he is born
to no vulgar destinies. But this is an erroneous notion, which is corrected by
daily experience. The same equality which allows every citizen to conceive these
lofty hopes, renders all the citizens less able to realize them: it circumscribes
their powers on every side, whilst it gives freer scope to their desires. Not only
are they themselves powerless, but they are met at every step by immense obstacles, which they did not at first perceive. They have swept away the privileges of
some of their fellow-creatures which stood in their way, but they have opened
the door to universal competition: the barrier has changed its shape rather than
its position. When men are nearly alike, and all follow the same track, it is very
difficult for any one individual to walk quick and cleave a way through the
dense throng which surrounds and presses him. This constant strife between the
propensities springing from the equality of conditions and the means it supplies
to satisfy them, harasses and wearies the mind.

It is possible to conceive men arrived at a degree of freedom which should
completely content them; they would then enjoy their independence without
anxiety and without impatience. But men will never establish any equality
with which they can be contented. Whatever efforts a people may make, they
will never succeed in reducing all the conditions of society to a perfect level;
and even if they unhappily attained that absolute and complete depression, the
inequality of minds would still remain, which, coming directly from the hand
of God, will forever escape the laws of man. However democratic then the
social state and the political constitution of a people may be, it is certain that
every member of the community will always find out several points about him
which command his own position; and we may foresee that his looks will be
doggedly fixed in that direction. When inequality of conditions is the common
law of society, the most marked inequalities do not strike the eye: when every-

thing is nearly on the same level, the slightest are marked enough to hurt it. Hence the desire of equality always becomes more insatiable in proportion as equality is more complete.

Amongst democratic nations men easily attain a certain equality of conditions: they can never attain the equality they desire. It perpetually retires from before them, yet without hiding itself from their sight, and in retiring draws them on. At every moment they think they are about to grasp it; it escapes at every moment from their hold. They are near enough to see its charms, but too far off to enjoy them; and before they have fully tasted its delights they die. To these causes must be attributed that strange melancholy which oftentimes will haunt the inhabitants of democratic countries in the midst of their abundance, and that disgust at life which sometimes seizes upon them in the midst of calm and easy circumstances. Complaints are made in France that the number of suicides increases; in America suicide is rare, but insanity is said to be more common than anywhere else. These are all different symptoms of the same disease. The Americans do not put an end to their lives, however disquieted they may be, because their religion forbids it; and amongst them materialism may be said hardly to exist, notwithstanding the general passion for physical gratification. The will resists—reason frequently gives way.

In democratic ages enjoyments are more intense than in the ages of aristocracy, and especially the number of those who partake in them is larger: but, on the other hand, it must be admitted that man's hopes and his desires are oftener blasted, the soul is more stricken and perturbed, and care itself more keen.

Note

[1] [I adopt the expression of the original, however strange it may seem to the English ear, partly because it illustrates the remark on the introduction of general terms into democratic language which was made in a preceding chapter, and partly because I know of no English word exactly equivalent to the expression. The chapter itself defines the meaning attached to it by the author.—*Translator's Note.*]

Women Miners in England

Industrialization is the *sine qua non* of the Modern World, altering relations between individuals and communities, between the West and the rest of the World, and between humankind and nature. Commentators in the nineteenth and twentieth centuries have pondered the effects, good or ill, of the industrial revolution as it moved out from England, first to North America in the West and to France and Germany in the East. From Europe, industrialization has continued to spread throughout most of the world.

Wherever industrialization has occurred, men, women, and children have all borne its hardships. While nineteenth-century reformers and critics such as Marx analyzed the effects of industrial work on all workers, some commentators directed their attention to the exploitation of women and children, appealing to the reading public's belief that a man's dependents should be protected in the family home. The way of life of the industrial working class would sharply conflict with middle-class mores.

Women and children were desirable laborers because they could be paid less and because their smaller bodies and nimbler fingers enabled them to squeeze into tight spaces. This was especially true in the mines. Parliamentary reports, a product of citizen agitation, galvanized British opinion and would eventually lead to an improvement in working conditions. In the following example, the plight of women working in England's coal mines is graphically told in their own words as well as those of the investigators. Rarely do we have an opportunity to hear the voices of the illiterate. In what ways is the discourse of the women miners effective? Ineffective? How do their middle-class interlocutors shape that discourse? What might be the long-term social consequences of these working conditions on large numbers of women and children?

Women Miners in the English Coal Pits
Parliamentary Papers of Great Britain (1842)

In England, exclusive of Wales, it is only in some of the colliery districts of Yorkshire and Lancashire that female Children of tender age and young and adult women are allowed to descend into the coal mines and regularly to perform the same kinds of underground work, and to work for the same number of hours, as boys and men; but in the East of Scotland their employment in the pits is general; and in South Wales it is not uncommon.

West Riding of Yorkshire: Southern Part. (In many of the collieries in this district, as far as relates to the underground employment, there is no distinction of sex, but the labour is distributed indifferently among both sexes, except that it is comparatively rare for the women to hew or get the coals, although there are numerous instances in which they regularly perform even this work. In great numbers of the coalpits in this district the men work in a state of perfect nakedness, and are in this state assisted in their labour by females of all ages, from girls of six years old to women of twenty-one, these females being themselves quite naked down to the waist.

"Girls," says the Sub-Commissioner [J. C. Symons], "regularly perform all the various offices of trapping, hurrying [Yorkshire terms for drawing the loaded coal corves[1]], filling, riddling, tipping, and occasionally getting, just as they are performed by boys. One of the most disgusting sights I have ever seen was that of young females, dressed like boys in trousers, crawling on all fours, with belts round their waists and chains passing between their legs, at day pits at Hunshelf Bank, and in many small pits near Holmfirth and New Mills: it exists also in several other places. I visited the Hunshelf Colliery on the 18th of January: it is a day pit; that is, there is no shaft or descent; the gate or entrance is at the side of a bank, and nearly horizontal. The gate was not more than a yard high, and in some places not above 2 feet.

"When I arrived at the board or workings of the pit I found at one of the sideboards down a narrow passage a girl of fourteen years of age in boy's clothes, picking down the coal with the regular pick used by the men. She was half sitting half lying at her work, and said she found it tired her very much, and 'of course she didn't like it.' The place where she was at work was not 2 feet high. Further on were men lying on their sides and getting. No less than six girls out of eighteen men and children are employed in this pit.

"Whilst I was in the pit the Rev Mr Bruce, of Wadsley, and the Rev Mr Nelson, of Rotherham, who accompanied me, and remained outside, saw another girl of ten years of age, also dressed in boy's clothes, who was employed in hurrying, and these gentlemen saw her at work. She was a nice-looking little child, but of course as black as a tinker, and with a little necklace round her throat.

"In two other pits in the Huddersfield Union I have seen the same sight. In one near New Mills, the chain, passing high up between the legs of two of these girls, had worn large holes in their trousers; and any sight more disgustingly indecent or revolting can scarcely be imagined than these girls at work—no brothel can beat it.

"On descending Messrs Hopwood's pit at Barnsley, I found assembled round a fire a group of men, boys, and girls, some of whom were of the age of puberty; the girls as well as the boys stark naked down to the waist, their hair bound up with a tight cap, and trousers supported by their hips. (At Silkstone and at Flockton they work in their shifts and trousers.) Their sex was recognizable only by their breasts, and some little difficulty occasionally arose in pointing out to me which were girls and which were boys, and which caused a good deal of laughing and joking. In the Flockton and Thornhill pits the system is even more indecent; for though the girls are clothed, at least three-fourths of the men for whom they "hurry" work *stark naked*, or with a flannel waistcoat only, and in this state they assist one another to fill the corves 18 or 20 times a day: I have seen this done myself frequently.

"When it is remembered that these girls hurry chiefly for men who are not their parents; that they go from 15 to 20 times a day into a dark chamber (the bank face), which is often 50 yards apart from any one, to a man working naked, or next to naked, it is not to be supposed but that where opportunity thus prevails sexual vices are of common occurrence. Add to this the free intercourse, and the rendezvous at the shaft or bullstake, where the corves are brought, and consider the language to which the young ear is habituated, the absence of religious instruction, and the early age at which contamination begins, and you will have before you, in the coal-pits where females are employed, the picture of a nursery for juvenile vice which you will go far and wide above ground to equal."

Two Women Miners

Betty Harris, age 37: I was married at 23, and went into a colliery when I was married. I used to weave when about 12 years old; can neither read nor write. I work for Andrew Knowles, of Little Bolton (Lancs.), and make sometimes 7s a week, sometimes not so much. I am a drawer, and work from 6 in the morning to 6 at night. Stop about an hour at noon to eat my dinner; have bread and butter for dinner; I get no drink. I have two children, but they are too young to work. I worked at drawing when I was in the family way. I know a woman who has gone home and washed herself, taken to her bed, been delivered of a child, and gone to work again under the week.

I have a belt round my waist, and a chain passing between my legs, and I go on my hands and feet. The road is very steep, and we have to hold by a rope; and when there is no rope, by anything we can catch hold of. There are six women and about six boys and girls in the pit I work in; it is very hard work for a woman. The pit is very wet where I work, and the water comes over our clog-tops always, and I have seen it up to my thighs; it rains in at the roof terribly. My clothes are wet through almost all day long. I never was ill in my life, but when I was lying in.

My cousin looks after my children in the day time. I am very tired when I get home at night; I fall asleep sometimes before I get washed. I am not so strong as I was, and cannot stand my work so well as I used to. I have drawn till I have had the skin off me; the belt and chain is worse when we are in the family way. My feller (husband) has beaten me many a time for not being ready. I were not used to it at first, and he had little patience.

I have known many a man beat his drawer. I have known men take liberties with the drawers, and some of the women have bastards.

Patience Kershaw, age 17, Halifax: I go to pit at 5 o'clock in the morning and come out at 5 in the evening; I get my breakfast, porridge and milk, first; I take my dinner with me, a cake, and eat it as I go; I do not stop or rest at any time for the purpose, I get nothing else until I get home, and then have potatoes and meat, not every day meat.

I hurry in the clothes I have now got on—trousers and a ragged jacket; the bald place upon my head is made by thrusting the corves; I hurry the corves a mile and more under ground and back; they weigh 3 cwt. I hurry eleven a day. I wear a belt and chain at the workings to get the corves out. The getters that I work for are naked except their caps; they pull off all their clothes; I see them at work when I go up.

Sometimes they beat me if I am not quick enough, with their hands; they strike me upon my back. The boys take liberties with me sometimes; they pull me about. I am the only girl in the pit; there are about 20 boys and 15 men; all the men are naked. I would rather work in mill than in coal-pit.

Note by Sub-Commissioner Scriven: This girl is an ignorant, filthy, ragged, and deplorable looking object, and such a one as the uncivilized natives of the prairies would be shocked to look upon.

Note

[1] Baskets to carry the hewn coal.

Flora Tristan

1803–1844

Flora Tristan was born of a French woman and her Peruvian noble lover. Her lifelong concern for the plight of poor women no doubt derived in part from her personal experience of poverty and illegitimacy. She not only published works meant to inspire women workers to organize; she also toured France making speeches and helping women form their own unions.

Tristan's ideas influenced Marx and Engels. Long before them, she called for a universal union of male and female workers. However, she specifically addressed the problems of women workers and believed that organizing them, *as workers*, was only half the battle. She argued for women's rights, and thus adds a powerful working class voice to the bourgeois women's rights discourse taking shape in France and elsewhere in the middle of the nineteenth century.

In this excerpt, Tristan specifically tackles the interlocking problems of class and gender, thus bridging the socialist analysis of Marx and the liberal analysis of Mill. She attempts to appeal to men workers, reminding them of the centrality of women in their lives, and reminding us that socialist women voiced a powerful counter-narrative to the prevailing ideology of bourgeois liberalism. In her tone as well, she is far more Romantic than Enlightenment: identify instances of this. How does she, despite her working-class socialism, reinforce ideas of middle-class domesticity? In what ways does she challenge it? How will rights for all women, regardless of class, create greater harmony in the home and in society?

from *The Female Worker's Union* (1843)

Woman is everything in the life of the worker: as mother she an influence over him during his childhood, it is from her and her alone that he learns the first notions of the science of life, so important to master because it teaches us to live decently for ourselves and for others in whatever walk of life fate has placed us. As lover she has an influence over him during his youth, and what powerful influence has a beautiful girl who is loved! As wife she has an influence on three-quarters of his life, and finally, as daughter she has an influence on his old age.

You will observe that the workers' position is quite different from that of the rich. If a rich child's mother is incapable of raising him, he is sent to a boarding school or given a governess. If a rich young man has no mistress, he can study art or science to keep his heart and imagination occupied. If a rich man has no wife, he will easily find pleasures in society. If a rich old man has no daughter, he can find some old friends or young nephews who will gladly come and play cards with him. Whereas the worker, to whom all these advantages are denied, has only the company of the women of his family—his fellow sufferers—for his sole joy and comfort.

As a result it is imperative, in order to improve the intellectual, moral, and material condition of the working class, that women of the lower classes be given a rational and solid education, conducive to the development of their good inclinations, so that they may become skillful workers, good mothers capable of raising and guiding their children, and of tutoring them in their school work, and so that they may also act as moralizing agents in the life of the men on whom they exert an influence from the cradle to the grave.

Do you begin to understand, you, men, who cry shame before even looking into the question, why I demand rights for woman? Why I should like her to be placed on a footing of absolute equality with man in society, and that she should be so by virtue of the legal right every human being brings at birth?

I demand rights for women because I am convinced that all the misfortunes in the world result from the neglect and contempt in which woman's natural and inalienable rights have so far been held. I demand rights for woman because it is the only way she will get an education, and because the education of man in general and man of the lower classes in particular depends on the education of woman. I demand rights for woman because it is the only way to obtain her rehabilitation in the Church, the law, and society, and because this preliminary rehabilitation is necessary to achieve the rehabilitation of the workers themselves. All the woes of the working class can be summed up in these two words: poverty and ignorance, ignorance and poverty. Now, I see only one way out of this labyrinth: begin by educating women, because women have the responsibility for educating male and female children.

Workers, the way things stand now, you know what is going on in your homes. You, man—the master—with rights over your wife, do you like living with her? Tell me: are you happy? No, no, it is easy to see that despite your rights you are neither content nor happy. Between master and slave there can be nothing but the weariness caused by the weight of the chain that binds them together. Whenever freedom is lacking there can be no happiness.

Men keep on complaining about the surliness, the sly and underhandedly mean character that woman reveals in nearly all her relationships. Oh, I would indeed have a very poor opinion of the female race if, in the state of abjection in which the law and customs have maintained them, women submitted to the yoke that weighs upon them without uttering a word. Thank heavens, it is not so; their protest has been continuous since the beginning of time. But since the *Declaration of the Rights of Man*—a solemn act that proclaimed the neglect and contempt of the new men for them—their protest has become vigorous and vehement, which proves that the exasperation of the slave has reached its peak.

Workers, you have good sense and one can reason with you because your minds are not stuffed with a bunch of systems, as Fourier[1] says, would you imagine for a moment that woman is by right the equal of man? Well, what would happen?

As soon as the dangerous consequences of the development of the moral and physical faculties of women—dangerous because of women's current slave status—are no longer feared, woman can be taught with great care so as to make the best possible use of her intelligence and work. Then, you, men of the lower classes, will have as mothers skillful workers who earn a decent salary, are educated, well brought up, and quite capable of raising you, of educating you, the workers, as is proper for free men. You will have well brought up and well educated sisters, lovers, wives, friends, with whom daily contacts will be most pleasant for you. Nothing is sweeter or more agreeable to a man's heart than the sensible and gracious conversation of good and well educated women.

We have given a brief outline of what takes place currently in workers' households. Let us now see what will take place in these same households when woman is equal to man.

The husband who knows that his wife's rights are equal to his does not treat her with the disdain and scorn that are shown to inferiors; on the contrary, he treats her with the respect and regard due to one's equal. Then, the woman has no more cause for irritation, and once the cause of irritation is removed the woman is no longer brutal, sly, surly, angry, exasperated, or mean. She is no longer considered as the husband's servant in the house, but rather as the man's partner, his friend and companion. She naturally takes an interest in their association and does her best to make the household prosper. Thanks to her practical experience and theoretical knowledge, she runs her house intelligently, economically, and methodically. Because she is well educated and aware of the usefulness of education, her highest ambition is to raise her children well, she lovingly instructs them herself, supervises their school work, and apprentices them to good employers. Finally she guides them in all manner of things with solicitude, affection, and good judgment.

The man, the worker, the husband who has such a wife, enjoys great peace of mind, satisfaction, and happiness. Aware of his wife's intelligence, good sense, and high-mindedness, he is able to discuss important matters with her, communicate his plans, work with her on ways to improve their position. Flattered by his trust, she helps him in his undertakings and business either with good advice or by her activity. The worker, who is himself well educated and well brought up, finds great joy in educating and developing the minds of his children. Workers, in general, are quite warm-hearted and love children.

●　●　●

Workers, I have barely sketched a picture of the life the proletarian class would enjoy if woman were recognized as the equal of man. This should make you think about the existing evil and about the well-being that could exist. It should make you greatly determined.

Workers, you have no power to repeal old laws and make new ones; no, indeed; but you have the power to protest against the inequity and absurdity of laws that hinder the progress of humanity and make you suffer, you in particular. Thus you can—it is even your sacred duty—you can protest strongly with your ideas, your words, and your writings against all the laws that oppress you. Now, be sure you understand this well: the law that enslaves woman and deprives her of an education also oppresses you, proletarian men.

To raise him, educate him, and teach him the science of the world, the son of the rich has learned governesses and teachers, clever head-mistresses, and finally, beautiful marquises, witty and elegant women, whose function consists in educating the youths of the upper class when they leave college. It is a most useful function for the well-being of those gentlemen of the high nobility. The ladies teach them politeness, tact, subtlety, open-mindedness, and good manners; in a word, they make of them men who know how to live, men of good breeding. If a young man shows any ability, if he has the good fortune to be under the protection of one of those lovely ladies, his success is assured. At thirty-five, he is certain to be an ambassador or a minister. Meanwhile, you, poor workers, to raise you, to educate you, you have only your mothers; to make of you men who know how to live, you have only the women of your class, your companions in ignorance and poverty.

Therefore it is not in the name of the superiority of woman (of which I shall no doubt be accused) that I tell you to demand rights for woman; no, indeed. To begin with, woman must be recognized as a full member of society before we can discuss her superiority. I rely on more solid arguments than that. It is in the name of your own interest, men, of your own improvement, men, and lastly, it is in the name of the universal well-being of all men and women that I urge you to demand rights for women and, in the meantime, to acknowledge them yourselves, at least in principle.

Thus, it is up to you, workers, victims of *de facto* inequality and injustice, finally to establish on earth the reign of justice and absolute equality between woman and man. Give a great example to the world, an example that will show your oppressors that you wish to triumph by right and not by brute force; you, the 7, 10, 15 millions of proletarians who could use that brute force.

While demanding justice for yourselves, show that you are just and fair; proclaim—you, the strong men, the men with bare arms—that you recognize woman as your equal, and that, as such, you recognize for her an equal right to the benefits of the UNIVERSAL UNION OF WORKING MEN AND WOMEN.

Note

[1] Charles Fourier (1772–1837), socialist.

Friedrich Engels

1820–1895

Friedrich Engels was born in Barmen, in the Rhineland, Germany's key industrial region in the early nineteenth century. Raised in a wealthy Protestant household, Engels never finished his formal education beyond high school, his father placing him instead in the family textile business. Primarily self-educated, the young Engels read widely and by the time he was nineteen he had begun writing for a number of periodicals. Between 1842 and 1844, Engels made the acquaintance of several Chartist intellectuals, supporters of extending suffrage to workers. By 1844, his studies had persuaded him that economic inequities and the problems arising out of the ownership of private property were the driving forces behind politics and history. In that same year, he wrote and published *The Condition of the Working Class in England*, in which he detailed the suffering occasioned by the development of large-scale industry and resulting urbanization.

Later that same year, Engels traveled to Paris, so that he might meet Karl Marx, who had been publishing on similar topics. From this time on, until Marx's death in 1883, the two political economists worked together, developing the principles of a scientific socialism—now known as communism—that they felt would address the oppressive conditions faced by the working poor. In 1848, the year of workers' revolutions across most of Europe, Engels and Marx collaborated on *The Communist Manifesto*, the classic articulation of the communist agenda. After the failure of the revolutions of 1848, Engels worked at a Manchester textile mill and was the primary financial support of the Marx family. He retired from the mill in 1869 and moved to London, where he employed himself by directing the operations of the General Council of the International Workingmen's Association.

In the selection below, consider Engels's description of the alienation and brutality engendered by industrialization and the flow of workers into the cities of England. In what ways does Engels capture the fundamental nature of the modern experience? Is the atomization he observes in the London of 1844 the inevitable result of modernization?

See p. 534 for accompanying map.

from *Condition of the Working Class in England in 1844*

The Great Towns

A town, such as London, where a man may wander for hours together without reaching the beginning of the end, without meeting the slightest hint which could lead to the inference that there is open country within reach, is a strange thing. This colossal centralization, this heaping together of two and a half millions of human beings at one point, has multiplied the power of this two and a half millions a hundredfold; has raised London to the commercial capital of the world, created the giant docks and assembled the thousand vessels that continually cover the Thames. I know nothing more imposing than the view which the Thames offers during the ascent from the sea to London Bridge. The masses of buildings, the wharves on both sides, especially from Woolwich upwards, the countless ships along both shores, crowding ever closer and closer together, until, at last, only a narrow passage remains in the middle of the river, a passage through which hundreds of steamers shoot by one another; all this is so vast, so impressive, that a man cannot collect himself, but is lost in the marvel of England's greatness before he sets foot upon English soil.

But the sacrifices which all this has cost become apparent later. After roaming the streets of the capital a day or two, making headway with difficulty through the human turmoil and the endless lines of vehicles, after visiting the slums of the metropolis, one realizes for the first time that these Londoners have been forced to sacrifice the best qualities of their human nature, to bring to pass all the marvels of civilization which crowd their city; that a hundred powers which slumbered within them have remained inactive, have been suppressed in order that a few might be developed more fully and multiply through union with those of others. The very turmoil of the streets has something repulsive, something against which human nature rebels. The hundreds of thousands of all classes and ranks crowding past each other, are they not all human beings with the same qualities and powers, and with the same interest in being happy? And have they not, in the end, to seek happiness in the same way, by the same means? And still they crowd by one another as though they had nothing in common, nothing to do with one another, and their only agreement is the tacit one, that each keep to his own side of the pavement, so as not to delay the opposing streams of the crowd, while it occurs to no man to honour another with so much as a glance. The brutal indifference, the unfeeling isolation of each in his private interest becomes the more repellent and offensive, the more these individuals are crowded together, within a limited space. And, however much one may be aware that this isolation of the individual, this narrow self-seeking, is the fundamental principle of our society everywhere, it is nowhere so shamelessly barefaced, so self-conscious as just here in the crowding of the great city. The dissolution of mankind into monads, of which each one has a separate essence, and a separate purpose, the world of atoms, is here carried out to its utmost extreme.

Hence it comes, too, that the social war, the war of each against all, is here openly declared. Just as in Stirner's recent book,[1] people regard each other only as useful objects; each exploits the other, and the end of it all is, that the stronger treads the weaker under foot, and that the powerful few, the capitalists, seize everything for themselves, while to the weak many, the poor, scarcely a bare existence remains.

What is true of London, is true of Manchester, Birmingham, Leeds, is true of all great towns. Everywhere barbarous indifference, hard egotism on one hand, and nameless misery on the other, everywhere social warfare, every man's house in a state of siege, everywhere reciprocal plundering under the protection of the law, and all so shameless, so openly avowed that one shrinks before the consequences of our social state as they manifest themselves here undisguised, and can only wonder that the whole crazy fabric still hangs together.

Since capital, the direct or indirect control of the means of subsistence and production, is the weapon with which this social warfare is carried on, it is clear that all the disadvantages of such a state must fall upon the poor man. For him no one has the slightest concern. Cast into the whirlpool, he must struggle through as well as he can. If he is so happy as to find work, i.e. if the bourgeoisie does him the favour to enrich itself by means of him, wages await him which scarcely suffice to keep body and soul together; if he can get no work he may steal, if he is not afraid of the police, or starve, in which case the police will take care that he does so in a quiet and inoffensive manner. During my residence in England, at least twenty or thirty persons have died of simple starvation under the most revolting circumstances, and a jury has rarely been found possessed of the courage to speak the plain truth in the matter. Let the testimony of the witnesses be never so clear and unequivocal, the bourgeoisie, from which the jury is selected, always finds some back-door through which to escape the frightful verdict, death from starvation. The bourgeoisie dare not speak the truth in these cases, for it would speak its own condemnation. But indirectly, far more than directly, many have died of starvation, where long-continued want of proper nourishment has called forth fatal illness, when it has produced such debility that causes which might otherwise have remained inoperative brought on severe illness and death. The English working men call this 'social murder', and accuse our whole society of perpetrating this crime perpetually. Are they wrong?

True, it is only individuals who starve, but what security has the working man that it may not be his turn tomorrow? Who assures him employment, who vouches for it that, if for any reason or no reason his lord and master discharges him tomorrow, he can struggle along with those dependent upon him, until he may find some one else 'to give him bread'? Who guarantees that willingness to work shall suffice to obtain work, that uprightness, industry, thrift, and the rest of the virtues recommended by the bourgeoisie, are really his road to happiness? No one. He knows that he has something today, and that it does not depend upon himself whether he shall have something tomorrow. He knows that every breeze that blows, every whim of his employer, every bad turn of trade may hurl him back into the fierce whirlpool from which he has temporarily saved himself, and in which it is hard and often impossible to keep his head above water. He knows that, though he may have the means of living today, it is very uncertain whether he shall tomorrow.

• • •

Every great city has one or more slums, where the working class is crowded together. True, poverty often dwells in hidden alleys close to the palaces of the rich; but, in general, a separate territory has been assigned to it, where, removed from the sight of the happier classes, it may struggle along as it can. These slums are pretty equally arranged in all the great towns of England, the worst houses in the worst quarters of the towns; usually one or two-storied cottages in long rows, perhaps with cellars used as dwellings, almost always irregularly built. These houses of three or four rooms and a kitchen form, throughout England, some parts of London excepted, the general dwellings of the working class. The streets are generally unpaved, rough, dirty, filled with vegetable and animal refuse, without sewers or gutters, but supplied with foul, stagnant pools instead. Moreover, ventilation is impeded by the bad, confused method of building of the whole quarter, and since many human beings here live crowded into a small space, the atmosphere that prevails in these workingmen's quarters may readily be imagined. Further, the streets serve as drying grounds in fine weather; lines are stretched across from house to house, and hung with wet clothing.

Let us investigate some of the slums in their order. London comes first, and in London the famous rookery of St Giles which is now, at last, about to be penetrated by a couple of broad streets. St Giles is in the midst of the most populous part of the town, surrounded by broad, splendid avenues in which the gay world of London idles about, in the immediate neighbourhood of Oxford

Street, Regent Street, of Trafalgar Square and the Strand. It is a disorderly collection of tall, three or four-storied houses, with narrow, crooked, filthy streets, in which there is quite as much life as in the great thoroughfares of the town, except that, here, people of the working class only are to be seen. A vegetable market is held in the street, baskets with vegetables and fruits, naturally all bad and hardly fit to use, obstruct the sidewalk still further, and from these, as well as from the fish-dealers' stalls, arises a horrible smell. The houses are occupied from cellar to garret, filthy within and without, and their appearance is such that no human being could possibly wish to live in them. But all this is nothing in comparison with the dwellings in the narrow courts and alleys between the streets, entered by covered passages between the houses, in which the filth and tottering ruin surpass all description. Scarcely a whole window-pane can be found, the walls are crumbling, door-posts and window-frames loose and broken, doors of old boards nailed together, or altogether wanting in this thieves' quarter, where no doors are needed, there being nothing to steal. Heaps of garbage and ashes lie in all directions, and the foul liquids emptied before the doors gather in stinking pools. Here live the poorest of the poor, the worst paid workers with thieves and the victims of prostitution indiscriminately huddled together, the majority Irish, or of Irish extraction, and those who have not yet sunk in the whirlpool of moral ruin which surrounds them, sinking daily deeper, losing daily more and more of their power to resist the demoralizing influence of want, filth, and evil surroundings.

• • •

But in spite of all this, they who have some kind of a shelter are fortunate, fortunate in comparison with the utterly homeless. In London 50,000 human beings get up every morning, not knowing where they are to lay their heads at night. The luckiest of this multitude, those who succeed in keeping a penny or two until evening, enter a lodging-house, such as abound in every great city, where they find a bed. But what a bed! These houses are filled with beds from cellar to garret, four, five, six beds in a room; as many as can be crowded in. Into every bed four, five, or six human beings are piled, as many as can be packed in, sick and well, young and old, drunk and sober, men and women, just as they come, indiscriminately. Then come strife, blows, wounds, or, if these bed-fellows agree, so much the worse; thefts are arranged and things done which our language, grown more humane than our deeds, refuses to record. And those who cannot pay for such a refuge? They sleep where they find a place, in passages, arcades, in corners where the police and the owners leave them undisturbed. A few individuals find their way to the refuges which are managed, here and there, by private charity, others sleep on the benches in the parks close under the windows of Queen Victoria. . . .

Note

[1] Engels is referring to Max Stirner, a pseudonym for Johann Kaspar Schmidt (1806–1856), author of *The Ego and His Own* (1845).

John Stuart Mill

1806–1873

In the following excerpt of *On Liberty*, Mill eloquently presents his liberal argument for freedom of action and freedom of speech. A central problem for Mill in considering this issue is how to mediate between the rights of one individual and those of another. When, according to Mill, is it permissible to use force or restraint upon another? What is meant by the contention that "[t]he moral good of the person is not sufficient warrant"? What reasons does Mill give for allowing the voicing of an unpopular opinion? What is his reasoning for allowing freedom of the press?

For biographical information, see p. 222.

from *On Liberty* (1859)

Chapter I
Introductory

● ● ●

The object of this essay is to assert one very simple principle, as entitled to govern absolutely the dealings of society with the individual in the way of compulsion and control, whether the means used be physical force in the form of legal penalties, or the moral coercion of public opinion. That principle is, that the sole end for which mankind are warranted, individually or collectively, in interfering with the liberty of action of any of their number, is self-protection. That the only purpose for which power can be rightfully exercised over any member of a civilized community, against his will, is to prevent harm to others. His own good, either physical or moral, is not a sufficient warrant. He cannot rightfully be compelled to do or forbear because it will be better for him to do so, because it will make him happier, because, in the opinions of others, to do so would be wise or even right. These are good reasons for remonstrating with him, or reasoning with him, or persuading him, or entreating him, but not for compelling him, or visiting him with any evil, in case he do otherwise. To justify that, the conduct from which it is desired to deter him must be calculated to produce evil to someone else. The only part of the conduct of anyone, for which he is amenable to society, is that which concerns others. In the part which merely concerns himself, his independence is, of right, absolute. Over himself, over his own body and mind, the individual is sovereign.

● ● ●

It is proper to state that I forego any advantage which could be derived to my argument from the idea of abstract right as a thing independent of utility. I regard utility as the ultimate appeal on all ethical questions; but it must be utility in the largest sense, grounded on the permanent interests of man as a progressive being. Those interests, I contend, authorize the subjection of individual spontaneity to external control only in respect to those actions of each which concern the interest of other people. If anyone does an act hurtful to others, there is a *prima facie*[1] case for punishing him by law or, where legal penalties are not safely applicable, by general disapprobation. There are also many positive acts for the benefit of others which he may rightfully be compelled to perform, such as to give evidence in a court of justice, to bear his fair share in the common defense or in any other joint work necessary to the interest of the society of which he enjoys the protection; and to perform certain acts of individual beneficence, such as saving a fellow creature's life or interposing to protect the defenseless against ill-usage—things which whenever it is obviously a man's duty to do he may rightfully be made responsible to society for not doing. A person may cause evil to others not only by his actions but by his inaction, and in either case he is justly accountable to them for the injury. The latter case, it is true, requires a much more cautious exercise of compulsion than the former. To make any one answerable for doing evil to others is the rule; to make him answerable for not preventing evil is, comparatively speaking, the exception. Yet there are many cases clear enough and grave enough to justify that exception. In all things which regard the external relations of the individual, he is *de jure*[2] amenable to those whose interests are concerned, and, if need be, to society as their protector.

• • •

This, then, is the appropriate region of human liberty. It comprises, first, the inward domain of consciousness; demanding liberty of conscience in the most comprehensive sense, liberty of thought and feeling, absolute freedom of opinion and sentiment on all subjects, practical or speculative, scientific, moral, or theological.

• • •

Chapter 2
Of the Liberty of Thought and Discussion

The time, it is to be hoped, is gone by when any defense would be necessary of the "liberty of the press" as one of the securities against corrupt or tyrannical government. No argument, we may suppose, can now be needed against permitting a legislature or an executive, not identified in interest with the people, to prescribe opinions to them and determine what doctrines or what arguments they shall be allowed to hear. This aspect of the question, besides, has been so often and so triumphantly enforced by preceding writers that it needs not be specially insisted on in this place. . . . Let us suppose, therefore, that the government is entirely at one with the people, and never thinks of exerting any power of coercion unless in agreement with what it conceives to be their voice. But I deny the right of the people to exercise such coercion, either by themselves or by their government. The power itself is illegitimate. The best government has no more title to it than the worst. It is as noxious, or more noxious, when exerted in accordance with public opinion than when in opposition to it. If all mankind minus one were of one opinion, mankind would be no more justified in silencing that one person than he, if he had the power, would be justified in silencing mankind. Were an opinion a personal possession of no value except to the owner, if to be obstructed in the enjoyment of it were simply a private injury, it would make some difference whether the injury was inflicted only on a few persons or on many. But the peculiar evil of silencing the expression of an opinion is that it is robbing the human race, posterity as well as the existing generation—those who dissent from the opinion, still more than those who hold it. If the opinion is right, they are deprived of the opportunity of exchanging error for truth; if wrong, they lose, what is almost as great a benefit, the clearer perception and livelier impression of truth produced by its collision with error.

•   •   •

First, the opinion which it is attempted to suppress by authority may possibly be true. Those who desire to suppress it, of course, deny its truth; but they are not infallible. They have no authority to decide the question for all mankind and exclude every other person from the means of judging. To refuse a hearing to an opinion because they are sure that it is false is to assume that *their* certainty is the same thing as *absolute* certainty. All silencing of discussion is an assumption of infallibility. Its condemnation may be allowed to rest on this common argument, not the worse for being common.

•   •   •

It is the duty of governments, and of individuals, to form the truest opinions they can; to form them carefully, and never impose them upon others unless they are quite sure of being right. But when they are sure (such reasoners may say), it is not conscientiousness but cowardice to shrink from acting on their opinions and allow doctrines which they honestly think dangerous to the welfare of mankind, either in this life or in another, to be scattered abroad without restraint, because other people, in less enlightened times, have persecuted opinions now believed to be true. Let us take care, it may be said, not to make the same mistake; but governments and nations have made mistakes in other things which are not denied to be fit subjects for the exercise of authority: they have laid on bad taxes, made unjust wars. Ought we therefore to lay on no taxes and, under whatever provocation, make no wars? Men and governments must act to the best of their ability. There is no such thing as absolute certainty, but there is assurance sufficient for the purposes of human life. We may, and must, assume our opinion to be true for the guidance of our own conduct; and it is assuming no more when we forbid bad men to pervert society by the propagation of opinions which we regard as false and pernicious.

I answer, that it is assuming very much more. There is the greatest difference between presuming an opinion to be true because, with every opportunity for contesting it, it has not been refuted, and assuming its truth for the purpose of not permitting its refutation. Complete liberty of contradicting and disproving our opinion is the very condition which justifies us in assuming its truth for purposes of action; and on no other terms can a being with human faculties have any national assurance of being right.

• • •

We have now recognized the necessity to the mental well-being of mankind (on which all their other well-being depends) of freedom of opinion, and freedom of the expression of opinion, on four distinct grounds, which we will now briefly recapitulate:

First, if any opinion is compelled to silence, that opinion may, for aught we can certainly know, be true. To deny this is to assume our own infallibility.

Secondly, though the silenced opinion be an error, it may, and very commonly does, contain a portion of truth; and since the general or prevailing opinion on any subject is rarely or never the whole truth, it is only by the collision of adverse opinions that the remainder of the truth has any chance of being supplied.

Thirdly, even if the received opinion be not only true, but the whole truth; unless it is suffered to be, and actually is, vigorously and earnestly contested, it will, by most of those who receive it, be held in the manner of a prejudice, with little comprehension or feeling of its rational grounds. And not only this, but, fourthly, the meaning of the doctrine itself will be in danger of being lost or enfeebled, and deprived of its vital effect on the character and conduct: the dogma becoming a mere formal profession, inefficacious for good, but cumbering the ground and preventing the growth of any real and heartfelt conviction from reason or personal experience.

• • •

Chapter 4
Of the Limits to the Authority of Society over the Individual

What, then, is the rightful limit to the sovereignty of the individual over himself? Where does the authority of society begin? How much of human life should be assigned to individuality, and how much to society?

Each will receive its proper share if each has that which more particularly concerns it. To individuality should belong the part of life in which it is chiefly the individual that is interested; to society, the part which chiefly interests society.

Though society is not founded on a contract, and though no good purpose is answered by inventing a contract in order to deduce social obligations from it, everyone who receives the protection of society owes a return for the benefit, and the fact of living in society renders it indispensable that each should be bound to observe a certain line of conduct toward the rest. This conduct consists, first, in not injuring the interests of one another, or rather certain interests which, either by express legal provision or by tacit understanding, ought to be considered as rights; and secondly, in each person's bearing his share (to be fixed on some equitable principle) of the labors and sacrifices incurred for defending the society or its members from injury and molestation. These conditions society is justified in enforcing at all costs to those who endeavor to withhold fulfillment. Nor is this all that society may do. The acts of an individual may be hurtful to others or wanting in due consideration for their welfare, without going to the length of violating any of their constituted rights. The offender may then be justly punished by opinion, though not by law. As soon as any part of a person's conduct affects prejudicially the interests of others, society has jurisdiction over it, and the question whether the general welfare will or will not be promoted by interfering with it becomes open to discussion. But there is no room for entertaining any such question when a person's conduct affects the interests of no persons besides himself, or needs not affect them unless they like (all the persons concerned being of full age and the ordinary amount of understanding). In all such cases, there should be perfect freedom, legal and social, to do the action and stand the consequences.

● ● ●

Notes

[1] Self-evident.

[2] By right or by law.

Elizabeth Garrett Anderson

1836–1917

Elizabeth Garrett Anderson was the first woman licensed to practice medicine in England. First and last—for several decades—for after Anderson successfully passed her exams, schools expressly prohibited women from sitting for them. Throughout Europe and North America women were denied access to higher education or professional training until late in the nineteenth century, with some institutions, such as Oxford, discriminating against women until the 1940s. Doctors like Harvard professor Edward Clarke and his British counterpart, Dr. Maudsley, to whom Anderson's "Sex in Mind and in Education: A Reply" is addressed, believed that the intense intellectual strain of study adversely affected women's nervous and reproductive systems. Clarke's ideas were widely known in the anglophone world, especially after his retirement when he dedicated himself to a veritable crusade against equal education for girls and boys.

As a doctor herself, Anderson fought fire with fire. She attacked Clarke's premises with logic and facts, pointing out on the one hand that some strain is inevitable as long as every obstacle is put in women's way, and on the other that far greater threats to women's health stem from the mental and physical idleness to which the cult of domesticity consigned them. As well, she observes that immature women marry too young and make poor marriage choices which also could be seen as unhealthy. She concludes that Clarke's ignorance about women's physiology illustrates one final point: the need for more women physicians.

Anderson's ideas supported women's rights movements, especially those of the middle class for whom access to education and the professions was one leg of a trio of demands essential to women's independence, including the vote and fertility control. How do her ideas compare with those of other advocates for women's rights? Would any of Clarke's ideas find support today? How does this debate highlight the bias behind "scientific" knowledge?

from "Sex in Mind and in Education: A Reply" (1874)

Hitherto most of the women who have "contended with men for the goal of man's ambition" have had no chance of being any the worse for being allowed to do so on equal terms. They have had all the benefit of being heavily handicapped. Over and above their assumed physical and mental inferiority, they have had to start in the race without a great part of the training men have enjoyed, or they have gained what training they have been able to obtain in an atmosphere of hostility, to remain in which has taxed their strength and endurance far more than any amount of mental work could tax it. Would, for instance, the ladies who for five years have been trying to get a medical education at Edinburgh find their task increased, or immeasurably lightened, by being allowed to contend "on equal terms with men" for that goal? The intellectual work required from other medical students is nothing compared with what it has been made to them by obliging them to spend time and energy in contesting every step of their course, and yet in spite of this heavy additional burden they have not at present shown any signs of enfeebled health or of inadequate mental power.

• • •

In estimating the possible consequences of extending the time spent in education, and even those of increasing somewhat the pressure put upon girls under eighteen, it should be borne in mind that even if the risk of overwork, pure and simple, work unmixed with worry, is more serious than we are disposed to think it, it is not the only, nor even the most pressing, danger during the period of active physiological development. The newly developed functions of womanhood awaken instincts which are more apt at this age to make themselves unduly prominent than to be hidden or forgotten. Even were the dangers of continuous mental work as great as Dr. Maudsley thinks they are, the dangers of a life adapted to develop only the specially and consciously feminine side of the girl's nature would be much greater. From the purely physiological point of view, it is difficult to believe that study much more serious than that usually pursued by young men would do a girl's health as much harm as a life directly calculated to over-stimulate the emotional and sexual instincts, and to weaken the guiding and controlling forces which these instincts so imperatively need. The stimulus found in novel-reading, in the theatre and ball-room, the excitement which attends a premature entry into society, the

269

competition of vanity and frivolity, these involve far more real dangers to the health of young women than the competition for knowledge, or for scientific or literary honors, ever has done, or is ever likely to do. And even if, in the absence of real culture, dissipation be avoided, there is another danger still more difficult to escape, of which the evil physical results are scarcely less grave, and this is dulness. It is not easy for those whose lives are full to overflowing of the interests which accumulate as life matures, to realise how insupportably dull the life of a young woman just out of the schoolroom is apt to be, nor the powerful influence for evil this dulness has upon her health and morals. There is no tonic in the pharmacopoeia to be compared with happiness, and happiness worth calling such is not known where the days drag along filled with make-believe occupations and dreary sham amusements.

The cases that Dr. Clarke brings forward in support of his opinion against continuous mental work during the period of development could be outnumbered many times over even in our own limited experience, by those in which the break-down of nervous and physical health seems at any rate to be distinctly traceable to want of adequate mental interest and occupation in the years immediately succeeding school life. Thousands of young women, strong and blooming at eighteen, become gradually languid and feeble under the depressing influence of dulness, not only in the special functions of womanhood, but in the entire cycle of the processes of nutrition and innervation, till in a few years they are morbid and self-absorbed, or even hysterical. If they had had upon leaving school some solid intellectual work which demanded real thought and excited genuine interest, and if this interest had been helped by the stimulus of an examination, in which distinction would have been a legitimate source of pride, the number of such cases would probably be indefinitely smaller than it is now. It may doubtless be objected that even if this plan were pursued, and young women were allowed and expected to continue at tolerably hard mental work till they were twenty-one or twenty-two, it would only be postponing the evil day, and that when they left college they would dislike idleness as much, and be as much injured by it as when they left school. This is true, but by this time they would have more internal resources against idleness and dulness, and they would have reached an age in which some share in practical work and responsibility—the lasting refuge from dulness—is more easily obtained than it is in girlhood. Moreover, by entering society at a somewhat less immature age, a young woman is more able to take an intelligent part in it; is prepared to get more real pleasure from the companionship it affords, and suffering less from *ennui*, she is less apt to make a hasty and foolish marriage. From the physiological point of view this last advantage is no small or doubtful one. Any change in the arrangements of young women's lives which tends to discourage very early marriages will probably do more for their health and for the health of their children than any other change could do. But it is hopeless to expect girls, who are at heart very very dull, to wait till they are physiologically fit for the wear and tear consequent upon marriage if they see their way to it at eighteen or nineteen. There is always a hope that the unknown may be less dull than the known, and in the mean time the mere mention of a change gives life a fillip. It is also hopeless to expect them to be even reasonably critical in their choice. Coleridge[1] says, "If Ferdinand hadn't come, Miranda *must* have married Caliban"; and many a Miranda finds her fate by not being free to wait a little longer for her Ferdinand.

But Dr. Maudsley supports his argument by references to American experience. He says in effect, "That which the English educational reformers advocate has been tried in America and has failed; the women there go through the same educational course as the men, and the result is that they are nervous, specially prone to the various ailments peculiar to their sex, not good at bearing children, and unable to nurse them." These are grave charges, and we can scarcely wonder at Dr. Maudsley's thinking "it is right to call attention to them." But it is also right to see if they are true. One fact certainly seems to be plain, and that is, that American women are frequently nervous, and do too often break down in the particular ways described in the quotation, though, if we judge at all from those whom we have an opportunity of seeing in Europe, it may be hoped that the race is not quite in such a bad plight as Dr. Maudsley's quotations would lead us to fear. But granting that the facts are stated correctly, the doubtful point is, what causes this condition of things? Dr. Clarke says that, among other causes, it is due to an education which is at once too continuous, too exciting, too much pressed, and which is taken at too early an age. But against this we have to notice the testimony of many independent witnesses to the effect that the evils complained of are seen to a much greater extent among the fashionable and idle American women—those guiltless of ever having passed an examination—than they are among those who have gone through the course of study complained of. Then, again, it is notorious that the American type in both sexes is "nervous." The men show it as distinctly, if not even more distinctly than the women, and not those men only who have any claim to be considered above the average in intellect or culture. If Dr. Clarke's explanation of the existence of this type in women is correct, what is its explanation in men?

Dr. Clarke himself gives us some valuable hints as to possible causes, other than study. He says: "We live in a zone of perpetual pie and doughnut"; "our girls revel in these unassimilable abominations." He also justly blames the dress of American women, "its stiff corsets and its heavy skirts"; but somewhat inconsequently, as it seems to us, he says, "these cannot be supposed to affect directly the woman's special functions." If one thing more than another is likely to do a woman harm in these directions, we should say it is heavy skirts; and it certainly shakes our faith in Dr. Clarke's acumen to find him attributing less direct influence to them than to mental occupation. Our own notion would be that till American girls wear light dresses and thick boots, and spend as much time out of doors as their brothers, no one knows how many examinations they could pass not only without injury but with positive benefit to their health and spirits. We find, however, no mention made by Dr. Clark of the influence of the stove-heated rooms in which American women live, nor of the indoor lives they lead. These two things only would, we believe, suffice to explain the general and special delicacy of which he complains, and the inferiority in point of health of American to English women.

Note

[1] Samuel Coleridge (1772–1834), poet.

Susan B. Anthony

1820–1906

Susan B. Anthony was born 100 years before the ratification of the 19th Amendment enfranchising women, an achievement she worked toward for a half century but did not live to witness. Anthony and her longtime friend Elizabeth Cady Stanton were the two leading nineteenth-century proponents for women's rights in America. Anthony received an excellent education from her father, a Quaker abolitionist, proving herself a brilliant student, reading and writing at the age of three. However, she soon discovered that, unlike her father, society at large did not support or recognize a woman's intellectual development. Earning as a teacher about one-fourth the amount her male colleagues were paid, her passion for justice intensified.

Anthony was a superb organizer, assisting in the establishment of many reform associations involving the temperance movement, the abolition of slavery, and equal pay and political rights for women, with a special emphasis later in life on women's suffrage. Dismayed when the 15th Amendment (1870) extended the right to vote to African-American males but not to women, she voted in the 1872 presidential election, pushing the interpretation of the 14th Amendment, which grants personal liberties to citizens. She was arrested, tried, found guilty, and fined $100. In an act of civil disobedience, she successfully refused to pay the fine, claiming that "resistance to tyranny is obedience to God." From 1882 to 1890, she was president of the National American Woman Suffrage Association, a position that offered her a platform on which to advocate for the extension of basic social and political liberties to women. Her last spoken words in a public address, during the last year of her life, were "Failure is impossible!"

Anthony wrote *The Declaration of Rights for Women by the National Woman Suffrage Association* (1876) after Elizabeth Cady Stanton, then president of the NWSA, was denied a voice in the Centennial celebration of the Declaration of Independence. She read the Declaration to a small group, in protest of the planned celebration. What are some of the specific examples given by Anthony concerning the lack of rights afforded to women during the first century since the Declaration of Independence? In what ways does the Declaration—and Anthony's challenges to the U.S. government—capture the intellectual and political climate in 1876?

273

from "The Declaration of Rights for Women by the National Woman Suffrage Association" (1876)

July 4, 1876

While the nation is buoyant with patriotism, and all hearts are attuned to praise, it is with sorrow we come to strike the one discordant note, on this one-hundredth anniversary of our country's birth. When subjects of kings, emperors, and czars, from the old world join in our national jubilee, shall the women of the republic refuse to lay their hands with benedictions on the nation's head? Surveying America's exposition, surpassing in magnificence those of London, Paris, and Vienna, shall we not rejoice at the success of the youngest rival among the nations of the earth? May not our hearts, in unison with all, swell with pride at our great achievements as a people; our free speech, free press, free schools, free church, and the rapid progress we have made in material wealth, trade, commerce and the inventive arts? And we do rejoice in the success, thus far, of our experiment of self-government. Our faith is firm and unwavering in the broad principles of human rights proclaimed in 1776, not only as abstract truths, but as the corner stones of a republic. Yet we can-not forget, even in this glad hour, that while all men of every race, and clime, and condition, have been invested with the full rights of citizenship under our hospitable flag, all women still suffer the degradation of disfranchisement.

The history of our country the past hundred years has been a series of assumptions and usurpations of power over woman, in direct opposition to the principles of just government, acknowledged by the United States as its foundation. . . .

And for the violation of these fundamental principles of our government, we arraign our rulers on this Fourth day of July, 1876,—and these are our arti-cles of impeachment: *Bills of attainder* have been passed by the introduction of the word "male" into all the State constitutions, denying to women the right of suffrage, and thereby making sex a crime—an exercise of power clearly for-bidden in article I, sections 9, 10 of the United States constitution. . . .

The right of trial by a jury of one's peers was so jealously guarded that States refused to ratify the original constitution until it was guaranteed by the sixth amendment. And yet the women of this nation have never been allowed a jury of their peers—being tried in all cases by men, native and foreign, educated and ignorant, virtuous and vicious. Young girls have been arraigned in our courts for the crime of infanticide; tried, convicted, hanged—victims, per-chance, of judge, jurors, advocates—while no woman's voice could be heard in their defense. . . .

Taxation without representation, the immediate cause of the rebellion of the colonies against Great Britain, is one of the grievous wrongs the women of this country have suffered during the century. Deploring war, with all the demoralization that follows in its train, we have been taxed to support stand-ing armies, with their waste of life and wealth. Believing in temperance, we have been taxed to support the vice, crime and pauperism of the liquor traffic. While we suffer its wrongs and abuses infinitely more than man, we have no power to protect our sons against this giant evil. . . .

Unequal codes for men and women. Held by law a perpetual minor, deemed incapable of self-protection, even in the industries of the world, woman is denied equality of rights. The fact of sex, not the quantity or quali-ty of work, in most cases, decides the pay and position; and because of this injustice thousands of fatherless girls are compelled to choose between a life of shame and starvation. Laws catering to man's vices have created two codes of morals in which penalties are graded according to the political status of the offender. Under such laws, women are fined and imprisoned if found alone in the streets, or in public places of resort, at certain hours. Under the pretense of regulating public morals, police officers seizing the occupants of disreputable houses, march the women in platoons to prison, while the men, partners in their guilt, go free. . . .

Representation of woman has had no place in the nation's thought. Since the incorporation of the thirteen original States, twenty-four have been admit-ted to the Union, not one of which has recognized woman's right of self-gov-ernment. On this birthday of our national liberties, July Fourth, 1876, Colorado, like all her elder sisters, comes into the Union with the invidious word "male" in her constitution. . . .

The judiciary above the nation has proved itself but the echo of the party in power, by holding and enforcing laws that are opposed to the spirit and let-ter of the constitution. When the slave power was dominant, the Supreme Court decided that a black man was not a citizen, because he had not the tight to vote; and when the constitution was so amended to make all persons citizens, the same high tribunal decided that a woman, though a citizen, had not the right to vote. Such vacillating interpretations of constitutional law unsettle our faith in judicial authority, and undermine the liberties of the whole people.

These articles of impeachment against our rulers we now submit to the impartial judgment of the people. To all these wrongs and oppressions woman has not submitted in silence and resignation. From the beginning of the century, when Abigail Adams, the wife of one president and mother of another, said, "We will not hold ourselves bound to obey laws in which we have no voice or representation," until now, woman's discontent has been steadily increasing, culminating nearly thirty years ago in a simultaneous movement among the women of the nation, demanding the right of suffrage. In making our just demands, a higher motive than the pride of sex inspires us; we feel that national safety and stability depend on the complete recognition of the broad principles of our government. Woman's degraded, helpless position is the weak point in our institutions today; a disturbing force everywhere, severing family ties, filling our asylums with the deaf, the dumb, the blind; our prisons with criminals, our cities with drunkenness and prostitution; our homes with disease and death. It was the boast of the founders of the republic, that the rights for which they contended were the rights of human nature. If these rights are ignored in the case of one-half the people, the nation is surely preparing for its downfall. Governments try themselves. The recognition of a governing and a governed class is incompatible with the first principles of freedom. Woman has not been a heedless spectator of the events of this century, nor a dull listener to the grand arguments for the equal rights of humanity. From the earliest history of our country woman has shown equal devotion with man to the cause of freedom, and has stood firmly by his side in its defense. Together they have made this country what it is. Woman's wealth, thought and labor have cemented the stones of every monument man has reared to liberty.

And now, at the close of a hundred years, as the hour-hand of the great clock that marks the centuries points to 1876, declare our faith in the principles of self-government: our full equality with man in natural rights; that woman was made first for her own happiness, with the absolute right to herself—to all the opportunities and advantages life affords for her complete development; and we deny that dogma of the centuries, incorporated in the codes of all nations—that woman was made for man—her best interests, in all cases, to be sacrificed to his will. We ask of our rulers, at this hour, no special privileges, no special legislation. We ask justice, we ask equality, we ask that all the civil and political rights that belong to citizens of the United States, be guaranteed to us and our daughters forever.

Andrew Carnegie

1835–1919

The American industrialist Andrew Carnegie was born in Fife, Scotland.
His father, William Carnegie, was a handloom weaver and an active Chartist,
a supporter of voting rights for workers. The increasingly widespread use of the
power loom in the Scottish textile industry spelled economic ruin for the
Carnegie family and in 1848 they immigrated to the United States. Settling in
Pennsylvania, the twelve-year-old Andrew worked in a cotton factory and
eventually enrolled in night school. In 1853, Carnegie got work at the
Pennsylvania Railroad Company, starting as a secretary and rising within six
years to the position of superintendent of the company's Pittsburgh division.
By 1873, Carnegie had started his own steelmaking company, pioneering new
manufacturing and accounting procedures that fed his growing success, and
within fifteen years his firm dominated the American steel market. In retirement, he immersed himself in philanthropic work, establishing such foundations as the Carnegie Trust, the Carnegie Corporation of New York, the
Carnegie Institution of Washington, and the Carnegie Endowment for
International Peace. Through these organizations, Carnegie worked to
improve educational institutions locally and nationally, to promote scientific
and medical research and development, and to assist libraries, museums, and
theaters across the country.

In the following excerpt of *The Gospel of Wealth*, Carnegie writes about
the success of capitalism and what it means for the modern individual, echoing in many ways the Enlightenment ideas of Adam Smith. What meaning
emerges from the title Carnegie gave this work? How does Carnegie define
progress? What benefits and problems arise from his conception of "the duty
of the man of wealth"?

from *The Gospel of Wealth* (1889)

The Problem of the Administration of Wealth

The problem of our age is the proper administration of wealth, that the ties of brotherhood may still bind together the rich and poor in harmonious relationship. The conditions of human life have not only been changed, but revolutionized, within the past few hundred years. In former days there was little difference between the dwelling, dress, food, and environment of the chief and those of his retainers. The Indians are to-day where civilized man then was. When visiting the Sioux, I was led to the wigwam of the chief. It was like the others in external appearance, and even within the difference was trifling between it and those of the poorest of his braves. The contrast between the palace of the millionaire and the cottage of the laborer with us to-day measures the change which has come with civilization. This change, however, is not to be deplored, but welcomed as highly beneficial. It is well, nay, essential, for the progress of the race that the houses of some should be homes for all that is highest and best in literature and the arts, and for all the refinements of civilization, rather than that none should be so. Much better this great irregularity than universal squalor. Without wealth there can be no Mæcenas.[1] The "good old times" were not good old times. Neither master nor servant was as well situated then as to-day. A relapse to old conditions would be disastrous to both—not the least so to him who serves—and would sweep away civilization with it. But whether the change be for good or ill, it is upon us, beyond our power to alter, and, therefore, to be accepted and made the best of. It is a waste of time to criticize the inevitable.

It is easy to see how the change has come. One illustration will serve for almost every phase of the cause. In the manufacture of products we have the whole story. It applies to all combinations of human industry, as stimulated and enlarged by the inventions of this scientific age. Formerly, articles were manufactured at the domestic hearth, or in small shops which formed part of the household. The master and his apprentices worked side by side, the latter living with the master, and therefore subject to the same conditions. When these apprentices rose to be masters, there was little or no change in their mode of life, and they, in turn, educated succeeding apprentices in the same routine. There was, substantially, social equality, and even political equality, for those engaged in industrial pursuits had then little or no voice in the State.

278

The inevitable result of such a mode of manufacture was crude articles at high prices. To-day the world obtains commodities of excellent quality at prices which even the preceding generation would have deemed incredible. In the commercial world similar causes have produced similar results, and the race is benefited thereby. The poor enjoy what the rich could not before afford. What were the luxuries have become the necessaries of life. The laborer has now more comforts than the farmer had a few generations ago. The farmer has more luxuries than the landlord had, and is more richly clad and better housed. The landlord has books and pictures rarer and appointments more artistic than the king could then obtain.

The price we pay for this salutary change is, no doubt, great. We assemble thousands of operatives in the factory, and in the mine, of whom the employer can know little or nothing, and to whom he is little better than a myth. All intercourse between them is at an end. Rigid castes are formed, and, as usual, mutual ignorance breeds mutual distrust. Each caste is without sympathy with the other, and ready to credit anything disparaging in regard to it. Under the law of competition, the employer of thousands is forced into the strictest economies, among which the rates paid to labor figure prominently, and often there is friction between the employer and the employed, between capital and labor, between rich and poor. Human society loses homogeneity.

The price which society pays for the law of competition, like the price it pays for cheap comforts and luxuries, is also great; but the advantages of this law are also greater still than its cost—for it is to this law that we owe our wonderful material development, which brings improved conditions in its train. But, whether the law be benign or not, we must say of it, as we say of the change in the conditions of men to which we have referred: It is here; we cannot evade it; no substitutes for it have been found; and while the law may be sometimes hard for the individual, it is best for the race, because it insures the survival of the fittest in every department. We accept and welcome, therefore, as conditions to which we must accommodate ourselves, great inequality of environment; the concentration of business, industrial and commercial, in the hands of a few; and the law of competition between these, as being not only beneficial, but essential to the future progress of the race. Having accepted these, it follows that there must be great scope for the exercise of special ability in the merchant and in the manufacturer who has to conduct affairs upon a great scale. That this talent for organization and management is rare among men is proved by the fact that it invariably secures enormous rewards for its possessor, no matter where or under what laws or conditions. The experienced in affairs always rate the MAN whose services can be obtained as a partner as not only the first consideration, but such as render the question of his capital scarcely worth considering: for able men soon create capital; in the hands of those without the special talent required, capital soon takes wings. Such men become interested in firms or corporations using millions; and, estimating only simple interest to be made upon the capital invested, it is inevitable that their income must exceed their expenditure and that they must, therefore, accumulate wealth. Nor is there any middle ground which such men can occupy, because the great manufacturing or commercial concern which does not earn at least interest upon its capital soon becomes bankrupt. It must either go forward or fall behind; to stand still is impossible. It is a condition essential to its successful operation that it should be thus far profitable, and even that, in addition to interest on capital, it should make profit. It is a law, as certain as any of the others named, that men possessed of this peculiar talent for affairs, under the free play of economic forces must, of necessity, soon be in receipt of more revenue than can be judiciously expended upon themselves; and this law is as beneficial for the race as the others.

Objections to the foundations upon which society is based are not in order, because the condition of the race is better with these than it has been with any other which has been tried. Of the effect of any new substitutes proposed we cannot be sure. The Socialist or Anarchist who seeks to overturn present conditions is to be regarded as attacking the foundation upon which civilization itself rests, for civilization took its start from the day when the capable, industrious workman said to his incompetent and lazy fellow, "If thou dost not sow, thou shalt not reap," and thus ended primitive Communism by separating the drones from the bees. One who studies this subject will soon be brought face to face with the conclusion that upon the sacredness of property civilization itself depends—the right of the laborer to his hundred dollars in the savings-bank, and equally the legal right of the millionaire to his millions. Every man must be allowed "to sit under his own vine and fig-tree, with none to make afraid," if human society is to advance, or even to remain so far advanced as it is. To those who propose to substitute Communism for this intense Individualism, the answer therefore is: The race has tried that. All progress from that barbarous day to the present time has resulted from its displacement. Not evil, but good, has come to the race from the accumulation of wealth by those who have had the ability and energy to produce it. But even if we admit for a moment that it might be better for the race to discard its present foundation, Individualism,—that it is a nobler ideal that man should labor, not for himself alone, but in and for a brotherhood of his fellows, and share with them all in common, realizing Swedenborg's[2] idea of heaven, where, as he says, the angels derive their happiness, not from for laboring self, but for each other,—even admit all this, and a sufficient answer is, This is not evolution, but revolution.

It necessitates the changing of human nature itself—a work of eons, even if it were good to change it, which we cannot know.

It is not practicable in our day or in our age. Even if desirable theoretically, it belongs to another and long-succeeding sociological stratum. Our duty is with what is practicable now—with the next step possible in our day and generation. It is criminal to waste our energies in endeavoring to uproot, when all we can profitably accomplish is to bend the universal tree of humanity a little in the direction most favorable to the production of good fruit under existing circumstances. We might as well urge the destruction of the highest existing type of man because he failed to reach our ideal as to favor the destruction of Individualism, Private Property, the Law of Accumulation of Wealth, and the Law of Competition; for these are the highest result of human experience, the soil in which society, so far, has produced the best fruit. Unequally or unjustly, perhaps, as these laws sometimes operate, and imperfect as they appear to the Idealist, they are, nevertheless, like the highest type of man, the best and most valuable of all that humanity has yet accomplished.

• • •

This, then, is held to be the duty of the man of wealth: To set an example of modest, unostentatious living, shunning display or extravagance; to provide moderately for the legitimate wants of those dependent upon him; and, after doing so, to consider all surplus revenues which come to him simply as trust funds, which he is called upon to administer, and strictly bound as a matter of duty to administer in the manner which, in his judgment, is best calculated to produce the most beneficial results for the community—the man of wealth thus becoming the mere trustee and agent for his poorer brethren, bringing to their service his superior wisdom, experience, and ability to administer, doing for them better than they would or could do for themselves.

• • •

In bestowing charity, the main consideration should be to help those who will help themselves; to provide part of the means by which those who desire to improve may do so; to give those who desire to rise the aids by which they may rise; to assist, but rarely or never to do all. Neither the individual nor the race is improved by almsgiving. Those worthy of assistance, except in rare cases, seldom require assistance. The really valuable men of the race never do, except in case of accident or sudden change. Every one has, of course, cases of individuals brought to his own knowledge where temporary assistance can do genuine good, and these he will not overlook. But the amount which can be wisely given by the individual for individuals is necessarily limited by his lack of knowledge of the circumstances connected with each. He is the only true reformer who is as careful and as anxious not to aid the unworthy as he is to aid the worthy, and, perhaps, even more so, for in almsgiving more injury is probably done by rewarding vice than by relieving virtue.

• • •

The best means of benefiting the community is to place within its reach the ladders upon which the aspiring can rise—free libraries, parks, and means of recreation, by which men are helped in body and mind; works of art, certain to give pleasure and improve the public taste; and public institutions of various kinds, which will improve the general condition of the people; in this manner returning their surplus wealth to the mass of their fellows in the forms best calculated to do them lasting good.

Thus is the problem of rich and poor to be solved. The laws of accumulation will be left free, the laws of distribution free. Individualism will continue, but the millionaire will be but a trustee for the poor, intrusted for a season with a great part of the increased wealth of the community, but administering it for the community far better than it could or would have done for itself. The best minds will thus have reached a stage in the development of the race in which it is clearly seen that there is no mode of disposing of surplus wealth creditable to thoughtful and earnest men into whose hands it flows, save by using it year by year for the general good. . . .

Notes

[1] Roman statesman and literary patron (c.70–8 B.C.). Carnegie is arguing that without wealth there can be no philanthropy.

[2] Emanuel Swedenborg (1688–1772), Christian theologain, mystic, and philosopher.

Charlotte Perkins Gilman

1860–1935

Charlotte Perkins Gilman had an unhappy childhood and an unconventional upbringing. Her father, a member of the famous Beecher family, left her mother when Charlotte was just an infant. Her great aunt was Harriet Beecher Stowe, author of *Uncle Tom's Cabin* (1852). Gilman's mother did not show her much affection, of necessity preoccupied with the struggle to support her family without a husband. The family was always moving and Gilman received little education. She studied for a short time at the Rhode Island School of Design, but in general was self-educated. She fell into depression after agreeing to marry a persistent suitor, the artist Charles D. Stetson. Throughout her life, she found social expectations for women, and particularly their confinement to the domestic sphere, to be truly debilitating; her antipathy to such restrictions only intensified after the birth of her daughter.

In her famous short story "The Yellow Wall-Paper" (1892), Gilman vividly portrays the gradual psychological deterioration of a young woman married to a doctor. Confined by her new domestic roles, this woman sees ghost-like images of women trapped behind the barred wall paper of her room. Eventually, she herself joins the imprisoned women. Hoping to escape the fate of her character, Gilman left her husband and child, experiencing much social disapproval. But she was pleased when her husband married her best friend, providing what she considered to be the best home for her daughter. Later, in 1900, she married George Gilman, a cousin. When her second husband died, Gilman moved in with her daughter's family in California. Gilman committed suicide by chloroform after she was told that she had incurable cancer and would thus be a burden to her daughter's family.

Gilman's most theoretical work is *Women and Economics* (1898), in which she maintains that to become free of society's imposed domestic constraints, women need to be independent economically. Only then will women be able to define what they would like to be, instead of settling for the stereotypical and subservient roles assigned to them by social conventions. What does Gilman mean when she describes the current state of a woman as a non-producing consumer? What effect does this state of being have on women? According to Gilman, what is essential to socially-organized beings? What is Gilman's assessment of the future for women?

from *Women and Economics* (1898)

• • •

Besides this maintenance of primeval individualism in the growing collectivity of social economic process and the introduction of the element of sex-combat into the narrowing field of industrial competition, there is another side to the evil influence of the sexuo-economic relation upon social development. This is in the attitude of woman as a non-productive consumer.

In the industrial evolution of the human race, that marvellous and subtle drawing out and interlocking of special functions which constitute the organic life of society, we find that production and consumption go hand in hand; and production comes first. One cannot consume what has not been produced. Economic production is the natural expression of human energy,—not sex-energy at all, but race-energy,—the unconscious functioning of the social organism. Socially organized human beings tend to produce, as a gland to secrete: it is the essential nature of the relation. The creative impulse, the desire to make, to express the inner thought in outer form, "just for the work's sake, no use at all i' the work!" this is the distinguishing character of humanity, "I want to mark!" cries the child, demanding the pencil. He does not want to eat. He wants to mark. He is not seeking to get something into himself, but to put something out of himself. He generally wants to do whatever he sees done,—to make pie-crust or to make shavings, as it happens. The pie he may eat, the shavings not; but he likes to make both. This is the natural process of production, and is followed by the natural process of consumption, where practicable. But consumption is not the main end, the governing force. Under this organic social law, working naturally, we have the evolution of those arts and crafts in the exercise of which consists our human living, and on the product of which we live. So does society evolve within itself—secrete as it were—the social structure with all its complex machinery; and we function therein as naturally as so many glands, other things being equal.

But other things are not equal. Half the human race is denied free productive expression, is forced to confine its productive human energies to the same channels as its reproductive sex-energies. Its creative skill is confined to the level of immediate personal bodily service, to the making of clothes and preparing of food for individuals. No social service is possible. While its power of production is checked, its power of consumption is inordinately increased by the showering upon it of the "unearned increment" of masculine gifts. For the woman there is, first, no free production allowed; and, second, no relation maintained between what she does produce and what she consumes. She is forbidden to make, but encouraged to take. Her industry is not the natural output of creative energy, not the work she does because she has the inner power and strength to do it; nor is her industry even the measure of her gain. She has, of course, the natural desire to consume; and to that is set no bar save the capacity or the will of her husband.

Thus we have painfully and laboriously evolved and carefully maintain among us an enormous class of non-productive consumers,—a class which is half the world, and mother of the other half. We have built into the constitution of the human race the habit and desire of taking, as divorced from its natural precursor and concomitant of making. We have made for ourselves this endless array of "horse-leech's daughters, crying, Give! give!" To consume food, to consume clothes, to consume houses and furniture and decorations and ornaments and amusements, to take and take and take forever,—from one man if they are virtuous, from many if they are vicious, but always to take and never to think of giving anything in return except their womanhood,—this is the enforced condition of the mothers of the race. What wonder that their sons go into business "for what there is in it"! What wonder that the world is full of the desire to get as much as possible and to give as little as possible! What wonder, either, that the glory and sweetness of love are but a name among us, with here and there a strange and beautiful exception, of which our admiration proves the rarity!

Between the brutal ferocity of excessive male energy struggling in the market-place as in a battlefield and the unnatural greed generated by the perverted condition of female energy, it is not remarkable that the industrial evolution of humanity has shown peculiar symptoms. One of the minor effects of this last condition—this limiting of female industry to close personal necessities, and this tendency of her over-developed sex-nature to overestimate the so-called "duties of her position"—has been to produce an elaborate devotion to individuals and their personal needs,—not to the understanding and developing of their higher natures, but to the intensification of their bodily tastes and pleasure. The wife and mother, pouring the rising tide of racial power into the same old channels that were allowed her primitive ancestors, constantly ministers to the physical needs of her family with a ceaseless and concentrated intensity. They like it, of course. But it maintains in the individuals of the race an exaggerated sense of the importance of food and clothes and ornaments to themselves, without at all including a knowledge of their right use and value to us all. It develops personal selfishness.

Again, the consuming female, debarred from any free production, unable to estimate the labor involved in the making of what she so lightly destroys, and her consumption limited mainly to those things which minister to physical pleasure, creates a market for sensuous decoration and personal ornament, for all that is luxurious and enervating, and for a false and capricious variety in such supplies, which operates as a most deadly check to true industry and true art. As the priestess of the temple of consumption, as the limitless demander of things to use up, her economic influence is reactionary and injurious. Much, very much, of the current of useless production in which our economic energies run waste—man's strength poured out like water on the sand—depends on the creation and careful maintenance of this false market, this sink into which human labor vanishes with no return. Woman, in her false economic position, reacts injuriously upon industry, upon art, upon science, discovery, and progress. The sexuo-economic relation in its effect on the constitution of the individual keeps alive in us the instincts of savage individualism which we should otherwise have well outgrown. It sexualizes our industrial relation and commercializes our sex-relation. And, in the external effect upon the market, the over-sexed woman, in her unintelligent and ceaseless demands, hinders and perverts the economic development of the world.

●　　●　　●

The popular thought of our day is voiced in fiction, fluent verse, and an incessant play of humor. By what is freely written by most authors and freely read by most people is shown our change in circumstances and change in feeling. In old romances the woman was nothing save beautiful, high-born, virtuous, and perhaps "accomplished." She did nothing but love and hate, obey or disobey, and be handed here and there among villain, hero, and outraged parent, screaming, fainting, or bursting into floods of tears as seemed called for by the occasion.

In the fiction of to-day women are continually taking larger place in the action of the story. They are given personal characteristics beyond those of physical beauty. And they are no longer content simply to *be*: they *do*. They are showing qualities of bravery, endurance, strength, foresight, and power for the swift execution of well-conceived plans. They have ideas and purposes of their own; and even when, as in so many cases described by the more reactionary novelists, the efforts of the heroine are shown to be entirely futile, and she comes back with a rush to the self-effacement of marriage with economic dependence, still the efforts were there. Disapprove as he may, use his art to oppose and contemn as he may, the true novelist is forced to chronicle the distinctive features of his time; and no feature is more distinctive of this time than the increasing individualization of women. With lighter touch, but with equally unerring truth, the wit and humor of the day show the same development. The majority of our current jokes on women turn on their "new-ness," their advance.

No sociological change equal in importance to this clearly marked improvement of an entire sex has ever taken place in one century. Under it all, the *crux* of the whole matter goes on the one great change, that of the economic relation. This follows perfectly natural lines. Just as the development of machinery constantly lowers the importance of mere brute strength of body and raises that of mental power and skill, so the pressure of industrial conditions demands an ever-higher specialization, and tends to break up that relic of the patriarchal age,—the family as an economic unit.

Women have been led under pressure of necessity into a most reluctant entrance upon fields of economic activity. The sluggish and greedy disposition bred of long ages of dependence has by no means welcomed the change. Most women still work only as they "have to," until they can marry and "be supported." Men, too, liking the power that goes with money, and the poor quality of gratitude and affection bought with it, resent and oppose the change; but all this disturbs very little the course of social progress.

A truer spirit is the increasing desire of young girls to be independent, to have a career of their own, at least for a while, and the growing objection of countless wives to the pitiful asking for money, to the beggary of their position. More and more do fathers give their daughters, and husbands their wives, a definite allowance,—a separate bank account,—something which they can play is all their own. The spirit of personal independence in the women of to-day is sure proof that a change has come.

•   •   •

VI. IMPERIALISM AND THE CONFLICT OF CULTURES

Lord William Bentinck

1774–1839

Conflicts between cultures, exacerbated by the spread of Imperialism in the nineteenth century, can be glimpsed in this document. While the British had established a commercial and military presence in India's port cities during the first half of the 18th century, no attempts were made to disrupt or "Europeanize" Indian civilization. In fact, religious toleration, consistent with Enlightenment principles, was essential to Indian cooperation. Moreover, early colonists taking up residence in India tended to adopt Indian lifestyles and cultural forms.

By the first decades of the nineteenth century, Christian missionaries began to call for reforms in India. Two practices in particular were abhorrent to Christians: female infanticide, and "sati" or Hindu widow-burning. Hinduism placed a high premium on female chastity and tried to prevent widows from shaming their husbands after their deaths by encouraging widows to immolate themselves voluntarily on the funeral pyre. Such an act of sacrifice would also be rewarded in the afterlife.

Lord Bentink castigates Indians in the following selection and succeeded in passing laws against these practices in British-controlled India. This signaled, however, the disruption of one of the world's oldest cultures, and thereby fed traditionalist opposition to British rule even as it divided Indians amongst themselves: western-oriented elites versus anti-Imperialist nationalists.

Imperialism entailed the military conquest of nations, but to be thoroughly successful, minds had to be conquered as well. How is advocacy on the basis of western-defined "rights" an extension of imperialism? Is this moral intervention justified? If so, when? What are the limits of religious toleration? How can cultural distinctiveness be maintained if all cultures are measured by one "universal" (i.e., Western) standard?

Comments on Ritual Murder and the
Limits of Religious Toleration (1829)

Whether the question be to continue or to discontinue the practice of *sati*, the decision is equally surrounded by an awful responsibility. To consent to the consignment year after year of hundreds of innocent victims to a cruel and untimely end, when the power exists of preventing it, is a predicament which no conscience can contemplate without horror. But, on the other hand, if heretofore received opinions are to be considered of any value, to put to hazard by a contrary course the very safety of the British Empire in India, and to extinguish at once all hopes of those great improvements—affecting the condition not of hundreds and thousands but of millions—which can only be expected from the continuance of our supremacy, is an alternative which even in the light of humanity itself may be considered as a still greater evil. It is upon this first and highest consideration alone, the good of mankind, that the tolerance of this inhuman and impious rite can in my opinion be justified on the part of the government of a civilized nation. While the solution of this question is appalling from the unparalleled magnitude of its possible results, the considerations belonging to it are such as to make even the stoutest mind distrust its decision. On the one side, Religion, Humanity, under the most appalling form, as well as vanity and ambition—in short, all the most powerful influences over the human heart—are arrayed to bias and mislead the judgment. On the other side, the sanction of countless ages, the example of all the Mussulman conquerors, the unanimous concurrence in the same policy of our own most able rulers, together with the universal veneration of the people, seem authoritatively to forbid, both to feeling and to reason, any interference in the exercise of their natural prerogative. In venturing to be the first to deviate from this practice it becomes me to show that nothing has been yielded to feeling, but that reason, and reason alone, has governed the decision.

• • •

We have now before us two reports of the Nizamat Adalat, with statements of *satis* in 1827 and 1828, exhibiting a decrease of 54 in the latter year as compared with 1827, and a still greater proportion as compared with former years. If this diminution could be ascribed to any change of opinion upon the question produced by the progress of education or civilization the fact would be most satisfactory, and to disturb this sure though slow process of self-correction would be most impolitic and unwise. But I think it may be safely

affirmed that, though in Calcutta truth may be said to have made a considerable advance among the higher orders, yet in respect to the population at large
no change whatever has taken place, and that from these causes at least no
hope of the abandonment of the rite can be rationally entertained. The
decrease, if it be real, may be the result of less sickly seasons, as the increase in
1824 and 1825 was of the greater prevalence of cholera. But it is probably in
a greater measure due to the more open discouragement of the practice given
by the greater part of the European functionaries in latter years, the effect of
which would be to produce corresponding activity in the police officers, by
which either the number would be really diminished or would be made to
appear so in the returns.

It seems to be the very general opinion that our interference has hitherto
done more harm than good by lending a sort of sanction to the ceremony,
while it has undoubtedly tended to cripple the efforts of magistrates and others to prevent the practice.

•   •   •

It might be very difficult to make a stranger to India understand, much
less believe that in a population of so many millions of people as the Calcutta
Division includes, and the same may be said of all the Lower Provinces, so
great is the want of courage and of vigour of character, and such the habitual
submission of centuries, that insurrection or hostile opposition to the will of
the ruling power may be affirmed to be an impossible danger. I speak of the
population taken separately from the army, and I may add for the information
of the stranger, and also in support of my assertion, that few of the natives of
the Lower Provinces are to be found in our military ranks. I therefore at once
deny the danger *in toto* in reference to this part of our territories, where the
practice principally obtains.

If, however, security was wanting against extensive popular tumult or revolution, I should say that the Permanent Settlement, which, though a failure
in many other respects and in its most important essentials, has this great
advantage at least, of having created a vast body of rich landed proprietors
deeply interested in the continuance of the British Dominion and having complete command over the mass of the people.

•   •   •

Were the scene of this sad destruction of human life laid in the Upper
instead of the Lower Provinces, in the midst of a bold and manly people, I
might speak with less confidence upon the question of safety. In these
Provinces the *satis* amount to forty-three only upon a population of nearly
twenty millions. It cannot be expected that any general feeling, where combi-

nation of any kind is so unusual, could be excited in defence of a rite in which so few participate, a rite also notoriously made too often subservient to views of personal interest on the part of the other members of the family.

• • •

But I have taken up too much time in giving my own opinion when those of the greatest experience and highest official authority are upon our records. In the report of the Nizamat Adalat for 1828, four out of five of the Judges recommended to the Governor-General in Council the immediate abolition of the practice, and attest its safety. The fifth Judge, though not opposed to the opinions of the rest of the Bench, did not feel then prepared to give his entire assent. In the report of this year the measure has come up with the unanimous recommendation of the Court. The two Superintendents of Police for the Upper and Lower Provinces (Mr. Walter Ewer and Mr. Charles Barwell) have in the strongest terms expressed their opinion that the suppression might be effected without the least danger. The former officer has urged the measure upon the attention of Government in the most forcible manner. No documents exist to show the opinions of the public functionaries in the interior, but I am informed that nine-tenths are in favour of the abolition.

• • •

Having made inquiries, also, how far *satis* are permitted in the European foreign settlements, I find from Dr. Carey that at Chinsurah no such sacrifices had ever been permitted by the Dutch Government. That within the limits of Chandarnager itself they were also prevented, but allowed to be performed in the British territories. The Danish Government of Serampur has not forbidden the rite, in conformity to the example of the British Government.

It is a very important fact that, though representations have been by the disappointed party to superior authority, it does not appear that a single instance of direct opposition to the executive of the prohibitory orders of our civil functionaries has ever occurred. How, then, can it be reasonably feared that to the Government itself, from whom all authority is derived, and whose power is now universally considered to be irresistible, anything bearing the semblance of resistance can be manifested? Mr. Wilson also is of opinion that no immediate overt act of insubordination would follow the publication of the edict. The Regulation of Government may be evaded, the police may be corrupted, but even here the price paid as hush money will operate as a penalty, indirectly forwarding the object of Government.

I venture, then, to think it completely proved that from the native population nothing of extensive combination, or even of partial opposition, may be expected from the abolition.

•   •   •

I have now to submit for the consideration of Council the draft of a regulation enacting the abolition of *satis*. It is accompanied by a paper containing the remarks and suggestions of the Judges of the Nizamut Adalat. In this paper is repeated the unanimous opinion of the Court in favour of the proposed measure. The suggestions of the Nizamat Adalat are in some measure at variance with a principal object I had in view, of preventing collision between the parties to the *sati* and the officers of police. It is only in the previous processes, or during the actual performance of the rite, when the feelings of all may be more or less roused to a high degree of excitement, that I apprehend the possibility of affray or of acts of violence through an indiscreet and injudicious exercise of authority. It seemed to me prudent, therefore, that the police, in the first instance, should warn and advise, but not forcibly prohibit, and if the *sati*, in defiance of this notice, were performed, that a report should be made to the magistrate, who would summon the parties and proceed as in any other case of crime. The Indian Court appears to think these precautions unnecessary, and I hope they may be so, but in the beginning we cannot, I think, proceed with too much circumspection. Upon the same principle, in order to guard against a too hasty or severe a sentence emanating from extreme zeal on the part of the local judge, I have proposed that the case should only be cognizable by the Commissioners of circuit. These are, however, questions which I should wish to see discussed in Council.

•   •   •

The first and primary object of my heart is benefit of the Hindus. I know nothing so important to the improvement of their future condition as the establishment of a purer morality, whatever their belief, and a more just conception of the will of God. The first step to this better understanding will be dissociation of religious belief and practice from blood and murder. They will then, when no longer under this brutalizing excitement, view with more calmness acknowledged truths. They will see that there can be no inconsistency in the ways of Providence, that to the command received as divine by all races of men, 'No innocent blood shall be spilt,' there can be no exception; and when they shall have been convinced of the error of this first and most criminal of their customs, may it not be hoped that others, which stand in the way of their improvement, may likewise pass away, and that, thus emancipated from those chains and shackles upon their minds and actions, they may no longer continue, as they have done, the slaves of every foreign conqueror, but that they may assume their first places among the great families of mankind? I disown in these remarks, or in this measure, any view whatever to conversion to our own faith. I write and feel as a legislator for the Hindus, and as I believe many enlightened Hindus think and feel.

Descending from these higher considerations, it cannot be a dishonest ambition that the Government of which I form a part should have the credit of an act which is to wash out a foul stain upon British rule, and to stay the sacrifice of humanity and justice to a doubtful expediency; and finally, as a branch of the general administration of the Empire, I may be permitted to feel deeply anxious that our course shall be in accordance with the noble example set to us by the British Government at home, and that the adaptation, when practicable to the circumstances of this vast Indian population, of the same enlightened principles, may promote here as well as there the general prosperity, and may exalt the character of our nation.

November 8th, 1829

Olive Schreiner

1855–1920

Olive Schreiner was truly cosmopolitan in a way that only a "new" woman in the age of imperialism could be. A member of a German Lutheran missionary family, Schreiner grew up in South Africa, the backdrop for many of her novels including this one. Desiring to pursue writing as a profession, she moved to England in her twenties and began to publish successfully under the pseudonym, Ralph Iron. Though her novels sold well in her lifetime, she then fell into relative obscurity but has benefited from contemporary efforts to include more women in literary canons.

From her experience of imperialism in South Africa, Schreiner became a pacifist and was an outspoken opponent of the Boer War (1899–1902) fought in South Africa between the British and the Dutch settlers. In the following excerpt from *Trooper Peter Halket of Mashonaland*, Schreiner offers keen insight into the motives of Europeans who went to Africa. Unlike powerful adventurers such as Cecil Rhodes, her protagonist is a man of humble origins. Peter Halket craves not only the riches of Africa but also the power his whiteness gives him, power he could not have as a member of the working class in England. At the same time he cannot escape the memories of atrocities perpetrated against the Mashona. At the close of this excerpt, Peter, exhausted from his night of wandering alone in the wilderness, has a conversation with a mysterious "stranger" who challenges him to justify white supremacy.

By inviting us into one man's delirium, Schreiner explores both the perceived attractions to and actual repulsion of imperialism. Which side is she ultimately on and which Peter Halket? Who is the "stranger" and how is this encounter a turning point for Peter? How might her novel have influenced public opinion in England? How does Peter's aloneness in a strange landscape lay bare the horror of the isolated individual?

See p. 536 for accompanying map.

from *Trooper Peter Halket of Mashonaland* (1897)

He sat there staring into the blaze. He resolved he would make a great deal of money, and she should live with him. He would build a large house in the West End of London, the biggest that had ever been seen, and another in the country, and they should never work any more.

Peter Halket sat as one turned into stone, staring into the fire.

All men made money when they came to South Africa,—Barney Barnato, Rhodes—they all made money out of the country, eight millions, twelve millions, twenty-six millions, forty millions; why should not he!

Peter Halket started suddenly and listened. But it was only the wind coming up the koppje like a great wheezy beast creeping upwards; and he looked back into the fire.

He considered his business prospects. When he had served his time as volunteer he would have a large piece of land given him, and the Mashonas and Matabeles would have all their land taken away from them in time, and the Chartered Company would pass a law that they had to work for the white men; and he, Peter Halket, would make them work for him. He would make money.

• • •

Then, after a while, Peter Halket's thoughts became less clear: they became at last, rather, a chain of disconnected pictures, painting themselves in irrelevant order on his brain, than a line of connected ideas. Now, as he looked into the crackling blaze, it seemed to be one of the fires they had made to burn the natives' grain by, and they were throwing in all they could not carry away: then, he seemed to see his mother's fat ducks waddling down the little path with the green grass on each side. Then, he seemed to see his huts where he lived with the prospectors, and the native women who used to live with him; and he wondered where the women were. Then—he saw the skull of an old Mashona blown off at the top, the hands still moving. He heard the loud cry of the native women and children as they turned the maxims on to the kraal; and then he heard the dynamite explode that blew up a cave. Then again he was working a maxim gun, but it seemed to him it was more like the reaping machine he used to work in England, and that what was going down before it was not yellow corn, but black men's heads; and he thought when he looked back they lay behind him in rows, like the corn in sheaves.

The logs sent up a flame clear and high, and, where they split, showed a burning core inside: the crackling and spluttering sounded in his brain like the discharge of a battery of artillery. Then he thought suddenly of a black woman he and another man caught alone in the bush, her baby on her back, but young and pretty. Well, they didn't shoot her!—and a black woman wasn't white! His mother didn't understand these things; it was all so different in England from South Africa. You couldn't be expected to do the same sort of things here as there. He had an unpleasant feeling that he was justifying himself to his mother, and that he didn't know how to.

• • •

"If these men," said the stranger, "would rather be free, or be under the British Government, than under the Chartered Company, why, when they resist the Chartered Company, are they more rebels than the Armenians when they resist the Turk? Is the Chartered Company God, that every knee should bow before it, and before it every head be bent? Would you, the white men of England, submit to its rule for a day?"

"Ah," said Peter, "no of course we shouldn't, but we are white men, and so are the Armenians—almost—" Then he glanced at the stranger's dark face, and added quickly, "At least, it's not the colour that matters, you know. I rather like a dark face, my mother's eyes are brown—but the Armenians, you know, they've got long hair like us."

"Oh, it is the hair, then, that matters," said the stranger softly.

"Oh, well," said Peter, "it's not altogether, of course. But it's quite a different thing, the Armenians wanting to get rid of the Turks, and these bloody niggers wanting to get rid of the Chartered Company. Besides, the Armenians are Christians, like us !"

"Are *you* Christians?" A strange storm broke across the stranger's features; he rose to his feet.

"Why, of course, we are!" said Peter. "We're all Christians, we English. Perhaps you don't like Christians, though? Some Jews don't, I know," said Peter, looking up soothingly at him.

"I neither love nor hate any man for that which it is called," said the stranger; "the name boots nothing."

José Rizal

1861–1896

Independence movements against European Imperialism spread rapidly in the Americas in the first half of the nineteenth century. Though Spain in particular suffered serious losses in Latin America, it maintained its other possessions late into the century, including the Philippines. Its refusal to grant concessions there stimulated a revolution which culminated in the foundation of a republic in 1886. However, the United States, which had supported the rebels, became the new possessors of the Philippines and the fighting continued. Not until 1946 were the Philippines finally independent.

José Rizal, a doctor, novelist, and revolutionary, lost his life in the first struggle, when he was captured by the Spanish in Manila and executed before a firing squad. In his first novel, *The Lost Eden*, Rizal reveals the plight of his people suffering under the yoke of imperialism. Its protagonist, Juan Ibarra, returns from foreign study with great dreams for his country. In this excerpt, he tells his old friend and mentor, Tasio, of his plans. Tasio cautions Ibarra that the government and the Church have become so entrenched that reform is impossible and that people, cowed into silence by fear, will be reluctant to embrace change.

In their dialogue, important themes emerge that are common to many colonial situations. Can positive change come from Imperialist forces or even be based on Imperialist models? How can indigenous, nationalist movements emerge under oppressive circumstances? What is the role of the romantic hero in bringing about such change?

from *The Lost Eden*
(*Noli Me Tangere*) (1886)

Ibarra told him briefly of his plan for a school, which was to be a gift to his fiancée, and put before the impressed scholar the building plans he had received from Manila.

'Now I should like you to tell me whom in town I should win over to make my plan as successful as possible. You know everyone here. I have just arrived and I am almost a stranger in my own country.'

Old Tasio carefully examined the plans before him with eyes moist with tears.

'You're going to do what I once dreamed of doing; a poor madman's dream!' he exclaimed greatly moved. 'And my first advice is never to ask my advice!'

Ibarra looked surprised.

•   •   •

'The Government! The Government you say!' muttered the scholar [Tasio], and raised his eyes to the ceiling. 'However desirous it may be of improving the country for its own sake and that of the Mother Country, however much this or that official may remember the generous spirit of Ferdinand and Isabella and pledge himself to it, the Government itself sees nothing, hears nothing, and decides nothing except what the parish priest or the head of a religious Order makes it see, hear, and decide. It is convinced that it rests on them alone; that it stands because they support it; that it lives because they allow it to live; and that the day they are gone, it will fall like a discarded puppet. The Government is intimidated with threats to raise the people against it, and the people cowed with the Government's armed forces. This is the basis of a strategy that is quite simple, but it works for the same reason that cowards in cemeteries take their own shadows for ghosts and the echoes of their own voices for calls from the dead. So long as the Government does not deal directly with the people it will not cease to be a ward, and will live like those idiots who tremble at the sound of their keeper's voice and curry his favour. The Government does not plan a better future; it is only an arm, the convent is the head. Because of the inertia with which it allows itself to be dragged from failure to failure, it becomes a shadow, loses its identity, and, weak and incapable, entrusts everything to selfish interests. If you don't believe me, compare our governmental system with that of the countries you have visited. . . .'

300

'Oh,' interrupted Ibarra, 'that's asking too much! Surely it's enough to satisfy us that our people don't complain or suffer like those of other countries, thanks to the Church and the benevolence of our rulers.'

'The people do not complain because they have no voice; they do not move because they are in a stupor; and you say that they do not suffer because you have not seen how their hearts bleed. But some day you will see and hear! Then woe unto those who draw their strength from ignorance and fanaticism, who take their pleasure in fraud, and who work under cover of night, confident that all are asleep! When the light of day reveals the monstrous creatures of the night, the reaction will be terrifying. All the forces stifled for centuries, the poisons distilled drop by drop, all the repressed emotions, will come to light in a great explosion. Who shall then settle the accounts, such accounts as the peoples of the world have presented from time to time in those revolutions that history records in blood-stained pages?'

'God, the Government, and the Church will not allow such a thing to happen!' replied Crisóstomo, greatly moved in spite of himself. 'The Philippines is religious and loves Spain, and she will realise how much the Mother Country is doing for her. Of course there are abuses; I won't deny there are shortcomings; but Spain is working out reforms to remedy them; she is developing a programme; she is not selfish.'

'I know it, and that's the worst of it. The reforms which come from above are annulled below by the vices of all, by, for example, the get-rich-quick madness, and the ignorance of the people who let everything pass. Abuses cannot be corrected by royal decree if zealous authorities do not watch over its execution, and while freedom of speech against the excesses of petty tyrants is not granted. Otherwise plans will stay plans, the abuses will continue, which will not prevent the cabinet member in Madrid from enjoying the sleep of one who has done his duty. Furthermore, if a high official comes with great and generous ideas, he soon hears such advice as this, while behind his back he is taken for a fool: "Your Excellency does not know the country, and the character of the natives; Your Excellency will spoil them; Your Excellency will do well to trust So and So, and so on." And as His Excellency really does not know the country, which heretofore he had thought was somewhere in America, and besides, has weaknesses and faults of his own like any other mortal, he finally allows himself to be convinced. His Excellency also keeps in mind that he has worked hard and endured even more to obtain his office, that he will hold it only for three years, and that he is getting old and must think of his future rather than quixotic enterprises—a modest house in Madrid, a little country lodge, a good income on which to make a show at Court, those are the things he must work for in the Philippines. Let us not ask for miracles; let us not expect the foreigner who comes only to make his fortune and then go home, to take an interest in the welfare of the country. What does he care about the blessings or the curses of a country which he does not know and where he has no memories or loved ones? To be satisfying, glory must ring in the ears of those we love, within the walls of our homes, in the air of our native country where we shall be laid to rest. We want glory to warm our graves, so that we may not be reduced to nothing and something of ourselves may yet endure. We cannot promise any of these things to those who come to guide our destinies. And the worst of it is that, just when they have begun to learn what their duty is, it is time for them to leave. But we are getting away from our subject.'

'Before returning to it, I must first get something clear,' interrupted the young man excitedly. 'I grant you that the Government does not understand the people, but I also think that the people understand the Government even less. There are officials who are useless, even bad, if you will, but there are also good ones, and, if the latter can do nothing, it is because they are faced with an inert mass, the people, who take scant interest in the matters which concern them. However, I did not come here to argue with you on this point; I came to ask your advice. You say I should bow my head before grotesque idols. . . .'

'Yes, and I repeat it because in this country you have either to bow your head or . . . lose it.'

'Bow my head or lose it,' repeated Ibarra thoughtfully. 'It is a hard dilemma. But why should it be so? Is my love of country incompatible with love for Spain? Is it necessary to humiliate oneself to be a good Christian, and to betray one's conscience to achieve a good objective? I love my county, the Philippines, because I owe her my life and happiness, and because every man should love his country. I love Spain, the country of my forefathers, because after all the Philippines owe and will owe to Spain both happiness and future. I am a Catholic and keep pure the faith of my fathers. I don't see why I should bow my head when I can hold it high, or place it in the hands of my enemies when I can defeat them.'

'The reason is that the field in which you want to work is in the power of your enemies, and you cannot prevail against them. You must first kiss the hand that—'

'Kiss it!' Ibarra interrupted him passionately. 'You forget that between them they killed my father and then threw his body out of the grave. But I am his son and do not forget it, and, if I do not avenge him, it is to protect the good name of the Church.'

The old scholar bent his head.

'Mr Ibarra,' he replied slowly, 'if you remember such things, and indeed I cannot advise you to forget them, you had better renounce the enterprise you plan and look for some other way to promote the welfare of our countrymen. The undertaking needs another man, because, to put it through, money and goodwill are not enough. In our country abnegation, tenacity, and faith are also required; the field is not ready for sowing, it is full of weeds.'

Ibarra realised the value of this advice, but could not allow himself to be discouraged. The memory of María Clara was in his mind, and it was necessary to keep his promise.

'Does not your experience suggest a way out that would be less painful?' he asked in a subdued voice.

The old man took him by the arm and led him to the window. A chilly wind, forerunner of the north wind, was blowing. Before them was the garden stretching out to the dense wood that served the house as a park.

'Why shouldn't we do as that weak stem loaded with roses and buds?' asked the scholar, pointing to a beautiful rose bush. 'The wind blows and shakes it and it bows down as if to hide its precious burden. If the stem were to stay straight it would break, and the wind would scatter the flowers, and the buds would die unopened. But the wind passes on, and then the stem straightens up again, proud of its treasure. Who will blame it for having bowed to necessity? Take that giant tree. The eagle builds its nest in those swaying stately branches. I transplanted it from the forest as a weak sapling. For months I had to prop it up with bamboo stakes. But if I had transplanted instead some full-grown vigorous tree, I am sure it would not have survived. The wind would have blown it down before its roots could have taken a firm grip, and before the ground had settled round it and given it the sustenance proper to its size and height. So might you come to an end, a tree transplanted from Europe to this stony soil, unless you look for support and make yourself small. You are in a bad situation, alone, high up. The earth shakes; there are storm signals in the skies; your family tree has been known to attract lightning. To fight alone against the world is not courage but foolhardiness. No one blames a pilot who takes refuge in port when the storm begins to blow. It is not cowardice to duck under a bullet; what is wrong is to defy it only to fall and never rise again.'

● ●. ●

Simon Pokagon

1830–1899

Born in Indiana, Simon Pokagon moved with his family to Dowagiac, Michigan, when he was still a boy. Pokagon studied at a manual labor school attached to Notre Dame and then at the Twinsburg Institute in Ohio. Pokagon lectured extensively throughout the 1850s, following his participation in a Potawatomi delegation visit to Washington. As a result of treaty agreements, the Potawatomi of Michigan were allowed to remain in southwest Michigan and continue to this day to live in the region. They were refused tribal status when they applied as required by the Indian Reorganization Act of 1934, but sixty years later were granted federal recognition. His tribe became known as the Pokagon Potawatomi in acknowledgment of his political and cultural efforts on their behalf.

Pokagon wrote numerous books and articles, including *The Red Man's Rebuke* (1893), "An Indian on the Problems of His Race" (1895), and *Algonquin Legends of South Haven* (1900). In "The Future of the Red Man" and elsewhere, he asks the reader to look for universal qualities and values when seeking to understand human nature, whether Christian or Native American. He laments the ignorance in which both whites and Native Americans live, when it comes to their dealings with one another. In his critique of Native-American responsibility for successful adaptation to a white worldview, he anticipates contemporary debates on the nature of cultural difference and the problem of preserving the heritage of marginalized peoples, in the face of such pressures as mass culture, intermarriage, and the rise of modern capitalism. How do Pokagon's contributions to our thinking about human nature compare with those of eighteenth- and nineteenth-century intellectuals, such as Mary Wollstonecraft and John Stuart Mill? What points of contact are there between Pokagon's political and cultural views and those expressed by writers such as Frederick Douglass, Booker T. Washington, W. E. B. DuBois, and Marcus Garvey?

from "The Future of the Red Man" (1897)

Often in the stillness of the night, when all nature seems asleep about me, there comes a gentle rapping at the door of my heart. I open it; and a voice inquires, "Pokagon, what of your people? What will their future be?" My answer is: "Mortal man has not the power to draw aside the veil of unborn time to tell the future of his race. That gift belongs to the Divine alone. But it is given to him to closely judge the future by the present and the past." Hence, in order to approximate the future of our race, we must consider our natural capabilities and our environments, as connected with the dominant race which outnumbers us—three hundred to one—in this land of our fathers.

First, then, let us carefully consider if Mis-ko-au-ne-ne-og' (the red man) possesses, or is devoid of, loyalty, sympathy, benevolence, and gratitude,—those heaven-born virtues requisite for Christian character and civilization. But, in doing so, let us constantly bear in mind that the character of our people has always been published to the world by the dominant race, and that human nature is now the same as when Solomon declared that "He that is first in his own cause seemeth just; but his neighbor cometh and searcheth him." In our case we have ever stood as dumb to the charges brought against us as did the Divine Master before His false accusers; hence all charges alleged against us in history should be cautiously considered, with Christian charity. There have been, and still are, too many writers who, although they have never seen an Indian in their lives, have published tragical stories of their treachery and cruelty. Mothers, for generations past, have frightened their children into obedience with that dreaded scarecrow, "Look out, or the Injuns will get you!"; creating in the infant mind a false prejudice against our race, which has given birth to that base slander, "There is no good Injun but a dead one." It is therefore no wonder that we are hated by some worse than Satan hates the salvation of human souls.

Let us glance backward to the year 1492. Columbus and his officers and crew are spending their first Christmas on the border-islands of the New World. It is not a merry, but a sad, Christmas to them. They stand crowded on the deck of the tiny ship "Nina." Four weeks since, Pinson, with the "Pinta" and her crew, deserted the squadron; and last night the flagship, "Santa Maria," that had safely borne the Admiral across an unknown sea to a strange land, was driven before the gale and stranded near the shore of Hispaniola. Deserted by her crew and left to the mercy of the breakers, she lies prostrate on the perilous sands, shivering and screaming in the wind like a wounded creature of life responsive to every wave that smites her.

It is early morning. Columbus sends Diego de Arna and Pedro Guthene to the great Chief of the Island, telling him of their sad disaster, and requesting that he come and help to save their goods from being swept into the sea. The Chief listens with all attention to the sad news; his heart is touched; he answers with his tears; and orders his people to go at once, with their canoes well manned, and help to save the stranger's goods. He also sends one of his servants to the Admiral with a message of sincere regrets for his misfortunes, offering all the aid in his power. Columbus receives the servant on shipboard; and, while he listens with gratitude to the cheering message delivered in signs and broken words, he rejoices to see coming to his relief along the shore a hundred boats, manned by a thousand men, mostly naked, bearing down upon the wrecked "Santa Maria," and swarming about her like bees around their hive. The goods disappear from the ship as by magic, are rowed ashore, and safely secured. Not one native takes advantage of the disaster for his own profit. Spanish history declares that in no part of the civilized world could Columbus have received warmer or more cordial hospitality.

Touched by such tender treatment, Columbus, writing to the King and Queen of Spain, pays this beautiful tribute to the native Carib race:—

> They are a loving, uncovetous people, so docile in all things that I swear to your Majesties there is not in all the world a better race, or more delightful country. They love their neighbors as themselves; their talk is ever sweet and gentle, accompanied with smiles; and though they be naked, yet their manners are decorous and praiseworthy.

Peter Martyr, a reliable historian, has left on record the following:—

> It is certain the land among these people is as common as sun and water, and that 'mine and thine,' the seed of all misery, have no place with them. They are content with so little that in so large a country they have rather a superfluity than a scarceness, so that they seem to live in the golden world, without toil, living in open gardens not intrenched or defended with walls. They deal justly one with another without books, without laws, without judges. They take him for an evil and mischievous man who taketh pleasure in doing hurt to another; and although they delight not in superfluities, yet they make provision for the increase of such roots whereof they make bread, content with such simple diet wherewith health is preserved and disease avoided.
>
> —Peter Martyr, Decade 1, Book 3.

Does not this quotation most emphatically show that the red men of the New World did originally possess every virtue necessary for Christian civilization and enlightenment?

The question is often asked, "What became of the numerous Caribs of those islands? They seemed to have vanished like leaves in autumn; for within a few years we find them supplanted by foreign slaves. The noble Bishop Las Casas tells us, in pity, "With mine own eyes, I saw kingdoms as full of people as hives are of bees; and now, where are they?" Almost all, he says, have perished by the sword and under the lash of cruel Spanish taskmasters, in the greedy thirst for gold.

Certain it is that in those days, which tried the souls of the Carib race, some fled from the lust and lash of their oppressors by sea to the coast of Florida, and reported to the natives there that *Wau-be-au'-ne-ne-og* (white men), who fought with *Awsh-kon-tay' Au-ne-me-kee'* (thunder and lightning), who were cruel, vindictive, and without love, except a thirsty greed for gold, had come from the other side of *Kons-ke-tchi-saw-me'* (the ocean) and made slaves of *Mis-ko-au-ne-ne-og'* (the red man) of the islands, which was reported from tribe to tribe across the continent.

Scarcely a quarter-century passes since the enslavement of the Carib race, and Ponce de Leon, a Spanish adventurer, is landing from his squadron a large number of persons to colonize the coast of Florida. A few years previously, while in pursuit of the fountain of youth, he had been here for the first time, on the day of the "Feast of Flowers." Then, he was kindly received and welcomed by the sons of the forest. Now, as then, the air is perfumed with the odor of fruits and flowers; and all on shore appears pleasing and inviting. The Spaniards land, and slowly climb the terrace that bounds the sea. Here they pause, planting side by side the Spanish standard and the cross. But hark! War-whoops are heard close by. And there they come,—long lines of savages from the surrounding woods, who, with slings and darts, with clubs and stones, fall upon the dreaded Spaniards. The onslaught is terrible. Many are killed; and Ponce de Leon is mortally wounded. He now begins to realize that among the savage hosts are Caribs who have escaped from slavery and death. He well knows the bitter story of their wrong, and that this bloody chastisement is but the returning boomerang of Spanish cruelty. They flee from the avengers of blood to the ships. The report they give of the savage attack, on their return to Spain, is so terrible that years pass before another attempt is made to colonize the land of fruits and flowers.

I deem it unnecessary to explain why these peaceful natives so soon became so warlike and vindictive. Suffice it to say: "Enslave a good man and, like the wasp which stings the hand that holds it fast, he will make use of all the means which nature has placed in his power to regain his liberty." During the first century of American history, many adventurers from different European countries sailed along the eastern coast of North America,—all reporting the natives peaceable and kind when not misused.

There was a tradition among our fathers that, before the colonization of North America, an armed band of *Wau-be-au'-ne-ne-og'* (white men), gorgeously clad, came on the war-path from the East, reaching the Dakotas, which then extended south as far as the mouth of the Arkansas River; that they were vindictive and cruel, destroying the natives wherever they went with *Awsh-kon-tay' Au-ne-me-kee'* (thunder and lightning). They were looking for gold, their *Man-i-to* (god), and, not finding him, went down *Mi-che-se-pe* (the great river) and were seen no more. Those cruel adventurers, who came among us by sea and land, must have awakened hatred and revenge in the hearts of our fathers, which may have been transmitted to their children.

• • •

At one time I felt that our race was doomed to extermination. There was an awful unrest among the western tribes who had been pushed by the cruel march of civilization into desert places, where subsistence was impossible. Starvation drove many to steal cattle from adjacent ranches; and when some of our people were killed by the cowboys, their friends were determined to take the war-path. I never failed on such occasions to declare most emphatically, "You might as well march your warriors into the jaws of an active volcano, expecting to shut off its fire and smoke, as to attempt to beat back the westward trend of civilization. You must teach your sons everywhere that the war-path will lead them but to the grave."

Having briefly reviewed some of our past history, the fact must be admitted that, when the white men first visited our shores, we were kind and confiding; standing before them like a block of marble before the sculptor, ready to be shaped into noble manhood. Instead of this, we were oftener hacked to pieces and destroyed. We further find in our brief review that the contending Powers of the Old World, striving for the mastery in the New, took advantage of our trustful, confiding natures, placing savage weapons of warfare in our hands to aid us in butchering one another.

• • •

While I most heartily endorse the present policy of the Government in dealing with our people, I must admit—to be true to my own convictions—that I am worried over the ration system, under which so many of our people are being fed on the reservations. I greatly fear it may eventually vagabondize many of them beyond redemption. It permits the gathering of lazy, immoral white men of the worst stamp, who spend their time in idleness and in corrupting Indian morality. I do hope the Government will provide something for them to do for their own good, although it should pay her little or nothing. Again: I fear for the outcome of the Indian nations. Our people in their native state were not avaricious. They were on a common level; and, like the osprey that divides her last fish with her young, so they acted toward each other. But I find, to my sorrow, that, when you associate them with squaw men, and place them in power, they develop the wolfish greed of civilization, disregarding the rights of their less fortunate brothers. I must admit that it staggers my native brain to understand what reason, equity, or justice there is in allowing independent powers to exist within the bounds of this Republic. If the "Monroe doctrine," which has been so much petted of late years, should be enforced anywhere, it would certainly be in the line of good statesmanship to carry it out, at least in principle, at home.

• • •

I have made diligent inquiries of the headmen of different tribes as to what estimate they place on the half-breeds among them. Their general reply has been, "They are certainly an improvement on the pale face, but not on the red man." Which no doubt is the case; for it is a lamentable fact that criminals, outlaws, and vagabonds are generally the first who seek homes among us, bringing with them nearly all the vices and diseases, and but few of the virtues, of civilization. Yet, notwithstanding such an unfortunate mixture, we find some grand characters who have been able to rise high above the sins of parentage. I have further found, by close observation, that those tinctured with our blood are far less subject to nervous diseases; but whether at the expense of intellectual force or otherwise, I am not so certain. Be that as it may, we cannot safely ignore the fact, that it is the physical development of the people of a nation that gives it strength and stability; that physical decay brings loss of executive ability, and has proved the overthrow of ancient kingdoms. I do not wish it to be understood that I advocate or desire the amalgamation of our people with the white race. But I speak of it as an event that is almost certain; and we had much better rock with the boat that oars us on than fight against the inevitable. I am frequently asked, "Pokagon, do you believe that the white man and the red man were originally of one blood?" My reply has been: "I do not know. But from the present outlook, they surely will be."

The index-finger of the past and present is pointing to the future, showing most conclusively that by the middle of the next century all Indian reservations and tribal relations will have passed away. Then our people will begin to scatter; and the result will be a general mixing up of the races. Through intermarriage the blood of our people, like the waters that flow into the great ocean, will be forever lost in the dominant race; and generations yet unborn will read in history of the red men of the forest, and inquire, "Where are they?"

Zitkala-Ša

1876–1938

Zitkala-Ša was born Gertrude Simmons, on the Yankton Reservation in South Dakota. Her mother was a Native American Sioux and her father was white. Simmon's father left the family before she was born, and so her mother, who never learned English and kept the customs of the Sioux, raised her daughter on the Yankton Reservation. Gertrude received her education at a Quaker mission school and at Earlham College in Indiana. Later, she became a violinist at the New England Conservatory. In 1902 she married a Sioux, Raymond T. Bonnin, after which she changed her name to Gertrude Simmons Bonnin. The Sioux name Zitkala-Ša, which translates as Red Bird, was one that she had given herself. During her lifetime she distinguished herself as a musician, reciter, author, and activist for Native-American rights. She collaborated with William E. Hanson on the prize-winning Native-American opera *Sun Dance* and she founded the National Council of American Indians.

Zitkala-Ša sought to preserve the rich legends of her ancestors, whose stories were handed down through oral tradition. As Native-American tribes fractured and disappeared, she committed herself to putting these stories into writing. In 1901, she published a collection of Sioux stories in *Old Indian Legends*. Her writings captured the sadness and hardship of the dual life of a Native American in mainstream society, especially during a time when Native-American culture was disintegrating under the pressure of contemporary politics and social practice.

Zitkala-Ša's "Why I Am a Pagan" (1902) is one of her autobiographical essays, originally published in the *Atlantic Monthly*. In this selection, she examines the confrontation of cultures and religious worldviews, in this case Native American and Christian, when a Sioux convert and preacher (referred to as "cousin" in the essay) criticizes her for not attending church services. Her essay challenges the concept of acculturation of the Native American. What is Zitkala-Ša's response to the preacher's Christian zeal to convert her? How is Zitkala-Ša's spirituality similar to that of Pascal or the later Romantics?

Why I Am a Pagan (1902)

When the spirit swells my breast I love to roam leisurely among the green hills; or sometimes, sitting on the brink of the murmuring Missouri, I marvel at the great blue overhead. With half closed eyes I watch the huge cloud shadows in their noiseless play upon the high bluffs opposite me, while into my ear ripple the sweet, soft cadences of the river's song. Folded hands lie in my lap, for the time forgot. My heart and I lie small upon the earth like a grain of throbbing sand. Drifting clouds and tinkling waters, together with the warmth of a genial summer day, bespeak with eloquence the loving Mystery round about us. During the idyll while I sat upon the sunny river brink, I grew somewhat, though my response be not so clearly manifest as in the green grass fringing the edge of the high bluff back of me.

At length retracing the uncertain footpath scaling the precipitous embankment, I seek the level lands where grow the wild prairie flowers. And they, the lovely little folk, soothe my soul with their perfumed breath.

Their quaint round faces of varied hue convince the heart which leaps with glad surprise that they, too, are living symbols of omnipotent thought. With a child's eager eye I drink in the myriad star shapes wrought in luxuriant color upon the green. Beautiful is the spiritual essence they embody.

I leave them nodding in the breeze but take along with me their impress upon my heart. I pause to rest me upon a rock embedded on the side of a foothill facing the low river bottom. Here the Stone-Boy, of whom the American aborigine tells, frolics about, shooting his baby arrows and shouting aloud with glee at the tiny shafts of lightning that flash from the flying arrow-beaks. What an ideal warrior he became, baffling the siege of the pests of all the land till he triumphed over their united attack. And here he lay,—Invan, our great-great-grandfather, older than the hill he rested on, older than the race of men who love to tell of his wonderful career.

Interwoven with the thread of this Indian legend of the rock, I fain would trace a subtle knowledge of the native folk which enabled them to recognize a kinship to any and all parts of this vast universe. By the leading of an ancient trail, I move toward the Indian village.

With the strong, happy sense that both great and small are so surely enfolded in His magnitude that, without a miss, each has his allotted individual ground of opportunities, I am buoyant with good nature.

Yellow Breast, swaying upon the slender stem of a wild sunflower, warbles a sweet assurance of this as I pass near by. Breaking off the clear crystal

312

song, he turns his wee head from side to side eyeing me wisely as slowly I plod with moccasined feet. Then again he yields himself to his song of joy. Flit, flit hither and yon, he fills the summer sky with his swift, sweet melody. And truly does it seem his vigorous freedom lies more in his little spirit than in his wing.

With these thoughts I reach the log cabin whither I am strongly drawn by the tie of a child to an aged mother. Out bounds my four-footed friend to meet me, frisking about my path with unmistakable delight. Chan is a black shaggy dog, "a thorough-bred little mongrel," of whom I am very fond. Chan seems to understand many words in Sioux, and will go to her mat even when I whisper the word, though generally I think she is guided by the tone of the voice. Often she tries to imitate the sliding inflection and long drawn out voice to the amusement of our guests, but her articulation is quite beyond my ear. In both my hands I hold her shaggy head and gaze into her large brown eyes. At once the dilated pupils contract into tiny black dots, as if the roguish spirit within would evade my questioning.

Finally resuming the chair at my desk I feel in keen sympathy with my fellow creatures, for I seem to see clearly again that all are akin.

The racial lines, which once were bitterly real, now serve nothing more than marking out a living mosaic of human beings. And even here men of the same color are like the ivory keys of one instrument where each represents all the rest, yet varies from them in pitch and quality of voice. And those creatures who are for a time mere echoes of another's note are not unlike the fable of the thin sick man whose distorted shadow, dressed like a real creature, came to the old master to make him follow as a shadow. Thus with a compassion for all echoes in human guise, I greet the solemn-faced "native preacher" whom I find awaiting me. I listen with respect for God's creature, though he mouth most strangely the jangling phrases of a bigoted creed.

As our tribe is one large family, where every person is related to all the others, he addressed me:—

"Cousin, I came from the morning church service to talk with you."

"Yes," I said interrogatively, as he paused for some word from me.

Shifting uneasily about in the straight-backed chair he sat upon, he began: "Every holy day (Sunday) I look about our little God's house, and not seeing you there, I am disappointed. This is why I come to-day. Cousin, as I watch you from afar, I see no unbecoming behavior and hear only good reports of you, which all the more burns me with the wish that you were a church member. Cousin, I was taught long years ago by kind missionaries to read the holy book. These godly men taught me also the folly of our old beliefs.

"There is one God who gives reward or punishment to the race of dead men. In the upper region the Christian dead are gathered in unceasing song and prayer. In the deep pit below, the sinful ones dance in torturing flames.

"Think upon these things, my cousin, and choose now to avoid the after-doom of hell fire!" Then followed a long silence in which he clasped tighter and unclasped again his interlocked fingers.

Like instantaneous lightning flashes came pictures of my own mother's making, for she, too, is now a follower of the new superstition.

"Knocking out the chinking of our log cabin, some evil hand thrust in a burning taper of braided dry grass, but failed of his intent, for the fire died out and the half burned brand fell inward to the floor. Directly above it, on a shelf, lay the holy book. This is what we found after our return from a several days' visit. Surely some great power is hid in the sacred book!"

Brushing away from my eyes many like pictures, I offered midday meal to the converted Indian sitting wordless and with downcast face. No sooner had he risen from the table with "Cousin, I have relished it," than the church bell rang.

Thither he hurried forth with his afternoon sermon. I watched him as he hastened along, his eyes bent fast upon the dusty road till he disappeared at the end of a quarter of a mile.

The little incident recalled to mind the copy of a missionary paper brought to my notice a few days ago, in which a "Christian" pugilist commented upon a recent article of mine, grossly perverting the spirit of my pen. Still I would not forget that the pale-faced missionary and the hoodooed aborigine are both God's creatures, though small indeed their own conceptions of Infinite Love. A wee child toddling in a wonder world, I prefer to their dogma my excursions into the natural gardens where the voice of the Great Spirit is heard in the twittering of birds, the rippling of mighty waters, and the sweet breathing of flowers. If this is Paganism, then at present, at least, I am a Pagan.

Ohiyesa

1858–1939

Ohiyesa was born a Santee Sioux in Redwood Falls, Minnesota. He was named Hadakah, which translates as "pitiful last," because his mother—Mary Nancy Eastman, herself of mixed parentage—died during his birth. His grandmother renamed him Ohiyesa, "the winner," after he distinguished himself in a sports event at age four. For his first fifteen years he lived according to the customs and traditions of the Sioux. Ohiyesa and his father, Ite Wakanhdi Ota (Many Lightnings), were forced to separate after the 1862 Sioux Uprising. Ohiyesa escaped to Canada, where he lived in the belief that his father had been caught and executed with 38 other Sioux warriors. In fact, Many Lightnings had been captured with the other Sioux, but had had his sentence commuted by President Abraham Lincoln to three years in a federal penitentiary in Davenport, Iowa. Returning home a convert to Christianity, Ohiyesa's father had him baptized and given the name Charles Alexander Eastman.

Many Lightnings wanted his son educated within the dominant white culture. Ohiyesa went first to a mission school, then to a series of other schools, leading eventually to Dartmouth College, where he excelled in both academics and athletics. He enrolled in Boston University's School of Medicine and received his medical degree in 1890 at the age of 32. Following the Native-American custom that individual achievement must be directed to the benefit of the tribe, Ohiyesa became the physician at the Pine Ridge reservation just months before the massacre at Wounded Knee. Ohiyesa witnessed firsthand the slaughter of his people as the United States pushed westward under the principle of "Manifest Destiny." He also experienced white prejudice in less historic ways, which nonetheless affected him deeply.

In this excerpt of *The Soul of the Indian* (1911), what does Ohiyesa convey about Native-American life and culture that draws from his childhood experience? What is morality according to Ohiyesa? Describe some of the changes he experienced as he came into contact with white civilization. How might these changes have shaped his worldview?

from *The Soul of the Indian* (1911)

I. The Great Mystery

The original attitude of the American Indian toward the Eternal, the "Great Mystery" that surrounds and embraces us, was as simple as it was exalted. To him it was the supreme conception, bringing with it the fullest measure of joy and satisfaction possible in this life.

The worship of the "Great Mystery" was silent, solitary, free from all self-seeking. It was silent, because all speech is of necessity feeble and imperfect; therefore the souls of my ancestors ascended to God in wordless adoration. It was solitary, because they believed that He is nearer to us in solitude, and there were no priests authorized to come between a man and his Maker. None might exhort or confess or in any way meddle with the religious experience of another. Among us all men were created sons of God and stood erect, as conscious of their divinity. Our faith might not be formulated in creeds, nor forced upon any who were unwilling to receive it; hence there was no preaching, proselyting, nor persecution, neither were there any scoffers or atheists.

There were no temples or shrines among us save those of nature. Being a natural man, the Indian was intensely poetical. He would deem it sacrilege to build a house for Him who may be met face to face in the mysterious, shadowy aisles of the primeval forest, or on the sunlit bosom of virgin prairies, upon dizzy spires and pinnacles of naked rock, and yonder in the jeweled vault of the night sky! He who enrobes Himself in filmy veils of cloud, there on the rim of the visible world where our Great-Grandfather Sun kindles his evening camp-fire, He who rides upon the rigorous wind of the north, or breathes forth His spirit upon aromatic southern airs, whose war-canoe is launched upon majestic rivers and inland seas—He needs no lesser cathedral!

That solitary communion with the Unseen which was the highest expression of our religious life is partly described in the word *bambeday*, literally "mysterious feeling," which has been variously translated "fasting" and "dreaming." It may better be interpreted as "consciousness of the divine."

The first *bambeday*, or religious retreat, marked an epoch in the life of the youth, which may be compared to that of confirmation or conversion in Christian experience.

• • •

In every religion there is an element of the supernatural, varying with the influence of pure reason over its devotees. The Indian was a logical and clear thinker upon matters within the scope of his understanding, but he had not yet charted the vast field of nature or expressed her wonders in terms of science. With his limited knowledge of cause and effect, he saw miracles on every hand,—the miracle of life in seed and egg, the miracle of death in lightning flash and in the swelling deep! Nothing of the marvelous could astonish him; as that a beast should speak, or the sun stand still. The virgin birth would appear scarcely more miraculous than is the birth of every child that comes into the world, or the miracle of the loaves and fishes excite more wonder than the harvest that springs from a single ear of corn.

Who may condemn his superstition? Surely not the devout Catholic, even Protestant missionary, who teaches Bible miracles as literal fact! The logical man must either deny all miracles or none, and our American Indian myths and hero stories are perhaps, in themselves, quite as credible as those of the Hebrews of old. If we are of the modern type of mind, that sees in natural law a majesty and grandeur far more impressive than any solitary infraction of it could possibly be, let us not forget that, after all, science has not explained everything. We have still to face the ultimate miracle,—the origin and principle of life! Here is the supreme mystery that is the essence of worship, without which there can be no religion, and in the presence of this mystery our attitude cannot be very unlike that of the natural philosopher, who beholds with awe the Divine in all creation.

It is simple truth that the Indian did not, so long as his native philosophy held sway over his mind, either envy or desire to imitate the splendid achievements of the white man. In his own thought he rose superior to them! He scorned them, even as a lofty spirit absorbed in its stern task rejects the soft beds, the luxurious food, the pleasure-worshiping dalliance of a rich neighbor. It was clear to him that virtue and happiness are independent of these things, if not incompatible with them.

There was undoubtedly much in primitive Christianity to appeal to this man, and Jesus' hard sayings to the rich and about the rich would have been entirely comprehensible to him. Yet the religion that is preached in our churches and practiced by our congregations, with its element of display and self-aggrandizement, its active proselytism, and its open contempt of all religions but its own, was for a long time extremely repellent. To his simple mind, the professionalism of the pulpit, the paid exhorter, the moneyed church, was unspiritual and unedifying, and it was not until his spirit was broken and his moral and physical constitution undermined by trade, conquest, and strong drink, that Christian missionaries obtained any real hold upon him. Strange as it may seem, it is true that the proud pagan in his secret soul despised the good men who came to convert and to enlighten him!

Nor were its publicity and its Phariseeism the only elements in the alien religion that offended the red man. To him, it appeared shocking and almost incredible that there were among this people who claimed superiority many irreligious, who did not even pretend to profess the national faith. Not only did they not profess it, but they stooped so low as to insult their God with profane and sacrilegious speech! In our own tongue His name was not spoken aloud, even with utmost reverence, much less lightly or irreverently.

More than this, even in those white men who professed religion we found much inconsistency of conduct. They spoke much of spiritual things, while seeking only the material. They bought and sold everything: time, labor, personal independence, the love of woman, and even the ministrations of their holy faith! The lust for money, power, and conquest so characteristic of the Anglo-Saxon race did not escape moral condemnation at the hands of his untutored judge, nor did he fail to contrast this conspicuous trait of the dominant race with the spirit of the meek and lowly Jesus.

He might in time come to recognize that the drunkards and licentious among white men, with whom he too frequently came in contact, were condemned by the white man's religion as well, and must not be held to discredit it. But it was not so easy to overlook or to excuse national bad faith. When distinguished emissaries from the Father at Washington, some of them ministers of the gospel and even bishops, came to the Indian nations, and pledged to them in solemn treaty the national honor, with prayer and mention of their God; and when such treaties, so made, were promptly and shamelessly broken, is it strange that the action should arouse not only anger, but contempt? The historians of the white race admit that the Indian was never the first to repudiate his oath.

It is my personal belief, after thirty-five years' experience of it, that there is no such thing as "Christian civilization." I believe that Christianity and modern civilization are opposed and irreconcilable, and that the spirit of Christianity and of our ancient religion is essentially the same.

IV. Barbarism and the Moral Code

Long before I ever heard of Christ, or saw a white man, I had learned from an untutored woman the essence of morality. With the help of dear Nature herself, she taught me things simple but of mighty import. I knew God. I perceived what goodness is. I saw and loved what is really beautiful. Civilization has not taught me anything better!

As a child, I understood how to give; I have forgotten that grace since I became civilized. I lived the natural life, whereas I now live the artificial. Any pretty pebble was valuable to me then; every growing tree an object of reverence. Now I worship with the white man before a painted landscape whose value is estimated in dollars! Thus the Indian is reconstructed, as the natural rocks are ground to powder, and made into artificial blocks which may be built into the walls of modern society.

The first American mingled with his pride a singular humility. Spiritual arrogance was foreign to his nature and teaching. He never claimed that the power of articulate speech was proof of superiority over the silent creation; on the other hand, it is to him a perilous gift. He believes profoundly in silence—the sign of a perfect equilibrium. Silence is the absolute poise or balance of body, mind, and spirit. The man who preserves his selfhood ever calm and unshaken by the storms of existence—not a leaf, as it were, astir on the tree; not a ripple upon the surface of shining pool—his, in the mind of the unlettered sage, is the ideal attitude and conduct of life.

If you ask him: "What is silence?" he will answer: "It is the Great Mystery! The holy silence is His voice!" If you ask: "What are the fruits of silence?" he will say: "They are self-control, true courage or endurance, patience, dignity, and reverence. Silence is the corner-stone of character."

"Guard your tongue in youth," said the old chief, Wabashaw, "and in age you may mature a thought that will be of service to your people!"

The moment that man conceived of a perfect body, supple, symmetrical, graceful, and enduring—in that moment he had laid the foundation of a moral life! No man can hope to maintain such a temple of the spirit beyond the period of adolescence, unless he is able to curb his indulgence in the pleasures of the senses. Upon this truth the Indian built a rigid system of physical training, a social and moral code that was the law of his life.

There was aroused in him as a child a high ideal of manly strength and beauty, the attainment of which must depend upon strict temperance in eating and in the sexual relation, together with severe and persistent exercise. He desired to be a worthy link in the generations, and that he might not destroy by his weakness that vigor and purity of blood which had been achieved at the cost of much self-denial by a long line of ancestors.

He was required to fast from time to time for short periods, and to work off his superfluous energy by means of hard running, swimming, and the vapor-bath. The bodily fatigue thus induced, especially when coupled with a reduced diet, is a reliable cure for undue sexual desires.

Personal modesty was early cultivated as a safeguard, together with a strong self-respect and pride of family and race. This was accomplished in part by keeping the child ever before the public eye, from his birth onward. His entrance into the world, especially in the case of the first-born, was often publicly announced by the herald, accompanied by a distribution of presents to the old and needy. The same thing occurred when he took his first step, when his ears were pierced, and when he shot his first game, so that his childish exploits and progress were known to the whole clan as to a larger family, and he grew into manhood with the saving sense of a reputation to sustain.

The youth was encouraged to enlist early in the public service, and to develop a wholesome ambition for the honors of a leader and feastmaker, which can never be his unless he is truthful and generous, as well as brave, and ever mindful of his personal chastity and honor. There were many ceremonial customs which had a distinct moral influence; the woman was rigidly secluded at certain periods, and the young husband was forbidden to approach his own wife when preparing for war or for any religious event. The public or tribal position of the Indian is entirely dependent upon his private virtue, and he is never permitted to forget that he does not live to himself alone, but to his tribe and his clan. Thus habits of perfect self-control were early established, and there were no unnatural conditions or complex temptations to beset him until he was met and overthrown by a stronger race.

•   •   •

Mahatma Gandhi

1869–1948

Born to middle-class parents of the Vaishya, or trading, caste in India, Mohandas Gandhi was sent at the age of eighteen to study law in London. In 1893, he went to South Africa to begin his legal practice and, after experiencing first-hand the racist treatment of the Indian minority by the South-African government, he was moved to become politically active, establishing one year later the Natal Indian Congress. During this time, Gandhi studied the texts of the great world religions—the Koran, the Bible, the Upanishads, the Bhagavad Gita—and gave up his career in the law, choosing instead a life of voluntary poverty and self-denial. Returning to India in 1915, he created a *satayagraha ashram*, a place for the spiritual study of nonviolence and freedom: he and his followers, whose numbers grew incredibly over the years, vowed to commit themselves to truth, chastity, and simplicity. Gandhi also practiced civil disobedience, often accompanied by large groups of supporters; often he was sentenced to prison for his protest, where he engaged in hunger strikes in order to highlight the injustice of British imperialism. In 1939, when war broke out in Europe, Gandhi refused to back the Allies and took an uncompromising anti-war stance. India, he argued, should neither support military forces nor respond to external aggression: if the Japanese invaded India, nonviolence would be the only appropriate response. With the conclusion of World War II, through Gandhi's political leadership and activism, India was freed from British control and gained its independence in 1946. On 30 January 1948, while on the way to his weekly prayer session, Gandhi was shot to death by a Hindu nationalist.

Gandhi drew on many Western philosophical traditions in shaping his own intellectual and moral outlook. During the time he spent as a student in London, he read the works of Marx and Darwin; later he would study Tolstoy, Ruskin, and Thoreau. Still, by the time he wrote *Indian Home Rule* in 1909, Gandhi had rejected western materialism and political methods, which he thought were incompatible with Indian history, culture and tradition.

In reading the selection below, consider the points of contact between Gandhi's position on Indian self-sufficiency and Emerson's views on American self-reliance. In what ways are their values similar? What are their significant differences? On what points does Gandhi take issue with ideas of enlightened self-interest and material progress, so central to our sense of identity in the West?

from *Indian Home Rule* (1909)

Chapter VI
Civilization

READER: . . . Now will you tell me something of what you have read and thought of this civilization?

EDITOR: Let us first consider what state of things is described by the word "civilization." Its true test lies in the fact that people living in it make bodily welfare the object of life. We will take some examples. The people of Europe today live in better-built houses than they did a hundred years ago. This is considered an emblem of civilization, and this is also a matter to promote bodily happiness. Formerly, they wore skins, and used spears as their weapons. Now, they wear long trousers, and, for embellishing their bodies, they wear a variety of clothing, and, instead of spears, they carry with them revolvers containing five or more chambers. If people of a certain country, who have hitherto not been in the habit of wearing much clothing, boots, etc., adopt European clothing, they are supposed to have become civilized out of savagery. Formerly, in Europe, people ploughed their lands mainly by manual labor. Now, one man can plough a vast tract by means of steam engines and can thus amass great wealth. This is called a sign of civilization. Formerly, only a few men wrote valuable books. Now, anybody writes and prints anything he likes and poisons people's minds. Formerly, men traveled in wagons. Now, they fly through the air in trains at the rate of four hundred and more miles per day. This is considered the height of civilization. It has been stated that, as men progress, they shall be able to travel in airships and reach any part of the world in a few hours. Men will not need the use of their hands and feet. They will press a button, and they will have their clothing by their side. They will press another button, and they will have their newspaper. A third, and a motor-car will be in waiting for them. They will have a variety of delicately dished up food. Everything will be done by machinery. Formerly, when people wanted to fight with one another, they measured between them their bodily strength; now it is possible to take away thousands of lives by one man working behind a gun from a hill. This is civilization.

•　•　•

This civilization takes note neither of morality nor of religion. Its votaries calmly state that their business is not to teach religion. Some even consider it

322

to be a superstitious growth. Others put on the cloak of religion, and prate about morality. Even a child can understand that in all I have described above there can be no inducement to morality. Civilization seeks to increase bodily comforts, and it fails miserably even in doing so.

This civilization is irreligion, and it has taken such a hold on the people in Europe that those who are in it appear to be half mad. They lack real physical strength or courage. They keep up their energy by intoxication. They can hardly be happy in solitude. Women, who should be the queens of households, wander in the streets or they slave away in factories. For the sake of a pittance, half a million women in England alone are laboring under trying circumstances in factories or similar institutions. This awful fact is one of the causes of the daily growing suffragette movement.

This civilization is such that one has only to be patient and it will be self-destroyed. According to the teaching of Mahomed this would be considered a Satanic Civilization. Hinduism calls it the Black Age. I cannot give you an adequate conception of it. It is eating into the vitals of the English nation. It must be shunned. Parliaments are really emblems of slavery. If you will sufficiently think over this, you will entertain the same opinion and cease to blame the English. They rather deserve our sympathy. They are a shrewd nation and I therefore believe that they will cast off the evil. They are enterprising and industrious, and their mode of thought is not inherently immoral. Neither are they bad at heart. I therefore respect them. Civilization is not an incurable disease, but it should never be forgotten that the English people are at present afflicted by it.

Chapter XIII
What Is True Civilization?

READER: You have denounced railways, lawyers and doctors. I can see that you will discard all machinery. What, then, is civilization?

EDITOR: The answer to that question is not difficult. I believe that the civilization India has evolved is not be beaten in the world. Nothing can equal the seeds sown by our ancestors. Rome went, Greece shared the same fate; the might of the Pharaohs was broken; Japan has become westernized; of China nothing can be said; but India is still, somehow or other, sound at the foundation. The people of Europe learn their lessons from the writings of the men of Greece or Rome, which exist no longer in their former glory. In trying to learn from them, the Europeans imagine that they will avoid the mistakes of Greece and Rome. Such is their pitiable condition. In the midst of all this India remains immovable and that is her glory. It is a charge against India that her people are so uncivilized, ignorant and stolid, that it is not possible to induce them to adopt any changes. It is a charge really against our merit. What we have tested and found true on the anvil of experience, we dare not change. Many thrust their advice upon India, and she remains steady. This is her beauty: it is the sheet-anchor of our hope.

Civilization is that mode of conduct which points out to man the path of duty. Performance of duty and observance of morality are convertible terms. To observe morality is to attain mastery over our mind and our passions. So doing, we know ourselves. The Gujarati equivalent for civilization means "good conduct."

If this definition be correct, then India, as so many writers have shown, has nothing to learn from anybody else, and this is as it should be.

• • •

In no part of the world, and under no civilization, have all men attained perfection. The tendency of the Indian civilization is to elevate the moral being, that of the Western civilization is to propagate immorality. The latter is godless, the former is based on a belief in God. So understanding and so believing, it behooves every lover of India to cling to the old Indian civilization even as a child clings to the mother's breast.

Chapter XVII
Passive Resistance

READER: Is there any historical evidence as to the success of what you have called soul-force or truth-force? No instance seems to have happened of any nation having risen through soul-force. I still think that the evil-doers will not cease doing evil without physical punishment.

EDITOR: The poet Tulsidas has said: "Of religion, pity, or love, is the root, as egotism of the body. Therefore, we should not abandon pity so long as we are alive." This appears [is the root] to me to be a scientific truth. I believe in it as much as I believe in two and two being four. The force of love is the same as the force of the soul or truth. We have evidence of its working at every step. The universe would disappear without the existence of that force. But you ask for historical evidence. It is, therefore, necessary to know what history means. The Gujarati equivalent means: "It so happened." If that is the meaning of history, it is possible to give copious evidence. But, if it means the doings of kings and emperors, there can be no evidence of soul-force or passive resistance in such history. You cannot expect silver ore in a tin mine. History, as we know it, is a record of the wars of the world, and so there is a proverb among Englishmen that a nation which has no history, that is, no wars, is a happy nation. How kings played, how they became enemies of one another, how they murdered one another, is found accurately recorded in history, and if this were all that had happened in the world, it would have been ended long ago. If the story of the universe had commenced with wars, not a man would have been found alive today. Those people who have been warred against have disappeared as, for instance, the natives of Australia of whom hardly a man was left alive by the intruders. Mark, please, that these natives did not use soul-force in self-defense, and it does not require much foresight to know that the Australians will share the same fate as their victims. "Those that take the sword shall perish by the sword." With us the proverb is that professional swimmers will find a watery grave.

The fact that there are so many men still alive in the world shows that it is based not on the force of arms but on the force of truth or love. Therefore, the greatest and most unimpeachable evidence of the success of this force is to be found in the fact that, in spite of the wars of the world, it still lives on.

Thousands, indeed tens of thousands, depend for their existence on a very active working of this force. Little quarrels of millions of families in their daily lives disappear before the exercise of this force. Hundreds of nations live in peace. History does not and cannot take note of this fact. History is really a record of every interruption of the even working of the force of love or of the soul. Two brothers quarrel; one of them repents and re-awakens the love that was lying dormant in him; the two again begin to live in peace; nobody takes note of this. But if the two brothers, through the intervention of solicitors or some other reason, take up arms or go to law—which is another form of the exhibition of brute force—their doings would be immediately noticed in the press, they would be the talk of their neighbors and would probably go down to history. And what is true of families and communities is true of nations. There is no reason to believe that there is one law for families and another for nations. History, then, is a record of an interrruption of the course of nature. Soul-force, being natural, is not noted in history.

READER: According to what you say, it is plain that instances of this kind of passive resistance are not to be found in history. It is necessary to understand this passive resistance more fully. It will be better, therefore, if you enlarge upon it.

EDITOR: Passive resistance is a method of securing rights by personal suffering; it is the reverse of resistance by arms. When I refuse to do a thing that is repugnant to my conscience, I use soul-force. For instance, the Government of the day has passed a law which is applicable to me. I do not like it. If by using violence I force the Government to repeal the law, I am employing what may be termed body-force. If I do not obey the law and accept the penalty for its breach, I use soul-force. It involves sacrifice of self.

Everybody admits that sacrifice of self is infinitely superior to sacrifice of others. Moreover, if this kind of force is used in a cause that is unjust, only the person using it suffers. He does not make others suffer for his mistakes. Men have before now done many things which were subsequently found to have been wrong. No man can claim that he is absolutely in the right or that a particular thing is wrong because he thinks so, but it is wrong for him so long as that is his deliberate judgment. It is therefore meet that he should not do that which he knows to be wrong, and suffer the consequence whatever it may be. This is the key to the use of soul-force.

READER: You would then disregard laws—this is rank disloyalty. We have always been considered a law-abiding nation. You seem to be going even beyond the extremists. They say that we must obey the laws that have been passed, but that if the laws be bad, we must drive out the law-givers even by force.

EDITOR: Whether I go beyond them or whether I do not is a matter of no consequence to either of us. We simply want to find out what is right and to act accordingly. The real meaning of the statement that we are a law-abiding nation is that we are passive resisters. When we do not like certain laws, we do not break the heads of law-givers but we suffer and do not submit to the laws. That we should obey laws whether good or bad is a new-fangled notion. There was no such thing in former days. The people disregarded those laws they did not like and suffered the penalties for their breach. It is contrary to our manhood if we obey laws repugnant to our conscience. Such teaching is opposed to religion and means slavery. If the Government were to ask us to go about without any clothing, should we do so? If I were a passive resister, I would say to them that I would have nothing to do with their law. But we have so forgotten ourselves and become so compliant that we do not mind any degrading law.

A man who has realized his manhood, who fears only God, will fear no one else. Man-made laws are not necessarily binding on him. Even the Government does not expect any such thing from us. They do not say: "You must do such and such a thing," but they say: "If you do not do it, we will punish you." We are sunk so low that we fancy that it is our duty and our religion to do what the law lays down. If man will only realize that it is unmanly to obey laws that are unjust, no man's tyranny will enslave him. This is the key to self-rule or home-rule.

Ito Hirobumi

1841–1909

The central drama of nineteenth century world history is the conflict of cultures as European nations used military might to dominate the globe. Indeed, by 1914, those nations directly or indirectly controlled 85 percent of the world. Even countries like Japan, which had resisted deliberate European incursions, were forced to react to economic trends that increasingly drew the nations of the world into Europe's orbit. Some western-style reforms were adopted in those areas seeking to retain political autonomy: Japan during the Meiji Restoration, the Ottomans in Turkey with the Tanzimat reforms, and even the Romanovs in Russia. In each of these states, new ideas confronted old and the more successful reforms were always blends of both.

Japan had long experienced the conflict of cultures because of its histori-cally tumultuous relations with its powerful neighbor, China. At times sinified (rendered Chinese) and at others more faithful to its indigenous heritage, Japan had to develop a flexible, if hybrid identity which enabled it to maintain internal cohesion while undergoing global change. This balance was most suc-cessfully achieved during the Meiji period (1867–1912).

The Meiji Emperor's prime minister, Ito, oversaw the promulgation of a new constitution which brought to Japan a series of liberal reforms. Note how these derive from the liberal tradition of the Western Enlightenment, yet at the same time are rooted in Japanese tradition. Where is the potential for balance between Western and Japanese cultures? For conflict? Note, too, how the con-stitution balances rights with autocracy, self-consciously similar to that of Germany. Within a few decades of the drafting of this constitution, Japan became a world superpower. Could this strategy, then, of adopting Western reforms to stave off conquest by the West be deemed successful? At what cost? How was Japan able to do this while so many other nations succumbed to Western domination?

from *Sources of Japanese Tradition* (1909)

• • •

The advent of Commodore Perry,[1] followed by a rapid succession of great events too well known to be repeated here, roughly awakened us to the consciousness of mighty forces at work to change the face of the outside world. We were ill-prepared to bear the brunt of these forces, but once awakened to the need, were not slow to grapple with them. So, first of all the whole fabric of the feudal system, which with its obsolete shackles and formalities hindered us in every branch of free development, had to be uprooted and destroyed. The annihilation of centrifugal forces taking the form of autocratic feudal provinces was a necessary step to the unification of the country under a strong central government, without which we would not have been able to offer a united front to the outside forces or stand up as a united whole to maintain the country's very existence.

Sources of Japanese Civilization and Culture

I must, however, disabuse my readers of the very common illusion that there was no education and an entire absence of public spirit during feudal times. It is this false impression which has led superficial observers to believe that our civilization has been so recent that its continuance is doubtful—in short, that our civilization is nothing but a hastily donned, superficial veneer. On the contrary, I am not exaggerating when I say that, for generations and centuries, we have been enjoying a moral education of the highest type. The great ideals offered by philosophy and by historical examples of the golden ages of China and India, Japanicized in the form of a "crust of customs," developed and sanctified by the continual usage of centuries under the comprehensive name *bushido*, offered us splendid standards of morality, rigorously enforced in the everyday life of the educated classes. The result, as everyone who is acquainted with Old Japan knows, was an education which aspired to the attainment of Stoic heroism, a rustic simplicity and a self-sacrificing spirit unsurpassed in Sparta, and the aesthetic culture and intellectual refinement of Athens. Art, delicacy of sentiment, higher ideals of morality and of philosophy, as well as the highest types of valor and chivalry—all these we have tried to combine in the man as he ought to be. We laid great stress on the harmonious combination of all the known accomplishments of a developed human being, and it is only since the introduction of modern technical sciences that

328

we have been obliged to pay more attention to specialized technical attainments than to the harmonious development of the whole. Let me remark, *en passant*, that the humanitarian efforts which in the course of the recent war were so much in evidence and which so much surprised Western nations were not, as might have been thought, the products of the new civilization, but survivals of our ancient feudal chivalry. If further instance were needed, we may direct attention to the numbers of our renowned warriors and statesmen who have left behind them works of religious and moral devotions, of philosophical contemplations, as well as splendid specimens of calligraphy, painting, and poetry, to an extent probably unparalleled in the feudalism of other nations.

Thus it will be seen that what was lacking in our countrymen of the feudal era was not mental or moral fiber, but the scientific, technical, and materialistic side of modern civilization. Our present condition is not the result of the ingrafting of a civilization entirely different from our own, as foreign observers are apt to believe, but simply a different training and nursing of a strongly vital character already-existent.

Draft of the New Constitution

It was in the month of March, 1882, that His Majesty ordered me to work out a draft of a constitution to be submitted to his approval. No time was to be lost, so I started on the 15th of the same month for an extended journey to different constitutional countries to make as thorough a study as possible of the actual workings of different systems of constitutional government, of their various provisions, as well as of theories and opinions actually entertained by influential persons on the actual stage itself of constitutional life. I took young men with me, who all belonged to the élite of the rising generation, to assist and to cooperate with me in my studies. I sojourned about a year and a half in Europe, and having gathered the necessary materials, in so far as it was possible in so short a space of time, I returned home in September, 1883. Immediately after my return I set to work to draw up the Constitution. I was assisted in my work by my secretaries, prominent among whom were the late Viscount K. Inouyé, and the Barons M. Itō and K. Kanéko, and by foreign advisers, such as Professor Roesler, Mr. Piggott, and others.

Peculiar Features of the National Life

It was evident from the outset that mere imitation of foreign models would not suffice, for there were historical peculiarities of our country which had to be taken into consideration. For example, the Crown was, with us, an institution far more deeply rooted in the national sentiment and in our history than in other countries. It was indeed the very essence of a once theocratic State, so that in formulating the restrictions on its prerogatives in the new Constitution, we had to take care to safeguard the future realness or vitality of these prerogatives, and not to let the institution degenerate into an ornamental crowning piece of the edifice. At the same time, it was also evident that any form of constitutional régime was impossible without full and extended protection of honor, liberty, property, and personal security of citizens, entailing necessarily many important restrictions on the powers of the Crown.

Emotional Elements in Social Life of People

On the other hand, there was one peculiarity of our social conditions that is without parallel in any other civilized country. Homogeneous in race, language, religion, and sentiments, so long secluded from the outside world, with the centuries-long traditions and inertia of the feudal system, in which the family and quasi-family ties permeated and formed the essence of every social organization, and moreover with such moral and religious tenets as laid undue stress on duties of fraternal aid and mutual succor, we had during the course of our seclusion unconsciously become a vast village community where cold intellect and calculation of public events were always restrained and even often hindered by warm emotions between man and man. Those who have closely observed the effects of the commercial crises of our country—that is, of the events wherein cold-blooded calculation ought to have the precedence of every other factor—and compared them with those of other countries, must have observed a remarkable distinction between them. In other countries they serve in a certain measure as the scavengers of the commercial world, the solid undertakings surviving the shock, while enterprises founded solely on speculative bases are sure to vanish thereafter. But, generally speaking, this is not the case in our country. Moral and emotional factors come into play. Solid undertakings are dragged into the whirlpool, and the speculative ones are saved from the abyss—the general standard of prosperity is lowered for the moment, but the commercial fabric escapes violent shocks. In industry, also, in spite of the recent enormous developments of manufactures in our country, our laborers have not yet degenerated into spiritless machines and toiling beasts. There still survives the bond of patron and protégé between them and the capitalist employers. It is this moral and emotional factor which will, in the future, form a healthy barrier against the threatening advance of socialistic ideas. It must, of course, be admitted that this social peculiarity is not without beneficial influences. It mitigates the conflict, serves as the lubricator of social organisms, and tends generally to act as a powerful lever for the practical application of the moral principle of mutual assistance between fellow citizens. But unless curbed and held in restraint, it too may exercise baneful influences on society, for in a village community, where feelings and emotions hold a higher place than intellect, free discussion is apt to be smothered, attainment and transference of power liable to become a family question of a powerful oligarchy, and the realization of such a régime as constitutional monarchy to become an impossibility, simply because in any representative régime free discussion is a matter of prime necessity, because emotions and passions have to be stopped for the sake of the cool calculation of national welfare, and even the best of friends have often to be sacrificed if the best abilities and highest intellects are to guide the helm. Besides, the dissensions between brothers and relatives, deprived as they usually are of safety-valves for giving free and hearty vent to their own opinions or discontents, are apt to degenerate into passionate quarrels and overstep the bounds of simple differences of opinion. The good side of this social peculiarity had to be retained as much as possible, while its baneful influences had to be safeguarded. These and many other peculiarities had to be taken into account in order to have a constitution adapted to the actual condition of the country.

Conflict between the Old and New Thoughts

Another difficulty equally grave had to be taken into consideration. We were just then in an age of transition. The opinions prevailing in the country were extremely heterogeneous, and often diametrically opposed to each other. We had survivors of former generations who were still full of theocratic ideas, and who believed that any attempt to restrict an imperial prerogative amounted to something like high treason. On the other hand there was a large and powerful body of the younger generation educated at the time when the Manchester theory was in vogue, and who in consequence were ultra-radical in their ideas of freedom. Members of the bureaucracy were prone to lend willing ears to the German doctrinaires of the reactionary period, while, on the other hand, the educated politicians among the people having not yet tasted the bitter significance of administrative responsibility, were liable to be more influenced by the dazzling words and lucid theories of Montesquieu, Rousseau, and other similar French writers. A work entitled *History Of Civilization*, by Buckle, which denounced every form of government as an unnecessary evil, became the great favorite of students of all the higher schools, including the Imperial University. On the other hand, these same students would not have dared to expound the theories of Buckle before their own conservative fathers. At that time we had not yet arrived at the stage of distinguishing clearly between political opposition on the one hand and treason to the established order of things on the other. The virtues necessary for the smooth working of any constitution, such as love of freedom of speech, love of publicity of proceedings, the spirit of tolerance for opinions opposed to one's own, etc., had yet to be learned by long experience.

Draft of the Constitution Completed

It was under these circumstances that the first draft of the Constitution was made and submitted to His Majesty, after which it was handed over to the mature deliberation of the Privy Council. The Sovereign himself presided over these deliberations, and he had full opportunities of hearing and giving due consideration to all the conflicting opinions above hinted at. I believe nothing evidences more vividly the intelligence of our august Master than the fact that in spite of the existence of strong undercurrents of an ultra-conservative nature in the council, and also in the country at large, His Majesty's decisions inclined almost invariably towards liberal and progressive ideas, so that we have been ultimately able to obtain the Constitution as it exists at present.

Note

[1] Commodore Matthew Perry negotiated a treaty with Japan, opening the country to trade with the U.S. in 1854.

Vladimir Lenin

1870–1924

Lenin, born Vladimir Ilich Ulianov, was the first world leader to effect revolutionary change based on the theories of Karl Marx. His life circumstances, as well as the peculiar circumstances of early twentieth-century Russia, informed his interpretation of Marxism. Born into the intelligentsia, young Lenin and his brother espoused radical politics even in their teens; indeed, Lenin's older brother was executed for alleged acts of terrorism in 1887. Vladimir was also punished, but his exile years in Siberia only enabled him to develop his Marxist convictions.

Russia had begun to industrialize by the first decade of the twentieth century, but it lagged far behind the West. When defeat came at the hands of the Japanese in 1905, Russia's technological and bureaucratic inferiority was clearly in evidence. Reforms followed, but only enough to whet people's appetite for more. Defeat came again in 1917, when the people of Russia joined mutinying soldiers who refused to continue to be slaughtered by the Germans. The regime discredited, czar Nicolas abdicated and a provisional government formed. Within a few months, however, this government was also toppled—by Lenin and the Bolsheviks.

Lenin aimed for nothing less than the overthrow of capitalism. Yet Russia lacked a class-conscious proletariat (the force for revolutionary change, according to Marx), so he deployed the vanguard, the well-trained, armed elite who had been operating in secret cells for years. To bring about communism, Lenin modified Marx's description of revolutionary change in yet another way, "leapfrogging" over the stages of capitalist development necessary, in Marx's view, for the roots of communism to take hold.

Though he departed from central tenets of classic Marxist theory, Lenin also advanced Marxist economic analysis in *Imperialism: The Highest Stage of Capitalism* wherein he chronicles the replacement of free-trade ideology by monopoly capitalism. Seeing monopoly capitalism as a decadent form of pure capitalism, Lenin believed this stage indicated capitalism's imminent demise. He also noted how the "scramble for colonies" would lead to war. How are monopolies antithetical to the spirit of capitalism? Consider how his description of the world as divided between usurer and debtor states is strikingly modern.

from *Imperialism: The Highest Stage of Capitalism* (1916)

Chapter VII
Imperialism as a Special Stage of Capitalism

• • •

We must now try to sum up and put together what has been said above on the subject of imperialism. Imperialism emerged as the development and direct continuation of the fundamental attributes of capitalism in general. But capitalism only became capitalist imperialism at a definite and very high stage of its development, when certain of its fundamental attributes began to be transformed into their opposites, when the features of a period of transition from capitalism to a higher social and economic system began to take shape and reveal themselves all along the line. Economically, the main thing in this process is the substitution of capitalist monopolies for capitalist free competition. Free competition is the fundamental attribute of capitalism, and of commodity production generally. Monopoly is exactly the opposite of free competition; but we have seen the latter being transformed into monopoly before our very eyes, creating large-scale industry and eliminating small industry, replacing large-scale industry by still larger-scale industry, finally leading to such a concentration of production and capital that monopoly has been and is the result: cartels, syndicates and trusts, and merging with them, the capital of a dozen or so banks manipulating thousands of millions. At the same time monopoly, which has grown out of free competition, does not abolish the latter, but exists over it and alongside of it, and thereby gives rise to a number of very acute, intense antagonisms, friction and conflicts. Monopoly is the transition from capitalism to a higher system.

If it were necessary to give the briefest possible definition of imperialism we should have to say that imperialism is the monopoly stage of capitalism. Such a definition would include what is most important, for, on the one hand, finance capital is the bank capital of a few big monopolist banks, merged with the capital of the monopolist combines of manufacturers; and, on the other hand, the division of the world is the transition from a colonial policy which has extended without hindrance to territories unoccupied by any capitalist power, to a colonial policy of monopolistic possession of the territory of the world which has been completely divided up.

334

But very brief definitions, although convenient, for they sum up the main points, are nevertheless inadequate, because very important features of the phenomenon that has to be defined have to be especially deduced. And so, without forgetting the conditional and relative value of all definitions, which can never include all the concatenations of a phenomenon in its complete development, we must give a definition of imperialism that will embrace the following five essential features:

1) The concentration of production and capital developed to such a high stage that it created monopolies which play a decisive role in economic life.

2) The merging of bank capital with industrial capital, and the creation, on the basis of this "finance capital," of a "financial oligarchy."

3) The export of capital, which has become extremely important, as distinguished from the export of commodities.

4) The formation of international capitalist monopolies which share the world among themselves.

5) The territorial division of the whole world among the greatest capitalist powers is completed.

Imperialism is capitalism in that stage of development in which the dominance of monopolies and finance capital has established itself; in which the export of capital has acquired pronounced importance; in which the division of the world among the international trusts has begun; in which the division of all territories of the globe among the great capitalist powers has been completed.

• • •

Capitalism is growing with the greatest rapidity in the colonies and in overseas countries. Among the latter, *new* imperialist powers are emerging (*e.g.,* Japan). The struggle of world imperialism is becoming more acute. The tribute levied by finance capital on the most profitable colonial and overseas enterprises is increasing. In sharing out this "booty," an exceptionally large part goes to countries which, as far as the development of productive forces is concerned, do not always stand at the top of the list.

• • •

Chaper VIII
The Parasitism and Decay of Capitalism

• • •

As we have seen, the most deep-rooted economic foundation of imperialism is monopoly. This is capitalist monopoly, *i.e.,* monopoly which has grown out of capitalism and exists in the general environment of capitalism, commodity production and competition, and remains in permanent and insoluble contradiction to this general environment. Nevertheless, like all monopoly, this capitalist monopoly inevitably gives rise to a tendency to stagnation and decay. As monopoly prices become fixed, even temporarily, so the stimulus to technical and, consequently, to all progress, disappears to a certain extent, and to that extent, also, the *economic* possibility arises of deliberately retarding technical progress. For instance, in America, a certain Mr. Owens invented a machine which revolutionised the manufacture of bottles. The German bottle manufacturing cartel purchased Owens' patent, but pigeonholed it, refrained from utilising it. Certainly, monopoly under capitalism can never completely, and for a long period of time, eliminate competition in the world market (and this, by the by, is one of the reasons why the theory of ultra-imperialism is so absurd). Certainly the possibility of reducing cost of production and increasing profits by introducing technical improvements operates in the direction of change. Nevertheless, the *tendency* to stagnation and decay, which is the feature of monopoly, continues, and in certain branches of industry, in certain countries, for certain periods of time, it becomes predominant.

The monopoly of ownership of very extensive, rich or well-situated colonies, operates in the same direction.

Further, imperialism is an immense accumulation of money capital in a few countries, which, as we have seen, amounts to 100–150 billion francs in various securities. Hence the extraordinary growth of a class, or rather of a category, of *bondholders* (*rentiers*), *i.e.*, people who live by "clipping coupons," who take no part whatever in production, whose profession is idleness. The export of capital, one of the most essential economic bases of imperialism, still more completely isolates the *rentiers* from production and sets the seal of parasitism on the whole country that lives by the exploitation of the labour of several overseas countries and colonies.

• • •

The income of the bondholders is *five times greater* than the income obtained from the foreign trade of the greatest "trading" country in the world. This is the essence of imperialism and imperialist parisitism.

For that reason the term, "rentier state" (*Rentnerstaat*), or usurer state, is passing into current use in the economic literature that deals with imperialism. The world has become divided into a handful of usurer states on the one side, and a vast majority of debtor states on the other.

• • •

Chapter X
The Place of Imperialism in History

We have seen that the economic quintessence of imperialism is monopoly capitalism. This very fact determines its place in history, for monopoly that grew up on the basis of free competition, and precisely out of free competition, is the transition from the capitalist system to a higher social-economic order. We must take special note of the four principal forms of monopoly, or the four principal manifestations of monopoly capitalism, which are characteristic of the epoch under review.

Firstly, monopoly arose out of the concentration of production at a very advanced stage of development. This refers to the monopolist capitalist combines, cartels, syndicates and trusts. We have seen the important part that these play in modern economic life. At the beginning of the twentieth century, monopolies acquired complete supremacy in the advanced countries. And although the first steps towards the formation of the cartels were first taken by countries enjoying the protection of high tariffs (Germany, America), Great Britain, with her system of free trade, was not far behind in revealing the same basic phenomenon, namely, the birth of monopoly out of the concentration of production.

Secondly, monopolies have accelerated the capture of the most important sources of raw materials, especially for the coal and iron industries, which are the basic and most highly cartelised industries in capitalist society. The monopoly of the most important sources of raw materials has enormously increased the power of big capital, and has sharpened the antagonism between cartelised and non-cartelised industry.

Thirdly, monopoly has sprung from the banks. The banks have developed from modest intermediary enterprises into the monopolists of finance capital. Some three or five of the biggest banks in each of the foremost capitalist countries have achieved the "personal union" of industrial and bank capital, and have concentrated in their hands the disposal of thousands upon thousands of millions which form the greater part of the capital and income of entire countries. A financial oligarchy, which throws a close net of relations of dependence over all the economic and political institutions of contemporary bourgeois society without exception—such is the most striking manifestation of this monopoly.

Fourthly, monopoly has grown out of colonial policy. To the numerous "old" motives of colonial policy, finance capital has added the struggle for the sources of raw materials, for the export of capital, for "spheres of influence," *i.e.*, for spheres for profitable deals, concessions, monopolist profits and so on;

in fine, for economic territory in general. When the colonies of the European powers in Africa, for instance, comprised only one-tenth of that territory (as was the case in 1876), colonial policy was able to develop by methods other than those of monopoly—by the "free grabbing" of territories, so to speak. But when nine-tenths of Africa had been seized (approximately by 1900), when the whole world had been divided up, there was inevitably ushered in a period of colonial monopoly and, consequently, a period of particularly intense struggle for the division and the redivision of the world.

The extent to which monopolist capital has intensified all the contradictions of capitalism is generally known. It is sufficient to mention the high cost of living and the oppression of the cartels. This intensification of contradictions constitutes the most powerful driving force of the transitional period of history, which began from the time of the definite victory of world finance capital.

Monopolies, oligarchy, the striving for domination instead of the striving for liberty, the exploitation of an increasing number of small or weak nations by an extremely small group of the richest or most powerful nations—all these have given birth to those distinctive characteristics of imperialism which compel us to define it as parasitic or decaying capitalism. More and more prominently there emerges, as one of the tendencies of imperialism, the creation of the "bondholding" (rentier) state, the usurer state, in which the bourgeoisie lives on the proceeds of capital exports and by "clipping coupons." It would be a mistake to believe that this tendency to decay precludes the possibility of the rapid growth of capitalism. It does not. In the epoch of imperialism, certain branches of industry, certain strata of the bourgeoisie and certain countries betray, to a more or less degree, one or other of these tendencies. On the whole, capitalism is growing far more rapidly than before. But this growth is not only becoming more and more uneven in general; its unevenness also manifests itself, in particular, in the decay of the countries which are richest in capital (such as England).

Black Elk

1863–1950

Black Elk was an Oglala Sioux, a holy man and an important leader in the struggle against the U.S. Army's efforts to force the tribes of the American plains off their ancestral lands. Black Elk survived the wars of western expansion to offer an eyewitness account of the massacre at Wounded Knee, a village on the Pine Ridge Indian Reservation in South Dakota. On 29 December 1890, U.S. troops converged on the Sioux living there, killing 200 to 300 men, women, and children, most of whom were unarmed. Following this tragic incident, Black Elk continued to live near the reservation, where he worked to preserve the ways of his people. Beginning in 1930, the poet and novelist John G. Niehardt, who was writing about the Indian wars, met with Black Elk to study the traditions and practices of the Oglala. Over a two-year period he and a stenographer recorded the memoirs of Black Elk, publishing them in 1932 as *Black Elk Speaks: Being the Life Story of a Holy Man of the Oglala Sioux.*

The following excerpt is Black Elk's description of Lakota government, taken from interviews conducted in 1944 and published in *The Sixth Grandfather: Black Elk's Teachings Given to John G. Niehardt* (University of Nebraska Press, 1984). Black Elk discusses tribal political structure, the organization of Lakota bands, the roles of tribal leaders, and the centrality of law to the daily life of the Sioux. How is Black Elk's account reminiscent of the political thought developed by Enlightenment intellectuals such as Locke, Rousseau, and Burke? How does western political theory differ from what Black Elk offers here? What are the potential benefits and limits of the Lakota political model?

Lakota Government Interview (1944)

Next I want to go on about how they govern themselves. I don't know, but they must have had at that council all this planned out. Perhaps it was improved later. In order to have law and order among themselves they had to have a certain way of keeping order in the bands. Each band was for itself. Maybe the seven camps had different rules, but it is all similar. They had a chief who was the head man. They already had the so-called "highest *tipi*" and "next to the highest *tipi*." The highest *tipi* is where the chief lives; the next one is where the laws for governing are made. This is called *tipi iyokihe* [*tipi iyokiheya*, council lodge].

Any human being is the chief of everything. The people were first, and the next was where they made the laws—*tipi iyokihe*. It seems that the governing bodies of the seven camps were all similar but the people elected their chief. I don't know whether Slow Buffalo was elected by the people or not. But at that time you had to be a great warrior and a good man to attain the chieftanship. You had to prove yourself.

The chief ruled just like a president, but his actions had to be approved. If the chief had a son, he would be a chief, if he could prove himself worthy of the honor. Otherwise, the councilors would choose someone. They went into the second *tipi* [council lodge] and whatever they decide is the law. The councilors would get together, and if they are going to elect anyone, they know all the people and know who is worthy.

The word *akichita* [*akicita*] is something that the seven bands had when at the dispersement it was up to them to name everything. A certain medicine man had a vision of the Thunder-beings, and that is where the word akichita comes from. *Akichita* means if I tell you to do anything, it has to be done. When the medicine man had a vision the Thunder-beings said they and *akichita* would be relatives and the Thunder-beings would give their power to the people. The *akichita* saw to it that the laws made by the sub-chiefs were enforced. Just like the Thunder-beings, the *akichita* could not be stopped.

There were chiefs in every band (*tiospaya* [*tiyospaye*]). The chiefs of the bands are the ones that get together and elect the *akichita*. They sang a song to pick the men. As they went around singing they had a piece of charcoal and put a black spot [stripe] on the faces of the ones chosen. Then they brought them together and the people came and they had a dedicatory ceremony. Whenever you were elected for *akichita* you had a power almost like a chief, for they watched the chief. If the chief violated any rules he could be deposed.

340

The chiefs had to watch over the *akichita*, and if one of them did not do the right thing, the chief could have him removed.

There was the governing body. The chief is the head man, and between him and the soldiers are six councilors (*tipi iyokihe*) who make the laws but were not chiefs. There used to be one chief in each band, but it changed sometime and they had as many as four chiefs. That is, a head chief and three sub-chiefs. Each band had its own chief, sub-chief, and *akichita*.

But when the bands got together there were higher laws. When they were together and an important matter came up, then the third *tipi* came into consideration. They built one big *tipi* out of three and all the chiefs from all the bands, the *akichita*, the councilors, all got in there and decided what the whole tribe should do. *Akichita* is singular or plural (like [the English word] sheep). The *tipi iyokihe* from all the bands are taken together and made into one big *tipi* for the councils in which the whole tribe takes place. This is called "*tipi* thrown over together." When that happened, they took the *tipi* and put the poles in a way that it looked like a corral. Then they spread the *tipi* hides all around. They did not cover the top, for it was not permanent—maybe for just one day.

Ti (where we live) *ošpaye* (apart but not separated completely).

Whatever the six councilors agree on is a law, and the *akichita* take care of it. If anyone in the band breaks a law, the *akichita* go there and whip him or knock him out. If he gets made [mad] and tries to fight back, they kill him. A lot of them were killed. Rules were made so the people would benefit. For instance, in getting provision, everyone, especially the older ones, were to get alike. Younger men killed for the older ones. They went hunting at certain times, when the council said to go. When they said it was permissible to go on a war party, then they could. If one or two went on a warpath when the law says they could not go, when they got back the *akichita* would go to the home and take down the tipi and chop up the sticks [*tipi* poles] and cut up the hide [*tipi* cover]. If someone goes hunting when he should not, they knock him out and ruin his *tipi*. The *akichita* were like the ash, which can be bent but not broken. When the men were chosen for *akichita*, they were told, "You will resemble the ash. You have noticed it can not be broken. It is up to you to look after the people and take care of the laws." When there was to be a council meeting, the *akichita* would go around and get coffee, meat, etc., for the meeting. The people had to give what was asked for. If the councilors say you can't go on a war party or hunting then the whole tribe moves. Everyone has to have a fair share, and they could not let someone go out and scare the game away.

Another thing I forgot: besides the chiefs, sub-chiefs, councilors, and *akichita*, there were those who were next in line for the chiefs. The warriors earned that. Whenever they had done so many brave deeds, then they were eligible for next in line for the chieftains or councilors. You had to kill an enemy, count coup first, second, and third, and then get a scalp. Then you had to bring in meat for old people, be kind to everybody and good. No one could say you were a bad man, so you had earned the right to be a candidate for chief, councilman, *akichita*. *Wichasha yatapika* [*wicaša yatapika*]. Whenever there is a chieftain to be made, the *wichasha yatapika* are the ones who elect the chief, or chiefs.

The *wichasa yatapika* get together and elect four big chiefs out of their own members from the whole tribe. They are over all the others, and they have equal power among themselves. If one chief is ousted by the *akichita*, then the *akichita* have the power to choose one man from the candidates to be the new chief. For example, the last big chiefs we had, Red Cloud was one, but he left for the white men, so they ousted him and Spotted Tail out. So they elected Crazy Horse, American Horse, [Young Man] Afraid of His Horse and Knife [Sword]. Crazy Horse was the only real chief, because the other three left for the white men and were ousted. Crazy Horse is the last big chief, and then it's all over.

The four chiefs had the power to care for the people, for the tribe as a whole. Next is the land; look after the land. Next is the helpless; see that they are taken care of. Remember you probably [will] have your graves in four different places; you probably will die on a plain or on a hill; it might be in a gulch; it might be the woods. They were elected to give their lives for the people, so they may have to die for the people. They are called *nacha* [*naca*], head man, [and] *wichashitanacha* [*wicaša itancan*], principal man, higher than *nacha*.

Crazy Horse's grandfather and Black Elk's grandfather were two of five brothers. Great grandfather's name was Black Elk, grandfather, father, Nicholas Black Elk, Ben Black Elk [son], Henry Black Elk [grandson].

The biggest council consists of the candidates and the *akichita* and the chiefs and the councilors. They all take part in the council. Later on the *akichita* formed so-called societies. The chiefs also had a society called "Owns White" (*Ska Yoha* [*Ska Yuha*]), and the candidates and councilors belonged to this society too. The *akichita* formed five societies: the Brave Heart [*Cante T'inza*], the [Kit] Fox [*Tokala*], Packs White [*Wicinska*], Crowskin [*Kangi Yuha*, Crow Owners], [and] Eeyuptala [*Iyuptala*]—"Go Right on Through," Perseverance society. These societies are to build boys up to manhood. They guide the young and take care of the old people. There was a sort of rivalry among the societies as to which had produced more warriors than the others.

VII. RACE AND POLITICS IN MODERN AMERICA

Booker T. Washington

1856–1915

Booker T. Washington was born to a Virginia slave and an unknown white man who never took any responsibility for or interest in the young boy. After emancipation in 1865, Washington moved with his mother and stepfather to West Virginia, where he worked in the salt furnaces and began teaching himself to read from a book that his mother had found. He also worked regularly in the coal mines that supplied fuel for the salt-furnace operations. In order to escape such dehumanizing work, he eventually attended the Hampton Institute in Virginia and became a teacher there in 1879.

In 1881, he established the Tuskegee Normal and Industrial Institute in Alabama. Over the next three decades, he transformed the school into an institution consisting of more than one hundred buildings, with modern industrial equipment and a multi-million dollar endowment. The school changed its name to Tuskegee Institute and today is known as Tuskegee University. Washington's emphasis at the school centered on vocational training, in an effort to free its African-American students from the oppressive sharecropper system in the deep South. Washington's agenda during the early decades after emancipation was to enable former slaves to take advantage of the resources nearest to them, which included their own manual labor. This meant training in areas such as farming, mechanical industrial skills, and construction.

Washington's Address at the World's Fair in Atlanta (1895) contains the classic statement of his philosophy, that black Americans should not fixate on political rights but should first strive for economic equality. Full rights would come only after proving that they could be economically independent. In other words, African Americans should accommodate to the current views of the dominant white population, in order to secure the capital that would foster economic opportunity. Eventually, Washington believed, segregation would come to an end as African Americans developed their own economic institutions. Washington's views were controversial for they advocated a cautious approach to political and social parity, built from the ground up. African-American intellectuals and leaders, such as W. E. B. Du Bois, who found themselves struggling against aggressive economic and political oppression by the white community, eventually rejected Washington's approach to black success as accommodationism. Among many whites, however, Washington and his ideas were popular. Sometimes referred to as the "Atlanta

Compromise" because of its acceptance of restricted equality for economic gain, Washington's Address nonetheless argues for a self-reliance that would resonate for many African Americans. What central metaphors and images does Washington employ in his argument? Was his compromise adequate to the historical moment and the political climate in the South? Is economic power more important than political equality for minority groups trying to confront a dominant culture with a strong tradition of racism?

Address at the World's
Fair in Atlanta (1895)

Mr. President[1] and Gentlemen of the Board of Directors and Citizens:
One-third of the population of the South is of the Negro race. No enterprise
seeking the material, civil, or moral welfare of this section can disregard this
element of our population and reach the highest success. I but convey to you,
Mr. President and Directors, the sentiment of the masses of my race when I
say that in no way have the value and manhood of the American Negro been
more fittingly and generously recognized than by the managers of this magnificent Exposition at every stage of its progress. It is a recognition that will do
more to cement the friendship of the two races than any occurrence since the
dawn of our freedom.

Not only this, but the opportunity here afforded will awaken among us
a new era of industrial progress. Ignorant and inexperienced, it is not strange
that in the first years of our new life we began at the top instead of at the bottom; that a seat in Congress or the state legislature was more sought than real
estate or industrial skill; that the political convention or stump speaking had
more attractions than starting a dairy farm or truck garden.

A ship lost at sea for many days suddenly sighted a friendly vessel. From
the mast of the unfortunate vessel was seen a signal, "Water, water; we die of
thirst!" The answer from the friendly vessel at once came back, "Cast down
your bucket where you are." A second time the signal, "Water, water; send us
water!" ran up from the distressed vessel, and was answered, "Cast down your
bucket where you are." And a third and fourth signal for water was answered,
"Cast down your bucket where you are." The captain of the distressed vessel,
at last heeding the injunction, cast down his bucket, and it came up full of
fresh, sparkling water from the mouth of the Amazon River. To those of my
race who depend on bettering their condition in a foreign land or who under-
estimate the importance of cultivating friendly relations with the Southern
white man, who is their next-door neighbour, I would say: "Cast down your
bucket where you are"—cast it down in making friends in every manly way of
the people of all races by whom we are surrounded.

Cast it down in agriculture, mechanics, in commerce, in domestic service, and in the professions. And in this connection it is well to bear in mind
that whatever other sins the South may be called to bear, when it comes to
business, pure and simple, it is in the South that the Negro is given a man's

chance in the commercial world, and in nothing is this Exposition more eloquent than in emphasizing this chance. Our greatest danger is that in the great leap from slavery to freedom we may overlook the fact that the masses of us are to live by the productions of our hands, and fail to keep in mind that we shall prosper in proportion as we learn to dignify and glorify common labour, and put brains and skill into the common occupations of life; shall prosper in proportion as we learn to draw the line between the superficial and the substantial, the ornamental gewgaws of life and the useful. No race can prosper till it learns that there is as much dignity in tilling a field as in writing a poem. It is at the bottom of life we must begin, and not at the top. Nor should we permit our grievances to overshadow our opportunities.

To those of the white race who look to the incoming of those of foreign birth and strange tongue and habits for the prosperity of the South, were I permitted I would repeat what I say to my own race, "Cast down your bucket where you are." Cast it down among the eight millions of Negroes whose habits you know, whose fidelity and love you have tested in days when to have proved treacherous meant the ruin of your firesides. Cast down your bucket among these people who have, without strikes and labour wars, tilled your fields, cleared your forests, builded your railroads and cities, and brought forth treasures from the bowels of the earth, and helped make possible this magnificent representation of the progress of the South. Casting down your bucket among my people, helping and encouraging them as you are doing on these grounds, and to education of head, hand, and heart, you will find that they will buy your surplus land, make blossom the waste places in your fields, and run your factories. While doing this, you can be sure in the future, as in the past, that you and your families will be surrounded by the most patient, faithful, law-abiding, and unresentful people that the world has seen. As we have proved our loyalty to you in the past, in nursing your children, watching by the sick-bed of your mothers and fathers, and often following them with tear-dimmed eyes to their graves, so in the future, in our humble way, we shall stand by you with a devotion that no foreigner can approach, ready to lay down our lives, if need be, in defense of yours, interlacing our industrial, commercial, civil, and religious life with yours in a way that shall make the interests of both races one. In all things that are purely social we can be as separate as the fingers, yet one as the hand in all things essential to mutual progress.

There is no defense or security for any of us except in the highest intelligence and development of all. If anywhere there are efforts tending to curtail the fullest growth of the Negro, let these efforts be turned into stimulating, encouraging, and making him the most useful and intelligent citizen. Effort or means so invested will pay a thousand per cent interest. These efforts will be twice blessed—"blessing him that gives and him that takes."

There is no escape through law of man or God from the inevitable:—

The laws of changeless justice bind
  Oppressor with oppressed;
And close as sin and suffering joined
  We march to fate abreast.

Nearly sixteen millions of hands will aid you in pulling the load upwards, or they will pull against you the load downward. We shall constitute one-third and more of the ignorance and crime of the South, or one-third its intelligence and progress; we shall contribute one-third to the business and industrial prosperity of the South, or we shall prove a veritable body of death, stagnating, depressing, retarding every effort to advance the body politic.

Gentlemen of the Exposition, as we present to you our humble effort at an exhibition of our progress, you must not expect overmuch. Starting thirty years ago with ownership here and there in a few quilts and pumpkins and chickens (gathered from miscellaneous sources), remember the path that has led from these to the inventions and production of agricultural implements, buggies, steam-engines, newspapers, books, statuary, carving, paintings, the management of drug stores and banks, has not been trodden without contact with thorns and thistles. While we take pride in what we exhibit as a result of our independent efforts, we do not for a moment forget that our part in this exhibition would fall far short of your expectations but for the constant help that has come to our educational life, not only from the Southern states, but especially from Northern philanthropists, who have made their gifts a constant stream of blessing and encouragement.

The wisest among my race understand that the agitation of questions of social equality is the extremest folly, and that progress in the enjoyment of all the privileges that will come to us must be the result of severe and constant struggle rather than of artificial forcing. No race that has anything to contribute to the markets of the world is long in any degree ostracized. It is important and right that all privileges of the law be ours, but it is vastly more important that we be prepared for the exercise of these privileges. The opportunity to earn a dollar in a factory just now is worth infinitely more than the opportunity to spend a dollar in an opera-house.

In conclusion, may I repeat that nothing in thirty years has given us more hope and encouragement, and drawn us so near to you of the white race, as this opportunity offered by the Exposition; and here bending, as it were, over the altar that represents the results of the struggles of your race and mine, both starting practically empty-handed three decades ago, I pledge that in your effort to work out the great and intricate problem which God has laid at the doors of the South, you shall have at all times the patient, sympathetic help of my race; only let this be constantly in mind, that, while from representations in these buildings of the product of field, of forest, of mine, of factory, letters, and art, much good will come, yet far above and beyond material benefits will be that higher good, that, let us pray God, will come, in a blotting out of sectional differences and racial animosities and suspicions, in a determination to administer absolute justice, in a willing obedience among all classes to the mandates of law. This, coupled with our material prosperity, will bring into our beloved South a new heaven and a new earth.

Note

[1] President of the Atlanta Exposition (Cotton States Exposition).

Frederick Douglass

1817–1895

In "The Race Problem," Douglass explores the dilemma that slavery poses for freed blacks and for Christianity, which, despite its central role in the abolitionist movement, is nonetheless implicated historically in the institution of slavery in the South. Douglass raises a number of difficult questions: Is the history of slavery in this country one which we can evade or resolve? What ought to be our response to this troubling past? Does our nation have "sufficient moral stamina" to address the legacy of slavery and its impact on today's black community?

from "The Race Problem" (1890)

The application of these homely truths and familiar examples will become apparent in the discussion I propose of what is popularly but improperly called the race problem. It seems that the American people have a special liking for this mathematical formula as applied to the Negro. They seem determined to keep his brain forever employed and his time forever occupied in solving a great variety of problems, and generally to his disadvantage.

As soon as he solves one another is propounded to him, and when he thinks, good, easy soul, his work is done he finds a new one invented, a new burden imposed, and a new hardship inflicted. There may be rest for the weary, but there seems at present no rest for the Negro. He has been solving problems during all his history.

I have before referred in this place, I think, to the fact that the Negro was confronted 200 years ago by what was considered a great religious problem, one which was very difficult of solution. That problem was: Ought the Negro to be baptized in water and admitted to membership in the Christian church?

This was, as I have often said, considering time of it, a tremendous problem. As in our day in regard to Negro problems, the opinions of the wise and great were strongly pronounced and much divided. The right of the Negro to baptism was fiercely disputed, especially by those who owned them as slaves. What is plain to all now was dark and doubtful to many then. It is easy to fancy that men spoke of it with bated breath, and saw in the Negro's baptism a menace to the peace and stability of society, as well as of slavery.

For to baptize the Negro and admit him to membership in the Christian church was to recognize him as a man, a child of God, an heir of Heaven, redeemed by the blood of Christ, a temple of the Holy Ghost, a standing type and representative of the Saviour of the world, one who, according to the apostle Paul, must be treated no longer as a servant, but as a brother beloved. Viewed in this light, his admission to baptism, and to the church was a matter for the gravest consideration.

It touched the money nerve of the Christians of that day, for their wealth was largely invested in Negro flesh and blood. It was well said that the proposition was novel, extraordinary, and full of danger. It would impair the value of the slave, and it would put in jeopardy the authority of the master: they were right, and if the Negro is to be regarded as a Christian, he could not be regarded as a heathen, and as the Bible sanctioned only the enslavement of heathen, the Negro Christian could not be bought and sold, enslaved and, whipped,

351

according to the requirements of the relation of master and slave. From every view they could then take of the proposition to baptize the Negro was rank radicalism and deserved stern resistance at its inception.

To the credit of the church and its ministers, it must be said that one learned and able divine, in the person of Dr. Godwin, was equal to the situation. He met the arguments of the opposition to Negro baptism in a book of 200 pages, in which he endeavored to show that baptism would not impair either the value of the slave or the authority of the master. His argument was a curious one. It divided the Negro into two separate parts, giving one to the Lord and the other to the slaveholder, and leaving nothing whatever of soul, body or spirit to himself. Baptism, he said, freed the Negro from the bondage of the devil, but not from the bondage of his earthly master.

The controversy over this problem was long and furious, and the Negro only won a partial victory after all. The matter was finally settled, as usual, by a kind of compromise. The Negro was baptized and admitted to the church, but a sort of second table was set for him. He could take the Lord's supper only after his white brethren had finished eating the bread and drinking the wine. He was not even allowed to enter the same door of the sanctuary by which his white brethren entered. A separate door was cut for him in the wall, a sort of hole in the wall, leading to a high and dark place in the gallery, where his presence could give no offense to the Lord's white children on the floor.

It is strange that this state of things did not disgust and repel the Negro, make him an infidel, and drive him from religion altogether, but it did not. He clung to religion all the same. Believing that half a loaf was better than no bread, he took what he could get of the church, kept on praying and singing, and sometimes shouting. He could pray as fervently for the conversion of the scoundrel who tore his flesh with the lash, as for his best friend. He was made to think that his offensive black skin on earth would be changed for a white one in Heaven. It was a strange fancy, but quite a natural one when we see the importance given to color in the problems before us in our day.

● ● ●

Another troublesome problem presented to our Christian country was whether the Negro should have the help of the Bible with which to get to Heaven; whether, in fact, the command to search the Scriptures imposed any obligation or duty on him. Our Southern brethren, with whom we have always been profoundly sympathetic even unto this day, decided this problem against the Bible, and against the Negro, as usual. They made it a crime, to be punished with banishment, imprisonment, and stripes, for any one to teach the Negro to read.

• • •

They tell us that they know the Negro, and that they can manage him better than anybody else. They can manage his wages, his voting, and his education, and all that pertains to him. I hope the nation will not let them do any such thing. They have shown a strange inaptitude for such a task. The point with them is not what is right, but what will best suit themselves.

But again, in the history of the Negro we had another perplexing problem. It was this, and this was in some sense a national problem: Can the Negro be made a soldier? This, too, was very serious problem for the country, for it was a matter of Union or no Union, of life or death. For at one time it needed all the material which the nation could command to settle the problem of our national existence. It will be remembered that at the beginning of the war it was given out that no Negro need apply.

He was not to be allowed to shoulder a musket, carry a knapsack, or wear a Union uniform. The glory of the battle-field was to be won wholly by white men. The Negro might dig but not fight. He might be a servant, but not a soldier. He might carry a pick-ax, but never a musket.

In considering this problem the nation, strangely enough, shut its eyes to the fact that in the history of the Revolution the Negro fought bravely for American independence, and in the war of 1812 he even extorted praise for his valor from the stern lips of General Andrew Jackson. His fighting qualities were nobly admitted by the hero of New Orleans. In spite of this it was insisted that the Negro was a born coward; that he could never make a soldier: that he would run at the sight of a gun. . . .

Whether the Negro could be educated, was another problem, and I think this has been solved to the satisfaction of all candid men. He would be a dishonest man, or an amazingly stupid one who, in the face of the thousands of Negro teachers, the hundreds of Negro preachers, doctors, lawyers, authors, and editors, with which the country is now studded, should insist, as it was once insisted, that education was impossible to the Negro.

But the greatest problem for the Negro was whether he could with safety be made free. Good men knew that slavery was wrong, but how to get rid of it was the great question. Neither the pulpit, nor the press, nor the statesman could see a solution of the great problem, and yet that problem has been solved. The Negro is free, and the country is cleansed of its greatest curse, crime, and scandal.

• • •

But now, though all this has been done, though slavery has been abolished, though the Negro has been freed, though he has become a citizen, though the Union has been saved, in part by his valor, the Negro is not to be let off quite yet. He is to be made the victim of a new deal by precipitating upon the country a false issue. He is to face another problem.

Now that the Union is no longer in danger, now that the North and South are no longer enemies: now that they have ceased to scatter, tear, and slay each other, but sit together in halls of Congress, commerce, religion, and in brotherly love, it seems that the negro is to lose by their sectional harmony and good will all the rights and privileges that he gained by their former bitter enmity. . . .

The true problem is not the negro, but the nation. Not the law-abiding blacks of the South, but the white men of that section, who by fraud, violence, and persecution, are breaking the law, trampling on the Constitution, corrupting the ballot-box, and defeating the ends of justice. The true problem is whether these white ruffians shall be allowed by the nation to go on in their lawless and nefarious career, dishonoring the Government and making its very name a mockery. It is whether this nation has in itself sufficient moral stamina to maintain its own honor and integrity by vindicating its own Constitution and fulfilling its own pledges, or whether it has already touched that dry rot of moral depravity by which nations decline and fall, and governments fade and vanish.

The United States Government made the negro a citizen, will it protect him as a citizen? This is the problem. It made him a soldier, will it honor him as a patriot? This is the problem. It made him a voter, will it defend his right to vote? This is the problem. This, I say, is more a problem for the nation than for the negro, and this is the side of the question far more than the other which should be kept in view by the American people. . . .

Ida B. Wells

(1862–1931)

Ida B. Wells was born in Mississippi in 1862, a child of slavery. Over the next seven decades Wells would lead a public crusade to fight racism, discrimination, and the lynching of black men and women. In 1882, Wells first entered the public record as an activist when a railroad conductor forcibly removed her from the ladies' car of a train. Claiming that she had paid the full price of a ticket and was thus entitled to her seat, Wells sued the Chesapeake and Ohio Railroad and won $500 in damages. Her victory against racial segregation on the railroad was cut short when a higher court ruled in favor of the railroad.

After this event, Wells began to write about racial issues for local African-American newspapers in Memphis and across the South. In 1892, Wells wielded the power of her pen when a white mob lynched her friend Thomas Lynch for operating a grocery store that successfully competed against white businesses. In an editorial she wrote for the *Free Speech* following the horrific lynching, Wells accused white southerners of perpetuating the myth that black men raped white women and thus needed to be lynched in order to maintain order. She argued that white southern men lynched black men to suppress African-American political and economic clout, not to protect white womanhood. Perhaps most inflammatory was Wells' claim that African-American men and white women often had consensual relationships. As she wrote in her editorial, "Nobody in this section believes the old thread-bare lie that Negro men rape white women. If Southern white men are not careful, they will overreach themselves. . . . A conclusion will then be reached which will be very damaging to the moral reputation of their women." With this accusation Wells exposed the complicated nature of race and gender politics and power relations in the post-Reconstruction South.

As a result of this editorial Wells was forced to abandon Memphis and she moved to New York City. She began a crusade against lynching that brought her into contact with the emerging African-American women's club movement. She also went to England where she was instrumental in organizing British support for her anti-lynching campaign. Wells continued to research and write about lynching and in 1895 she published *A Red Record: Tabulated Statistics and Alleged Causes of Lynchings in the United States, 1892–1893–1894,* from which the following selection is taken. In this excerpt Wells is challenging the sexual basis of white supremacy. She points out that while white men accused black men of rape, it was more likely the case that white men raped black women. Thus those white men who claimed to be lynching black men out of chivalrous concern for white women were assuming "a chivalry they did not possess."

Wells settled in Chicago and married Ferdinand Barnett in 1895. Together they had four children but this did not keep Wells from continuing her activism and her writing. In addition to her lifelong fight against lynching, Wells was involved with the women's suffrage movement, the African-American women's club movement, workers rights campaigns, the NAACP, and the Republican Party. When Ida B. Wells-Barnett died in 1931 she left a powerful legacy for us in her fight to protect, maintain, and ensure African-American citizenship.

Speaking Out against Lynching (1895)

Humanity abhors the assailant of womanhood, and this charge upon the Negro at once placed him beyond the pale of human sympathy. With such unanimity, earnestness and apparent candor was this charge made and reiterated that the world has accepted the story that the Negro is a monster which the Southern white man has painted him. And to-day, the Christian world feels, that while lynching is a crime, and lawlessness and anarchy the certain precursors of a nation's fall, it can not by word or deed, extend sympathy or help to a race of outlaws, who might mistake their plea for justice and deem it an excuse for their continued wrongs.

The Negro has suffered much and is willing to suffer more. He recognizes that the wrongs of two centuries can not be righted in a day, and he tries to bear his burden with patience for to-day and be hopeful for to-morrow. But there comes a time when the veriest worm will turn, and the Negro feels to-day that after all the work he has done, all the sacrifices he has made, and all the suffering he has endured, if he did not, now, defend his name and manhood from this vile accusation, he would be unworthy even of the contempt of mankind. It is to this charge he now feels he must make answer.

If the Southern people in defense of their lawlessness, would tell the truth and admit that colored men and women are lynched for almost any offense, from murder to a misdemeanor, there would not now be the necessity for this defense. But when they intentionally, maliciously and constantly belie the record and bolster up these falsehoods by the words of legislators, preachers, governors and bishops, then the Negro must give to the world his side of the awful story.

A word as to the charge itself. In considering the third reason assigned by the Southern white people for the butchery of blacks, the question must be asked, what the white man means when he charges the black man with rape. Does he mean the crime which the statutes of the civilized states describe as such? Not by any means. With the Southern white man, any mesalliance existing between a white woman and a colored man is a sufficient foundation for the charge of rape. The Southern white man says that it is impossible for a voluntary alliance to exist between a white woman and a colored man, and therefore, the fact of an alliance is a proof of force. In numerous instances where colored men have been lynched on the charge of rape, it was positively known at the time of lynching, and indisputably proven after the victim's death, that the relationship sustained between the man and woman was voluntary and clandestine, and that in no court of law could even the charge of assault have been successfully maintained.

It was for the assertion of this fact, in the defense of her own race, that the writer hereof became an exile; her property destroyed and her return to her home forbidden under penalty of death, for writing the following editorial which was printed in her paper, the Free Speech, in Memphis, Tenn., May 21, 1892:

"Eight Negroes lynched since last issue of the 'Free Speech' one at Little Rock, Ark., last Saturday morning where the citizens broke (?) into the penitentiary and got their man; three near Anniston, Ala., one near New Orleans; and three at Clarksville, Ga., the last three for killing a white man, and five on the same old racket—the new alarm about raping white women. The same programme of hanging, then shooting bullets into the lifeless bodies was carried out to the letter. Nobody in this section of the country believes the old threadbare lie that Negro men rape white women. If Southern white men are not careful, they will over-reach themselves and public sentiment will have a reaction; a conclusion will then be reached which will be very damaging to the moral reputation of their women."

But threats cannot suppress the truth, and while the Negro suffers the soul deformity, resultant from two and a half centuries of slavery, he is no more guilty of this vilest of all vile charges than the white man who would blacken his name.

During all the years of slavery, no such charge was ever made, not even during the dark days of the rebellion, when the white man, following the fortunes of war went to do battle for the maintenance of slavery. While the master was away fighting to forge the fetters upon the slave, he left his wife and children with no protectors save the Negroes themselves. And yet during those years of trust and peril, no Negro proved recreant to his trust and no white man returned to a home that had been despoiled.

Likewise during the period of alleged "insurrection," and alarming "race riots," it never occurred to the white man, that his wife and children were in danger of assault. Nor in the Reconstruction era, when the hue and cry was against "Negro Domination," was there ever a thought that the domination would ever contaminate a fireside or strike to death the virtue of womanhood. It must appear strange indeed, to every thoughtful and candid man, that more than a quarter of a century elapsed before the Negro began to show signs of such infamous degeneration.

In his remarkable apology for lynching, Bishop Haygood, of Georgia, says: "No race, not the most savage, tolerates the rape of woman, but it may be said without reflection upon any other people that the Southern people are now and always have been most sensitive concerning the honor of their women—their mothers, wives, sisters and daughters." It is not the purpose of this defense to say one word against the white women of the South. Such need not be said, but it is their misfortune that the chivalrous white men of that section, in order to escape the deserved execration of the civilized world, should shield themselves by their cowardly and infamously false excuse, and call into question that very honor about which their distinguished priestly apologist claims they are most sensitive. To justify their own barbarism they assume a chivalry which they do not possess. True chivalry respects all womanhood, and no one who reads the record, as it is written in the faces of the million mulattoes in the South, will for a minute conceive that the Southern white man had a very chivalrous regard for the honor due the women of this own race or respect for the womanhood which circumstances placed in his power. That chivalry which is "most sensitive concerning the honor of women" can hope for but little respect from the civilized world, when it confines itself entirely to the women who happen to be white. Virtue knows no color line, and the chivalry which depends upon complexion of skin and texture of hair can command no honest respect.

W. E. B. Du Bois

1868–1963

W. E. B. Du Bois graduated from Fisk University and, in 1895, became the first African American to receive a doctorate from Harvard. He was a brilliant scholar, trained in history with a broad background in the social sciences. An outspoken critic of Booker T. Washington's accommodationism, Du Bois believed that only a direct political response was adequate to counter Jim Crow legislation, the barriers to black voting rights, and the tragic violence of lynching that punctuated the African-American experience in the South. At best, he contended, the dominant racist culture would always expect African-Americans to do manual and domestic work under the supervision of whites. In the end, Du Bois could not accept the social segregation and restricted educational program advanced in Washington's "Atlanta Compromise."

Du Bois believed that it was necessary to protest racial inequality and to work vigorously through the legal system. He argued for integration, not accommodation, co-founding the National Association for the Advancement of Colored People (NAACP) in 1909. However, the process of achieving integration and political equality was slow. For example, it took until 1954 for the Supreme Court finally to outlaw segregation in the public schools. And with racism still strong across United States, the segregation problem was far from solved. The Supreme Court ruling was not enforced, and, eventually, having suffered a number of political disappointments and setbacks, Du Bois became frustrated with the American system, drifting instead toward socialism and communism. When he was in his nineties, he renounced his American citizenship and lived the last years of his life in Ghana.

In "Strivings of the Negro People," first published in the *Atlantic Monthly* (1897), Du Bois directly confronts the issue of racial integration and black identity. The goal of integration, he argues, is neither to Africanize America nor for African Americans to be lost in a sea of white Americanism. How does Du Bois describe the modern black experience? What sort of balance between the races does he want to achieve in American society? How might different cultural traditions enrich each other? What contributions of African culture does Du Bois find enriching for all Americans?

from "Strivings of the Negro People" (1897)

Between me and the other world there is ever an unasked question: unasked by some through feelings of delicacy; by others through the difficulty of rightly framing it. All, nevertheless, flutter round it. They approach me in a half-hesitant sort of way, eye me curiously or compassionately, and then, instead of saying directly, How does it feel to be a problem? they say, I know an excellent colored man in my town; or, I fought at Mechanicsville; or, Do not these Southern outrages make your blood boil? At these I smile, or am interested, or reduce the boiling to a simmer, as the occasion may require. To the real question, How does it feel to be a problem? I answer seldom a word.

And yet, being a problem is a strange experience,—peculiar even for one who has never been anything else, save perhaps in babyhood and in Europe. It is in the early days of rollicking boyhood that the revelation first bursts upon one, all in a day, as it were. I remember well when the shadow swept across me. I was a little thing, away up in the hills of New England, where the dark Housatonic[1] winds between Hoosac[2] and Taghanic[3] to the sea. In a wee wooden schoolhouse, something put it into the boys' and girls' heads to buy gorgeous visiting-cards—ten cents a package—and exchange. The exchange was merry, till one girl, a tall newcomer, refused my card,—refused it peremptorily, with a glance. Then it dawned upon me with a certain suddenness that I was different from the others; or like, mayhap, in heart and life and longing, but shut out from their world by a vast veil. I had thereafter no desire to tear down that veil, to creep through; I held all beyond it in common contempt, and lived above it in a region of blue sky and great wandering shadows. That sky was bluest when I could beat my mates at examination-time, or beat them at a foot-race, or even beat their stringy heads. Alas, with the years all this fine contempt began to fade; for the world I longed for, and all its dazzling opportunities, were theirs, not mine. But they should not keep these prizes, I said; some, all, I would wrest from them. Just how I would do it I could never decide: by reading law, by healing the sick, by telling the wonderful tales that swam in my head,—some way. With other black boys the strife was not so fiercely sunny: their youth shrunk into tasteless sycophancy, or into silent hatred of the pale world about them and mocking distrust of everything white; or wasted itself in a bitter cry. Why did God make me an outcast and a stranger in mine own house? The "shades of the prison-house" closed round about us all: walls strait and stubborn to the whitest, but relentlessly narrow, tall, and unscalable to sons of night who must plod darkly on in resignation, or beat unavailing palms against the stone, or steadily, half hopelessly watch the streak of blue above.

After the Egyptian and Indian, the Greek and Roman, the Teuton and Mongolian, the Negro is a sort of seventh son, born with a veil, and gifted with second-sight in this American world,—a world which yields him no self-consciousness, but only lets him see himself through the revelation of the other world. It is a peculiar sensation, this double-consciousness, this sense of always looking at one's self through the eyes of others, of measuring one's soul by the tape of a world that looks on in amused contempt and pity. One ever feels his two-ness,—an American, a Negro; two souls, two thoughts, two unreconciled strivings; two warring ideals in one dark body, whose dogged strength alone keeps it from being torn asunder. The history of the American Negro is the history of this strife,—this longing to attain self-conscious manhood, to merge his double self into a better and truer self. In this merging he wishes neither of the older selves to be lost. He does not wish to Africanize America, for America has too much to teach the world and Africa; he does not wish to bleach his Negro blood in a flood of white Americanism, for he believes—foolishly, perhaps, but fervently—that Negro blood has yet a message for the world. He simply wishes to make it possible for a man to be both a Negro and an American without being cursed and spit upon by his fellows, without losing the opportunity of self-development.

This is the end of his striving: to be a co-worker in the kingdom of culture, to escape both death and isolation, and to husband and use his best powers. These powers, of body and of mind, have in the past been so wasted and dispersed as to lose all effectiveness, and to seem like absence of all power, like weakness. The double-aimed struggle of the black artisan, on the one hand to escape white contempt for a nation of mere hewers of wood and drawers of water, and on the other hand to plough and nail and dig for a poverty-stricken horde, could only result in making him a poor craftsman, for he had but half a heart in either cause. By the poverty and ignorance of his people the Negro lawyer or doctor was pushed toward quackery and demagogism, and by the criticism of the other world toward an elaborate preparation that overfitted him for his lowly tasks. The would-be black savant was confronted by the paradox that the knowledge his people needed was a twice-told tale to his white neighbors, while the knowledge which would teach the white world was Greek to his own flesh and blood. The innate love of harmony and beauty that set the ruder souls of his people a-dancing, a-singing, and a-laughing raised but confusion and doubt in the soul of the black artist; for the beauty revealed to him was the soul-beauty of a race which his larger audience despised, and he could not articulate the message of another people.

This waste of double aims, this seeking to satisfy two unreconciled ideals, has wrought sad havoc with the courage and faith and deeds of eight thousand thousand people, has sent them often wooing false gods and invoking false means of salvation, and has even at times seemed destined to make them ashamed of themselves. In the days of bondage they thought to see in one divine event the end of all doubt and disappointment; eighteenth-century Rousseauism never worshiped freedom with half the unquestioning faith that the American Negro did for two centuries. To him slavery was, indeed, the sum of all villainies, the cause of all sorrow, the root of all prejudice; emancipation was the key to a promised land of sweeter beauty than ever stretched before the eyes of wearied Israelites. In his songs and exhortations swelled one refrain, liberty; in his tears and curses the god he implored had freedom in his right hand. At last it came,—suddenly, fearfully, like a dream. With one wild carnival of blood and passion came the message in his own plaintive cadences:—

> Shout, O children!
> Shout, you're free!
> The Lord has bought your liberty!

Years have passed away, ten, twenty, thirty. Thirty years of national life, thirty years of renewal and development, and yet the swarthy ghost of Banquo sits in its old place at the national feast. In vain does the nation cry to its vastest problem,—

> Take any shape but that, and my firm nerves
> Shall never tremble!

The freedman has not yet found in freedom his promised land. Whatever of lesser good may have come in these years of change, the shadow of a deep disappointment rests upon the Negro people,—a disappointment all the more bitter because the unattained ideal was unbounded save by the simple ignorance of a lowly folk.

The first decade was merely a prolongation of the vain search for freedom, the boom that seemed ever barely to elude their grasp,—like a tantalizing will-o'-the-wisp, maddening and misleading the headless host. The holocaust of war, the terrors of the Kuklux Klan, the lies of carpet-baggers, the disorganization of industry, and the contradictory advice of friends and foes left the bewildered serf with no new watchword beyond the old cry for freedom. As the decade closed, however, he began to grasp a new idea. The ideal of liberty demanded for its attainment powerful means, and these the Fifteenth Amendment gave him. The ballot, which before he had looked upon as a visible sign of freedom, he now regarded as the chief means of gaining and perfecting the liberty with which war had partially endowed him. And why not? Had not votes made war and emancipated millions? Had not votes enfranchised the freedmen? Was anything impossible to a power that had done all this? A million black men started with renewed zeal to vote themselves into the kingdom. The decade fled away,—a decade containing, to the freedman's mind, nothing but suppressed votes, stuffed ballot-boxes, and election outrages that nullified his vaunted right of suffrage. And yet that decade from 1875 to 1885 held another powerful movement, the rise of another ideal to guide the unguided, another pillar of fire by night after a clouded day. It was the ideal of "book-learning"; the curiosity, born of compulsory ignorance, to know and test the power of the cabalistic[4] letters of the white man, the longing to know. Mission and night schools began in the smoke of battle, ran the gauntlet of reconstruction, and at last developed into permanent foundations. Here at last seemed to have been discovered the mountain path to Canaan; longer than the highway of emancipation and law, steep and rugged, but straight, leading to heights high enough to overlook life.

Up the new path the advance guard toiled, slowly, heavily, doggedly; only those who have watched and guided the faltering feet, the misty minds, the dull understandings of the dark pupils of these schools know how faithfully, how piteously, this people strove to learn. It was weary work. The cold statistician wrote down the inches of progress here and there, noted also where here and there a foot had slipped or some one had fallen. To the tired climbers, the horizon was ever dark, the mists were often cold, the Canaan was always dim and far away. If, however, the vistas disclosed as yet no goal, no resting-place, little but flattery and criticism, the journey at least gave leisure for reflection and self-examination; it changed the child of emancipation to the youth with dawning self-consciousness, self-realization, self-respect. In those sombre forests of his striving his own soul rose before him, and he saw himself,—darkly as through a veil; and yet he saw in himself some faint revelation of his power, of his mission. He began to have a dim feeling that, to attain his place in the world, he must be himself, and not another. For the first time he sought to analyze the burden he bore upon his back, that dead-weight of social degradation partially masked behind a half-named Negro problem. He felt his poverty; without a cent, without a home, without land, tools, or savings, he had entered into competition with rich, landed, skilled neighbors. To be a poor man is hard, but to be a poor race in a land of dollars is the very bottom of hardships. He felt the weight of his ignorance,—not simply of letters, but of life, of business, of the humanities; the accumulated sloth and shirking and awkwardness of decades and centuries shackled his hands and feet. Nor was his burden all poverty and ignorance. The red stain of bastardy, which two centuries of systematic legal defilement of Negro women had stamped upon his race, meant not only the loss of ancient African chastity, but also the hereditary weight of a mass of filth from white whoremongers and adulterers, threatening almost the obliteration of the Negro home.

A people thus handicapped ought not to be asked to race with the world, but rather allowed to give all its time and thought to its own social problems. But alas! while sociologists gleefully count his bastards and his prostitutes, the very soul of the toiling, sweating black man is darkened by the shadow of a vast despair. Men call the shadow prejudice, and learnedly explain it as the natural defense of culture against barbarism, learning against ignorance, purity against crime, the "higher" against the "lower" races. To which the Negro cries Amen! and swears that to so much of this strange prejudice as is founded on just homage to civilization, culture, righteousness, and progress he humbly bows and meekly does obeisance. But before that nameless prejudice that leaps beyond all this he stands helpless, dismayed, and well-nigh speechless; before that personal disrespect and mockery, the ridicule and systematic humiliation, the distortion of fact and wanton license of fancy, the cynical ignoring of the better and boisterous welcoming of the worse, the all-pervading desire to inculcate disdain for everything black, from Toussaint to the devil,—before this there rises a sickening despair that would disarm and discourage any nation save that black host to whom "discouragement" is an unwritten word.

They still press on, they still nurse the dogged hope,—not a hope of nauseating patronage, not a hope of reception into charmed social circles of stock-jobbers, pork-packers, and earl-hunters, but the hope of a higher synthesis of civilization and humanity, a true progress, with which the chorus "Peace, good will to men,"

May make one music as before,
But vaster.

Thus the second decade of the American Negro's freedom was a period of conflict, of inspiration and doubt, of faith and vain questionings, of Sturm and Drang.[5] The ideals of physical freedom, of political power, of school training, as separate all-sufficient panaceas for social ills, became in the third decade dim and overcast. They were the vain dreams of credulous race childhood; not wrong, but incomplete and over-simple. The training of the schools we need to-day more than ever,—the training of deft hands, quick eyes and ears, and the broader, deeper, higher culture of gifted minds. The power of the ballot we need in sheer self-defense, and as a guarantee of good faith. We may misuse it, but we can scarce do worse in this respect than our whilom[6] masters. Freedom, too, the long-sought, we still seek,—the freedom of life and limb, the freedom to work and think. Work, culture, and liberty,—all these we need, not singly, but together; for to-day these ideals among the Negro people are gradually coalescing, and finding a higher meaning in the unifying ideal of race,—the ideal of fostering the traits and talents of the Negro, not in opposition to, but in conformity with, the greater ideals of the American republic, in order that some day, on American soil, two world races may give each to each those characteristics which both so sadly lack. Already we come not altogether empty-handed: there is to-day no true American music but the sweet wild melodies of the Negro slave; the American fairy tales are Indian and African; we are the sole oasis of simple faith and reverence in a dusty desert of dollars and smartness. Will America be poorer if she replace her brutal, dyspeptic blundering with the light-hearted but determined Negro humility; or her coarse, cruel wit with loving, jovial good humor; or her Annie Rooney[7] with Steal Away?[8]

Merely a stern concrete test of the underlying principles of the great republic is the Negro problem, and the spiritual striving of the freedmen's sons is the travail of souls whose burden is almost beyond the measure of their strength, but who bear it in the name of an historic race, in the name of this land of their fathers' fathers, and in the name of human opportunity.

Notes

[1] New England river.

[2] Southern range of the Green Mountains in New England.

[3] Another New England mountain range.

[4] Cryptic; also can pertain to knowledge possessed only by a small group of people.

[5] German: "Storm and Stress," a late eighteenth-century literary movement emphasizing nature, individualism, and passion. The Sturm and Drang artists and intellectuals were critical of Enlightenment rationalism.

[6] Former.

[7] "Little Annie Rooney," a popular song first appearing in England (1890) and then a hit song in the U.S.

[8] "Steal Away to Jesus," an African-American spiritual (c. 1870).

Marcus Garvey

1887–1940

Born in Jamaica, Marcus Garvey became one of the leading African-American political thinkers of early twentieth century. In contrast to Booker T. Washington, the accommodationist, and W. E. B. Du Bois, the integrationist, Garvey conceived of himself as a separatist, heading the Black Nationalist movement of the 1920s. Black Nationalism celebrates African cultural identity, encouraging economic independence and political self-governance within black communities. The more extreme separatist positions call for a black nation either in the United States or as part of a relocation to Africa. W. E. B. Du Bois had entertained pan-African ideas, whereby individuals of African descent but living in different continents would work together for a common cause. However, Garvey developed a black nationhood movement with the founding of the Universal Negro Improvement Association.

Garvey established the Black Star Line, which was intended to promote trade, internationally, between black communities, with the aim of establishing a foundation for a worldwide black economy. His radical beliefs—including his views in favor of racial purity—made him unpopular with more conservative African-American leaders. After a controversial mail fraud conviction, and subsequent jail term, President Calvin Coolidge pardoned Garvey, but deported him back to Jamaica. Garvey's movement lost momentum; however, the seeds were planted for the resurgence of Black Nationalism following World War II.

How is Black Nationalism reflected in Garvey's "Negro Progress Postulates Negro Government" (1929)? What social perceptions work against African-American cultural identity, as Garvey articulates this problem in his essays "The World as It Is: Insulting Negro Womanhood" (1930) and "The World as It Is: The Internal Prejudices of Negroes" (1930)? What is the value of self-determination as Garvey conceives it in "Let the Negro Accumulate Wealth: It Will Bring Him Power" (1935)?

Selections from the
Writings of Marcus Garvey

Negro Progress Postulates
Negro Government (1929)

Whether it be viewed from the moral, legal, industrial and economic, social or political standpoint, there is no reasonable ground of objection to the establishment of a system of government by Negroes for Negroes. And such a system will not be characterized, as some persons fear, by the primitivism of intertribal strife and savage, perpetual warfare for temporary supremacy of this or that tribal leader. For the race is endowed with the instincts of government that bore the marks of a high standard of civilization, to which, in certain features, our boasted Western Culture has not made a worthy approach.

The Race has fallen but her instincts are not dead. The silence of centuries has been broken. Her winter has passed and her springtime is here with the promise of a bountiful harvest, for Negro genius has again been fanned into activity, and is ready to infuse into Negro life the qualities and characteristics that made Negroes great in their institutions of the past.

The Seat of Empire Northward Moves was true to history and poetry during the period of Negro decline. But its Northern limit has been reached, and with the revival of Negro activity its path has again turned South. For Empire has not only a Seat but a Home and that Home is Africa.

It is well for black men to think on these things and to notice the movements that are contributory to this end. Jamaica is to be favored in August with the General Convention of the UNIA movement. And while we can make only the briefest reference to that subject today we would ask Negroes to say what is their mind upon the matter. What do they expect to see and hear? They possibly have read concerning former conventions held in New York. These have been wonderful happenings in a wonderful country. What is their conjecture concerning that to be held in Jamaica? Hundreds and hundreds of Negro delegates from all parts of the world will meet from day to day for a whole month in discussion on Negro problems, and world issues as they affect the Negro. What is the aim? What will be the effect? Can Jamaica Negroes and the Jamaica community be the same after the convention?

And will not this convention in its implications and bearings be significant in regard to the growing consciousness of kinship of Negroes in whatev-

368

er part of the world they are found? Can it leave us without a strong, irresistible urge to realize the meaning of a common, permanent government, with a fixed habitation and a name? The convention will be a demonstration of the possibilities of Negro Government that no one can deny.

The World as It Is: Insulting
Negro Womanhood (1930)

It is an unfortunate thing that the Negro womanhood of Jamaica in particular and of the West Indies in general can be abused without any protection
given them or interest taken in the matter. We have before us the case of a
prominent man, who is only one of many, who has taken gross advantage of
a Negro girl, yet he continues to enjoy public respect. Unfortunately, the man
himself is a Negro; his action toward a member of his own race is worse than
if it were committed by a man of any other race. This man is wealthy, he was
not always so, he was once a poor man. When he was poor, he got engaged to
a colored girl probably with the best intention; when he started to get rich, he
started to ignore this colored fiancée, to "put her off" and tell her all kinds of
false tales with the object of breaking his pledge. According to the man's way
of thinking he had become sufficiently prominent and rich to enter "into society" and so he wanted a white wife, apparently, as most successful Negro men
of a certain turn of mind do after amassing fortunes. The colored girl refused
to release him from his obligation and so because he feared a suit for breach of
promise he has not yet married a white woman but he doesn't want to marry
a colored girl any more, yet during the time he has been taking advantage of
colored girls and in one instance has made one a mother.

The World as It Is: The Internal Prejudices of Negroes (1930)

According to the arrangement of the "colored" leaders, the following plan is decided and acted upon; it is made very successful in the West Indies and is now being successfully fostered in America and elsewhere. In countries where the blacks outnumber the whites, the "colored" build up a buffer society through the financial assistance and patronage of the minority whites. They convince the minority whites that the blacks are dangerous and vicious, and that their only chance of successfully living among them is to elevate to positions of trust, superiority and overseership of the "colored" element who will directly deal with the blacks and exploit them for the general benefit of the whites. The whites being not strong enough to stand alone accept our acquiescence and thus the "colored" element is elevated to a superior position and naturally becomes attached to the whites. The skillful group, however, by its ability to acquire wealth through the privileged position allowed, immediately starts out to socially equip itself educationally and culturally to meet the whites on equal terms. They also skillfully strengthen their positions by stirring up the blacks against the whites explaining to the former that all their ills are caused by the whites, then they go back to the whites and intimidate them by drawing their attention to the great danger of the dissatisfied blacks, and offer as a solution the uniting of the whites and "colored" in a social and economic union to offset the supposed common danger from the blacks. By this artful method the "colored" elements of the colonies have socially subdued the white man, who now looks on and sees the prosperous "colored" gentleman leading away his sister or daughter in the bonds of marriage without the ability to raise the voice of protest.

The "colored" elements have arranged it so that the blacks are always kept down, so that they can use their dissatisfaction and disaffection as an argument to strengthen and further perpetuate their positions of social equality and economic privilege and preferment with the whites.

Such is the game that is being played over in America by the Du Bois–Weldon Johnson group of "colored" persons of the National Association for the Advancement of Colored People. The Universal Negro Improvement Association stands in opposition to this association on the miscegenation question, because we believe in the racial purity of both the Negro and white races. We feel that the moral disadvantage of slavery should not be perpetuated. That where our slave masters were able to abuse our slave mothers and thereby cre-ate a hybrid bastardy, we ourselves, at this time of freedom and culture, should not perpetuate the crime of nature.

We desire to standardize our race morally, hence our advocacy of all ele-ments and shades within the race coming together and by well understood and defined codes build up a strong and healthy Negro race with pride and respect in itself, rather than seeking, as the Du Bois group does, to practice an unre-stricted intercourse of miscegenation.

All the hate that the leaders of the small "colored" group can find has been levied at me for my interference with and interruption of their plans. My indictment, conviction and imprisonment are but a small effort of theirs to help destroy and ruin me because of my effort to save the Negro race from extinction through miscegenation.

That "colored" group has scientifically arranged their method of propa-ganda. In America and the colonies, they hold out certain baits and hopes to the educated and financially prosperous men of the darker groups, such as encouraging them to marry the very lightest element of their women and adopting them into their society. These darker men for the special privilege and "honor" are used as active propagandists to deceive the great mass of dark peo-ple so that they would not suspect the motive or the design of the "colored" ele-ment. Generally the darker men, who marry the very lightest "colored" women who sometimes pass off as white, become more hostile to their kind in the mass as well as by individual contact than the very leaders, as the leaders are general-ly careful not to attract or arouse suspicion of their motive. The majority of the "colored" leaders who seek after white women and the darker men who marry very light "colored" women are seldom on social terms with their own mothers if they are dark. If they have their mothers in their homes, which is generally never so, they hide them away either in the kitchen or a back room where they do not come in contact with either their light "colored" or white guests. Such is the great problem that I have sought to solve, and no one will wonder why I have been made a criminal in the struggle to rescue and save the Negro race from itself and from continuous suffering and ultimate extermination.

This treatment to colored girls is common among us and it is time a halt be called—if by no one else, by the *Blackman* in exposing such cases to the public. It is a dirty trick on the part of successful Negroes to spend two-thirds of their lives amassing wealth from among the Negro people, [that] then when they become rich they marry people outside of their own race to die shortly after, leaving their fortunes, made from the Negro people, to go into the cof-fers of other people who are sufficiently independent and provided for, while the Negro race still remains in poverty. It is a shame, and so we shall make it a point of our duty to at all times bring any abuse of our womanhood to the attention of the public.

Not long ago a prominent doctor died and left a fortune. The fortune went to the white lady he married and, naturally, to her relatives. The doctor, like most of our successful men, came up through difficulties; his poor Negro parents labored hard to give him an education. Nearly everything he got by way of education and start in life came through Negroes. The success of his profession was insured through Negroes because all his patients were Negroes, yet when he became rich instead of marrying a Negro woman like his mother, he married a white woman, and now that he is dead all of his wealth is gone out of the race.

There is one thing that we have to admire the white man for and that is he is never found disloyal to his race. We find isolated cases where individuals of the white race marry Negro women, but not where they have to give their fortunes to these women or their relatives; it is always the case [that] the Negro women are rich when marriages take place between them and white men. We hope that public sentiment will be stirred as to make it impossible for successful Negro men to so insult our womanhood, and we hope the gentleman we have in mind will marry the poor nurse he has dishonored.

Let the Negro Accumulate Wealth: It Will Bring Him Power (1935)

Our economic condition seems, to a great extent, to affect our general status. When it is considered that twentieth century civilization pays homage to and worships peoples and nations only on the basis of wealth, it should not be surprising to understand why the Negro is universally ignored. Economic independence or wealth is the recommendation of a people in the full consideration of others. With all that may be said of the morals and ethics of our time, carrying with it the suggestion of rights, liberty and justice, the whole fabric is based upon economic wealth. Either the wealth of the individual, the race, or the nation. So it behooves the Negro to think in terms of economic expansion through which he may enforce the consideration that is necessary for his political, social and other betterment.

The Universal Negro Improvement Association, as everyone will admit—the most thoughtful Negro movement in the world is now, according to the need of time, emphasizing economic expansion and solidarity among Negroes. We have to make more conquests in the economic field. We have to bring under control every available resource to which the Negro is allied on his natural ground or wheresoever he happens to find himself in its midst. Be assured of this, that in the Negro's rise to wealth will come the adjustment of most of the wrongs inflicted upon him. We must have wealth in culture, wealth in education and solidly wealth of real economic values.

The program laid down by the last Convention of the Universal Negro Improvement Association in Jamaica, 1934, covers a wide range of economic expansion. This is a program that every sensible Negro, in affiliation with the Universal Negro Improvement Association, must work for, and so the urge is for greater loyalty to the work, because it is only through proper organization that the real work can be done. Be not deceived, wealth is strength, wealth is power, wealth is influence, wealth is justice, is liberty, is real human rights. The system of our world politics suggests such and as a fact it is. Show wealth to your statesmen and they will couch their language in terms satisfactory, show wealth to the soldiers and they will enlist in your army, show wealth to the neutral populations and they will turn on your side. It is by the accumulated wealth of the Jew that he is winning support from a hostile world, it is the accumulated wealth of the Negro that will force him to the front and compel men and nations to think of him in terms of human justice. All this is achievable through a greater economic expansion. That must be our purpose and to this the Universal Negro Improvement Association dedicates itself.

P.S. No message of mine would be complete to the Negro peoples of the world without again reminding them of their obligations to the parent body of the Universal Negro Improvement Association. Divisions, branches, chapters and members must do their duty. The greatest duty now is to report regularly each month and for each member to pay in his Assessment Tax; if not convenient to pay it to the divisions pay it direct to the parent body, Universal Negro Improvement Association, 2, Beaumont Crescent, West Kensington, London, W. 14, England.

Langston Hughes

1902–1967

Langston Hughes was born in Joplin, Missouri, and started college in 1921. He left due to racial problems on campus and spent from 1923 to 1925 working his way around West Africa and Europe. When he returned he published his first book, *The Weary Blues* (1926), and returned to school at Lincoln University. As a writer Hughes created poems, short stories, novels, plays, musicals and nonfiction. His work is popular as portraying realistic views of African-American culture and he always insisted that his characters were common but noble. In 1960 he received the Spingarn Medal from the National Association for the Advancement of Colored People (NAACP).

The poem we have selected was written in 1925. This was the era of open lynching in the United States and anti-lynching bills that failed to pass the Senate. It was a time when huge numbers of Blacks went north looking for something better. Hughes was perhaps the most famous of the poets of the Harlem Renaissance, a period of heightened productivity by black artists and receptivity of their work by white audiences that reached its peak in the 1920s. Hughes's work from that time demonstrates a racial awareness and effort to deal with the negative stereotypes of African Americans that were prevalent. His poetry uses the rhythms and styles of jazz and blues, musical styles that were also growing in the Harlem of the 1920s.

To whom was Hughes writing? What does the poem say about what it was like to be an African American in 1925? What does the poem say about the value of any human being?

I, Too (1925)

I, too, sing America.

I am the darker brother.
They send me to eat in the kitchen
When company comes,
But I laugh,
And eat well,
And grow strong.

Tomorrow,
I'll be at the table
When company comes.
Nobody'll dare
Say to me,
"Eat in the kitchen,"
Then.

Besides,
They'll see how beautiful I am
And be ashamed—

I, too, am America.

Anne Bethel Spencer

1882–1975

Anne Spencer was born in Henry County, Virginia. She attended
Virginia Theological Seminary and College, earning her degree in 1899. She
married one of her fellow students, Edward A. Spencer, and they had three
children, two girls and a boy. Recognizing Spencer as one of the central
Harlem Renaissance poets, James Weldon Johnson published her work in *The
Book of American Negro Poetry* in 1922. The frequent visitors who came to
spend time with her in Lynchburg, Virginia, made her home much like the
Parisian *salons* of the 1700s. Over the years, Spencer brought together such
diverse people as George Washington Carver, W. E. B. Du Bois and Claude
McKay, placing her in the center of early twentieth-century African-American
thought and culture.

In her poems, she often used nature imagery taken from the garden where
she did so much of her writing. Her themes included racial discrimination,
human relations, class issues, and rights for women. Although there were
African-American women poets both before and after the Harlem Renaissance,
Spencer's work is presented here as an example of the ideas and values in the
African-American community in her time. Artists of the Harlem Renaissance
were indeed prolific, steadfastly interrogating the racial situation in which they
lived and reflecting their critical awareness of identity and social justice.

In what ways is this work similar to that of the Romantic movement of
the late eighteenth and early nineteenth centuries? How is this twentieth-century American poem different from those of the Enlightenment and
Romanticism? To whom is Anne Spencer writing? Explore the significance of
the last line—"Man-maker, make white!"

White Things (c. 1922)

Most things are colorful things—the sky, earth, and sea.
Black men are most men; but the white are free!
White things are rare things; so rare, so rare
They stole from out a silvered world—somewhere.
Finding earth-plains fair plains, save greenly grassed,
They strewed white feathers of cowardice, as they passed;
The golden stars with lances fine
The hills all red and darkened pine,
They blanched with their wand of power;
And turned the blood in a ruby rose
To a poor white poppy-flower.
They pyred a race of black, black men,
And burned them to ashes white; then,
Laughing, a young one claimed a skull,
For the skull of a black is white, not dull,
But a glistening awful thing;
Made, it seems, for this ghoul to swing
In the face of God with all his might,
And swear by the hell that sired him:
"Man-maker, make white!"

VIII. Intellectual Uncertainty and the Rise of Modernism

Charles Darwin

1809–1883

Charles Darwin, the initiator of what is sometimes called the Second Scientific Revolution, was born into a life of relative affluence at Shrewsbury, England. His father was a successful physician and his mother was the daughter of the celebrated potter Josiah Wedgwood. As a result, his youth was directed by personal interest, not material need, and what interested him from his earliest years was the natural world. An indifferent student, Darwin first studied medicine—which appalled him—at the University of Edinburgh and then prepared for the ministry at Cambridge University, graduating in 1831. But his life immediately took a different direction when he joined H.M.S. Beagle as the naturalist and gentleman companion of its captain. There he spent nearly five years as it circled the globe, years that were decisive for his intellectual development. After twenty-three more years of study and reflection—largely brought to an end by the competing work of British naturalist Alfred Russell Wallace—he published *On the Origin of Species* on 24 November 1859. Darwin's theory of evolution by means of natural selection was an immediate sensation and it has occupied the minds of men and women ever since. The remainder of his life was filled with family (he was the father of ten children) and the writing of a series of impressive works, the most controversial of which was *The Descent of Man* (1871). Darwin died at home in Downe, England, having had a life of intellectual adventure experienced by few.

The following selection is drawn from Chapter IV of the sixth, definitive edition of *On the Origin of Species* (1872). It is the culmination of Darwin's core argument, the stage for which is set by the three chapters which precede it (not included here). Chapter I establishes the fact of "Variation under Domestication" by examining the experiences of animal breeders who select animals to breed in order to attain characteristics they desire. Darwin had a particular affinity for pigeons. Chapter II establishes the fact of "Variation under Nature" by reviewing the variability of life in natural settings. It is here that Darwin's study of the finches of the Galapagos Islands was especially important. Chapter III describes "The Struggle for Existence" in which all life is engaged. Darwin's initial understanding of this struggle grew out of his reading of *An Essay on the Principle of Population* (1798), by Thomas Robert Malthus. Chapter IV describes how "Natural Selection" works in nature. Its essential point is that given the fundamental variability of all life, natural selection does for life in nature what the breeder does for domesticated animals. What roles do variability, persistent action and time play in natural selection?

No brief statement can summarize the influence of Darwin's work. Just as it has provided the framework for an enormous, variegated and ongoing research program in the biological sciences, so too *On the Origin of Species* is the book that launched a thousand sermons (and still does). How has Darwin's work contributed to the biological sciences? Why has it been the source of so much religious controversy? What, if anything, stands in the way of reconciling these views?

from *The Origin of Species* (1859)

How will the struggle for existence, briefly discussed in the last chapter, act in regard to variation? Can the principle of selection, which we have seen is so potent in the hands of man, apply under nature? I think we shall see that it can act most efficiently. Let the endless number of slight variations and individual differences occurring in our domestic productions, and, in a lesser degree, in those under nature, be borne in mind; as well as the strength of the hereditary tendency. Under domestication, it may truly be said that the whole organisation becomes in some degree plastic. But the variability, which we almost universally meet with in our domestic productions is not directly produced, as Hooker and Asa Gray have well remarked, by man; he can neither originate varieties nor prevent their occurrence; he can only preserve and accumulate such as do occur. Unintentionally he exposes organic beings to new and changing conditions of life, and variability ensues; but similar changes of conditions might and do occur under nature. Let it also be borne in mind how infinitely complex and close-fitting are the mutual relations of all organic beings to each other and to their physical conditions of life; and consequently what infinitely varied diversities of structure might be of use to each being under changing conditions of life. Can it then be thought improbable, seeing that variations useful to man have undoubtedly occurred, that other variations useful in some way to each being in the great and complex battle of life, should occur in the course of many successive generations? If such do occur, can we doubt (remembering that many more individuals are born than can possibly survive) that individuals having any advantage, however slight, over others, would have the best chance of surviving and procreating their kind? On the other hand, we may feel sure that any variation in the least degree injurious would be rigidly destroyed. This preservation of favourable individual differences and variations, and the destruction of those which are injurious, I have called Natural Selection, or the Survival of the Fittest. Variations neither useful nor injurious would not be affected by natural selection, and would be left either a fluctuating element, as perhaps we see in certain polymorphic species, or would ultimately become fixed, owing to the nature of the organism and the nature of the conditions.

Several writers have misapprehended or objected to the term Natural Selection. Some have even imagined that natural selection induces variability, whereas it implies only the preservation of such variations as arise and are beneficial to the being under its conditions of life. No one objects to agriculturists speaking of the potent effects of man's selection; and in this case the individual differences given by nature, which man for some object selects, must of necessity first occur. Others have objected that the term selection implies conscious choice in the animals which become modified; and it has even been urged that, as plants have no volition, natural selection is not applicable to them! In the literal sense of the word, no doubt, natural selection is a false term; but who ever objected to chemists speaking of the elective affinities of the various elements?—and yet an acid cannot strictly be said to elect the base with which it in preference combines. It has been said that I speak of natural selection as an active power or Deity; but who objects to an author speaking of the attraction of gravity as ruling the movements of the planets? Every one knows what is meant and is implied by such metaphorical expressions; and they are almost necessary for brevity. So again it is difficult to avoid personifying the word Nature; but I mean by nature, only the aggregate action and product of many natural laws, and by laws the sequence of events as ascertained by us. With a little familiarity such superficial objections will be forgotten.

We shall best understand the probable course of natural selection by taking the case of a country undergoing some slight physical change, for instance, of climate. The proportional numbers of its inhabitants will almost immediately undergo a change, and some species will probably become extinct. We may conclude, from what we have seen of the intimate and complex manner in which the inhabitants of each country are bound together, that any change in the numerical proportions of the inhabitants, independently of the change of climate itself, would seriously affect the others. If the country were open on its borders, new forms would certainly immigrate, and this would likewise seriously disturb the relations of some of the former inhabitants. Let it be remembered how powerful the influence of a single introduced tree or mammal has been shown to be. But in the case of an island, or of a country partly surrounded by barriers, into which new and better adapted forms could not freely enter, we should then have places in the economy of nature which would assuredly be better filled up, if some of the original inhabitants were in some manner modified; for, had the area been open to immigration, these same places would have been seized on by intruders. In such cases, slight modifications, which in any way favoured the individuals of any species, by better adapting them to their altered conditions, would tend to be preserved; and natural selection would have free scope for the work of improvement.

We have good reason to believe, as shown in the first chapter, that changes in the conditions of life give a tendency to increased variability; and in the foregoing cases the conditions have changed, and this would manifestly be favourable to natural selection, by affording a better chance of the occurrence of profitable variations. Unless such occur, natural selection can do nothing. Under the term of "variations," it must never be forgotten that mere individual differences are included. As man can produce a great result with his domestic animals and plants by adding up in any given direction individual differences, so could natural selection, but far more easily from having incomparably longer time for action. Nor do I believe that any great physical change, as of climate, or any unusual degree of isolation, to check immigration, is necessary in order that new and unoccupied places should be left for natural selection to fill up by improving some of the varying inhabitants. For as all the inhabitants of each country are struggling together with nicely balanced forces, extremely slight modifications in the structure or habits of one species would often give it an advantage over others; and still further modifications of the same kind would often still further increase the advantage, as long as the species continued under the same conditions of life and profited by similar means of subsistence and defence. No country can be named in which all the native inhabitants are now so perfectly adapted to each other and to the physical conditions under which they live, that none of them could be still better adapted or improved; for in all countries, the natives have been so far conquered by naturalised productions that they have allowed some foreigners to take firm possession of the land. And as foreigners have thus in every country beaten some of the natives, we may safely conclude that the natives might have been modified with advantage, so as to have better resisted the intruders.

As man can produce, and certainly has produced, a great result by his methodical and unconscious means of selection, what may not natural selection effect? Man can act only on external and visible characters: Nature, if I may be allowed to personify the natural preservation or survival of the fittest, cares nothing for appearances, except in so far as they are useful to any being. She can act on every internal organ, on every shade of constitutional difference, on the whole machinery of life. Man selects only for his own good; Nature only for that of the being which she tends. Every selected character is fully exercised by her, as is implied by the fact of their selection. Man keeps the natives of many climates in the same country. He seldom exercises each selected character in some peculiar and fitting manner; he feeds a long and a short-beaked pigeon on the same food; he does not exercise a long-backed or long-legged quadruped in any peculiar manner; he exposes sheep with long and short wool to the same climate; does not allow the most vigorous males to struggle for the females; he does not rigidly destroy all inferior animals, but protects during each varying season, as far as lies in his power, all his productions. He often begins his selection by some half-monstrous form; or at least by some modification prominent enough to catch the eye or to be plainly useful to him. Under nature, the slightest differences of structure or constitution may well turn the nicely-balanced scale in the struggle for life, and so be preserved. How fleeting are the wishes and efforts of man! How short his time, and consequently how poor will be his results, compared with those accumulated by Nature during whole geological periods! Can we wonder, then, that Nature's productions should be far "truer" in character than man's productions; that they should be infinitely better adapted to the most complex conditions of life, and should plainly bear the stamp of far higher workmanship?

It may metaphorically be said that natural selection is daily and hourly scrutinising, throughout the world, the slightest variations; rejecting those that are bad, preserving and adding up all that are good; silently and insensibly working, WHENEVER AND WHEREVER OPPORTUNITY OFFERS, at the improvement of each organic being in relation to its organic and inorganic conditions of life. We see nothing of these slow changes in progress, until the hand of time has marked the long lapse of ages, and then so imperfect is our view into long-past geological ages that we see only that the forms of life are now different from what they formerly were.

•   •   •

Illustrations of the Action of Natural Selection, or the Survival of the Fittest.

In order to make it clear how, as I believe, natural selection acts, I must beg permission to give one or two imaginary illustrations. Let us take the case of a wolf, which preys on various animals, securing some by craft, some by strength, and some by fleetness; and let us suppose that the fleetest prey, a deer for instance, had from any change in the country increased in numbers, or that other prey had decreased in numbers, during that season of the year when the wolf was hardest pressed for food. Under such circumstances the swiftest and slimmest wolves have the best chance of surviving, and so be preserved or selected,—provided always that they retained strength to master their prey at this or some other period of the year, when they were compelled to prey on other animals. I can see no more reason to doubt that this would be the result, than that man should be able to improve the fleetness of his greyhounds by careful and methodical selection, or by that kind of unconscious selection which follows from each man trying to keep the best dogs without any thought of modifying the breed. I may add that, according to Mr. Pierce, there are two varieties of the wolf inhabiting the Catskill Mountains, in the United States, one with a light greyhound-like form, which pursues deer, and the other more bulky, with shorter legs, which more frequently attacks the shepherd's flocks.

Even without any change in the proportional numbers of the animals on which our wolf preyed, a cub might be born with an innate tendency to pursue certain kinds of prey. Nor can this be thought very improbable; for we often observe great differences in the natural tendencies of our domestic animals; one cat, for instance, taking to catch rats, another mice; one cat, according to Mr. St. John, bringing home winged game, another hares or rabbits, and another hunting on marshy ground and almost nightly catching woodcocks or snipes. The tendency to catch rats rather than mice is known to be inherited. Now, if any slight innate change of habit or of structure benefited an individual wolf, it would have the best chance of surviving and of leaving offspring. Some of its young would probably inherit the same habits or structure, and by the repetition of this process, a new variety might be formed which would either supplant or coexist with the parent-form of wolf. Or, again, the wolves inhabiting a mountainous district, and those frequenting the lowlands, would naturally be forced to hunt different prey; and from the continued preservation of the individuals best fitted for the two sites, two varieties might slowly be formed.

• • •

Circumstances Favourable for the Production of New Forms through Natural Selection.

• • •

Isolation, also, is an important element in the modification of species through natural selection. In a confined or isolated area, if not very large, the organic and inorganic conditions of life will generally be almost uniform; so that natural selection will tend to modify all the varying individuals of the same species in the same manner. Intercrossing with the inhabitants of the surrounding districts, will also be thus prevented. Moritz Wagner has lately published an interesting essay on this subject, and has shown that the service rendered by isolation in preventing crosses between newly-formed varieties is probably greater even than I supposed. But from reasons already assigned I can by no means agree with this naturalist, that migration and isolation are necessary elements for the formation of new species. The importance of isolation is likewise great in preventing, after any physical change in the conditions, such as of climate, elevation of the land, etc., the immigration of better adapted organisms; and thus new places in the natural economy of the district will be left open to be filled up by the modification of the old inhabitants. Lastly, isolation will give time for a new variety to be improved at a slow rate; and this may sometimes be of much importance. If, however, an isolated area be very small, either from being surrounded by barriers, or from having very peculiar physical conditions, the total number of the inhabitants will be small; and this will retard the production of new species through natural selection, by decreasing the chances of favourable variations arising.

The mere lapse of time by itself does nothing, either for or against natural selection. I state this because it has been erroneously asserted that the element of time has been assumed by me to play an all-important part in modifying species, as if all the forms of life were necessarily undergoing change through some innate law. Lapse of time is only so far important, and its importance in this respect is great, that it gives a better chance of beneficial variations arising and of their being selected, accumulated, and fixed. It likewise tends to increase the direct action of the physical conditions of life, in relation to the constitution of each organism.

If we turn to nature to test the truth of these remarks, and look at any small isolated area, such as an oceanic island, although the number of the species inhabiting it is small, as we shall see in our chapter on Geographical Distribution; yet of these species a very large proportion are endemic,——that is, have been produced there and nowhere else in the world. Hence an oceanic island at first sight seems to have been highly favourable for the production of new species. But we may thus deceive ourselves, for to ascertain whether a small isolated area, or a large open area like a continent, has been most favourable for the production of new organic forms, we ought to make the comparison within equal times; and this we are incapable of doing.

Although isolation is of great importance in the production of new species, on the whole I am inclined to believe that largeness of area is still more important, especially for the production of species which shall prove capable of enduring for a long period, and of spreading widely. Throughout a great and open area, not only will there be a better chance of favourable variations, arising from the large number of individuals of the same species there supported, but the conditions of life are much more complex from the large number of already existing species; and if some of these many species become modified and improved, others will have to be improved in a corresponding degree, or they will be exterminated. Each new form, also, as soon as it has been much improved, will be able to spread over the open and continuous area, and will thus come into competition with many other forms. Moreover, great areas, though now continuous, will often, owing to former oscillations of level, have existed in a broken condition, so that the good effects of isolation will generally, to a certain extent, have concurred. Finally, I conclude that, although small isolated areas have been in some respects highly favourable for the production of new species, yet that the course of modification will generally have been more rapid on large areas; and what is more important, that the new forms produced on large areas, which already have been victorious over many competitors, will be those that will spread most widely, and will give rise to the greatest number of new varieties and species. They will thus play a more important part in the changing history of the organic world.

• • •

That natural selection generally acts with extreme slowness I fully admit. It can act only when there are places in the natural polity of a district which can be better occupied by the modification of some of its existing inhabitants. The occurrence of such places will often depend on physical changes, which generally take place very slowly, and on the immigration of better adapted forms being prevented. As some few of the old inhabitants become modified the mutual relations of others will often be disturbed; and this will create new places, ready to be filled up by better adapted forms; but all this will take place very slowly. Although all the individuals of the same species differ in some slight degree from each other, it would often be long before differences of the right nature in various parts of the organisation might occur. The result would often be greatly retarded by free intercrossing. Many will exclaim that these several causes are amply sufficient to neutralise the power of natural selection. I do not believe so. But I do believe that natural selection will generally act very slowly, only at long intervals of time, and only on a few of the inhabitants of the same region. I further believe that these slow, intermittent results accord well with what geology tells us of the rate and manner at which the inhabitants of the world have changed.

Slow though the process of selection may be, if feeble man can do much by artificial selection, I can see no limit to the amount of change, to the beauty and complexity of the coadaptations between all organic beings, one with another and with their physical conditions of life, which may have been effected in the long course of time through nature's power of selection, that is by the survival of the fittest.

Emily Dickinson

1830–1886

Emily Dickinson was born in Amherst, Massachusetts. She attended Amherst Academy and then Mount Holyoke Female Seminary, which integrated a strong religious training with its academic studies and required students to be active in the Church. Though steeped in the tradition of New England Puritanism and spirituality, she never underwent a "conversion experience" as so many of her schoolmates did. Leaving the seminary after one year, she turned for inspiration to Emerson's transcendentalism, which challenged the very conception of the mechanistic universe. For Dickinson, such views were a welcome alternative to the reductive determinisms of her age. Among her other influences were the writings of the Brontë sisters, especially the poems of Emily Brontë.

Apart from occasional trips to Boston and Philadelphia, she remained with her family always and never married (though she formed passionate attachments, the nature and number of which are debated by scholars). As she grew older she spent most of her time at home, and has been viewed by some critics and biographers as a recluse. She wrote prolifically and aspired to see her verses in print, but she was discouraged by Thomas Wentworth Higginson, a critic friend from publishing. Though appreciating her originality, he felt that her innovative poetic forms, derived from hymn meters and filled with emotional intensity, were too unconventional for print. It wasn't until after her death that her poetry was finally published and recognized.

Dickinson's poem "This World is not Conclusion" (c. 1860) expresses an awareness that the transcendent coexists alongside persistent doubt, anticipating the themes of intellectual uncertainty and alienation that will become so prevalent in the works of twentieth-century modernist writers. The second poem included here, "I Felt a Funeral in My Brain" (1861), illustrates how Dickinson can capture with compelling intensity a psychological breakdown. How does Dickinson portray the various authorities who try to explain the mysteries of the spiritual? What kind of imagery does she employ to take us gradually deeper and deeper into a profound despair and beyond?

501

This World is not Conclusion.
A Species stands beyond—
Invisible, as Music—
But positive, as Sound—
It beckons, and it baffles—
Philosophy—don't know—
And through a Riddle, at the last—
Sagacity, must go—
To guess it, puzzles scholars—
To gain it, Men have borne
Contempt of Generations
And Crucifixion, shown—
Faith slips—and laughs, and rallies—
Blushes, if any see—
Plucks at a twig of Evidence—
And asks a Vane, the way—
Much Gesture, from the Pulpit—
Strong Hallelujahs roll—
Narcotics cannot still the Tooth
That nibbles at the soul—

c. 1860

280

I felt a Funeral, in my Brain,
And Mourners to and fro
Kept treading—treading—till it seemed
That Sense was breaking through—

And when they all were seated,
A Service, like a Drum—
Kept beating—beating—till I thought
My Mind was going numb—

And then I heard them lift a Box
And creak across my Soul
With those same Boots of Lead, again,
Then Space—began to toll,

As all the Heavens were a Bell,
And Being, but an Ear,
And I, and Silence, some strange Race
Wrecked, solitary, here—

And then a Plank in Reason, broke,
And I dropped down, and down—
And hit a World, at every plunge,
And Finished knowing—then—

c. 1861

Fyodor Dostoevsky

1821–1881

Fyodor Mikhailovich Dostoevsky was born in Moscow. His father had served in the Franco-Russian War of 1812 and later became a physician; his mother was the daughter of a Moscow merchant. From 1837 to 1843, Dostoevsky studied at the St. Petersburg Engineering Academy. Unhappy in school, he began a course of self-study in the literatures of Russia, England, and continental Europe, finding himself drawn especially to the works of Goethe, Shakespeare, Hugo, and Dickens. In 1839, Dostoevsky's father was killed by peasants living and working on his small estate, who revolted against his cruel treatment. Dostoevsky began his writing career in 1844, publishing a translation of Balzac's *Eugénie Grandet*; within a year he had also completed his own first novel, *Poor Folk*. By 1848, the year of the workers' revolutions across Europe, Dostoevsky had become involved with the radical Petrashevsky socialists; it was also about this time that he began to experience his first epileptic seizures, from which he would suffer throughout his lifetime.

In 1849, Dostoevsky was convicted of participating with the Petrashevsky circle in illegal political activity and was sentenced to death. The death sentence was commuted to hard labor, but Dostoevsky was not informed of this; instead, he was subjected to a mock execution and only when the firing squad had been readied was he informed that he was to be transferred to a labor camp in Siberia. This barbarism affected Dostoevsky deeply, leading him to reject socialism and to find solace in the teachings of Russian Orthodoxy. From 1864 to 1880, Dostoevsky would write his greatest novels, including *Notes from Underground* (1864), *Crime and Punishment* (1866), *The Idiot* (1868), *Demons* (1872), and *The Brothers Karamazov* (1880). In many ways, Dostoevsky writes in the style of the European realists: he wishes to engage the social realities of his time and to explore the psychological experiences and motivations of his characters. His themes include the suffering of the urban poor, the brutality and alienation of the modern human condition, and the tragedy of life spent without the moral underpinning of spiritual fulfillment.

In this excerpt of *The Brothers Karamazov*, entitled "The Grand Inquisitor," Dostoevsky contends that human beings are too weak and too ruled by material necessity to achieve true spiritual freedom and salvation; and, for its part, Dostoevsky claims, the Roman Catholic Church has rejected Christ's teachings as beyond the ability of humanity to master and offers up instead its authority as a salve for our spiritual wounds. What are the Inquisitor's views about human nature? To what extent is he accurate in his estimation? What issues or problems underlie the Inquisitor's explanations of our needs for worship and community?

from *The Brothers Karamazov* (1880)

The Grand Inquisitor

"Even this must have a preface—that is, a literary preface," laughed Ivan, "and I am a poor hand at making one. You see, my action takes place in the sixteenth century, and at that time, as you probably learnt at school, it was customary in poetry to bring down heavenly powers on earth. Not to speak of Dante, in France, clerks, as well as the monks in the monasteries, used to give regular performances in which the Madonna, the saints, the angels, Christ, and God Himself were brought on the stage. In those days it was done in all simplicity. In Victor Hugo's[1] 'Notre Dame de Paris' an edifying and gratuitous spectacle was provided for the people in the Hotel de Ville of Paris in the reign of Louis XI.[2] in honour of the birth of the dauphin. It was called *Le bon jugement de la très sainte et gracieuse Vierge Marie,*[3] and she appears herself on the stage and pronounces her *bon jugement.* Similar plays, chiefly from the Old Testament, were occasionally performed in Moscow too, up to the times of Peter the Great.[4] But besides plays there were all sorts of legends and ballads scattered about the world, in which the saints and angels and all the powers of Heaven took part when required. In our monasteries the monks busied themselves in translating, copying, and even composing such poems—and even under the Tatars.[5] There is, for instance, one such poem (of course, from the Greek), 'The Wanderings of Our Lady through Hell,' with descriptions as bold as Dante's. Our Lady visits Hell, and the Archangel Michael leads her through the torments. She sees the sinners and their punishment. There she sees among others one noteworthy set of sinners in a burning lake; some of them sink to the bottom of the lake so that they can't swim out, and 'these God forgets'—an expression of extraordinary depth and force. And so Our Lady, shocked and weeping, falls before the throne of God and begs for mercy for all in Hell—for all she has seen there, indiscriminately. Her conversation with God is immensely interesting. She beseeches Him, she will not desist, and when God points to the hands and feet of her Son, nailed to the Cross, and asks, 'How can I forgive His tormentors?' she bids all the saints, all the martyrs, all the angels and archangels to fall down with her and pray for mercy on all without distinction. It ends by her winning from God a respite of suffering every year from Good Friday till Trinity Day, and the sinners at once raise a cry of thankfulness from hell, chanting, 'Thou art just, O Lord, in this judgment.' Well, my poem would have been of that kind if it had appeared at that time. He comes on the scene in my poem, but He says nothing, only appears and passes on. Fifteen centuries have passed since He promised to come in His glory, fifteen centuries since His prophet wrote, 'Behold, I come quickly'; 'Of that day and that hour knoweth no man, neither the Son, but the Father,' as He Himself predicted on earth. But humanity awaits him with the same faith and with the same love. Oh, with greater faith, for it is fifteen centuries since man has ceased to see signs from heaven.

> No signs from heaven come to-day
> To add to what the heart doth say.

There was nothing left but faith in what the heart doth say. It is true there were many miracles in those days. There were saints who performed miraculous cures; some holy people, according to their biographies, were visited by the Queen of Heaven herself. But the devil did not slumber, and doubts were already arising among men of the truth of these miracles. And just then there appeared in the north of Germany a terrible new heresy. 'A huge star like to a torch' (that is, to a church) 'fell on the sources of the waters and they became bitter.' These heretics began blasphemously denying miracles. But those who remained faithful were all the more ardent in their faith. The tears of humanity rose up to Him as before, awaited His coming, loved Him, hoped for Him, yearned to suffer and die for Him as before. And so many ages mankind had prayed with faith and fervour, 'O Lord our God, hasten Thy coming,' so many ages called upon Him, that in His infinite mercy He deigned to come down to His servants. Before that day He had come down, He had visited some holy men, martyrs, and hermits, as is written in their Lives. Among us, Tyutchev,[6] with absolute faith in the truth of his words, bore witness that

> Bearing the Cross, in slavish dress,
> Weary and worn, the Heavenly King
> Our mother, Russia, came to bless,
> And through our land went wandering.

And that certainly was so, I assure you.

"And behold, He deigned to appear for a moment to the people, to the tortured, suffering people, sunk in iniquity, but loving Him like children. My story is laid in Spain, in Seville, in the most terrible time of the Inquisition, when fires were lighted every day to the glory of God, and 'in the splendid *auto da fé*[7] the wicked heretics were burnt.' Oh, of course, this was not the coming in which He will appear according to His promise at the end of time in all His heavenly glory, and which will be sudden 'as lightning flashing from east to west.' No, He visited His children only for a moment, and there where the flames were crackling round the heretics. In His infinite mercy He came once more among men in that human shape in which He walked among men for three years fifteen centuries ago. He came down to the 'hot pavement' of the southern town in which on the day before almost a hundred heretics had, *ad majorem gloriam Dei*,[8] been burnt by the cardinal, the Grand Inquisitor, in a magnificent *auto da fé*, in the presence of the king, the court, the knights, the cardinals, the most charming ladies of the court, and the whole population of Seville.

"He came softly, unobserved, and yet, strange to say, every one recognised Him. That might be one of the best passages in the poem. I mean, why they recognised Him. The people are irresistibly drawn to Him, they surround Him, they flock about Him, follow Him. He moves silently in their midst with a gentle smile of infinite compassion. The sun of love burns in His heart, light and power shine from His eyes, and their radiance, shed on the people, stirs their hearts with responsive love. He holds out His hands to them, blesses them, and a healing virtue comes from contact with Him, even with His garments. An old man in the crowd, blind from childhood, cries out, 'O Lord, heal me and I shall see Thee!' and, as it were, scales fall from his eyes and the blind man sees Him. The crowd weeps and kisses the earth under His feet. Children throw flowers before Him, sing, and cry hosannah. 'It is He—it is He!' all repeat. 'It must be He, it can be no one but Him!' He stops at the steps of the Seville cathedral at the moment when the weeping mourners are bringing in a little open white coffin. In it lies a child of seven, the only daughter of a prominent citizen. The dead child lies hidden in flowers. 'He will raise your child,' the crowd shouts to the weeping mother. The priest, coming to meet the coffin, looks perplexed, and frowns, but the mother of the dead child throws herself at His feet with a wail. 'If it is Thou, raise my child!' she cries, holding out her hands to Him. The procession halts, the coffin is laid on the steps at His feet. He looks with compassion, and His lips once more softly pronounce, 'Maiden, arise!' and the maiden arises. The little girl sits up in the coffin and looks round, smiling with wide-open wondering eyes, holding a bunch of white roses they had put in her hand.

"There are cries, sobs, confusion among the people, and at that moment the cardinal himself, the Grand Inquisitor, passes by the cathedral. He is an old man, almost ninety, tall and erect, with a withered face and sunken eyes, in which there is still a gleam of light. He is not dressed in his gorgeous cardinal's robes, as he was the day before, when he was burning the enemies of the Roman Church—at this moment he was wearing his coarse, old, monk's cassock. At a distance behind him come his gloomy assistants and slaves and the 'holy guard.' He stops at the sight of the crowd and watches it from a distance. He sees everything; he sees them set the coffin down at His feet, sees the child rise up, and his face darkens. He knits his thick grey brows and his eyes gleam with a sinister fire. He holds out his finger and bids the guards take Him. And such is his power, so completely are the people cowed into submission and trembling obedience to him, that the crowd immediately makes way for the guards, and in the midst of deathlike silence they lay hands on Him and lead him away. The crowd instantly bows down to the earth, like one man, before the old inquisitor. He blesses the people in silence and passes on. The guards lead their prisoner to the close, gloomy vaulted prison in the ancient palace of the Holy Inquisition and shut Him in it. The day passes and is followed by the dark, burning 'breathless' night of Seville. The air is 'fragrant with laurel and lemon.' In the pitch darkness the iron door of the prison is suddenly opened and the Grand Inquisitor himself comes in with a light in his hand. He is alone; the door is closed at once behind him. He stands in the doorway and for a minute or two gazes into His face. At last he goes up slowly, sets the light on the table and speaks.

"'Is it Thou? Thou?' but receiving no answer, he adds at once, 'Don't answer, be silent. What canst Thou say, indeed? I know too well what Thou wouldst say. And Thou hast no right to add anything to what Thou hadst said of old. Why, then, art Thou come to hinder us? For Thou hast come to hinder us, and Thou knowest that. But dost Thou know what will be to-morrow? I know not who Thou art and care not to know whether it is Thou or only a semblance of Him, but to-morrow I shall condemn Thee and burn Thee at the stake as the worst of heretics. And the very people who have to-day kissed Thy feet, to-morrow at the faintest sign from me will rush to heap up the embers of Thy fire. Knowest Thou that? Yes, maybe Thou knowest it,' he added with thoughtful penetration, never for a moment taking his eyes off the Prisoner."

"I don't quite understand, Ivan. What does it mean?" Alyosha, who had been listening in silence, said with a smile. "Is it simply a wild fantasy, or a mistake on the part of the old man—some impossible *quiproquo*?"[9]

"Take it as the last," said Ivan, laughing, "if you are so corrupted by modern realism and can't stand anything fantastic. If you like it to be a case of mistaken identity, let it be so. It is true," he went on, laughing, "the old man was ninety, and he might well be crazy over his set idea. He might have been struck by the appearance of the Prisoner. It might, in fact, be simply his ravings, the delusion of an old man of ninety, over-excited by the *auto da fé* of a hundred heretics the day before. But does it matter to us after all whether it was a mistake of identity or a wild fantasy? All that matters is that the old man should speak out, that he should speak openly of what he has thought in silence for ninety years."

"And the Prisoner too is silent? Does He look at him and not say a word?"

"That's inevitable in any case," Ivan laughed again. "The old man has told Him He hasn't the right to add anything to what He has said of old. One may say it is the most fundamental feature of Roman Catholicism, in my opinion at least. 'All has been given by Thee to the Pope,' they say, 'and all, therefore, is still in the Pope's hands, and there is no need for Thee to come now at all. Thou must not meddle for the time, at least.' That's how they speak and write too—the Jesuits,[10] at any rate. I have read it myself in the works of their theologians. 'Hast Thou the right to reveal to us one of the mysteries of that world from which Thou hast come?' my old man asks Him, and answers the question for Him. 'No, Thou hast not; that Thou mayest not add to what has been said of old, and mayest not take from men the freedom which Thou didst exalt when Thou wast on earth. Whatsoever Thou revealest anew will encroach on men's freedom of faith; for it will be manifest as a miracle, and the freedom of their faith was dearer to Thee than anything in those days fifteen hundred years ago. Didst Thou not often say then, "I will make you free"? But now Thou hast seen these "free" men,' the old man adds suddenly, with a pensive smile. 'Yes, we've paid dearly for it,' he goes on, looking sternly at Him, 'but at last we have completed that work in Thy name. For fifteen centuries we have been wrestling with Thy freedom, but now it is ended and over for good. Dost Thou not believe that it's over for good? Thou lookest meekly at me and deignest not even to be wroth with me. But let me tell Thee that now, to-day, people are more persuaded than ever that they have perfect freedom, yet they have brought their freedom to us and laid it humbly at our feet. But that has been our doing. Was this what Thou didst? Was this Thy freedom?'"

"I don't understand again," Alyosha broke in. "Is he ironical, is he jesting?"

"Not a bit of it! He claims it as a merit for himself and his Church that at last they have vanquished freedom and have done so to make men happy. 'For now' (he is speaking of the Inquisition, of course) 'for the first time it has become possible to think of the happiness of men. Man was created a rebel; and how can rebels be happy? Thou wast warned,' he says to Him. 'Thou hast had no lack of admonitions and warnings, but Thou didst not listen to those warnings; Thou didst reject the only way by which men might be made happy. But, fortunately, departing Thou didst hand on the work to us. Thou hast promised, Thou hast established by Thy word, Thou hast given to us the right to bind and to unbind, and now, of course, Thou canst not think of taking it away. Why, then, hast Thou come to hinder us?'"

"And what's the meaning of 'no lack of admonitions and warnings'?" asked Alyosha.

"Why, that's the chief part of what the old man must say.

"'The wise and dread spirit, the spirit of self-destruction and non-existence,' the old man goes on, 'the great spirit talked with Thee in the wilderness, and we are told in the books that he "tempted" Thee.[11] Is that so? And could anything truer be said than what he revealed to Thee in three questions and what Thou didst reject, and what in the books is called "the temptation"? And yet if there has ever been on earth a real stupendous miracle, it took place on that day, on the day of the three temptations. The statement of those three questions was itself the miracle. If it were possible to imagine simply for the sake of argument that those three questions of the dread spirit had perished utterly from the books, and that we had to restore them and to invent them anew, and to do so had gathered together all the wise men of the earth—rulers, chief priests, learned men, philosophers, poets—and had set them the task to invent three questions, such as would not only fit the occasion, but express in three words, three human phrases, the whole future history of the world and of humanity—dost Thou believe that all the wisdom of the earth united could have invented anything in depth and force equal to the three questions which were actually put to Thee then by the wise and mighty spirit in the wilderness? From those questions alone, from the miracle of their statement, we can see that we have here to do not with the fleeting human intelligence, but with the absolute and eternal. For in those three questions the whole subsequent history of mankind is, as it were, brought together into one whole, and foretold, and in them are united all the unsolved historical contradictions of human nature. At the time it could not be so clear, since the future was unknown; but now that fifteen hundred years have passed, we see that everything in those three questions was so justly divined and foretold, and has been so truly fulfilled, that nothing can be added to them or taken from them.

"'Judge Thyself who was right—Thou or he who questioned Thee then? Remember the first question; its meaning, in other words, was this: "Thou wouldst go into the world, and art going with empty hands, with some promise of freedom which men in their simplicity and their natural unruliness cannot even understand, which they fear and dread—for nothing has ever been more insupportable for a man and a human society than freedom. But seest Thou these stones in this parched and barren wilderness? Turn them into bread, and mankind will run after Thee like a flock of sheep, grateful and obedient, though for ever trembling, lest Thou withdraw Thy hand and deny them Thy bread." But Thou wouldst not deprive man of freedom and didst reject the offer, thinking, what is that freedom worth, if obedience is bought with bread? Thou didst reply that man lives not by bread alone. But dost Thou know that for the sake of that earthly bread the spirit of the earth will rise up against Thee and will strive with Thee and overcome Thee, and all will follow him, crying, "Who can compare with this beast? He has given us fire from heaven!" Dost Thou know that the ages will pass, and humanity will proclaim by the lips of their sages that there is no crime, and therefore no sin; there is only hunger? "Feed men, and then ask of them virtue!" that's what they'll write on the banner, which they will raise against Thee, and with which they will destroy Thy temple. Where Thy temple stood will rise a new building; the terrible tower of Babel will be built again, and though, like the one of old, it will not be finished, yet Thou mightest have prevented that new tower and have cut short the sufferings of men for a thousand years; for they will come back to us after a thousand years of agony with their tower. They will seek us again, hidden underground in the catacombs, for we shall be again persecuted and tortured. They will find us and cry to us, "Feed us, for those who have promised us fire from heaven haven't given it!" And then we shall finish building their tower, for he finishes the building who feeds them. And we alone shall feed them in Thy name, declaring falsely that it is in Thy name. Oh, never, never can they feed themselves without us! No science will give them bread so long as they remain free. In the end they will lay their freedom at our feet, and say to us, "Make us your slaves, but feed us." They will understand themselves, at last, that freedom and bread enough for all are inconceivable together, for never, never will they be able to share between them! They will be convinced, too, that they can never be free, for they are weak, vicious, worthless and rebellious. Thou didst promise them the bread of Heaven, but, I repeat again, can it compare with earthly bread in the eyes of the weak, ever sinful and ignoble race of man? And if for the sake of the bread of Heaven thousands and tens of thousands shall follow Thee, what is to become of the millions and tens of thousands of millions of creatures who will not have the strength to forego the earthly bread for the sake of the heavenly? Or dost Thou care only for the tens of thousands of the great and strong, while the millions, numerous as the sands of the sea, who are weak but love Thee, must exist only for the sake of the great and strong? No, we care for the weak too. They are sinful and rebellious, but in the end they too will become obedient. They will marvel at us and look on us as gods, because we are ready to endure the freedom which they have found so dreadful and to rule over them—so awful it will seem to them to be free. But we shall tell them that we are Thy servants and rule them in Thy name. We shall deceive them again, for we will not let Thee come to us again. That deception will be our suffering, for we shall be forced to lie.

"'This is the significance of the first question in the wilderness, and this is what Thou hast rejected for the sake of that freedom which Thou hast exalted above everything. Yet in this question lies hid the great secret of this world. Choosing "bread," Thou wouldst have satisfied the universal and everlasting craving of humanity—to find some one to worship. So long as man remains free he strives for nothing so incessantly and so painfully as to find some one to worship. But man seeks to worship what is established beyond dispute, so that all men would agree at once to worship it. For these pitiful creatures are concerned not only to find what one or the other can worship, but to find something that all would believe in and worship; what is essential is that all may be *together* in it. This craving for *community* of worship is the chief misery of every man individually and of all humanity from the beginning of time. For the sake of common worship they've slain each other with the sword. They have set up gods and challenged one another, "Put away your gods and come and worship ours, or we will kill you and your gods!" And so it will be to the end of the world, even when gods disappear from the earth; they will fall down before idols just the same. Thou didst know, Thou couldst not but have known, this fundamental secret of human nature, but Thou didst reject the one infallible banner which was offered Thee to make all men bow down to Thee alone—the banner of earthly bread; and Thou hast rejected it for the sake of freedom and the bread of Heaven. Behold what Thou didst further. And all again in the name of freedom! I tell Thee that man is tormented by no greater anxiety than to find some one quickly to whom he can hand over that gift of freedom with which the ill-fated creature is born. But only one who can appease their conscience can take over their freedom. In bread there was offered Thee an invincible banner; give bread, and man will worship Thee, for nothing is more certain than bread. But if some one else gains possession of his conscience—oh! then he will cast away Thy bread and follow after him who has ensnared his conscience. In that Thou wast right. For the secret of man's being is not only to live but to have something to live for. Without a stable conception of the object of life, man would not consent to go on living, and would rather destroy himself than remain on earth, though he had bread in abundance. That is true. But what happened? Instead of taking men's freedom from them, Thou didst make it greater than ever! Didst Thou forget that man prefers peace, and even death, to freedom of choice in the knowledge of good and evil? Nothing is more seductive for man than his freedom of conscience, but nothing is a greater cause of suffering. And behold, instead of giving a firm foundation for setting the conscience of man at rest for ever, Thou didst choose all that is exceptional, vague and enigmatic; Thou didst choose what was utterly beyond the strength of men, acting as though Thou didst not love them at all—Thou who didst come to give Thy life for them! Instead of taking possession of men's freedom, Thou didst increase it, and burdened the spiritual kingdom of mankind with its sufferings for ever. Thou didst desire man's free love, that he should follow Thee freely, enticed and taken captive by Thee. In place of the rigid ancient law, man must hereafter with free heart decide for himself what is good and what is evil, having only Thy image before him as his guide. But didst Thou not know that he would at last reject even Thy image and Thy truth, if he is weighed down with the fearful burden of free choice? They will cry aloud at last that the truth is not in Thee, for they could not have been left in greater confusion and suffering than Thou hast caused, laying upon them so many cares and unanswerable problems.

"'So that, in truth, Thou didst Thyself lay the foundation for the destruction of Thy kingdom, and no one is more to blame for it. Yet what was offered Thee? There are three powers, three powers alone, able to conquer and to hold captive forever the conscience of these impotent rebels for their happiness—those forces are miracle, mystery and authority. Thou hast rejected all three and hast set the example for doing so. When the wise and dread spirit set Thee on the pinnacle of the temple and said to Thee, "If Thou wouldst know whether Thou art the Son of God then cast Thyself down, for it is written: the angels shall hold him up lest he fall and bruise himself, and Thou shalt know then whether Thou art the Son of God and shalt prove then how great is Thy faith in Thy Father." But Thou didst refuse and wouldst not cast Thyself down. Oh! of course, Thou didst proudly and well, like God; but the weak, unruly race of men, are they gods? Oh, Thou didst know then that in taking one step, in making one movement to cast Thyself down, Thou wouldst be tempting God and have lost all Thy faith in Him, and wouldst have been dashed to pieces against that earth which Thou didst come to save. And the wise spirit that tempted Thee would have rejoiced. But I ask again, are there many like Thee? And couldst Thou believe for one moment that men, too, could face such a temptation? Is the nature of men such, that they can reject miracle, and at the great moments of their life, the moments of their deepest, most agonising spiritual difficulties, cling only to the free verdict of the heart? Oh, Thou didst know that Thy deed would be recorded in books, would be handed down to remote times and the utmost ends of the earth, and Thou didst hope that man, following Thee, would cling to God and not ask for a miracle. But Thou didst not know that when man rejects miracles he rejects God too; for man seeks not so much God as the miraculous. And as man cannot bear to be without the miraculous, he will create new miracles of his own for himself, and will worship deeds of sorcery and witchcraft, though he might be a hundred times over a rebel, heretic and infidel. Thou didst not come down from the Cross when they shouted to Thee, mocking and reviling Thee, "Come down from the cross and we will believe that Thou art He." Thou didst not come down, for again Thou wouldst not enslave man by a miracle, and didst crave faith given freely, not based on miracle. Thou didst crave for free love and not the base raptures of the slave before the might that has overawed him for ever. But Thou didst think too highly of men therein, for they are slaves, of course, though rebellious by nature. Look round and judge; fifteen centuries have passed, look upon them. Whom hast Thou raised up to Thyself? I swear, man is weaker and baser by nature than Thou hast believed him! Can he, can he do what Thou didst? By showing him so much respect,

Thou didst, as it were, cease to feel for him, for Thou didst ask far too much from him—Thou who hast loved him more than Thyself! Respecting him less, Thou wouldst have asked less of him. That would have been more like love, for his burden would have been lighter. He is weak and vile. What though he is everywhere now rebelling against our power, and proud of his rebellion? It is the pride of a child and a schoolboy. They are little children rioting and barring out the teacher at school. But their childish delight will end; it will cost them dear. They will cast down temples and drench the earth with blood. But they will see at last, the foolish children, that, though they are rebels, they are impotent rebels, unable to keep up their own rebellion. Bathed in their foolish tears, they will recognise at last that He who created them rebels must have meant to mock at them. They will say this in despair, and their utterance will be a blasphemy which will make them more unhappy still, for man's nature cannot bear blasphemy, and in the end always avenges it on itself. And so unrest, confusion and happiness—that is the present lot of man after Thou didst bear so much for their freedom! Thy great prophet tells in vision and in image, that he saw all those who took part in the first resurrection and that there were of each tribe twelve thousand. But if there were so many of them, they must have been not men but gods. They had borne Thy cross, they had endured scores of years in the barren, hungry wilderness, living upon locusts and roots—and Thou mayest indeed point with pride at those children of freedom, of free love, of free and splendid sacrifice for Thy name. But remember that they were only some thousands; and what of the rest? And how are the other weak ones to blame, because they could not endure what the strong have endured? How is the weak soul to blame that it is unable to receive such terrible gifts? Canst Thou have simply come to the elect and for the elect? But if so, it is a mystery and we cannot understand it. And if it is a mystery, we too have a right to preach a mystery, and to teach them that it's not the free judgment of their hearts, not love that matters, but a mystery which they must follow blindly, even against their conscience. So we have done. We have corrected Thy work and have founded it upon miracle, mystery and authority. And men rejoiced again that they were led like sheep, and that the terrible gift that had brought them such suffering, was, at last, lifted from their hearts. Were we right teaching them this? Speak! Did we not love mankind, so meekly acknowledging their feebleness, lovingly lightening their burden, and permitting their weak nature even sin with our sanction? Why hast Thou come now to hinder us? And why dost Thou look silently and searchingly at me with Thy mild eyes? Be angry. I don't want Thy love, for I love Thee not. And what use is it for me to hide anything from Thee? Don't I know to Whom I am speaking? All that I can say is known to Thee already. And is it for me to conceal from Thee our mystery? Perhaps it is Thy will to hear it from my lips. Listen, then. We are not working with Thee, but with him—that is our mystery. It's long—eight centuries—since we have been on his side and not on Thine. Just eight centuries ago, we took from him what Thou didst reject with scorn, that last gift he offered Thee, showing Thee all the kingdoms of the earth. We took from him Rome and the sword of Cæsar, and proclaimed ourselves sole rulers of the earth, though hitherto we have not been able to complete our work. But whose fault is that? Oh, the work is only beginning, but it has begun. It has long to wait completion and the earth has yet much to suffer, but we shall triumph and shall be Cæsars, and then we shall plan the universal happiness of man. But Thou mightest have taken even then the sword of Cæsar. Why didst Thou reject that last gift? Hadst Thou accepted that last counsel of the mighty spirit, Thou wouldst have accomplished all that man seeks on earth—that is, some one to worship, some one to keep his conscience, and some means of uniting all in one unanimous and harmonious ant-heap, for the craving for universal unity is the third and last anguish of men. Mankind as a whole has always striven to organise a universal state. There have been many great nations with great histories, but the more highly they were developed the more unhappy they were, for they felt more acutely than other people the craving for worldwide union. The great conquerors, Timours[12] and Ghenghis-Khans,[13] whirled like hurricanes over the face of the earth striving to subdue its people, and they too were but the unconscious expression of the same craving for universal unity. Hadst Thou taken the world and Cæsar's purple,[14] Thou wouldst have founded the universal state and have given universal peace. For who can rule men if not he who holds their conscience and their bread in his hands? We have taken the sword of Caesar, and in taking it, of course, have rejected Thee and followed him. Oh, ages are yet to come of the confusion of free thought, of their science and cannibalism. For having begun to build their tower of Babel without us, they will end, of course, with cannibalism. But then the beast will crawl to us and lick our feet and spatter them with tears of blood. And we shall sit upon the beast and raise the cup, and on it will be written, "Mystery." But then, and only then, the reign of peace and happiness will come for men. Thou art proud of Thine elect, but Thou hast only the elect, while we give rest to all. And besides, how many of those elect, those mighty ones who could become elect, have grown weary waiting for Thee, and have transferred and will transfer the powers of their spirit and the warmth of their heart to the other camp, and end by raising their free banner against Thee. Thou didst Thyself lift up that banner. But with us all will be happy and will no more rebel nor destroy one another as under Thy freedom. Oh, we shall persuade them that they will only become free when they renounce their freedom to us and submit to us. And shall we be right or shall we be lying? They will be convinced that we are right, for they will remember the horrors of slavery and confusion to which Thy freedom brought them. Freedom, free thought and science, will lead them into such straits and will bring them face to face with such marvels and insoluble mysteries, that some of them, the fierce and rebellious, will destroy themselves, others, rebellious but weak, will destroy one another, while the rest, weak and unhappy, will crawl fawning to our feet and whine to us: "Yes, you were right, you alone possess His mystery, and we come back to you, save us from ourselves!"

"'Receiving bread from us, they will see clearly that we take the bread made by their hands from them, to give it to them, without any miracle. They will see that we do not change the stones to bread, but in truth they will be more thankful for taking it from our hands than for the bread itself! For they will remember only too well that in old days, without our help, even the bread they made turned to stones in their hands, while since they have come back to us, the very stones have turned to bread in their hands. Too, too well they know the value of complete submission! And until men know that, they will be unhappy. Who is most to blame for their not knowing it, speak? Who scattered the flock and sent it astray on unknown paths? But the flock will come together again and will submit once more, and then it will be once for all. Then we shall give them the quiet humble happiness of weak creatures such as they are by nature. Oh, we shall persuade them at last not to be proud, for Thou didst lift them up and thereby taught them to be proud. We shall show them that they are weak, that they are only pitiful children, but that childlike happiness is the sweetest of all. They will become timid and will look to us and huddle close to us in fear, as chicks to the hen. They will marvel at us and will be awe-stricken before us, and will be proud at our being so powerful and clever, that we have been able to subdue such a turbulent flock of thousands of millions. They will tremble impotently before our wrath, their minds will grow fearful, they will be quick to shed tears like women and children, but they will be just as ready at a sign from us to pass to laughter and rejoicing, to happy mirth and childish song. Yes, we shall set them to work, but in their leisure hours we shall make their life like a child's game, with children's songs and innocent dance. Oh, we shall allow them even sin, they are weak and helpless, and they will love us like children because we allow them to sin. We shall tell them that every sin will be expiated, if it is done with our permission, that we allow them to sin because we love them, and the punishment for these sins we take upon ourselves. And we shall take it upon ourselves, and they will adore us as their saviours who have taken on themselves their sins before God. And they will have no secrets from us. We shall allow or forbid them to live with their wives and mistresses, to have or not to have children—according to whether they have been obedient or disobedient—and they will submit to us gladly and cheerfully. The most painful secrets of their conscience, all, all they will bring to us, and we shall have an answer for all. And they will be glad to believe our answer, for it will save them from the great anxiety and terrible agony they endure at present in making a free decision for themselves. And all will be happy, all the millions of creatures except the hundred thousand who rule over them. For only we, we who guard the mystery, shall be unhappy. There will be thousands of millions of happy babes, and a hundred thousand sufferers who have taken upon themselves the curse of the knowledge of good and evil. Peacefully they will die, peacefully they will expire in Thy name, and beyond the grave they will find nothing but death. But we shall keep the secret, and for their happiness we shall allure them with the reward of heaven and eternity. Though if there were anything in the other world, it certainly would not be for such as they. It is prophesied that Thou wilt come again in victory, Thou wilt come with Thy chosen, the proud and strong, but we will say that they have only saved themselves, but we have saved all. We are told that the harlot who sits upon the beast, and holds in her hands the *mystery*, shall be put to shame, that the weak will rise up again, and will rend her royal purple and will strip naked her loathsome body. But then I will stand up and point out to Thee the thousand millions of happy children who have known no sin. And we who have taken their sins upon us for their happiness will stand up before Thee and say: "Judge us if Thou canst and darest." Know that I fear Thee not. Know that I too have been in the wilderness, I too have lived on roots and locusts, I too prized the freedom with which Thou hast blessed men, and I too was striving to stand among Thy elect, among the strong and powerful, thirsting "to make up the number." But I awakened and would not serve madness. I turned back and joined the ranks of those *who have corrected Thy work*. I left the proud and went back to the humble, for the happiness of the humble. What I say to Thee will come to pass, and our dominion will be built up. I repeat, to-morrow Thou shalt see that obedient flock who at a sign from me will hasten to heap up the hot cinders about the pile on which I shall burn Thee for coming to hinder us. For if any one has ever deserved our fires, it is Thou. To-morrow I shall burn Thee. Dixi.'"[15]

Ivan stopped. He was carried away as he talked and spoke with excitement; when he had finished, he suddenly smiled.

Alyosha had listened in silence; towards the end he was greatly moved and seemed several times on the point of interrupting, but restrained himself. Now his words came with a rush.

"But . . . that's absurd!" he cried, flushing. "Your poem is in praise of Jesus, not in blame of Him—as you meant it to be. And who will believe you about freedom? Is that the way to understand it? That's not the idea of it in the Orthodox Church . . . That's Rome, and not even the whole of Rome, it's false—those are the worst of the Catholics, the Inquisitors, the Jesuits! . . . And there could not be such a fantastic creature as your Inquisitor. What are these sins of mankind they take on themselves? Who are these keepers of the mystery who have taken some curse upon themselves for the happiness of mankind? When have they been seen? We know the Jesuits, they are spoken ill of, but surely they are not what you describe? They are not that at all, not at all. . . . They are simply the Romish army for the earthly sovereignty of the world in the future, with the Pontiff of Rome for Emperor . . . that's their ideal, but there's no sort of mystery or lofty melancholy about it. . . . It's simple lust of power, of filthy earthly gain, of domination—something like a universal serfdom with them as masters—that's all they stand for. They don't even believe in God perhaps. Your suffering Inquisitor is a mere fantasy."

"Stay, stay," laughed Ivan, "how hot you are! A fantasy you say, let it be so! Of course it's a fantasy. But allow me to say: do you really think that the Roman Catholic movement of the last centuries is actually nothing but the lust of power, of filthy earthly gain? Is that Father Païssy's[16] teaching?"

"No, no, on the contrary, Father Païssy did once say something rather the same as you. . . but of course it's not the same, not a bit the same," Alyosha hastily corrected himself.

"A precious admission, in spite of your 'not a bit the same.' I ask you why your Jesuits and Inquisitors have united simply for vile material gain? Why can there not be among them one martyr oppressed by great sorrow and loving humanity? You see, only suppose that there was one such man among all those who desire nothing but filthy material gain—if there's only one like my old Inquisitor, who had himself eaten roots in the desert and made frenzied efforts to subdue his flesh to make himself free and perfect. But yet all his life he loved humanity, and suddenly his eyes were opened, and he saw that it is no great moral blessedness to attain perfection and freedom, if at the same time one gains the conviction that millions of God's creatures have been created as a mockery, that they will never be capable of using their freedom, that these poor rebels can never turn into giants to complete the tower, that it was not for such geese that the great idealist dreamt his dream of harmony. Seeing all that he turned back and joined—the clever people. Surely that could have happened?"

"Joined whom, what clever people?" cried Alyosha, completely carried away. "They have no such great cleverness and no mysteries and secrets. . . . Perhaps nothing but Atheism, that's all their secret. Your Inquisitor does not believe in God, that's his secret!"

"What if it is so! At last you have guessed it. It's perfectly true that that's the whole secret, but isn't that suffering, at least for a man like that, who has wasted his whole life in the desert and yet could not shake off his incurable love of humanity? In his old age he reached the clear conviction that nothing but the advice of the great dread spirit could build up any tolerable sort of life for the feeble, unruly, 'incomplete, empirical creatures created in jest.' And so, convinced of this, he sees that he must follow the counsel of the wise spirit, the dread spirit of death and destruction, and therefore accept lying and deception, and lead men consciously to death and destruction, and yet deceive them all the way so that they may not notice where they are being led, that the poor blind creatures may at least on the way think themselves happy. And note, the deception is in the name of Him in Whose ideal the old man had so fervently believed all his life long. Is not that tragic? And if only one such stood at the head of the whole army 'filled with the lust of power only for the sake of filthy gain'—would not one such be enough to make a tragedy? More than that, one such standing at the head is enough to create the actual leading idea of the Roman Church with all its armies and Jesuits, its highest idea. I tell you frankly that I firmly believe that there has always been such a man among those who stood at the head of the movement. Who knows, there may have been some such even among the Roman Popes. Who knows, perhaps the spirit of that accursed old man who loves mankind so obstinately in his own way, is to be found even now in a whole multitude of such old men, existing not by chance but by agreement, as a secret league formed long ago for the guarding of the mystery, to guard it from the weak and the unhappy, so as to make them happy. No doubt it is so, and so it must be indeed. I fancy that even among the Masons there's something of the same mystery at the bottom, and that that's why the Catholics so detest the Masons[17] as their rivals breaking up the unity of the idea, while it is so essential that there should be one flock and one shepherd. . . . But from the way I defend my idea I might be an author impatient of your criticism. Enough of it."

"You are perhaps a Mason yourself!" broke suddenly from Alyosha. "You don't believe in God," he added, speaking this time very sorrowfully. He fancied besides that his brother was looking at him ironically. "How does your poem end?" he asked, suddenly looking down. "Or was it the end?"

"I meant to end it like this. When the Inquisitor ceased speaking he waited some time for his Prisoner to answer him. His silence weighed down upon him. He saw that the Prisoner had listened intently all the time, looking gently in his face and evidently not wishing to reply. The old man longed for Him to say something, however bitter and terrible. But He suddenly approached the old man in silence and softly kissed him on his bloodless aged lips. That was all his answer. The old man shuddered. His lips moved. He went to the door, opened it, and said to Him: 'Go, and come no more. . . . come not at all, never, never!' And he let Him out into the dark alleys of the town. The Prisoner went away."

"And the old man?"

"The kiss glows in his heart, but the old man adheres to his idea."

"And you with him, you too?" cried Alyosha, mournfully.

Ivan laughed.

"Why, it's all nonsense, Alyosha. It's only a senseless poem of a senseless student, who could never write two lines of verse. Why do you take it so seriously? Surely you don't suppose I am going straight off to the Jesuits, to join the men who are correcting His work? Good Lord, it's no business of mine. I told you, all I want is to live on to thirty, and then . . . dash the cup to the ground!"

"But the little sticky leaves, and the precious tombs, and the blue sky, and the woman you love! How will you live, how will you love them?" Alyosha cried sorrowfully. "With such a hell in your heart and your head, how can you? No, that's just what you are going away for, to join them . . . if not, you will kill yourself, you can't endure it!"

"There is a strength to endure everything," Ivan said with a cold smile.

"The strength of the Karamazov—the strength of the Karamazov baseness."

"To sink into debauchery, to stifle your soul with corruption, yes?"

"Possibly even that . . . only perhaps till I am thirty I shall escape it, and then."

"How will you escape it? By what will you escape it? That's impossible with your ideas."

"In the Karamazov way, again."

"'Everything is lawful,' you mean? Everything is lawful, is that it?"

Ivan scowled, and all at once turned strangely pale.

"Ah, you've caught up yesterday's phrase, which so offended Miüsov[18]— and which Dmitri pounced upon so naïvely and paraphrased!" he smiled queerly. "Yes, if you like, 'everything is lawful' since the word has been said, I won't deny it. And Mitya's[19] version isn't bad."

Alyosha looked at him in silence.

"I thought that going away from here I have you at least," Ivan said suddenly, with unexpected feeling; "but now I see that there is no place for me even in your heart, my dear hermit. The formula, 'all is lawful,' I won't renounce—will you renounce me for that, yes?"

Alyosha got up, went to him and softly kissed him on the lips.

"That's plagiarism," cried Ivan, highly delighted. "You stole that from my poem. Thank you though. Get up, Alyosha, it's time we were going, both of us."

They went out, but stopped when they reached the entrance of the restaurant.

"Listen, Alyosha," Ivan began in a resolute voice, "if I am really able to care for the sticky little leaves I shall only love them, remembering you. It's enough for me that you are somewhere here, and I shan't lose my desire for life yet. Is that enough for you? Take it as a declaration of love if you like. And now you go to the right and I to the left. And it's enough, do you hear, enough. I mean even if I don't go away to-morrow (I think I certainly shall go) and we meet again, don't say a word more on these subjects. I beg that particularly. And about Dmitri too, I ask you especially never speak to me again," he added, with sudden irritation; "it's all exhausted, it has all been said over and over again, hasn't it? And I'll make you one promise in return for it. When at thirty, I want to 'dash the cup to the ground,' wherever I may be I'll come to have one more talk with you, even though it were from America, you may be sure of that. I'll come on purpose. It will be very interesting to have a look at you, to see what you'll be by that time. It's rather a solemn promise, you see. And we really may be parting for seven years or ten. Come, go now to your Pater Seraphicus,[20] he is dying. If he dies without you, you will be angry with me for having kept you. Good-bye, kiss me once more; that's right, now go."

Ivan turned suddenly and went his way without looking back. It was just as Dmitri had left Alyosha the day before, though the parting had been very different. The strange resemblance flashed like an arrow through Alyosha's mind in the distress and dejection of that moment. He waited a little, looking after his brother. He suddenly noticed that Ivan swayed as he walked and that his right shoulder looked lower than his left. He had never noticed it before. But all at once he turned too, and almost ran to the monastery. It was nearly dark, and he felt almost frightened; something new was growing up in him for which he could not account. The wind had risen again as on the previous evening, and the ancient pines murmured gloomily about him when he entered the hermitage copse. He almost ran. "Pater Seraphicus—he got that name from somewhere—where from?" Alyosha wondered. "Ivan, poor Ivan, and when shall I see you again? . . . Here is the hermitage. Yes, yes, that he is, Pater Seraphicus, he will save me—from him and for ever!"

Several times afterwards he wondered how he could, on leaving Ivan, so completely forget his brother Dmitri, though he had that morning, only a few hours before, so firmly resolved to find him and not to give up doing so, even should he be unable to return to the monastery that night.

Notes

[1] French novelist (1802–1885).

[2] King of France (reigned 1461–1483).

[3] French: "The good sense of the very holy and gracious Virgin Mary."

[4] Czar of Russia (reigned 1689–1725).

[5] A group of Turkish-speaking peoples living along Russia's Volga River and in the Ural mountain range to the east. During the medieval period, the Tatars ruled over a large part of Russia.

[6] Russian poet and rationalist (1803–1873).

[7] The reading of sentences upon individuals sanctioned by the Spanish Inquisition, after which punishment was executed as a spectacle for public consumption.

[8] Latin: "to the greater glory of God."

[9] i.e., *quid quo pro*: Latin for "an exchange of this for that, of one thing for another."

[10] Roman Catholic order, known for its emphasis on education and charitable work as focal points of the Christian mission.

[11] See Matthew 4:1–11, Luke 4:1–13.

[12] Timour, or Tamerlane (1336–1405), the Turkish conqueror of vast territories including lands we now know as Russia, India, and portions of the Middle East.

[13] Ghengis Kahn (c.1162–1227), Mongol conqueror of Asia and portions of what is now modern-day Russia.

[14] Purple is the color symbolic of Roman power and authority.

[15] Latin: "I have spoken."

[16] Father Païssy, described elsewhere in the novel as "the silent and learned monk."

[17] Also referred to as Freemasons, a fraternal society whose members share secret rituals and mystical traditions.

[18] Pyotr Alexandrovitch Miusov, a character in the novel, the cousin of Dmitri Karamazov's mother. Dmitri is the half-brother of Ivan and Alyosha Karamozov.

[19] Mitya is a nickname for Dmitri.

[20] Pater Seraphicus refers to the novel's Father Zossimov, a former soldier who has become an elder in the Russian church. He is a mentor to Alyosha.

Friedrich Nietzsche

1844–1900

Friedrich Nietzsche was born in Röcken, Prussia. His father was a Lutheran minister, as were both of his grandfathers. Following his father's death in 1849, Nietzsche and his sister were raised by his mother. After finishing his studies in classical philology at the Universities of Bonn and Leipzig at the age of 24, he was appointed professor at the University of Basel. At the beginning of the Franco-Prussian War, in 1870, Nietzsche took leave from the university, in order to serve in a military hospital. He returned to Basel and continued to teach, but poor health—he suffered his whole life from severe headaches, an affliction which worsened after the war—compelled his early retirement in 1879. He experienced a complete mental collapse in 1889 and never recovered; he died eleven years later in Weimar, Germany.

Nietzsche was a writer of terrific range and profound insight. His major works include *The Birth of Tragedy* (1872), *Thus Spoke Zarathustra* (1883–1885), *Beyond Good and Evil* (1886), *On the Genealogy of Morals* (1887), *Ecce Homo* (1889), and *The Will to Power* (1901). Nietzsche believed that there existed no transcendent meaning to support our lives in the world; rather, values are shaped by those in power to serve their own interests. Because of this relationship between traditional value systems and power, the weak would always suffer at the hands of the mighty. And yet there are individuals who, because of their independence, intellect, and originality, can liberate themselves from the tyranny of oppressive conventions and enslaving moralities: these are the *Übermenschen*, or supermen, who can create and live by their own values. This desire to create new ideals, to master oneself and to transform the world, Nietzsche calls "the will to power." The greatest figures of history, Nietzsche argues, display the qualities of the superman precisely by manifesting this will to power: among them he includes Socrates, Jesus, Michelangelo, Shakespeare, and Napoleon.

In the selection of *Beyond Good and Evil* below, Nietzsche questions the Enlightenment notion that morality liberates us to live good and creative lives. In what senses do our values erect barriers to personal and social transformation? Whose interests do our values and beliefs reflect? How is morality, as Nietzsche contends, the product of fear? What are the limits of Nietzsche's ideas about moral thought?

414

from *Beyond Good and Evil* (1886)

200

The man of an age of dissolution which mixes the races with one another, who has the inheritance of a diversified descent in his body—that is to say, contrary, and often not only contrary, instincts and standards of value, which struggle with one another and are seldom at peace—such a man of late culture and broken lights, will, on an average, be a weak man. His fundamental desire is that the war which is *in him* should come to an end; happiness appears to him in the character of a soothing medicine and mode of thought (for instance, Epicurean[1] or Christian), as above all things the happiness of repose, of undisturbedness, of repletion, of final unity—as the "Sabbath of Sabbaths," to use the expression of the holy rhetorician, St Augustine,[2] who was himself such a man.—Should, however, the contrariety and conflict in such natures operate as an *additional* incentive and stimulus to life—and if, on the other hand, in addition to their powerful and irreconcilable instincts, they have also inherited and indoctrinated into them a proper mastery and subtlety for carrying on the conflict with themselves (that is to say, the faculty of self-control and self-deception), there then arise those marvellously incomprehensible, and inexplicable beings, those enigmatical men, predestined for conquering and circumventing others, the finest examples of which are Alcibiades[3] and Caesar (with whom I should like to associate the *first* of Europeans according to my taste, the Hohenstaufen, Frederick the Second[4]), and amongst artists, perhaps Lionardo da Vinci. They appear precisely in the same periods when that weaker type, with its longing for repose, comes to the front; the two types are complementary to each other, and spring from the same causes.

201

As long as the utility which determines moral estimates is only gregarious utility, as long as the preservation of the community is only kept in view, and the immoral is sought precisely and exclusively in what seems dangerous to the maintenance of the community, there can be no "morality of love to one's neighbour." Granted even that there is already a little constant exercise of consideration, sympathy, fairness, gentleness, and mutual assistance, granted that even in this condition of society all those instincts are already active which are latterly distinguished by honourable names as "virtues," and eventually almost coincide with the conception "morality": in that period they do not as yet

415

belong to the domain of moral valuations—they are still *ultra-moral*. A sympathetic action, for instance, is neither called good nor bad, moral nor immoral, in the best period of the Romans; and should it be praised, a sort of resentful disdain is compatible with this praise, even at the best, directly the sympathetic action is compared with one which contributes to the welfare of the whole, to the *res publica*.[5] After all, "love to our neighbour" is always a secondary matter, partly conventional and arbitrarily manifest in relation to our *fear of our neighbour*. After the fabric of society seems on the whole established and secured against external dangers, it is this fear of our neighbour which again creates new perspectives of moral valuation. Certain strong and dangerous instincts, such as the love of enterprise, foolhardiness, revengefulness, astuteness, rapacity, and love of power, which up till then had not only to be honoured from the point of view of general utility—under other names, of course, than those here given—but had to be fostered and cultivated (because they were perpetually required in the common danger against the common enemies), are now felt in their dangerousness to be doubly strong—when the outlets for them are lacking—and are gradually branded as immoral and given over to calumny. The contrary instincts and inclinations now attain to moral honour; the gregarious instinct gradually draws its conclusions. How much or how little dangerousness to the community or to equality is contained in an opinion, a condition, an emotion, a disposition, or an endowment—that is now the moral perspective; here again fear is the mother of morals. It is by the loftiest and strongest instincts, when they break out passionately and carry the individual far above and beyond the average, and the low level of the gregarious conscience, that the self-reliance of the community is destroyed; its belief in itself, its backbone, as it were, breaks; consequently these very instincts will be most branded and defamed. The lofty independent spirituality, the will to stand alone, and even the cogent reason, are felt to be dangers; everything that elevates the individual above the herd, and is a source of fear to the neighbour, is henceforth called *evil*; the tolerant, unassuming, self-adapting, self-equalising disposition, the *mediocrity* of desires, attains to moral distinction and honour. Finally, under very peaceful circumstances, there is always less opportunity and necessity for training the feelings to severity and rigour; and now every form of severity, even in justice, begins to disturb the conscience; a lofty and rigorous nobleness and self-responsibility almost offends, and awakens distrust, "the lamb," and still more "the sheep," wins respect. There is a point of diseased mellowness and effeminacy in the history of society, at which society itself takes the part of him who injures it, the part of the *criminal* and does so, in fact, seriously and honestly. To punish, appears to it to be somehow unfair—it is certain that the idea of "punishment" and "the obligation to punish" are then painful and alarming to people. "Is it not sufficient if the criminal be rendered *harmless*? Why should we still punish? Punishment itself is terrible!"—with these questions gregarious morality, the morality of fear, draws its ultimate conclusion. If one could at all do away with danger, the cause of fear, one would have done away with this morality at the same time, it would no longer be necessary, it *would not consider itself* any longer necessary!—Whoever examines the conscience of the present-day European, will always elicit the same imperative from its thousand moral folds and hidden recesses, the imperative of the timidity of the herd: "we wish that some time or other there may be *nothing more to fear!*" Some time or other—the will and the way *thereto* is nowadays called "progress" all over Europe.

202

Let us at once say again what we have already said a hundred times, for people's ears nowadays are unwilling to hear such truths—*our* truths. We know well enough how offensively it sounds when any one plainly, and without metaphor, counts man amongst the animals; but it will be accounted to us almost a *crime*, that it is precisely in respect to men of "modern ideas" that we have constantly applied the terms "herd," "herd-instincts," and such like expressions. What avail is it? We cannot do otherwise, for it is precisely here that our new insight is. We have found that in all the principal moral judgments Europe has become unanimous, including likewise the countries where European influence prevails: in Europe people evidently *know* what Socrates thought he did not know, and what the famous serpent of old once promised to teach—they "know" to-day what is good and evil. It must then sound hard and be distasteful to the ear, when we always insist that that which here thinks it knows, that which here glorifies itself with praise and blame, and calls itself good, is the instinct of the herding human animal: the instinct which has come and is ever coming more and more to the front, to preponderance and supremacy over other instincts, according to the increasing physiological approximation and resemblance of which it is the symptom. *Morality in Europe at present is herding animal morality*; and therefore, as we understand the matter, only one kind of human morality, beside which, before which, and after which many other moralities, and above all *higher* moralities, are or should be possible. Against such a "possibility," against such a "should be," however, this morality defends itself with all its strength; it says obstinately and inexorably: "I am morality itself and nothing else is morality!"—indeed, with the help of a religion which has humoured and flattered the sublimest desires of the herding-animal, things have reached such a point that we always find a more visible expression of this morality even in political and social arrangements: the *democratic* movement is the inheritance of the Christian movement. That its *tempo*, however, is much too slow and sleepy for the more impatient ones, for those who are sick and distracted by the herding-instinct, is indicated by the increasingly furious howling, and always less disguised teeth-gnashing of the anarchist dogs, who are now roving through the highways of European culture, apparently in opposition to the peacefully industrious democrats and Revolution-ideologues, and still more so to the awkward philosophasters and fraternity-visionaries who call themselves Socialists and want a "free society"; but in reality at one with them all in their thorough and instinctive hostility to every form of society other than that of the *autonomous* herd (to the extent even of repudiating the notions "master" and "servant"— *ni dieu ni maître,*[6] says a socialist formula); at one in their tenacious opposition to every special claim, every special right and privilege (this means ultimately opposition to *every* right, for when all are equal, no one needs "rights" any longer); at one in their distrust of punitive justice (as though it were a violation of the weak, a wrong to the *necessary* consequences of all former society); but equally at one in their religion of sympathy, in their compassion for all that feels, lives, and suffers (down to the very animals, up even to "God"—the extravagance of "sympathy for God" belongs to a democratic age); altogether at one in the cry and impatience of their sympathy, in their deadly hatred of suffering generally, in their almost feminine incapacity for witnessing it or *allowing* it; at one in their involuntary beglooming and besoftening, under the spell of which Europe seems to be threatened with a new Buddhism; at one in their belief in the morality of *mutual* sympathy, as though it were morality in itself, the climax, the *attained* climax of mankind, the sole hope of the future, the consolation of the present, the great discharge from all the obligations of the past; altogether at one in their belief in the community as the *deliverer*, in the herd, and therefore in "themselves."

• • •

241

We "good Europeans," we also have hours when we allow ourselves a warm-hearted patriotism, a plunge and relapse into old loves and narrow views—I have just given an example of it—hours of national excitement, of patriotic anguish, and all other sorts of old-fashioned floods of sentiment. Duller spirits may perhaps only get done with what confines its operations in us to hours and plays itself out in hours—in a considerable time: some in half a year, others in half a lifetime, according to the speed and strength with which they digest and "change their material." Indeed, I could think of sluggish, hesitating races, which, even in our rapidly moving Europe, would require half a century ere they could surmount such atavistic attacks of patriotism and soil-attachment, and return once more to reason, that is to say, to "good Europeanism." And while digressing on this possibility, I happen to become an ear-witness of a conversation between two old patriots—they were evidently both hard of hearing and consequently spoke all the louder. "*He* has as much, and knows as much, philosophy as a peasant or a corps-student," said the one— "he is still innocent. But what does that matter nowadays! It is the age of the masses: they lie on their belly before everything that is massive. And so also *in politicis*. A statesman who rears up for them a new Tower of Babel, some monstrosity of empire and power, they call 'great'—what does it matter that we more prudent and conservative ones do not meanwhile give up the old belief that it is only the great thought that gives greatness to an action or affair. Supposing a statesman were to bring his people into the position of being obliged henceforth to practise 'high politics,' for which they were by nature badly endowed and prepared, so that they would have to sacrifice their old and reliable virtues, out of love to a new and doubtful mediocrity;—supposing a statesman were to condemn his people generally to 'practise politics,' when they have hitherto had something better to do and think about, and when in the depths of their souls they have been unable to free themselves from a prudent loathing of the restlessness, emptiness, and noisy wranglings of the essentially politics-practising nations;—supposing such a statesman were to stimulate the slumbering passions and avidities of his people, were to make a stigma out of their former diffidence and delight in aloofness, an offence out of their exoticism and hidden permanency, were to depreciate their most radical proclivities, subvert their consciences, make their minds narrow, and their tastes 'national'— what! a statesman who should do all this, which his people would have to do penance for throughout their whole future, if they had a future, such a statesman would be *great*, would he?"—"Undoubtedly!" replied the other old patriot vehemently; "otherwise he *could not* have done it! It was mad perhaps to wish such a thing! But perhaps everything great has just been mad at its commencement!"—"Misuse of words!" cried his interlocutor, contradictorily—"strong! strong! Strong and mad! *Not* great!"—The old men had obviously become heated as they thus shouted their "truths" in each other's faces; but I, in my happiness and apartness, considered how soon a stronger one may become master of the strong; and also that there is a compensation for the intellectual superficialising of a nation—namely, in the deepening of another.

242

Whether we call it "civilisation," or "humanising," or "progress," which now distinguishes the European; whether we call it simply, without praise or blame, by the political formula: the *democratic* movement in Europe—behind all the moral and political foregrounds pointed to by such formulas, an immense *physiological* process goes on, which is ever extending: the process of the assimilation of Europeans; their increasing detachment from the conditions under which, climatically and hereditarily, united races originate; their increasing independence of every definite *milieu*, that for centuries would fain inscribe itself with equal demands on soul and body;—that is to say, the slow emergence of an essentially *super-national* and nomadic species of man, who possesses, physiologically speaking, a maximum of the art and power of adaptation as his typical distinction. This process of the *evolving European*, which can be retarded in its *tempo* by great relapses, but will perhaps just gain and grow thereby in vehemence and depth—the still raging storm and stress of "national sentiment" pertains to it, and also the anarchism which is appearing at present—this process will probably arrive at results on which its naïve propagators and panegyrists, the apostles of "modern ideas," would least care to reckon. The same new conditions under which on an average a levelling and mediocrising of man will take place—a useful, industrious, variously serviceable and clever gregarious man—are in the highest degree suitable to give rise to exceptional men of the most dangerous and attractive qualities. For, while the capacity for adaptation, which is ever trying changing conditions, and begins a new work with every generation, almost with every decade, makes the *powerfulness* of the type impossible; while the collective impression of such future Europeans will probably be that of numerous, talkative, weak-willed, and very handy workmen who *require* a master, a commander, as they require their daily bread; while, therefore, the democratising of Europe will tend to the production of a type prepared for *slavery* in the most subtle sense of the term: the *strong* man will necessarily in individual and exceptional cases, become stronger and richer than he has perhaps ever been before—owing to the unprejudicedness of his schooling, owing to the immense variety of practice, art, and disguise. I meant to say that the democratising of Europe is at the same time an involuntary arrangement for the rearing of *tyrants*—taking the word in all its meanings, even in its most spiritual sense.

• • •

256

Owing to the morbid estrangement which the nationality-craze has induced and still induces among the nations of Europe, owing also to the short-sighted and hasty-handed politicians, who with the help of this craze, are at present in power, and do not suspect to what extent the disintegrating policy they pursue must necessarily be only an interlude policy—owing to all this, and much else that is altogether unmentionable at present, the most unmistakable signs that *Europe wishes to be one,* are now overlooked, or arbitrarily and falsely misinterpreted. With all the more profound and large-minded men of this century, the real general tendency of the mysterious labour of their souls was to prepare the way for that new *synthesis,* and tentatively to anticipate the European of the future; only in their simulations, or in their weaker moments, in old age perhaps, did they belong to the "fatherlands"—they only rested from themselves when they became "patriots." I think of such men as Napoleon, Goethe, Beethoven, Stendhal, Heinrich Heine, Schopenhauer: it must not be taken amiss if I also count Richard Wagner among them, about whom one must not let oneself be deceived by his own misunderstandings (geniuses like him have seldom the right to understand themselves), still less, of course, by the unseemly noise with which he is now resisted and opposed in France: the fact remains, nevertheless, that Richard Wagner and the *later French Romanticism* of the forties, are most closely and intimately related to one another. They are akin, fundamentally akin, in all the heights and depths of their requirements; it is Europe, the *one* Europe, whose soul presses urgently and longingly, outwards and upwards, in their multifarious and boisterous art—whither? into a new light? towards a new sun? But who would attempt to express accurately what all these masters of new modes of speech could not express distinctly? It is certain that the same storm and stress tormented them, that they *sought* in the same manner, these last great seekers! All of them steeped in literature to their eyes and ears—the first artists of universal literary culture—for the most part even themselves writers, poets, intermediaries and blenders of the arts and the senses (Wagner, as musician is reckoned among painters, as poet among musicians, as artist generally among actors); all of them fanatics for *expression* "at any cost"—I specially mention Delacroix, the nearest related to Wagner; all of them great discoverers in the realm of the sublime, also of the loathsome and dreadful, still greater discoverers in effect, in display, in the art of the show-shop; all of them talented far beyond their genius, out and out *virtuosi,* with mysterious accesses to all that seduces, allures, constrains, and upsets; born enemies of logic and of the straight line, hankering after the strange, the exotic, the monstrous, the crooked, and the self-contradictory; as men, Tantaluses of the will, plebeian parvenus, who knew themselves to be incapable of a noble *tempo* or of a *lento* in life and action—think of Balzac, for instance,—unrestrained workers, almost destroying themselves by work; antinomians and rebels in manners, ambitious and insatiable, without equilibrium and enjoyment; all of them finally shattering and sinking down at the Christian cross (and with right and reason, for who of them would have been sufficiently profound and sufficiently original for an *Antichristian* philosophy?);—on the whole, a boldly daring, splendidly overbearing, high-flying, and aloft-up-dragging class of higher men, who had first to teach their century—and it is the century of the *masses*—the conception "higher man." . . . Let the German friends of Richard Wagner advise together as to whether there is anything purely German in the Wagnerian art, or whether its distinction does not consist precisely in coming from *super-German* sources and impulses: in which connection it may not be underrated how indispensable Paris was to the development of his type, which the strength of his instincts made him long to visit at the most decisive time—and how the whole style of his proceedings, of his self-apostolate, could only perfect itself in sight of the French socialistic original. On a more subtle comparison it will perhaps be found, to the honour of Richard Wagner's German nature, that he has acted in everything with more strength, daring, severity, and elevation than a nineteenth-century Frenchman could have done—owing to the circumstance that we Germans are as yet nearer to barbarism than the French;—perhaps even the most remarkable creation of Richard Wagner is not only at present, but for ever inaccessible, incomprehensible, and inimitable to the whole latter-day Latin race: the figure of Siegfried, that *very free* man, who is probably far too free, too hard, too cheerful, too healthy, too *anti-Catholic* for the taste of old and mellow civilised nations. He may even have been a sin against Romanticism, this anti-Latin Siegfried: well, Wagner atoned amply for this sin in his old sad days, when—anticipating a taste which has meanwhile passed into politics—he began, with the religious vehemence peculiar to him, to preach, at least, *the way to Rome*, if not to walk therein.—That these last words may not be misunderstood, I will call to my aid a few powerful rhymes, which will even betray to less delicate ears what I mean—what I mean *counter to* the "last Wagner" and his Parsifal music:

—Is this our mode ?—
From German heart came this vexed ululating?
From German body, this self-lacerating?
Is ours this priestly hand-dilation,
This incense-fuming exaltation?
Is ours this faltering, falling, shambling,
This quite uncertain ding-dong-dangling?
This sly nun-ogling, Ave-hour-bell ringing,
This wholly false enraptured heaven-o'erspringing?
—Is this our mode?—
Think well!—ye still wait for admission—
For what ye hear is *Rome—Rome's faith by intuition!*

Notes

[1] A follower of Epicurus, the Greek philosopher (341–270 B.C.).

[2] Church father (354–430).

[3] Athenian general and statesman (c. 450–404 B.C.).

[4] Holy Roman Emperor (reigned 1220–1250).

[5] Republic, commonwealth, state.

[6] French: "neither God nor master."

Gertrude Stein

1874–1946

Gertrude Stein was born in Pennsylvania, but spent the first four years of her life living in Austria and France. Her family moved to California in 1879, where she spent the remainder of her childhood. Afterwards, she attended the annex of Harvard that later became Radcliffe College, studying psychology with William James and philosophy with George Santayana. She then spent some time in medical school at John Hopkins. After the death of her parents, an inheritance allowed her to live independently. She moved to Paris where she shared an apartment with her brother Leo at first, then with Alice B. Toklas, her lifelong companion. In her home, she created an atmosphere where innovative artistic and literary friends gathered, forming a modern-day *salon* during the interwar years. At this time, she became an art collector, one of the first to buy paintings of the cubists and their contemporaries.

Stein was fascinated by the art of the impressionists, postimpressionists, and modernists. These new aesthetic approaches deviated from representational depictions of the world and created striking visual effects through the innovative use of color and form. Modernism calls upon the viewer to move beyond the ways of seeing reinforced by more traditional art-forms, to experience new perceptions and inner states. Just as bold techniques in painting were defining the visual world in new ways, she set out to find a way to capture in words a sense of the fragmented "presentness" or immediacy of lived experience. This emphasis upon the individual's particularized consciousness eventually became an integral part of modernist artworks, in expressionist painting, for example, or the stream-of-consciousness narrative method of James Joyce. In a series of lectures presented at Oxford and Cambridge—appearing in 1926 as *Composition and Explanation*—Stein details her theories about literature and the creative act.

In "Picasso" (1912), Stein places us in the present moment of a master painter at work, drawing upon her own observations of Picasso at close range, from the time when he had painted a portrait of her. Stein uses language unconventionally, in order to capture the spirit and meaning of each moment. Her methods include repetition and heavily reinforced rhythmic structure, designed to generate states of being rather than to convey content alone. Such departures from conventional form, modernists believed, should at once alienate and rivet the reader's attention. In studying this piece, have someone read it aloud to you. How does the prose seem to structure your experience? How do the elements of fragmentation and restructuring, artistic ingredients found in modernism, play an integral part in this work?

Picasso (1912)

One whom some were certainly following was one who was completely charming. One whom some were certainly following was one who was charming. One whom some were following was one who was completely charming. One whom some were following was one who was certainly completely charming.

Some were certainly following and were certain that the one they were then following was one working and was one bringing out of himself then something. Some were certainly following and were certain that the one they were then following was one bringing out of himself then something that was coming to be a heavy thing, a solid thing and a complete thing.

One whom some were certainly following was one working and certainly was one bringing something out of himself then and was one who had been all his living had been one having something coming out of him.

Something had been coming out of him, certainly it had been coming out of him, certainly it was something, certainly it had been coming out of him and it had meaning, a charming meaning, a solid meaning, a struggling meaning, a clear meaning.

One whom some were certainly following and some were certainly following him, one whom some were certainly following was one certainly working.

One whom some were certainly following was one having something coming out of him something having meaning and this one was certainly working then.

This one was working and something was coming then, something was coming out of this one then. This one was one and always there was something coming out of this one and always there had been something coming out of this one. This one had never been one not having something coming out of this one. This one was one having something coming out of this one. This one had been one whom some were following. This one was one whom some were following. This one was being one whom some were following. This one was one who was working.

This one was one who was working. This one was one being one having something being coming out of him. This one was one going on having something come out of him. This one was one going on working. This one was one whom some were following. This one was one who was working.

This one always had something being coming out of this one. This one was working. This one always had been working. This one was always having something that was coming out of this one that was a solid thing, a charming thing, a lovely thing, a perplexing thing, a disconcerting thing, a simple thing, a clear thing, a complicated thing, an interesting thing, a disturbing thing, a repellant thing, a very pretty thing. This one was one certainly being one having something coming out of him. This one was one whom some were following. This one was one who was working.

This one was one who was working and certainly this one was needing to be working so as to be one being working. This one was one having something coming out of him. This one would be one all his living having something coming out of him. This one was working and then this one was working and this one was needing to be working, not to be one having something coming out of him something having meaning, but was needing to be working so as to be one working.

This one was certainly working and working was something this one was certain this one would be doing and this one was doing that thing, this one was working. This one was not one completely working. This one was not ever completely working. This one certainly was not completely working.

This one was one having always something being coming out of him, something having completely a real meaning. This one was one whom some were following. This one was one who was working. This one was one who was working and he was one needing this thing needing to be working so as to be one having some way of being one having some way of working. This one was one who was working. This one was one having something come out of him something having meaning. This one was one always having something come out of him and this thing the thing coming out of him always had real meaning. This one was one who was working. This one was one who was almost always working. This one was not one completely working. This one was one not ever completely working. This one was not one working to have anything come out of him. This one did have something having meaning that did come out of him. He always did have something come out of him. He was working, he was not ever completely working. He did have some following. They were always following him. Some were certainly following him. He was one who was working. He was one having something coming out of him something having meaning. He was not ever completely working.

Franz Kafka

1883–1924

Franz Kafka was born in Prague, Czechoslovakia, to Julie Löwy and Hermann Kafka, a middle-class shopowner. Kafka's upbringing was only nominally Jewish, despite the historical ties of his mother's family to the rabbinic tradition. Alienated from the Jewish community in Prague, the Kafkas saw themselves as secular Germans in language and in culture. Kafka's relations with his father, an exacting and tyrannical man, were difficult and, later, in 1919, Kafka would write (but never send) an autobiographical "Letter to Father," in which he accuses Hermann of filling him with a dread of life. As a teen, Franz attended the Altstäder Staatsgymnasium and then studied law at the University of Prague, taking his doctorate in 1906. After graduation, he started work for the Workers' Accident Insurance Institute for the Kingdom of Bohemia, where he stayed until his retirement in 1922. His final years found him struggling with the effects of tuberculosis and he died in 1924, outside Vienna.

Kafka spent nearly all his free time writing, but during his lifetime published only a few works, including *Betrachtung* (1913; trans. *Meditation*), *Das Urteil* (1916; trans. *The Judgment*), *Die Verwandlung* (1915; trans. *Metamorphosis*), and two collections, *In der Strafkolonie* (1919; trans. *In the Penal Colony*) and *Ein Landarzt* (1919; trans. *A Country Doctor*). Though Kafka requested that his editor, Max Brod, destroy his unfinished work after his death, Brod instead published the most famous of the novels over a three-year period: *Der Prozess* (1925; trans. *The Trial*), *Das Schloss* (1926; trans. *The Castle*), and *Amerika* (1927). Kafka's writing is known for its irrational and dreamlike texture, in which characters find themselves in situations they cannot comprehend and engage a world that always resists their attempts to create meaning. Though Kafka would probably not have labeled himself either an existentialist or a modernist, his work shares much in common with both traditions: it explores the absurdity of the human condition in an increasingly mechanized and alienating world, one in which reality presents itself as no more than nightmarish perceptions and in which the only possible response is guilt and despair.

In "The Country Doctor," Kafka combines the strategies of realism and of fantasy in order to explore the problems of knowledge, authority, and salvation. How does Kafka capture, through his technique, the qualities of modern experience? In what ways are we like the villagers in the story, or like the country doctor himself? To what historical, cultural, or intellectual issues does this story respond?

A Country Doctor (1919)

I was in great perplexity; I had to start on an urgent journey; a seriously
ill patient was waiting for me in a village ten miles off; a thick blizzard of snow
filled all the wide spaces between him and me; I had a gig, a little gig with big
wheels, exactly right for our country roads; muffled in furs, my bag of instruments in my hand, I was in the courtyard all ready for the journey; but there
was no horse to be had, no horse. My own horse had died in the night, worn
out by the fatigues of this icy winter; my servant girl was now running around
the village trying to borrow a horse; but it was hopeless, I knew it, and I stood
there forlornly, with the snow gathering more and more thickly upon me,
more and more unable to move. In the gateway the girl appeared, alone, and
waved a lantern; of course, who would lend a horse at this time for such a journey? I strode through the courtyard once more; I could see no way out; in my
confused distress I kicked at the dilapidated door of the yearlong uninhabited
pigsty. It flew open and flapped to and fro on its hinges. A steam and smell as
of horses came out from it. A dim stable lantern was swinging inside from a
rope. A man, crouching on his hams in that low space, showed an open blue-
eyed face. "Shall I yoke up?" he asked, crawling out on all fours. I did not
know what to say and merely stooped down to see what else was in the sty.
The servant girl was standing beside me. "You never know what you're going
to find in your own house," she said, and we both laughed. "Hey there,
Brother, hey there, Sister!" called the groom, and two horses, enormous creatures with powerful flanks, one after the other, their legs tucked close to their
bodies, each well-shaped head lowered like a camel's, by sheer strength of but-
tocking squeezed out through the door hole which they filled entirely. But at
once they were standing up, their legs long, and their bodies steaming thickly. "Give me a hand," I said, and the willing girl hurried to help the groom
with the harnessing. Yet hardly was she beside him when the groom clipped
hold of her and pushed his face against hers. She screamed and fled back to
me; on her cheek stood out in red the marks of two rows of teeth. "You brute,"
I yelled in fury, "do you want a whipping?" but in the same moment reflected
that the man was a stranger; that I did not know where he came from, and
that of his own free will he was helping me out when everyone else had failed
me. As if he knew my thoughts he took no offense at my threat but, still busied with the horses, only turned around once toward me. "Get in," he said
then, and indeed: everything was ready. A magnificent pair of horses, I
observed, such as I had never sat behind, and I climbed in happily. "But I'll

430

drive, you don't know the way," I said. "Of course," said he, "I'm not coming with you anyway, I'm staying with Rose." "No," shrieked Rose, fleeing into the house with a justified presentiment that her fate was inescapable; I heard the door chain rattle as she put it up; I heard the key turn in the lock; I could see, moreover, how she put out the lights in the entrance hall and in further flight all through the rooms to keep herself from being discovered. "You're coming with me," I said to the groom, "or I won't go, urgent as my journey is. I'm not thinking of paying for it by handing the girl over to you." "Gee up!" he said; clapped his hands; the gig whirled off like a log in a freshet; I could just hear the door of my house splitting and bursting as the groom charged at it and then I was deafened and blinded by a storming rush that steadily buffeted all my senses. But this only for a moment, since, as if my patient's farmyard had opened out just before my courtyard gate, I was already there; the horses had come quietly to a standstill; the blizzard had stopped; moonlight all around; my patient's parents hurried out of the house, his sister behind them; I was almost lifted out of the gig; from their confused ejaculations I gathered not a word; in the sickroom the air was almost unbreathable; the neglected stove was smoking; I wanted to push open a window; but first I had to look at my patient. Gaunt, without any fever, not cold, not warm, with vacant eyes, without a shirt, the youngster heaved himself up from under the feather bedding, threw his arms around my neck, and whispered in my ear: "Doctor, let me die." I glanced around the room; no one had heard it; the parents were leaning forward in silence waiting for my verdict; the sister had set a chair for my handbag; I opened the bag and hunted among my instruments; the boy kept clutching at me from his bed to remind me of his entreaty; I picked up a pair of tweezers, examined them in the candlelight, and laid them down again. "Yes," I thought blasphemously, "in cases like this the gods are helpful, send the missing horse, add to it a second because of the urgency, and to crown everything bestow even a groom—" And only now did I remember Rose again; what was I to do, how could I rescue her, how could I pull her away from under that groom at ten miles' distance, with a team of horses I couldn't control. These horses, now, they had somehow slipped the reins loose, pushed the windows open from outside, I did not know how; each of them had stuck a head in at a window and, quite unmoved by the startled cries of the family, stood eyeing the patient. "Better go back at once," I thought, as if the horses were summoning me to the return journey, yet I permitted the patient's sister, who fancied that I was dazed by the heat, to take my fur coat from me. A glass of rum was poured out for me, the old man clapped me on the shoulder, a familiarity justified by this offer of his treasure. I shook my head; in the narrow confines of the old man's thoughts I felt ill; that was my only reason for refusing the drink. The mother stood by the bedside and cajoled me toward it;

I yielded, and, while one of the horses whinnied loudly to the ceiling, laid my head to the boy's breast, which shivered under my wet beard. I confirmed what I already knew; the boy was quite sound, something a little wrong with his circulation, saturated with coffee by his solicitous mother, but sound and best turned out of bed with one shove. I am no world reformer and so I let him lie. I was the district doctor and did my duty to the uttermost, to the point where it became almost too much. I was badly paid and yet generous and helpful to the poor. I had still to see that Rose was all right, and then the boy might have his way and I wanted to die too. What was I doing there in that endless winter! My horse was dead, and not a single person in the village would lend me another. I had to get my team out of the pigsty; if they hadn't chanced to be horses I should have had to travel with swine. That was how it was. And I nodded to the family. They knew nothing about it, and, had they known, would not have believed it. To write prescriptions is easy, but to come to an understanding with people is hard. Well, this should be the end of my visit, I had once more been called out needlessly, I was used to that, the whole district made my life a torment with my night bell, but that I should have to sacrifice Rose this time as well, the pretty girl who had lived in my house for years almost without my noticing her—that sacrifice was too much to ask, and I had somehow to get it reasoned out in my head with the help of what craft I could muster, in order not to let fly at this family, which with the best will in the world could not restore Rose to me. But as I shut my bag and put an arm out for my fur coat, the family meanwhile standing together, the father sniffing at the glass of rum in his hand, the mother, apparently disappointed in me—why, what do people expect?—biting her lips with tears in her eyes, the sister fluttering a blood-soaked towel, I was somehow ready to admit conditionally that the boy might be ill after all. I went toward him, he welcomed me smiling as if I were bringing him the most nourishing invalid broth—ah, now both horses were whinnying together; the noise, I suppose, was ordained by heaven to assist my examination of the patient—and this time I discovered that the boy was indeed ill. In his right side, near the hip, was an open wound as big as the palm of my hand. Rose-red, in many variations of shade, dark in the hollows, lighter at the edges, softly granulated, with irregular clots of blood, open as a surface mine to the daylight. That was how it looked from a distance. But on a closer inspection there was another complication. I could not help a low whistle of surprise. Worms, as thick and as long as my little finger, themselves rose-red and blood-spotted as well, were wriggling from their fastness in the interior of the wound toward the light, with small white heads and many little legs. Poor boy, you were past helping. I had discovered your great wound; this blossom in your side was destroying you. The family was pleased; they saw me busying myself; the sister told the mother, the mother the father, the father told several guests who were coming in, through the moonlight at the open door, walking on tiptoe, keeping their balance with outstretched arms. "Will you save me?" whispered the boy with a sob, quite blinded by the life within his wound. That is what people are like in my district. Always expecting the impossible from the doctor. They have lost their ancient beliefs; the parson sits at home and unravels his vestments, one after another; but the doctor is supposed to be omnipotent with his merciful surgeon's hand. Well, as it pleases them; I have not thrust my services on them; if they misuse me for sacred ends, I let that happen to me too; what better do I want, old country doctor that I am, bereft of my servant girl! And so they came, the family and the village elders, and stripped my clothes off me; a school choir with the teacher at the head of it stood before the house and sang these words to an utterly simple tune:

Strip his clothes off, then he'll heal us,
If he doesn't, kill him dead!
Only a doctor, only a doctor.

Then my clothes were off and I looked at the people quietly, my fingers in my beard and my head cocked to one side. I was altogether composed and equal to the situation and remained so, although it was no help to me, since they now took me by the head and feet and carried me to the bed. They laid me down in it next to the wall, on the side of the wound. Then they all left the room; the door was shut; the singing stopped; clouds covered the moon; the bedding was warm around me; the horses' heads in the open windows wavered like shadows. "Do you know," said a voice in my ear, "I have very little confidence in you. Why, you were only blown in here, you didn't come on your own feet. Instead of helping me, you're cramping me on my deathbed. What I'd like best is to scratch your eyes out." "Right," I said, "it is a shame. And yet I am a doctor. What am I to do? Believe me, it is not too easy for me either." "Am I supposed to be content with this apology? Oh, I must be, I can't help it. I always have to put up with things. A fine wound is all I brought into the world; that was my sole endowment." "My young friend," said I, "your mistake is: you have not a wide enough view. I have been in all the sickrooms, far and wide, and I tell you: your wound is not so bad. Done in a tight corner with two strokes of the ax. Many a one proffers his side and can hardly hear the ax in the forest, far less that it is coming nearer to him." "Is that really so, or are you deluding me in my fever?" "It is really so, take the word of honor of an official doctor." And he took it and lay still. But now it was time for me to think of escaping. The horses were still standing faithfully in their places. My clothes, my fur coat, my bag were quickly collected; I didn't want to waste time dressing; if the horses raced home as they had come, I should only be springing, as it were, out of this bed into my own. Obediently a horse backed away from the window; I threw my bundle into the gig; the fur coat missed its mark and was caught on a hook only by the sleeve. Good enough. I swung myself onto the horse. With the reins loosely trailing, one horse barely fastened to the other, the gig swaying behind, my fur coat last of all in the snow. "Gee up!" I said, but there was no galloping; slowly, like old men, we crawled through the snowy wastes; a long time echoed behind us the new but faulty song of the children:

> O be joyful, all you patients,
> The doctor's laid in bed beside you!

Never shall I reach home at this rate; my flourishing practice is done for; my successor is robbing me, but in vain, for he cannot take my place; in my house the disgusting groom is raging; Rose is his victim; I do not want to think about it anymore. Naked, exposed to the frost of this most unhappy of ages, with an earthly vehicle, unearthly horses, old man that I am, I wander astray. My fur coat is hanging from the back of the gig, but I cannot reach it, and none of my limber pack of patients lifts a finger. Betrayed! Betrayed! A false alarm on the night bell once answered—it cannot be made good, not ever.

Radclyffe Hall

1880–1943

The "roaring" 1920s were a decade of unprecedented freedom of expression for women and African Americans in Europe and North America. Another group, largely silenced and marginalized by mainstream culture, which asserted its voice in these years was gays and lesbians. While modernist artists responded to Freud's ideas, "sexologists" began using them to develop theories of human sexuality. Sexologists were among the first to name, study, and draw public attention to alternative sexual orientations, which they labelled as "inversion." These findings in turn inspired artists to consider homosexuality in their texts.

The Well of Loneliness, by British writer Radclyffe Hall, is widely regarded as the first openly lesbian-themed novel. The story revolves around the protagonist Stephen whose torment in a homophobic family and society results in terrible self-hatred. Only when she confronts her mother is Stephen able to begin to affirm her identity. In modernist fashion, readers are invited into the interior spaces of Stephen's self-image. And like the more daring works of modernist fiction, *The Well of Loneliness* was the subject of public outcry resulting in a censorship trial.

In the following excerpts, Hall wrestles with one of the ultimate dilemmas of identity formation: nature versus nurture. What "makes" Stephen a lesbian in Hall's view? Why is ultimate happiness denied to Stephen? As Stephen's misery turns outward, to a desire for understanding and then to rage, a confrontation with homophobia is imminent. Particularly in the moving dialogue between Stephen and her mother, we see the homophobe's refusal to accept alternate sexualities even to the point of denying the humanity of her own daughter. Cast out, likening herself to Cain, there seems to be no hope for Stephen. But the novel does not end on that note. In what ways does her life-long servant, Puddle, encourage her to forge a new path? This novel poses one of the central dilemmas of modernity: how can the lone individual thrive outside the community? Can communities be built among those "outcast?"

from *The Well of Loneliness* (1928)

Sir Philip never knew how much he longed for a son until, some ten years after marriage, his wife conceived a child; then he knew that this thing meant complete fulfilment, the fulfilment for which they had both been waiting. When she told him, he could not find words for expression, and must just turn and weep on her shoulder. It never seemed to cross his mind for a moment that Anna might very well give him a daughter; he saw her only as a mother of sons, nor could her warnings disturb him. He christened the unborn infant Stephen, because he admired the pluck of that Saint. He was not a religious man by instinct, being perhaps too much of a student, but he read the Bible for its fine literature, and Stephen had gripped his imagination. Thus he often discussed the future of their child: 'I think I shall put Stephen down for Harrow,' or: 'I'd rather like Stephen to finish off abroad, it widens one's outlook on life.'

But: 'Man proposes—God disposes,' and so it happened that on Christmas Eve, Anna Gordon was delivered of a daughter; a narrow-hipped, wide-shouldered little tadpole of a baby, that yelled and yelled for three hours without ceasing as though outraged to find itself ejected into life.

• • •

Pacing restlessly up and down her bedroom, Stephen [now in late adolescence] would be thinking of Angela Crossby—haunted, tormented by Angela's words that day in the garden: 'Could you marry me, Stephen?' and then by those other pitiless words: 'Can I help it if you're—what you obviously are?'

She would think with a kind of despair: 'What am I in God's name—some kind of abomination?' And this thought would fill her with very great anguish, because, loving much, her love seemed to her sacred. She could not endure that the slur of those words should come anywhere near her love. So now night after night she must pace up and down, beating her mind against a blind problem, beating her spirit against a blank wall—the impregnable wall of non-comprehension: 'Why am I as I am—and what am I?' Her mind would recoil while her spirit grew faint. A great darkness would seem to descend on her spirit—there would be no light wherewith to lighten that darkness.

• • •

That night she stared at herself in the glass; and even as she did so she hated her body with its muscular shoulders, its small compact breasts, and its slender flanks of an athlete. All her life she must drag this body of hers like a monstrous fetter imposed on her spirit. This strangely ardent yet sterile body that must worship yet never be worshipped in return the creature of its adoration. She longed to maim it, for it made her feel cruel; it was so white, so strong and so self-sufficient; yet withal so poor and unhappy a thing that her eyes filled with tears and her hate turned to pity. She began to grieve over it, touching her breasts with pitiful fingers, stroking her shoulders, letting her hands slip along her straight thighs—Oh, poor and most desolate body!

Then, she, for whom Puddle [her servant] was actually praying at that moment, must now pray also, but blindly; finding few words that seemed worthy of prayer, few words that seemed to encompass her meaning—for she did not know the meaning herself. But she loved, and loving groped for the God who had fashioned her, even unto this bitter loving.

● ● ●

Anna began to speak very slowly as though nothing of what she would say must be lost; and that slow, quiet voice was more dreadful than anger: 'All your life I've felt very strangely towards you;' she was saying, 'I've felt a kind of physical repulsion, a desire not to touch or to be touched by you—a terrible thing for a mother to feel—it has often made me deeply unhappy. I've often felt that I was being unjust, unnatural—but now I know that my instinct was right; it is you who are unnatural, not I. . . . '

'Mother—stop!'

'It is you who are unnatural, not I. And this thing that you are is a sin against creation. Above all is this thing a sin against the father who bred you, the father whom you dare to resemble. You dare to look like your father, and your face is a living insult to his memory, Stephen. I shall never be able to look at you now without thinking of the deadly insult of your face and your body to the memory of the father who bred you. I can only thank God that your father died before he was asked to endure this great shame. As for you, I would rather see you dead at my feet than standing before me with this thing upon you—this unspeakable outrage that you call love in that letter which you don't deny having written. In that letter you say things that may only be said between man and woman, and coming from you they are vile and filthy words of corruption—against nature, against God who created nature. My gorge rises; you have made me feel physically sick—,

'Mother—you don't know what you're saying—you're my mother—'

'Yes, I am your mother, but for all that, you seem to me like a scourge. I ask myself what I have ever done to be dragged down into the depths by my daughter. And your father—what had he ever done? And you have presumed to use the word love in connection with this—with these lusts of your body; these unnatural cravings of your unbalanced mind and undisciplined body— you have used that word. I have loved—do you hear? I have loved your father, and your father loved me. That was *love*.'

Then, suddenly, Stephen knew that unless she could, indeed, drop dead at the feet of this woman in whose womb she had quickened, there was one thing that she dared not let pass unchallenged, and that was this terrible slur upon her love. And all that was in her rose up to refute it; to protect her love from such unbearable soiling. It was part of herself and unless she could save it, she could not save herself anymore. She must stand or fall by the courage of that love to proclaim its right to toleration.

She held up her hand, commanding silence; commanding that slow, quiet voice to cease speaking, and she said: 'As my father loved you, I loved. As a man loves a woman, that was how I loved—protectively, like my father. I wanted to give all I had in me to give. It made me feel terribly strong . . . and gentle. It was good, good, *good*—I'd have laid down my life a thousand times over for Angela Crossby. If I could have I'd have married her and brought her home—I wanted to bring her home here to Morton. If I loved her the way a man loves a woman, it's because I can't feel that I am a woman. All my life I've never felt like a woman, and you know it—you say you've always disliked me, that you've always felt a strange physical repulsion . . . . I don't know what I am; no one's ever told me that I'm different and yet I know that I'm differ-ent—that's why, I suppose, you've felt as you have done. And for that I forgive you, though whatever it is, it was you and my father who made this body— but what I will never forgive is your daring to try and make me ashamed of my love. I'm not ashamed of it, there's no shame in me.' And now she was stam-mering a little wildly, 'Good and—and fine it was' she stammered, 'the best part of myself—I gave all and I asked nothing in return—I just went on hope-lessly loving—' she broke off, she was shaking from head to foot, and Anna's cold voice fell like icy water on that angry and sorely tormented spirit.

'You have spoken, Stephen. I don't think there's much more that needs to be said between us except this, we two cannot live together at Morton—not now, because I might grow to hate you. Yes, although you're my child, I might grow to hate you. The same roof mustn't shelter us both any more; one of us must go—which of us shall it be?' And she looked at Stephen and waited.

Morton! They could not both live at Morton. Something seemed to catch hold of the girl's heart and twist it. She stared at her mother, aghast for a moment, while Anna stared back—she was waiting for her answer.

But quite suddenly Stephen found her manhood and she said: 'I under-stand. I'll leave Morton.'

Then Anna made her daughter sit down beside her, while she talked of how this thing might be accomplished in a way that would cause the least possible scandal: 'For the sake of your father's honourable name, I must ask you to help me Stephen.' It was better, she said, that Stephen should take Puddle with her, if Puddle would consent to go. They might live in London or somewhere abroad, on the pretext that Stephen wished to study. From time to time Stephen would come back to Morton and visit her mother, and during those visits, they two would take care to be seen together for appearances' sake, for the sake of her father. She could take from Morton whatever she needed, the horses, and anything else she wished. Certain of the rent-rolls would be paid over to her, should her own income prove insufficient. All things must be done in a way that was seemly—no undue haste, no suspicion of a breach between mother and daughter: 'For the sake of your father I ask this of you, not for your sake or mine, but for his. Do you consent to this, Stephen?'

And Stephen answered: 'Yes, I consent.'

Then Anna said: 'I'd like you to leave me now—I feel tired and I want to be alone for a little—but presently I shall send for Puddle to discuss her living with you in the future.' So Stephen got up, and she went away, leaving Anna Gordon alone.

• • •

[Stephen went to her father's study where she found a sexology text.] Then suddenly she had got to her feet and was talking aloud—she was talking to her father: 'You knew! All the time you knew this thing, but because of your pity you wouldn't tell me. Oh, Father—and there are so many of us—thousands of miserable, unwanted people, who have no right to love, no right to compassion because they're maimed, hideously maimed and ugly—God's cruel; He let us get flawed in the making.'

And then, before she knew what she was doing, she had found her father's old, well-worn Bible. There she stood demanding a sign from heaven—nothing less than a sign from heaven she demanded. The Bible fell open near the beginning. She read: 'And the Lord set a mark upon Cain. . . .

Then Stephen hurled the Bible away, and she sank down completely hopeless and beaten, rocking her body backwards and forwards with a kind of abrupt yet methodical rhythm: 'And the Lord set a mark upon Cain, upon Cain....' she was rocking now in rhythm to those words, 'And the Lord set a mark upon Cain—upon Cain—upon Cain. And the Lord set a mark upon Cain. . . .'

That was how Puddle came in and found her, and Puddle said: 'Where you go, I go, Stephen. All that you're suffering at this moment I've suffered. It was when I was very like you—but I still remember.'

Stephen looked up with bewildered eyes: 'Would you go with Cain whom God marked?' she said slowly, for she had not understood Puddle's meaning, so she asked her once more: 'Would you go with Cain?'

Puddle put an arm around Stephen's bowed shoulders, and she said: 'You've got work to do—come and do it! Why, just because you are what you are, you may actually find that you've got an advantage. You may write with a curious double insight—write both men and women from a personal knowledge. Nothing's completely misplaced or wasted, I'm sure of that—and we're all part of nature. Some day the world will recognize this, but meanwhile there's plenty of work that's waiting. For the sake of all the others who are like you, but less strong and less gifted perhaps, many of them, it's up to you to have the courage to make good, and I'm here to help you do it, Stephen.'

● ● ●

Carl Gustav Jung

1885–1961

Carl Jung was born in Kesswil, Switzerland. The son of a pastor and literary scholar, he was drawn to both science and spirituality, eventually finding in psychiatry a field that for him incorporated both passions. In his autobiography he wrote: "Here was the empirical field common to biological and spiritual facts, which I had everywhere sought and nowhere found. Here at last was the place where the collision of nature and spirit became a reality." Jung began as a disciple of Freud in the new field of psychoanalysis; however, he eventually rejected Freud's emphasis on sexuality, developing his own analytic psychology, the theoretical framework of which depended deeply on the symbols and structures implicit in mythic narratives and folk legends.

Jung believed that the psyche was a self-regulating system and that disunity in the personality causes or characterizes mental illness. On the other hand, unity, toward which the personality strives, is a sign of mental health. He defined neurosis as "the suffering of the soul which has not discovered its meaning." In search of a solution to the fragmented personality, he directed his attention to the deep meanings that underlie mythology, believing that different cultures shared a common set of psychic motifs, which he called "archetypes." These common, embedded psychological features of the psyche comprise the "collective unconscious," an understanding of which we can only unlock through mythological representation. Jung's works include *The Psychology of the Unconscious* (1916), *Modern Psychological Types* (1923), *Man in Search of a Soul* (1933), *Psychology and Religion* (1938), *The Undiscovered Self* (1957) and the posthumously published *Man and His Symbols* (1964).

In "The Spiritual Problem of Modern Man" (*Europäische Revue*, Berlin, IV, 1928), Jung addresses the spiritual bankruptcy of modern life, which he believes has led us to lose touch with our inner selves. For Jung and others, scientific determinism had replaced the universe of purpose and meaning that existed in earlier centuries. And this problem is deeply historical: the mass killing of World War I numbed our consciousness; the interwar years fractured traditional political systems and gave rise to the totalitarian annihilation of the individual; modernism severed us from the power of representational art, leaving us with fragmented and disjoined abstraction. What does Jung challenge us to do in the midst of this intellectual and political chaos? Where do we turn when our guiding traditions become obsolete? How can we recapture our spirituality in an age that does not value the spirit?

from *The Spiritual Problem of Modern Man* (1928)

The spiritual problem of modern man is one of those questions which belong so intimately to the present in which we are living that we cannot judge of them fully. The modern man is a newly formed human being; a modern problem is a question which has just arisen and whose answer lies in the future. In speaking, therefore, of the spiritual problem of modern man we can at most state a question—and we should perhaps put this statement in different terms if we had but the faintest inkling of the answer. The question, moreover, seems rather vague; but the truth is that it has to do with something so universal that it exceeds the grasp of any single human being. We have reason enough, therefore, to approach such a problem with true moderation and with the greatest caution. I am deeply convinced of this, and wish it stressed the more because it is just such problems which tempt us to use high-sounding words—and because I shall myself be forced to say certain things which may sound immoderate and incautious.

• • •

The revolution in our conscious outlook, brought about by the catastrophic results of the World War, shows itself in our inner life by the shattering of our faith in ourselves and our own worth. We used to regard foreigners—the other side—as political and moral reprobates; but the modern man is forced to recognize that he is politically and morally just like anyone else. Whereas I formerly believed it to be my bounden duty to call other persons to order, I now admit that I need calling to order myself. I admit this the more readily because I realize only too well that I am losing my faith in the possibility of a rational organization of the world, that old dream of the millennium, in which peace and harmony should rule, has grown pale. The modern man's scepticism regarding all such matters has chilled his enthusiasm for politics and world-reform; more than that, it does not favour any smooth application of psychic energies to the outer world. Through his scepticism the modern man is thrown back upon himself; his energies flow towards their source and wash to the surface those psychic contents which are at all times there, but lie hidden in the silt as long as the stream flows smoothly in its course. How totally different did the world appear to mediæval man! For him the earth was eternally fixed and at rest in the centre of the universe, encircled by the course of a sun that solicitously bestowed its warmth. Men were all children of God

443

under the loving care of the Most High, who prepared them for eternal blessedness; and all knew exactly what they should do and how they should conduct themselves in order to rise from a corruptible world to an incorruptible and joyous existence. Such a life no longer seems real to us, even in our dreams. Natural science has long ago torn this lovely veil to shreds. That age lies as far behind as childhood, when one's own father was unquestionably the handsomest and strongest man on earth.

The modern man has lost all the metaphysical certainties of his mediæval brother, and set up in their place the ideals of material security, general welfare and humaneness. But it takes more than an ordinary dose of optimism to make it appear that these ideals are still unshaken. Material security, even, has gone by the board, for the modern man begins to see that every step in material "progress" adds just so much force to the threat of a more stupendous catastrophe. The very picture terrorizes the imagination. What are we to imagine when cities today perfect measures of defence against poison-gas attacks, and practise them in "dress rehearsals"? We cannot but suppose that such attacks have been planned and provided for—again on the principle "in time of peace prepare for war." Let man but accumulate his materials of destruction and the devil within him will soon be unable to resist putting them to their fated use. It is well known that fire-arms go off of themselves if only enough of them are together.

An intimation of the law that governs blind contingency, which Heraclitus[1] called the rule of *enantiodromia* (conversion into the opposite), now steals upon the modern man through the by-ways of his mind, chilling him with fear and paralysing his faith in the lasting effectiveness of social and political measures in the face of these monstrous forces. If he turns away from the terrifying prospect of a blind world in which building and destroying successively tip the scale, and if he then turns his gaze inward upon the recesses of his own mind, he will discover a chaos and a darkness there which he would gladly ignore. Science has destroyed even the refuge of the inner life. What was once a sheltering haven has become a place of terror.

And yet it is almost a relief for us to come upon so much evil in the depths of our own minds. We are able to believe, at least, that we have discovered the root of the evil in mankind. Even though we are shocked and disillusioned at first, we yet feel, because these things are manifestations of our own minds, that we hold them more or less in our own hands and can therefore correct or at least effectively suppress them. We like to assume that, if we succeeded in this, we should have rooted out some fraction of the evil in the world. We like to think that, on the basis of a widespread knowledge of the unconscious and its ways, no one could be deceived by a statesman who was unaware of his own bad motives; the very newspapers would pull him up: "Please have yourself analysed; you are suffering from a repressed father-complex."

I have purposely chosen this grotesque example to show to what absurdities we are led by the illusion that because something is psychic it is under our control. It is, however, true that much of the evil in the world is due to the fact that man in general is hopelessly unconscious, as it is also true that with increasing insight we combat this evil at its source in ourselves. As science enables us to deal with injuries inflicted from without, so it helps us to treat those arising from within.

The rapid and world-wide growth of a "psychological" interest over the last two decades shows unmistakably that modern man has to some extent turned his attention from material things to his own subjective processes. Should we call this mere curiosity ? At any rate, art has a way of anticipating future changes in man's fundamental outlook, and expressionist art has taken this subjective turn well in advance of the more general change.

This "psychological" interest of the present time shows that man expects something from psychic life which he has not received from the outer world: something which our religions, doubtless, ought to contain, but no longer do contain—at least for the modern man. The various forms of religion no longer appear to the modern man to come from within—to be expressions of his own psychic life; for him they are to be classed with the things of the outer world. He is vouchsafed no revelation of a spirit that is not of this world; but he tries on a number of religions and convictions as if they were Sunday attire, only to lay them aside again like worn-out clothes.

Yet he is somehow fascinated by the almost pathological manifestations of the unconscious mind. We must admit the fact, however difficult it is for us to understand, that something which previous ages have discarded should suddenly command our attention. That there is a general interest in these matters is a truth which cannot be denied. Their offence to good taste notwithstanding. I am not thinking merely of the interest taken in psychology as a science, or of the still narrower interest in the psychoanalysis of Freud, but of the widespread interest in all sorts of psychic phenomena as manifested in the growth of spiritualism, astrology, theosophy, and so forth. The world has seen nothing like it since the end of the seventeenth century. We can compare it only to the flowering of Gnostic thought in the first and second centuries after Christ. The spiritual currents of the present have, in fact, a deep affinity with Gnosticism. There is even a Gnostic church in France today, and I know of two schools in Germany which openly declare themselves Gnostic. The modern movement which is numerically most impressive is undoubtedly Theosophy, together with its continental sister, Anthroposophy; these are pure

Gnosticism in a Hindu dress. Compared with these movements the interest in scientific psychology is negligible. What is striking about Gnostic systems is that they are based exclusively upon the manifestations of the unconscious, and that their moral teachings do not baulk at the shadow-side of life. Even in the form of its European revival, the Hindu *Kundalini-Yoga* shows this clearly. And as every person informed on the subject of occultism will testify, the statement holds true in this field as well.

The passionate interest in these movements arises undoubtedly from psychic energy which can no longer be invested in obsolete forms of religion. For this reason such movements have a truly religious character, even when they pretend to be scientific. It changes nothing when Rudolf Steiner[2] calls his Anthroposophy "spiritual science," or Mrs. Eddy[3] discovers a "Christian Science." These attempts at concealment merely show that religion has grown suspect—almost as suspect as politics and world-reform.

I do not believe that I am going too far when I say that modern man, in contrast to his nineteenth-century brother, turns his attention to the psyche with very great expectations; and that he does so without reference to any traditional creed, but rather in the Gnostic sense of religious experience. We should be wrong in seeing mere caricature or masquerade when the movements already mentioned try to give themselves scientific airs; their doing so is rather an indication that they are actually pursuing "science" or knowledge instead of the *faith* which is the essence of Western religions. The modern man abhors dogmatic postulates taken on faith and the religions based upon them. He holds them valid only in so far as their knowledge-content seems to accord with his own experience of the deeps of psychic life. He wants to know—to experience for himself. Dean Inge of St. Paul's has called attention to a movement in the Anglican Church with similar objectives.

Notes

[1] Greek philosopher.

[2] Rudolf Steiner (1861–1925), founder of Anthroposophy, a twentieth-century religious system focused on principles of human development.

[3] Mary Baker Eddy (1821–1910), founder of Christian Science.

[4] William Ralph Inge (1860–1959), British clergyman, author of *Truth and Falsehood in Religion* (1906) and *Faith* (1909).

Margaret Sanger

1879–1966

Born Margaret Louise Higgins in 1879 in Corning, New York, Sanger was the sixth of eleven children in a struggling Irish family. She recalls in her *Autobiography* that her father, a stonemason, "was a nonconformist through and through" who taught his children to make the world a better place. Sanger's mother, who was frail and suffered from tuberculosis, worked unceasingly to meet the needs of a growing family. The inspiration of her father's free-thinking approach to life and awareness of the struggles of her own mother, caused by multiple pregnancies and poverty, had a profound impact on the work Sanger eventually chose to do.

After her marriage to an architect, William Sanger, and the birth of her three children, Sanger took a job with Lillian Wald's visiting nursing service in New York City in 1910. There she met women, like her mother, who were dealing with the health risks and economic problems of frequent pregnancies. These women often appealed to Sanger for information about family planning. In this selection, from her *Autobiography*, Sanger describes her personal experience with these women and their anguish. They became more than a social problem, but flesh and blood women without hope. She vowed to help these women even though the Comstock laws passed by Congress in 1873 banned the dissemination of information about birth control as obscene. In her state of New York, she faced fines and lengthy prison terms.

Having decided that "something had to be done to rescue these women who were voiceless" (*Autobiography* 106), Sanger lectured about her experiences as a nurse working with the poor and coined the term, birth control. In 1914 Sanger founded the National Birth Control League and began to publish her own newspaper, *The Woman Rebel*, which led to her arrest for writing indecent material. Later, charges were dropped, but she was again arrested in 1916 and served thirty days in the penitentiary for women when she opened a birth control clinic in Brooklyn. Sanger continued the struggle to make birth control available to women by founding the American Birth Control League in 1921 (which became the Planned Parenthood Foundation in 1942) and by organizing international conferences on birth control throughout the twenties, which eventually led to establishment of the International Planned Parenthood Federation in 1953.

Sanger was a pioneer in the movement to give women control over reproduction and parents the right to make responsible decisions about the size of their families. In *Woman and the New Race* (1920), she wrote, "No woman can call herself free who does not own and control her own body. No woman can call herself free until she can choose consciously whether she will or will not be a mother." Sanger's work changed the face of modern life. According to Gloria Steinem, H. G. Wells said in 1931 that "When the history of our civilization is written, it will be a biological history, and Margaret Sanger will be its heroine."

Inherent in this essay is the idea that parents have the right and responsibility to determine how many children they will have. What is the interest of the state in reproduction? Do parents have this individual right? As a nurse, what responsibilities did Sanger have to her patients? Do these responsibilities override the legal law that prohibited the distribution of information about birth control? What role does a woman's right to control her own body have in the larger fight for women's suffrage or equal rights?

The Turbid Ebb and Flow of Misery (1938)

"Every night and every morn
Some to misery are born,
Every morn and every night
Some are born to sweet delight.
Some are born to sweet delight,
Some are born to endless night."
William Blake

During these years in New York trained nurses were in great demand. Few people wanted to enter hospitals; they were afraid they might be "practiced" upon, and consented to go only in desperate emergencies. Sentiment was especially vehement in the matter of having babies. A woman's own bedroom, no matter how inconveniently arranged, was the usual place for her lying-in. I was not sufficiently free from domestic duties to be a general nurse, but I could ordinarily manage obstetrical cases because I was notified far enough ahead to plan my schedule. And after serving my two weeks I could get home again.

Sometimes I was summoned to small apartments occupied by young clerks, insurance salesmen, or lawyers, just starting out, most of them under thirty and whose wives were having their first or second baby. They were always eager to know the best and latest method in infant care and feeding. In particular, Jewish patients, whose lives centered around the family, welcomed advice and followed it implicitly.

But more and more my calls began to come from the Lower East Side, as though I were being magnetically drawn there by some force outside my control. I hated the wretchedness and hopelessness of the poor, and never experienced that satisfaction in working among them that so many noble women have found. My concern for my patients was now quite different from my earlier hospital attitude. I could see that much was wrong with them which did not appear in the physiological or medical diagnosis. A woman in childbirth was not merely a woman in childbirth. My expanded outlook included a view of her background, her potentialities as a human being, the kind of children she was bearing, and what was going to happen to them.

The wives of small shopkeepers were my most frequent cases, but I had carpenters, truck drivers, dishwashers, and pushcart vendors. I admired intensely the consideration most of these people had for their own. Money to

449

pay doctor and nurse had been carefully saved months in advance—parents-in-law, grandfathers, grandmothers, all contributing.

As soon as the neighbors learned that a nurse was in the building they came in a friendly way to visit, often carrying fruit, jellies, or gefüllter fish made after a cherished recipe. It was infinitely pathetic to me that they, so poor themselves, should bring me food. Later they drifted in again with the excuse of getting the plate, and sat down for a nice talk; there was no hurry. Always back of the little gift was the question, "I am pregnant (or my daughter, or my sister is). Tell me something to keep from having another baby. We cannot afford another yet."

I tried to explain the only two methods I had ever heard among the middle classes, both of which were invariably brushed aside as unacceptable. They were of no certain avail to the wife because they placed the burden of responsibility solely upon the husband—a burden which he seldom assumed. What she was seeking was self-protection she could herself use, and there was none.

Below this stratum of society was one in truly desperate circumstances. The men were sullen and unskilled, picking up odd jobs now and then, but more often unemployed, lounging in and out of the house at all hours of the day and night. The women seemed to slink on their way to market and were without neighborliness.

These submerged, untouched classes were beyond the scope of organized charity or religion. No labor union, no church, not even the Salvation Army reached them. They were apprehensive of everyone and rejected help of any kind, ordering all intruders to keep out; both birth and death they considered their own business. Social agents, who were just beginning to appear, were profoundly mistrusted because they pried into homes and lives, asking questions about wages, how many were in the family, had any of them ever been in jail. Often two or three had been there or were now under suspicion of prostitution, shoplifting, purse snatching, petty thievery, and, in consequence, passed furtively by the big blue uniforms on the corner.

The utmost depression came over me as I approached this surreptitious region. Below Fourteenth Street I seemed to be breathing a different air, to be in another world and country where the people had habits and customs alien to anything I had ever heard about.

There were then approximately ten thousand apartments in New York into which no sun ray penetrated directly; such windows as they had opened only on a narrow court from which rose fetid odors. It was seldom cleaned, though garbage and refuse often went down into it. All these dwellings were pervaded by the foul breath of poverty, that moldy, indefinable, indescribable smell which cannot be fumigated out, sickening to me but apparently unnoticed by those who lived there. When I set to work with antiseptics, their pungent sting, at least temporarily, obscured the stench.

I remember one confinement case to which I was called by the doctor of an insurance company. I climbed up the five flights and entered the airless rooms, but the baby had come with too great speed. A boy of ten had been the only assistant. Five flights was a long way; he had wrapped the placenta in a piece of newspaper and dropped it out the window into the court.

Many families took in "boarders," as they were termed, whose small contributions paid the rent. These derelicts, wanderers, alternately working and drinking, were crowded in with the children; a single room sometimes held as many as six sleepers. Little girls were accustomed to dressing and undressing in front of the men, and were often violated, occasionally by their own fathers or brothers, before they reached the age of puberty.

Pregnancy was a chronic condition among the women of this class. Suggestions as to what to do for a girl who was "in trouble" or a married woman who was "caught" passed from mouth to mouth—herb teas, turpentine, steaming, rolling downstairs, inserting slippery elm, knitting needles, shoe-hooks. When they had word of a new remedy they hurried to the drugstore, and if the clerk were inclined to be friendly he might say, "Oh, that won't help you, but here's something that may." The younger druggists usually refused to give advice because, if it were to be known, they would come under the law; midwives were even more fearful. The doomed women implored me to reveal the "secret" rich people had, offering to pay me extra to tell them; many really believed I was holding back information for money. They asked everybody and tried anything, but nothing did them any good. On Saturday nights I have seen groups of from fifty to one hundred with their shawls over their heads waiting outside the office of a five-dollar abortionist.

Each time I returned to this district, which was becoming a recurrent nightmare, I used to hear that Mrs. Cohen "had been carried to a hospital, but had never come back," or that Mrs. Kelly "had sent the children to a neighbor and had put her head into the gas oven." Day after day such tales were poured into my ears—a baby born dead, great relief—a death of an older child, sorrow but again relief of a sort—the story told a thousand times of death from abortion and children going into institutions. I shuddered with horror as I listened to the details and studied the reasons back of them—destitution linked with excessive childbearing. The waste of life seemed utterly senseless. One by one worried, sad, pensive, and aging faces marshaled themselves before me in my dreams, sometimes appealingly, sometimes accusingly.

These were not merely "unfortunate conditions among the poor" such as we read about. I knew the women personally. They were living, breathing, human beings, with hopes, fears, and aspirations like my own, yet their weary, misshapen bodies, "always ailing, never failing," were destined to be thrown on the scrap heap before they were thirty-five. I could not escape from the facts of their wretchedness; neither was I able to see any way out. My own cozy and comfortable family existence was becoming a reproach to me.

Then one stifling mid-July day of 1912 I was summoned to a Grand Street tenement. My patient was a small, slight Russian Jewess, about twenty-eight years old, of the special cast of features to which suffering lends a madonna-like expression. The cramped three-room apartment was in a sorry state of turmoil. Jake Sachs, a truck driver scarcely older than his wife, had come home to find the three children crying and her unconscious from the effects of a self-induced abortion. He had called the nearest doctor, who in turn had sent for me. Jake's earnings were trifling, and most of them had gone to keep the none-too-strong children clean and properly fed. But his wife's ingenuity had helped them to save a little, and this he was glad to spend on a nurse rather than have her go to a hospital.

The doctor and I settled ourselves to the task of fighting the septicemia. Never had I worked so fast, never so concentratedly. The sultry days and nights were melted into a torpid inferno. It did not seem possible there could be such heat, and every bit of food, ice, and drugs had to be carried up three flights of stairs.

Jake was more kind and thoughtful than many of the husbands I had encountered. He loved his children, and had always helped his wife wash and dress them. He had brought water up and carried garbage down before he left in the morning, and did as much as he could for me while he anxiously watched her progress.

After a fortnight Mrs. Sachs' recovery was in sight. Neighbors, ordinarily fatalistic as to the results of abortion, were genuinely pleased that she had survived. She smiled wanly at all who came to see her and thanked them gently, but she could not respond to their hearty congratulations. She appeared to be more despondent and anxious than she should have been, and spent too much time in meditation.

At the end of three weeks, as I was preparing to leave the fragile patient to take up her difficult life once more, she finally voiced her fears, "Another baby will finish me, I suppose?"

"It's too early to talk about that," I temporized.

But when the doctor came to make his last call, I drew him aside. "Mrs. Sachs is terribly worried about having another baby."

"She well may be," replied the doctor, and then he stood before her and said, "Any more such capers, young woman, and there'll be no need to send for me."

"I know, doctor," she replied timidly, "but," and she hesitated as though it took all her courage to say it, "what can I do to prevent it?"

The doctor was a kindly man, and he had worked hard to save her, but such incidents had become so familiar to him that he had long since lost whatever delicacy he might once have had. He laughed good-naturedly. "You want to have your cake and eat it too, do you? Well, it can't be done."

Then picking up his hat and bag to depart he said, "Tell Jake to sleep on the roof."

I glanced quickly at Mrs. Sachs. Even through my sudden tears I could see stamped on her face an expression of absolute despair. We simply looked at each other, saying no word until the door closed behind the doctor. Then she lifted her thin, blue-veined hands and clasped them beseechingly. "He can't understand. He's a man. But you do, don't you? Please tell me the secret, and I'll never breathe it to a soul. *Please!*"

What was I to do? I could not speak the conventionally comforting phrases which would be of no comfort. Instead, I made her as physically easy as I could and promised to come back in a few days to talk with her again. A little later, when she slept, I tiptoed away.

Night after night the wistful image of Mrs. Sachs appeared before me. I made all sorts of excuses to myself for not going back. I was busy on other cases; I really did not know what to say to her or how to convince her of my own ignorance; I was helpless to avert such monstrous atrocities. Time rolled by and I did nothing.

The telephone rang one evening three months later, and Jake Sachs' agitated voice begged me to come at once; his wife was sick again and from the same cause. For a wild moment I thought of sending someone else, but actually, of course, I hurried into my uniform, caught up my bag, and started out. All the way I longed for a subway wreck, an explosion, anything to keep me from having to enter that home again. But nothing happened, even to delay me. I turned into the dingy doorway and climbed the familiar stairs once more. The children were there, young little things.

Mrs. Sachs was in a coma and died within ten minutes. I folded her still hands across her breast, remembering how they had pleaded with me, begging so humbly for the knowledge which was her right. I drew a sheet over her pallid face. Jake was sobbing, running hands through his hair and pulling it out like an insane person. Over and over again he wailed, "My God! My God! My God!"

I left him pacing desperately back and forth, and for hours I myself walked and walked and walked through the hushed streets. When I finally arrived home and let myself quietly in, all the household was sleeping. I looked out my window and down upon the dimly lighted city. Its pains and griefs crowded in upon me, a moving picture rolled before my eyes with photographic clearness: women writhing in travail to bring forth little babies; the babies themselves naked and hungry, wrapped in newspapers to keep them from the cold; six-year-old children with pinched, pale, wrinkled faces, old in concentrated wretchedness, pushed into gray and fetid cellars, crouching on stone floors, their small scrawny hands scuttling through rags, making lamp shades, artificial flowers; white coffins, black coffins, coffins, coffins interminably passing in never-ending succession. The scenes piled one upon another on another. I could bear it no longer.

As I stood there the darkness faded. The sun came up and threw its reflection over the house tops. It was the dawn of a new day in my life also. The doubt and questioning, the experimenting and trying, were now to be put behind me. I knew I could not go back merely to keeping people alive.

I went to bed, knowing that no matter what it might cost, I was finished with palliatives and superficial cures; I was resolved to seek out the root of evil, to do something to change the destiny of mothers whose miseries were vast as the sky.

IX. Crisis in the Years of World War

Helena Marie Swanwick

1864–1939

The British Feminist movement was severed in two by the outbreak of World War I. The more militant wing of the movement (associated with the Pankhursts' Women's Social and Political Union) declared a truce with the government and ceased its pro-suffrage agitation in order to support the war effort. Other feminists believed it was women's duty to oppose war on behalf of motherhood and in protest against women's continued exclusion from decision-making.

Helena Maria Sickert Swanwick was one of the latter. Daughter of a Danish father and British mother, she graduated from one of England's new women's colleges (Girton). Swanwick made her living as a journalist, even gaining employment with the nationally prominent *Manchester Guardian*. She also edited *The Common Cause*, the main women's suffrage publication, and published numerous pamphlets.

In the following selection, Swanwick gives voice to the maternalism common to feminist-pacifists: the deaths, not just of soldiers but of farm animals and the land itself, would forever render women grief-stricken. She appealed to widows deprived of husbands and perhaps sons, and to other women deprived of the chance to ever have either. Swanwick's feminism also contains equal-rights strands. She expresses concern not only for the women who lost their loved ones during the war, but also for those who would lose the new-found independence war afforded them. She insists that "all human questions effect all humanity," and that therefore war is women's business just as care for children is men's.

Swanwick's anti-war publications were censored by the government, while other pacifists of both genders were jailed for treason. On what grounds do governments suppress citizens' freedom of expression? How does women's lack of rights render them above the law? Is maternalist-feminism one possible way to reconcile individual rights with the needs of community?

from *The War and Its Effect upon Women* (1915)

How has the war affected women? How will it affect them? Women, as half the human race, are compelled to take their share of evil and good with men, the other half. The destruction of property, the increase of taxation, the rise of prices, the devastation of beautiful things in nature and art—these are felt by men as well as by women. Some losses doubtless appeal to one or the other sex with peculiar poignancy, but it would be difficult to say whose sufferings are the greater, though there can be no doubt at all that men get an exhilaration out of war which is denied to most women. When they see pictures of soldiers encamped in the ruins of what was once a home, amidst the dead bodies of gentle milk cows, most women would be thinking too insistently of the babies who must die for need of milk to entertain the exhilaration which no doubt may be felt at "the good work of our guns." When they read of miles upon miles of kindly earth made barren, the hearts of men may be wrung to think of wasted toil, but to women the thought suggests a simile full of an even deeper pathos; they will think of the millions of young lives destroyed, each one having cost the travail and care of a mother, and of the millions of young bodies made barren by the premature death of those who should have been their mates. The millions of widowed maidens in the coming generation will have to turn their thoughts away from one particular joy and fulfillment of life. While men in war give what is, at the present stage of the world's development, the peculiar service of men, let them not forget that in rendering that very service they are depriving a corresponding number of women of the opportunity of rendering what must, at all stages of the world's development, be the peculiar service of women. After the war, men will go on doing what has been regarded as men's work; women, deprived of their own, will also have to do much of what has been regarded as men's work. These things are going to affect women profoundly, and one hopes that the reconstruction of society is going to be met by the whole people—men and women—with a sympathetic understanding of each other's circumstances. When what are known as men's questions are discussed, it is generally assumed that the settlement of them depends upon men only; when what are known as women's questions are discussed, there is never any suggestion that they can be settled by women independently of men. Of course they cannot. But, then, neither can "men's questions" be rightly settled so. In fact, life would be far more truly envisaged if we dropped the silly phrases "men's and women's questions"; for, indeed, there are no such matters, and all human questions affect all humanity.

Now, for the right consideration of human questions, it is necessary for humans to understand each other. This catastrophic war will do one good thing if it opens our eyes to real live women as they are, as we know them in workaday life, but as the politician and the journalist seem not to have known them. . . .

Women are, through the war, becoming good "copy." But women have not suddenly become patriotic, or capable, or self-sacrificing; the great mass of women have always shown these qualities in their humble daily life. Now that their services are asked for in unfamiliar directions, attention is being attracted to them, and many more people are realising that, with extended training and opportunity, women's capacity for beneficent work would be extended. The fiction of women's incapacity must have indeed bitten deep, when it could be supposed that it required a "superwoman" to clip a ticket![1]

There never was any justification for that sort of sentimentalism, but we are now in some danger of sentimentalism of the opposite kind. Extravagant writers are filling the papers with assertions that women in engineering works can do two or three times as much work as men, and that raw female hands can plough a straighter and deeper furrow in heavy soil than practised men are able. All this does nothing but harm. If unpractised women have turned out more work at a lathe than practised men, it is most assuredly not because the men could not have turned out more than they did; we must seek for other reasons. The problem of the readjustment of men's and women's work after the war is going to be so difficult and so great that we want none of this frivolous sentimentality in dealing with it. We want facts. We want a sober judgment. We want an alert mind, which will meet the problems with no dead obstructive prejudices, but with the single intention to make the very best use of the men and women who will emerge from this ghastly catastrophe. To condemn any section of the people to inaction, to restrict or cramp their powers of production and of healing, is going to cripple the nation and be the most unpatriotic course conceivable.

It is often forgotten that for full prosperity a country needs to be producing as much wealth as possible, consistently with the health, freedom, and happiness of its people. To arrive at this desired result, it is quite clear that as many people as possible should be employed productively, and it is one of the unhappy results of our economic anarchy that employers have found it profitable to have a large reserve class of unemployed and that wage-earners have been driven to try and diminish their own numbers and to restrict their own output. To keep women out of the "labour market" (by artificial restrictions, such as the refusal to work with them, or the refusal to allow them to be trained, or the refusal to adapt conditions to their health requirements) is in truth anti-social. But it is easy to see how such anti-social restrictions have been forced upon the workers, and it is futile to blame them. A way must be found out of industrial war before we can hope that industry will be carried on thriftily. Men and women must take counsel together and let the experience of the war teach them how to solve economic problems by co-operation rather than conflict. Women have been increasingly conscious of the satisfaction to be got from economic independence, of the sweetness of earned bread, of the dreary depression of subjection. They have felt the bitterness of being "kept out"; they are feeling the exhilaration of being "brought in." They are ripe for instruction and organisation in working for the good of the whole. . . .

The return of millions of men to civil life and work will tax the goodwill and organising capacity of the whole nation. The change from war production to peace production will possibly be even greater. The readjustments required must necessarily be slow and difficult, and unless there can be co-operation between employers and employed, and between all sections of employed, there will be friction to the raw and many disastrous mistakes.

Because it will obviously be impossible for all to find work quickly (not to speak of the right kind of work), there is almost certain to be an outcry for the restriction of work in various directions, and one of the first cries (if we may judge from the past) will be to women: "Back to the Home!" This cry will be raised whether the women have a home or not. All who care for the good of the whole must meet this cry and all that it implies with a sympathetic understanding of all sides of the problem, and a grasp, not only of present difficulties, but of the needs of the future, and there must be no hurried rushing into emergency measures which will seriously cripple future development. We must understand the unimpeachable right of the man who has lost his work and risked his life for his country, to find decent employment, decent wages and conditions, on his return to civil life. We must also understand the enlargement and enhancements of life which women feel when they are able to live by their own productive work, and we must realise that to deprive women of the right to live by their work is to send them back to a moral imprisonment (to say nothing of physical and intellectual starvation), of which they become now for the first time fully conscious. And we must realise the exceeding danger that conscienceless employers may regard women's labour as preferable, owing to its cheapness and its docility, and that women, if unsympathetically treated by their male relatives and fellow workers, may be tempted to continue to be cheap and docile in the hands of those who have no desire except that of exploiting them and the community. The kind of man who likes "to keep women in their place" may find he has made slaves who will be used by his enemies against him. Men need have no fear of free women; it is the slaves and the parasites who are a deadly danger.

The demand for equal wage for equal work has been hotly pressed by men since the war began, and it is all to the good so far as it goes. But most men are still far from realising the solidarity of their interests with those of women in all departments of life, and are still too placidly accepting the fact that women are sweated over work which is not the same as that of men. They don't realise yet that starved womanhood means starved manhood, and they don't enough appreciate the rousing and infectious character of a generous attitude on the part of men, who, in fighting the women's battles unselfishly and from a love of right, would stimulate the women to corresponding generosity. There are no comrades more staunch and loyal than women, where men have engaged their truth and courage. But men must treat them as comrades; they must no longer think only of how they can "eliminate female labour"; they must take the women into their trade unions and other organisations, and they must understand that the complexities of a woman's life are not of her invention or choosing, but are due to her function as mother of men.

The sexual side of a woman's life gravely affects the economic side, and we can never afford to overlook this. As mothers and home-makers women are doing work of the highest national importance and economic value, but this value is one which returns to the nation as a whole and only in small and very uncertain part to the women themselves. The fact that a woman is a wife and mother diminishes her value in the "labour market," and even the fact that she is liable to become a wife and mother has done so in the past. Unless men are prepared to socialise the responsibilities of parenthood, one does not see how women's labour is ever to be organised for the welfare of the whole, nor does one see how women are to perform their priceless functions of motherhood as well as possible if they are to be penalised for them in the future as they have been in the past. I do not overlook the complexity of the problem of the reconcilement of women's work as mothers with their work as home-makers and wage-earners, but I plead that the problem should be treated as a whole and not in scraps, as hitherto. . . .

Note

[1] A published snapshot of the first women ticket collectors on English buses had been captioned "Superwomen."

Adolf Hitler

1889–1945

Born in Austria, Adolf Hitler was the son of Alois Hitler, a customs official in Linz. Hitler left school at the age of sixteen, having done poorly and failing to graduate; he aspired to become an artist, but was refused admission
twice by the Academy of Fine Arts in Vienna. For a time, he made a living
painting postcards and designing advertisements. In 1913, he was rejected by
the Austrian military as unfit to serve, but joined the German army reserves
shortly after the start of World War I. When the war ended, Hitler joined the
German Workers' Party, which was renamed the National Socialist (Nazi)
Party in 1920. Germany's defeat in World War I had shattered the spirit of the
German people, who had been led to believe that the war was going well. The
punitive terms handed down by the Treaty of Versailles aggravated the economic hardship and overall discontent in Germany. Hitler was quickly able to
capitalize on German disillusionment, rising to the presidency of the Nazi
Party by July 1921. Under his leadership, the Party played on the widespread
public perception that Germany had been politically and economically undermined by Jews, liberals, Marxists, and others. Nazi leaders advanced an
extremist agenda of ethnocentric nationalism and a revitalized German mili-
tary-industrial complex.

Hitler was imprisoned in 1923 after the failed Munich *putsch*, a coup to
overthrow the existing government. However, the right-wing judicial system
was sympathetic to his political program and sentenced him to five years, so
that he would be freed in less than a year. During his time in prison, Hitler
wrote *Mein Kampf* (1923–1924; trans. *My Struggle*), which outlines his ultra-
rightist philosophy and anticipates much of his future political vision for
Germany. In *Mein Kampf,* Hitler articulates his conception of the German
people as descendants of a superior "Aryan race," advocating an aggressive foreign policy and identifying the enemies of Nazism. Released from prison, he
took advantage of the deepening depression and growing popularity of right-
wing politics. Hitler opposed Paul von Hindenburg in the presidential election
of 1932 and lost, but nonetheless found his way to leadership, when President
von Hindenburg appointed him Chancellor, with the expectation that he
could be brought under control. Hitler quickly seized dictatorial powers and
the totalitarian rule of Germany was underway.

Hitler's ideas were simple and had great appeal to the unhappy German masses. As an orator, he mesmerized audiences, offering them a renewed sense of purpose through his idea of the Third Reich as a transformative epoch in German history. Their true destiny, he contended, was to rule Europe and the first stage in this plan was to expand eastward by wresting away *Lebensraum* ("living space") from the "inferior" Slavic nations. This military strategy touched off World War II, which lasted from 1939 to 1945, leaving scores of millions dead and changing irrevocably our modern worldview. Hitler's program of conquest and expansion found its most terrifying expression in its demand for the systematic extermination of "lesser" peoples, including Poles, Gypsies, homosexuals, the disabled, and most insistently all of European Jewry, whom he vilified as the cause of nearly all the world's evil. On April 4, 1945, as the invading Soviets neared the capital of his defeated country, Hitler committed suicide.

Mein Kampf challenges us to examine our own willingness to follow the charismatic individual, to demonize those we have cast on the margins of society, and to glorify reductive solutions to complex political difficulties. According to Hitler, what is the function of blame in a propaganda campaign and to what audience should leaders direct their propaganda? What role does "the big lie" play in shaping ideology and its expression in political propaganda? What are the core principles Hitler employed so effectively and how might we recognize them at work in our own politics?

from *Mein Kampf* (1923–1924)

III. General Political Considerations Based on My Vienna Period

• • •

But the power which has always started the greatest religious and political avalanches in history rolling has from time immemorial been the magic power of the spoken word, and that alone.

Particularly the broad masses of the people can be moved only by the power of speech. And all great movements are popular movements, volcanic eruptions of human passions and emotional sentiments, stirred either by the cruel Goddess of Distress or by the firebrand of the word hurled among the masses; they are not the lemonade-like outpourings of literary aesthetes and drawing-room heroes.

• • •

A movement with great aims must therefore be anxiously on its guard not to lose contact with the broad masses.

It must examine every question primarily from this standpoint and make its decisions accordingly.

It must, furthermore, avoid everything which might diminish or even weaken its ability to move the masses, not for 'demagogic' reasons, but in the simple knowledge that without the mighty force of the mass of a people, no great idea, however lofty and noble it may seem, can be realized.

• • •

In general the art of all truly great national leaders at all times consists among other things primarily in not dividing the attention of a people, but in concentrating it upon a single foe. The more unified the application of a people's will to fight, the greater will be the magnetic attraction of a movement and the mightier will be the impetus of the thrust. It belongs to the genius of a great leader to make even adversaries far removed from one another seem to belong to a single category, because in weak and uncertain characters the knowledge of having different enemies can only too readily lead to the beginning of doubt in their own right.

VI. War Propaganda

• • •

The second really decisive question was this: To whom should propaganda be addressed? To the scientifically trained intelligentsia or to the less educated masses?

It must be addressed always and exclusively to the masses.

• • •

All propaganda must be popular and its intellectual level must be adjusted to the most limited intelligence among those it is addressed to. Consequently, the greater the mass it is intended to reach, the lower its purely intellectual level will have to be. But if, as in propaganda for sticking out a war, the aim is to influence a whole people, we must avoid excessive intellectual demands on our public, and too much caution cannot be exerted in this direction.

The more modest its intellectual ballast, the more exclusively it takes into consideration the emotions of the masses, the more effective it will be. And this is the best proof of the soundness or unsoundness of a propaganda campaign, and not success in pleasing a few scholars or young aesthetes.

The art of propaganda lies in understanding the emotional ideas of the great masses and finding, through a psychologically correct form, the way to the attention and thence to the heart of the broad masses. The fact that our bright boys do not understand this merely shows how mentally lazy and conceited they are.

Once we understand how necessary it is for propaganda to be adjusted to the broad mass, the following rule results:

It is a mistake to make propaganda many-sided, like scientific instruction, for instance.

The receptivity of the great masses is very limited, their intelligence is small, but their power of forgetting is enormous. In consequence of these facts, all effective propaganda must be limited to a very few points and must harp on these in slogans until the last member of the public understands what you want him to understand by your slogan. As soon as you sacrifice this slogan and try to be many-sided, the effect will piddle away, for the crowd can neither digest nor retain the material offered. In this way the result is weakened and in the end entirely cancelled out.

• • •

X. Causes of the Collapse

• • •

It required the whole bottomless falsehood of the Jews and their Marxist fighting organization to lay the blame for the collapse on that very man who alone, with superhuman energy and will power, tried to prevent the catastrophe he foresaw and save the nation from its time of deepest humiliation and disgrace. By branding Ludendorff[1] as guilty for the loss of the World War, they took the weapon of moral right from the one dangerous accuser who could have risen against the traitors to the fatherland. In this they proceeded on the sound principle that the magnitude of a lie always contains a certain factor of credibility, since the great masses of the people in the very bottom of their hearts tend to be corrupted rather than consciously and purposely evil, and that, therefore, in view of the primitive simplicity of their minds, they more easily fall a victim to a big lie than to a little one, since they themselves lie in little things, but would be ashamed of lies that were too big.

• • •

XI. Nation and Race

• • •

No more than Nature desires the mating of weaker with stronger individuals, even less does she desire the blending of a higher with a lower race, since, if she did, her whole work of higher breeding, over perhaps hundreds of thousands of years, night be ruined with one blow.

Historical experience offers countless proofs of this. It shows with terrifying clarity that in every mingling of Aryan blood with that of lower peoples the result was the end of the cultured people. North America, whose population consists in by far the largest part of Germanic elements who mixed but little with the lower colored peoples, shows a different humanity and culture from Central and South America, where the predominantly Latin immigrants often mixed with the aborigines on a large scale. By this one example, we can clearly and distinctly recognize the effect of racial mixture. The Germanic inhabitant of the American continent, who has remained racially pure and unmixed, rose to be master of the continent; he will remain the master as long as he does not fall a victim to defilement of the blood.

The result of all racial crossing is therefore in brief always the following:

(a) lowering of the level of the higher race;

(b) physical and intellectual regression and hence the beginning of a slowly but surely progressing sickness.

To bring about such a development is, then, nothing else but to sin against the will of the eternal creator.

• • •

Everything we admire on this earth today—science and art, technology and inventions—is only the creative product of a few peoples and originally perhaps of *one* race. On them depends the existence of this whole culture. If they perish, the beauty of this earth will sink into the grave with them.

However much the soil, for example, can influence men, the result of the influence will always be different depending on the races in question. The low fertility of a living space may spur the one race to the highest achievements; in others it will only be the cause of bitterest poverty and final undernourishment with all its consequences. The inner nature of peoples is always determining for the manner in which outward influences will be effective. What leads the one to starvation trains the other to hard work.

All great cultures of the past perished only because the originally creative race died out from blood poisoning.

The ultimate cause of such a decline was their forgetting that all culture depends on men and not conversely; hence that to preserve a certain culture the man who creates it must be preserved. This preservation is bound up with the rigid law of necessity and the right to victory of the best and stronger in this world.

Those who want to live, let them fight, and those who do not want to fight in this world of eternal struggle do not deserve to live.

• • •

If we were to divide mankind into three groups, the founders of culture, the bearers of culture, the destroyers of culture, only the Aryan could be considered as the representative of the first group. From him originate the foundations and walls of all human creation, and only the outward form and color are determined by the changing traits of character of the various peoples. He provides the mightiest building stones and plans for all human progress and only the execution corresponds to the nature of the varying men and races.

• • •

Thus, the Jew of all times has lived in the states of other peoples, and there formed his own state, which, to be sure, habitually sailed under the disguise of 'religious community' as long as outward circumstances made a complete revelation of his nature seem inadvisable. But as soon as he felt strong enough to do without the protective cloak, he always dropped the veil and suddenly became what so many of the others previously did not want to believe and see: the Jew.

The Jew's life as a parasite in the body of other nations and states explains a characteristic which once caused Schopenhauer, as has already been mentioned, to call him the 'great master in lying.' Existence impels the Jew to lie, and to lie perpetually, just as it compels the inhabitants of the northern countries to wear warm clothing.

His life within other peoples can only endure for any length of time if he succeeds in arousing the opinion that he is not a people but a 'religious community,' though of a special sort.

And this is the first great lie.

• • •

But even more: all at once the Jew also becomes liberal and begins to rave about the necessary progress of mankind.

Slowly he makes himself the spokesman of a new era.

Also, of course, he destroys more and more thoroughly the foundations of any economy that will really benefit the people. By way of stock shares he pushes his way into the circuit of national production which he turns into a purchasable or rather tradable object, thus robbing the enterprises of the foundations of a personal ownership. Between employer and employee there arises that inner estrangement which later leads to political class division.

Finally, the Jewish influence on economic affairs grows with terrifying speed through the stock exchange. He becomes the owner, or at least the controller, of the national labor force.

• • •

Since the Jew is not the attacked but the attacker, not only anyone who attacks passes as his enemy, but also anyone who resists him. But the means with which he seeks to break such reckless but upright souls is not honest warfare, but lies and slander.

Here he stops at nothing, and in his vileness he becomes so gigantic that no one need be surprised if among our people the personification of the devil as the symbol of all evil assumes the living shape of the Jew.

The ignorance of the broad masses about the inner nature of the Jew, the lack of instinct and narrow-mindedness of our upper classes, make the people an easy victim for this Jewish campaign of lies.

• • •

With satanic joy in his face, the black-haired Jewish youth lurks in wait for the unsuspecting girl whom he defiles with his blood, thus stealing her from her people. With every means he tries to destroy the racial foundations of the people he has set out to subjugate. Just as he himself systematically ruins women and girls, he does not shrink back from pulling down the blood barriers for others, even on a large scale. It was and it is Jews who bring the Negroes into the Rhineland, always with the same secret thought and clear aim of ruining the hated white race by the necessarily resulting bastardization, throwing it down from its cultural and political height, and himself rising to be its master.

For a racially pure people which is conscious of its blood can never be enslaved by the Jew. In this world he will forever be master over bastards and bastards alone.

And so he tries systematically to lower the racial level by a continuous poisoning of individuals.

And in politics he begins to replace the idea of democracy by the dictatorship of the proletariat.

In the organized mass of Marxism he has found the weapon which lets him dispense with democracy and in its stead allows him to subjugate and govern the peoples with a dictatorial and brutal fist.

• • •

Volume Two
The Socialist Movement

I. Philosophy and Party

• • •

Human culture and civilization on this continent are inseparably bound up with the presence of the Aryan. If he dies out or declines, the dark veils of an age without culture will again descend on this globe.

The undermining of the existence of human culture by the destruction of its bearer seems in the eyes of a folkish philosophy the most execrable crime. Anyone who dares to lay hands on the highest image of the Lord commits sacrilege against the benevolent creator of this miracle and contributes to the expulsion from paradise.

And so the folkish philosophy of life corresponds to the innermost will of Nature, since it restores that free play of forces which must lead to a continuous mutual higher breeding, until at last the best of humanity, having achieved possession of this earth, will have a free path for activity in domains which will lie partly above it and partly outside it.

We all sense that in the distant future humanity must be faced by problems which only a highest race, become master people and supported by the means and possibilities of an entire globe, will be equipped to overcome.

● ● ●

Note

¹ Erich Ludendorff (1865–1937), a high-ranking World War I German military commander who insisted on an armistice after it became clear to him that Germany would lose the war.

John Maynard Keynes

1883–1946

John Maynard Keynes was born into an intellectual, well-to-do family in England. He developed quickly into a brilliant student, studying at Eton and Cambridge. He served as an economic advisor at the Versailles Peace Conference following World War I, but protested the harsh economic sanctions imposed upon Germany and finally resigned his position at the conference. His publication of *The Economic Consequences of the Peace* (1919) provided a probing economic and political analysis of the conditions of the Versailles Treaty, concluding that they would have disastrous repercussions in Europe.

In 1936, Keynes's *The General Theory of Unemployment, Interest and Money* provided a theoretical explanation for the observation some economists were making that classical economic theory was not working in modern capitalist systems. The stock market crash of 1929 and the ensuing Great Depression of the 1930s posed a serious threat to industrial societies shaped by *laissez-faire* theory, as articulated by Adam Smith, that economies performed best when left alone by governments so that the natural forces of supply and demand might bring about low unemployment and continued growth. Persistent faith in this classical hands-off policy prevented President Hoover from doing anything in response to the crash, leading to the landslide victory of Franklin D. Roosevelt. Working from intuition and common sense, Roosevelt crafted his "New Deal," in which government would become more involved in economic decision-making and would take a more direct role in creating economic opportunity.

In the *General Theory*, Keynes offered a detailed analysis showing that government intervention, in the form of increased government spending, was justified in order to address conditions of high unemployment, even if this meant deficit spending. In times of economic difficulty, he argued, private expenditures, if left unsupplemented, would be insufficient to generate necessary demand for goods, resulting in production cutbacks, greater unemployment, and spiraling depression.

In the following excerpt of *The End of Laissez-Faire* (1926), how does Keynes describe the limitations of classical economics? How is Keynes critical of the roles played by one's natural liberty and self-interest? What does Keynes say about Marxist socialism?

from *The End of Laissez-Faire* (1926)

The parallelism between economic *laissez-faire* and Darwinism, already briefly noted, is now seen, as Herbert Spencer was foremost to recognise, to be very close indeed. Just as Darwin invoked sexual love, acting through sexual selection, as an adjutant to Natural Selection by competition, to direct evolution along lines which should be desirable as well as effective, so the individualist invokes the love of money, acting through the pursuit of profit, as an adjutant to bring about the production on the greatest possible scale of what is most strongly desired as measured by exchange value.

The beauty and the simplicity of such a theory are so great that it is easy to forget that it follows not from the actual facts, but from an incomplete hypothesis introduced for the sake of simplicity. Apart from other objections to be mentioned later, the conclusion that individuals acting independently for their own advantage will produce the greatest aggregate of wealth, depends on a variety of unreal assumptions to the effect that the processes of production and consumption are in no way organic, that there exists a sufficient foreknowledge of conditions and requirements, and that there are adequate opportunities of obtaining this foreknowledge. For economists generally reserve for a later stage of their argument the complications which arise—(1) when the efficient units of production are large relatively to the units of consumption, (2) when overhead costs or joint costs are present, (3) when internal economies tend to the aggregation of production, (4) when the time required for adjustments is long, (5) when ignorance prevails over knowledge, and (6) when monopolies and combinations interfere with equality in bargaining—they reserve, that is to say, for a later stage their analysis of the actual facts. Moreover, many of those who recognise that the simplified hypothesis does not accurately correspond to fact conclude that it does not represent what is "natural" and therefore ideal. They regard the simplified hypothesis as health, and the further complications as disease.

Yet, besides this question of fact, there are other considerations, familiar enough, which rightly bring into the calculation the cost and character of the competitive struggle itself, and the tendency for wealth to be distributed where it is not appreciated most. If we have the welfare of the giraffes at heart, we must not overlook the sufferings of the shorter necks who are starved out, or the sweet leaves which fall to the ground and are trampled underfoot in the struggle, or the overfeeding of the long-necked ones, or the evil look of anxiety of struggling greediness which overcasts the mild faces of the herd.

But the principles of *laissez-faire* have had other allies besides economic text-books. It must be admitted that they have been confirmed in the minds of sound thinkers and the reasonable public by the poor quality of the opponent proposals—Protectionism on one hand, and Marxian Socialism on the other. Yet these doctrines are both characterised, not only or chiefly by their infringing the general presumption in favour of *laissez-faire*, but by mere logical fallacy. Both are examples of poor thinking, of inability to analyse a process and follow it out to its conclusion. The arguments against them, though reinforced by the principle of *laissez-faire*, do not strictly require it. Of the two, Protectionism is at least plausible, and the forces making for its popularity are nothing to wonder at. But Marxian Socialism must always remain a portent to the historians of Opinion—how a doctrine so illogical and so dull can have exercised so powerful and enduring an influence over the minds of men, and, through them, the events of history. At any rate, the obvious scientific deficiencies of these two schools greatly contributed to the prestige and authority of nineteenth-century *laissez-faire*.

Nor has the most notable divergence into centralised social action on a great scale—the conduct of the late war—encouraged reformers or dispelled old-fashioned prejudices. There is much to be said, it is true, on both sides. War experience in the organisation of socialised production has left some near observers optimistically anxious to repeat it in peace conditions. War socialism unquestionably achieved a production of wealth on a scale far greater than we even knew in Peace, for though the goods and services delivered were destined for immediate and fruitless extinction, none the less they were wealth. Nevertheless the dissipation of effort was also prodigious, and the atmosphere of waste and not counting the cost was disgusting to any thrifty of provident spirit.

Finally, Individualism and *laissez-faire* could not, in spite of their deep roots in the political and moral philosophies of the late eighteenth and early nineteenth centuries, have secured their lasting hold over the conduct of public affairs, if it had not been for their conformity with the needs and wishes of the business world of the day. They gave full scope to our erstwhile heroes, the great business men. "At least one-half of the best ability in the Western world," Marshall used to say, "is engaged in business." A great part of "the higher imagination" of the age was thus employed. It was on the activities of these men that our hopes of Progress were centred. "Men of this class," Marshall wrote, "live in constantly shifting visions, fashioned in their own brains, of various routes to their desired end; of the difficulties which Nature will oppose to them on each route, and of the better of her opposition. This imagination gains little credit with the people, because it is not allowed to run riot; its strength is disciplined by a stronger will; and its highest glory is to have attained great ends by means so simple that no one will know, and none but experts will even guess, how a dozen other expedients, each suggesting as much brilliancy to the hasty observer, were set aside in favour of it. The imagination of such a man is employed, like that of the master chess-player, in forecasting the obstacles which may be opposed to the successful issue of his far-reaching projects, and constantly rejecting brilliant suggestions because he has pictured to himself the counter-strokes to them. His strong nervous force is at the opposite extreme of human nature from that nervous irresponsibility which conceives hasty Utopian schemes, and which is rather to be compared to the bold facility of a weak player, who will speedily solve the most difficult chess problem by taking on himself to move the black men as well as the white."

This is a fine picture of the great Captain of Industry, the Master-Individualist, who serves us in serving himself, just as any other artist does. Yet this one, in his turn, is becoming a tarnished idol. We grow more doubtful whether it is he who will lead us into Paradise by the hand.

These many elements have contributed to the current intellectual bias, the mental make-up, the orthodoxy of the day. The compelling force of many of the original reasons has disappeared, but, as usual, the vitality of the con-clusions outlasts them. To suggest social action for the public good to the City of London[1] is like discussing the *Origins of Species* with a Bishop sixty years ago. The first reaction is not intellectual, but moral. An orthodoxy is in ques-tion, and the more persuasive the arguments the graver the offence. Nevertheless, venturing into the den of the lethargic monster, at any rate I have traced his claims and pedigree so as to show that he has ruled over us rather by hereditary right than by personal merit.

IV

Let us clear from the ground the metaphysical or general principles upon which, from time to time, *laissez-faire* has been founded. It is *not* true that individuals possess a prescriptive "natural liberty" in their economic activities. There is *no* "compact" conferring perpetual rights on those who Have or on those who Acquire. The world is *not* so governed from above that private and social interest always coincide. It is *not* so managed here below that in practice they coincide. It is *not* a correct deduction from the Principles of Economics that enlightened self-interest always operates in the public interest. Nor is it true that self-interest generally *is* enlightened; more often individuals acting separately to promote their own ends are too ignorant or too weak to attain even these. Experience does *not* show that individuals, when they make up a social unit, are always less clear-sighted than when they act separately.

We cannot therefore settle on abstract grounds, but must handle on its merits in detail what Burke termed "one of the finest problems in legislation, namely, to determine what the State ought to take upon itself to direct by the public wisdom, and what it ought to leave, with as little interference as possible, to individual exertion." We have to discriminate between what Bentham, in his forgotten but useful nomenclature, used to term *Agenda* and *Non-Agenda*, and to do this without Bentham's prior presumption that interference is, at the same time, "generally needless" and "generally pernicious." Perhaps the chief task of Economists at this hour is to distinguish afresh the *Agenda* of Government from the *Non-Agenda*; and the companion task of Politics is to devise forms of Government within a Democracy which shall be capable of accomplishing the *Agenda*.

Note

[1] This refers to the financial district, not to the city itself.

Winifred Holtby

1898–1935

Winifred Holtby was a member of that extraordinary generation of "new" women, including Virginia Woolf, who benefited from unprecedented access to educational and professional opportunities, and whose lives were shaped by WWI—women who were among the first to articulate what it meant to be "modern." Like all members of that generation, Holtby survived the horrors of one war, only to witness the rise of another as Fascism spread. She did not live to see WWII, which makes the prescience of her comments on her generation that much more striking. A dedicated activist and journalist, Holtby did not focus exclusively on "women's" issues; indeed, for her, the situation of women was inextricably linked to the larger forces sweeping the later 1920s and '30s.

In the following excerpt, Holtby explores what she calls the "slump complex." She refers in part to the "slump" in the economy due to the Depression, but her keenest insights shed light on the psychological ramifications of the slump. Hopelessness and hedonism characterized the attitudes of her generation. What are some of the causes and consequences of the slump? Does this characterization describe other generations of young people? How did high unemployment pit men and women against each other? Does the "slump" help explain people's acceptance of totalitarianism?

from *Women and a Changing Civilisation* (1934)

These disadvantages are further accentuated by a group of reactions which I shall call the "slump complex." They have been particularly conspicuous during the past five years, and affect especially those young men and women who grew into maturity since the Armistice. Their condition is natural; it is directly attributable to the circumstances of their epoch, but they are apt to overlook this and mistake it for an unalterable law of nature ignored with naïve ignorance by their elders.

The effect of the slump upon women's economic position is most obvious, not only in the problems of unemployment among both industrial and professional women, but still more in the bitterness surrounding the question of married women's paid employment, "pin money" office girls, unorganised casual female factory labour, and claims to alimony, maintenance and separation allowances. These are the dilemmas of scarcity. It is here that the shoe pinches when national purchasing power has failed to distribute adequately the products of industry.

During the War, women entered almost every branch of industry and most of the professions. Even the Diplomatic Service, still, when this book is written, closed to women (though a committee is inquiring into future possibilities) was temporarily invaded by the adventurous Gertrude Bell who, under the modest title of Temporary Assistant Political Officer, really acted as British representative in Iraq. In transport, engineering, chemicals, textiles, tailoring and woodwork, women took the places which, ever since the sorting-out process which followed the first disorganised scramble of the Industrial Revolution, had been reserved to men. They took and they enjoyed them.

Then the men returned, and on demobilisation demanded again the jobs which they had left. The position was not simple.

Some of the men had received promises that their work should be kept for them; but of these, some did not return. Some women surrendered their shovels, lathes and hoes without a grievance. Their work had been "for the duration of the war" and they had no desire to retain it.

But others thought differently. Women, they told themselves, had been excluded from the more highly-skilled and better-paid industrial posts for two or more generations. They had been told that certain processes were beyond their power. It was a lie. During the war they had proved it to be so, by their own skill and efficiency. Why surrender without a word opportunities closed

476

to them by fraud and falsehood? They had as much right to wheel, loom or cash-register as any man. Why then pretend that they were intruders in a world which was as much their own as their brothers?

Some of these malcontents were nevertheless driven out; some stayed because their employers found then cheaper, and became willing blacklegs. One notable example of this was the case of "writing assistants" in the Civil Service, the lowest-graded category of clerks, engaged on purely mechanical and routine tasks. Organisations of ex-service men repeatedly petitioned that men should be admitted to this work; but the refusal was justified on the grounds that the work—besides being inadequately paid—was "too mechanical" for men.

The boon came; the new industries of the South sprang up like mushrooms; cities grew. For six or seven years it seemed as though production was infinite in expansion and the presence of women at unfamiliar tasks, though arousing occasional local criticism, was not nationally disturbing.

The slump changed that. After 1928, jobs became not duties which wartime propaganda taught girls that it was patriotic to perform, but privileges to be reserved for potential bread-winners and fathers of families. Women were commanded to go back to the home.

The bitterness began which has lasted ever since—the women keeping jobs and the men resenting it—the men regaining the jobs and the women resenting it.

On November 14th, 1933, the Central Hall, Westminster, was crowded for a mass meeting of women's organisations to claim the right of married women to paid employment. The crowds, the banners, the enthusiasm, echoed, faintly but unmistakably the spirit of pre-war suffrage meetings. The following March the Hall was nearly filled again when a similar demand was made for "Equal Pay for Equal Work."

In January 1934 the *News-Chronicle* published an article on Women Secretaries by a well-known writer, pleading the advantages of higher payment in order that the girls might not only be better fed and housed, but neater in appearance, more self-respecting and therefore more efficient. On the next day a correspondent had written in to the paper, bitterly complaining: "Better pay and smarter clothes for women: unemployment and patched pants for men."

The men have a real grievance. So long as women are content to accept lower wages, to remain unorganised, and to regard wage-earning as a "meanwhile" occupation till marriage, their cheap labour will continue to blackleg; and during any widespread contraction of trade, under a system of competitive capitalism, employers will deliberately use them for this purpose.

But the trouble is complex. The slump did not only depress the economic life of the country; it depressed its political, its intellectual and spiritual life.

Just after the war, society was infected by a rush of idealism to the head. Democracy and reason, equality and co-operation were acclaimed as uncontested virtues. In the new constitutions of Europe and America were incorporated splendid statements about the freedom of opinion, equality of the sexes, accessibility of education. We were about to build a brave new world upon the ruins of catastrophe.

The children to-day who are young men and women were assured at school of a good time coming. Everything evil was the result of four years' war; that horror has passed; they were to inherit the benefits purchased by sacrifice. Old hampering conventions had broken down; superstitions were destroyed; the young had come into their kingdom.

It was under the influence of this optimism that young women cherished ambitions for the wider exercise of their individual powers, and saw no limit to the kind and quality of service which they might offer to the community.

About 1926, after the General Strike in England and its failure, after the entry of Germany into the League of Nations and the delay by the Powers in making good their promises, the slump in idealism began to set in. Reason, democracy, the effort of the individual human will, liberty and equality were at a discount. As economic opportunities shrank, so the hopefulness and idealism of the early post-war period dwindled.

In Italy, Germany and Ireland a new dream of natural instinctive racial unity was arising, which designed for women a return to their "natural" functions of housekeeping and child-bearing; while in the English-speaking countries a new anti-rational philosophy combined with economic fatalism, militated against the ebullient hopes which an earlier generation had pinned to education, effort, and individual enterprise.

All generalisations are false. In every civilised country are little groups of older women with memories of suffrage struggles, and young women who grew up into the post-war optimism, and whose ideas remain unchanged by the fashions of the hour. It is they who still organise protests against the reaction; who in national and international societies defend the political, civil and economic equality of men and women; who invade new territories of achievement; who look towards a time when there shall be no wrangling over rights and wrongs, man's place and woman's place, but an equal and co-operative partnership, the individual going unfettered to the work for which he is best suited, responsibilities and obligations shared alike.

But these groups of professional women, organisers, artists, writers, members of societies like the Equal Rights International, the Open Door Council, the National Women's Party of America, the Women's International League of Peace and Freedom, are now in a minority and they know it.

The younger women more closely resemble a description recently given of the newly-adult generation in modern France. "They are fatalists. They are sensible. They are not interested in ideas. They believe that a war is coming against Germany which will destroy all individual plans, and they say 'Que faire?' They do not choose their work. They have to take what they can get and be glad of that. They marry early, feeling that life being so short and uncertain they must make sure of posterity while they can. They are completely indifferent to large general principles or long-distance hopes of social amelioration. They have stoical courage but no enterprise, no hope, and no idealism. They ask for discipline, not freedom; for security, not for opportunity. Many of them are returning to orthodox religion; but few of them seem to have experienced religious ardour."

One man I know, an ex-minister of the Crown in this country, gave an explanation that the young generation just recently adult has grown up in a time of huge impersonal events—the War, the Boom, the Slump. News is reported daily of immense catastrophes over which they can have no control, the Japanese and Indian earthquakes, Chinese famine, African drought. The cheap daily press and wireless bring these facts vividly home to them in a way their ancestors never knew. The individual will seems unimportant, the individual personality is dwarfed, by happenings on so large a scale. The world is too much for them. They give it up, content to be passive passengers in a vehicle which they cannot steer.

This is the slump complex—this narrowing of ambition, this closing-in alike of ideas and opportunities. Somewhere, a spring of vitality and hope has failed. As though it required too great an effort against such odds to assume responsibility for their own individual destiny, they fall back upon tradition, instinct, orthodoxy. The slump is really a general resignation by humanity of its burden of initiative, and women fall under its influence as much as men.

Benito Mussolini

1883–1945

The son of a blacksmith, Benito Mussolini spent his early years as a teacher, a journalist, and a draftee in the Italian army. Later, he served as a volunteer enlisted man during World War I. During the postwar period, he worked again as a journalist and as a political agitator on his way to becoming Prime Minister of Italy in 1922. His political allegiance had been to socialism during his prewar journalism career, but afterwards, exasperated with parliamentarism and the Treaty of Versailles, which did not reward Italy sufficiently for joining the victorious Allies, he became the leader of the new Fascist movement.

In writing for such newspapers as *La Lotta di Classe* (trans. *The Class Struggle*) and *Il Populo d'Italia* (trans. *The Italian People*), Mussolini began shaping his plan for Italy's political rise to dominance. A powerful orator and skillful propagandist, he acquired the support of anarchists, frustrated republicans, ultra-conservatives and other disillusioned radicals, who came to be known as the *Fasci di Combattimento*, self-styled warriors for the Italian state, conceived so as to evoke in the public mind the age of Imperial Rome. Through these tactics, Mussolini was able to achieve enormous power: despite the failure of the fascists to gain any seats in the Parliamentary election of 1919, he and his followers, also called Black Shirts, continued their political agitation. In the unstable atmosphere they helped to create, they marched on Rome in 1922 to demand that the king appoint Mussolini to save the nation. The king agreed, naming Mussolini to form a new cabinet and granting him temporary dictatorial powers, which he extended by changing the electoral laws.

Mussolini's program was nationalist—aimed at reviving the glory of Italy—and populist, representing him as the defender of the little man. He glorified the State and embarked on elaborate public works projects. Originally antagonistic towards Hitler, he later allied Italy with Germany; as a result, his political agenda incorporated anti-Semitism, which had never before been part of his appeal, and drew Italy into World War II, for which it was badly unprepared. In 1943, after the Allies invaded Italy, Mussolini was deposed, but he was established as the puppet leader of a new German regime which fought on in northern Italy. He was finally captured and killed by Italian partisans.

Mussolini insists that the natural state of human existence is war, which serves to purify both the individual and the nation. *The Political and Social Doctrine of Fascism* (1935) demonstrates the appeal that romantic rhetoric has for the body politic, wherein individuals find their purpose in the glory of the State. Mussolini forces us to evaluate our own sentiments and ideas regarding our political values. How does Mussolini define fascism in this work? What is the role of violence in his worldview? Why does individual freedom as found in democracy or Marx's economic solution through class struggle fail, according to Mussolini? How does he argue that the individual is enhanced under Fascism?

from *The Political and Social Doctrine of Fascism* (1935)

•   •   •

The years which preceded the march to Rome were years of great difficulty, during which the necessity for action did not permit of research or any
complete elaboration of doctrine. The battle had to be fought in the towns and
villages. There was much discussion, but—what was more important and
sacred—men died. They knew how to die. Doctrine, beautifully defined and
carefully elucidated, with headlines and paragraphs, might be lacking; but
there was to take its place something more decisive—Faith. Even so, anyone
who can recall the events of the time through the aid of books, articles, votes
of congresses, and speeches of great and minor importance—anyone who
knows how to research and weigh evidence—will find that the fundamentals
of doctrine were cast during the years of conflict. It was precisely in those years
that Fascist thought armed itself, was refined, and began the great task of
organization. The problem of the relation between the individual citizen and
the State; the allied problems of authority and liberty; political and social
problems as well as those specifically national—a solution was being fought for
all these while at the same time the struggle against Liberalism, Democracy,
Socialism, and the Masonic bodies was being carried on, contemporaneously
with the "punitive expedition." But, since there was inevitably some lack of
system, the adversaries of Fascism have disingenuously denied that it had any
capacity to produce a doctrine of its own, though that doctrine was growing
and taking shape under their very eyes, even though tumultuously; first, as
happens to all ideas in their beginnings, in the aspect of a violent and dogmatic
negation, and then in the aspect of positive construction which has found its
realization in the laws and institutions of the régime as enacted successively in
the years 1926, 1927, and 1928.

Fascism is now a completely individual thing, not only as a régime but as
a doctrine. And this means that today Fascism, exercising its critical sense
upon itself and upon others, has formed its own distinct and peculiar point of
view, to which it can refer and upon which, therefore, it can act in the face of
all problems, practical or intellectual, which confront the world.

And above all, Fascism, the more it considers and observes the future and
the development of humanity quite apart from political considerations of the
moment, believes neither in the possibility nor the utility of perpetual peace.

It thus repudiates the doctrine of Pacificism—born of a renunciation of the struggle and an act of cowardice in the face of sacrifice. War alone brings up to its highest tension all human energy and puts the stamp of nobility upon the peoples who have the courage to meet it. All other trials are substitutes, which never really put men into the position where they have to make the great decision—the alternative of life or death. Thus a doctrine which is founded upon this harmful postulate of peace is hostile to Fascism. And thus hostile to the spirit of Fascism, though accepted for what use they can be in dealing with particular political situations, are all the international leagues and societies which, as history will show, can be scattered to the winds when once strong national feeling is aroused by any motive—sentimental, ideal, or practical. This anti-Pacifist spirit is carried by Fascism even into the life of the individual; the proud motto of the *Squadrista*, "Me ne frego,"[1] written on the bandage of the wound, is an act of philosophy not only stoic, the summary of a doctrine not only political—it is the education for combat, the acceptation of the risks which combat implies, and a new way of life for Italy. Thus the Fascist accepts life and loves it, knowing nothing of and despising suicide: he rather conceives of life as duty and struggle and conquest, life which should be high and full, lived for oneself, but above all for others—those who are at hand and those who are far distant, contemporaries, and those who will come after.

This "demographic" policy of the régime is the result of the above premise. Thus the Fascist loves in actual fact his neighbor, but this "neighbor" is not merely a vague and undefined concept, this love for one's neighbor puts no obstacle in the way of necessary educational severity, and still less to differentiation of status and to physical distance. Fascism repudiates any universal embrace, and in order to live worthily in the community of civilized peoples watches its contemporaries with vigilant eyes, takes good note of their state of mind and, in the changing trend of their interests, does not allow itself to be deceived by temporary and fallacious appearances.

Such a conception of life makes Fascism the complete opposite of that doctrine, the base of so-called scientific and Marxian Socialism, the materialist conception of history; according to which the history of human civilization can be explained simply through the conflict of interests among the various social groups and by the change and development in the means and instruments of production. That the changes in the economic field—new discoveries of raw materials, new methods of working them, and the inventions of science—have their importance no one can deny; but that these factors are sufficient to explain the history of humanity excluding all others is an absurd delusion. Fascism, now and always, believes in holiness and in heroism; that is to say, in actions influenced by no economic motive, direct or indirect. And if the economic conception of history be denied, according to which theory men are no more than puppets, carried to and fro by the waves of chance, while the real directing forces are quite out of their control, it follows that the existence of an unchangeable and unchanging class-war is also denied—the natural progeny of the economic conception of history. And above all Fascism denies that class-war can be the preponderant force in the transformation of society. These two fundamental concepts of Socialism being thus refuted, nothing is left of it but the sentimental aspiration—as old as humanity itself—towards a social convention in which the sorrows and sufferings of the humblest shall be alleviated. But here again Fascism repudiates the conception of "economic" happiness, to be realized by Socialism and, as it were, at a given moment in economic evolution to assure to everyone the maximum of well-being. Fascism denies the materialist conception of happiness as a possibility, and abandons it to its inventors, the economists of the first half of the nineteenth century: that is to say, Fascism denies the validity of the equation, well-being-happiness, which would reduce men to the level of animals, caring for one thing only—to be fat and well-fed—and would thus degrade humanity to a purely physical existence.

After Socialism, Fascism combats the whole complex system of democratic ideology, and repudiates it, whether in its theoretical premises or in its practical application. Fascism denies that the majority, by the simple fact that it is a majority, can direct human society; it denies that numbers alone can govern by means of a periodic consultation, and it affirms the immutable, beneficial, and fruitful inequality of mankind, which can never be permanently leveled through the mere operation of a mechanical process such as universal suffrage. The democratic régime may be defined as from time to time giving the people the illusion of sovereignty, while the real effective sovereignty lies in the hands of other concealed and irresponsible forces. Democracy is a régime nominally without a king, but it is ruled by many kings—more absolute, tyrannical, and ruinous than one sole king, even though a tyrant. This explains why Fascism, having first in 1922 (for reasons of expediency) assumed an attitude tending towards republicanism, renounced this point of view before the march to Rome; being convinced that the question of political form is not today of prime importance, and after having studied the examples of monarchies and republics past and present reached the conclusion that monarchy or republicanism are not to be judged, as it were, by an absolute standard; but that they represent forms in which the evolution—political, historical, traditional, or psychological—of a particular country has expressed itself. Fascism supersedes the antithesis monarchy or republicanism, while democracy still tarries beneath the domination of this idea, forever pointing out the insufficiency of the first and forever praising the second as the perfect régime. Today, it can be seen that there are republics innately reactionary and absolutist, and also monarchies which incorporate the most ardent social and political hopes of the future.

• • •

The foundation of Fascism is the conception of the State, its character, its duty, and its aim. Fascism conceives of the State as an absolute, in comparison with which all individuals or groups are relative, only to be conceived of in their relation to the State. The conception of the Liberal State is not that of a directing force, guiding the play and development, both material and spiritual, of a collective body, but merely a force limited to the function of recording results: on the other hand, the Fascist State is itself conscious, and has itself a will and a personality—thus it may be called the "ethic" State. In 1929, at the first five-yearly assembly of the Fascist régime, I said:

"For us Fascists, the State is not merely a guardian, preoccupied solely with the duty of assuring the personal safety of the citizens; nor is it an organization with purely material aims, such as to guarantee a certain level of well-being and peaceful conditions of life; for a mere council of administration would be sufficient to realize such objects. Nor is it a purely political creation, divorced from all contact with the complex material reality which makes up the life of the individual and the life of the people as a whole. The State, as conceived of and as created by Fascism, is a spiritual and moral fact in itself, since its political, juridical, and economic organization of the nation is a concrete thing: and such an organization must be in its origins and development a manifestation of the spirit. The State is the guarantor of security both internal and external, but it is also the custodian and transmitter of the spirit of the people, as it has grown up through the centuries in language, in customs, and in faith. And the State is not only a living reality of the present, it is also linked with the past and above all with the future, and thus transcending the brief limits of individual life, it represents the immanent spirit of the nation. The forms in which States express themselves may change, but the necessity for such forms is eternal. It is the State which educates its citizens in civic virtue, gives them a consciousness of their mission and welds them into unity; harmonizing their various interests through justice, and transmitting to future generations the mental conquests of science, of art, of law and the solidarity of humanity. It leads men from primitive tribal life to that highest expression of human power which is Empire: it links up through the centuries the names of those of its members who have died for its existence and in obedience to its laws, it holds up the memory of the leaders who have increased its territory and the geniuses who have illumined it with glory as an example to be followed by future generations. When the conception of the State declines, and disunifying and centrifugal tendencies prevail, whether of individuals or of particular groups, the nations where such phenomena appear are in their decline."

From 1929 until today, evolution, both political and economic, has everywhere gone to prove the validity of these doctrinal premises. Of such gigantic importance is the State. It is the force which alone can provide a solution to the dramatic contradictions of capitalism, and that state of affairs which we call the crisis can only be dealt with by the State, as between other States. Where is the shade of Jules Simon,[2] who in the dawn of Liberalism proclaimed that, "The State must labor to make itself unnecessary, and prepare the way for its own dismissal"? Or of McCulloch,[3] who, in the second half of the last century, affirmed that the State must guard against the danger of governing too much? What would the Englishman, Bentham, say today to the continual and inevitably-invoked intervention of the State in the sphere of economics, while according to his theories industry should ask no more of the State than to be left in peace? Or the German, Humboldt,[4] according to whom the "lazy" State should be considered the best? It is true that the second wave of Liberal economists were less extreme than the first, and Adam Smith himself opened the door—if only very cautiously—which leads to State intervention in the economic field: but whoever says Liberalism implies individualism, and whoever says Fascism implies the State. Yet the Fascist State is unique, and an original creation. It is not reactionary, but revolutionary, in that it anticipates the solution of the universal political field by the rivalry of parties, the excessive power of the parliamentary régime and the irresponsibility of political assemblies; while it meets the problems of the economic field by a system of syndicalism which is continually increasing in importance, as much in the sphere of labor as of industry: and in the moral field enforces order, discipline, and obedience to that which is the determined moral code of the country. Fascism desires the State to be a strong and organic body, at the same time reposing upon broad and popular support. The Fascist State has drawn into itself even the economic activities of the nation, and, through the corporative social and educational institutions created by it, its influence reaches every aspect of the national life and includes, framed in their respective organizations, all the political, economic and spiritual forces of the nation. A State which reposes upon the support of millions of individuals who recognize its authority, are continually conscious of its power and are ready at once to serve it, is not the old tyrannical State of the medieval lord nor has it anything in common with the absolute governments either before or after 1789. The individual in the Fascist State is not annulled but rather multiplied, just in the same way that a soldier in a regiment is not diminished but rather increased by the number of his comrades. The Fascist State organizes the nation, but leaves a sufficient margin of liberty to the individual; the latter is deprived of all useless and possibly harmful freedom, but retains what is essential; the deciding power in this question cannot be the individual, but the State alone.

Notes

[1] A Blackshirt slogan that translates as "I don't give a damn."

[2] Jules Simon (1814–1896), French Premier (1876–1877) who favored the establishment of a republic.

[3] John Ramsey McCulloch (1789–1864), political economist who argued for *laissez-faire*.

[4] Wilhelm von Humboldt (1767–1835), statesman and Prussian scholar who was critical of state control of education and religion.

Gertrude Scholtz-Klink

1902–?

Despite Fascism's mandate of female subordination, Hitler occasionally trusted women with some power. Hitler's official filmaker, Leni Riefensthal, is perhaps the best known example. Another is Gertrude Scholtz-Klink who was appointed "National Women's Leader" in order to coordinate women's organizations and rouse support for Nazis among homemakers.

Scholtz-Klink was well suited to this task. An early devotée of Hitler, Scholtz-Klink gave up her employment as a social worker and devoted herself to raising her eleven children. Though she never enjoyed much formal power in her post (it was more of a supporting role), her organization did oversee the establishment of over 32,000 day care centers which served over a million children. These centers were of vital importance after 1939 when wartime demands for production necessitated the employment of large numbers of women. Thus, in Germany as elsewhere in the industrialized world, women were clearly seen as a disposable labor force, charged with devoting themselves to children and home under normal circumstances, forced to abandon them when the needs of the state demanded it.

Though in many speeches Hitler himself emphasized women's importance to the state as childbearers, Scholtz-Klink's speech is featured here. She employs a wide-range of emotional and psychological images and arguments to appeal to women, addressing issues likely to be of concern to them. She also strives not to alienate non-childbearing women, urging them to use their special talents to serve the nation as well. Why would this strategy be effective? In what ways is it propagandistic? Are there precedents for her arguments? Are they peculiarly Nazi?

from "A Speech to the Nazi's Women's Organization" (1935)

A year has passed since the day we met here for the first time as a unified group of German women, to demonstrate our willingness to cooperate in our Führer's work of reconstruction.

This year has been inspired by the desire to mark our times with our best efforts so that our descendants will be able to forget our nation's fourteen years of weakness and sickness. We women knew, quite as well as German men, that we had to teach a people, partially sunk in self-despair, attitudes requiring those very qualities that had been deliberately suppressed in our nation. In order to carry out our intention to unite and to march shoulder to shoulder, we demanded honor and loyalty, strength and sincerity, humility and respect—such virtues appeal to the soul people. In matters of the soul, however, it is no longer the majority who decide, but the strength and inner freedom of upright individuals. Therefore, we could only fulfill our task if it enabled us to penetrate the soul of the individual. . . .

When we came to the point of recognizing that the human eye reflected a nation's soul, we had to reach the women of our nation, once and for all, through our labor on women's behalf. Because as mothers our women have carried the heavy burden of the past fourteen years—and the ruins of the war and post-war period—in their hearts; and as future mothers other women must presently develop an understanding of the demands of our times—to both of these groups we dedicated the first important path that we built to the hearts of German women: our Reichs-Maternity Service.

Urged on by the tired eyes of many overburdened mothers and the responsibility for the coming generation of mothers, we joined together under the leadership of the National Socialist Women's Association [*N.S Frauenschaft*] and appealed to the German women especially trained for this work. When I tell you today that, between the 1st of October 1934 and the 1st of April 1935, we enrolled more than 201,700 women in 7,653 maternity school courses in about 2,000 locations throughout the German Reich, it may not seem much at first glance. But we must not forget that we had no funds and met with much opposition, and that we had no patronage since we were quite unknown. But we did have absolute and unshakable faith. None of our traveling teachers asked: How much will I earn? or, What are my pension rights? We have done this work out of a sense of duty to our nation—and our

489

nation has responded. On Mothers' Day this year we were presented with 3.5 million marks for this work of maternity training. Moreover, on this day of honor for the mothers of Germany, when we all collected money in the streets, we found that our humblest fellow-countrymen were the most generous. This was surely the most wonderful reward for all of us, but it also gave practical evidence of where our major efforts must be directed. And when, only one or two months from now, we open our Reichs-Maternity School in Wedding, formerly one of the most solidly "red" quarters of Berlin, we will be able to congratulate ourselves on having prepared a place, on behalf of our Party and our State, that will reveal to all of you how we are solving our problems.

In this place, mothers of all ages and classes discuss their problems and their needs. Here they will become acquainted with the aims of the National Socialist state and will receive inspiration to pass them on from woman to woman, and thus to recover our national faith in ourselves. If by means of the Reichs-Maternity Service we gradually succeed in brightening the eyes of our mothers and in bringing some joy into their often difficult lives, perhaps even a song to their lips, we may consider that have accomplished our task, because happy mothers will raise happy children. But our Reichs-Maternity Service must also make a point of teaching our young and future mothers those things that a liberal era did not teach them—for the omission of which our nation has had to pay dearly—namely, that through marriage we consciously become mothers of the nation; that is, we understand and share every national requirement laid upon German men, and that, therefore, as wives we must unconditionally become the companions of our men—not merely in personal terms, but in all national requirements.

First we pursued our task by appealing to the mothers of the nation, and then to that generation closest to the mothers, the girls between eighteen and twenty-five years of age. We called upon them to join voluntarily in the chain of helping hands and to create a relationship of unbreakable trust among German women. And they came, our girls of the German Women's Labor Service.

You, my girls, who have now spent two years with me in the struggle for the autonomy of the German people, have learned to carry every responsibility and have become the inspiration of our mothers. No matter whether our girls are cheerfully helping German settlers on the moors in their difficult work of creating new homes; or whether they are working in Rhön, Spessart, or in eastern Bavaria, hand in hand with the National Socialist Welfare Organization in giving help to careworn adults and joyless children, in reawakening a taste for beauty and a belief in themselves or whether they are helping German peasant women harvest from dawn to dusk—one thing unites them all, for they know: We are needed, we are of some use, and we are playing our part in the rebirth of our nation. And what is perhaps even more important, they come to know themselves, because the German land or the German plight confronted them with inexorable demands. Faced with the realities of life, neither beauty nor examinations, neither wealth nor connections suffice— only the value of personal character will stand the test. Because we have experienced all of this so deeply, we have demanded compulsory labor service for girls exactly as for German men.

Since at present we cannot satisfy all these demands, owing to financial and organizational difficulties, we have begun by making only those demands that professional and university women can take the lead in supporting. German women students have accepted the demand for compulsory labor service with the utmost readiness. But in spite of this, for the next few years our principal task will be to keep German women students constantly in touch with the vital realities of our nation, in contrast to the detachment of their private academic existence that was formerly so common. At one time, it was considered the height of achievement in Germany to know everything and thereby to lose the simplemindedness of childhood. We wish to impress on our women at the universities that as university students, they must place the intellectual abilities entrusted to them at the disposal of their nation with the same humility as that with which women workers and mothers fulfill their duties. . . . This summer our women students began to live in this manner and thereby joined the chain of helping hands we have created among ourselves. They went into German factories and replaced working women and mothers, enabling them to have a real vacation in order to regain strength for their hard day-to-day existence. For it is these women, these mothers of families, who are hardest hit by the short working hours or unemployment of their husbands, because at home their children sap their strength. We were able to carry out this work of mutual assistance without great expenditure, owing to the solidarity of German women students and the cooperation of industrial management, the Labor Front, the Nation Socialist Welfare Organization, and the National-Socialist Women's League.

This brings us to the point where we must consider the millions of German women who perform heavy labor in factories day in and day out. If we consider the human eye as the measure of a people's soul, it is here that we find the deepest imprints of that fourteen-year-long attempt to strangle our national soul. We know that a great deal of industrial work must always be done by women, but it is essential that the woman at the machine should feel that she, in her position, represents her nation, in common with all other women. That is to say, we awaken her consciousness so that she will say to herself: "This is my responsibility, my attitude determines the attitude of the nation." In recent times, this very basic consciousness of recognition of the importance of the tight mesh of joint national labor of individuals was not instilled. For this reason, we in the Women's Section of the German Labor Front have given the women workers their own women trustees and their own district and regional superintendents chosen from their own ranks, in order that they too may play their part in the labor of the nation. We are well aware that it is most difficult to include the working woman in the general scheme of responsibilities, because she is hardest hit by problems of unemployment and reduced working hours. But since we women are not directly concerned with financial relief, the help we can give must be indirect, though equally effective. We begin by giving advice to women and girls in the form of courses in cooking, sewing, and child-care in the maternity schools. In this way we have given considerable assistance to over 80,000 women workers and workers' wives in the past year. . . .

Our most important effort, however, toward the education of working women for a National Socialist life-style has been our appointment of female social workers among the women working in factories. These female social workers (upon whom we are forced to make extraordinary demands, both human and political) must stand by the side of the factory managers and counsellors responsible for the welfare of the workers and as comrades of the women workers, they must help to introduce them to all other women's organizations and to ensure that the individual woman factory worker feels truly committed to her own labor. . . .

I must deal briefly with a question that is constantly brought to our attention, that is, how our present attitude toward life differs from that of the previous women's movement. First, in principle we permit only Germans to be leaders of German women and to concern themselves with matters of importance to Germans. Second, as a matter of principle we never have demanded, nor shall we ever demand, equal rights for women with the men of our nation. Instead we shall always make women's special interests dependent upon the needs of our entire nation. All further considerations will follow from this unconditional intertwining of the collective fate of the nation. . . .

Lázaro Cárdenas

1895–1970

While the 1930s saw increasing conservatism, indeed Fascism, spreading throughout Europe, Socialist-inspired reforms prevailed in the Americas. In particular, certain visionary Latin American leaders spurned totalitarian solutions to the problems of modernity. Wishing to realize the full independence that their postcolonial status promised, such leaders combined concern for the poor with a rejection of global capitalism.

Mexican President Lázaro Cárdenas, in office from 1934–1940, was dedicated to implementing reforms demanded during Mexico's revolution which ended in 1917. He upheld the constitutional rights enacted in 1917 including universal suffrage and free speech. Above all, he aimed to improve the lot of Mexico's poor, and to this end embarked on massive land redistribution, confiscating millions of acres from large estates. He also introduced social legislation which provided free education and unemployment and health insurance to all. As conditions improved, workers organized to gain still more rights. In 1936 a labor dispute in Mexico's oil refineries ended with a supreme court judgment in favor of the workers' unions. However, the British and U.S.-owned oil companies refused to recognize the Mexican court's ruling. Cárdenas's solution was to nationalize the oil industry, thus delivering a harsh blow to neo-imperialist interests.

In this "Speech to the Nation," Cárdenas justifies his decision with nationalist rhetoric. He also demonstrates that foreign ownership did not bring the prosperity it promised. His rationale seems especially relevant today—for Mexico, and for other countries whose resources are monopolized by corporations backed by industrial countries. How was Cárdenas's solution radical? Essential? What were the potential and actual consequences of his decision? How is his program an alternative to those programs attempted elsewhere?

Speech to the Nation (1938)

In each and every one of the various attempts of the Executive to arrive at a final solution of the conflict within conciliatory limits . . . the intransigence of the companies was clearly demonstrated.

Their attitude was therefore premeditated and their position deliberately taken, so that the Government, in defense of its own dignity, had to resort to application of the Expropriation Act, as there were no means less drastic or decision less severe that might bring about a solution of the problem.

For additional justification of the measure herein announced, let us trace briefly the history of the oil companies' growth in Mexico and of the resources with which they have developed their activities.

It has been repeated *ad nauseam* that the oil industry has brought additional capital for the development and progress of the country. This assertion is an exaggeration. For many years throughout the major period of their existence, oil companies have enjoyed great privileges for development and expansion, including customs and tax exemptions and innumerable prerogatives; it is these factors of special privilege, together with the prodigious productivity of the oil deposits granted them by the Nation often against public will and law, that represent almost the total amount of this so-called capital.

Potential wealth of the Nation; miserably underpaid native labor; tax exemptions; economic privileges; governmental tolerance—these are the factors of the boom of the Mexican oil industry.

Let us now examine the social contributions of the companies. In how many of the villages bordering on the oil fields is there a hospital, or school or social center, or a sanitary water supply, or an athletic field, or even an electric plant fed by the millions of cubic meters of natural gas allowed to go to waste?

What center of oil production, on the other hand, does not have its company police force for the protection of private, selfish, and often illegal interests? These organizations, whether authorized by the Government or not, are charged with innumerable outrages, abuses, and murders, always on behalf of the companies that employ them.

Who is not aware of the irritating discrimination governing construction of the company camps? Comfort for the foreign personnel; misery, drabness, and insalubrity for the Mexicans. Refrigeration and protection against tropical insects for the former; indifference and neglect, medical service and supplies always grudgingly provided, for the latter; lower wages and harder, more exhausting labor for our people.

494

The tolerance which the companies have abused was born, it is true, in the shadow of the ignorance, betrayals, and weakness of the country's rulers; but the mechanism was set in motion by investors lacking in the necessary moral resources to give something in exchange for the wealth they have been exploiting.

Another inevitable consequence of the presence of the oil companies, strongly characterized by their anti-social tendencies, and even more harmful than all those already mentioned, has been their persistent and improper intervention in national affairs.

The oil companies' support to strong rebel factions against the constituted government in the Huasteca region of Veracruz and in the Isthmus of Tehuantepec during the years 1917 to 1920 is no longer a matter for discussion by anyone. Nor is anyone ignorant of the fact that in later periods and even at the present time, the oil companies have almost openly encouraged the ambitions of elements discontented with the country's government, every time their interests were affected either by taxation or by the modification of their privileges or the withdrawal of the customary tolerance. They have had money, arms, and munitions for rebellion, money for the antipatriotic press which defends them, money with which to enrich their unconditional defenders. But for the progress of the country, for establishing an economic equilibrium with their workers through a just compensation of labor, for maintaining hygienic conditions in the districts where they themselves operate, or for conserving the vast riches of the natural petroleum gases from destruction, they have neither money, nor financial possibilities, nor the desire to subtract the necessary funds from the volume of their profits.

Nor is there money with which to meet a responsibility imposed upon them by judicial verdict, for they rely on their pride and their economic power to shield them from the dignity and sovereignty of a Nation which has generously placed in their hands its vast natural resources and now finds itself unable to obtain the satisfaction of the most elementary obligations by ordinary legal means.

As a logical consequence of this brief analysis, it was therefore necessary to adopt a definite and legal measure to end this permanent state of affairs in which the country sees its industrial progress held back by those who hold in their hands the power to erect obstacles as well as the motive power of all activity and who, instead of using it to high and worthy purposes, abuse their economic strength to the point of jeopardizing the very life of a Nation endeavoring to bring about the elevation of its people through its own laws, its own resources, and the free management of its own destinies.

With the only solution to this problem thus placed before it, I ask the entire Nation for moral and material support sufficient to carry out so justified, important, and indispensable a decision.

The Government has already taken suitable steps to maintain the constructive activities now going forward throughout the Republic, and for that purpose it asks the people only for its full confidence and backing in whatever dispositions the Government may be obliged to adopt.

Nevertheless, we shall, if necessary, sacrifice all the constructive projects on which the Nation has embarked during the term of this Administration in order to cope with the financial obligations imposed upon us by the application of the Expropriation Act to such vast interests; and although the subsoil of the country will give us considerable economic resources with which to meet the obligation of indemnization which we have contracted, we must be prepared for the possibility of our individual economy also suffering the indispensable readjustments, even to the point, should the Bank of Mexico deem it necessary, of modifying the present exchange rate of our currency, so that the whole country may be able to count on sufficient currency and resources with which to consolidate this act of profound and essential economic liberation of Mexico.

It is necessary that all groups of the population be imbued with a full optimism and that each citizen, whether in agricultural, industrial, commercial, transportation, or other pursuits, develop a greater activity from this moment on, in order to create new resources which will reveal that the spirit of our people is capable of saving the nation's economy by the efforts of its own citizens.

And, finally, as the fear may arise among the interests now in bitter conflict in the field of international affairs that a deviation of raw materials fundamentally necessary to the struggle in which the most powerful nations are engaged might result from the consummation of this act of national sovereignty and dignity, we wish to state that our petroleum operations will not depart a single inch from the moral solidarity maintained by Mexico with the democratic nations, whom we wish to assure that the expropriation now decreed has as its only purpose the elimination of obstacles erected by groups who do not understand the evolutionary needs of all peoples and who would themselves have no compunction in selling Mexican oil to the highest bidder, without taking into account the consequences of such action to the popular masses and the nations in conflict.

Hannah Arendt

1906–1975

A political scientist and philosopher, Hannah Arendt was born in Hannover, Germany, and received her university education at schools in Marburg, Freiburg, and Heidelberg, taking her Ph.D. in 1928. During this period she had been both the student and lover of Martin Heidegger, the famous German philosopher and eventual member of the Nazi Party. In 1933, when Hitler came to power, she left the country with the first wave of German-Jewish refugees and fled to Paris; in 1941, she was forced to leave again, this time heading for New York City. In America, she worked as research director for the Conference on Jewish Relations and as an editor for Schocken Books. In the 1960s, she served on the faculties of the University of Chicago and of the New School for Social Research in New York.

In 1951, Arendt published her comprehensive study *The Origins of Totalitarianism*, in which she examines the history and structures of European antisemitism, imperialism, and totalitarianism. She is particularly interested in analyzing the institutional organization of the totalitarian governments of Nazi Germany and Stalinist Russia, exploring how the political systems in each of these countries managed to dominate every aspect of the individual's life through ideology and terror. In 1961, she published a series of highly controversial articles for the *New Yorker* on the trial in Jerusalem of the Nazi war criminal Adolf Eichmann, the architect of the so-called Final Solution, the extermination of six million Jews and countless millions of other Europeans. These articles were revised, enlarged, and then republished in 1963 as *Eichmann in Jerusalem: A Report on the Banality of Evil*. For her, the most critical point to understanding what Eichmann represented lay precisely in the fact that he was not a monster, but a bureaucrat doing his job and acting on the orders of superiors. Arendt argues that evil is not a special case; rather, it resides like a darkness within us all. Other works of significance include *The Human Condition* (1958), *Between Past and Future* (1961), *On Revolution* (1963), and *On Violence* (1970).

In the selection below, taken from a chapter of *The Origins of Totalitarianism* entitled "A Classless Society," Hannah Arendt examines the means by which totalitarian countries atomize their citizens. How is ideology used to isolate individuals and thereby seize power? What, according to

Arendt, are the central qualities and functions of the totalitarian leader? Do the same structures or conditions that allow such isolation and control to exist in totalitarian governments exist in governments we typically regard as democratic?

from *The Origins of Totalitarianism* (1951)

Totalitarian movements are mass organizations of atomized, isolated individuals. Compared with all other parties and movements, their most conspicuous external characteristic is their demand for total, unrestricted, unconditional, and unalterable loyalty of the individual member. This demand is made by the leaders of totalitarian movements even before they seize power. It usually precedes the total organization of the country under their actual rule and it follows from the claim of their ideologies that their organization will encompass, in due course, the entire human race. Where, however, totalitarian rule has not been prepared by a totalitarian movement (and this, in contradistinction to Nazi Germany, was the case in Russia), the movement has to be organized afterward and the conditions for its growth have artificially to be created in order to make loyalty—the psychological basis for total domination—at all possible. Such loyalty can be expected only from the completely isolated human being who, without any other social ties to family, friends, comrades, or even mere acquaintances, derives his sense of having a place in the world only from his belonging to a movement, his membership in the party.

Total loyalty is possible only when fidelity is emptied of all concrete content, from which changes of mind might naturally arise. The totalitarian movements, each in its own way, have done their utmost to get rid of the party programs which specified concrete content and which they inherited from earlier, nontotalitarian stages of development. No matter how radically they might have been phrased, every definite political goal which does not simply assert or circumscribe the claim to world rule, every political program which deals with issues more specific than "ideological questions of importance for centuries" is an obstruction to totalitarianism. Hitler's greatest achievement in the organization of the Nazi movement, which he gradually built up from the obscure crackpot membership of a typically nationalistic little party, was that he unburdened the movement of the party's earlier program, not by changing or officially abolishing it, but simply by refusing to talk about it or discuss its points, whose relative moderateness of content and phraseology were very soon outdated.[1] Stalin's task in this as in other respects was much more formidable; the socialist program of the Bolshevik party was a much more troublesome burden[2] than the 25 points of an amateur economist and a crackpot politician.[3] But Stalin achieved eventually, after having abolished the factions of the Russian party, the same result through the constant zigzag of the Communist Party lines, and the constant reinterpretation and application of Marxism which voided the doctrine of all its content because it was no longer possible to predict what course or action it would inspire. The fact that the most perfect education in Marxism and Leninism was no guide whatsoever for political behavior—that, on the contrary, one could follow the party line only if one repeated each morning what Stalin had announced the night before—naturally resulted in the same state of mind, the same concentrated obedience, undivided by any attempt to understand what one was doing, that Himmler's ingenious watchword for his SS-men expressed: "My honor is my loyalty."[4]

Lack of, or ignoring of, a party program is by itself not necessarily a sign of totalitarianism. The first to consider programs and platforms as needless scraps of paper and embarrassing promises, inconsistent with the style and impetus of a movement, was Mussolini with his Fascist philosophy of activism and inspiration through the historical moment itself.[5] Mere lust for power combined with contempt for "talkative" articulation of what they intend to do with it is characteristic of all mob leaders, but does not come up to the standards of totalitarianism. The true goal of Fascism was only to seize power and establish the Fascist "elite" as uncontested ruler over the country. Totalitarianism is never content to rule by external means, namely, through the state and a machinery of violence; thanks to its peculiar ideology and the role assigned to it in this apparatus of coercion, totalitarianism has discovered a means of dominating and terrorizing human beings from within. In this sense it eliminates the distance between the rulers and the ruled and achieves a condition in which power and the will to power, as we understand them, play no role, or at best, a secondary role. In substance, the totalitarian leader is nothing more nor less than the functionary of the masses he leads; he is not a power-hungry individual imposing a tyrannical and arbitrary will upon his subjects. Being a mere functionary, he can be replaced at any time, and he depends just as much on the "will" of the masses he embodies as the masses depend on him. Without him they would lack external representation and remain an amorphous horde; without the masses the leader is a nonentity. Hitler who was fully aware of this interdependence, expressed it once in a speech addressed to the SA:[6] "All that you are, you are through me; all that I am, I am through you alone."[7] We are only too inclined to belittle such statements or to misunderstand them in the sense that acting is defined here in terms of giving and executing orders, as has happened too often in the political tradition and history of the West.[8] But this idea has always presupposed someone in command who thinks and wills, and then imposes his thought and will on a thought- and will-deprived group—be it by persuasion, authority, or violence. Hitler, however, was of the opinion that even "thinking . . . [exists] only by virtue of giving or executing orders,"[9] and thereby eliminated even theoretically the distinction between thinking and acting on one hand, and between the rulers and the ruled on the other. Neither National Socialism nor Bolveshism has ever proclaimed a new form of government or asserted that its goals were reached with the seizure of power and the control of the state machinery. Their idea of domination was something that no state and no mere apparatus of violence can ever achieve, but only a movement that is constantly kept in motion: namely, the permanent domination of each single individual in each and every sphere of life.[10] The seizure of power through the means of violence is never an end in itself but only the means to an end, and the seizure of power in any given country is only a welcome transitory stage but never the end of the movement. The practical goal of the movement is to organize as many people as possible within its framework and to set and keep them in motion; a political goal that would constitute the end of the movement simply does not exist.

Notes

[1] Hitler stated in *Mein Kampf* (2 vols., 1st German ed., 1925 and 1927 respectively. Unexpurgated translation, New York, 1939) that it was better to have an antiquated program than to allow a discussion of program (Book II, chapter v). Soon he was to proclaim publicly: "Once we take over the government, the program will come of itself. . . . The first thing must be an inconceivable wave of propaganda. That is a political action which would have little to do with the other problems of the moment." See Heiden, op. cit., p. 203.

[2] Souvarine, in our opinion wrongly, suggests that Lenin had already abolished the role of a party program: "Nothing could show more clearly the non-existence of Bolshevism as a doctrine except in Lenin's brain; every Bolshevik left to himself wandered from 'the line' of his faction . . . for these men were bound together by their temperament and by the ascendancy of Lenin rather than by ideas" (op. cit., p. 85).

[3] Gottfried Feder's Program of the Nazi Party with its famous 25 points has played a greater role in the literature about the movement than in the movement itself.

[4] The impact of the watchword, formulated by Himmler himself, is difficult to render. Its German equivalent: "*Meine Ehre heisst Treue,*" indicates an absolute devolution and obedience which transcends the meaning of mere discipline or personal faithfulness. *Nazi Conspiracy*, whose translations of German documents and Nazi literature are indispensable source material but, unfortunately, are very uneven, renders the SS watchword: "My honor signifies faithfulness" (V, 346).

[5] Mussolini was probably the first party leader who consciously rejected a formal program and replaced it with inspired leadership and action alone. Behind this act lay the notion that the actuality of the moment itself was the chief element of inspiration, which would only be hampered by a party program. The philosophy of Italian Fascism has been expressed by Gentile's "actualism" rather than by Sorel's "myths."

Compare also the article "Fascism" in the *Encyclopedia of the Social Sciences*. The Program of 1921 was formulated when the movement had been in existence two years and contained, for the most part, its nationalist philosophy.

[6] Editor's note: *SA*, an abbreviation for *die Sturmabteilung*, or Brownshirts, Hitler's infamous storm troops.

[7] Ernst Bayer, *Die SA*, Berlin, 1938. Translation quoted from *Nazi Conspiracy*, IV, 783.

[8] For the first time in Plato's *Statesman*, 305, where acting is interpreted in terms of *archein* and *prattein*—of ordering the start of an action and of executing this order.

[9] *Hitlers Tischgespräche*, p. 198.

[10] *Mein Kampf*, Book I, chapter xi. See also, for example, Dieter Schwarz, *Angriffe auf die nationalsozialistische Weltanschauung. Aus dem Schwarzen Korps*, No. 2, 1936, who answers the obvious criticism that National Socialists after their rise to power continued to talk about "a struggle": "National Socialism as an ideology [Weltanschauung] will not abandon its struggle until . . . the way of life of each individual German has been shaped by its fundamental values and these are realized every day anew."

X. World War II, the Holocaust Experience, and the Response of Existentialism

Bruno Bettelheim

1903–1990

Born a Jew in Vienna, Austria, Bruno Bettelheim was 35 at the time of his imprisonment in the concentration camps at Dachau and Buchenwald. In 1939, he was released and allowed to immigrate to the United States, where he worked first as a research associate at the Progressive Education Association at the University of Chicago and then as a professor at Rockford College in Illinois. In 1943, he won attention for his essay "Individual and Mass Behavior in Extreme Situations," a study based on his concentration-camp experience and the observations he made there. Claiming to have earned his doctorate at the University of Vienna, he found a place on the faculty of the University of Chicago as an assistant professor in the Department of Psychology. He came to specialize in the treatment of autistic children and later wrote on a wide range of psychological and social problems as they relate to the raising of emotionally disturbed children. After Bettelheim's death by suicide, it was revealed that his doctorate from Vienna was spurious, sparking a controversy over the status of his scholarship.

Nonetheless, Bettelheim's writings have continued to offer insight. They include such works as *The Informed Heart* (1960); *The Empty Fortress* (1967), a study of autism in children; *Children of the Dream* (1967), on the lives of children raised on Israeli kibbutzim; and *The Uses of Enchantment* (1976), on fairy tales and their impact on child development.

In this excerpt from *The Informed Heart*, Bettelheim recounts the dehumanizing experience of life in the concentration camp and the ways in which our identities are, in part, shaped by the perceptions of others; in Bettelheim's story, it is the Jew's identity which is shaped by an SS guard. What connections do you see between the tale Bettelheim relates and the themes explored by Sartre in "Republic of Silence"? In what sense was Bettelheim's experience a powerfully existential one? How do we experience a similar sort of relationship between our sense of self and the "Other" in our daily lives?

See p. 535 for accompanying map.

from *The Informed Heart:*
Autonomy in a Mass Age (1960)

Aggression toward minorities was not an outlet open to all prisoners, since some belonged to minorities themselves, while others could not accept it either in the SS or themselves. For them an alternative outlet was to extrapolate it and project it into the SS man. This relieved them of some of their hostility and at the same time protected them from aggression toward the enemy, whose overpowering strength they had to stress. It was a most ineffective system of defense, and may be compared with delusional efforts to master inner pressures by externalizing them.

Psychologically, reality-testing might have destroyed the fiction of the all-powerful SS which they needed for restraining themselves; but reality-testing had to be avoided at all cost. Any attempt to test the actual dangerousness of the SS would have endangered survival.

Thus the combination and interaction of an imaginary system with reality made it hard for such prisoners to escape the psychotic tendencies many of them were forced to develop. The imaginary system was built up out of infantile fears and the prisoner's rage reactions at being forced into infantile patterns; these he projected into the fictitious SS man. The reality interacting with it was the actually overpowering might of the SS. Real helplessness, the need to block every revengeful tendency, and the need to hang on to some narcissism were all motives for creating this fictional image of the persecutor.

Many students of discrimination are aware that the victim often reacts in ways as undesirable as the actions of the aggressor. Less attention is paid to this because it is easier to excuse a defendant than an offender, and because they assume that once the aggression stops the victim's reactions will stop too. But I doubt if this is of real service to the persecuted. His main interest is that the persecution cease. But that is less apt to happen if he lacks a real understanding of the phenomenon of persecution, in which victim and persecutor are inseparably interlocked.

Let me illustrate with the following example: in the winter of 1938 a Polish Jew murdered the German attaché in Paris, vom Rath. The Gestapo used the event to step up anti-Semitic actions, and in the camp new hardships were inflicted on Jewish prisoners. One of these was an order barring them from the medical clinic unless the need for treatment had originated in a work accident.

Nearly all prisoners suffered from frostbite which often led to gangrene and then amputation. Whether or not a Jewish prisoner was admitted to the clinic to prevent such a fate depended on the whim of an SS private. On reaching the clinic entrance, the prisoner explained the nature of his ailment to the SS man, who then decided if he should get treatment or not.

I too suffered from frostbite. At first I was discouraged from trying to get medical care by the fate of Jewish prisoners whose attempts had ended up in no treatment, only abuse. Finally things got worse and I was afraid that waiting longer would mean amputation. So I decided to make the effort.

When I got to the clinic, there were many prisoners lined up as usual, a score of them Jews suffering from severe frostbite. The main topic of discussion was one's chances of being admitted to the clinic. Most Jews had planned their procedure in detail. Some thought it best to stress their service in the German army during World War I: wounds received or decorations won. Others planned to stress the severity of their frostbite. A few decided it was best to tell some "tall story," such as that an SS officer had ordered them to report at the clinic.

Most of them seemed convinced that the SS man on duty would not see through their schemes. Eventually they asked me about my plans. Having no definite ones, I said I would go by the way the SS man dealt with other Jewish prisoners who had frostbite like me, and proceed accordingly. I doubted how wise it was to follow a preconceived plan, because it was hard to anticipate the reactions of a person you didn't know.

The prisoners reacted as they had at other times when I had voiced similar ideas on how to deal with the SS. They insisted that one SS man was like another, all equally vicious and stupid. As usual, any frustration was immediately discharged against the person who caused it, or was nearest at hand. So in abusive terms they accused me of not wanting to share my plan with them, or of intending to use one of theirs; it angered them that I was ready to meet the enemy unprepared.

No Jewish prisoner ahead of me in line was admitted to the clinic. The more a prisoner pleaded, the more annoyed and violent the SS became. Expressions of pain amused him; stories of previous services rendered to Germany outraged him. He proudly remarked that he could not be taken in by Jews, that fortunately the time had passed when Jews could reach their goal by lamentations.

When my turn came he asked me in a screeching voice if I knew that work accidents were the only reason for admitting Jews to the clinic, and if I came because of such an accident. I replied that I knew the rules, but that I couldn't work unless my hands were freed of the dead flesh. Since prisoners were not allowed to have knives, I asked to have the dead flesh cut away. I tried to be matter-of-fact, avoiding pleading, deference, or arrogance. He replied: "If that's all you want, I'll tear the flesh off myself." And he started to pull at the festering skin. Because it did not come off as easily as he may have expected, or for some other reason, he waved me into the clinic.

Inside, he gave me a malevolent look and pushed me into the treatment room. There he told the prisoner orderly to attend to the wound. While this was being done, the guard watched me closely for signs of pain but I was able to suppress them. As soon as the cutting was over, I started to leave. He showed surprise and asked why I didn't wait for further treatment. I said I had gotten the service I asked for, at which he told the orderly to make an exception and treat my hand. After I had left the room, he called me back and gave me a card entitling me to further treatment, and admittance to the clinic without inspection at the entrance.

• • •

Because my behavior did not correspond to what he expected of Jewish prisoners on the basis of his projection, he could not use his prepared defenses against being touched by the prisoner's plight. Since I did not act as the dangerous Jew was expected to, I did not activate the anxieties that went with his stereotype. Still he did not altogether trust me, so he continued to watch while I received treatment.

Throughout these dealings, the SS felt uneasy with me, though he did not unload on me the annoyance his uneasiness aroused. Perhaps he watched me closely because he expected that sooner or later I would slip up and behave the way his projected image of the Jew was expected to act. This would have meant that his delusional creation had become real.

To act in line with his delusional expectations of the Jew meant threatening him with the panic we all experience when our magical thinking suddenly materializes. He would then have been forced to defend himself against the terrible power he originally projected into that figure. Nothing is more threatening than a delusional figure that suddenly assumes body, appears in reality. For it must be remembered that the SS projection contained not only the cowardly and cunning Jew but also the overpowering international Jewish conspiracy bent on destroying him, and people like him.

To summarize then, most one-to-one interactions between prisoner and SS resulted only in a clashing of stereotypes. This was most exaggerated when the SS interacted with prisoners who were not even their own countrymen, but Jewish or Russian, etc. But pitting one delusional system against its delusional counterpart precluded any real interaction as between real persons, and the odds were always heavily against the prisoners.

• • •

Primo Levi

1919–1987

Born in Turin, Italy, Primo Levi was educated as a chemist. He became involved with a group of anti-Fascist partisans and was arrested in 1944 by the Gestapo on one of his first missions for the Italian resistance. He was interned at Auschwitz, where his chemistry training was put to use in a I.G. Farbenindustrie synthetic-rubber factory, thus sparing him from death in the gas chambers. After Soviet troops liberated Auschwitz in 1945, Levi wandered through Eastern Europe with other war refugees and camp survivors, finally returning home to Turin, where he spent the rest of his life. Levi then worked as a manager of a chemical factory, retiring in 1977, after which he spent his time chronicling his wartime experiences and writing fiction. He committed suicide in 1987.

Levi's works include *Se questo è un uomo* (1947; trans. *If This Is a Man*, or *Survival at Auschwitz*), *La tregua* (1963; trans. *The Truce*, or *The Reawakening*), *Il sistema periodico* (1975; trans. *The Periodic Table*), and *I sommersi e I salvati* (1986; trans. *The Drowned and the Saved*). In addition, he wrote short stories, novels, and a collection of poetry.

In the selection below, an excerpt from *Survival at Auschwitz* entitled "The Drowned and the Saved," Levi writes of "two particularly well differentiated categories among men," those who would survive the camps and those who would not. How, according to Levi, must one reörient oneself in order to survive this catastrophe? What sorts of connections can we draw between Levi's experience here and that of Bettelheim? What are the significant points of contact between the structure of experience in the German Lager and the structures Hannah Arendt describes in her account of totalitarian movements?

See p. 535 for accompanying map.

from "The Drowned and the Saved" (1986)

What we have so far said and will say concerns the ambiguous life of the Lager. In our days many men have lived in this cruel manner, crushed against the bottom, but each for a relatively short period; so that we can perhaps ask ourselves if it is necessary or good to retain any memory of this exceptional human state.

To this question we feel that we have to reply in the affirmative. We are in fact convinced that no human experience is without meaning or unworthy of analysis, and that fundamental values, even if they are not positive, can be deduced from this particular world which we are describing. We would also like to consider that the *Lager*[1] was pre-eminently a gigantic biological and social experiment.

Thousands of individuals, differing in age, condition, origin, language, culture and customs are enclosed within barbed wire: there they live a regular, controlled life which is identical for all and inadequate to all needs, and which is much more rigorous than any experimenter could have set up to establish what is essential and what adventitious to the conduct of the human animal in the struggle for life.

We do not believe in the most obvious and facile deduction: that man is fundamentally brutal, egoistic and stupid in his conduct once every civilized institution is taken away, and that the *Häftling*[2] is consequently nothing but a man without inhibitions. We believe, rather, that the only conclusion to be drawn is that in the face of driving necessity and physical disabilities many social habits and instincts are reduced to silence.

But another fact seems to us worthy of attention: there comes to light the existence of two particularly well-differentiated categories among men—the saved and the drowned. Other pairs of opposites (the good and the bad, the wise and the foolish, the cowards and the courageous, the unlucky and the fortunate) are considerably less distinct, they seem less essential, and above all they allow for more numerous and complex intermediary gradations.

This division is much less evident in ordinary life; for there it rarely happens that a man loses himself. A man is normally not alone, and in his rise or fall is tied to the destinies of his neighbours; so that it is exceptional for anyone to acquire unlimited power, or to fall by a succession of defeats into utter ruin. Moreover, everyone is normally in possession of such spiritual, physical and even financial resources that the probabilities of a shipwreck, of total inadequacy in the face of life, are relatively small. And one must take into account

509

a definite cushioning effect exercised both by the law, and by the moral sense which constitutes a self-imposed law; for a country is considered the more civilized the more the wisdom and efficiency of its laws hinder a weak man from becoming too weak or a powerful one too powerful.

But in the *Lager* things are different: here the struggle to survive is without respite, because everyone is desperately and ferociously alone. If some *Null Achtzehn*[3] vacillates, he will find no one to extend a helping hand; on the contrary, someone will knock him aside, because it is in no one's interest that there be one more *"mussulman"*[4] dragging himself to work every day; and if someone, by a miracle of savage patience and cunning, finds a new method of avoiding the hardest work, a new art which yields him an ounce of bread, he will try to keep his method secret, and he will be esteemed and respected for this, and will derive from it an exclusive, personal benefit; he will become stronger and so will be feared, and who is feared is, *ipso facto*, a candidate for survival.

In history and in life one sometimes seems to glimpse a ferocious law which states: "To he that has, will be given; to he that has not, will be taken away." In the *Lager*, where man is alone and where the struggle for life is reduced to its primordial mechanism, this unjust law is openly in force, is recognized by all. With the adaptable, the strong and astute individuals, even the leaders willingly keep contact, sometimes even friendly contact, because they hope later to perhaps derive some benefit. But with the mussulmans, the men in decay, it is not even worth speaking, because one knows already that they will complain and will speak about what they used to eat at home. Even less worthwhile is it to make friends with them, because they have no distinguished acquaintances in camp, they do not gain any extra rations, they do not work in profitable *Kommandos*[5] and they know no secret method of organizing. And in any case, one knows that they are only here on a visit, that in a few weeks nothing will remain of them but a handful of ashes in some near-by field and a crossed-out number on a register. Although engulfed and swept along without rest by the innumerable crowd of those similar to them, they suffer and drag themselves along in an opaque intimate solitude, and in solitude they die or disappear, without leaving a trace in anyone's memory.

The result of this pitiless process of natural selection could be read in the statistics of *Lager* population movements. At Auschwitz, in 1944, of the old Jewish prisoners (we will not speak of the others here, as their condition was different) *"kleine Nummer,"* low numbers less than 150,000, only a few hundred had survived; not one was an ordinary *Häftling*, vegetating in the ordinary *Kommandos*, and subsisting on the normal ration. There remained only the doctors, tailors, shoemakers, musicians, cooks, young attractive homosexuals, friends or compatriots of some authority in the camp; or they were particularly pitiless, vigorous and inhuman individuals, installed (following an investiture by the SS command, which showed itself in such choices to possess satanic knowledge of human beings) in the posts of *Kapos, Blockältester,*[6] etc.; or finally, those who, without fulfilling particular functions, had always succeeded through their astuteness and energy in successfully organizing, gaining in this way, besides material advantages and reputation, the indulgence and esteem of the powerful people in the camp. Whosoever does not know how to become an *"Organisator," "Kombinator," "Prominent"* (the savage eloquence of these words!) soon becomes a *"mussulman."* In life, a third way exists, and is in fact the rule; it does not exist in the concentration camp.

To sink is the easiest of matters; it is enough to carry out all the orders one receives, to eat only the ration, to observe the discipline of the work and the camp. Experience showed that only exceptionally could one survive more than three months in this way. All the mussulmans who finished in the gas chambers have the same story, or more exactly, have no story; they followed the slope down to the bottom, like streams that run down to the sea. On their entry into the camp, through basic incapacity, or by misfortune, or through some banal incident, they are overcome before they can adapt themselves; they are beaten by time, they do not begin to learn German, to disentangle the infernal knot of laws and prohibitions until their body is already in decay, and nothing can save them from selections or from death by exhaustion. Their life is short, but their number is endless; they, the *Musselmänner*, the drowned, form the backbone of the camp, an anonymous mass, continually renewed and always identical, of non-men who march and labour in silence, the divine spark dead within them, already too empty to really suffer. One hesitates to call them living: one hesitates to call their death death, in the face of which they have no fear, as they are too tired to understand.

They crowd my memory with their faceless presences, and if I could enclose all the evil of our time in one image, I would choose this image which is familiar to me: an emaciated man, with head dropped and shoulders curved, on whose face and in whose eyes not a trace of a thought is to be seen.

If the drowned have no story, and single and broad is the path to perdition, the paths to salvation are many, difficult and improbable.

The most travelled road, as we have stated, is the *"Prominenz."* *"Prominenten"* is the name for the camp officials, from the Häftling-director (*Lagerältester*) to the *Kapos*, the cooks, the nurses, the night-guards, even to the hut-sweepers and to the *Scheissminister* and *Bademeister* (superintendents of the latrines and showers). We are more particularly interested in the Jewish prominents, because while the others are automatically invested with offices as they enter the camp in virtue of their natural supremacy, the Jews have to plot and struggle hard to gain them.

The Jewish prominents form a sad and notable human phenomenon. In them converge present, past and atavistic sufferings, and the tradition of hostility towards the stranger makes of them monsters of asociality and insensitivity. They are the typical product of the structure of the German *Lager*: if one offers a position of privilege to a few individuals in a state of slavery, exacting in exchange the betrayal of a natural solidarity with their comrades, there will certainly be someone who will accept. He will be withdrawn from the common law and will become untouchable; the more power that he is given, the more he will be consequently hateful and hated. When he is given the command of a group of unfortunates, with the right of life or death over them, he will be cruel and tyrannical, because he will understand that if he is not sufficiently so, someone else, judged more suitable, will take over his post. Moreover, his capacity for hatred, unfulfilled in the direction of the oppressors, will double back, beyond all reason, on the oppressed; and he will only be satisfied when he has unloaded onto his underlings the injury received from above.

Notes

[1] Concentration camp.

[2] Prisoner, concentration-camp inmate.

[3] "zero eighteen," the last three numbers tattooed on the forearm of Levi's hypothetical prisoner.

[4] Levi's note: "This word 'Musselmann' I do not know why, was used by the old ones of the camp to describe the weak, the inept, those doomed to selection." *Mussulman*: muslim. *Selection*: being chosen for the gas chambers and the ovens.

[5] Work squads, consisting of prisoners assigned to particular duties or jobs. These duties could involve either skilled or unskilled labor.

[6] *Kapo*: one who oversees a kommando. *Blockältester*: the senior prisoner in a block, or set, of barracks, who received privileges and a certain authority as a result of his longevity and experience.

Albert Camus

1913–1960

Albert Camus was born in Mondovi, Algeria, a colony of France at the time. His father, a manual laborer unable to lift his family out of poverty, died in World War I, in the First Battle of the Marne. His mother worked as a servant and, following her husband's death, she moved Albert and his older brother Lucien into a small apartment in a working-class neighborhood in Algiers. As a boy, Camus was intensely passionate about sports—as a teenager and young adult, he was competitive in soccer and boxing—but his teacher Louis Germain stirred in him a desire to learn and helped him gain a scholarship to the *lycée*. After studying literature and philosophy at the University of Algiers, Camus became involved with the Workers' Theater as an actor, director, and writer. At the outset of World War II, he left for France in order to edit the underground periodical *Combat*, a journal published by the French Resistance; it was also during the war years that he wrote the novel *L'Etranger* (1942; trans. *The Stranger*) and a collection of essays entitled *The Myth of Sisyphus* (1943). After the war, Camus continued writing, publishing the novels *La Peste* (1947; trans. *The Plague*) and *La Chute* (1956; trans. *The Fall*), along with *L'Homme révolté* (1951; trans. *The Rebel*), a long essay critical of Christianity and Communism, which brought about his break with the French existential philosopher Jean-Paul Sartre. Camus won the Nobel Prize for Literature in 1957, just three years before his death in an automobile accident.

In his essays and novels, Camus examined the alienation characteristic of modern life. Much of Camus's work engages the themes of nihilism, a philosophy that denied the existence of transcendent meaning and advocated a skepticism toward political, religious, and cultural institutions. In rejecting such nihilism, Camus insisted on the meaning of humanity and on action in the face of suffering and despair. In *The Myth of Sisyphus*, Camus argues that, in a world without meaning, the "one truly serious philosophical problem . . . is suicide"; that is to say, we must ask why—when truth and meaning seem to slip forever through our fingers, and when justice seems always to succumb to pain—we continue to want to live. Camus describes our condition as that of the Absurd, which he defines as a sense that we are alienated or disconnected from the world and our lives in it. In his essay "The Absurd Man," he recalls Dostoevsky's character Ivan Karamazov, who declares that in an absurd world, one without meaning, "Everything is permitted," to which Camus responds:

"The absurd does not liberate; it binds. It does not authorize all actions. 'Everything is permitted' does not mean that nothing is forbidden."

In the following selection, consider the predicament of Sisyphus. How is our condition like the one he faces? How might his punishment be relevant to our lives? Sisyphus is for Camus the "absurd hero": in what senses is he heroic? Why must we imagine Sisyphus happy?

from *The Myth of Sisyphus* (1943)

The gods had condemned Sisyphus to ceaselessly rolling a rock to the top of a mountain, whence the stone would fall back of its own weight. They had thought with some reason that there is no more dreadful punishment than futile and hopeless labor.

If one believes Homer, Sisyphus was the wisest and most prudent of mortals.[1] According to another tradition, however, he was disposed to practice the profession of highwayman. I see no contradiction in this. Opinions differ as to the reasons why he became the futile laborer of the underworld. To begin with, he is accused of a certain levity in regard to the gods. He stole their secrets. Ægina, the daughter of Æsopus, was carried off by Jupiter. The father was shocked by that disappearance and complained to Sisyphus. He, who knew of the abduction, offered to tell about it on condition that Æsopus would give water to the citadel of Corinth. To the celestial thunderbolts he preferred the benediction of water. He was punished for this in the underworld. Homer tells us also that Sisyphus had put Death in chains. Pluto could not endure the sight of his deserted, silent empire. He dispatched the god of war, who liberated Death from the hands of her conqueror.

It is said that Sisyphus, being near to death, rashly wanted to test his wife's love. He ordered her to cast his unburied body into the middle of the public square. Sisyphus woke up in the underworld. And there, annoyed by an obedience so contrary to human love, he obtained from Pluto permission to return to earth in order to chastise his wife. But when he had seen again the face of this world, enjoyed water and sun, warm stones and the sea, he no longer wanted to go back to the infernal darkness. Recalls, signs of anger, warnings were of no avail. Many years more he lived facing the curve of the gulf, the sparkling sea, and the smiles of earth. A decree of the gods was necessary. Mercury came and seized the impudent man by the collar and, snatching him from his joys, lead him forcibly back to the underworld, where his rock was ready for him.

You have already grasped that Sisyphus is the absurd hero. He *is*, as much through his passions as through his torture. His scorn of the gods, his hatred of death, and his passion for life won him that unspeakable penalty in which the whole being is exerted toward accomplishing nothing. This is the price that must be paid for the passions of this earth. Nothing is told us about Sisyphus in the underworld. Myths are made for the imagination to breathe life into them. As for this myth, one sees merely the whole effort of a body straining to

515

raise the huge stone, to roll it, and push it up a slope a hundred times over; one sees the face screwed up, the cheek tight against the stone, the shoulder bracing the clay-covered mass, the foot wedging it, the fresh start with arms outstretched, the wholly human security of two earth-clotted hands. At the very end of his long effort measured by skyless space and time without depth, the purpose is achieved. Then Sisyphus watches the stone rush down in a few moments toward that lower world whence he will have to push it up again toward the summit. He goes back down to the plain.

It is during that return, that pause, that Sisyphus interests me. A face that toils so close to stones is already stone itself! I see that man going back down with a heavy yet measured step toward the torment of which he will never know the end. That hour like a breathing-space which returns as surely as his suffering, that is the hour of consciousness. At each of those moments when he leaves the heights and gradually sinks toward the lairs of the gods, he is superior to his fate. He is stronger than his rock.

If this myth is tragic, that is because its hero is conscious. Where would his torture be, indeed, if at every step the hope of succeeding upheld him? The workman of today works everyday in his life at the same tasks, and his fate is no less absurd. But it is tragic only at the rare moments when it becomes con-scious. Sisyphus, proletarian of the gods, powerless and rebellious, knows the whole extent of his wretched condition: it is what he thinks of during his descent. The lucidity that was to constitute his torture at the same time crowns his victory. There is no fate that can not be surmounted by scorn.

• • •

If the descent is thus sometimes performed in sorrow, it can also take place in joy. This word is not too much. Again I fancy Sisyphus returning toward his rock, and the sorrow was in the beginning. When the images of earth cling too tightly to memory, when the call of happiness becomes too insistent, it happens that melancholy rises in man's heart: this is the rock's vic-tory, this is the rock itself. The boundless grief is too heavy to bear. These are our nights of Gethsemane. But crushing truths perish from being acknowl-edged. Thus, Œdipus at the outset obeys fate without knowing it. But from the moment he knows, his tragedy begins. Yet at the same moment, blind and desperate, he realizes that the only bond linking him to the world is the cool hand of a girl. Then a tremendous remark rings out: "Despite so many ordeals, my advanced age and the nobility of my soul make me conclude that all is well." Sophocles' Œdipus, like Dostoevsky's Kirilov, thus gives the recipe for the absurd victory. Ancient wisdom confirms modern heroism.

One does not discover the absurd without being tempted to write a man-ual of happiness. "What!—by such narrow ways—?" There is but one world, however. Happiness and the absurd are two sons of the same earth. They are inseparable. It would be a mistake to say that happiness necessarily springs from the absurd discovery. It happens as well that the feeling of the absurd springs from happiness. "I conclude that all is well," says Œdipus, and that remark is sacred. It echoes in the wild and limited universe of man. It teaches that all is not, has not been, exhausted. It drives out of this world a god who had come into it with dissatisfaction and a preference for futile sufferings. It makes of fate a human matter, which must be settled among men.

All Sisyphus' silent joy is contained therein. His fate belongs to him. His rock is his thing. Likewise, the absurd man, when he contemplates his torment, silences all the idols. In the universe suddenly restored to its silence, the myriad wondering little voices of the earth rise up. Unconscious, secret calls, invitations from all the faces, they are the necessary reverse and price of victory. There is no sun without shadow, and it is essential to know the night. The absurd man says yes and his efforts will henceforth be unceasing. If there is a personal fate, there is no higher destiny, or at least there is but one which he concludes is inevitable and despicable. For the rest, he knows himself to be the master of his days. At that subtle moment when man glances backward over his life, Sisyphus returning toward his rock, in that slight pivoting he contemplates that series of unrelated actions which becomes his fate, created by him, combined under his memory's eye and soon sealed by his death. Thus, convinced of the wholly human origin of all that is human, a blind man eager to see who knows that the night has no end, he is still on the go. The rock is still rolling.

I leave Sisyphus at the foot of the mountain! One always finds one's burden again. But Sisyphus teaches the higher fidelity that negates the gods and raises rocks. He too concludes that all is well. This universe henceforth without a master seems to him neither sterile nor futile. Each atom of that stone, each mineral flake of that night-filled mountain, in itself forms a world. The struggle itself toward the heights is enough to fill a man's heart. One must imagine Sisyphus happy.

Note

[1] Homer's story about Sisyphus and his punishment is found in *The Odyssey*, XI. 625 ff.

Jean-Paul Sartre

1905–1980

Philosopher, novelist, and playwright, Jean-Paul Sartre was born in Paris, France, and following the death of his father he was raised by Carl Schweitzer, his maternal grandfather and uncle of the famous missionary Albert Schweitzer. He studied philosophy at the École Normale Supérieure, graduating in 1929, and then went on to teach at a number of French schools until 1939, when he was drafted into the army to serve in World War II. In 1940, Sartre was captured by the Germans. Freed a year later, he became involved with the French resistance, where he met and worked with Albert Camus. Sartre's long-term companion was the existentialist writer Simone de Beauvior, whose monumental work *The Second Sex* (1949) shaped much of twentieth-century feminist thought.

Sartre published his first novel, *La Nausée* (trans. *Nausea*), in 1938; it tells the story of Roquentin, a historian who suffers physically because of his sense that existence is impermanent and experience is uncertain, finally coming to doubt the possibility of meaning at all. In 1943, he published *L'Etre et Neant* (trans. *Being and Nothingness*), his seminal work of philosophy, in which he develops, among many other ideas, his phenomenological analysis of consciousness. For Sartre, consciousness manifests itself in terms of the choices individuals make. That is, prior to choice and action, consciousness—and therefore our being itself—is possibility; through engaging our freedom responsibly, through enacting our choices, we come to be, we come to shape who we are. In Sartre's words, "existence precedes essence." Sartre's major novels include *L'Âge de raison* (1945; trans. *The Age of Reason*), *Le Sursis* (1945; *The Reprieve*), and *La Mort dans l'âme* (1949; trans. *Troubled Sleep*); his major plays include *Les Mouches* (1943; trans. *The Flies*) and *Huis-clos* (1944; trans. *No Exit*). He also wrote several biographies and critical studies, including works on Baudelaire and Jean Genet. In 1964, he won the Nobel Prize for Literature, but turned it down, saying that such an award would forever limit his freedom.

In "The Republic of Silence," Sartre analyzes the concepts of freedom and responsibility. In what ways are we never more free than when we are under literal (and possibly figurative) occupation, as Sartre claims? How does Sartre's conception of freedom change the way we must conduct our lives?

How does his idea of freedom reshape our sense of responsibility? What are the points of contact between Sartre's thesis in this essay and that of Camus in "The Myth of Sisyphus"?

The Republic of Silence (1949)

We have never been so free as under German occupation. We had lost every right, and above all the right of speech: we were insulted every day and we had to remain silent; we were deported as laborers, as Jews, as political prisoners; everywhere, on the walls, in the newspapers, and on the screen, we saw the foul and listless face which our oppressors wanted to give us. Because of all this we were free. Since the Nazi venom penetrated our very thoughts, every true thought was a victory. Since an all-powerful police tried to force us to be silent, each word became as precious as a declaration of principle. Since we were hounded, every one of our movements had the importance of commitment. The often atrocious circumstances of our struggle had at last put us in a position to live our life without pretenses—to live in this torn, unbearable condition which we call the human condition. Exile, captivity, and above all death, which is ably disguised in periods of happiness, became the perpetual object of our concern; we discovered that they were not evitable accidents or even constant but external threats: they had become our *lot*, our destiny, the source of our reality as men. Each second we fully realized the meaning of the trite little phrase "All men are mortal." And the choice which each man made on his own was genuine, since he made it in the presence of death, since he would always have been able to express it in terms of "better death than . . ." And I'm not talking of the elite formed by the true resistants, but of every Frenchman who, at every hour of the day and night, for four years, said no. The cruelty of the enemy pushed us to the extremes of our condition by forcing us to ask these questions which we avoid in peacetime: each of us—and what Frenchman did not at one point find himself in this position?—who knew certain details concerning the Resistance wondered anxiously: "If I were tortured, would I hold out?" Thus the question of liberty was raised and we were on the brink of the deepest knowledge that man can have of himself. Because man's secret is not his Oedipus complex or his inferiority complex, it is the limit of his freedom, it is his power to resist torture and death. To those who were active in the underground, the circumstances of this struggle were a new experience: they did not fight in the open, like soldiers; they were hunted in solitude, arrested in solitude, and it was all alone that they resisted torture: alone and naked before well-shaved, well-fed, well-dressed executioners who laughed at their wretched flesh, who, with clean consciences and unlimited power, looked as though they were in the right. And yet at the depths of this solitude it was the others, all the others, all the comrades of the Resistance whom they defended. One word was enough to cause ten, a hundred arrests. Is not total responsibility in total solitude the revelation of our liberty? The need, the solitude, the enormous risk were the same for everybody, for the leaders and the men. For those who carried messages and did not know what they contained as for those who organized the whole Resistance, there was only one sentence: imprisonment, deportation, death. There is no army in the world with such equal risks for the soldiers and the general. And that is why the Resistance was a real democracy: for the soldier and for the leader there was the same danger, the same responsibility, the same absolute liberty in discipline. Thus, in darkness and in blood, the strongest republic was formed. Each of its citizens knew that he owed himself to everyone and could only count on himself; each one performed his historic part in total solitude. Each one, in defiance of the oppressor, undertook to be himself; irremediably and by freely choosing himself, he chose freedom for everybody. This republic without institutions, without army or police, had to be conquered by each Frenchman and established at every moment against Nazism. We are now on the brink of another Republic: can't we preserve by day the austere virtues of the Republic of Silence and Night?

Ralph Ellison

1914–1994

Born in Oklahoma City, Ralph Ellison's earliest creative interest was music, particularly jazz and the blues. He studied music at Tuskeegee Institute, a school for African Americans founded by Booker T. Washington, and in 1936 moved to New York City, intent on continuing his music education and on studying sculpture, as well. In New York, Ellison met other black artists, including the poet Langston Hughes and the novelist Richard Wright, who urged him to turn his talents to writing. In 1952, Ellison published *Invisible Man*, for which he won the National Book Award the next year. *Invisible Man* tells the story of an unnamed African-American man who travels from the Deep South—he attends a school much like Tuskeegee—to Harlem, experiencing firsthand the racial gulf that separates whites from blacks in America. At the same time, he confronts his own growing inner alienation. Among his other works are *Shadow and Act* (1964) and *Going to the Territory* (1986), both collections of essays, interviews, and reviews about the African-American experience in literature, music, and culture.

In the "Prologue" to *Invisible Man*, Ellison begins to develop his theme of "invisibility," exploring the ways in which blacks are made to "disappear" in American society. Consider carefully the symbolism of the scene in which the main character realizes that the tall blond man has actually *not seen him*. What are the facets of his "invisibility," as Ellison describes them? What are the meanings—social, political, philosophical—of this invisibility?

from *Invisible Man* (1953)

I am an invisible man. No, I am not a spook like those who haunted Edgar Allan Poe; nor am I one of your Hollywood-movie ectoplasms. I am a man of substance, of flesh and bone, fiber and liquids—and I might even be said to possess a mind. I am invisible, understand, simply because people refuse to see me. Like the bodiless heads you see sometimes in circus sideshows, it is as though I have been surrounded by mirrors of hard, distorting glass. When they approach me they see only my surroundings, themselves, or figments of their imagination—indeed, everything and anything except me.

Nor is my invisibility exactly a matter of a biochemical accident to my epidermis. That invisibility to which I refer occurs because of a peculiar disposition of the eyes of those with whom I come in contact. A matter of the construction of their *inner* eyes, those eyes with which they look through their physical eyes upon reality. I am not complaining, nor am I protesting either. It is sometimes advantageous to be unseen, although it is most often rather wearing on the nerves. Then too, you're constantly being bumped against by those of poor vision. Or again, you often doubt if you really exist. You wonder whether you aren't simply a phantom in other people's minds. Say, a figure in a nightmare which the sleeper tries with all his strength to destroy. It's when you feel like this that, out of resentment, you begin to bump people back. And, let me confess, you feel that way most of the time. You ache with the need to convince yourself that you do exist in the real world, that you're a part of all the sound and anguish, and you strike out with your fists, you curse and you swear to make them recognize you. And, alas, it's seldom successful.

One night I accidentally bumped into a man, and perhaps because of the near darkness he saw me and called me an insulting name. I sprang at him, seized his coat lapels and demanded that he apologize. He was a tall blond man, and as my face came close to his he looked insolently out of his blue eyes and cursed me, his breath hot in my face as he struggled. I pulled his chin down sharp upon the crown of my head, butting him as I had seen the West Indians do, and I felt his flesh tear and the blood gush out, and I yelled, "Apologize! Apologize!" But he continued to curse and struggle, and I butted him again and again until he went down heavily, on his knees, profusely bleeding. I kicked him repeatedly, in a frenzy because he still uttered insults though his lips were frothy with blood. Oh yes, I kicked him! And in my outrage I got out my knife and prepared to slit his throat, right there beneath the lamplight in the deserted street, holding him in the collar with one hand, and opening the knife with my teeth—when it occurred to me that the man had not *seen* me, actually; that he, as far as he knew, was in the midst of a walking nightmare! And I stopped the blade, slicing the air as I pushed him away, letting him fall back to the street. I stared at him hard as the lights of a car stabbed through the darkness. He lay there, moaning on the asphalt; a man almost killed by a phantom. It unnerved me. I was both disgusted and ashamed. I was like a drunken man myself, wavering about on weakened legs. Then I was amused: Something in this man's thick head had sprung out and beaten him within an inch of his life. I began to laugh at this crazy discovery. Would he have awakened at the point of death? Would Death himself have freed him for wakeful living? But I didn't linger. I ran away into the dark, laughing so hard I feared I might rupture myself. The next day I saw his picture in the *Daily News*, beneath a caption stating that he had been "mugged." Poor fool, poor blind fool, I thought with sincere compassion, mugged by an invisible man!

Most of the time (although I do not choose as I once did to deny the violence of my days by ignoring it) I am not so overtly violent. I remember that I am invisible and walk softly so as not to awaken the sleeping ones. Sometimes it is best not to awaken them; there are few things in the world as dangerous as sleepwalkers. I learned in time though that it is possible to carry on a fight against them without their realizing it. For instance, I have been carrying on a fight with Monopolated Light & Power for some time now. I use their service and pay them nothing at all, and they don't know it. Oh, they suspect that power is being drained off, but they don't know where. All they know is that according to the master meter back there in their power station a hell of a lot of free current is disappearing somewhere into the jungle of Harlem. The joke, of course, is that I don't live in Harlem but in a border area. Several years ago (before I discovered the advantages of being invisible) I went through the routine process of buying service and paying their outrageous rates. But no more. I gave up all that, along with my apartment, and my old way of life: That way based upon the fallacious assumption that I, like other men, was visible. Now, aware of my invisibility, I live rent-free in a building rented strictly to whites, in a section of the basement that was shut off and forgotten during the nineteenth century, which I discovered when I was trying to escape in the night from Ras the Destroyer.[1] But that's getting too far ahead of the story; almost to the end, although the end is in the beginning and lies far ahead.

The point now is that I found a home—or a hole in the ground, as you will. Now don't jump to the conclusion that because I call my home a "hole" it is damp and cold like a grave; there are cold holes and warm holes. Mine is a warm hole. And remember, a bear retires to his hole for the winter and lives until spring; then he comes strolling out like the Easter chick breaking from its shell. I say all this to assure you that it is incorrect to assume that, because I'm invisible and live in a hole, I am dead. I am neither dead nor in a state of suspended animation. Call me Jack-the-Bear, for I am in a state of hibernation.

My hole is warm and full of light. Yes, *full* of light. I doubt if there is a brighter spot in all New York than this hole of mine, and I do not exclude Broadway. Or the Empire State Building on a photographer's dream night. But that is taking advantage of you. Those two spots are among the darkest of our whole civilization—pardon me, our whole *culture* (an important distinction, I've heard)—which might sound like a hoax, or a contradiction, but that (by contradiction, I mean) is how the world moves: Not like an arrow, but a boomerang. (Beware of those who speak of the *spiral* of history; they are preparing a boomerang. Keep a steel helmet handy.) I know; I have been boomeranged across my head so much that I now can see the darkness of lightness. And I love light. Perhaps you'll think it strange that an invisible man should need light, desire light, love light. But maybe it is exactly because I *am* invisible. Light confirms my reality, gives birth to my form. A beautiful girl once told me of a recurring nightmare in which she lay in the center of a large dark room and felt her face expand until it filled the whole room, becoming a formless mass while her eyes ran in bilious jelly up the chimney. And so it is with me. Without light I am not only invisible, but formless as well; and to be unaware of one's form is to live a death. I myself, after existing some twenty years, did not become alive until I discovered my invisibility.

That is why I fight my battle with Monopolated Light & Power. The deeper reason, I mean: It allows me to feel my vital aliveness. I also fight them for taking so much of my money before I learned to protect myself. In my hole in the basement there are exactly 1,369 lights. I've wired the entire ceiling, every inch of it. And not with fluorescent bulbs, but with the older, more-expensive-to-operate kind, the filament type. An act of sabotage, you know. I've already begun to wire the wall. A junk man I know, a man of vision, has supplied me with wire and sockets. Nothing, storm or flood, must get in the way of our need for light and ever more and brighter light. The truth is the light and light is the truth. When I finish all four walls, then I'll start on the floor. Just how that will go, I don't know. Yet when you have lived invisible as long as I have you develop a certain ingenuity. I'll solve the problem. And maybe I'll invent a gadget to place my coffee pot on the fire while I lie in bed, and even invent a gadget to warm my bed—like the fellow I saw in one of the picture magazines who made himself a gadget to warm his shoes! Though invisible, I am in the great American tradition of tinkers. That makes me kin to Ford, Edison and Franklin. Call me, since I have a theory and a concept, a "thinker-tinker." Yes, I'll warm my shoes; they need it, they're usually full of holes. I'll do that and more.

Note

[1] A character who appears later in the novel. He represents the black separatism of Marcus Garvey. *Ras* is a shortening of *rastafarian*, a member of the religious and political movement important among black Jamaicans particularly, the central tenets of which stress return to Africa as part of a struggle for liberation and redemption.

Monica Sone

(1919–)

In 1942 President Franklin Delano Roosevelt signed Executive Order 9022 thereby consigning 110,000 Japanese-Americans to internment camps for the duration of World War II. Following the bombing of Pearl Harbor by the Japanese Army, government and military officials claimed that the internment of Japanese Americans was a justifiable act during wartime. This abridgement of civil liberties was particularly striking since it was based solely on national origin. As General John L. De Witt, chief of the West Coast Defense Command argued, "The Japanese race is an enemy race. It makes no difference whether he is an American citizen or not."

Historically, Japanese Americans have had an ambivalent relationship with the United States government. Beginning in the late nineteenth century, immigration restrictions prevented *Issei*, or Japanese immigrants, from attaining U.S. citizenship. Despite these obstacles, *Issei* had created vibrant and prosperous Japanese American communities throughout the West Coast. Their children, or *Nisei*, were citizens since they had been born in the United States. Together, immigrants and their children were forced to leave thriving businesses and farms and relocate to one of the ten internment camps. Despite the U.S. government's disregard for their rights as citizens, many Japanese Americans were drafted and left the camps to serve in a segregated regiment. This regiment, the 442nd Regimental Combat Team, was the most decorated unit in the U.S. army. Ironically the 442nd helped liberate the concentration camp Dachau, even as their families resided in a prison camp. As a result of their internment *Issei* and *Nisei* lost thousands of dollars of property and in 1988 the federal government apologized and made a small financial reparation to camp residents and their families.

In the following selection, Monica Sone describes her introduction to camp life. In this passage one gets a sense of the resilience of Japanese-American families who were forced to leave normal life for the setting of a prison camp. Monica also calls into question the seemingly arbitrary nature of American citizenship. Can citizenship be so easily removed because of one's race? She highlights the age-old problem of what happens when governments stop believing in their creeds and start relying on repressive laws and prison camps to ensure loyalty. What are the ethics and implications of the Japanese-American experience in this historical moment?

Japanese Relocation (1953)

When our bus turned a corner and we no longer had to smile and wave, we settled back gravely in our seats. Everyone was quiet except for a chattering group of university students who soon started singing college songs. A few people turned and glared at them, which only served to increase the volume of their singing. Then suddenly a baby's sharp cry rose indignantly above the hubbub. The singing stopped immediately, followed by a guilty silence. Three seats behind us, a young mother held a wailing red-faced infant in her arms, bouncing it up and down. Its angry little face emerged from multiple layers of kimonos, sweaters and blankets, and it, too, wore the white pasteboard tag pinned to its blanket. A young man stammered out an apology as the mother gave him a wrathful look. She hunted frantically for a bottle of milk in a shopping bag, and we all relaxed when she had found it.

We sped out of the city southward along beautiful stretches of farmland, with dark, newly turned soil. In the beginning we devoured every bit of scenery which flashed past our window and admired the massive-muscled work horses plodding along the edge of the highway, the rich burnished copper color of a browsing herd of cattle, the vivid spring green of the pastures, but eventually the sameness of the country landscape palled on us. We tried to sleep to escape from the restless anxiety which kept bobbing up to the surface of our minds. I awoke with a start when the bus filled with excited buzzing. A small group of straw-hatted Japanese farmers stood by the highway, waving at us. I felt a sudden warmth toward them, then a twinge of pity. They would be joining us soon.

About noon we crept into a small town. Someone said, "Looks like Puyallup, all right." Parents of small children babbled excitedly, "Stand up quickly and look over there. See all the chick-chicks and fat little piggies?" One little city boy stared hard at the hogs and said tersely, "They're *bachi*—dirty!"

Our bus idled a moment at the traffic signal and we noticed at the left of us an entire block filled with neat rows of low shacks, resembling chicken houses. Someone commented on it with awe, "Just look at those chicken houses. They sure go in for poultry in a big way here." Slowly the bus made a left turn, drove through a wire-fenced gate, and to our dismay, we were inside the oversized chicken farm. The bus driver opened the door, the guard stepped out and stationed himself at the door again. Jim, the young man who had shepherded us into the busses, popped his head inside and sang out, "Okay, folks, all off at Yokohama, Puyallup."

We stumbled out, stunned, dragging our bundles after us. It must have rained hard the night before in Puyallup, for we sank ankle deep into gray, gluttinous mud. The receptionist, a white man, instructed us courteously, "Now, folks, please stay together as family units and line up. You'll be assigned your apartment."

We were standing in Area A, the mammoth parking lot of the state fairgrounds. There were three other separate areas, B, C and D, all built on the fair grounds proper, near the baseball field and the race tracks. This camp of army barracks was hopefully called Camp Harmony.

We were assigned to apartment 2-I-A, right across from the bachelor quarters. The apartments resembled elongated, low stables about two blocks long. Our home was one room, about 18 by 20 feet, the size of a living room. There was one small window in the wall opposite the one door. It was bare except for a small, tinny wood-burning stove crouching in the center. The flooring consisted of two by fours laid directly on the earth, and dandelions were already pushing their way up through the cracks. Mother was delighted when she saw their shaggy yellow heads. "Don't anyone pick them. I'm going to cultivate them."

Father snorted, "Cultivate them! If we don't watch out, those things will be growing out of our hair."

Just then Henry stomped inside, bringing the rest of our baggage. "What's all the excitement about?"

Sumi replied laconically, "Dandelions."

Henry tore off a fistful. Mother scolded, "*Arra! Arra!* Stop that. They're the only beautiful things around here. We could have a garden right in here."

"Are you joking, Mama?"

I chided Henry, "Of course, she's not. After all, she has to have some inspiration to write poems, you know, with all the '*nali keli's.*' I can think of a poem myself right now:

Oh, Dandelion, Dandelion,
Despised and uprooted by all,
Dance and bob your golden heads
For you've finally found your home
With your yellow fellows, *nali keli*, amen!"

Henry said, thrusting the dandelions in Mother's black hair, "I think you can do ten times better than that, Mama."

Sumi reclined on her seabag and fretted, "Where do we sleep? Not on the floor, I hope."

"Stop worrying," Henry replied disgustedly.

Mother and Father wandered out to see what the other folks were doing and they found people wandering in the mud, wondering what other folks were doing. Mother returned shortly, her face lit up in an ecstatic smile, "We're in luck. The latrine is right nearby. We won't have to walk blocks."

We laughed, marveling at Mother who could be so poetic and yet so practical. Father came back, bent double like a woodcutter in a fairy tale, with stacks of scrap lumber over his shoulder. His coat and trouser pockets bulged with nails. Father dumped his loot in a corner and explained, "There was a pile of wood left by the carpenters and hundreds of nails scattered loose. Everybody was picking them up, and I hustled right in with them. Now maybe we can live in style with tables and chairs."

The block leader knocked at our door and announced lunchtime. He instructed us to take our meal at the nearest mess hall. As I untied my seabag to get out my pie plate, tin cup, spoon and fork, I realized I was hungry. At the mess hall we found a long line of people. Children darted in and out of the line, skiing in the slithery mud. The young stood impatiently on one foot, then the other, and scowled, "The food had better be good after all this wait." But the Issei stood quietly, arms folded, saying very little. A light drizzle began to fall, coating bare black heads with tiny sparkling raindrops. The chow line inched forward.

Lunch consisted of two canned sausages, one lob of boiled potato, and a slab of bread. Our family had to split up, for the hall was too crowded for us to sit together. I wandered up and down the aisles, back and forth along the crowded tables and benches, looking for a few inches to squeeze into. A small Issei woman finished her meal, stood up and hoisted her legs modestly over the bench, leaving a space for one. Even as I thrust myself into the breach, the space had shrunk to two inches, but I worked myself into it. My dinner companion, hooked just inside my right elbow, was a bald headed, gruff-looking Issei man who seemed to resent nestling at mealtime. Under my left elbow was a tiny, mud-spattered girl. With busy runny nose, she was belaboring her sausages, tearing them into shreds and mixing them into the potato gruel which she had made with water. I choked my food down.

We cheered loudly when trucks rolled by, distributing canvas army cots for the young and hardy, and steel cots for the older folks. Henry directed the arrangement of the cots. Father and Mother were to occupy the corner nearest the wood stove. In the other corner, Henry arranged two cots in L shape and announced that this was the combination living room-bedroom area, to be occupied by Sumi and myself. He fixed a male den for himself in the corner nearest the door. If I had had my way, I would have arranged everyone's cots in one neat row as in Father's hotel dormitory.

We felt fortunate to be assigned to a room at the end of the barracks because we had just one neighbor to worry about. The partition wall separating the rooms was only seven feet high with an opening of four feet at the top, so at night, Mrs. Funai next door could tell when Sumi was still sitting up in bed in the dark, putting her hair up. "*Mah, Sumi-chan*," Mrs. Funai would say through the plank wall, "are you curling your hair tonight again? Do you put it up every night?" Sumi would put her hands on her hips and glare defiantly at the wall.

The block monitor, an impressive Nisei who looked like a star tackle with his crouching walk, came around the first night to tell us that we must all be inside our room by nine o'clock every night. At ten o'clock, he rapped at the door again, yelling, "Lights out!" and Mother rushed to turn the light off not a second later.

Throughout the barracks, there were a medley of creaking cots, whimpering infants and explosive night coughs. Our attention was riveted on the intense little wood stove which glowed so violently I feared it would melt right down to the floor. We soon learned that this condition lasted for only a short time, after which it suddenly turned into a deep freeze. Henry and Father took turns at the stove to produce the harrowing blast which all but singed our army blankets, but did not penetrate through them. As it grew quieter in the barracks, I could hear the light patter of rain. Soon I felt the "splat! splat!" of raindrops digging holes into my face. The dampness on my pillow spread like a mortal bleeding, and I finally had to get out and haul my cot toward the center of the room. In a short while Henry was up. "I've got multiple leaks, too. Have to complain to the landlord first thing in the morning."

All through the night I heard people getting up, dragging cots around. I stared at our little window, unable to sleep. I was glad Mother had put up a makeshift curtain on the window for I noticed a powerful beam of light sweeping across it every few seconds. The lights came from high towers placed around the camp where guards with Tommy guns kept a twenty-four hour vigil. I remembered the wire fence encircling us, and a knot of anger tightened in my breast. What was I doing behind a fence like a criminal? If there were accusations to be made, why hadn't I been given a fair trial? Maybe I wasn't considered an American anymore. My citizenship wasn't real, after all. Then what was I? I was certainly not a citizen of Japan as my parents were. On second thought, even Father and Mother were more alien residents of the United States than Japanese nationals for they had little tie with their mother country. In their twenty-five years in America, they had worked and paid their taxes to their adopted government as any other citizen.

Of one thing I was sure. The wire fence was real. I no longer had the right to walk out of it. It was because I had Japanese ancestors. It was also because some people had little faith in the ideas and ideals of democracy. They said that after all these were but words and could not possibly insure loyalty. New laws and camps were surer devices. I finally buried my face in my pillow to wipe out burning thoughts and snatch what sleep I could.

Appendix of Maps

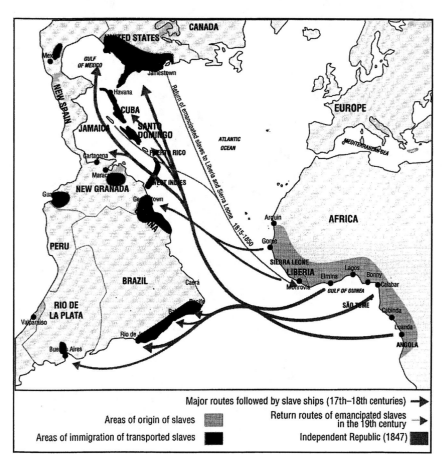

I. Slave trade routes from Africa to North America

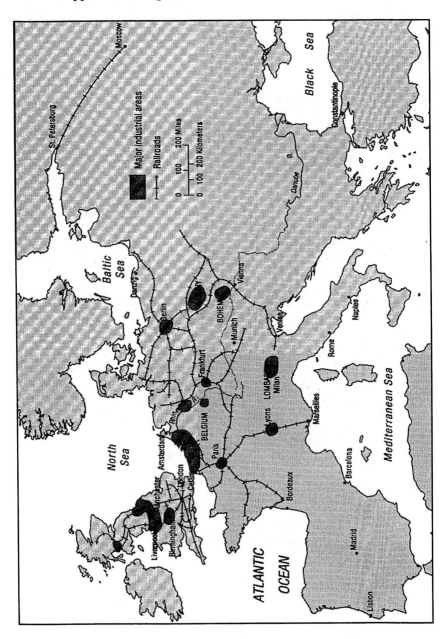

II. Railroads and the Industrialization of Europe

III. Concentration camp sites in Western Europe

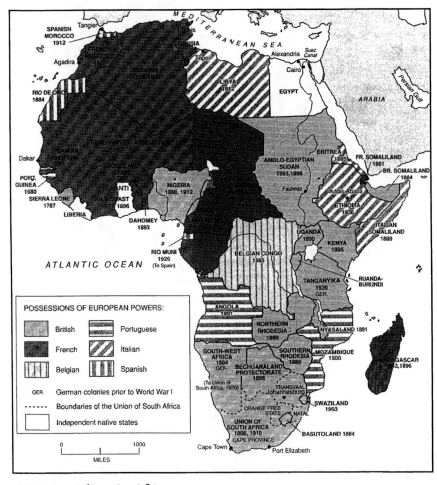

IV. Imperialism in Africa

Appendix of Publication Dates

Seventeenth Century

1615	Galileo Galilei "The Letter to the Grand Duchess Christina"
1670	Blaise Pascal *Thoughts*
1684	Isaac Newton Preface to *Principia* (Motte trans.) and The System of the World (Book III)
1690	John Locke *Two Treatises of Government*

Eighteenth Century

Early 18th c.	Emperor K'ang-hsi *Self-Portrait of K'ang-hsi*
1711	Alexander Pope *Essay on Criticism*
1729	Isaac Newton *Rules of Reasoning in Philosophy*
1734	Alexander Pope *Essay on Man*
1739–1740	David Hume *A Treatise of Human Nature*
1747	Françoise de Graffigny Letters from a Peruvian Woman
1763	Jean-Jacques Rousseau *The Social Contract*
1764	François Marie Arouet de Voltaire *Philosophical Dictionary*

1776 Abigail and John Adams
     Letters

1776 Thomas Jefferson
     The Declaration of Independence

1776 Adam Smith
     The Wealth of Nations

1784 Immanuel Kant
     What Is Enlightenment?

1786 Thomas Jefferson
     A Bill Establishing Religious Freedom

1787–1788 James Madison and Alexander Hamilton
     The Federalist Papers

1789 Jeremy Bentham
     Chapter 1 of *Introduction to the Principles of Morals and Legislation*

1789 Olaudah Equiano
     The Interesting Narrative of the Life of Olaudah Equiano or Gustavus Vassa, the African

1789 National Assembly of France
     Declaration of the Rights of Man and Citizen

1790 Edmund Burke
     Reflections on the Revolution in France

1791 Olympe de Gouges
     Declaration of the Rights of Woman and Citizen

1791 Benjamin Benneker
     Letter from Benjamin Benneker to Thomas Jefferson and Jefferson's Response

1792 Mary Wollstonecraft
     A Vindication of the Rights of Woman

1793 Emperor Ch'ien-lung
     Letter to George III

1795 Marquis de Condorcet
     The Future Progress of the Human Mind

1794   William Blake
        "London" and "The Sick Rose"

Nineteenth Century

1813–1814   Robert Owen
            A New View of Society

1819   Simón Bolívar
        Message to the Congress of Angostura

1829   Lord William Bentinck
        Comments on Ritual Murder and the Limits of Religious
        Toleration

1835–1840   Alexis de Tocqueville
            Democracy in America

1836   Angelina E. Grimke
        Appeal to the Christian Women of the South

1840   Emily Brontë
        "The Night-Wind"

1841   Ralph Waldo Emerson
        Self-Reliance

1842   Women Miners in the English Coal Pits
        "Parliamentary Papers of Great Britain"

1843   Flora Tristan
        "The Female Worker's Union"

1844   Friedrich Engels
        "Condition of the Working Class in England in 1844"

1845   Frederick Douglass
        *Narrative of the Life of Frederick Douglass, an American
        Slave*

1848   Elizabeth Cady Stanton
        "Declaration of Sentiments"

1851   Sojourner Truth
        "A'n't I a Woman"

1859   John Stuart Mill
        On Liberty

1897	Olive Schreiner *Trooper Peter Halket of Mashonaland*
1898	Charlotte Perkins Gilman *Women and Economics*

Twentieth Century

1902	Zitkala-Ša "Why I Am a Pagan"
1909	Mahatma Gandhi *Indian Home Rule*
1909	Ito Hirobumi *Sources of Japanese Tradition*
1911	Ohiyesa *The Soul of the Indian*
1912	Gertrude Stein "Picasso"
1915	Helena Marie Swanwick *The War and Its Effect upon Women*
1916	Vladimir Lenin *Imperialism: The Highest Stage of Capitalism*
1919	Franz Kafka "A Country Doctor"
c. 1922	Anne Spencer "White Things"
1923–1924	Adolf Hitler *Mein Kampf*
1926	Langston Hughes "I, Too, Sing America"
1926	John Maynard Keynes *The End of Laissez-faire*
1928	Radclyffe Hall *The Well of Loneliness*

1960	Bruno Bettelheim *The Informed Heart: Autonomy in a Mass Age*
1986	Primo Levi "The Drowned and the Saved"